JOURNAL FOR THE STUDY OF THE NEW TESTAMENT
SUPPLEMENT SERIES
176

Executive Editor
Stanley E. Porter

Sheffield Academic Press

Idol Food in Corinth

Jewish Background and Pauline Legacy

Alex T. Cheung

Journal for the Study of the New Testament
Supplement Series 176

Copyright © 1999 Sheffield Academic Press

Published by
Sheffield Academic Press Ltd
Mansion House
19 Kingfield Road
Sheffield S11 9AS
England

Typeset by Sheffield Academic Press
and
Printed on acid-free paper in Great Britain
by Biddles Ltd
Guildford, Surrey

British Library Cataloguing in Publication Data

A catalogue record for this book is available
from the British Library

ISBN 1-85075-904-9

CONTENTS

Preface   7
Abbreviations   11
Introduction   15

Chapter 1
THE SOCIAL MEANING OF EATING IDOL FOOD   27
  1. The Nature and Occasions of Eating Idol Food   28
  2. The Social Significance of Meals   35
  3. Some Implications for the Problem of Idol Food in Corinth   36

Chapter 2
THE BACKGROUND TO PAUL'S ATTITUDE TO IDOL FOOD
IN EARLY JUDAISM   39
  1. The Jewish Scriptures   41
  2. Jewish Apocryphal Writings   43
  3. Jewish Pseudepigraphical Writings   49
  4. Qumran   56
  5. Philo   56
    Excursus   60
  6. Josephus   65
  7. Rabbinic Writings   69
  8. Pagan Authors on Jewish Attitude   74
  9. Implications for our Understanding of Paul's Attitude
    to Idol Food   76

Chapter 3
EXEGETICAL INVESTIGATION OF 1 CORINTHIANS 8.1–11.1   82
  1. Literary Integrity of 1 Corinthians 8.1–11.1   82
  2. The Nature of the Problem in Corinth and Paul's
    Response   85
  3. An Alternative Understanding of Paul's Approach
    to εἰδωλόθυτα   108

    4. Conclusion   162
        Excursus   162

Chapter 4
THE EARLY CHRISTIANS' UNDERSTANDING OF PAUL'S
ATTITUDE TO IDOL FOOD   165
    1. The State of Research   165
    2. Assumptions and General Remarks   171
    3. The Book of Acts   177
    4. Revelation   197
    5. *6 Ezra*   209
    6. The Apostolic Fathers   210
    7. Pagan References to Early Christian Attitudes toward
        Idol Food   220
    8. The Apologists   236
    9. Irenaeus   242
   10. Marcion   247
   11. The Gnostics   253
   12. Tertullian   256
   13. Minucius Felix   261
   14. Clement of Alexandria   262
   15. Origen   267
   16. Novatian   272
   17. The Apostolic Constitutions   272
   18. Jewish Christianity   272
   19. Later Patristic Writers   275
   20. Conclusions   278
        Excursus   284

Chapter 5
SUMMARY AND CONCLUDING REFLECTIONS   296
    1. Summary   296
    2. The Origins of Paul's Approach   299
    3. Concluding Hermeneutical Reflections   303

Appendix
EVALUATION OF SOME MAJOR STUDIES   306

Bibliography   323
Index of References   350
Index of Authors   361

PREFACE

This study is a substantial revision of my doctoral dissertation at Westminster Theological Seminary. It represents a major milestone, but by no means the culmination, of my long pilgrimage towards an understanding of Paul's teaching on idol food. The origin of this pilgrimage goes back many years to the beginning of my Christian life.

I grew up in a home that worshiped idols and lived in a society and culture which, like Corinth, acknowledged many gods and many lords. The problem of idol food forced itself on me almost immediately after I had become a Christian. Over the years of grappling with Paul's teaching on this subject in 1 Corinthians 8–10, I came to the conclusion that Paul regarded the eating of idol food, *with the awareness of their idolatrous origins*, as a sinful act rather than a matter indifferent.

As I began formal theological studies, I naturally paid a great deal of attention to scholarly works on the issue. The experience was very unsettling. I was not able to find any discussion—let alone support—of my interpretation in scholarly literature. My excitement of having possibly discovered something original was tempered with nagging doubts that such originality might be nothing more than a result of my pre-critical *naïveté*.

Happily, when I studied early Christians' attitudes toward idol food as part of my dissertation research, my doubts vanished. What a relief to find that I have merely stumbled upon the virtually unanimous early Christian understanding of Paul's position! What is lost by way of the supposed originality of my interpretation is more than compensated for by solid ancient support for its substantiality.

The appearance of Peter Tomson's study was very reassuring in this regard,[1] as his conclusion and mine are clearly corollaries to each other.

---

1.   P.J. Tomson, *Paul and the Jewish Law: Halakha in the Letters of the Apostle to the Gentiles* (CRINT, 3.1; Jewish Traditions in Early Christian Literature; Assen: Van Gorcum; Minneapolis: Fortress Press, 1990).

Both of us agree that Paul intends a general prohibition of idol food—if the food can be established as idol food. On the other hand, my preliminary research was done and my preliminary conclusion was reached prior to and independent of Tomson's publication (which I read with great interest in late 1991). As a result, the evidence and reasons for my interpretation are sufficiently different from Tomson's that this work should not be redundant. The same can be said with regard to the relationship between this work and Gooch's dissertation (which was not available to me until early 1993).[2] While references will be made to the works of Tomson and Gooch throughout this dissertation, I will discuss their works as a whole in an appendix, after I have fully presented the results of my research.

This work—both in its dissertation stage and throughout the revision process—is in many respects a community effort. A great debt is owed to the faculty and library staff of Westminster Theological Seminary. It is a real pleasure to acknowledge the valuable advice and encouragement of Dr Moisés Silva, my dissertation advisor. He has shown constant interest in my research since I first broached the subject as a possible dissertation topic about eight years ago. He has continued to give me much appreciated input during the revision stage. From him I have learned how to do level-headed exegesis with a deep reverence for Scripture. Appreciation must also be given to Dr Vern Poythress for enriching my theological understanding of Scripture and instilling in me a hermeneutical self-consciousness as I approach God's Word; to Dr Tremper Longman, III for introducing me to the literary study of the Bible; and to Dr Richard Gaffin for his encouraging comments upon reading an early draft of chapter three. Ms. Grace Mullen has been tremendously helpful in tracking down hard-to-find works. For her cheerful and efficient service I can only say 'thank you'.

I would also like to thank Dr David Garland, Professor of Christian Scriptures at Truett Seminary, for his enthusiastic comments and for encouraging me to get my work published in a notable series. He has given me valuable suggestions how I may improve this work.

A special thank goes to Dr Robert Kraft, Professor of Religious Studies at the University of Pennsylvania, who despite his busy schedule

---

2. P.D. Gooch, 'Food and the Limits of Community: I Corinthians 8 to 10' (PhD dissertation, University of Toronto, 1988). I want to thank Dr Gooch for making available to me a copy of his dissertation, thus ending my great frustration at having to read his work on very poorly reproduced microfiche.

has given generously of his time to offer expert advice and constructive criticism on early drafts of chapters two and four. With the words, 'come and learn how to do research', he took me under his wings by introducing me to the monthly Philadelphia Seminar of Christian Origins meetings, where first-rate scholars and fledgling graduate students participated in lively discussions. Bob has added to his former kindness by agreeing to play the role of a devil's advocate during the revision process. He has greatly sharpened my thinking and argumentation.

Dr Simon Wong and many other friends have read various parts of the manuscript and offered constructive comments. There are also individuals from whose published works I learned much, even though I did not have the privilege to learn at their feet. Gordon Fee's commentary on 1 Corinthians is a model of excellence; working through it has been a tremendous education in exegesis for me. Martin Hengel's critical and yet respectful handling of primary sources is a great inspiration for me. I am touched by his kind letters of encouragement affirming the value and significance of the present study.

It is important in research, as in all human experience, to learn from those with whom we have disagreements and to be able to disagree with those from whom we learn much. I make no apology for saying that these friends do not agree with every detail of my interpretation—the experience of this revision taught me how much even I can disagree with myself after a few years! These friends are, however, entitled to share the accolades for virtually any part of the book which is deemed successful.

Yet more than academic efforts and advice make a dissertation. The actual completion of my dissertation would not have been possible except for the spiritual and practical support of many. For their loving concern and encouragement over the years, I want to thank my parents, Luen and Kee Hop Cheung; my mother-in-law, Betty Vitayatprapaiphan; my sister, Lisa; my brothers, Jarvis and Eric; my sisters-in-law, Gina, Portia, and Gloria; and my brother-in-law, Gary. I am also deeply indebted to Christian brothers and sisters in the Chinese Presbyterian Church and other Christian friends in Sydney, Australia, for their sacrificial giving in times of severe economic recession. The Presbyterian Theological Centre (Sydney), at which I began my theological studies, has graciously offered me its first postgraduate scholarship. Westminster Theological Seminary not only provided full-tuition scholarship, but also generously paid for my external study at the Institute for Holy Land Studies in Jerusalem.

I deem it appropriate to put on record here my deep appreciation for the late Dr Raymond Dillard, Professor of Old Testament at Westminster Theological Seminary. His friendship and encouragement, and his 'be sure to look up ...' notes informing me of potentially relevant new research, will always be treasured. My exhilaration for the conclusion of my arduous dissertation research was very much subdued by his (humanly speaking) untimely death.

I would like to thank Professor Stanley Porter for accepting this work for publication in the JSNTSup series and for encouraging me to develop the relatively brief exegetical section of the dissertation. I am impressed by Sheffield Academic Press's concern for quality rather than publication schedules. The skills, thoroughness, care and efficiency of the editorial staff left me in awe. I am also deeply grateful to Mrs Jean Allen, Managing Director, for her kindness and patience as I requested to postpone the manuscript submission deadline countless times because of the pressure and constraints of having a child with developmental disabilities.

Finally, I thank my wife, Rebecca, for her support and companionship throughout the years of study and beyond. She understands, and has shared with me, the struggles of how to keep a Christian witness in a society and culture (Asia) where there are many gods and many lords. She has also experienced with me the precious promise of 1 Cor. 10.13. I dedicate this work to her.

Above all, I thank my God who has redeemed me from 'the cosmic powers of this present darkness and the spiritual forces of evil in the heavenly places'. It is also he who has given me the strength to undertake and complete this work. May his holy name be praised.

Alex Cheung
San Francisco, 1998

ABBREVIATIONS

AAR	American Academy of Religion
AB	Anchor Bible
ACW	*Ancient Christian Writers*
AFNTC	The Apostolic Fathers: A New Translation and Commentary
AGJU	Arbeiten zur Geschichte des antiken Judentums und des Urchristentums
AIIFCS	The Book of Acts in its First Century Setting
AJS Review	*Association for Jewish Studies Review*
ALGHJ	Arbeiten zur Literatur und Geschichte des hellenistischen Judentums
ANF	Anti-Nicene Fathers
ANRW	Hildegard Temporini and Wolfgang Haase (eds.), *Aufstieg und Niedergang der römischen Welt: Geschichte und Kultur Roms im Spiegel der neueren Forschung* (Berlin: W. de Gruyter, 1972–)
ANTJ	Arbeiten zum Neuen Testament und Judentum
APOT	R.H. Charles (ed.), *Apocrypha and Pseudepigrapha of the Old Testament in English* (2 vols.; Oxford: Clarendon Press, 1913)
ATR	*Anglican Theological Review*
AusBR	*Australian Biblical Review*
BAGD	Walter Bauer, William F. Arndt, F. William Gingrich and Frederick W. Danker, *A Greek–English Lexicon of the New Testament and Other Early Christian Literature* (Chicago: University of Chicago Press, 2nd edn, 1958)
BBB	Bonner biblische Beiträge
BETL	Bibliotheca ephemeridum theologicarum lovaniensium
BHT	Beiträge zur historischen Theologie
Bib	*Biblica*
BJRL	*Bulletin of the John Rylands University Library of Manchester*
BJS	Brown Judaic Studies
BR	*Bible Review*
BSac	*Bibliotheca Sacra*
BTB	*Biblical Theology Bulletin*
BZ	*Biblische Zeitschrift*
CBC	*Cambridge Bible Commentary*

CBQ	*Catholic Biblical Quarterly*
CBQMS	*Catholic Biblical Quarterly*, Monograph Series
CChr	Corpus Christianorum
CP	*Classical Philology*
CQR	*Church Quarterly Review*
CRINT	Compendia rerum iudaicarum ad Novum Testamentum
CSEL	Corpus scriptorum ecclesiasticorum latinorum
EBib	Etudes bibliques
EKKNT	Evangelisch-Katholischer Kommentar zum Neuen Testament
ETL	*Ephemerides theologicae lovanienses*
EvQ	*Evangelical Quarterly*
EvT	*Evangelische Theologie*
FC	Fathers of the Church
FRLANT	Forschungen zur Religion und Literatur des Alten und Neuen Testaments
GCS	Griechische christliche Schriftsteller
GLA	*Greek and Latin Authors on Jews and Judaism* (3 vols; ed. M. Stern; Jerusalem: Israel Academy of Sciences and Humanities, 1974–84).
GNS	Good News Studies
HDR	Harvard Dissertations in Religion
HKNT	Handkommentar zum Neuen Testament
HNT	Handbuch zum Neuen Testament
HNTC	Harper's NT Commentaries
HSM	Harvard Semitic Monographs
HTKNT	Herders theologischer Kommentar zum Neuen Testament
HTR	*Harvard Theological Review*
HTS	Harvard Theological Studies
HUCA	*Hebrew Union College Annual*
ICC	International Critical Commentary
IEJ	*Israel Exploration Journal*
Int	*Interpretation*
JAAR	*Journal of the American Academy of Religion*
JBL	*Journal of Biblical Literature*
JEH	*Journal of Ecclesiastical History*
JETS	*Journal of the Evangelical Theological Society*
JJS	*Journal of Jewish Studies*
JNSL	*Journal of Northwest Semitic Languages*
JQR	*Jewish Quarterly Review*
JR	*Journal of Religion*
JRelS	*Journal of Religious Studies*
JRH	*Journal of Religious History*
JSJ	*Journal for the Study of Judaism in the Persian, Hellenistic and Roman Period*
JSNT	*Journal for the Study of the New Testament*

JSNTSup	*Journal for the Study of the New Testament*, Supplement Series
JSOT	*Journal for the Study of the Old Testament*
JSOTSup	*Journal for the Study of the Old Testament*, Supplement Series
JSP	*Journal for the Study of the Pseudepigrapha*
JTS	*Journal of Theological Studies*
LCC	Library of Christian Classics
LCL	Loeb Classical Library
LEC	Library of Early Christianity
LPGL	G.W.H. Lampe, *A Patristic Greek Lexicon* (Oxford: Clarendon Press, 1961)
LSJ	H.G. Liddell, Robert Scott and H. Stuart Jones, *Greek–English Lexicon* (Oxford: Clarendon Press, 9th edn, 1968)
MM	J.H. Moulton and G. Milligan, *The Vocabulary of the Greek Testament*
MeyerK	H.A.W. Meyer (ed.), Kritisch-exegetischer Kommetar über das Neue Testament
NCB	New Century Bible
NEB	Neue Echter Bibel. Kommentar zum Neuen Testament mit der Einheitsübersetzung
NHC	Nag Hammadi Codex
NHL	*Nag Hammadi Library* (ed. J.M. Robinson; New York: HarperCollins, rev. edn, 1990)
NHS	Nag Hammadi Studies
NICNT	New International Commentary on the New Testament
NIGTC	The New International Greek Testament Commentary
NovT	*Novum Testamentum*
NovTSup	*Novum Testamentum*, Supplements
NPNF	Nicene and Post-Nicene Fathers
NRSV	New Revised Standard Version
NTAbh	Neutestamentliche Abhandlungen
NTApoc	E. Hennecke and W. Schneemelcher (eds.), *New Testament Apocrypha*
NTF	Neutestamentliche Forschungen
NTL	New Testament Library
NumenSup	*Numen* Supplement Series
OTP	James Charlesworth (ed.), *Old Testament Pseudepigrapha*
PG	J.-P. Migne (ed.), *Patrologia cursus completa…Series graeca* (166 vols.; Paris: Petit-Montrouge, 1857–83)
PL	J.-P. Migne (ed.), *Patrologia cursus completus…Series prima [latina]* (221 vols.; Paris: J.-P. Migne, 1844–65)
PTMS	Pittsburgh Theological Monograph Series
RB	*Revue biblique*
RevExp	*Review and Expositor*
RHR	*Revue de l'histoire des religions*

RSR	*Recherches de science religieuse*
RSV	Revised Standard Version
SBLASP	SBL Abstracts and Seminar Papers
SBLDS	SBL Dissertation Series
SBLMS	SBL Monograph Series
SBLSBS	SBL Sources for Biblical Study
SBLSP	SBL Seminar Papers
SBT	Studies in Biblical Theology
SC	Sources chrétiennes
SE	*Studia Evangelica I, II, III* (= TU 73 [1959], 87 [1964], 88 [1964], etc.)
SecCent	Second Century
SNTSMS	Society for New Testament Studies Monograph Series
SR	*Studies in Religion/Sciences religieuses*
ST	*Studia theologica*
Str–B	[Hermann L. Strack and] Paul Billerbeck, *Kommentar zum Neuen Testament aus Talmud und Midrasch* (7 vols.; Munich: Beck, 1922–61)
TDNT	Gerhard Kittel and Gerhard Friedrich (eds.), *Theological Dictionary of the New Testament* (trans. Geoffrey W. Bromiley; 10 vols.; Grand Rapids: Eerdmans, 1964–)
ThStud	*Theologische Studiën*
TLG	*Thesaurus Linguae Graecae*
TrinJ	*Trinity Journal*
TRu	*Theologische Rundschau*
TU	Texte und Untersuchungen
TynBul	*Tyndale Bulletin*
TZ	*Theologische Zeitschrift*
VC	*Vigiliae christianae*
VCSup	Supplements to *Vigiliae christianae*
VTSup	*Vetus Testamentum*, Supplements
WBC	Word Biblical Commentary
WTJ	*Westminster Theological Journal*
WUNT	Wissenschaftliche Untersuchungen zum Neuen Testament
ZNW	*Zeitschrift für die neutestamentliche Wissenschaft*

INTRODUCTION

The Issue and its Importance

For Paul, Gentile conversion to Christianity meant a turning from the worship of 'dumb idols' (1 Cor. 12.2) to the service of 'a living and true God' (1 Thess. 1.9). Nevertheless, Gentile Christians still lived in cities like Corinth, which acknowledged 'many gods and many lords' (1 Cor. 8.5). There was no way they could avoid dealing with 'idolaters' other than by leaving this world (1 Cor. 5.9-10). In particular, in view of the almost ubiquitous use of idol food in Greco-Roman social contexts, the question of the proper Christian attitude towards idol food was bound to arise.[1] The Corinthian Christians simply could not have avoided taking a stand on this issue.

This problem was not unique to Paul's Gentile converts. Long before Paul came on the scene, Jews had been living in similar pluralistic environments for centuries under Babylonian, Persian, Greek, and Roman rule. Their attitude toward idols and idol food was one of the most important expressions of their identity as the chosen people of God vis-à-vis their pagan neighbors. Indeed, going further back, the Torah had to reckon with the problem of food offered to idols as the Israelites were settling down in the Promised Land. Important and specific instructions on this issue were given lest Israel compromise its monotheistic faith.

On the other hand, other Christian communities (Jewish or Gentile) roughly contemporary to Paul also had to deal with the problem of idol food (cf. Acts 15; Rev. 2). In the sub- and post-apostolic age, it was to

---

1. Many scholars refer to εἰδωλόθυτα as idol *meat*. This has support from 1 Cor. 8.13, where Paul says that he will never eat *meat* if food causes a brother to stumble. I find this argument probable but not conclusive. Since many sorts of non-meat products like grain, wine, honey were offered to idols in ancient times, I opt for the more inclusive term idol *food*. Cf. P.D. Gooch, 'Food and the Limits of Community: I Corinthians 8 to 10' (PhD dissertation, University of Toronto, 1988), pp. 180-83.

become a burning issue—sometimes literally during periods of persecutions. As early Christians sought to establish and assert their identity in a pagan world, the prohibition of idol food functioned as a boundary marker that defined the limits of the community.

Therefore, the problem of idol food in Corinth not only has implications for our understanding of Pauline ethics, but it is also crucial to the determination of his practical and theoretical relationship with early Jewish and Christian traditions. It touches upon, *inter alia*, perennial debates such as 'how Jewish was Paul?'; 'Paul's attitude to the law'; 'the relationship between Paul and Acts'; and 'the understanding of Paul in early Christianity'. Needless to say, this issue also has a significant bearing on the modern mission field.

The State of Research

Commentators have traditionally taken Paul's discussion in 1 Corinthians 8–10 as a response to an internal problem in Corinth between the 'weak' and the 'strong' over the question of eating idol food sold in the marketplace or at social meals at idol temples. According to this common view, Paul agrees in principle with the 'strong' that the issue of idol food is an *adiaphoron*. He urges abstention from idol food only when there is the danger of causing the weak to stumble.

This view became so entrenched in modern scholarship that, until recently, there has not been much incentive for substantive scholarly work on the passage. About a decade ago, Wendell Willis observed in the introduction to his study of the problem of idol food in Corinth that 'unlike some topics in Pauline studies, the problem ... has not been the object of extensive study. Beyond the treatments in various commentaries, there is only one monograph which deals in a thorough way with these chapters, the unpublished dissertation of W.T. Sawyer.'[2]

In the intervening decade the picture has changed dramatically. The current scholarly interest in sociological and rhetorical analyses of

2.   W.L. Willis, *Idol Meat in Corinth: The Pauline Argument in 1 Corinthians 8 and 10* (SBLDS, 68; Chico, CA: Scholars Press, 1985), p. 2; W.T. Sawyer, 'The Problem of Meat Sacrificed to Idols in the Corinthian Church' (ThD dissertation, Southern Baptist Theological Seminary, 1968). Willis has apparently overlooked the dissertation of J.C. Brunt, which is more thorough and penetrating than Sawyer's in many respects ('Paul's Attitude Toward and Treatment of Problems Involving Dietary Practice: A Case Study in Pauline Ethics' [PhD dissertation, Emory University, 1978]).

Pauline letters provides much impetus for renewed study of 1 Corinthians, which is an ideal test case for such analyses. Moreover, the recent paradigm shift occasioned by the works of E.P. Sanders and others on Paul's view of the law also leads to re-examination of the evidence of 1 Corinthians, a touchstone for the understanding of Paul's practical teaching on the law.[3] As a result, a plethora of studies on 1 Corinthians 8–10 has been produced in the past decade.[4]

On the other hand, Willis's observation is still true in a major respect: in spite of the bulk of material written on many topics associated with 1 Corinthians 8–10, there is still precious little effort devoted to Paul's

---

3.   E.P. Sanders, *Paul and Palestinian Judaism: A Comparison of Patterns of Religion* (Philadelphia: Fortress Press, 1977); *idem, Paul, the Law and the Jewish People* (Philadelphia: Fortress Press, 1983). See also the collection of J.D.G. Dunn's essays in *Jesus, Paul and the Law: Studies in Mark and Galatians* (Louisville, KY: Westminster/John Knox Press, 1990).

4.   Besides the study by Willis mentioned in n. 2 above, the following significant works deal extensively with these chapters: K. Yeo, *Rhetorical Interaction in 1 Corinthians 8 and 10: A Formal Analysis with Preliminary Suggestions for a Chinese, Cross-Cultural Hermeneutic* (Biblical Interpretation Series, 9; Leiden: E.J. Brill, 1995); P.D. Gardner, *The Gifts of God and the Authentication of a Christian: An Exegetical Study of 1 Corinthians 8.1–11.1* (Lanham, MD: University Press of America, 1994); C. Heil, *Die Ablehnung der Speisegebote durch Paulus: Zur Frage nach der Stellung des Apostels zum Gesetz* (BBB, 96; Weinheim: Beltz Athenäum, 1994); P.D. Gooch, *Dangerous Food: 1 Corinthians 8–10 in its Context* (Studies in Christianity and Judaism, 5; Waterloo, ON: Wilfred Laurier University Press, 1993) (a downsized version of his doctoral dissertation, 'Food and Limits'); H. Probst, *Paulus und der Brief: Die Rhetorik des antiken Briefes als Form der paulinischen Korintherkorrespondenz (1 Kor 8–10)* (WUNT, 2.45; Tübingen: Mohr Siebeck, 1991); M.M. Mitchell, *Paul and the Rhetoric of Reconciliation: An Exegetical Investigation of the Language and Composition of 1 Corinthians* (Tübingen: Mohr-Siebeck, 1991); Tomson, *Jewish Law*; B.R. Magee, 'A Rhetorical Analysis of First Corinthians 8.1–11.1 and Romans 14.1–15.13' (ThD dissertation, New Orleans Baptist Theological Seminary, 1988); H.-J. Klauck, *Herrenmahl und hellenistischer Kult: Eine religionsgeschichtliche Untersuchung zum ersten Korintherbrief* (NTAbh, NS 15; Münster: Aschendorff, 1982); G. Theissen, *The Social Setting of Pauline Christianity: Essays on Corinth* (Philadelphia: Fortress Press, 1982). The issue of idol food is also treated in great detail in major commentaries such as W. Schrage, *Der erste Brief an die Korinther* II. *1Kor 6,12–11,16* (EKKNT, 7.2; Zürich: Benziger Verlag, 1995), pp. 211-486, and G.D. Fee, *The First Epistle to the Corinthians* (Grand Rapids: Eerdmans, 1987), pp. 357-491. In addition, numerous articles have been written recently on various aspects and sections of 1 Cor. 8–10.

approach to the problem of idol food as a concrete historical issue. I cannot help having the nagging feeling that because idol food is not an issue in much of the history of Western society, many scholars simply see the problem of idol food per se as a historical curiosity, of interest only because of the perennial ethical principles derivable from Paul's discussion of it.

Since our exegesis cannot be separated from our own historicality, I make this observation as a statement of fact rather than as a wholesale condemnation of the works of previous scholars. Our own historicality entails that the very questions we ask (or fail to ask) of a text, and the answers we expect from it, are determined by our present concern and the cultural baggage we carry. Indeed, without concern for present application, many people would find little reason for exegeting a text at all. Nevertheless, while our exegesis is not necessarily invalidated by our historicality, our hermeneutical self-consciousness must be heightened because of it.

Most scholars are not so interested in the rightness or wrongness of the act of eating idol food as in the question of Christian freedom—a subsidiary concern in the text but a major concern for modern Westerners. The text of 1 Corinthians 8–10, which ostensibly deals with the concrete historical issue of idol food, has been approached with a view to extracting or developing the principles that underlie Paul's response.[5] The implicit assumption is that the value of Paul's discussion lies in its perennial ethical principles about Christian freedom rather than its concrete solution to the pressing social problem of idol food in early Christianity. Murphy-O'Connor surely speaks for many:

> The problem of the legitimacy of the eating of meat which had formed pagan sacrifices is, in itself, of *very limited interest.* Paul's treatment is of perennial value because he saw that fundamental principles were involved. The way in which the issue was raised forced him to deal with such basic questions as the nature of Christian freedom, the place of the believer in non-Christian society, and the education of conscience.[6]

5.   I am not disputing the value of such an approach. Many fine ethical conclusions are drawn from it. But most of these conclusions can be drawn from a similar study of Rom. 14–15 as well. My point is that while 1 Cor. 8–10 has been a very significant passage for the discussion of Christian ethics, there has not been enough research on the passage investigating the issue of idol food in terms of idolatry.

6.   J. Murphy-O'Connor, 'Freedom or the Ghetto (1 Cor. viii, 1-13; x, 23-xi.1)', *RB* 85 (1978), pp. 543-74 (543) (emphasis added; note the suggestive title of the article).

Likewise, Brunt asserts: 'Paul's basic concern is much more complex than the "rightness" or "wrongness" of certain actions... Paul is much less concerned with action as such than he is with *the way actions affect others*. The important themes of freedom, the priority of love, concern for the weaker brother, etc., all have to do with this central concern.'[7] Such an emphasis on ethics rather than the problem of idolatry informs most of the earlier scholarly literature on 1 Corinthians 8–10.[8]

While recent sociological and rhetorical analyses of 1 Corinthians 8–10 have produced much that is illuminating, the same lack of interest in idol food as a concrete historical problem can be discerned. The passage is often explored first and foremost as an illustration for certain sociological models or rhetorical techniques. The main outline of the traditional interpretation of the passage is usually assumed at the outset and is, not surprisingly, largely confirmed by the analyses. In particular, the traditional understanding of Paul's attitude toward idol food is seldom challenged. In view of the descriptive nature of such methods and the limited amount of data available for analysis, this phenomenon is not necessarily to be deplored. However, without the concomitant exegetical and historical re-examination of specific sources, such analyses may have merely put new packaging on a traditional interpretation that is fundamentally flawed.[9]

General Remarks on the Inadequacies of the Traditional View

In Chapter 3 I will address the traditional view and its variations in detail. Here I will simply make some general remarks on the inadequacies of the traditional understanding of Paul's approach. I find it disturbing that many commentators, while reconstructing the historical situation in Corinth with some plausibility and tackling the exegetical

7. Brunt, 'Paul's Attitude', p. 311.

8. The classic expression of such an emphasis is H.F. von Soden's 'Sakrament und Ethik bei Paulus: Zur Frage der literarischen und theologischen Einheitlichkeit von 1 Kor. 8–10', in H. von Campenhausen (ed.), *Urchristentum und Geschichte: Gesammelte Aufsätze und Vorträge* (2 vols.; Tübingen: Mohr-Siebeck, 1951–56), I, pp. 239-75.

9. Convinced as I am that much scholarly work on 1 Cor. 8–10 is not motivated by concerns to tackle the concrete problem of the rightness or wrongness of eating idol food, I feel that a discussion of the various approaches to the subject is best postponed until my own interpretation is fully presented. I critique some major studies on 1 Cor. 8–10 in the Appendix to this volume.

issues in great detail, give no or only minimal attention to the implications of their exegetical results for Paul's relationship with early Jewish and Christian traditions. As a result, their exegeses are often abstracted from Paul's Jewish background and from the broader context of early Christianity. For example, in his generally excellent commentary on 1 Corinthians, Fee admits in a footnote that 'Paul's response on this question makes his own relationship to the Decree a matter of some historical difficulty',[10] but does not explore that relationship in any detail.

Scholars who do study 1 Corinthians 8–10 in the broader context of early Judaism and Christianity almost invariably regard Paul's approach (as usually understood) as a singularity or anomaly. Paul's apparent disregard for Jewish sensibility concerning idol food leads Barrett to assert that 'in the matter of εἰδωλόθυτα... Paul was not a practising Jew'.[11] While Barrett does not deny that 'Paul's thought continued to work within a rabbinic framework', he argues on the basis of Paul's attitude toward idol food that the emphasis of Davies and others on Paul's essential Jewishness is unjustified.[12] By contrasting Paul's rule that anything sold at the market can be eaten without inquiring (1 Cor. 10.25) with 'the repeated investigations διὰ τὴν συνείδησιν that were incumbent upon the devout Jew', Barrett concludes that 'Paul is nowhere more un-Jewish than in this μηδὲν ἀνακρίνοντες'.[13]

Tomson notes that Barrett's assessment of Paul's approach to idol food represents a near-consensus of New Testament scholarship.[14] Paul's ideological position on idol food is seen as a clear indication of his radical liberation from his Jewish past. This understanding seems to cohere with an emphasis on justification by faith alone apart from the

10. Fee, *The First Epistle to the Corinthians*, p. 360 n. 10.

11. C.K. Barrett, 'Things Sacrificed to Idols', in *idem*, *Essays on Paul* (Philadelphia: Westminster Press, 1982), pp. 40-59 (50).

12. Barrett, 'Things Sacrificed', p. 51; W.D. Davies, *Paul and Rabbinic Judaism* (Philadelphia: Fortress Press, 4th edn, 1980 [1948]).

13. Barrett, 'Things Sacrificed', p. 49. As Brunt points out, even Davies, who emphasizes Paul's Jewishness, shies away from discussing Paul's attitude toward idol food: while Davies 'makes literally hundreds of references to Paul's letters, he...never mentions Rom. 14.23 or 1 Cor. 10.25, never discusses 1 Cor. 8.7-13, refers to Rom. 14.14 only once...and refers to 1 Cor. 10.27 only in a foot note...in the course of arguing that Paul probably did not know the Apostolic Decree' ('Paul's Attitude', p. 250 n. 1).

14. Tomson, *Jewish Law*, p. 187.

law. Apparently, it is also consistent with Paul's determination to eliminate boundaries separating Jews and Gentiles.

But there is a fundamental problem that refuses to go away: if Barrett's assessment is correct, Paul's handling of the problem of idol food would be unique not only vis-à-vis Judaism in the Hellenistic era, but also vis-à-vis early Christianity, for 'all other extant sources in early Christianity which discuss the issue oppose idol meat'.[15] Barrett himself admits that 'if...we set aside the Pauline material it appears that the eating of εἰδωλόθυτα was reprobated in the strongest possible terms...this attitude persisted in the primitive Church for centuries'.[16] This raises a serious historical problem: if Paul did condone eating idol food—a practice vehemently, and almost universally, condemned by Christians and Jews alike—he would have been the first, and in effect the only, early Christian authority to do so.[17] Apart from pure ignorance and misunderstanding, how could such a singularity exist? More incomprehensible is how the universal Christian prohibition of idol food—a 'triumph of Jewish Christianity' according to Barrett—could have arisen in a context where 'Jewish Christians became less important in the church'![18]

It is arguable that Paul's discussion of the issue of Jewish food laws in Romans 14 contributes largely to the above anomaly. Influenced by Paul's highly conciliatory approach in Romans 14 in maintaining the unity of Jewish and Gentile Christians, scholars tend to explain Paul's handling of the problem of idol food in terms of his masterful mediation between the 'strong' and the 'weak'. By allowing Paul's discussion of Jewish food laws in Romans 14 to dominate their

15. J.C. Brunt, 'Rejected, Ignored, or Misunderstood? The Fate of Paul's Approach to the Problem of Food Offered to Idols in Early Christianity', *NTS* 31 (1985), pp. 113-24 (120).

16. Barrett, 'Things Sacrificed', p. 43. A.F. Segal also points out that 'throughout early church history, the dominant position is more like the Didache or the Apostolic Decree than Paul's ideological position' (*Paul the Convert: The Apostolate and Apostasy of Saul the Pharisee* [New Haven: Yale University Press, 1990], p. 236). Brunt suggests that Paul's approach was first ignored and then misunderstood by early Christians ('Rejected', pp. 113-24).

17. Tomson, *Jewish Law*, p. 185. Tomson comments that if the traditional understanding of Paul's attitude towards idol food is correct, then 'indeed it would have been a miracle, resulting from pure misunderstanding, that First Corinthians was preserved at all by the early Church in its extant form'.

18. Barrett, 'Things Sacrificed', p. 56.

understanding of 1 Corinthians 8–10, insufficient attention is paid to the distinctive context of the latter. Thus, Brunt suggests in his dissertation that 'the overall thrust of both passages is the same'.[19] Sawyer goes even further to argue that the 'weak' in 1 Corinthians 8 were Jewish Christians.[20] The problem of idol food in Corinth is regarded as only a part of a general struggle in the early church between the freedom allowed by the Pauline gospel and the legalism of some 'Judaizing' Christians who opposed such freedom.

While it is true that in both letters Paul does advocate a similar principle of not causing fellow Christians to stumble, such blurring of his treatments of the two distinct issues is most unfortunate. It totally overlooks the strong contrast between the highly conciliatory tone of Romans 14 and Paul's combative style in 1 Corinthians 8–10. It also pays no attention to the fact that the Apostolic Decree in Acts 15 that prohibited idol food came *after* Peter's vision in Acts 10–11 which had already rejected the validity of Jewish food laws insofar as it created a barrier between Jewish and Gentile Christians. Evidently, the distinction between Jewish dietary laws and the idol food prohibition was made very early.

Willis's dissertation rightly sees that 1 Corinthians 8–10 does not reflect a debate over Jewish dietary laws. But, unfortunately, he draws the unwarranted conclusion that the relevance of Jewish laws about food is minimal in comparison with 'the very significant Hellenistic background'.[21] He also fails to write a single word on the early Christian attitude toward idol food and how it compared to Paul's own attitude.

In his impressive study on the role of Jewish halakha in Paul's thinking, Peter Tomson includes a substantive treatment of 1 Corinthians 8–10 which strongly challenges the traditional interpretation.[22] By affirming Paul's essential Jewishness and assuming that Paul operates within a halakhic framework, he comes to the conclusion that Paul 'does not teach a partial permission to eat idol food. He teaches a

19. Brunt, 'Paul's Attitude', p. 183.

20. Sawyer, 'Meat Sacrificed', pp. 122-40. However, despite Sawyer's ingenious justification of his interpretation by literary and structural arguments, 1 Cor. 8.7 makes it an impossible interpretation: how could Paul describe a Jew as 'accustomed to idols until now'?

21. Willis, *Idol Meat*, p. 3.

22. Tomson, *Jewish Law*, pp. 151-220.

rational, halakhic definition of what should be considered an idol offering in uncertain cases and what should not.'[23] If Tomson's understanding is correct, then Paul's approach to the problem of idol food would be consistent with Acts, Revelation, and other early Christian traditions, not to mention Jewish traditions. Whether or not Tomson has proven his thesis is, of course, a matter for debate; that he has marshaled impressive evidence in support of his conclusions is certain.

The traditional view is also challenged independently by Peter Gooch from completely different premises.[24] After analyzing massive archaeological and literary data and ascertaining the concrete settings and social meaning of idol food in Corinth at the time of Paul, he asks and answers very specific social-historical questions such as 'what was idol food?' and 'for whom was it a problem?' He concludes that, in Paul's Corinth, it is highly improbable that eating social meals in temples would be perceived in any other way than taking part in idolatry. Paul's prohibition against eating idol food on the grounds that it might harm the weak is only the first stage of his argument dissuading the Corinthian Christians from eating idol food. Based on his self-understanding as a Jew, Paul at root considered idol food dangerous and therefore urged avoidance of any food infected by non-Christian religious rites. In this way Paul's attitude toward idol food is reconciled to early Jewish and Christian views.

The Objective and Scope of my Study

I have made the common-sense assumption that Paul's attitude toward idol food is to be understood in its historical context. This means that Paul's discussion in 1 Corinthians 8–10 cannot be treated in isolation from his social, historical, and literary environment. The historical Paul is far more than his extant letters, which preserve only fragments of Paul. Even those letters we have must be understood as occasional literature, called forth by specific needs of specific Christian communities in situations often polemical. They do not readily reveal the non-polemical Paul or those aspects of his preaching that other Christian authorities found unobjectionable. Therefore an adequate assessment of Paul's position concerning idol food demands not only a reconstruction of the occasion of 1 Corinthians 8–10 (in the sense of what had

23. Tomson, *Jewish Law*, p. 217.
24. Gooch, 'Food and Limits'.

happened between Paul and the Corinthian Christians), and an under-standing of the concrete social context of idol food in the Hellenistic era, a sympathetic investigation of Paul's Jewish background, which possibly informed his approach, but also an effort to situate Paul within the spectrum of other early Christian material as part of the context for the illumination or determination of his attitude.

Accordingly, my investigation begins with an examination of the social meaning of idol food in the Hellenistic era. I will discuss the relationship between idol food and idolatry, the occasions for eating idol food, the social significance of meals, and the consequences for avoiding idol food. In view of Gooch's thorough analysis of literary and archaeological sources concerning such topics, this chapter will be brief.

Chapter 2 surveys a wide range of Jewish material on idolatry and idol food, in relation to the broader issue of the sociological balance of assimilation and resistance in maintaining Jewish identity in pagan environments. I will examine the Jewish Scriptures, the apocryphal and pseudepigraphical literature, Qumran, Philo, Josephus, rabbinic writings, as well as comments on Jewish attitudes by Greco-Roman authors. Some implications for our understanding of Paul's attitude toward idol food will be drawn from the results of the survey.

The third chapter consists of an exegetical investigation of the internal evidence of 1 Corinthians 8–10 for Paul's approach to idol food. After examining the traditional view and its variations in detail and setting forth arguments against them, I will present my own understanding of Paul's attitude toward idol food and tackle the key exegetical issues.

As Paul was *both* a Christian and a Jew, his approach to idol food must be seen in relation to early Christian traditions as well as his Jewish background. Therefore in the fourth and the lengthiest chapter, I will undertake an exhaustive examination of the early Christians' attitudes toward idol food and especially their understanding of Paul's own attitude. I will discuss pertinent New Testament passages and early Christian ('orthodox' or otherwise) documents. I want to see whether and how early Christian writers referred to, and understood, Paul's discussion. In particular I want to find out whether there is any evidence for the traditional view. My interest is not whether early Christians objected to the traditional interpretation of Paul's approach, but whether they were aware of such an interpretation at all. I also want to test the validity of the hypothesis that a distinction was made in early

Christianity between Jewish food laws and the idol food prohibition. If this hypothesis can be validated, it would give us reason to believe that Paul indeed treated the two issues differently.

The final chapter summarizes my conclusions and offers some hermeneutical reflections. In an appendix, I will interact in some depth with a number of major studies on 1 Corinthians 8–10.

Chapter 1

THE SOCIAL MEANING OF EATING IDOL FOOD

The fact of religious pluralism in Roman Corinth, borne out by extensive literary and archaeological evidence, is entirely uncontroversial.[1] Despite criticism by a handful of philosophers, sacrifices to pagan gods were widely practised. The importance of the issue of idol food becomes evident when one realizes the pervasive nature of pagan sacrifices in Greco-Roman society. MacMullen notes that

> For most people, to have a good time with their friends involved some contact with a god who served as guest of honor…meat was a thing never eaten and wine to surfeit never drunk save as some religious setting permitted. There existed—it is no exaggeration to say it of all but the fairly rich—no formal social life…that was entirely secular.[2]

It is generally agreed that many of these sacrifices were eaten by the worshipers, at the cultic sites or outside them. On the other hand, the role of food and dining in the cults is far from clear. Unhappy with the way commentators draw broad conclusions about the social significance of idol food from only a few literary sources,[3] Peter Gooch has

1.   For a detailed catalogue of pagan religions in Corinth, see R. Lisle, 'Cults of Corinth' (PhD dissertation, John Hopkins University, 1955), pp. 99-125. For a brief profile of religious pluralism in Corinth (and bibliography for major works), see B.W. Winter, 'Theological and Ethical Responses to Religious Pluralism: 1 Corinthians 8–10', *TynBul* 41 (1990), pp. 209-25 (210-15).

2.   R. MacMullen, *Paganism in the Roman Empire* (New Haven: Yale University Press, 1981), p. 40. See pp. 34-42 for a general description of the connections between eating and religious expression in the Roman period.

3.   Gooch, 'Food and Limits', pp. 2-4, esp. n. 5. Willis and Klauck are significant exceptions in that they pay considerable attention to the nature of cultic meals as reflected in a wide variety of sources (Willis, *Idol Meat*, pp. 21-61; Klauck, *Herrenmahl*, pp. 31-166). However, Willis's work is too much dictated by the agenda set by earlier scholarship. He approaches the sources with a narrow focus to determine whether cultic meals are sacramental or secular in character. But

analyzed extensive amounts of archaeological and literary data, with
specific focus on the nature and social meaning of idol food in Corinth
around Paul's time. Here I can do no better than refer the reader to his
pertinent findings.[4]

1. *The Nature and Occasions of Eating Idol Food*

a. *The Connection between Meals and Temples in Roman Corinth*
Whereas the sanctuaries of Apollo and Aphrodite were perhaps the
most impressive temples in ancient Corinth, the sanctuary of Demeter
and Kore on Acrocorinth is the natural place to begin our discussion, in
view of the large number of dining rooms excavated within its
precincts. After surveying the evidence concerning food in the cultus of
Demeter and Kore, Gooch concludes that the consumption of food was
not the central rite: 'the layout of the Sanctuary, with the dining rooms
on the lowest, least hallowed terrace, suggested that eating was not the
most important rite in the cultus practised there'.[5] On the other hand,
the sheer extent of the dining facilities in the Sanctuary indicates that
the consumption of sacrificed food was an integral and probably important part of the cultus.[6] 'To eat from the *kernos* in the Sanctuary of
Demeter, or to share in pork from a sacrifice offered to her, or to eat a
cake representing the fertility brought by Demeter would be to eat food
sacred to Demeter, and to share in the rites of her worship'.[7] Such eating would certainly qualify for what Paul would call τραπέζης
δαιμονίων μετέχειν (1 Cor. 10.21), for 'how could one eat in Demeter's Sanctuary and not remember, or be reminded by word or symbol
or ritual act, that the fruit of the fertile ground was her gift?'[8] Similar
conclusions can also be reached on the basis of evidence from Eleusis.
The two sets of evidence are thus mutually supporting.[9]

the imposition of such modern categories on the sources flattens the multidimen-
sional nature of the meals. Klauck does not directly address the social meaning of
idol food in the Greco-Roman world; he discusses the significance of pagan cultic
meals only to the extent they bear on the origins of the Lord's Supper.

4.   Gooch, 'Food and Limits', pp. 15-160. The following discussion is largely
based on the coverage of material presented in Gooch's study.

5.   Gooch, 'Food and Limits', p. 68.

6.   Gooch, 'Food and Limits', pp. 23-63.

7.   Gooch, 'Food and Limits', p. 69.

8.   Gooch, 'Food and Limits', p. 69.

9.   Gooch, 'Food and Limits', pp. 68-69.

However, the association between food and cultus was not always so plain in Paul's Corinth.[10] For example, the dining rooms of Lerna stood in a very ambiguous relationship with the adjacent Sanctuary of Asklepios.[11] It is clear that the association of the dining rooms of Lerna with the cultus of Asklepios is qualitatively different from that of the dining rooms in the Sanctuary of Demeter with that cultus. Roebuck concludes in his excavation report that the dining rooms of Lerna probably played no cultic role in the Asklepieion. Neither architecturally nor functionally related to the Sanctuary, they were probably a mere extension of the recreational function of the fountain of Lerna.[12]

On the other hand, since there was a clear association of water with the cultus of Asklepios, Lerna, being a fountain, was probably perceived by many as part of the Asklepieion. Vitruvius writes:

> For all temples there shall be chosen the most healthy sites with suitable springs...and especially for Asclepius... For when sick persons are moved from a pestilent to a healthy place and the water supply is from wholesome fountains, they will more quickly recover. So will it happen that the divinity (from the nature of the site) will gain a greater and higher reputation and authority (*On Architecture*, 1.2.7).[13]

One cannot overlook the importance of water in connection with healing in the cultus. As Gooch observes, virtually all sanctuaries of Asklepios were found near springs or wells. Since there were no other springs or fountains on the level of the *abaton* in Corinth, it raises the likelihood that, contrary to the suggestion of the excavation report,

10. Gooch, 'Food and Limits', p. 71-106.

11. Gooch's survey of the archaeological data about the Asklepieion and Lerna is largely based on C.A. Roebuck, *Corinth: Results of excavations conducted by the American School of Classical Studies in Athens*. XIV. *The Asklepieion and Lerna* (Princeton, NJ: American School of Classical Studies in Athens, 1951) and the summary of Roebuck's report in Mabel Lang, *Cure and Cult in Ancient Corinth: A Guide to the Asklepieion* (American Excavations in Old Corinth, Corinth Notes, 1; Princeton, NJ: American School of Classical Studies in Athens, 1977).

12. Roebuck, *Corinth*, XIV, pp. 24-26. Roebuck notes that the dining rooms were not easily accessible from the precinct for cult officials. Gooch also points out that in Pausanias's account (*Description of Greece* 2.4.5), Lerna is described not in conjunction with the sanctuary but in conjunction with the gymnasium ('Food and Limits', p. 107). However, Gooch thinks that there was still a clear link between the dining rooms of Lerna and the Sanctuary. See below.

13. Cited in J. Murphy-O'Connor, *St Paul's Corinth: Texts and Archaeology* (GNS, 6; Wilmington, DE: Michael Glazier, 1983), p. 162.

Lerna was closely associated with the Sanctuary of Asklepios in Corinth.[14]

Moreover, both the accessibility of the dining rooms to the Sanctuary, and the frequent use of these dining rooms by visitors to the Sanctuary, would have made the connection between Lerna and the Asklepieion an easy one to draw. Thus there might well have been an ambiguity concerning the religious status of these rooms in the eyes of the Corinthian Christians.[15] Gooch observes:

> The ambiguity of the status of Lerna—a public fountain and place of relaxation, and yet associated with the Asklepieion—might lead very easily to difficulties of interpretation among the group of Christians in Corinth. If there were Christians who were worried by any contact with other Gods and Lords, these might well find the dining rooms of Lerna too strongly associated with the Sanctuary of Asklepios. Yet the ambiguity of the status of Lerna would provide support to any Christians who found it desirable to eat there and wished to defend the practice (even if they accepted the premises of the first group, let alone if they rejected those premises). Even if there was unanimity concerning the wrongfulness of sharing in the table of demons, the dining rooms of Lerna would present an awkward case.[16]

The relation of the banqueting hall to the Sanctuary of Asklepios in Epidauros is also illustrative of the ambiguous status of the dining rooms.[17] The construction of the Sanctuary, which took place over more than a century, was undertaken only when funds were available.

---

14. Gooch, 'Food and Limits', p. 83.

15. Similar ambiguities can be found even today in the dining facilities adjacent to Buddhist or Taoist temples in Asia. Sometimes no formal or conscious worship is involved, and the food served there may not even be sacred food, yet the very location of the dining facilities inevitably confers a distinct religious flavor on all the meals. There is no doubt in the mind of most diners that they are having a 'sacred' rather than an ordinary meal. Therefore, while a dining facility is not an integral part of the temple, its relation to the temple puts a clear religious stamp, at least in the diners' perception, on meals served there.

16. Gooch, 'Food and Limits', p. 108. Murphy-O'Connor also makes similar but less developed arguments concerning the ambiguous religious status of the dining rooms of Lerna and its awkward implications (*Corinth*, pp. 162-65).

17. Gooch, 'Food and Limits', pp. 88-89. Gooch refers to R.A. Tomlinson, *Epidauros* (Archaeological Sites; London: Granada, 1983), pp. 27-29; and A. Burford, *The Greek Temple Builders at Epidauros* (Toronto: University of Toronto Press, 1969).

The sequence of construction thus indicates the relative importance of the various buildings in the Sanctuary to the cult and its worshippers. It is therefore highly significant that the dining hall was not built until the completion of all the various temples in the Sanctuary, the *abaton*, the athletic buildings, the Theater, and even the hostel for the accommodation of visitors! On the other hand, the sheer size and the quality of decorations, the elaborate entrance to the building, and the careful maintenance all suggest its importance in the Sanctuary.

Banqueting halls near other sanctuaries also give indications that they were not of central importance.[18] It is not even clear that all Asklepieia had banqueting rooms. The conclusion is inevitable: 'dining rooms were not integral to the performance of the cultus of Asklepios or necessary to those persons seeking the salvation of the God'.[19] Nevertheless, once dining rooms were built, they assumed considerable importance. They were clearly associated with the sanctuaries and were *perceived* as religiously significant in the popular mind.

Inasmuch as there was considerable ambiguity concerning the status of these dining facilities in relation to the sanctuaries, the religious import of dining in such facilities seemed to be different from that of cultic eating in the Sanctuary of Demeter and Kore, where the meal was integral to the cultus. The possibility of eating meals in a temple which were not necessarily connected to religious rites carried out there might underlie the apparent distinction Paul made between eating in an idol's temple and participating at the table of demons (8.10 and 10.21), as Paul seemed to provide distinct assessments of these: the table of demons is to be shunned, but eating in an idol's temple is to be avoided for the sake of the weak.[20] Indeed these two distinct contexts of eating might confirm what many interpreters posit (with little supporting evidence) in their attempts to resolve the apparent contradiction between

18. Banqueting halls were built after the completion of the main buildings of the sanctuaries (Athens), and set either outside the *temenos* (Athens, Corinth), or on its edge (Troizen). See Gooch, 'Food and Limits', p. 95.

19. Gooch, 'Food and Limits', p. 94.

20. Gooch raises this possibility but then rejects it after considering all the evidence. He concludes that an objective separation between meals eaten in an idol's temple and meals involving idolatrous rites was highly improbable in Paul's Corinth. Even if there was such a distinction in the mind of some, the distinction would not have been perceived by Paul himself ('Food and Limits', pp. 79-80, 242-45).

the attitudes of Paul expressed in 1 Cor. 8.1-13 and 10.1-22.[21] I will address this possibility later in the chapter.

b. *Where Was Sacrificed Food Eaten?*

Three broad categories of use of sacrificed food can be discerned in the literary and inscriptional sources and the archaeological evidence: the priestly portion, sacred food consumed by worshipers within the sanctuary, and sacred food consumed outside the sanctuary.[22]

The first two categories need not concern us, as they were clearly examples of partaking of the table of demons. The third category, however, is relevant to an understanding of Paul's discussion and will be discussed briefly.

The testimony of Pausanias concerning Epidauros and Titane and the inscription from Athens indicate that in these places sacrificed meat was not permitted to be removed from the sanctuary.[23] This prohibition perhaps reflected the idea that the food was still regarded as sacred after the rites and thus was not allowed to be removed from sacred places.

But in some other contexts sacred food could be and was removed. The most explicit evidence of this is found in one of the mimes of Herondas, *Women at the Temple*: In a scene at an Asklepieion, Kynno brings a rooster in thanksgiving for a cure (*Mime* 4.19), and, after a prayer, says to her companion Kokkale:[24]

> Carve a drumstick for [the priest], and give the snake a morsel, quietly, in sacred silence, there on the altar. We'll eat, don't forget, the rest at home. [To the priest] Stay well, my fellow. Here now, have some bread. We'll begin with you, close to the god, in passing it around on the way home (*Mime* 4.88-95).

---

21. For example, R.E. Oster, Jr, claims that 'when the modern exegete investigates and compares the counsel of Paul in 1 Cor. 8 with 10,1-22 he need no longer bemoan that 'Paul's argument appears to vacillate'... The dining facilities at Corinth provide architectural evidence for a situation in which "monotheistic" believers...could attend and participate in activities indigenous to their religio-cultural matrix but which did not require overt participation in the central *cultus* and sacrifices of the religion itself' ('Use, Misuse and Neglect of Archaeological Evidence in Some Modern Works on 1 Corinthians [1 Cor. 7, 1-5; 8, 10; 11, 2-16; 12, 14-26]', *ZNW* 83 [1992], pp. 52-73 [66-67]).

22. Gooch, 'Food and Limits', p. 99.

23. Gooch, 'Food and Limits', p. 103.

24. Herondas, *The Mimes of Herondas* (trans. Guy Davenport; San Francisco: Grey Fox, 1981), p. 23.

This passage indicates explicitly that sacrificial food could be shared with the priest in the precinct and with others that the worshiper might meet outside the precinct, and it could be consumed at home. There was no thought, however, that the food was somehow desecrated after being removed from the temple. On the contrary, the food was clearly regarded as special and sacred.[25]

c. *Idol Food in Social Meals at Private Homes*[26]

Gooch observes that the typical main meal, whether of the rich or of the poor, normally included not only food but also, whenever possible, songs and stories which often had clear religious overtones.[27]

As for the meals themselves, it is probable that not every meal involved the consumption of food used in religious rites. In the literature surveyed, meals are often mentioned without any overt or implicit reference to sacrifice or rites.[28]

On the other hand, there are also many references to meals in private homes which included sacrificed food, especially on occasions of social significance, such as weddings, birthdays, funerals, the visits of returning friends or important persons, religious holidays, and occasions of thanksgiving. Gooch emphasizes that these meals were both religious and social:

> Meals involving sacrifice in private homes were not occasions focussing exclusively on high religious ritual and demanding solemn religious dedication from participants, but they also were not simple common meals bracketed by habitual, formal and essentially empty rites. Rather they

25. This phenomenon is strongly analogous to the distribution of sacrificed food following the conclusion of important religious or social occasions in Asia. Those who receive portions of the sacred food treasure them as such. 'This is sacrificed food', my mother used to point out to me.

26. Gooch has carried out an extensive survey of literature dated from c. 200 BCE to c. 200 CE concerning social meals ('Food and Limits', pp. 113-60). Gooch's virtually exhaustive survey is limited only by the time period specified and by genre. He focuses his attention on biography, letters, romances and drama, which deal often with habits of social interaction in telling detail. He also includes sources that loosely might be called philosophical but which include materials that provide glimpses of table practices and the social significance of shared meals, such as Plutarch's *Convivial Questions*.

27. Gooch, 'Food and Limits', pp. 120-23. Cf. D.E. Smith's brief description of the typical courses and entertainment at a communal meal or banquet ('Meals and Morality in Paul and his World', *SBLSP* 20 [1981], pp. 319-39 [319-21]).

28. Gooch, 'Food and Limits', p. 124.

seem often to be meals of some social importance ... They are meals where quantities are eaten, wine flows free, and conviviality reigns—true meals and not simply ritual events. At the same time, the rites performed over the food were of significance: just as the occasions called for serious eating, they also called for authentic thanksgiving to the Gods.[29]

It would be a mistake to think that sacrificed food was consumed only in important occasions. Religious rites could be performed over 'any meal considered special, even if its special character derived simply from its occasion of good cheer among friends'.[30] In his *Convivial Questions*, Plutarch writes: 'Most of the dinners [at which the table-talk he records took place] were portion-banquets, and each man at the sacrifices was allotted his share of the meal' (*Quest. Conv.* 642F). In Horace's description of a meal when friends arrived or 'neighbors dropped in for a friendly visit on a wet day', host and guests would share a meal and play drinking games, 'and Ceres, receiving our prayer that she would rise high on the stalk, allowed the wine to smooth away our worried wrinkles' (*Satire* 2.2, lines 115-25). In all probability such a prayer would be accompanied by a libation or offering which would hallow the food and drink.[31] A more explicit reference to offering at meals is found in Horace's description of a meal which is remarkable for its simplicity and lack of social pretension: 'Ah, those evenings and dinners. What heaven! My friends and I have our own meal at my fireside. Then, after making an offering, I hand the rest to the cheeky servants' (*Satire* 2.6, lines 65-66).

Thus it is clear that, on whatever occasions friends met to eat, some oblation could readily occur to hallow the meal and the event.[32] Incidentally, this shows that the assumption of the Mishnah that a Gentile is always ready 'to contaminate the wine through idolatry, if he gets the chance', is not the result of xenophobic paranoia, but reflects typical Gentile practices.[33] This fear of the rabbis is indicative of the frequency of religious rites performed over meals by Gentiles.

29. Gooch, 'Food and Limits', p. 125.
30. Gooch, 'Food and Limits', p. 159.
31. Gooch, 'Food and Limits', p. 136.
32. Gooch, 'Food and Limits', pp. 136-37.
33. J. Neusner, *Judaism: The Evidence of the Mishnah* (Atlanta: Scholars Press, 1988), p. 202. Neusner does not give any rabbinic reference. Presumably, he is thinking of *m. 'Abod. Zar.* 5.5: 'If an Israelite was eating with a Gentile at a table, and, leaving in his presence a flagon [of wine] on the table...left him and went out, what is on the table is forbidden'.

2. *The Social Significance of Meals*

Meals in Greco-Roman society were a central focus of social intercourse. Not only was food a significant marker of social status, but dining was also the primary means for social advancement in winning favors and benefits from one's superiors. Thus Epictetus disapproves of social climbing through grasping for invitations for meals: 'You have not been invited to somebody's dinner party? Of course not; for you did not give the host the price at which he sells his dinner. He sells it for praise; he sells it for personal attention.'[34] Conversely, an effective way to retain control over another person is to 'give him all he wants to eat and drink every day, and he will never try to run away... The bonds of food and drink are very elastic, you know: the more you stretch them, the tighter they hold you.'[35]

Shared meals were also expressions of friendship. Plutarch refers to the 'friend-making character of the dining table' (*Quest. Conv.* 612D). Some claim that 'the drinking party is a passing of time over wine which, guided by gracious behavior, ends in friendship' (*Quest. Conv.* 621C). In a discussion of etymologies, one of Plutarch's characters comments: 'they say that *cena* has its name from κοινωνία' (*Quest. Conv.* 726E). In the same vein Lucian observes:

> nobody invites an enemy or unknown person to dinner; not even a slight acquaintance. A man must first, I take it, become a friend in order to share another's bowl and board [τράπεζα]... I have often heard people say: 'How much of a friend is he, when he has neither eaten or drunk with us?'[36]

As shared meals were the primary means of social intercourse and an important means of social advancement, so refusal of a meal or part of a meal was to give offense. Thus Epictetus advises: 'Now when we have been invited to a banquet, we take what is set before us; and if a person should bid his host to set before him fish or cakes, he would be regarded as eccentric [ἄτοπος]'.[37] Similarly, Seneca thinks that the ascetic diet (among other eccentric behaviors) of some philosophers

34. Epictetus, *Encheiridion* 25.4-5.
35. Plautus, *Twin Menaechmi* Act 1, Scene 1, lines 90-95.
36. Lucian, *Parasite* 22.
37. Epictetus, *Fragment* 17. Note Paul's instruction in 1 Cor. 10.27: 'If an unbeliever invites you ... eat whatever is set before you'.

would 'earn only hostility and ridicule' from the common people: 'The first thing philosophy promises us is the feeling of fellowship, of belonging to mankind and being members of a community; being different will mean the abandoning of that manifesto'.[38]

3. *Some Implications for the Problem of Idol Food in Corinth*

a. *Is it Possible to 'Eat in an Idol's Temple' and not Be Involved in Idolatry?*

I have earlier raised the possibility of whether meals could be eaten ἐν εἰδωλείῳ without τραπέζης δαιμονίων μετέχειν (p. 31). Gooch's survey of the use of sacred food in the Greco-Roman world allows a thorough answer to this question which is not available to earlier commentators.

On first impression, the ambiguous religious status of the dining rooms of Lerna in relation to the Asklepieion does lend support to this possibility. Moreover, Willis has shown convincingly the essentially social purpose of many meals where religious rites were performed.[39] This would add weight to the argument that some meals in temples were only nominally connected to idolatry, and then not in any material way.

The totality of Gooch's survey of archaeological and literary evidence, however, makes it very clear that an objective separation between social dining in temples and meals involving religious rites was extremely unlikely. First, one must recognize that many social meals took place in homes rather than in temples:

> The constant theme of the literary sources with regard to meals is the theme of host and guest, of shared meals at private homes as marks of social intimacy—so constant a theme that were it not for the archaeological evidence of the extensive use of dining rooms associated with cultic centres it might be concluded that no significant degree of social eating occurred there.[40]

38. Seneca, *Letter* 5.4.
39. Willis, *Idol Meat*, pp. 47-56.
40. Gooch, 'Food and Limits', pp. 242-43. Gooch complains that the only evidence commonly cited in commentaries on 1 Cor. 8–10 for social meals in temples is the papyrus inscriptions (noted by A. Deissmann, *New Light on the New Testament from Records of the Graeco-Roman Period* [Edinburgh: T. & T. Clark, 1908], p. 351) which extend invitations to dine at the table of the Lord Serapis. The frequent appeal to this evidence, and only this evidence, leaves the impression that

Secondly, whatever the precise relation of the dining rooms to the sanctuaries, the dining facilities were clearly an important part of the temple complex. The literary evidence strongly suggests that socially significant meals (and even not so significant ones), which were often held in homes,[41] involved explicit religious rites.[42] If libations might be poured by the host at even the most ordinary social dinner party in private homes, it would be most unlikely that there would not be some cultic acts associated with meals eaten in cultic settings where there was heightened consciousness of the gods.[43] Therefore, it is highly unrealistic to think that social meals in temples could be purely secular or only nominally connected to idolatry.

Thirdly, it is anachronistic to argue that social events and religious events could be tidily separated in the Greco-Roman world to the same extent that they can be in modern Western world.[44] One must not think in terms of 'either–or', but 'both–and'. While Willis is essentially correct in his assessment of the social import of meals in temples, he has seriously underestimated the religious import of such meals.

Therefore, an objective separation between purely social meals eaten ἐν εἰδωλείῳ and meals involving τραπέζης δαιμονίων μετέχειν was highly improbable in Paul's Corinth. On the contrary, such meals

sharing meals in temples was the norm for social dining. The bulk of evidence, not explored by New Testament scholars, gives an entirely different picture of the social context of shared meals ('Food and Limits', p. 242 n. 20).

41. The main exception seems to be when there was a lack of facilities in private homes to entertain all the guests. According to the calculation of Murphy-O'Connor (*Corinth*, pp. 153-58) dining rooms in large houses could usually accommodate only nine diners at a time, while the atrium could hold another 30 or 40 people. The communal facilities of temples would become necessary for hosting some prominent social occasions. See also MacMullen, *Paganism*, pp. 34-42.

42. Gooch notes that this conclusion is supported even by the selective evidence Willis uses ('Food and Limits', p. 244 n. 23). The rites occurred, whatever the participants' or Willis's assessment of their religious import.

43. Gooch, 'Food and Limits', p. 244. Cf. G.H.R. Horsley's claim that 'there is now a clear consensus that these banquets had a fundamentally religious character' (*New Documents Illustrating Early Christianity* [8 vols.; Sydney, Australia: Macquarie University Press, 1981], I, p. 6).

44. In a large part of the world where 'many gods and many lords' are still acknowledged, there continues to be an inseparable connection between religious rites and conviviality. Religious and social establishments are mutually supporting and legitimizing.

would naturally be perceived as idolatrous by most Christians, including Paul.

b. *The Social Impact of a Prohibition of Idol Food on the Corinthian Christians*

The occasions on which idol food was consumed at homes or temples were indeed many. It might have been possible to avoid religious festivals. But what about weddings, birthdays, funerals, or just a simple meal with a religiously-minded host who happened to be one's superior or relative? To refuse to eat idol food presented at such meals would mark one as antisocial and invite misunderstanding and hostility. It would be to risk ostracism. By forfeiting a major means of social advancement, it would also be economically detrimental. Therefore the potential social impact of a prohibition of idol food cannot be over-emphasized. It is not difficult to imagine that some of the Corinthians Christians might take issue with a prohibition of idol food, no matter who imposed such a prohibition. They would be tempted to compromise or even rationalize their behavior, which might conflict with apostolic teaching.

Another important observation can be made: since shared meals were major expressions of friendship and since many meals of social significance involved idol food, one can safely assume that most, if not all, of the Gentile Christians in Corinth had eaten idol food and taken part in pagan cults before they became Christians. They were 'accustomed to idols' (1 Cor. 8.7). Even after their conversion to the new faith, it would still be difficult to avoid eating idol food, whether they wanted to or not. Therefore, the problem over eating idol food was almost bound to arise as soon as Paul made his first converts. It is highly probable, if not certain, that Paul would have paid considerable attention to this important and urgent issue in his earliest missionary preaching in Corinth. In particular, during his lengthy ministry in Corinth, Paul could not have failed to tell the Corinthian Christians whether, or in what context, it was all right to eat idol food. In other words, 1 Corinthians 8–10 would not have been the first time Paul discussed the issue. This observation will be relevant for my exegesis of the passage.

Chapter 2

THE BACKGROUND TO PAUL'S ATTITUDE TO IDOL FOOD
IN EARLY JUDAISM

This chapter seeks to gather evidence concerning Jewish attitudes toward idol food in order to locate Paul's own position on the map of early Judaism.[1] I should perhaps state at the outset that some conclusions to which the sources lead are hardly disputed or unexpected. For example, I will argue that food was a significant boundary marker of Jewish identity and that idol food was strictly forbidden among most Jews. In fact, such conclusions are routinely regarded as givens by most commentators.[2]

On the other hand, precisely because scholars often take for granted the validity of these observations, only the barest minimum in the way of evidence, consisting mostly of generalities, has been supplied. Therefore one motivation for this survey of relevant sources is to set out well documented evidence that clearly substantiates my observations on attitudes toward idol food in early Judaism.

More importantly, I want to examine the primary texts to see what, if any, patterns emerge. I realize that norms and boundaries differed temporally, locally, and among different social groups and individuals. Moreover, as the extant sources available for us to examine are filtered

---

1. I am aware of the fact that 'Judaism at the turn of the era was a variegated and complex phenomenon' (R.A. Kraft and G.W.E. Nickelsburg [eds.], *Early Judaism and its Modern Interpreters* [Philadelphia: Fortress Press; Atlanta: Scholars Press, 1986], p. 3). Nevertheless, to avoid encumbrance of expression, I use 'Judaism' as a shorthand for the religion as a whole, which comprises a diverse number of groups with a reasonable commonality. The same holds true for 'Christianity'.

2. For example, assuming the validity of the traditional understanding of Paul's attitude toward idol food, Barrett asserts without much ado that 'in the matter of εἰδωλόθυτα... Paul was not a practising Jew' ('Things Sacrificed', p. 50).

through the interests of the surviving 'mainstream' and are to a considerable extent the product of historical coincidence, I do not expect such sources in themselves to yield a simple unbiased picture. Therefore I will examine not only what the authors said, but also why and in what context they said what they said. Some attempt will be made to determine whether and to what degree their statements corresponded to opinions held in their respective communities.[3] In other words, some measure of historical criticism of the sources is necessary. While this kind of survey rarely makes for elegant prose, it is indispensable if foundationless conjectures are to be avoided. I simply ask the reader's forbearance in the interests of sound conclusions resting on clear evidence.

In examining the evidence, I shall proceed in roughly chronological order. Since the textual–redactional histories of many documents are not well understood, it is simply impossible to be precise concerning dates and audiences. Consequently, I shall begin with the Jewish Scriptures, and move on to the apocryphal and pseudepigraphical literature, and then the Dead Sea Scrolls, Philo, Josephus, and the rabbinic writings. Supplementing these will be comments on Jewish attitudes by Greco-Roman authors. An exploration of the implications of the survey for our understanding of Paul's attitude towards idol food will round up the chapter.

A Jew's attitude toward idol food was part of the larger issue of how Jews were to maintain their Jewish identity in an environment dominated by Gentiles. Before proceeding to an examination of the sources, it will be appropriate to make a few preliminary remarks on the tendencies of integration and resistance in Jewish encounter with pagan culture.[4]

---

3. E.P. Sanders wisely warns (regarding rabbinic sayings about the impurities of Gentiles) that the question of whether something was officially 'decreed' must be carefully distinguished from that of what people actually did ('Jewish Association with Gentiles and Galatians 2.11-14', in R.T. Fortna and B.R. Gaventa [eds.], *The Conversation Continues: Studies in Paul and John in Honor of J. Louis Martyn* [Nashville: Abingdon Press, 1990], pp. 170-88 [172-76]).

4. For a clear and thorough investigation of such tendencies see J.J. Collins, *Between Athens and Jerusalem: Jewish Identity in the Hellenistic Diaspora* (New York: Crossroad, 1983). See also the helpful discussions in S. McKnight, *A Light among the Gentiles: Jewish Missionary Activity in the Second Temple Period* (Minneapolis: Fortress Press, 1991), pp. 11-29; P. Borgen, '"Yes", "No", "How Far?": The Participation of Jews and Christians in Pagan Cults', in *idem, Early Christianity*

It needs to be emphasized that there is no such thing as '*the* Jewish attitude toward Gentiles', as the degree of an individual Jew's openness toward Gentiles may vary considerably according to historical circumstances and individual visions. In fact, the extant literature in the Second Temple period gives evidence both of Jewish assimilation to pagan culture and of resistance to it. Doubtless many Jews who felt attached to their Jewish heritage and community also wanted to participate in the broader civilization of the Greco-Roman world. Compromise was inevitable. Moreover, as Jewish and pagan assessments of Jewish mores were often diametrically opposed, 'the plausibility of Judaism in the Hellenistic world came under strain' and there was pressure to eliminate such social dissonance.[5] Not many opted for the extremes of either abandoning Judaism altogether or virtually wholesale rejection of anything Gentile. Instead, most Jews both resisted non-Jewish culture and also integrated themselves into that culture. The degree of integration and resistance varied. As resistance might range from barely retaining a formal and theoretical monotheism to unmitigated hostility towards pagans, integration might range from a magnanimous universalism to total assimilation.

In view of the above remarks, it is impossible to draw a precise boundary line beyond which a Jew became a sure apostate. Nevertheless, it remains a fact that such lines were drawn, however tightly or loosely. Josephus mentions Jews who forsook their ancestral customs (*Ant.* 18.141, 20.100). Even the generally tolerant Philo could speak of essentials in Judaism for which Jews would be willing to die 'not once but a thousand times, if it were possible' (*Leg. Gai.* 209). The following survey will show that to eat idol food was, for most Jews, a clear example of apostasy.

1. *The Jewish Scriptures*

The stand of the Jewish Scriptures against idolatry and food offered to idols is clear and uncompromising. In the Torah, Yahweh is described as 'a jealous God' who demands Israel's total allegiance and cannot tolerate his people's devotion to any other god (Exod. 20.5; 34.14). Therefore, the Israelites are forbidden to partake of the sacrifices to

---

and Hellenistic Judaism (Edinburgh: T. & T. Clark, 1996), pp. 15-43.
    5.   Collins, *Athens and Jerusalem*, pp. 8-10 (quotation from p. 9).

other gods (Exod. 34.15).[6] Numbers 25 is a classic text which documents an early transgression against this prohibition by the Israelites (v. 2).[7] As a result, the 'jealousy' of God was kindled against Israel and many died in a plague (v. 11).

In Deuteronomy, idol food is deemed to be sacrifices to demons (Deut. 32.17)—a concept which also surfaces in Paul's attack on the practice of consuming idol food (1 Cor. 10.20).[8] In a commentary on the incident in Numbers 25, the Psalmist reiterates this concept with a variation: sacrifices to pagan gods are sacrifices to the dead (Ps. 106.28).

In the didactic story of Daniel 1,[9] we read: 'But Daniel resolved that he would not defile (ἀλισγέω in the LXX) himself with the royal rations of food and wine; so he asked the palace master to allow him not to defile himself' (1.8).[10] Daniel's refusal to eat the king's food was rewarded by God with better health than the other courtiers. Though the reason for Daniel's abstention is stated only generally in terms of avoiding defilement, the reference is probably to defilement by pagan deities. While it is true that royal food, being non-kosher, would be excluded by the dietary laws as well, the reference to *wine* as well as meat suggests dietary laws are not the focus. Nor can Daniel's abstention be adequately explained as merely an ascetic practice, because of the reference to defilement. The food and drink of the palace would in all likelihood have come from the temple of pagan deities.[11] It may be

6.   Indeed the explicit reason given for the prohibition of intermarriage with foreigners is the fear that such relations would lead Israel to idolatry.

7.   Note that the incident underlies Paul's strong warning against idolatry in 1 Cor. 10.1-13.

8.   Note also that 1 Cor. 10.22—'Shall we provoke the Lord to jealousy?'— echoes Deut. 32.21: 'They have provoked me to jealousy with what is no god'. It is clear that Paul has Deut. 32 and Num. 25 in mind in his discussion of the problem of idol food.

9.   The dating of the source for the story, as of the book of Daniel as a whole, is disputed. The concern with dietary defilement could fit any time since the exile. Cf. V. Tcherikover, *Hellenistic Civilization and the Jews* (New York: Atheneum, 1977), pp. 346-47, 460; J.J. Collins, *The Apocalyptic Vision of the Book of Daniel* (HSM, 16; Missoula, MT: Scholars Press, 1977), pp. 36-37; J.E. Goldingay, *Daniel* (WBC, 30; Dallas: Word Books, 1989), pp. 12-14.

10.   Note the use of ἀλίσγημα (*hapax legomenon* in the New Testament) in Acts 15.20.

11.   The fear of defilement by pagan deities perhaps leads to unease about all pagan food and drink, which epitomize pagan uncleanness (cf. Jdt. 10.5; 12.2; Add

noted that in *Joseph and Aseneth*, Aseneth's royal dinner is clearly identified with sacrifices to idols (*Jos. Asen.* 10.13; 13.8; cf. Dan. 5.2-4; Bel 3). The impression that idol food is involved is reinforced by the Israelite heroes' willingness to die rather than to engage in idolatrous practice (Daniel 3 and 6).

2. *Jewish Apocryphal Writings*

In the apocryphal and pseudepigraphical writings, the use of the term εἰδωλόθυτα is rare and is probably the result of Christian redaction.[12] Nevertheless, if the term εἰδωλόθυτα itself is not used, references to food offered to idols are certainly not lacking.[13] Moreover, in this period, a widespread tendency to avoid food prepared or sold by pagans is evident, and those Jews who abhorred pagan food would naturally also avoid idol food. After all, the idea of Gentile uncleanness had much to do with the Gentiles' presumed association with idolatry. This sort of connection is clearly attested in rabbinic writings, when rationales are often provided for the halakhot.[14] For example *m. 'Abod. Zar.*

Est. 14.17; Tob. 1.10-11). But note that Daniel does not refuse to eat from the royal table at all; in this sense he is less scrupulous.

12. εἰδωλόθυτον, being a polemical term, is naturally not used in pagan writings. In Jewish writings, it is used only in *4 Macc.* 5.2; *Pseudo-Phocylides* 31; and *Sib. Or.* 2.96. *Ps.-Phocy.* 31 is in all probability a Christian interpolation, as the line is found in only one inferior manuscript (P.W. van der Horst, *The Sentences of Pseudo-Phocylides* [VTSup, 4; Leiden: E.J. Brill, 1978], p. 135). As *Sib. Or.* 2.56-148 shows clear literary dependence on *Pseudo-Phocylides*, *Sib. Or.* 2.96 is also traceable to Christian redaction. On the other hand, textual evidence for Christian interpolation in *4 Macc.* 5.2 is lacking. Nevertheless, if *4 Macc.* postdates 1 Cor.— which is not impossible—then the use of εἰδωλόθυτον in the book can still be influenced by (Jewish) Christian terminology. See the discussion on *4 Macc.* 5.2 below.

13. E.g. *Jub.* 22.17; *6 Ezra* 16.69; and *Jos. Asen.* 8.5-7; 10.11-13; 11.8-9; 12.5; 21.13-14. θυσίαι τῶν εἰδώλων/θεῶν and its variants are found already in the LXX (the most notable being Num 25.2, which underlies Paul's discussion of εἰδωλόθυτα in 1 Cor. 8–10). There is some uncertainty whether *6 Ezra* 16 is a Jewish or Christian composition.

14. Gedalyahu Alon observes that, in rabbinic thinking, both 'the laws of Gentile uncleanness and the defilement of idols...have a single root, that is, that Gentile impurity was begotten of idol uncleanness' (*Jews, Judaism and the Classical World: Studies in Jewish History in the Times of the Second Temple and the Talmud* [Jerusalem: Magnes Press, 1977], p. 187). Thus Gentile impurity, unlike other categories of uncleanness which 'pertain essentially to the body of the defiled...is

4.9–5.10 explains that Gentile wine was prohibited because it might just possibly have been consecrated to a pagan deity.[15] What is remarkable in that passage is that it assumes that it is all right for a Jew to eat with a Gentile,[16] provided precaution is being taken to avoid any association with idolatry.

The admonitions against partaking of Gentile food are often introduced indirectly in exemplary tales rather than as direct commands. Like the story of Daniel, which I have already considered, many of these narrative accounts are concerned to show how pious Jews should maintain their purity in regard to food when they are in the midst of Gentiles (especially those Gentiles who hold political power). In their exhortation to live up to the ideal, such tales probably point towards the fear that the food laws were not being kept as strictly as the authors wished.

a. *1 Maccabees*
The author of 1 Maccabees tells the story of how, when coerced by Antiochus to 'give up their particular customs... Many even from Israel...sacrificed to idols and profaned the Sabbath' (1 Macc. 1.42-

due to a spiritual fact' (p. 188). Nevertheless, Alon himself believes that all such prohibitions in the rabbinic era were justified *post hoc*, being 'originally forbidden only on account of Gentile uncleanness' (p. 181). It seems to me that Alon's conclusion is too sweeping. While it is entirely possible that some Jews would avoid Gentile food just because it was *Gentile* food, it is hard to believe that, in view of the long biblical tradition of associating Gentiles with their idols, there were not other Jews who avoided Gentile food because of its association with idolatry. Perhaps some did not make distinction between the concept of idol uncleanness and the concept of Gentile uncleanness, but there is abundant evidence that some other Jews did. Cf. J. Klawans, 'Notions of Gentile Impurity in Ancient Judaism', *AJS Review* 20 (1995), pp. 293-97. Klawans argues from Second Temple Jewish evidence that Gentile uncleanness is often seen as being the result of idolatry and sexual immorality.

15. Note especially *m. 'Abod. Zar.* 5.5: 'If an Israelite was eating with a Gentile at a table, and, leaving in his presence a flagon [of wine] on the table...left him and went out, what is on the table is forbidden'. Neusner observes that the Mishnah assumes that a Gentile is always ready 'to contaminate the wine through idolatry, if he gets the chance' (*Judaism*, p. 202).

16. W.A.I. Elmslie infers from this passage that 'common meals [between Jews and Gentiles] must frequently have occurred' (*The Mishna on Idolatry: 'Aboda Zara'* [trans. J.A. Robinson; Text and Studies, 8.2; Cambridge: Cambridge University Press, 1911], p. 81).

43). Doubtless those Jews would not have refused to eat food offered to idols either. Even in the absence of active persecution, 'certain rene-gades came out from Israel and misled many, saying, "Let us go and make a covenant with the Gentiles around us, for since we separated from them many disasters have come upon us"' (1.11-15). On the other hand, the author also asserts that many heroic Jews 'stood firm and...chose to die rather than to be defiled by food' (1.62-3). In his opinion, steadfastness in observing the food laws, even when under persecution, was clearly one of the main distinguishing marks of a faithful Jew. Whether the majority of Jews shared the author's view is difficult to ascertain; it is probable that faithfulness to the food laws would at least be held, if only theoretically, as exemplary conduct by many.

b. *2 Maccabees*
There is no direct mention of idol food in 2 Maccabees, but an interest-ing incident throws some light on the attitude of some Jews in Tyre towards sacrifices to idols. The attempt of Jason to use the money obtained from the quadrennial gymnasium games at Tyre to pay for a sacrifice to Hercules was thwarted because the bearers of the money did not consider it appropriate (2 Macc. 4.18-20). It seems that some Jews who had no qualms in participating in the gymnasium were neverthe-less reluctant to be seen as patrons of idolatry. This naturally implies a negative attitude toward idol food.

c. *3 Maccabees*
In his account of Ptolemy's decree to put all Jews in his kingdom to death, the author of *3 Maccabees* mentions that Egyptian Jews 'steadily maintained their goodwill toward the kings and their unwavering loy-alty. But reverencing God and conducting themselves *according to his Law, they kept themselves apart in the matter of food*' (*3 Macc.* 3.3-4). The author is concerned to stress that Jews have been extremely friendly towards their Gentile overlords (7.7; cf. 5.31; 6.25) and only set themselves apart in the essential matter of food. The reference to the Law makes it likely that their conduct regarding 'food' here would include avoiding pagan sacrifices. Moreover, the charges of their ene-mies were that the Jews were different 'in regard to *worship* and food' (3.7) and that they rejected Ptolemy's 'good offer' of 'Alexandrian citi-zenship' and of participating 'in our regular religious rites' (3.22-23).

Even allowing for the author's tendency to exaggeration, it is evident that, in his view, the Alexandrian Jewish community as a whole would not be disposed to eating pagan sacrifices. This is significant in view of the special effort made in *3 Maccabees* to emphasize the amicable relations of the Alexandrian Jews to their Gentile neighbors.[17]

d. *4 Maccabees*

In *4 Maccabees*, we read that 'The tyrant Antiochus [IV]...ordered his guards to drag along every single one of the Hebrews and compel them to eat swine's flesh and food sacrificed to idols [εἰδωλόθυτα]. Whoever refused to eat the defiled food was to be tortured and put to death. Many were violently snatched away' (*4 Macc.* 5.1-4). Then follows the martyrological account of the aged Eleazar and seven young brothers with their mother, who all refused to eat the unclean food (*4 Macc.* 5.5-18.23; cf. 2 Macc. 7). The fact that pork and idol food were singled out for mention suggests that they were considered essential elements of the Law, which 'under no circumstances whatever do we ever deem it right to transgress' (*4 Macc.* 5.17). It is also apparent that Jewish abstention from such food was a well-established and well-known practice.

It is significant that although Eleazar gives allegorical meaning to the dietary laws in terms of Greek philosophy, he also observes the laws literally and is willing to die rather than transgress them. Thus, through allegorization, the dietary laws are justified rather than negated.

---

17. M. Hadas, *The Third and Fourth Books of Maccabees* (New York: Harper & Brothers, 1953), pp. 24-25. In Hadas's view, *3 Maccabees* supplies a moderate view amidst the extremes of 'tending to open hostility at one pole and to assimilation at the other'. Likewise, Collins maintains that while the book supports a strict observance of the Jewish law, it is 'designed to keep open a door to good relations with the gentile world' (*Athens and Jerusalem*, pp. 104-11; quotation from p. 111). Thus the attitude of *3 Maccabees* is in keeping with the general tenor of the so-called 'apologetic' writings of Alexandrian Judaism. On the other hand, V.A. Tcherikover takes an opposite view and refers to the author of the book as 'hating the gentiles in general' ('The Third Book of Maccabees as a Historical Source', *Scripta Hierosolymitana* 7 [1961], pp. 1-26 [21]). This seems difficult to maintain in view of the book's obvious effort to exculpate 'the Greeks' (even Tcherikover himself recognizes the lack of hostility toward the Greeks in the book) and to portray the Jews as very loyal supporters of the Ptolemies.

It is worth noting that after *4 Macc.* 5.2, εἰδωλόθυτα is not mentioned again in the book.[18] Instead, the account focuses on how Antiochus and his courtiers attempted to coerce the martyrs to eat pork. It is possible that the author of *4 Maccabees* considered eating pork a more heinous sin than eating idol sacrifices. But it is perhaps more likely that the author considered idol sacrifices so non-negotiable as to require no further comment, whereas the temptation for some Jews to eat pork under compulsion may be greater. If one may read between the lines, *4 Macc.* 5.20 seems to indicate that there were Jews who considered eating pork, especially when under compulsion, as a 'minor sin' (cf. 5.13) or even among 'harmless pleasures' (5.9).[19] When Eleazar (or, rather, the author of *4 Maccabees*) asserts that 'minor sins are just as weighty as great sins' (5.20), he is little short of admitting that eating

18. The lack of later mention of food sacrificed to idols in the book raises the question whether εἰδωλόθυτα is attributable to Christian redaction, though one must bear in mind that later references to unclean food may well encompass idol sacrifices. The reference to Antiochus's 'sitting in state with his counselors on a certain high place [προκαθίσας...ἐπί τινος ὑψηλοῦ τόπου]' (5.1) may indicate that the scene of the story is a cultic site. If this were the case, then, of course, εἰδωλόθυτα would likely have been an integral part of the story and not a gloss. On the other hand, *4 Maccabees*, as well as other parallel accounts, portrays the trial and the execution of the martyrs as taking place in Jerusalem. Therefore, the reference to a 'high place' may not have any cultic significance. Indeed the use of προκαθίσας...ἐπί makes it likely that the 'high place' is simply a reference to something like a raised platform rather than to any cultic site. In the Jewish Scriptures the idea of 'seated on high' is a metaphor for royal loftiness, with reference to God (Ps. 112.5: ἐν ὑψηλοῖς κατοικῶν) or those who would usurp God's place (Isa. 14.13: καθιῶ ἐν ὄρει ὑψηλῷ). One may also note that the LXX never refers to a cultic high place as ὑψηλός τόπος in numerous references to high places; the simpler τὸ ὑψηλόν (or another non-cognate term) is used instead. In any case, as there is no textual evidence suggesting that the word is a Christian gloss, any theory of Christian interpolation must be put forward with great caution.

19. Hadas thinks that eating pork is the 'lesser sin' (*Third and Fourth Maccabees*, pp. 168-69 n. 3; cf. pp. 118-19), but he cites only rabbinic material to substantiate this opinion. By contrast, E.P. Sanders proposes that 'some Jews regarded the minor, formal idolatry involved in eating sacrificial meat as less serious than transgressing either of two prohibitions which are among the strongest in the Bible: do not eat pork, shellfish, donkey etc.; do not consume blood' (*Jewish Law from Jesus to the Mishnah: Five Studies* [London: SCM Press; Philadelphia: Trinity Press International, 1990], pp. 281-82). However, Sanders's judgment seems solely based on an a priori view that Paul's approach in 1 Cor. 8–10 must have a precedent in Jewish sources. Cf. Winter, 'Religious Pluralism', p. 218 n. 32.

pork is not ranked among the major transgressions of the Law.

It is difficult to tell how many Jews actually remained faithful to the Law in this regard. The author claims that many did (5.4). Nevertheless, it is evident that some did not, otherwise the author would probably have said 'all' rather than 'many'. Moreover, as we have suggested above, there are indications that some Jews considered eating unclean food a minor sin. If the earnest exhortatory character of the book is somehow commensurate with the seriousness of the temptation, then the number of Jews in the author's time who transgressed the food Law might not be small. Whether those Jews also ate idol food cannot be determined with any certainty.

e. *Tobit*

The purpose of this sympathetic story of Israelites exiled to Assyria after the fall of Samaria in 722 BCE, which is couched in the form of an autobiography, is to exhort Jews to piety. Tobit claimed that when he and other Jews were taken captive to Nineveh, 'all my brethren and those that were of my kindred did eat of the bread of the Gentiles. But I kept myself from eating' (Tob. 1.10-11). Obviously Tobit regarded abstention from pagan food as essential to Jewish piety. The motivation behind this abstention seems to be the avoidance of idolatry, of which Gentiles are presumably guilty. Tobit's apocalyptic hope that 'all nations shall turn...and shall bury their idols' (13.6) suggests that rampant idolatry might have been bothering the author.

The story also mentions that many exiled Jews 'did eat of the bread of the Gentiles'. They either were not concerned with Jewish piety or did not regard it essential to keep away from Gentile food. However, since the author is purportedly describing the religious climate of Israelites exiled to Assyria—which was well known to be syncretistic according to the biblical book of Kings—one must not hastily jump to the conclusion that many Diaspora Jews in the author's time (c. 200 BCE) had no qualms about eating pagan food.[20] On the contrary, the author seemed able to assume that his audience would agree that to avoid pagan food was a trait of faithfulness to the traditions of Judaism. Therefore the number of transgressors in the author's community is not likely to have been large.

---

20. P. Deselaers (*Das Buch Tobit* [Düsseldorf: Patmos, 1990], p. 12) dates the book not long after mid-third century BCE.

f. *Judith*
In her mission to assassinate Holofernes, Judith took along her own wine, oil, grain, figs and bread so that she could avoid eating unclean food in the enemy's camp (Jdt. 10.5; 12.2, 9). Even in Holofernes's banquet, which she attended, she only 'ate and drank what her maid had prepared' (12.19). It is not clear whether the avoidance of Gentile food was due to the presumption that the food and wine would have been previously offered to idols. Perhaps the more general concept of Gentile uncleanness was in view.

g. *Additions to Esther*
In Add. Est. 14.17, Esther reminds God of her piety in that she had not eaten food from Haman's table nor graced the royal drinking party with her presence nor drunk the wine of libations. Here the motive of Esther's abstention seems to have more to do with the idolatrous association of the food and drink. But some unease about Gentile food in general cannot be ruled out. Such unease is probably reflective of periods of Jewish–Gentile tension in Egypt near the turn of the second–first century BCE.

Vigorous polemic against idolatry can be found in other apocryphal writings, whether in the form of legendary narratives (Bel and the Dragon) or didactic discourse (The Wisdom of Solomon; especially chs. 13–16). These may be considered implicit attacks on idol food.

3. *Jewish Pseudepigraphical Writings*

a. *Letter of Aristeas*
This letter, probably written in the second century BCE by an Alexandrian Jew, is remarkable in its openness and accommodation to Hellenism. It portrays the relationship between the Alexandrian Jewish community and the Ptolemaic intellectual and political establishment in a cordial light. Already in the beginning of the letter there is a blurring of national distinctions. In seeking the release of Jews forcibly deported to Egypt, Aristeas argues that 'these people worship God the overseer and creator of all, whom all men worship including ourselves, O King, except that we have a different name. Their name for him is Zeus and Jove' (*Ep. Arist.* 16). The pagan king Ptolemy is highly praised by the translators of the Law throughout the seven days of the banquet in which each of the translators was questioned by the King. Even

watching serious entertainment in the theater for leisure is considered to have therapeutic value (284-85).

On the other hand, a separatist attitude in the matter of food is also evident. In reply to the questions raised 'concerning meats and drink and beasts considered to be unclean' (128), Aristeas argues that human-kind as a whole shows some concern in such issues. He goes on to explain that the point of the Mosaic legislation is to protect Jews from idolatry. Moses 'hedged [the Jews] in on all sides with strict purities connected with meat and drink' (142) so that they might be 'kept pure in body and soul, preserved from false beliefs, worshipping the only God omnipotent over all creation' (139). It is significant that the polemic against idolatry is given before the allegorical explanation of some dietary laws. As in the case of *4 Maccabees*, the allegorical explanations serve to strengthen rather than void the literal observance of the food laws.

While Aristeas seems to have no qualms about Jews eating with Gentiles, he is painstaking in showing that the food laws are being maintained. An illuminating incident is Ptolemy's reception dinner for the delegates, in which other royal pages and the king's honored guests were present (180-86). 'Everything of which you partake', Ptolemy said, 'will be served in compliance of your [i.e. the Jews'] habits; it will be served to me as well as to you' (181). More significantly, Eleazar the priest, instead of 'the sacred heralds, the sacrificial ministers and the rest, whose habitual role was to offer the prayers', was asked to offer the prayer over the meal, 'in accordance with the customs practiced by all his [Ptolemy's] visitors from Judea' (184). In this way, every possible connection of the meal to idolatry was severed.

We may safely infer that Aristeas would strongly disapprove of the eating of idol sacrifices. Moreover, since Aristeas asserted that the maintenance of the food Law was the 'habits' and 'customs' of the Jews, there were probably not too many Jews who would deviate from the food laws. While one must allow for exaggeration in Aristeas' claim, it is probably not too far from the truth. The tone of the letter suggests that the letter is less an exhortation to purity in time of apostasy than an apologetic to some 'hardliners' in demonstrating how pious Jews could associate with Gentiles and prosper, as long as the laws of diet, ritual purity, and avoidance of idolatry are strictly observed.

b. *Joseph and Aseneth*

There is no consensus on whether *Joseph and Aseneth*[21] is a Jewish work with minimal Christian retouching, a Jewish work with extensive interpolations, or a Christian work incorporating Jewish traditions.[22] A major difficulty facing scholars in these kinds of decisions is, as R.A. Kraft puts it, that 'it is all but impossible to draw a clear line between Jewish and Christian ethical instructions and ideals'.[23]

21. See R. Doran, 'Narrative Literature', in R.A. Kraft and G.W.E. Nickelsburg (eds.), *Early Judaism and its Modern Interpreters* (Philadelphia: Fortress Press; Atlanta: Scholars Press, 1986), pp. 287-310 (290-92 and 305-10), for summary of and bibliography on issues of provenance, text, genre, and religious background. See also C. Burchard, 'The Importance of Joseph and Aseneth for the Study of the New Testament: A General Survey and a Fresh Look at the Lord's Supper', *NTS* 33 (1987), pp. 102-34.

22. Burchard attempts a detailed refutation of the theory of Christian authorship in *Untersuchungen zu Joseph und Aseneth* (WUNT, 8; Tübingen: Mohr/Siebeck, 1965), pp. 99-107; cf. M. Philonenko, *Joseph et Aséneth: Introduction, texte critique et notes* (Leiden: E.J. Brill, 1968), pp. 98-109. Burchard also asserts that 'every competent scholar has since [the review of Batiffol by Duchesne] affirmed that Joseph and Aseneth is Jewish, with perhaps some Christian interpolations' ('Joseph and Aseneth', *OTP*, II, pp. 177-247 [187]). This, however, seems an overstatement, as there was no lack of defenders of Christian authorship (or major Christian redactions) among participating scholars in the 1991–92 Philadelphia Seminar on Christian Origins on the topic of Joseph and Aseneth. In particular, Gordon Lathrop of Lutheran Theological Seminary perceives a ritual shape behind Joseph and Aseneth that corresponds with early Christian practices. In particular, he points out that the emphasis on the 'first day' and the 'eighth day', the identification of Joseph as the sun and as the son of God, Aseneth as virgin and the bride of God, the concept of marriage to the son of God, and the repeated accent on 'not returning evil for evil' (in language found only in Paul, 1 Peter and *Polycarp*) betrays Christian rather than Jewish interests. I am indebted to Dr Lathrop for providing me with a copy of detailed notes of his research for his seminar paper.

Lathrop does not address a major argument for Jewish authorship, namely, that Christians would not be concerned about Joseph's marriage to a Gentile woman. However, once we recognize that the issue at stake was religious exogamy rather than ethnic exogamy, this argument loses its force (this issue is covered in depth in Larry Kuenning, 'Would Early Christians Care whether Joseph Married an Outsider? A Possible Context for Joseph and Aseneth' [unpublished paper for Robert Kraft's doctoral seminar on 'Joseph and Aseneth', University of Pennsylvania, 1991]).

23. R.A. Kraft, 'The Multiform Jewish Heritage of Early Christianity', in J. Neusner (ed.), *Christianity, Judaism and Other Greco-Roman Cults: Studies for Morton Smith at Sixty* (3 vols.; Leiden: E.J. Brill, 1975), III, pp. 174-99 (185).

The textual history of the book is likewise complicated and not well understood.[24] Whatever its provenance, this idealized account of Aseneth's conversion is highly relevant for our study, since, by all accounts, the text is dated between early first century BCE and early second century CE.[25] It shows what some Jews or Christians expected of the converts: a radical departure from their previous idolatry, demonstrated by the destruction of idols and idol food. This radical expectation is all the more significant because, except on the issue of idolatry, the author does not seem to be hostilely disposed to Gentiles.[26]

Joseph refused to be kissed by Aseneth because she is an idolater:

οὐκ ἔστι προσῆκον ἀνδρὶ θεοσεβεῖ, ὃς εὐλογεῖ τῷ στόματι αὐτοῦ τὸν θεὸν ζῶντα καὶ ἐσθίει ἄρτον εὐλογημένον ζωῆς καὶ πίνει ποτήριον εὐλογημένον ἀθανασίας... φιλῆσαι γυναῖκα ἀλλοτρίαν, ἥτις εὐλογεῖ τῷ στόματι αὐτῆς εἴδωλα νεκρὰ καὶ κωφὰ καὶ ἐσθίει ἐκ τῆς τραπέζης

C. Burchard is quite certain that *Joseph and Aseneth* 'comes from a Jewish milieu similar to that from which many early Christians were recruited' ('Importance of Joseph and Aseneth', p. 104). But then most of the arguments for Jewish authorship can be used for Christian authorship as well, especially when the book's 'style and language bear a *prima facie* resemblance to at least some parts of the NT' and 'its main concern is with conversion which was a regular feature of early Christian life and is also the concern of many NT passages' (Burchard, 'Importance of Joseph and Aseneth', p. 104).

24. I will follow the text and versification in C. Burchard, 'Ein vorläufiger griechischer Text von Joseph und Aseneth', *Dielheimer Blätter zum Alten Testament* 14 (1979), pp. 2-53 and 'Verbesserungen zum vorläufigen Text von Joseph und Aseneth', *Dielheimer Blätter zum Alten Testament* 16 (1982), pp. 37-39. This text forms the basis for his English translation in 'Joseph and Aseneth', *OTP*, II, pp. 202-47, which will be used here. Burchard's eclectic text is usually considered to be superior to Philonenko's text (essentially the shorter d text), but without detailed examination and argumentation. Fortunately, whichever text is chosen, my own presentation is not materially affected.

25. See Collins, *Athens and Jerusalem*, pp. 89-91 for a succinct outline of the various options and the arguments in their support; see also Burchard's discussion in *OTP*, II, pp. 188-89. Collins himself argues for an early first century BCE dating, but virtually all his arguments presuppose pre-Christian Jewish authorship, which are largely worthless if the book is a Christian work.

26. For example, the author mentions the cordial relation between Joseph and Aseneth's father, who is highly praised (1.3; cf. 3.3). Note also that Joseph considered Pharaoh 'like a father to me' (20.9). Of course, one should not press a legendary romantic tale too hard on its details, especially when there are significant textual problems. Nevertheless, it is still a striking example of how a radical exclusivism on particular issues can coexist with a general openness.

αὐτῶν ἄρτον ἀγχόνης καὶ πίνει ἐκ τῆς σπονδῆς αὐτῶν ποτήριον ἐνέ-
δρας...ὁμοίως καὶ γυναικὶ θεοσεβεῖ οὐκ ἔστι προσῆκον φιλῆσαι
ἄνδρα ἀλλότριον, διότι βδέλυγμά ἐστι τοῦτο ἐνώπιον κυρίου τοῦ
θεοῦ (*Jos. Asen.* 8.5-7).

It is not fitting for a man who worships God, who will bless with his
mouth the living God and eat blessed bread of life and drink a blessed
cup of immortality...to kiss a strange woman who will bless with her
mouth dead and dumb idols and eat from their table bread of strangulation and drink from their libation a cup of insidiousness... Likewise, for
a woman who worships God it is not fitting to kiss a strange man,
because this is an abomination before the Lord God.

Moreover, the author regards idol food as defiling the mouth: μεμίαν-
ται τὸ στόμα μου ἀπὸ τῶν θυσιῶν εἰδώλων καὶ ἀπὸ τραπέζης τῶν
θεῶν Αἰγυπτίων (12.5; cf. 11.9). In Aseneth's confession of sin to the
Lord God of Joseph, the partaking of idol food epitomizes the worship
of strange gods (21.13-14; 11.8-9). The author's intense hatred of idol
sacrifices is unmistakably shown in the account of Aseneth's repentance. They are even more abominable than the idols themselves: while
Aseneth only destroyed the idols and threw them through the window
to the poor and needy (10.11-12), 'she took...all the sacrifices of her
gods and the vessels of their wine of libation and threw everything...to
the strange dogs. For Aseneth said to herself, "By no means must my
dogs eat from...the sacrifice of the idols, but let the strange dogs eat
those"' (10.13; cf. 13.8). It would be instructive to note here Alon's
observation that the Babylonian Talmud (e.g. *b. 'Abod. Zar.* 48b, 50a)
takes a more stringent attitude to idol food than to the idol itself.[27] Of
course, the author of *Joseph and Aseneth* is far from suggesting a conceptual separation of idol food from idolatry. On the contrary, inasmuch as the consumption of idol food is the epitome of idolatry, the
separate mention of the destruction of idol food is the author's rhetori-
cally effective way of highlighting Aseneth's final and climactic renunciation of idol worship. It is significant that even after the idols were
destroyed, Aseneth still considered food previously sacrificed to them
abominable. Thus it is clear that the author regards eating any idol food
as (sinful) eating from the table of the idols, even when the idols are no
longer present.

When Aseneth completed the process of repentance and met Joseph
again, he could not recognize her because of her transformed beauty.

27. Alon, *Jews*, pp. 170-71 and notes.

She told him: 'I am...Aseneth, and all the idols I have thrown away... And a man came to me from heaven today, and gave me bread of life and I ate, and a cup of blessing and I drank. And he said to me, "I have given you for a bride to Joseph today"' (19.4-5). It is clear that, for the author, the only valid scruple about Joseph's marriage to Aseneth is religious exogamy and not any consideration of ethnic origins. Conversion consists in the rejection of dead and dumb idols and the worship of the living God. Collins notes that 'the traditional criteria for Jewish identity...are no longer decisive' and 'while the religion of Joseph and Aseneth preserves sharp boundaries over against polytheism, it is, nevertheless, a universal religion freed from the restrictions of race. It is a distinct religion...which can appeal to the reasonable Gentile.'[28] But, then, it is difficult to see what is in such a religion that is not in Christianity.

There is much debate about whether the so-called 'meal formula' in *Jos. Asen.* 8.5-7 has reference to a cultic or sacramental meal or is simply a *theologoumenon* about Jewish (in contrast to Gentile) dietary practices.[29] In particular, much energy has been spent on its relation to the Lord's Supper. The constraints imposed on this study do not allow us to go into these issues in any detail. What is important for our purpose is the inescapable analogy of *Jos. Asen.* 8.5-7 to 1 Cor. 10.21, where Paul argues that 'you cannot drink the cup of the Lord and the cup of demons; you cannot partake of the table of the Lord and the table of demons'. The analogy is much strengthened when one considers also 1 Thess. 1.9-10 and 1 Cor. 12.1–2. For Paul, the conversion experience of the Thessalonians consists in that they 'turned to God from idols, to serve a living and true God' (ἐπεστρέψατε πρὸς τὸν θεὸν ἀπὸ τῶν εἰδώλων δουλεύειν θεῷ ζῶντι καὶ ἀληθινῷ)'. Likewise, 'when [the Corinthians] were pagans, [they] were led astray to dumb idols' (τὰ εἴδωλα τὰ ἄφωνα). The least that can be said is that Paul and *Joseph and Aseneth* share a common heritage, whether of

28. Collins, *Athens and Jerusalem*, p. 215. Cf. P.-G. Klumbies's observation on the insignificant role the law plays in *Joseph and Aseneth*: 'In dem jüdischen Bekehrungsroman Joseph und Aseneth spielt im Gegensatz zu der Mehrzahl der anderen Schriften aus hellenistisch-römischer Zeit das Gesetz keine Rolle' (*Die Rede von Gott bei Paulus in ihrem zeitgeschichtlichen Kontext* [Göttingen: Vandenhoeck & Ruprecht, 1992], p. 71).

29. For this see Burchard's discussion and thorough bibliography on major studies of the topic ('Importance of Joseph and Aseneth'); see also Collins, *Athens and Jerusalem*, pp. 213-14.

Jewish proselytism or of early Christian missionary preaching.[30] I think it is somewhat more likely that *Joseph and Aseneth* is influenced by the Christian traditions that also underlie Paul's missionary preaching, as it is arguable that expressions like 'blessed bread of life' and 'blessed cup of immortality' (8.5) betray Christian interests and are results of Christian redaction, if not Christian composition.[31] The wide popularity of the book in Christian circles and the lack of reference to it in Jewish literature tend to confirm this understanding.

If *Joseph and Aseneth* is indeed a Christian work or has undergone major Christian redaction, then it can be seen as an early (Jewish) Christian witness to Paul's negative attitude toward idol food. If, on the other hand, the influence is the other way round, then it shows that Paul's approach to idol food may be much more Jewish than scholars tend to think.

c. *Jubilees*

In this work which was probably written by a Palestinian Jew around the mid-second century BCE, a much more 'hardline' approach was taken regarding association with Gentiles. Gentiles are 'sinners' (23.24) who are portrayed as the main threat to Jewish purity (1.9,19). However, the reason for separation is not (solely) nationalistic conceit, but rather the fear that the children of Israel might 'forget the feast of the covenant and walk in the feasts of the Gentiles' (6.35), which are 'sacrifices to the dead' and demons (22.17)—echoing Deut. 32.17 and Ps. 105.28 [LXX]. For this reason Israel was charged not just to avoid idol sacrifices, but, more radically, to separate from the Gentiles and 'eat not with them' (22.16). Such an extreme attitude towards outsiders was certainly consistent with the author's apocalyptic outlook.[32]

---

30. Cf. the parallels between *Joseph and Aseneth* and Paul listed in Klumbies, *Die Rede*, pp. 71-74; and Klauck, *Herrenmahl*, pp. 187-96.

31. Note the verbal analogy, pointed out by Burchard ('Importance of Joseph and Aseneth', p. 119) between ἄρτος [εὐλογημένος] ζωῆς (*Jos. Asen.* 8.5, 9; 15.5; 16.16; 19.5; 21.21) and ὁ ἄρτος τῆς ζωῆς (Jn 6.35, 48; cf. 6.51). Note also the almost exact correspondence between *Jos. Asen.* 16.14: 'this is a comb of life, and everyone who eats of it will not die for ever and ever', and Jn 6.51: 'I am the living bread that came down from heaven. Whoever eats of this bread will live forever.' In particular, both passages clearly allude to the manna.

32. McKnight comments that this negative attitude toward Gentiles is an expression of 'religious convictions in social clothing' (*Light*, p. 28).

Strong polemic against idolatry (and hence, indirectly, idol food) can be found in other apocryphal and pseudepigraphical writings. I will not rehearse such evidence here as it does not add anything substantial to the picture.

4. *Qumran*

The Qumran covenanters are known for their sectarian nationalism and social separation.[33] Their meticulous observance of regulations of purity is so well known as to require little comment. As in the case of *Jubilees*, their separation from Gentiles, and also from unfaithful Israelites (that is, basically everybody outside the community), emerges as a sociological rule in order to avoid sin and idolatry.[34]

The covenanters' extreme abhorrence of sacrifices to idols was evident in the legal section of the Damascus Covenant: 'No man shall sell clean beasts or birds to the Gentiles *lest they offer them in sacrifice*. He shall refuse, with all his power, to sell them anything from his granary or wine-press' (4QD 12.9-11). The Community Rule forbids outsiders of the Covenant 'to partake of the pure Meal of the saints'. Conversely, members of the Covenant were not to 'eat or drink anything of theirs' (1QS 5.13,16). It is instructive to mention here Josephus's account of Essenes who were cast out from the community. Those expelled members often died of starvation because, 'being bound by their oaths and customs', they would not eat the food of outsiders—let alone idol food! (*War* 2.143).

5. *Philo*

Philo is an extremely important witness to Alexandrian Judaism in New Testament times as he wrote only two decades or so before Paul and left us with plenty of material to study. Above all Jewish writers we know, he was a Jew who fully assimilated Hellenistic culture and yet remained loyal enough to his Jewish heritage to risk his life in pleading

33. If they are indeed kindred to the Essenes, then Josephus's comments about the strictness of the Essenes are pertinent (See *War* 2.119-63).

34. Cf. McKnight, *Light*, p. 21. McKnight lists as supporting evidence the following passages: 4QD 6.14, 15; 7.13; 8.4, 8, 16; 11.4-5; 12.6-11; 13.14; 16.9; 19.17-29; 1QS 1.4; 5.1-2, 10-11; 6.15; 9.5, 8-9, 20-21; 1QH 14.21-22; 11QT 48.7-13; 60.16-21.

the cause of Alexandrian Judaism before Gaius Caligula.[35]

Philo did not directly comment on food offered to idols, but his position on this issue can be gauged from his attitude on other closely related issues such as idolatry, literal observance of the Law, and dietary laws.

Philo's disdain for idolatry has been pointed out by various scholars.[36] He assumes that even Gaius should be aware that Jewish monotheism precludes religious loyalty to any other deities or the emperor (*Leg. Gai.* 115-18, 162-64). A Jew will be prepared to die rather than let the emperor profane the sanctity of the Temple (*Leg. Gai.* 209). In one important passage Philo comes close to explicitly condemning the eating of idol sacrifices:

> If anyone cloaking himself under the name and guise of a prophet and claiming to be possessed by inspiration lead us on to the worship of the gods... And if a brother or son or daughter or wife... or anyone else who seems to be kindly disposed, urge us to a like course, bidding us fraternize with the multitude, resort to their temples, and *join in their libations and sacrifices*, we must punish him as a public and general enemy, taking little thought for the ties which bind us to him... and deem it a religious duty to seek his death (*Spec. Leg.* 1.315-16).[37]

Philo says in the same vein that 'if any members of the nation betray the honour due to the One they should suffer the utmost penalties... And... all who have a zeal for virtue should be permitted to exact the penalties offhand and with no delay' (*Spec. Leg.* 1.54-55). Then Philo justifies his call for zeal by referring to Phinehas's 'admirable courage' in Numbers 25, a *locus classicus* for Israel's lapse into idolatry which involves the eating of idol food (*Spec. Leg.* 56-57). It is doubtful whether the death sentence could be carried out in Philo's community. Nevertheless, the severity of the proposed punishment for idolatry was completely in line with biblical injunctions and was a measure of the threat (as perceived by Philo) idolatry posed to the Alexandrian Jewish community.

35. See Philo's *Legatio ad Gaium*. Note that Paul, like Philo, claimed to be loyal to the Jewish nation (Rom. 9.1-3).

36. See E.R. Goodenough, *An Introduction to Philo Judaeus* (New Haven: Yale University Press, 1962), pp. 68-74, 80-85; A. Mendelson, *Philo's Jewish Identity* (BJS, 161; Atlanta: Scholars Press, 1988), pp. 29-38.

37. It is possible that Philo is here thinking of members of his own family such as his nephew Tiberius Alexander (private communication from Robert Kraft).

Philo's disdain for idolatry makes it very unlikely that he would approve of the eating of idol sacrifices, but it does not by itself completely settle the issue. After all, Philo freely admitted he had watched contests of pancratiasts in the stadium and seen plays in the theater (*Omn. Prob. Lib.* 26, 141; cf. *Ebr.* 177). It can be argued that these activities included at least passive contact with idolatry. And yet Philo, in his willingness to participate in the broader civilization, apparently did not see it that way. Is it possible that Philo treated idol food the way he treated games?

To answer this question, it is important to note that, in contrast to eating food offered to idols, watching games is not explicitly forbidden in the Law and there is thus more room for rationalization. Bearing in mind this contrast, one expects that Philo's attitude to the literal observance of the Law would have a determining effect on whether Philo would abide by the scriptural prohibition of eating idol food.

From Philo's extant writing, it seems clear that he did endeavor to remain true both to the letter of the Law and to its deeper symbolic meaning.[38] Although he attempted to make Judaism more acceptable in an educated Hellenistic world by symbolically transforming elements of scriptural text into transcendent ideas of Hellenistic philosophies, his Jewish loyalty held him back from becoming one of those extreme allegorists 'who, regarding laws in their literal sense in the light of symbols of matters belonging to the intellect, are overpunctilious about the latter, while treating the former with easy-going neglect' (*Migr. Abr.* 89). In Philo's opinion, those allegorists 'ought to have given careful attention to both aims'. Philo reasoned that as the body was the abode of the soul, 'so we must pay heed to the letter of the laws' in order to 'gain a clearer conception of those things of which these are the symbols' (*Migr. Abr.* 93). 'And besides that, we would then not incur the censure of the many and the charges they are sure to bring against us'.[39]

Philo took up considerable space in providing rational explanations

---

38. Walter Houston notes that while Philo interpreted the purity laws as an allegory of virtues, he kept them literally because they were commanded. Therefore, 'in Philo purity continues as a symbolic system [of rituals] as well as a metaphor' (*Purity and Monotheism: Clean and Unclean Animals in Biblical Law* [JSOTSup, 140; Sheffield: JSOT Press, 1993], p. 267). On the importance Philo attached to the literal interpretation of Scripture, see the excursus at the end of this section.

39. Perhaps this was the more important reason!

and allegorical interpretations for the exclusions in the dietary laws (*Spec. Leg.* 4.100-31).[40] But there can be little doubt that Philo himself kept the dietary laws. In fact, he took the refusal to eat pork as a touchstone of faithfulness to Judaism. Two incidents he recorded are particularly interesting. The first describes Flaccus's persecution of the Jews. Some Jewish women were seized and ordered to eat pork:

> the women who in fear of punishment tasted the meat were dismissed and did not have to bear any further dire maltreatment. But the more resolute were delivered to the tormentors to suffer desperate ill-usage (*Flacc.* 95-6).

The second incident concerns Philo's defense of Jewish interests in an audience with Gaius. Gaius's question, 'Why do you refuse to eat pork?' was greeted by an outburst of laughter from Philo's opponents (*Leg. Gai.* 361). The answer Philo and other delegates gave, which led to more laughter, was in terms of faithfulness to Jewish customs rather than any rational explanation of the prohibition (362). Philo and his companions felt completely helpless in the situation (363). But they were willing to endure the mocking rather than compromise their Jewish loyalty.

In light of the above discussion, I can reasonably formulate my inference of Philo's opinion on eating idol food as follows.

1. Philo considered it important to keep the letter of the Law as well as fulfilling its symbolic meaning.
2. The Law prohibits eating pork, and Philo defended this prohibition despite being mocked.[41]
3. The Law also prohibits eating food offered to idols, and we expect Philo observed this prohibition as well.
4. Further, Philo had a strong disdain for idolatry and was outspokenly hostile against those who would lead other Jews into idolatry.
5. Therefore, it is highly unlikely that Philo would approve of the eating of idol food.[42]

---

40. For instance, he explained that pork, being the most delicious of land animals, is forbidden in order to discourage gluttony, 'an evil very dangerous both to soul and body' (*Spec. Leg.* 4.100-101).

41. Although one cannot always equate apologetics with actions, there is little reason to doubt that Philo himself obeyed the food laws.

42. Unfortunately, since there is no way to know if Philo *always* observed laws

That Philo did not condone eating idol food is an important witness to the attitude of Alexandrian Judaism. But it is an altogether different question whether Philo's attitude on this issue represents the majority view of Alexandrian Jews. As I have already mentioned, Philo knew of Jews for whom the symbolic meaning of the laws was all that mattered. It is conceivable that some of them would have argued that the point of the scriptural prohibition was to defend monotheism, hence they could eat whatever they liked as long as they gave thanks to God rather than to the idols!

Nevertheless, the Jews who might have taken such a position would probably have been confined to the educated and their number was not likely to have been large. Philo's writings give the impression that most Jews were of the uneducated mass who took a literal approach to the Law. They were content with the sensuous and took ancestral traditions for granted. Moreover, Philo's fear that the failure to keep the letter of the laws would 'incur the censure of the many' is surely a testimony to the strictness of many in Alexandrian Jewish society. Indeed, Flaccus's use of threats of punishment to coerce the Jews to eat pork would have been pointless if most Jews had not taken the prohibition seriously. Similarly, the stiff resistance to Gaius's attempt to foist emperor worship on the Jewish nation would scarcely have been possible unless there was a prevalent hatred of actual idolatry among the Jews. A strict concern to avoid idolatry could also been seen in the refusal of Alexandrian Jews who were guild members to join in the guild dinners in pagan temples.[43]

Excursus: The Importance of Literal Interpretation in Philo

The importance of literal interpretation in Philo has been largely overlooked in Philonic scholarship because of the almost exclusive focus on his allegorical explanations and the conception of Philo as a philosopher rather than an exegete. Happily, since the publication of Nikiprowetzky's monumental study on Philo as an exegete, Philonic scholarship has experienced a paradigm shift.[44] The importance of

of conduct literally and since what qualifies as literal interpretation to Philo may not appear literal to us, this series of arguments cannot be conclusive.

43. M. Wischnitzer, 'Notes to a History of the Jewish Guilds', *HUCA* 23.2 (1938), pp. 246-53; cited in Winter, 'Religious Pluralism', p. 218.

44. V. Nikiprowetzky, *Le commentaire de l'écriture chez Philo d'Alexandrie* (ALGHJ, 11; Leiden: E.J. Brill, 1977).

Philo's role as an interpreter of Scripture, especially of the Pentateuch, is increasingly recognized. Nikiprowetzky argues convincingly that Philo must be regarded first and foremost as an exegete of Scripture

> who does not express his ideas except as a function of the scriptural text. He does not propose to develop a system but wants to communicate the profound sense of the Mosaic Law which he follows verse by verse, watching closely the text on which he is working.[45]

Unfortunately, while some full-scale studies have been published on Philo's allegorical treatises,[46] very little work has been done on his verse-by-verse commentaries of Scripture (such as the *Quaestiones*), which can be most helpful in determining Philo's exegetical presuppositions and methods.[47] In view of this imbalance, I have conducted a

---

45. Nikiprowetzky, *Philo*, p. 181 (my own translation).

46. Notably J. Cazeaux, *La trame et la chaîne: Structures littéraires et exégèse dans cinq traités de Philon d'Alexandrie* (ALGHJ, 15; Leiden: E.J. Brill, 1983); and D. Winston and J. Dillon, *Two Treatises of Philo of Alexandria: A Commentary on De Gigantibus and Quod Deus Sit Immutabilis* (BJS, 25; Chico, CA: Scholars Press, 1983).

47. Other than the important study on the formal aspects of the *Quaestiones* by P. Borgen and R. Skarsten ('*Quaestiones et Solutiones*: Some Observations on the Form of Philo's Exegesis', *Studia Philonica* 4 [1976–77], pp. 1-16), I am unable to track down any other substantial treatment of the *Quaestiones*. This imbalance is perhaps due to a preconception that the allegorical treatises are the more representative works of Philo. Yehoshua Amir surely speaks for many when he writes, 'it is not the "Questions and Answers" that define Philo as a Bible commentator, but rather the great "Allegorical Commentary", in which his hermeneutic genius celebrates its most impressive triumph' ('Authority and Interpretation of Scripture in the Writings of Philo', in M.J. Mulder [ed.], *Mikra: Text, Translation, Reading and Interpretation of the Hebrew Bible in Ancient Judaism and Early Christianity* [CRINT, 2.1; Assen: Van Gorcum; Philadelphia: Fortress Press, 1988], p. 428). Ironically, these words are written immediately after a frank acknowledgment that it is in the *Quaestiones* that—'in contrast to the great allegorical commentary— Philo has doubtless *subordinated his own religious-philosophical thinking to his task as Bible exegete*' (emphasis added).

Peder Borgen notes that 'some scholars have suggested that *Questiones* is catechetical, while *Allegorical Interpretation* is more scholarly' but he is not convinced that this is supported by the evidence ('Philo of Alexandria', in M. Stone [ed.], *Jewish Writings of the Second Temple Period* [Philadelphia: Fortress Press, 1984], p. 242). We may also note Marcus's interesting suggestion that the *Quaestiones* is a later work than the *Allegoriae* (R. Marcus, *Philo. Supplement I: Questions and Answers on Genesis* [Cambridge, MA: Harvard University Press, 1953], p. x).

preliminary investigation of Philo's exegetical methods in Book One of
Quaestiones in Genesin to see if any pattern can be discerned.[48] Some
of the results regarding Philo's attitude to literal interpretation are
indeed surprising.

The common perception of Philo's exegesis is that Philo is primarily
interested in allegorical interpretation and pays only lip service to the
validity of literal interpretation. Longenecker writes,

> Philo usually treated the Old Testament as a body of symbols given by
> God for man's spiritual and moral benefit, which must be understood
> other than in a literal and historical fashion. The *prima facie* meaning
> must normally be pushed aside—even counted as offensive—to make
> room for the intended spiritual meaning underlying the obvious.[49]

While it is undeniable that Philo is more interested in those answers
that are of an allegorical nature, Longenecker's description simply does
not square with the data in *Quaest. in Gen.* 1. The most striking feature
revealed in my study of *Quaest. in Gen.* 1 is the preponderance of literal interpretations over the allegorical. In the one hundred sections of
the book, allegorical interpretation is given only in about thirty occa-
·sions,[50] whereas one or more literal interpretations are almost always
provided in every section. Only very infrequently is the literal interpretation disposed of in a few words.[51] On the other hand, about half of the
literal interpretations span one quarter of a page or more; often they are
as long as, if not longer than, the corresponding allegorical interpretations.

Perhaps troubled by the unusually large number of literal interpretations in the *Quaestiones*, T.H. Tobin suggests that 'many, if not most,
of the literal interpretations in *Questions and Answers on Genesis* are
not the work of Philo himself'.[52] This suggestion is supported by the
observation that 'a number of times Philo himself explicitly indicates

48. I would like to thank Robert Kraft for his helpful advice on undertaking this
investigation.

49. R.N. Longenecker, *Biblical Exegesis in the Apostolic Period* (Grand
Rapids: Eerdmans, 1975), p. 46.

50. *Quaest. in Gen.* 1.6, 8, 10-13, 25, 31, 37, 38?, 39, 41, 44-50, 52, 53, 56, 57,
70, 75?, 76, 77?, 82?, 87?, 88, 90, 94, 95.

51. *Quaest. in Gen.* 1.6, 11, 25, 31, 48, 49.

52. T.H. Tobin, *The Creation of Man: Philo and the History of Interpretation*
(CBQMS, 14; Washington, DC: Catholic Biblical Association of America, 1983),
p. 5.

that the literal interpretation is the work of others'.[53] In response, it must be noted that Philo does not cite those literal interpretations by others in order to refute them—he by and large regards them as valid and useful, and thus very much as his own interpretations. It is practically irrelevant whether he borrows them or not. We must always bear in mind that we simply do not know to what extent Philo also borrows from or attributes to others his allegorical interpretations. It is not valid to assume that if an interpretation is allegorical, it must have originated with Philo. Moreover, there are surely many allegorical interpretations which Philo knows but fails to incorporate into *Quaestiones in Genesin*. Thus the fact that Philo is drawing from traditions does not really account for the preponderance of literal interpretations in *Quaest. in Gen.* 1. The only reasonable explanation is that he indeed regards the literal interpretations as important.

It is also often asserted that Philo resorts to allegory primarily because it enables him to 'continue to bind himself to a textual passage that is both sacred and troubling'.[54] It provides a way out when the literal interpretation presents difficulties, contradictions, or something unworthy of God. However, in *Quaest. in Gen.* 1, the reasons behind Philo's use of allegory appear to be quite different. On many occasions Philo confronts squarely the difficulties presented by the text in his literal interpretation.[55] In *Quaest. in Gen.* 1.87, Philo goes as far as admitting that Noah's father Lamech made a false prophecy in saying, 'This one will give us rest from our labours': 'But in the realization of the prediction the prophecy spoke falsely, for...it was not so much a cessation of evils that took place but an intensification of violence'. Another good example is *Quaest. in Gen.* 1.3, where Philo accepts the description of God's planting Paradise in Gen. 2.8 literally. This is in sharp contrast with *Leg. All.* 1.43: 'Far be it from man's reasoning to be the victim of so great impiety as to suppose that God tills the soil and plants pleasaunces'. An even more striking example is Philo's comments on Gen. 3.1. In *Agr.* 97 the idea of a talking serpent belongs to the realm of the 'mythical' which needs to be 'removed out of our way'

---

53. Tobin, *Creation of Man*; Tobin gives the following references: *Quaest. in Gen.* 1.8, 10, 32, 57, 93; 2.28, 58, 64, 79; 3.8, 11, 13, 52; 4.2, 64, 145.

54. S. Sandmel, *Philo of Alexandria: An Introduction* (Oxford: Oxford University Press, 1979), p. 18.

55. *Quaest. in Gen.* 1.3, 12, 13, 14, 18, 19, 21, 32, 39, 45, 53, 55, 58, 59, 68, 74, 93.

so that 'the real sense becomes as clear as daylight'. In *Quaest. in Gen.* 1.32, to the question, 'Did the serpent speak in the manner of men?', there are given three answers which unmistakably indicate that Philo accepts the literal truth of the story. First, Philo suggests that animals could probably speak at the beginning of creation. Secondly, God can do what is miraculous in changing their inner nature. Thirdly, human beings had more accurate sense perception prior to the fall. Unlike what he does in *Agr.* 97, Philo finds no need for an allegorical interpretation here. This failure of Philo to allegorize (when he could easily have done so) can also be found in some other passages.[56]

Therefore Philo does not abandon his literal interpretation in difficult texts. On the other hand, he often introduces allegorical interpretation when there is no difficulty in the text at all. This phenomenon clearly shows that, at least for *Quaest. in Gen.* 1, Philo's reason for using allegorical interpretation is other than to remove difficulties in literal interpretations of scriptural texts.

Considering Philo's irenic tone in discussing various literal interpretations, it is possible that he is addressing a readership that is primarily concerned with literal interpretations.[57] While hoping to convince these literalists of the importance of the deeper allegorical meaning of scripture, he apparently does not want to overdo it.[58]

It is perhaps more probable that Philo may not always have had any particular reason for including an allegorical or literal interpretation in one place but not in another. Convinced as he was of the incomparable superiority and richness of the Mosaic text, he may simply have wanted to indicate the vast hermeneutical potential of a text by incorporating a variety of interpretations, literal or allegorical.[59] Thus Philo could let

56. E.g. *Quaest. in Gen.* 1.18, 19, 21, 32, 33.

57. R. Melnick suggests that much of the material in *Quaestiones in Genesin* is directed toward, not against, a literalist audience ('On the Philonic Conception of the Whole Man', *JSJ* 11 [1980], pp. 1-32 [8]). This contrasts with *Legum allegoriae*, where Philo chides the literalists on their unwillingness to see a deeper meaning in the text.

58. As Philo proceeds in *Quaestiones in Genesin*, there seems to be increasingly frequent use of allegorical interpretation.

59. One interesting indication of Philo's desire to exhibit the richness of the Mosaic Scripture is his treatment of texts involving numbers, where his comments often span a few pages, much longer than any non-numeric passages (e.g. *Quaest. in Gen.* 1.77, 83, 91). If, as Sandmel suggests (*Philo*, pp. 22-23), Philo has a strong Pythagorean background, it is only natural that, when he wants to show forth the

literal and allegorical interpretations sit side by side without attempting to remove any inconsistencies. Both were obviously important to him.[60]

6. *Josephus*

Like Philo, Josephus is very important for my purpose as he was roughly contemporary with Paul. He wrote only a few decades after Paul, and left us with plenty of material to study. While remaining a loyal Jew in terms of ancestral religious traditions, he was ready to fit himself, socially and politically, into the Greco-Roman world.

Josephus did not comment directly on food offered to idols. However, as in the case of Philo, Josephus has left us with enough material to infer his (and some other Jews') opinion on this issue with some plausibility.

Josephus's disdain for idolatry is evident in his writings, though outright condemnation is rare. Given that Josephus seemed concerned to commend Judaism to the Greco-Roman world (including his political supporters), harsh polemics against pagan idolatry was simply not politically correct.[61] Even when he did overtly criticize idolatry (*Apion* 2.239-49), he prefaced his criticism with a very diplomatic explanation: he would gladly avoid criticizing other gods, but it was impossible for him to remain silent because of the accusers of the Jews (2.237-38). In any case, the fact that he condemned idolatry at all in his writings is significant.

Josephus's criticism of idolatry is often indirect. In his narration of Israel's history, he follows the biblical practice of condemning the

richness of a text, he makes the fullest comments on subjects about which he knows most.

60. It is possible that Philo paid more attention to literal interpretation in his later works because he grew more conservative in certain issues as he aged and became more involved with the Jewish community (private communication from Kraft).

61. Since Josephus was supported by the Flavian family of emperors, he usually sought to portray Rome and, in particular, the Flavians in the best possible light. Josephus was more overt in his ridicule of the gods of the Egyptians (cf. *Apion* 2.128-29). This was perhaps due less to his contempt for idolatry than to his contempt for the Egyptians, who were considered socially inferior in the Greco-Roman world. It is instructive to note that a similar cultural and social bias also led Philo to ridicule the idolatry of Egyptians above that of all other pagans (Mendelson, *Philo*, pp. 36-38).

wicked kings for leading the Israelites into idolatry and bringing mis-
fortunes upon the nation (*Ant.* 9.99, 205, 243). Conversely, he com-
mends the good kings for destroying idolatry (9.273; 10.50, 65, 69). He
claims that Jews were loyal to their God and that his opponent Apion
should not be surprised that the Jews did not worship the same gods as
the Alexandrians (*Apion* 2.66-67).

It can scarcely be doubted that Josephus took the letter of the laws
and ancestral traditions very seriously. He was of priestly descent.
While a youth, he was attracted to the ascetic way of life and became 'a
devoted disciple' of Bannus for three years. Later, he 'began to engage
in public affairs by the rules of the Pharisees'.[62] He claimed that he and
other Jews regarded 'as the most essential task in life the observance of
our laws and of the pious practices...which we have inherited' (*Apion*
1.60). They 'hold it a point of honour to endure anything rather than
transgress them' (1.190), even 'in the face of death' (2.235; cf. 2.271-
72).[63] For Josephus, 'the only wisdom, the only virtue, consists in
refraining from every action, from every thought that is contrary to the
laws originally laid down' (2.183). Not to observe the Law would be
ranked impiety (2.184).

Josephus's attitude towards the food laws was highly positive. He
praised Moses who, as a wise legislator,[64] did not 'permit the letter of
the law to remain inoperative. Starting from the very beginning with
the *food* of which we partake from infancy...he left nothing...to the
discretion and caprice of the individual' (*Apion* 2.173). Josephus
claimed that no one should be surprised at the faithfulness of the Jews
to the food laws (2.234-35; cf. 2.137). Even the nations showed a keen
desire to imitate the Jewish religion. 'There is not one city, Greek or
barbarian,...to which...many of our prohibitions in the matter of food
are not observed' (2.283)!

As in the case with Philo, we may safely conclude that it is unlikely
that Josephus would condone eating food offered to idols. But what

62. See *Life* 1-12, for Josephus's description of his own background. We cannot
get into the subject of whether Josephus was actually a Pharisee or whether he was
'following' the Pharisees merely in the sense of deferring to them as he began to
engage in public affairs. See S.N. Mason's fine monograph, *Flavius Josephus on
the Pharisees: A Composition-Critical Study* (Leiden: E.J. Brill, 1991), esp. chapter
15 (pp. 342-56) which deals directly with the evidence in *Life* 1-12.

63. Josephus then cited a few examples from Hecataeus to illustrate the point.

64. Like Philo, Josephus praised Moses for having avoided the extremes of
other legislators (*Apion* 2.168-176; cf. Philo, *Op. Mund.* 1-2).

about other Jews? It seems that at least some Jews did not remain faithful to their ancestral traditions, as Josephus himself testified.[65] Josephus wrote of the descendants of Alexander, Herod's son: 'The offspring of Alexander abandoned from birth the observances of the ways of the Jewish land and ranged themselves with the Greek tradition' (*Ant.* 18.141). He also accused Tiberius Alexander, the nephew of Philo, of not continuing 'in the practices of his countrymen' (*Ant.* 20.100).

Indeed, Tiberius Alexander's abandonment of Jewish traditions was a revealing case. It would have been difficult for him, without compromising on the issue of food offered to idols, to climb so high up the political ladder.[66] He became the Roman Procurator of Judea (and later of Syria, it seems), then Prefect of Alexandria and Egypt and a staff general of Titus at the siege of Jerusalem.[67]

On the other hand, Josephus claimed that most Jews, like himself, knew the laws well and were meticulous in keeping them. He boasted that, in contrast to most people, who hardly knew what the laws of their nations were, 'should anyone of our nation be questioned about the laws, he would repeat them all more readily than his own name' (*Apion* 2.177-78). Moreover, there was 'a unity and identity of religious belief, perfect uniformity in habits and customs' (2.179). He even challenged

65. As Kraft observes, Josephus also gave evidence of a less than strict attitude toward literal observance of the law among some Jews. For example, the Sabbath could be broken for the sake of self defense (*Ant.* 12.276); Izates was advised by a leading Jew that he did not have to be circumcised to adopt the Jewish religion (*Ant.* 20.41). Though Josephus himself apparently took a stricter attitude, it is unlikely that he would consider those Jew apostates. See R.A. Kraft, 'Judaism on the World Scene', in S. Benko and J.J. O'Rourke (eds.), *The Catacombs and the Colosseum: The Roman Empire as the Setting of Primitive Christianity* (Valley Forge, PA: Judson Press, 1971), pp. 84-85.

66. Kraft thinks it is not hard to believe that Tiberius Alexander was not even circumcised ('Jewish Heritage', p. 191). For a concise summary of the career of Tiberius Alexander see Thackeray's notes on Josephus, *Wars* 2.220 (H. Thackeray *et al.* [ed. and trans.], *Josephus, with an English Translation* [10 vols; LCL; London: Heinemann, 1926–65], II, p. 409 n. R). For Josephus's attitude toward Tiberius Alexander, see R.A. Kraft, 'Tiberius Julius Alexander and The Crisis in Alexandria according to Josephus' in H.W. Attridge *et al.* (eds.), *Of Scribes and Scrolls: Studies on the Hebrew Bible, Intertestamental Judaism, and Christian Origins Presented to John Strugnell on the Occasion of his Sixtieth Birthday* (Lanham, MD: University Press of America, 1990), pp. 175-84.

67. Compare the reluctance of later Christians to join the military because of the possible association with idolatry.

Apion to produce 'a case of our people, merely two or three, proving traitors to their laws or afraid of death [i.e. death under torture for refusing to compromise the laws]' (2.232-35).

No doubt Josephus was exaggerating as he was carried away by his rhetoric, for even he himself testified that some Jews did not remain faithful to their ancestral traditions. However, if Josephus's writings can be trusted at all, the number of Jews who would eat food offered to idols is not likely to have been large. I have already noted Josephus's assertion that Jews generally kept the laws meticulously. He also asserted that they were fiercely opposed to idolatry.[68]

Several passages in Josephus show that many or most Jews were very concerned with the matter of purity. For example, they seemed to prefer not to use Gentile oil, the resort to which was viewed as an act of 'violating their legal ordinances', even when 'pure oil' was not available (*Life* 74; cf. *War* 2.591).[69] Even Jews of Antioch, who seemed ready enough to participate in the gymnasium, were apparently too pious to use the oil of Gentiles (*Ant.* 12.120).

Josephus also gives evidence of certain ultra-conservatives with regard to the food laws. Like the expelled Essenes, who would not eat food of outsiders which they considered impure, some priests starved to death because the tithes on which they depended were stolen (*Ant.* 20.181, 206-207).[70] Apparently to avoid food offered to idols, some

---

68. As L.H. Feldman (*Jew and Gentile in the Ancient World: Attitudes and Interactions from Alexander to Justinian* [Princeton, NJ: Princeton University Press, 1993], p. 41) observes, Jews were opposed to Herod's placing of an image of an eagle at the Temple gate (*Ant.* 17.149-54; *War* 1.641-50) and to Pilate's marching his troops into Jerusalem with images of the emperor (*Ant.* 18.55-59; *War* 1.648-50). They were ready to die rather than to allow the statue of Caligula to be brought into the Temple (*Ant.* 18.257-309; *War* 2.184-203) and destroyed the palace of Herod Antipas in Tiberius simply because it contained representations of animals (*Life* 66-67).

69. It is not clear just what was wrong with Gentile oil. Perhaps purity was at stake, as foreign oil was likely to be tainted by unclean vessels.

70. Those priests perhaps understood the biblical law about priestly tithes (e.g. Deut. 18.1-4) narrowly to mean that they should eat *only* holy food set aside for them. Josephus apparently shows admiration rather than contempt for these ultra-conservatives (*Life* 13-14). He also records that, in a Passover which occurred in the midst of a drought, some priests would not eat leavened bread even though it was the only bread available (*Ant.* 3.320).

priests who were imprisoned in Rome lived only on figs and nuts (*Life* 13-14).[71] Josephus praises them for not having 'forgotten the pious practices of religion'.

7. *Rabbinic Writings*

A caveat is needed before I embark on a discussion of rabbinic attitude toward idol food. As recent scholarship has emphasized, one is often on precarious ground in using rabbinic material (from the third century or later) to illustrate Jewish thoughts in the first century.[72] Because of the late codification of rabbinic teachings, any discussion of rabbinic doctrine in Paul's time—even if one can legitimately speak of 'rabbis' as an institution in the first century—necessarily raises the question of anachronism in attributions. In particular, the so-called Noachic commandments, which bear some resemblance to the Apostolic Decree in Acts 15, cannot be traced to earlier than the third century.[73] It is unreasonable to think that the two monumental crises that Jews went through in the first two centuries—the Great Rebellion against Rome and the Bar Kochba Revolt—did not profoundly affect their mindset and shape their literature.[74] We cannot simply assume that when the Rabbis quoted past masters they introduced no change to their material, nor that they did not incorrectly (whether consciously or unconsciously) attribute anonymous sayings to known masters. Even if all the attributions are accurate, the very decisions to include those attributions and exclude others might have altered the whole picture of pre-70 Pharisaism considerably.[75] In short, it may not be possible to know to what

71. Sanders, however, thinks that those priests took the extreme position of avoiding not only idol food, but all food that had been cooked because the cooking vessels had previously been used to cook non-kosher and possibly idolatrous food (*Jewish Law*, p. 26).

72. For the numerous critical issues confronting the use of rabbinic literature to determine first century Jewish thought see P.S. Alexander, 'Rabbinic Judaism and the New Testament', *ZNW* 74 (1983), pp. 237-46.

73. Segal, *Paul*, p. 195.

74. One need only consider the effect the Exodus, the division of the Kingdom, or the Babylonian exile had on the biblical writings to recognize the truth of this statement.

75. As is commonly recognized in current scholarship, 'im Gegensatz zu der…"Vereinheitlichung" des palästinischen Judentums unter der Führung der rabbinischen Schriftgelehrten nach 70 das geistige Gesicht Jerusalems vor seiner

extent rabbinic halakhot governing idolatry and relations with Gentiles reflect the situation in first-century Judaism.

On the other hand, it is also unreasonable to posit a complete discontinuity between first-century Jewish (Pharisaic) thoughts and rabbinic teachings reflected in later sources, especially when there is corroborating evidence for such thoughts in other early Jewish and Christian traditions. Since corroborating evidence for the prohibition of idol food is indeed overwhelming, we can safely assume the correctness of the general picture, though not always the details. Moreover, while there is no certainty that rabbinic teachings represent the whole or the dominant position of the Pharisees in Paul's time, the Rabbis' attitude toward idol food is probably reflective of the attitude of many Pharisees, and hence possibly that of the pre-Christian Paul.

As in other Jewish sources, many of the rabbinic prohibitions in the matter of food are explained in terms of the danger of the infiltration of idolatry. Thus it appears unlikely that the Rabbis would condone eating idol food. However, there is some uncertainty as to what qualifies as eating idol food.

That the rabbinic writings are strongly opposed to idolatry is undisputed.[76] But the issue of what constitutes idolatry and idol food seems

Zerstörung ein ausgesprochen *"pluralistisches"* war' (M. Hengel, 'Der vorchristliche Paulus', in M. Hengel and U. Heckel [eds.], *Paulus und das antike Judentum. Tübingen-Durham-Symposium im Gedenken an den 50. Todestag Adolf Schlatters* [WUNT, 58; Tübingen: Mohr Siebeck, 1991], p. 244; emphasis original). But Hengel also warns that we must not conveniently treat rabbinic material as *bedeutungslos* for the study of pre-70 Pharisaic teaching (pp. 242-48).

76. See E.E. Urbach's discussion on this issue (*The Sages: Their Concepts and Beliefs* [2 vols.; Jerusalem: Magnes Press, 2nd edn, 1979], I, pp. 19-36). Urbach also argues that actual idolatry was extremely rare in Palestine ('The Rabbinic Laws of Idolatry in the Second and Third Centuries in the Light of Archaeological and Historical Facts', *IEJ* 9 [1959], pp. 149-65, 229-45 [154-56]). Cf. Lieberman's observation that, in contrast to patristic writers who vehemently denounced images, the Rabbis seldom felt the need to ridicule idols (*Hellenism in Jewish Palestine: Studies in the Transmission, Beliefs, and Manners of Palestine in the 1 Century BCE–IV Century BCE* [New York: Jewish Theological Seminary of America, 1950], p. 116). Feldman regards this as 'a measure of their confidence that idol-worship by Jews was not an immediate problem or threat' (*Jew and Gentile*, pp. 40-41). Tomson, citing Tcherikover's study on the Diaspora situation, notes that Jewish idolatry was also rare outside Palestine (*Jewish Law*, p. 154 and n. 22; Tcherikover, *Hellenistic Civilization*, pp. 344-57). This last point is debatable. As E.R. Goodenough has shown, various Egyptian and Greek gods are invoked together on many magical

to be vigorously debated.[77] In an oft-quoted story (*m. 'Abod. Zar.* 3.4) Proklos asked R. Gamaliel III while the latter was bathing in the bath house of Aphrodite in Acre, 'It is written in your Law, "And nothing of the banned thing shall cleave to your hand". Why then are you bathing in the bath house of Aphrodite?' Gamaliel's answer is very revealing:

> I did not come to her domain, but she came into mine! They do not say, 'Let us make a bath house for Aphrodite', but 'Let us make an Aphrodite as an adornment for the bath house'. Moreover... you would not enter before your goddess naked or... urinate before her! Yet this goddess stands above the gutter and everyone urinates before her... That which is treated as a god is forbidden, but what is not treated as a god is permitted.

Thus the Rabbi justified his action on the ground that the image of Aphrodite in the bath house was a mere ornament. It was clearly desecrated and not treated as a god.[78] This reflects a rational view of idolatry that the idol itself has no reality. Urbach notes that such a rational view 'led to lenient [halakhic] decisions by most of the Rabbis in the period between the second and fourth centuries in all that related to the use of the art of imagery and its production'.[79] On the basis of the non-

---

amulets which are in all probability Jewish (*Jewish Symbols in the Greco-Roman Period* [13 vols.; New York: Bollingen Foundation, 1953–68], II, pp. 153-295). Kraft notes that the evidence suggests that even Jews in Palestine were not immune to magical practices ('Jewish Heritage', p. 197).

77. Cf. Tomson's important discussion on such debates in Tannaitic halakha (*Jewish Law*, pp. 154-76). See also Winter, 'Religious Pluralism', pp. 215-19; Liebermann, 'Heathen Idolatrous Rites in Rabbinic Literature', in *Hellenism in Jewish Palestine*, pp. 128-38.

78. The same rationale underlies R. Ishmael's judgments: 'If a garden or a bath house belonged to an idol, they may be used if there is no need to offer thanks, but not if there is need to offer thanks. If they belonged both to the idol and to others, they may be used whether there is need to offer thanks or no need' (*m. 'Abod. Zar.* 4.3); and 'An idol whose worshippers have abandoned it in time of peace is permitted, but if in time of war it is forbidden' (*m. 'Abod. Zar.* 4.6; the idea is that in time of peace the desertion of the idol is voluntary; in time of war it may not be).

79. Urbach, *Sages*, I, p. 25; cf. Urbach, 'Rabbinic Laws'. For the opposite view that such a leniency toward images is an indication of the decline of rabbinic tradition under the influence of Hellenism, see Goodenough, *Jewish Symbols*, IV, pp. 3-24. My feeling is that, inasmuch as rabbinic Judaism itself was probably influenced by Hellenism to a significant degree, one may set up a false dichotomy by asking which tradition triumphed. On the interpenetration of Judaism and Hellenism see Martin Hengel's magisterial study, *Judaism and Hellenism: Studies in their*

reality of idols some even justified Jewish possession or manufacturing of idols provided the owner or manufacturer did not worship them.[80] Such an attempt 'to find a sanction *post factum*...clearly shows the reality with which the sages had to reckon, even if they did not approve'.[81]

On the other hand, that questions were raised at all about R. Gamaliel's bathing in the bath house of Aphrodite suggests that the Rabbi's practice may be somewhat unusual according to typical Gentile perceptions of pious Jews.[82] That many sages held a stricter attitude than Gamaliel did is apparent in a discussion of what counted as desecration of an idol:

> [R. Ishmael says.] A Gentile can desecrate his own or his fellow's idol, but an Israelite cannot desecrate a Gentile's idol...How is an idol desecrated? If a Gentile cut off the tip of its ear or the end of its nose or the tip of its finger...he has desecrated it. But if he spat in its face, or urinated before it, or dragged it about, or threw filth at it, he has *not* desecrated it. If he sold it or gave it in pledge, Rabbi says: He has desecrated it. But the Sages say: He has not desecrated it (*m. 'Abod. Zar.* 4.4-5).

Given such a divergence of opinions concerning what counted as desecration of idols, one cannot assume without further reflection that idol food was always forbidden in all circumstances by all the sages. Conceivably, some Jews could argue that since idol food was sold in the market, it was desecrated, and hence could be bought and eaten. The buyer could claim that 'I did not come into the domain of idol food; it came into mine!' In principle, this kind of reasoning is not very different from that of R. Gamaliel for justifying his bathing in the bath house of Aphrodite.

Such an argument would have been persuasive if not for the fact that rabbinic writings register no debate whatever on whether one can eat idol food. Idol food is strictly forbidden if it is identified as such. Discussions only exist in doubtful cases where one is not certain if the

Encounter in Palestine during the Early Hellenistic Period (2 vols.; Philadelphia: Fortress Press, 1974).

80. 'The idol of a gentile is straightly forbidden, but that of an Israelite is not forbidden unless it has been worshipped' (*m. 'Abod. Zar.* 4.4).

81. Urbach, 'Rabbinic Laws', pp. 160-61. It is interesting to find that Tertullian, who knew little about the halakhot, also had to struggle with the problem of Christian manufacturing of idols (*De idol.* 5).

82. Cf. Tomson's observation that Onkelos the Proselyte (*t. Ḥag.* 3.3) preferred to bathe in the sea rather than in the bath houses (*Jewish Law*, pp. 159-60 n. 61).

food has been sacrificed to idols. Here opinions vary greatly.

On the one extreme is the ban on the sale of animals or other sacrificial items to Gentiles, especially when the time of pagan festivals approaches, lest they use them for sacrifices.[83] Likewise, R. Eliezer rules that a Jew should not slaughter for a Gentile, since 'the unexpressed intention of a Gentile is directed to idolatry' (*m. Ḥul.* 2.7). It is clear that, in the opinion of those conservative sages, not only are Jews forbidden to buy or eat idol food, but they must not even in any way assist in any possible production of idol food.

Not all Rabbis, however, are so conservative. R. Judah rules that while it is forbidden to sell a single white cock to a Gentile during pagan festivals—since it is clearly intended for idolatrous use—one may sell a Gentile a white cock among other cocks. The general principle behind this is: 'if [any idolatrous use is] not specified, it is permitted; but if [any idolatrous use is] specified, it is forbidden' (*m. 'Abod. Zar.* 1.5).

A more lenient attitude seems to be taken by R. Jose, who disputes R. Eliezer's ruling and claims that intention (whether the Jewish slaughterer's or the Gentile owner's) has nothing to do with the validity of the slaughtering of non-consecrated animals. It is a situation in which (improper) intention does not invalidate. Even if, for argument's sake, intention is important, then drawing on the analogy of the rites of slaughtering sacrificial animals (where improper intention does invalidate) what counts is the slaughterer's but not the owner's (*m. Ḥul.* 2.7).[84]

---

83. E.g. 'It is forbidden to sell these things to the Gentiles [during pagan festivals]: fir-cones, white figs with their stalks, frankincense, or a white cock' (*m. 'Abod. Zar.* 1.5). Cf. G. J. Blidstein, 'The Sale of Animals to Gentiles in Talmudic Law', *JQR* 61 (1970–71), pp. 188-98; Winter, 'Religious Pluralism', pp. 218-19. Such a strict attitude recalls that of the Qumran covenanters: 'No man shall sell clean beasts or birds to the Gentiles lest they offer them in sacrifice. He shall refuse, with all his power, to sell them anything from his granary or winepress' (4QD 12.9-11).

84. Tomson, *Jewish Law*, p. 161 appeals to this text to show that 'R. Yose argued from the case of sacrificial slaughtering, where not the intention of the owner of the sacrificial animal, but only that of the slaughterer counts'. He draws the conclusion that if the Gentile did express an intention towards idolatry, 'all would agree with R. Eliezer that the slaughtering was invalid'. But this is missing the main point of R. Jose, namely, that intention (even the slaughterer's) does not count in this case.

Rabbi Akiba is yet more lenient. He rules that Jews are permitted even to profit from the sale of animals used by Gentiles for sacrifices to idols. Nevertheless the bottom line is that once the meat has been sacrificed, Jews must have nothing to do with it: 'Flesh that is entering in unto an idol is permitted, but what comes forth is forbidden, for it is as the sacrifices of the dead' (*m. 'Abod. Zar.* 2.3).

It is not certain why the Rabbis took a more stringent attitude toward idol food than toward images and idols. Perhaps it has something to do with the importance of dietary laws for rabbinic Judaism.[85] But whatever the reason, such an attitude is certainly consistent with the rest of early Jewish literature which regards the consumption of idol food as the prime and representative act of idolatry.

8. *Pagan Authors on Jewish Attitude*

Greco-Roman writers did not directly comment on the attitude of Jews to food offered to idols, but some pertinent observations may be made.[86] To begin with, it is significant that pagan writers hardly men-

85. The whole tractate *Ḥullin* is devoted to the issue of the purity of animals killed for food. Jacob Neusner says of the rabbinic traditions about the pre-70 Pharisees: 'Approximately 67% of all legal pericopae deal with dietary laws: ritual purity for meals and agricultural rules governing the fitness of food for Pharisaic consumption. Observance of Sabbaths and festivals is a distant third' (*Rabbinic Traditions about the Pharisees before 70* [3 vols.; Leiden: E.J. Brill, 1971], III, pp. 303-304). In relation to this observation, Neusner develops his view of the history of Pharisees, which involves a transformation from politics to piety: the originally political party was later transformed into an apolitical table-fellowship sect which tried to eat its everyday meals in a state of purity as if one were a Temple priest (*From Politics to Piety: The Emergence of Pharisaic Judaism* (Englewood Cliffs, NJ: Prentice–Hall, 1973]). See also Neusner, *The Idea of Purity in Ancient Judaism* (Leiden: E.J. Brill, 1973), pp. 65-69. Sanders is critical of Neusner for attributing too much importance to the purity laws in Pharisaic thinking, but he agrees that the Pharisees did have a positive concern for purity—just as most Jews, including Paul, did (*Jewish Law*; especially the chapter 'Did the Pharisees Eat Ordinary Food in Purity?', pp. 131-254). Note also E. Rivkin's view, in opposition to Neusner's, that the Pharisees were concerned with issues ranging far beyond ritual purity; they were revolutionaries (*A Hidden Revolution: The Pharisees' Search for the Kingdom Within* [Nashville: Abingdon Press, 1978], pp. 72-75, 242).

86. For references concerning Jews and Judaism in Greco-Roman literature see M. Stern, *Greek and Latin Authors on Jews and Judaism* (3 vols.; Jerusalem: Israel Academy of Sciences and Humanities, 1974–84), which is a collection of virtually

tion Jews who have rejected the authority of the Torah.[87] Moreover, many writers often found Jewish dietary laws (especially the prohibition to eat pork) incomprehensible and deserving ridicule.[88]

On the other hand, what Gentiles found particularly offensive about the Jews was not the oddness of their food laws. The peculiar dietary exclusions of the Jews certainly intrigued the ancients, but perhaps no more than did the practices of the Pythagoreans and other races.[89] In all likelihood they were tolerated as ethnic oddities.[90] It was chiefly the Jews' refusal to recognize pagan gods (which, Josephus notes in *Apion* 2.148, earned them the appellation 'atheists') and the reluctance to engage in normal social intercourse with outsiders that marked them as misanthropic.

In his account of the clash between Antiochus VII and the Jews, Diodorus (first century BCE) mentions that Jews were accused by the advisors of Antiochus VII of introducing 'utterly outlandish laws: not to break bread with any other race, nor to show them any good will at all'.[91] Likewise Tacitus (c. 56–120 CE) felt offended by Jews because

all such references with extensive annotation. See also E. Gabba, 'The Growth of Anti-Judaism or the Greek Attitude towards Jews', in W.D. Davies and L. Finkelstein (eds.), *The Cambridge History of Judaism*. II. *The Hellenistic Age* (Cambridge: Cambridge University Press, 1989), pp. 614-56.

87. J. Goldstein, 'Jewish Acceptance and Rejection of Hellenism', in E.P. Sanders and A.I. Baumgarten (eds.), *Jewish and Christian Self-Definition* (3 vols.; Philadelphia: Fortress Press, 1981), II, pp. 64-87 (65) n. 8. Note also Juvenal's (c. 60–130 CE) assertion that Jews 'learn and practice and revere the Jewish law, and all that Moses handed down in his secret tome' (*Satire* 301, in *GLA*, II, p. 103).

88. See M. Whittaker, *Jews and Christians: Greco-Roman Views* (Cambridge: Cambridge University Press, 1984), pp. 73-80, for documentation of some of the more significant pagan writings about Jewish food laws.

89. R.M. Grant notes that food laws were very scarce among pagans and when they appeared they were as a rule allegorized ('Dietary Laws among Pythagoreans, Jews, and Christians', *HTR* 73 [1980], pp. 299-310).

90. Sextus Empiricus notes that 'a Jew or Egyptian priest would prefer to die instantly rather than eat pork, while to taste mutton is reckoned an abomination in the eyes of a Libyan, and Syrians think the same about pigeons, and others about cattle' (*GLA*, II, p. 159). Similarly, Celsus observes that the Egyptian priests abstain from pork, goats, sheep, oxen, and fish (in Origen, *Contra Cels.* 5.41).

91. Diodorus, *Bibliotheca historica* 34.1.2, in *GLA*, I, p. 183. Diodorus apparently agrees with the advisors' assessment but praises the 'magnanimous' Antiochus for not following their recommendation to exterminate the Jews; cf. Josephus, *Ant.* 13.246.

'they sit apart at meals' due to their 'hate and enmity' towards outsiders. They 'conceive of one god only, and...regard as impious those
who make...representations of gods in man's image'. The 'earliest
lesson' they taught Gentile converts was 'to despise the gods, to disown
their country, and to regard their parents, children and brothers as of
little account'.[92]

It would be unwise to conclude from these charges that many Jews in
the Greco-Roman world were antisocial and idol-bashing fundamental-
ists. Charges like these could easily have arisen through ignorance or
social or racial bias. Nevertheless, they probably contain a kernel of
truth that many Jews, perhaps like Christians, did not consider association with pagans a top priority, nor were they well disposed to the worship of other gods. Their avoidance of non-kosher and idolatrous food
could easily have led to a hesitation or even unwillingness to eat with
Gentiles. In any case, it is fair to say that pagan references regarding
Jews do not give the impression that the number of Jews who would eat
idol food is significant.

9. Implications for our Understanding of Paul's Attitude to Idol Food

From this survey of Jewish attitudes, it seems that most Jews, especially those in Palestine, would not condone eating idol food. Of
course, it should not be surprising that there is explicit evidence for
negative attitude toward idol food among Jews. What is surprising is
the pervasiveness of this negative attitude. This is seen both in the
range of the sources which attest it and also in the familiarity with the
prohibition of idol food that is assumed by the authors.

The fear of inadvertent involvement with idolatry seems to lie behind
the popular Jewish unease about eating Gentile food and association
with Gentiles. It is probable that, for some Jews, the avoidance of
Gentiles and their food stemmed from a hateful, nationalistic disposition towards outsiders. But such Jews were definitely in the minority.
Most Jews seemed willing, though not always eager, to participate in
the social life of the Gentile world, provided such participation did not
force them to disobey Yahweh and the Jewish laws. In particular, there
are clear indications in some Jewish writings—both in Palestine and in

---

92. Tacitus, *Historiae* 5.5.1-4, in *GLA*, II, p. 26. Cf. Josephus's mention of a
similar charge in *Apion* 2.258.

the Diaspora—that it is all right for a Jew to eat with a Gentile, provided precaution is being taken to avoid any association with idolatry.

In attempts to justify or promote Judaism before Gentiles, it is significant that the dietary laws were often allegorized. To be sure, the allegorical explanations usually did not set aside, but served to reinforce, the literal observance of the dietary regulations commanded in the law. Nevertheless, that Jewish authors felt the need to give allegorical explanations for the food laws at all is an indication of the intellectual difficulties in regarding non-kosher foods as inherently unclean.[93] In fact, such feelings may well stand in the background of Paul's opinion that 'nothing is unclean in itself'.

In contrast, there is no evidence that allegorization of the idol food prohibition was ever attempted in early Judaism. In the minds of most Jews, idol food was so inextricably bound up with idolatry that they were instinctively repulsed by it. Idol food simply epitomized idol worship. It was no accident that the Jewish attitude toward idol food reflected in these sources was more stringent than attitudes concerning other matters which involved at least passive contact with idolatry.

Paul speaks vociferously of his Jewish—and probably Pharisaic—credentials: he was 'a Hebrew of Hebrews; in regard to the law, a Pharisee' (Phil. 3.5).[94] According to Acts 22.3, he studied in Jerusalem

---

93. On the sociological explanation of purity laws as a symbolic system for protecting holiness and marking boundaries, see M. Douglas, *Purity and Danger: An Analysis of the Concepts of Pollution and Taboo* (London: Routledge & Kegan Paul, 1966) and Housten, *Purity and Monotheism*. Housten notes that such purity laws 'could operate with a perfectly arbitrary definition of the permitted and forbidden species' (p. 15). Because of this, monotheism without purity (as a ritual system) is possible, as the case of Christianity shows (pp. 259-82). For an understanding of the priesthood and purity laws as types and symbols of the restored creation, see A.T.M. Cheung, 'The Priest as a Redeemed Man: A Biblical-Theological Study of the Priesthood', *JETS* 29 (1986), pp. 265-75.

94. Cf. Rom. 9.3, 11.1; Gal. 2.15; 2 Cor. 11.22. See also Acts 23.6, 26.5. In his masterful study on the upbringing and education of the pre-Christian Paul, Hengel hypothesizes that Paul was born in Tarsus but grew up in a strict Jewish (Pharisaic) family with connections with Palestine. He studied in the school of Gamaliel I and perhaps with other Pharisaic teachers. His spiritual home was in one of the Greek-speaking synagogues in Jerusalem, where 'er vermutlich seine Aufgabe darin sah, sein pharisäisches Gesetzesverständnis als Lehrer und Prediger den in großer Zahl nach Jerusalem strömenden Diasporajuden zu vermitteln' ('Vorchristliche Paulus', pp. 212-91; see especially his 'Zusammenfassende Hypothese' on pp. 237-39 and 265 [265]). It is not possible to discuss here the issues of authenticity of Philippians

under the famous (proto-)rabbi Gamaliel I. He claims that he 'was advancing in Judaism beyond many Jews of [his] own age and was extremely zealous for the traditions of [his] fathers' (Gal. 1.14).[95] Moreover, even after Paul's call to be an apostle to the Gentiles, his writings exhibit numerous and stunning parallels to the Tanak and other writings in early Judaism (especially those coming from the rabbinic milieu).[96] Since Jewish attitudes toward idol food were almost entirely negative in both rabbinic and non-rabbinic sources, can we conclude from the above observations that Paul would not condone eating idol food?

Unfortunately, the issue is not that simple. For one thing, the equation of rabbinic Judaism with Pharisaic teachings is far from certain. For another, one cannot simply assume that Paul would follow the prevalent Jewish attitude. Paul's vision of the risen Christ and his calling as the apostle to the Gentiles introduced a profound discontinuity with his Jewish past. For the newly enlightened Paul it was not such boundary marking requirements as circumcision, Sabbath, and the dietary laws, but repentance from paganism and faith in the death, resurrection, and coming of Jesus Christ (1 Thess. 1.9-10), that defined membership in God's covenant community. To the extent that they separated Jews and Gentiles, the *kashrut* must be declared invalid. No matter how important they were in Paul's Pharisaic past, they lost their binding significance in his Christian present. Hence, at least in regard to food, Paul's attitude was atypical among Jews. Would the difference between Paul and his fellow Jews also pertain to idol food?

We recall that Jews who avoided idol food avoided it mainly for one or both of two reasons: fear of Gentile uncleanness and fear of

or whether Paul was in fact from Tarsus. In any case, Gal. 1.14 and the numerous contacts of Paul's writings with Jewish Scripture clearly indicate Paul's strong Jewish background.

95. Sometimes claims are made that the dominant influence on Paul's thinking was not Judaism but Hellenism. For example, John Knox is extremely skeptical about Luke's claim that Paul studied under Gamaliel in Jerusalem (*Chapters in a Life of Paul* [London: A. & C. Black, 1954] chapter 2). But such claims seriously underestimate the interpenetration of Hellenism and Judaism. Most of the Hellenistic elements discernible in Paul's writing were in all probability already prepackaged in the Judaism that Paul knew. On the falsehood of the traditional convenient dichotomy between Hellenism and Judaism see Hengel's well-documented study, *Judaism and Hellenism*.

96. Hengel, 'Vorchristliche Paulus', pp. 248-54.

involvement with idolatry. Crucial in our understanding of Paul's attitude to idol food is the question of whether Paul associated idol food
with Gentile uncleanness or with idolatry. Had Paul associated idol
food with the concept of Gentile uncleanness, he would probably have
rejected the prohibition of idol food—as he rejected the *kashrut* as a
barrier separating Jews and Gentiles. However, it is clear that Paul did
not consider Gentiles *qua* Gentiles unclean; if they were unclean, it was
by reason of idolatry (and immorality). Thus, the significance of the
pervasive negative attitude toward idol food in early Judaism for Paul's
own position cannot legitimately be down-played by an uncritical
appeal to Paul's rejection of the validity of Jewish dietary laws for
Gentile Christians.

It is instructive to compare Paul's combative style in 1 Corinthians
8–10 with his highly conciliatory tone in Romans 14, where the issue
was not idol food but Jewish dietary laws. It is evident that, in contrast
to his attitude to the dietary laws, Paul did not see the issue of idol food
as one concerning sociological interaction between Jews and Gentiles.[97]
Rather, he saw it as the issue that separated Christians from pagans.[98]

97. It is often asserted that the idol food prohibition created a social barrier
between Jewish and Gentile Christians. The remarks of Ben Witherington (*Conflict
and Community in Corinth: A Socio-rhetorical Commentary on 1 and 2 Corinthians* [Grand Rapids: Eerdmans, 1995], p. 200), who thinks that Paul permitted
Christians to eat idol food, are typical: 'Paul believed that Christianity could not be
an ethnically specific religion…Paul did not accept the alternative advocated by
proselytizing Jews, that of turning Gentiles into Jews, culturally speaking… It is no
accident that it is precisely in those areas of action that would ethnically mark off a
group from others that Paul says a Christian is free either to act in that way or not.'
However, there is no evidence at all to support the common notion that idol food is
an issue in Jew–Gentile relationships. Even a cursory reading of patristic writings
reveals the readiness, indeed eagerness, with which Gentile Christians, like their
Jewish counterparts, refuse to eat idol food (see Chapter 4 below). Therefore, the
idol food prohibition was not a boundary marker that separated Gentile Christians
from Jewish Christians. On the contrary, it was something that defined the limits of
the new covenant community—comprising Jews and Gentiles—vis-à-vis the pagan
world.

98. J.T. Sanders ('Paul Between Jews and Gentiles in Corinth', *JSNT* 65 [1997],
pp. 67-83 [83]) insightfully remarks that 'Paul was engaging in boundary definition
for nascent Christianity' and that he 'forged a Christianity that was Jewish to the
degree that it forbade idolatry and extra-marital sex and was Gentile to the degree
that it forbade circumcision, Sabbath, and dietary laws. It was thus both and
neither.'

Therefore, he set his discussion of idol food squarely in the context of idolatry and covenant allegiance to God, thus adopting a typical Jewish stance against Greco-Roman culture.[99] Because of this, one would not expect Paul to condone eating idol food without some strong reasons (as yet unknown to us).

Like Philo, Paul considered the spirit of the law more important than its letter. But, as we have seen in the case of Philo, there is no necessary link between such enlightened piety and the setting aside of specific laws. In particular, Paul's creativity alone would not explain why his (Jewish) disdain for idolatry should somehow change after he became a Christian. In Paul's exposition of his gospel, he placed idolatry at the head of his long list of vices (Rom. 1.21-32). Indeed, idolatry is the sin that leads to all sins. And whatever the meaning of 'robbing temples' might be, Paul clearly considered abhorrence of idols to be a characteristic virtue of every pious Jew (Rom. 2.22). No Jew should ever derive any profit from a pagan temple. There could be absolutely no agreement between the temple of God and idols (2 Cor. 6.16). Because of this, Gentile conversion to Christianity meant a release from the 'bondage to beings that by nature are no gods' (Gal. 4.8) and the turning from the worship of 'dumb idols' (1 Cor. 12.2) to the service of 'a living and true God' (1 Thess. 1.9). Paul clearly views idols as no gods, dumb gods, and dead gods, in line with biblical and Jewish traditions. In fact, it is demonstrable that Paul's earliest missionary preaching has much in common with Jewish literature for proselytism or the bolstering of self identity.[100] While Paul did not consider the Law to be

99. Cf. Gooch's comment that 'Paul's "liberalism" thus may extend to kashrut and to circumcision, but it extends no further, and in no way abandons the centre of Judaism's conception of the relationship between God and his people' ('Food and Limits', p. 401).

100. For the close connection between Paul's missionary preaching and Jewish apologetic and proselyte traditions see J.Y.-S. Pak, *Paul as Missionary: A Comparative Study of Missionary Discourse in Paul's Epistles and Selected Contemporary Jewish Texts* (European University Studies, 23; New York: Peter Lang, 1991). For example, in the *Sibylline Oracles*, the readers are exhorted to worship the one God, forsake demon worship, and offer their cultic service to the true and eternal God (*Sib. Or.* 1.15-22; cf. 1 Thess. 1.9). The sibyl also argues that men's refusal to honor God leads them to offer religious worship to his creatures (*Sib. Or.* 3.29-35; cf. Rom. 1.21-23) and that idolatry, immorality and infanticide are the cause of God's judgment (*Sib. Or.* 3.762-66; cf. Rom. 1.24-32). Pak also notes that the *Sibylline Oracles* emphasize the recognition of the one true God rather than the

the instrument of salvation, he did not abrogate its moral imperatives. His converts were expected to refrain from idolatry, no less than from other vices like sexual immorality, greed, drunkenness, murder, and the like, which were strongly forbidden in the Law.

I conclude that nothing in Paul's Jewish background would encourage Paul to condone eating idol food. If Paul was influenced by his Jewish heritage against idolatry in any significant ways, his attitude toward idol food was likely to be negative. Indeed, as F. Siegert points out, the polemics against idolatry in Hellenistic Jewish preaching exemplified in Pseudo-Philo's sermons seems very mild compared to Paul's denunciation of pagan gods.[101] Given Paul's strong disdain for idolatry, one is hard put to find a motive for his condoning the consumption of idol food. Nothing in his encounter with the risen Christ or in his calling as an apostle to the Gentiles leads us to believe otherwise.

keeping of the distinctive Jewish laws such as circumcision, Sabbath, and the dietary laws (though this recognition is a first step that does not exclude further steps toward Jewish observances). See also Collins's discussion of the 'common ethic' in *Athens and Jerusalem*, pp. 137-74, where he points out that monotheism and sexual ethics are given much more prominent places in the literature of the Hellenistic Diaspora than the distinctive Jewish observances such as circumcision and the food laws. Cf. Klumbies, *Die Rede*; R.M. Grant, *Gods and the One God* (ed. W.A. Meeks; LEC, 1; Philadelphia: Westminster Press, 1986), pp. 45-53; U. Heckel, 'Das Bild der Heiden und die Identität der Christen bei Paulus', in R. Feldmeier and U. Heckel (eds.), *Die Heiden: Juden, Christen und das Problem des Fremden* (WUNT, 70; Tubingen: Mohr Siebeck, 1992), pp. 269-96. For the question of whether, and to what extent, missionary style proselytism was practiced by Jews in the Second Temple period see McKnight, *Light*.

101. F. Siegert, 'Die Heiden in der pseudo-philonischen Predigt *De Jona*', in Feldmeier and Heckel (eds.), *Die Heiden*, pp. 55-59 (55-56 n. 5). In another work, Siegert notes the parallels between Paul's letters and Hellenistic Jewish preaching in the stereotypical use of catalogs of Gentile vices (*Drei hellenistisch-jüdische Predigten* [2 vols.; WUNT, 61; Tubingen: Mohr Siebeck, 1992], II, p. 172).

Chapter 3

EXEGETICAL INVESTIGATION OF 1 CORINTHIANS 8.1–11.1

1. *Literary Integrity of 1 Corinthians 8.1–11.1*

While the Pauline authorship of 1 Corinthians has never been seriously questioned, the literary integrity of the letter is a controversial issue in modern scholarship. Much of the debate centers on Paul's treatment of the issue of food offered to idols (1 Cor. 8.1–11.1), which is regarded as the 'keystone of the various attempts to divide 1 Corinthians into two or more letters'.[1] The alleged conflict between the theology expressed in 1 Cor. 10.1-22 and that of the rest of the section, coupled with the fact that 1 Corinthians 9 seems only loosely connected with its context, is seen as evidence for the composite nature of the section. Schmithals's proposal is representative of those who challenge the literary integrity of the section:

> The unity of…8.1–11.1 is to be contested…a continuous train of thought is formed by…8.1-13, 9.1-23, and 10.23–11.1. At first Paul speaks in principle about the occasionally necessary renunciation of the freedom to eat meat sacrificed to idols and of Christian freedom in general, then he presents himself as example and model, and finally he gives instructions for the attitude of the Corinthians toward the problem of eating meat sacrificed to idols, for which in fact they had asked him by letter. The statements about the *worship* of idols (10.1-22) by no means fit into this connection. They concern a basically different theme. In the treatment of the profane eating of meat sacrificed to idols there is nothing to indicate that at the same time some in Corinth had the inclination to take part in the pagan worship. Conversely, 10.1-22 treats only *cultic* meals.[2]

---

1. J.C. Hurd, Jr, *The Origin of 1 Corinthians* (Macon, GA: Mercer University Press, new edn, 1983), p. 115.

2. W. Schmithals, *Gnosticism in Corinth* (Nashville: Abingdon Press, 1971), p. 92. See Hurd, *Origins*, pp. 43-47, for the list of prominent scholars who divide the passage similarly.

Since Schmithals sees a connection between 9.24-27 and 10.1-22, he assigns 9.24-10.22 to Epistle A. He assigns the rest of the section to Epistle B (later than A) as he further argues that 'the principle of 10.23 can sensibly be joined only with 9.19-23, where it moreover fits *very well*, while in connection with 10.14-22 it is simply impossible'.[3] In Epistle A Paul gives a warning against εἰδωλολατρία because some members of the Corinthian congregation are exhibiting Gnostic tendencies to participate in pagan cults. The church accepts Paul's anti-Gnostic position, but then the new problem of εἰδωλόθυτα is raised and demands a different answer from Paul in a subsequent letter (B).[4] The inconsistency in the flow of logic of 8.1–11.1 is the result of the juxtaposition of the two letter fragments.

Furthermore, as Brunt notes, 1 Cor. 10.1-22 is often seen as being more 'magical' in its teaching than the rest.[5] Here, eating and drinking assume a sacramental dimension. Moreover, the argument against the eating of idol food is motivated by a fear of demons that is not present in the rest of the passage, where the concern is for the weak. In addition, 10.22 seems to contradict both 10.27 and 8.10.

It must be admitted that it is not easy to understand the flow of Paul's logic in this section. However, most modern scholars do not consider the difficulties insurmountable. The apparent inconsistencies, while significant, are not deemed evidence enough for the composite nature of the section. In particular, Barrett maintains that the alleged inconsistencies can be explained when one understands that Paul is dealing with a complex situation.[6] In fact, the majority of scholars see 1 Corinthians as a single, unified composition.[7] This commitment to the integrity of the section results in various attempts to explain the overall structure of the passage and the connections that can be seen between its various parts.[8]

3. Schmithals, *Gnosticism*, p. 93.

4. Schmithals, *Gnosticism*, p. 227.

5. Brunt, 'Paul's Attitude', p. 55.

6. C. K. Barrett, *The First Epistle to the Corinthians* (HNTC; New York: Harper & Row, 1968), p. 16.

7. For a summary of the issues and a defense of the integrity of the letter, see W. G. Kümmel, *Introduction to the New Testament* (Nashville: Abingdon Press, 3rd edn, 1975), pp. 276-78; Hurd, *Origins*, pp. 43-47, 131-42.

8. For recent major attempts to demonstrate the unity of the passage with good bibliography, see Mitchell, *Rhetoric*; and Probst, *Paulus*. A main objective of

A full defense of the integrity of the section must await detailed exegesis of the passage. In particular, one must attempt a plausible reconstruction of the problem of εἰδωλόθυτα in Corinth that makes sense of Paul's discussion. Nevertheless, I note here some general arguments against the partition theories.

First, there is no textual evidence whatsoever for the composite nature of the section in a comparatively full manuscript tradition. This consideration takes on much added weight as the evidence for the use of 1 Corinthians is more early, frequent, and widespread than any other New Testament writings. Thus the onus must be on those who favor partition theories to give a plausible account of how such a juxtaposition took place from a text-critical point of view.[9]

Secondly, the partition theories assume that the discrepancies between the purported letter fragments are great enough to show that they are from separate letters but small enough for them to be both Pauline. In other words, Paul is allowed to be inconsistent from one letter to another—even though the time span between them is small—but not in the course of a single letter. This distinction, while possible, is much too subtle.[10]

Thirdly, as argued in the previous chapter, it is historically unrealistic

Probst's monograph is to show that 1 Cor. 8–10 exhibits the form and structure of an ancient letter.

9. W. Walker, Jr, claims that 'the emerging Catholic leadership in the churches "standardized" the text of the Pauline corpus in the light of "orthodox" views and practices, *suppressing and even destroying all deviant texts and manuscripts*' so that 'the manuscript evidence can tell us nothing about the state of the Pauline literature prior to the third century' ('The Burden of Proof in Identifying Interpolations in the Pauline Letters', *NTS* 33 [1987], pp. 610-18 [614]; emphasis added). I think it is historically improbable, and contrary to evidence in our extant manuscripts of New Testament writings, that all indications of such major textual disturbance like interpolations and translocations could have disappeared without trace. As Paul's letters (especially 1 Corinthians) were quickly copied, it is highly unlikely that later interpolations or combinations would appear in *all* extant manuscripts. See K. Aland, 'Neutestamentliche Textkritik und Exegese', in K. Aland and S. Meurer; Bielefeld and W. Germany (eds.), *Wissenschaft und Kirche: Festschrift für Eduard Lohse* (Luther-Verlag, 1989), pp. 132-48. For an introduction to the issues on the text–canon intersection at the compositional stage of the New Testament, see E.J. Epp, 'Textual Criticism in the Exegesis of the New Testament, with an Excursus on Canon', in S.E. Porter (ed.), *Handbook to Exegesis of the New Testament* (Leiden: E.J. Brill, 1997), pp. 45-97, esp. pp. 73-91.

10. Brunt, 'Paul's Attitude', p. 132.

to think that Paul did not discussed the issue of idol food with the Corinthian Christians during his lengthy ministry there. Moreover, he had been preaching to Gentiles for many years by the time he penned 1 Corinthians (or the letters that it allegedly comprises). At this mature stage of his ministry, it is highly unlikely that Paul changed his opinion drastically on this important subject over a very brief span of time as the partition theories suggest.

More damaging to the partition theories is Hurd's observation that 10.19 ('What do I imply then…that an idol is anything?') seems to be Paul's conscious attempt to avoid contradicting 8.4-6 ('an idol is nothing…for us there is one God, the Father…').[11] Thus if the section must be partitioned, 10.1-22 would have to come later, rather than earlier, than 8.1-13! That even Paul himself recognized a certain tension between his statements in chapters 8 and 10 suggests strongly that the two parts were composed on the same occasion. Weiss, whose partition theory has shaped much of the subsequent debate over the literary integrity of 1 Corinthians, is obviously troubled by 1 Cor. 10.19. Thus he sees the verse as a mere aside in the earlier letter, which was seized upon by the strong and developed into the slogans that occasioned Paul's response in the later letter.[12] Such an attempt to salvage the partition theory is as *ad hoc* as it is ingenious. It only serves to underline the strong interconnections between the two allegedly distinct Pauline letters which refuse to be explained away.

2. *The Nature of the Problem in Corinth and Paul's Response*

a. *The Traditional or Majority View*
Most interpreters consider Paul's discussion to be a response to an internal problem in Corinth between the 'weak' and the 'strong' parties over the question of eating marketplace idol food and/or social meals at idol temples.[13] As a result, the Corinthian Christians sought Paul's advice on the issue in their letter.

---

11. Hurd, *Origins*, p. 134. Hurd notes that this point has been appreciated by von Soden ('Sakrament und Ethik', pp. 246-47, 257). See also H. Conzelmann, *1 Corinthians* (Hermeneia; Philadelphia: Fortress Press, 1975), p. 175 n. 6, for connections between 8.1-13 and 10.1-22.

12. Johannes Weiss, *Der erste Korintherbrief* (MeyerK; Göttingen: Vandenhoeck & Ruprecht, 1910), p. 261.

13. The following outline is an adaptation of G.D. Fee's presentation of the traditional view in 'Εἰδωλόθυτα Once Again: An Interpretation of 1 Corinthians 8–

It is usually understood that the 'strong' Christians are those who claim 'knowledge' and 'freedom' (8.1-4, 7-13) to eat idol food without qualms. Some even attend cultic meals at the temples (8.10; 10.14-22). The 'weak', on the other hand, are either over-scrupulous Jewish Christians or Gentile Christians who continue to be haunted by their former pagan religious experience. They argue against eating idol food because such an act goes against their conscience. However, these weak Christians are feeling the pressure from the strong to be 'built up' by eating idol food. In imitating the strong, they violate their own conscience and are in danger of being destroyed.

Paul's advice shows 'an attitude of extraordinary liberalism' that disregards traditional Jewish sensibilities.[14] In principle, he agrees with the strong that an idol is nothing and hence no food can be contaminated by virtue of its having been sacrificed to an idol. Hence, the issue of idol food is an ἀδιάφορον. However, as they advocate eating such food on the basis of knowledge and freedom, these strong Christians are placing a stumbling-block before those with uninformed conscience. Therefore, while acknowledging their freedom to eat, Paul cautions them to be more considerate, lest they inflict spiritual damage on the weak. In a digression, he relates his own example of how he has forgone his freedom for the sake of others (ch. 9). Some scholars believe that Paul is also making a defense of his apostleship here.[15]

Almost as an aside, Paul again digresses to warn those who are so bold as to actually enter pagan temples and participate in cultic feasts (10.1-22). Paul prohibits such an act either as a concession to the weak or because it represents idol worship (εἰδωλολατρία), which the eating of εἰδωλόθυτα does not in itself imply. He is thus distinguishing the mere eating of consecrated food from actual idolatry, in the sense of participation in pagan feasts.

After this second digression, Paul reaffirms his position that idol food is a matter of indifference and encourages the weak to take a broader

10', *Bib* 61 (1980), pp. 173-74, and *The First Epistle to the Corinthians*, pp. 358-59. Fee notes that 'this is the position assumed or advocated in the commentaries (Parry excepted), as well as in most of the other literature' (*The First Epistle to the Corinthians*, p. 358). Fee's description of the traditional view is fair on the whole, though recent scholarly opinion has become more nuanced—no doubt influenced in part by Fee's works. My presentation of the traditional view attempts to reflect this recent shift and allows for a wider range of scholarly opinion.

14. Barrett, 'Things Sacrificed', p. 50.
15. See Mitchell, *Rhetoric*, pp. 243-50 and notes.

view regarding it (10.23–11.1). At the same time, he also takes the opportunity to remind the strong again not to scandalize the weak.

The apparent vacillation and confusion in Paul's treatment of the issue is due to the complexity of the situation, as Paul has to 'walk the tightrope between the legalism of Jewish Christianity and the false liberalism of gnostic rationalism'.[16]

Evaluation of the Traditional View. The traditional interpretation regards Paul's ideological position on idol food as a clear indication of his radical liberation from his Jewish past. This understanding seems to cohere with an emphasis on justification by faith alone apart from the law. It also enables a reading of 1 Corinthians 8–10 that is consistent with Paul's clearly conciliatory approach in Romans 14 in maintaining the unity of Jewish and Gentile Christians. Moreover, the problem of idol food in Corinth can then be seen as a part of the general struggle in early Christianity between the freedom allowed by the Pauline gospel and the legalism of some 'Judaizing' Christians who opposed such freedom.

However, this traditional reconstruction is shaky at its very foundation, namely, the idea that there is a dispute between two parties on the issue of idol food. In fact, there is no evidence that the Corinthians' question about εἰδωλόθυτα represents a division of opinion within the church.[17] The element of internal strife has simply been read into the text from 1 Corinthians 1–4 or under the influence of Rom. 14.1–15.13.

There is no hint in our passage that the weak ever challenge the right of the strong to eat idol food.[18] On the contrary, it is clear that the weak

16. Barrett, 'Things Sacrificed', p. 56.

17. It is beyond the scope of this work to investigate the nature of the 'parties' or that of 'Paul's opponents' in Corinth. Scholarly opinion is divided between those who hold that 1 Corinthians is aimed at a single, more or less unified, group of Paul's opponents and those who think it deals with intra-church conflicts between the Corinthian Christians. For a brief survey of the history of research and the basic issues involved see W. Baird, ' "One Against the Other": Intra-Church Conflict in 1 Corinthians', in R.T. Fortna and B.R. Gaventa (eds.), *The Conversation Continues: Studies in Paul and John in Honor of J. Louis Martyn* (Nashville: Abingdon Press, 1990), pp. 116-36. If the 'one-front' hypothesis can be validated for the entire epistle, it automatically follows that Paul is not merely responding to an internal dispute in 1 Cor. 8.1–11.1. Even if not, it does not preclude the possibility that Paul's discussion of εἰδωλόθυτα is addressed to a single group.

18. Some interpreters understand the informant in 10.28 as a weak Christian. I

wish to be seen to be like the strong, even to the point of eating idol food in spite of their συνείδησις (1 Cor. 8.7-10). If they do advocate a conservative position in opposition to the strong it is hardly likely that they would be tempted to follow their example; it is more likely that they will judge the strong, who will in turn despise the weak (as in Rom. 14.1–15.13). Yet what Paul fears here is not factionalism but that the weak would be destroyed in imitating the strong. Moreover, unlike 1 Corinthians 1–4, there is no indication in 1 Cor. 8-10 that the unity of the church is being threatened. If there is any quarrel, it is between Paul and the Corinthians.

To be sure, Paul mentions the weak and pleads for their welfare. However it is important to note that he never addresses the weak but only describes them—using third person plural.[19] On the other hand, he does not describe those who have knowledge but addresses them directly—using second person plural.[20] This is in marked contrast to Rom. 14.1–15.13, where both the weak and the strong are addressed in a more conciliatory manner. In fact, the 'weak' seem so shadowy in 1 Cor. 8.1–11.1 that Hurd, followed by not a few scholars, considers them a mere hypothetical construction by Paul to prove a point to those who claim to have knowledge.[21]

The Corinthians' seeking of Paul's advice over an internal dispute hardly calls for the 'vigorous, combative nature' of Paul's response.[22] Is it believable that Paul is engaging in such an awful lot of vehement rhetoric simply to play the role of an adjudicator for two parties who ask and supposedly value his advice? Moreover, though it is often

will show later that this is unlikely. Even if that understanding is correct, the text does not indicate that the informant *disputes* the eating, but only that attention is drawn to the idolatrous origin of the food.

19. It is true that 10.23-29 (or part of it) has been taken as Paul's instruction to the weak. I will refute this dubious suggestion later.

20. Paul does not address those who have 'knowledge' as the 'strong' in his discussion, nor does he identify himself with them as he does with the strong in Rom. 15.1.

21. Hurd does not deny that some Corinthians were 'less secure in their new faith than others' (hence they were weak in this sense), but he emphasizes that there is no evidence that they as a party had communicated their point of view to Paul (*Origins*, p. 125); cf. Gooch, *Dangerous Food*, pp. 66-67; J.F.M. Smit, 'The Rhetorical Disposition of First Corinthians 8.7–9.27', *CBQ* 59 (1997), pp. 476-91 [480].

22. Fee, *The First Epistle to the Corinthians*, p. 477.

asserted that Paul's own position is closer to that of the strong, his language hardly suggests that he is in basic agreement with them, but strongly suggests that he and they are at odds on the issue. Paul's attack seems solely directed at those over-wise and over-confident shapers of opinion in the Corinthian church. He seems totally uninterested in changing the weak.[23] Indeed, he exhibits no concern to change the weak while he has every concern to change the strong. It is telling that while Paul is willing to 'become weak to the weak', he does not say he becomes strong to the strong. If a 'weak' party ever existed, Paul would only have increased the discord at Corinth by standing so completely behind them against the strong.[24]

When the basically one-front nature of Paul's response to the Corinthians is recognized, it becomes obvious that scholarly attempts to identify and define the parties in conflict over the issue of idol food are futile. In particular, the identification of the 'weak' as over-scrupulous Jewish Christians[25] associated with the anti-Pauline 'Cephas party' bears little semblance to historical reality.[26]

---

23. Many defenders of the traditional view *assume* that Paul, while condemning the strong's harsh approach in 'building up' the conscience of the weak, intends to educate the weak with a gradual and indirect approach. See Jewett, *Anthropological Terms*, pp. 428, 459; Barrett, *The First Epistle to the Corinthians*, pp. 194-95; J. Moffatt, *The First Epistle of Paul to the Corinthians* (New York: Harper and Brothers, 1938), p. 111. For a elaborate proposal of Paul's psychagogic adaptability in educating the weak, see C.E. Glad, *Paul and Philodemus: Adaptability in Epicurean and Early Christian Psychagogy* (NovTSup, 81; Leiden: E.J. Brill, 1995), pp. 277-95.

24. Hurd, *Origins*, p. 119.

25. An implicit anti-Judaism seems to lie behind much of this kind of reconstruction. Weiss, whose commentary on 1 Corinthians has shaped the basic contour both of the traditional view and of the partition-theories, suggests that Paul's warnings about the danger of demons, made on behalf of the weak in the earlier letter (1 Cor. 10.1-22), reflected the superstitions of Judaism (*Der Erste Korintherbrief*, p. 264). In Weiss's view, Paul was liberated from earlier superstitious Jewish fear of demons when he wrote the second letter (1 Cor. 8.1-13; 10.23–11.1).

26. The attempt to link the weak with a Petrine party (either Jewish Christian or strongly influenced by Jewish Christians) in Corinth goes as far back as F.C. Baur. Barrett suggests that 'the problem of εἰδωλόθυτα would never have arisen in a Gentile Church like that of Corinth if the Jewish Christians (the Cephas·group perhaps) had not raised it' ('Things Sacrificed', p. 49). This cannot be further from the truth. In view of the significant social meaning of εἰδωλόθυτα in the Greco-Roman world, it would be one of the first issues to arise in a Gentile church! Conzelmann's

My caution against the undue influence of Romans 14 on the interpretation of 1 Corinthians 8–10 must not be taken as a denial of the
strong relationship and similarity between the passages. Romans 14 is
clearly an adaptation of 1 Corinthians 8–10. The correspondence of the
two passages in terms of vocabulary and concept is truly impressive.[27]
Moreover, the length and the prominence of the discussion of the
'weaker brethren' principle in both passages show unmistakably the
importance of this principle in Paul's community ethics. Nevertheless,
the fact that this same principle is operative in more contexts than one
does not mean the contexts are necessarily the same. In addition, we
must recognize that while the weaker brethren principle establishes the
illegitimacy of eating in some circumstances, it does not in itself establish the legitimacy of eating in other circumstances.[28] The theoretical
rightness or wrongness of eating is not a necessary part of the principle,
and hence must be determined by other factors.

As we shall see, Romans 14 can shed light on our exegesis of
1 Corinthians 8–10. But we cannot import wholesale our understanding
of the former into our interpretation of the latter, as the historical and
rhetorical situations of the passages are very different. To begin with,
Romans 14 is concerned with the problem of unclean food (in the context of Jews–Gentiles relationship), not idol food (in the context of
idolatry). Paul's treatment there cannot simply be read into his discussion of idol food in 1 Corinthians 8–10 without further ado. Gooch
rightly maintains that the vocabulary of Romans 14 'falls naturally...into the arena of disputes over whether the laws of *kashrut* were
still valid, and would not be connected, but for 1 Corinthians 8–10,

conclusion is much more sober: 'It is impossible for the specific positions which
Paul combats to be assigned to any specific group [of 1.12]' (*1 Corinthians*, p. 14).

27. The parallels between the two passages are conveniently set forth in R.J.
Karris, 'Romans 14.1–15.3 and the Occasion of Romans', *CBQ* 35 (1973), pp. 155-
178; cf. Magee's 'Rhetorical Analysis'.

28. For an instructive parallel, consider Paul's use of the principle 'all things
are lawful' in 1 Cor. 6.12 and 1 Cor. 10.23. No serious scholar who thinks that Paul
treats εἰδωλόθυτα as a matter indifferent would argue that, since the principle is
invoked in both passages, Paul also permits πορνεία in theory. To do so is to
commit the fallacy of false analogies (which is like guilt by association). It is true
that if two entities share some common characteristics, it gives us reason to believe
that they may be similar in other respects. But simply because two entities have
something in common, one must not hastily conclude that they are alike in other
ways without weighing other factors such as known dissimilarities.

with the problem of food offered to idols'.[29] Moreover, as Dunn points out, different criteria are used in the two discussions: ' "faith", so central in Romans 14, does not feature in 1 Corinthians 8–10; and "conscience", so determinative in 1 Corinthians 8–10, does not appear in Romans 14'.[30] Apparently, one was the appropriate criterion for an internal issue and, the other, a boundary-crossing issue.[31]

Once the foundational premise of an internal dispute is removed, the whole traditional reconstruction crumbles. For example, it fails to resolve the apparent contradiction between 8.1-13 (where Paul argues for abstinence) and 10.23-29 (where Paul permits eating, without asking questions and without concern for the weak, unless the idolatrous origin of the food is known). 'If the "gnostic's" eating of marketplace idol food endangers a brother's life in 8.7-13, then how possibly can Paul be so relaxed about their eating the same food in 10.23-30, even to the point of making it an imperative in 10.25?'[32] The only way out—which I have ruled out—is to assume that Paul is actually addressing two different groups, the 'strong' in 8.1-13, and the 'weak' in 10.23-29.

The traditional view also fails to resolve satisfactorily the apparent inconsistency between 8.1-13 and 10.1-22 that gives rise to the partition theories. The usual solution turns on differentiating and dissociating the consumption of εἰδωλόθυτα (eating marketplace idol food or social meals at temples) from εἰδωλολατρία (actual worship of idols).[33] Paul condones the former but condemns the latter. Paul is thus addressing two different, though (loosely) related, situations. But in this way those who avoid partitioning the section do so at the cost of making

---

29. Gooch, 'Food and Limits', p. 378. There is some debate about whether the subject of Rom. 14 is Jewish food laws or other problems such as asceticism. For a concise discussion of the issues and arguments involved, see C.E.B. Cranfield, *The Epistle to the Romans* (ICC; 2 vols.; Edinburgh: T. & T. Clark, 1979), pp. 690-98; cf. J.D.G. Dunn, *Romans 9–16* (WBC, 38B; Dallas: Word Books, 1988), pp. 797-810. In any case, most commentators agree that the passage has nothing to do with idol food. As Cranfield points out, 'it is scarcely credible, in view of its prominence in 1 Corinthians 8 and 10, that Paul should never once have used the word εἰδωλόθυτος in this passage, had he had this problem in mind' (*Romans*, p. 692).

30. J.G.D. Dunn, *The Theology of Paul the Apostle* (Grand Rapids: Eerdmans, 1998), p. 703.

31. Dunn, *Theology of Paul*, p. 703.

32. Fee, 'Εἰδωλόθυτα', p. 178.

33. Brunt, 'Paul's Attitude', p. 118, maintains that one must draw 'a sharp distinction...between idol meat and idolatry'.

Paul vacillate so much and so abruptly that in substance their solution is not very different from the partition theories.[34] Conzelmann, who maintains the literary integrity of 1 Cor. 8.1–11.1, admits that

> Paul's argument appears to vacillate. In chaps. 8 and 10.23–11.1 he adopts in principle the standpoint of the 'strong'... The restriction on freedom is imposed not by meat, but by the conscience, by the bond with the 'weak' brother... In 10.1-22, on the other hand, Paul appears to vote in favor of the weak. Eating is dangerous ...
>
> Now both forms of argumentation are Pauline in content. The question is, however, whether Paul can argue both ways in the same breath.[35]

It is arguable that the attraction of the partition theories lies precisely in the feeling that Paul jumps from one subject (εἰδωλόθυτα) to another (εἰδωλολατρία) too abruptly and without warning. However the relation between 8.4-6 and 10.14-22 (especially 10.19-20) is in fact much closer than the traditional view admits. I have already mentioned above that in 10.19 Paul consciously avoids contradicting what he says in 8.4-6. Presumably Paul is dealing with the same subject in both passages. The contrast between one God/Christ and 'many gods and many lords' also corresponds with the sustained contrast between fellowship with God/Christ and fellowship with demons.

It must also be pointed out that the purported dissociation of εἰδωλόθυτα from εἰδωλολατρία is nowhere to be found in early Judaism or Christianity. On the contrary, as I have already demonstrated in the previous chapter, εἰδωλόθυτον epitomizes εἰδωλολατρία in Jewish traditions.[36] If Paul is influenced by his Jewish hostility to idolatry in any significant ways, he is unlikely to make such a distinction. In contrast to his handling of the issue of *kashrut* in Romans 14, Paul does not see the issue of idol food as one concerning sociological interaction between Jews and Gentiles. Rather, he sets his discussion of idol food squarely in the context of idolatry. In fact, in the only place in the whole of 1 Corinthians 8–10 where Paul comes close to identifying the nature of εἰδωλόθυτον, he links it unmistakably to idolatry: 'What do I

34. This is not surprising when one remembers that Weiss, whose reconstruction of the problem of idol food in Corinth set the agenda for subsequent debates, argued in the same breath for the partition theory and the traditional view.

35. Conzelmann, *1 Corinthians*, p. 137.

36. As I will demonstrate in the next chapter, the same holds true for early Christian traditions.

imply then? That idol food is anything? Or that an idol is anything? No, but...they offer to demons and not to God. I do not want you to be sharers in demons' (10.19-20)! There idol food is clearly set in apposition to the idol itself.

The attempt to differentiate εἰδωλόθυτα from εἰδωλολατρία is made more difficult when one considers the possible contexts for the eating of εἰδωλόθυτα in 1 Corinthians 8. Presumably, dining in an idol temple is included (8.10). If the eating envisaged in chapter 8 is permissible in principle provided the weak are not caused to stumble, then Paul's strong warning against cultic meals in the idol temple becomes inexplicable unless 'some activities and meals within a pagan temple are morally objectionable for Christians while others are not. 1 Cor. 8.10 describes permissible temple attendance, while 10.19-22 clearly portrays what is off limits'.[37] Fisk, a defender of the traditional view, considers this the only possible explanation of the apparent contradiction between chapters 8 and 10.

Defenders of such a view often point out that temple meals had very diverse functions and significance in the Greco-Roman world.[38] A meal at the temple can be anything from a 'harmless' social gathering with minimal religiosity to full-fledged idolatry. It has been suggested that Paul allows the former but prohibits the latter.[39]

I have already argued in Chapter 1 that, if social meals at private homes often involved explicit religious rites, it is most unlikely that there would not be some cultic acts associated with meals eaten in temples where there was heightened consciousness of the gods. Therefore, such an objective distinction between purely social meals eaten ἐν εἰδωλείῳ and meals involving τραπέζης δαιμονίων μετέχειν was highly improbable in Paul's Corinth. On the contrary, such meals would naturally be perceived as idolatrous by most Christians, including Paul.

---

37. B.N. Fisk, 'Eating Meat Offered to Idols: Corinthian Behavior and Pauline Response in 1 Corinthians 8–10 (A Response to Gordon Fee)', *Trinity Journal* 10 NS (1989), pp. 49-70 (62).

38. See especially Willis, *Idol Meat*, pp. 17-64. Willis himself argues that even cultic meals were essentially social in character.

39. See, e.g., Conzelmann, *1 Corinthians*, p. 177; J.C. Brunt, 'Love, Freedom, and Moral Responsibility: The Contribution of 1 Cor 8–10 to an Understanding of Paul's Ethical Thinking', *SBLSP* 20 (1981), pp. 19-33 (25); von Soden, 'Sacrament and Ethics in Paul', in W.A. Meeks (ed.), *The Writings of St Paul* (trans. W. Meek; New York: W.W. Norton, 1972), pp. 257-68 (264).

Moreover, on closer examination, the recognition of the diverse functions of temple meals, rather than aiding the traditional view, makes it improbable: if there is a broad spectrum for the significance of temple meals ranging from social to religious, where is one to draw the line beyond which eating becomes idolatry? Even if such a line could be drawn, there is no evidence in 1 Cor. 8.1–11.1 that Paul ever draws it. It is of little help to make conscious worship of deities during those meals the deciding criterion, for how can one tell such conscious intent? Moreover, those who have 'knowledge' can argue (and probably have argued) that for them there is never any conscious worship in any cultic meal because idols are non-existent.

When we look at the situation of Corinth in particular, it is also difficult to find a suitable candidate for the idol temple referred to in 8.10 where 'permissible temple dining' could occur. For the few scholars who ask which particular temple is in view in 8.10, the choice is basically between the sanctuary of Demeter and the *Asklepion*, which have extensive dining facilities. Archeological evidence suggests that there was a break in dining activities at the Demeter sanctuary in the Roman period and that the restoration occurred later than the writing of 1 Corinthians.[40] Moreover, as Gooch argues, when eating occurred, it was an integral part of the cultus and would qualify for what Paul would call 'sharing the table of demons' (10.21).[41] As for the *Asklepion*, dining, like the use of the fountain, in nearby Lerna is probably related to specific dietary requirements in connection with individual healing. If the inscription from the sanctuary of Asklepios in Epidaurus is any guide, it is doubtful that dining with an exclusive social purpose took place in Lerna.[42] There is also some uncertainty as to whether the dining rooms in Lerna were functioning at the time of Paul.[43]

Noting the obstacles of identifying either of these sanctuaries as the idol temple in 8.10, Winter suggests that Paul refers rather to the eating at the feasts in connection with the imperial cult in the temple of Poseidon in Isthmia during the quadrennial Caesarian Games.[44] If Winter is

---

40. B.W. Winter, *Seek the Welfare of the City: Early Christians as Benefactors and Citizens* (Grand Rapids: Eerdmans, 1994), p. 170.

41. Gooch, 'Food and Limits', p. 69.

42. Winter, *Welfare*, p. 171 n. 13. See also the earlier discussion on the ambiguous status of dining rooms in Lerna.

43. Murphy-O'Connor, *Corinth*, p. 162.

44. Winter, *Welfare*, pp. 166-77; *idem*, 'The Achaean Federal Imperial Cult II:

correct, such eating would still hardly be 'permissible' in Paul's view. On the other hand, if we do not assume that Paul is tacitly permitting temple dining in 8.10, then we do not need to search for temple meal contexts that are somewhat innocuous. 1 Cor. 8.10 can then be taken as a general reference to any temple dining, whether the focus is cultic (as it seems, for example, in the cult of Dionysus or Isis) or social.

It is entirely possible that some Corinthians participated in social meals at temples without seeing it as idolatry.[45] But a careful distinction must be made between Paul's assessment and the Corinthians' assessment of the situation. There is no evidence, and no reason to believe, that Paul himself perceived the eating of meals in idol temples as anything but idolatry, whatever the Corinthians' assessment of it. In fact, where Paul discusses permissible contexts for eating (10.23-28), temple dining is conspicuous by its absence. The apostle mentions only marketplace food and private meals, in which cases the link to idolatry is neither necessary nor obvious.

The traditional view assumes—probably under the influence of Rom. 14.1–15.13—that the issue of εἰδωλόθυτα is an ἀδιάφορον. An almost insurmountable difficulty with this assumption is that in 1 Cor. 10.20 Paul clearly condemns the eating of idol food as 'sharing in demons'. In 1 Cor. 10.14-22, Paul does not speak against idolatry in general but against the specific act of eating idol food. It is worth noting that, because 1 Cor. 10.1-22 scarcely supports the traditional view that Paul condones the practice of eating idol food, Brunt considers the passage 'the most difficult to fit into the course of the overall argument', whereas Barrett calls it an 'apparently confused and inconsistent treatment of idolatry and idolatrous practices'.[46] Others go even further in identifying 1 Cor. 10.1-22 as 'Jewish', having its origin in a different letter, or in a different 'Paul' altogether.[47] Such theories are faulty methodologically. Aside from the complete lack of textual support, it is circular reasoning of the worst sort to begin with the assumption that Paul's approach to the issue is not Jewish and then to conclude that the passage is too Jewish to be consistent with Paul!

The Corinth Church', *TynBul* 46 (1995), pp. 169-81 (172-76).

45. Murphy-O'Connor, 'Freedom', p. 549.

46. Brunt, 'Paul's Attitude', p. 100; Barrett, 'Things Sacrificed', p. 52.

47. See Hurd, *Origins*, pp. 43-46, 118-19, 126-42 for discussion of the various theories on the integrity issue.

It must be noted that, in 1 Corinthians 8, Paul nowhere explicitly acknowledges the legitimacy of the Corinthian believers to eat idol food.[48] To be sure, Paul's ostensible position is that if the Corinthians eat idol food, they will hurt the weak. However, it does not follow that it is wrong to eat idol food only if someone is hurt by such an act. It is possible, but by no means necessary, that Paul's prohibition of eating is conditioned upon the harmful effects of such eating on the weak. One cannot conclude without further ado that he permits the Corinthians to eat idol food if no one is caused to stumble. A teacher who finds it difficult to convince the recalcitrant students of the virtue of study may say, 'if you are lazy, you will fail your test'. But the statement in no way implies that the teacher thinks that the students can be lazy provided they do not fail their test. Once this *non sequitur* is recognized, the main ground for seeing 10.1-22 as an intrusion is removed. There is no difficulty in the text that would prevent one from seeing Paul as arguing in two different—but compatible—ways against the eating of idol food in both 8.1-13 and 10.1-22. Abstention for the sake of the weak and abstention in order to avoid idolatry are not mutually exclusive arguments. On the contrary, they are mutually reinforcing in their prohibition of the consumption of idol food.[49] This is clearly how native Greek speakers and rhetoricians such as Origen and Chrysostom understood Paul's argument.

Perhaps most damaging to the traditional understanding of Paul's attitude of the issue of εἰδωλόθυτα is the fact that such an attitude can

---

48. Whether he does so implicitly is a matter of interpretation.

49. J.F.M. Smit ('1 Corinthians 8, 1-6, a Rhetorical Partitio: A Contribution to the Coherence of 1 Cor. 8, 1–11, 1', in R. Bieringer [ed.], *The Corinthian Correspondence* [BETL, 125; Leuven: Peeters, 1996], pp. 577-91) argues that Paul addresses two different aspects of the single problem of temple dining: the human aspect in 8.7–9.27, and the theological aspect in 10.1-22. Similarly, Fee, *The First Epistle to the Corinthians*, p. 360. This is in basic agreement with my own view as far as rhetorical strategy is concerned. I differ from them in that I believe the problem of idol food is more extensive than temple dining. Peter Gooch ('Food and Limits', pp. 238-50) agrees with me that idol food in general, not just temple dining, is the problem and that Paul is using two arguments to make a single point. However, I do not share his view that Paul is unconcerned about consistency and logical development: 'a series of unrelated arguments, developed to varying degrees, sometimes in tension with one another, linked only by their common conclusion in support of Paul's central point' (249). I believe that Paul's arguments are carefully and skilfully crafted to deliver maximal rhetorical impact.

be found neither in Paul's Jewish heritage nor in his Christian legacy. I have already considered the evidence of early Judaism in the previous chapter. In the next chapter, I will show that the current consensus view could not be found in early Christianity. The point is not that early Christians opposed that view, but that they were not even aware of its existence! They felt no need whatsoever to defend Paul against those who themselves had no qualms about eating idol food. As Dunn puts it, 'when those closer to the thought world of Paul and closer to the issue of idol food show no inkling of the current interpretation, that interpretation is probably wrong'.[50]

Moreover, there was a virtually uniform opposition to the eating of any food identified as εἰδωλόθυτα in early Christianity and most early Christian authors appealed to Paul in justifying this prohibition. Of course, early Christians are not necessarily correct in their interpretation of Paul. Sometimes they are notorious for their misinterpretation of the apostle. Nonetheless, is it historically plausible that the 'correct' understanding of Paul's approach to such an important issue vanishes without trace, when 'the evidence for the use of 1 Corinthians is older, clearer, and more widespread than that for any other book of the New Testament'?[51] I will return later to this issue of external evidence. Here it will suffice to say that when there is absolutely no external evidence for any competing interpretations, the uniform appeal to Paul in the prohibition of idol food in early Christianity cannot be set aside except by internal argument of the most persuasive sort. But, as we have argued above, the internal evidence for the current majority view is hardly compelling.

b. *An Alternative to the Traditional View: John Hurd's Proposal*
John Hurd's monograph is an invaluable study of the history of the relationship between Paul and the Corinthian Christians leading to the composition of 1 Corinthians.[52] Working backward in time, stage by stage, from the evidence in 1 Corinthians, Hurd attempts to reconstruct the content of the Corinthians' letter to Paul, then Paul's previous letter, and, finally, all the way back to Paul's first preaching at Corinth. The

---

50. Dunn, *Theology of Paul*, p. 704. Dunn refers to the results of my investigation of early Christian material.
51. Barrett, *The First Epistle to the Corinthians*, pp. 11-12.
52. Hurd, *Origins*. Hurd deals with with the issue of idol food in pp. 114-49.

basic outline of Hurd's reconstruction is this: when the 'younger, more vigorous Paul' first came to Corinth, he was 'fired with enthusiasm in his new faith' and quite unguarded in his theological statements emphasizing Christian freedom. His enthusiastically oriented preaching included many of the Corinthian slogans found in 1 Corinthians. Later on, however, 'in his understandable desire to strengthen the Gentile mission' by seeking the goodwill of the Jerusalem Church, Paul moved in a conservative direction. In his 'previous letter' to the Corinthians (1 Cor. 5.9) he demanded, *inter alia*, the observance of the Apostolic Decree. Such a reversal of stance 'puzzled and angered' the Corinthians, who in their reply to Paul voiced their objection to the restriction of their freedom, (mis)quoting Paul's own slogans in his earlier preaching back to him, and charging him with inconsistency. In response, Paul wrote 1 Corinthians, in which he avoided the excessive strictness of his previous letter and returned to his former position on most points of actual practice. At the same time, he became more cautious in his theological statements and sought to qualify the liberal extremes of his earlier preaching.[53]

Hurd's reading of 1 Corinthians 8–10 is central to his reconstruction of the exchange between Paul and the Corinthian Christians. Challenging the traditional view at its very foundation, Hurd argues that there is no evidence for a dispute over idol meat in Corinth.[54] Instead, the real dispute was between Paul and the Corinthians. The Corinthians' question to Paul was in response to the prohibition of idol food that Paul had imposed on them in his previous letter. They were not asking, 'can we eat idol food?' but, 'why can't we eat idol food?' Moreover, their objections 'stem from a single point of view at Corinth opposed in some degree to Paul's. There was no "weak" or "scandalized" second party'.[55]

The problem of idol food did not arise from intra-community conflicts among the Corinthians. Instead it arose from the conflict between Paul's earlier teaching on the indifference of idol food and his

---

53. A convenient summary of Hurd's conclusions can be found in *Origins*, pp. 287-88 and 290-93 (Table 7).

54. Hurd, *Origins*, pp. 117-25.

55. Hurd, *Origins*, p. 147. Hurd does not deny that some individual Corinthian Christians were weak in faith; he simply denies that they as a party opposed the strong (p. 125).

subsequent command in the 'previous letter' forbidding it. Hurd reconstructs the content of the Corinthians' question concerning εἰδωλόθυτα as follows:

> We find nothing wrong with eating idol meat. After all, we have knowledge. We know that an idol has no real existence. We know that there is no God but one. For those in Christ all things are lawful, and as far as food is concerned everyone knows that 'food is meant for the stomach and the stomach for food'. We fail to see what is to be gained by the avoidance of idol meat. You know yourself that when you were with us you never questioned what you ate and drank. Moreover, what of the markets? Are we to be required to inquire as to the history of each piece of meat we buy? And what of our friends? Are we to decline their invitations to banquets because of possible contamination by idol meat?[56]

Hurd believes that Paul in fact agrees with the Corinthians in principle, for their objection is based on Paul's own earlier preaching. Nevertheless, in order to justify his previous prohibition, Paul offers two qualifications, which correspond to two hypothetical cases of 'abuse of Christian freedom so obvious that the Corinthians would surely agree with him'.[57] These qualifications on their freedom are: that they 'must not offend a weaker Christian', and that they 'must not commit an act of idolatry'.[58] In each case Paul seeks to 'generalize the particular occasion on which idol meat should be avoided to include all occasions'.[59] In this way these hypothetical qualifications are offered solely for the purpose of dissuading the Corinthians from eating idol meat.[60]

Evaluation. Hurd's reconstruction is more defensible than the traditional view in many respects. He is correct in his assumption that Paul's response in 1 Cor. 8.1–11.1 must be related to the 'Previous Letter' and Paul's earliest preaching. I also find his reconstruction of the Corinthians' question persuasive. However, his understanding of Paul's approach on the issue of idol food is very problematic. In order to allow enough time for Paul's instructions on idol food to vacillate as much as his proposal demands, Hurd has to disregard completely the evidence

56. Hurd, *Origins*, p. 146.
57. Hurd, *Origins*, p. 143.
58. Hurd, *Origins*, p. 148.
59. Hurd, *Origins*, p. 143.
60. Hurd, *Origins*, pp. 143, 148.

of Acts on Pauline chronology.[61] This really creates more problems than it solves.[62]

Hurd maintains that Paul is in essential agreement with the Corinthians and that the qualifications of the weak and of temple attendance are hypothetical. However, it is difficult to understand how Paul's argument can carry any plausibility, let alone conviction, unless it is based on reality. It is scarcely conceivable that the emotional appeal for the welfare of the weak in 8.7-13, not to mention the vehement denunciation of idolatry in 10.1-22, is mere rhetoric. As Fee points out, 'there is simply too much urgency in all of this for temple attendance to be purely hypothetical'.[63]

Hurd's serious underrating of the urgency of 10.1-22 leaves him scrambling for a motive why Paul prohibited idol food at all in his previous letter. He speculates that such a prohibition is part of an uncomfortable compromise struck between Paul and the Jerusalem Christian leadership in order for the latter to legitimize Paul's Gentile mission. But the explicit evidence for Paul's motive—namely, to eat idol food is to hurt the weak and to have fellowship with demons—is set aside as hypothetical in favor of his own speculative hypothesis.

---

61. Assuming the usual Pauline chronology, Barrett considers Hurd's reconstruction improbable because there is not enough time for Paul's thought to move 'from thesis through antithesis to synthesis' (*The First Epistle to the Corinthians*, pp. 8-9). While this criticism of Hurd is valid in other respects, it misses Hurd's central point. See Hurd, *Origins*, pp. 1-42, for his misgivings about 'the usual chronology of Paul's letters'.

62. Unfortunately, due to the large number of exegetical and historical judgments involved, it is well beyond the scope of this work to address the problem of Pauline chronology in any detail. Hurd's approach to Pauline chronology is deeply influenced by John Knox, *Chapters*. Because of the fragmentary nature of the data in Paul's letters and the lack of consensus in revisionist chronologies, most scholars, especially those who have some respect for the historicity of Acts, do not agree to Knox's practice of constructing the events of Paul's life almost exclusively from the Pauline letters. See W.W. Gasque, *A History of the Interpretation of the Acts of the Apostles* (Peabody, MA: Hendrickson, 1989), pp. 197-99. For a thorough, critical, yet respectful use of the evidence from Acts in establishing Pauline chronology, see R. Riesner *Die Frühzeit des Apostels Paulus: Studien zur Chronologie, Missionsstrategie und Theologie* (Tübingen: J.C.B. Mohr, 1994); cf. M. Hengel and A.M. Schwemer, *Paul between Damascus and Antioch: The Unknown Years* (Louisville, KY: Westminster/John Knox Press, 1997).

63. Fee, 'Εἰδωλόθυτα', p. 176.

Moreover, if his interpretation is correct, then, by Hurd's own admission, Paul's lengthy and vehement discussion will have

> limited the conduct of the Corinthians only slightly, if at all... Therefore, we reach the somewhat strange conclusion that Paul appears to have permitted the Corinthians to continue their current practices concerning idol meat virtually unchanged... Paul devoted the major part of his reply to vigorous disagreement with them, and only at the close did he give them permission to behave as in fact they had been behaving.[64]

I submit that such a conclusion is not only 'somewhat strange'; it is inherently improbable.

Like the traditional view, Hurd assumes without justification the dissociation of εἰδωλόθυτα from εἰδωλολατρία. Thus it is likewise vulnerable to the criticism that Paul's background and legacy are completely ignored. In fact, a major weakness of Hurd's work is that it pays far too little attention to the religious and social backgrounds of the first century which may shed light on the situation of the Corinthian community.[65]

c. *Gordon Fee's Proposal*

Gordon Fee considers the traditional view to be 'filled with nearly insuperable difficulties'.[66] He adopts Hurd's proposals that there were no actual weak and strong *as parties* in Corinth, and that the Corinthian church as a whole is responsible for the letter to Paul in which they have taken a somewhat anti-Pauline stance.[67] However, Fee does not agree with Hurd that the problem of temple attendance was only hypothetical. On the contrary, he sees cultic meals at temples as the main issue that Paul is dealing with in 1 Cor. 8.1–11.1. Following the lead of Parry, Fee suggests that εἰδωλόθυτον does not refer primarily to marketplace food (which is first mentioned only in 10.23), but to the partaking of idol food at cultic meals in pagan temples.[68] The basic problem Paul wishes to address is already suggested in 8.10, where dining

64. Hurd, *Origins*, pp. 147-48.
65. This weakness is probably related to his excessive concern to depend primarily on the Pauline letters for any historical reconstruction, thus downplaying other evidence like Acts and other early Christian writings.
66. Fee, *The First Epistle to the Corinthians*, p. 359.
67. Fee, 'Εἰδωλόθυτα', p. 176.
68. Fee, *The First Epistle to the Corinthians*, pp. 359-61; cf. Willis, *Idol Meat*, pp. 76-77.

in an idol's temple is mentioned. The same act is in view in 10.1-22. Paul argues that such an act is forbidden first on ethical (8.1-13), and then on theological (10.14-22), grounds. In 10.23–11.1 Paul concludes by tightening up some loose ends regarding marketplace idol food and dinner invitations by pagan friends. Paul permits the eating of 'marketplace idol food, which apparently Paul himself had been known to eat (cf. 9.19-23) and for which he had been judged (9.3; 10.29)'.[69] Paul also allows the eating of idol food at pagan homes unless attention is called to the idolatrous origins of the food.[70]

In Fee's view, the *referent* of the term εἰδωλόθυτα in 1 Corinthians 8 is temple dining, even though its *meaning* can be broader (which includes marketplace food) in other contexts.[71] Some scholars go further and insist that εἰδωλόθυτα is a technical term for that which is eaten ἐν εἰδωλείῳ.[72] As a corollary, the term ἱερόθυτον, usually taken to be the proper non-pejorative pagan equivalent to εἰδωλόθυτον, has to be understood as sacrificed food eaten outside the cultic context because in 1 Cor. 10.28 ἱερόθυτον definitely does not refer to temple dining. Ben Witherington is the most vocal proponent of such an interpretation: 'εἰδωλόθυτον in all its 1st century AD occurrences means an animal sacrificed in the presence of an idol *and eaten in the temple precints*. It does not refer to a sacrifice which has come *from* the temple and is eaten elsewhere, for which the Christian sources rather use the

69. Fee, *The First Epistle to the Corinthians*, p. 476.

70. Fee, *The First Epistle to the Corinthians*, pp. 482-85.

71. For example, he thinks that in Acts 15 'it probably refers to marketplace food' (*The First Epistle to the Corinthians*, pp. 357-78 n. 1; pp. 425, 481) He also notes that second-century Christian writers 'almost certainly' understood the term in this sense. Fisk's charge that Fee confuses meaning with referent is unmerited ('Eating', pp. 55-56).

72. B. Witherington, III, 'Not so Idle Thoughts about *Eidolothuton*', *TynBul* 44 (1993), pp. 237-54; *idem*, 'Why Not Idol Meat? Is It What You Eat or Where You Eat It?', *BR* (1994), pp. 38-43, 54-55; *idem*, *The Acts of the Apostles: A Socio-Rhetorical Commentary* (Grand Rapids: Eerdmanns; Cambridge: Paternoster Press, 1998), pp. 460-67; Gardner, *Gifts*, pp. 183-85. C.A. Kennedy ('The Cult of the Dead in Corinth', in J.H. Marks and R.M. Good [eds.], *Love and Death in the Ancient Near East: Essays in Honor of Marvin H. Pope* [Guilford, CN: Four Quarters, 1987], pp. 227-36) proposes another meaning for εἰδωλόθυτα: funerary meals. However, as Fee (*The First Epistle to the Corinthians*, p. 358 n. 6) points out, neither the text of 1 Cor. 8–10 itself nor early Jewish and Christian usage gives any hints that the word was used for funerary rites.

term ἱερόθυτον'.[73] In this way, ἱερόθυτον takes the meaning of εἰδωλόθυτον usually assigned by commentators and the conflict between
1 Corinthians 8–10 and Acts 15 is resolved: Paul followed the injunction of the Jerusalem Council on εἰδωλόθυτον completely, and he
could take a liberal attitude to ἱερόθυτον since it was not an issue
addressed by the Council.[74]

Evaluation. In the Appendix, I will examine and refute Witherington's
suggestion that εἰδωλόθυτον, per se, means temple dining and that it is
to be distinguished from ἱερόθυτον. I will show that such an understanding is the result of doubtful interpretation of unrepresentative
evidence. However, Fee's argument is not significantly affected, for
it does not critically depend on understanding the meaning of εἰδωλόθυτα to be temple dining; it only requires that the referent of
εἰδωλόθυτα is temple dining in 1 Corinthians 8.

Fee's reading of 1 Corinthians 8–10 seems to be gaining popularity
in current scholarship. I myself find it on the whole very persuasive.
His interpretation has many of Hurd's strong points and few of his
weaknesses. It takes seriously into account Paul's vigorous rhetoric and
his explicit condemnation of the act of eating food sacrificed to idols in
10.1-22. By understanding both 8.1-13 and 10.1-22 as dealing with the
single issue of meals at temples, it resolves the apparent inconsistencies
between the two passages that give rise to the partition theories and has
the advantage of reading Paul's argument as a consistent whole. By
considering marketplace idol food as a matter of indifference, it seems
to be consistent with Paul's statements elsewhere regarding Christian
liberty on matters of food and drink.

I am convinced that Fee is on the right track and it will be obvious to
my readers how much my own interpretation is indebted to Fee's
exegetical efforts. Nevertheless, his view has some significant weaknesses and thus requires considerable modification. First of all, like the
traditional view it gives too little attention to Paul's relationship with
early Jewish and Christian traditions as it attempts to dissociate (marketplace) idol food from actual idolatry. This makes Paul's approach to
εἰδωλόθυτα a singularity, with no historical evidence whatsoever to

73. Witherington, 'Idle Thoughts', p. 240. Gardner also thinks that this is the
distinction Paul made and cautiously raises the possibility that such a distinction is
inherent in the words εἰδωλόθυτον and ἱερόθυτον (*Gifts*, pp. 183-85).

74. Gardner, *Gifts*, p. 184.

support it. That Paul himself had eaten, or had condoned eating, idol food was an unimaginable scenario for early Christians. Not even the anti-Pauline pseudo-Clementine writings give us any hint that such was the case. In fact, Fee himself frankly admits that his view makes 'Paul's own relationship with the Decree a matter of some historical difficulty'.[75] There is no indication in the decree itself that εἰδωλόθυτα had reference only to cultic meals. On the contrary, given the input from the Jerusalem leaders to the Decree, one has every reason to believe that a more general prohibition of idol food was in view. Whatever is said about Luke's historical accuracy there is little doubt that he viewed the eating of idol food with disfavor. This is significant in light of Luke's obviously positive attitude toward Paul. Brunt is understandably puzzled that 'Luke writes in support of Paul, addresses an issue which Paul discussed, yet makes no mention of Paul's discussion, does not even show awareness of it, and appears to take an attitude which is very different from it'.[76]

Moreover, it is precarious to put too much weight on a single phrase in 1 Cor. 8.10. One would like more explicit references to temple dining in Paul's discussion. Fee, like the proponents of the traditional view, *assumes* that 10.14-22 refers only to cultic meals at idol temples. This is possible, but by no means proven. One has to bear in mind that, given the intimate association between εἰδωλόθυτα and εἰδωλολατρία, any first-century Jew could easily have referred—and did refer—to εἰδωλόθυτα with appellations like 'table of demons' even apart from a temple setting. The author of *Joseph and Aseneth* clearly regards eating any idol food as eating from the table of the idols, even when the food is no longer in a temple.[77] After all, it is the idol altar from which εἰδωλόθυτα originate![78] Not only that, any meal over which grace has not been said is viewed as 'the sacrifice of the dead (= demons)' by some rabbis.[79]

In any case, while the Corinthians' problem probably involves temple dining, Fee has not supplied any conclusive argument that *only* temple dining is in view. In fact, 8.10 seems to argue against this:

75. Fee does not explore this relationship any further.
76. Brunt, 'Rejected', pp. 115-16.
77. *Jos. Asen.* 8.5-7; 10.1-13; 11.8-9; 21.13-14.
78. Note *m. 'Abod. Zar.* 2.3: 'Flesh that is entering in unto an idol is permitted, but what comes forth is forbidden, for it is as the sacrifices of the dead'.
79. *m. Ab.* 3.3.

Paul's concern is that if those who have 'knowledge' dine in an idol temple, the weak will be 'built up' to eat εἰδωλόθυτα. This sounds like an argument from the greater to the lesser: if the strong are so bold as to eat in idol temples, then the weak, who are more timid, might be tempted to take the not-so-bold step of eating idol food in less overtly idolatrous setting. If, as many commentators believe, the weak do not have the same right and opportunities as the 'strong' to attend temple feasts (even if they wish to attend), then this inference is made more probable. Paul's statement assumes that to eat εἰδωλόθυτα, as far as opportunities for eating are concerned, is something the weak can do without any difficulty. Moreover, if only temple dining is in view here, why does Paul need to go to the extreme to say that he will never, ever eat meat under any circumstance to avoid causing the ruin of the weak brother.[80] It seems that eating in a more general context is presupposed. A similar impression is given by Paul's reference to his own example of not exercising his rights to eat and drink in order to dissuade the Corinthians from eating idol food. It is probably better to see cultic meals at the temple as the extreme act of eating εἰδωλόθυτα, which may include eating that is less overtly idolatrous.

Paul could easily have opened his discussion with περὶ δὲ τῶν ἐν εἰδωλείῳ κατακειμένων instead of περὶ δὲ τῶν εἰδωλοθύτων. However, Paul's main concern seems to be with εἰδωλόθυτα, rather than with idol temples. It is perhaps better to take the phrase ἐν εἰδωλείῳ κατακείμενον as a hyperbole, that is, as the logical extreme of the Corinthians' position: if any behavior consistent with the Corinthians' 'knowledge' would most easily cause the 'weak' to stumble, this is it! But there is no need to suppose that Paul is *only* forbidding this extreme behavior. Rather, Paul, like any good debater, is launching his attack at where his opponents are most vulnerable. It is understandable that he brings out the 'worst case' scenario to show what evil the strong's knowledge and behavior can lead to.

Tomson, following Hurd's lead, believes that in 8.10 Paul describes a hypothetical situation for rhetorical purposes.[81] As I have argued earlier, there is simply too much urgency in Paul's rhetoric for temple dining to be purely hypothetical. Had the Corinthians not been actually dining in temples, they would have easily dismissed Paul's whole discussion as not based on factuality. Such hypothetical construct would

---

80. Note the extremely emphatic οὐ μὴ ... εἰς τὸν αἰῶνα (1 Cor. 8.13).
81. Tomson, *Jewish Law*, p. 196.

have undermined rather than enhanced the strength of Paul's persuasion. In fact, I suspect that the Corinthians' participation in temple meals might have been the last straw that set off Paul's vehement rhetoric. Nevertheless, I believe Tomson is correct in understanding 8.10 as a rhetorical tactic intended to shock the Corinthian Christians into realizing the potential harm their action may cause the weak.[82] In this regard, 8.10 is clearly hyperbolic. We can compare 8.10 with Paul's statement a few verses later that he will never eat meat[83] again if food causes his brother to stumble—a statement that is equally hyperbolic, but in the opposite direction! To adopt this extreme behavior of abstinence from all meat (not just idol food) is to bring the probability of stumbling the 'weak' to a minimum, just as to dine in pagan temples is to bring this probability to a maximum.

The question may be raised whether the emphasis in chapter 10 on 'sharing' indicates a focus more on actual attendance at a meal where the god/idol was host, rather than on idol food in general.[84] In response, I maintain that while the Corinthians' problem involved cultic meals, temple dining was probably not the exclusive focus. As pointed out in chapter one, the bulk of literary evidence suggests that sharing meals in homes, rather than in temples, was the norm for social dining. Even at religious significant occasions, Sarapis can be invoked as a host to a dinner at home as well as at the temple.[85] Moreover, in ancient culture, meals were by far the most common context for fellowship, whether or not there was overt presence of the god/idol. It is instructive to compare Paul's emphasis on sharing with *m. A b.* 3.3: (R. Shimon ben Yohai says) 'If three have eaten at one table and not spoken words of Torah

82. Tomson, *Jewish Law*, p. 196.

83. Some commentators assume that the reason why Paul said he would never eat meat if it caused a brother to stumble is that virtually all meat sold in the markets was εἰδωλόθυτον, sacrificed probably in nearby temples. However, the extent to which Christians shopping in the markets would be forced to purchase εἰδωλόθυτον must not be exaggerated. In any case, Paul's telling the Christians not to ask any questions should have been sufficient indication that non-sacrificed food was available. See my discussion below on 1 Cor. 10.25.

84. Private communication from Professor Stanley Porter; cf. Dunn, *Theology of Paul*, p. 605.

85. Out of the nine papyrus invitations to sacred meals that Willis (*Idol Meat*, pp. 40-42) lists, six refer to temple meals (P. Oxy. 110, 1484, 1755, 2791; P. Colon 2555; P. Fouad 76) and three to meals at the host's house (P. Oslo 157; P. Oxy. 523; P. Yale 85).

on it, it is as though they had eaten of the sacrifices of the dead. But if three have eaten at one table and have spoken words of Torah on it, it is as if they had eaten from the table of God.' The emphasis on 'three have eaten' (rather than 'one has eaten') underlines the communal character of meals. Thus the emphasis on 'sharing' gives no indication of the presence of the idol as host. Moreover, if only temple dining is in view, why would Paul need to argue in 10.18 that eating idol food amounts to participating in the altar, as the altar is in such a close proximity? It seems that the food has been removed from the sacrificial setting so the connection becomes less obvious and has to be pointed out. Again, why would Paul need to comment in 10.20 that idol food is sacrificed to demons and not to God if the Corinthians are eating in the presence of the idols/demons? Though I cannot prove it, I suspect that Paul's comment might be occasioned in part by the practice of some Corinthians of bringing idol food to the Lord's Supper for feasting. This would be consistent with Paul's antithesis between idol food and the Lord's Supper and his strong warning against provoking God to jealousy. In any case, even if Paul is focusing on temple dining, it does not necessarily imply that he condones eating idol food in more general contexts. It may simply mean that, in the context of his vehement rhetoric, Paul denounces this obvious evil of the Corinthians to score a palpable debating point.

Finally, it is difficult to account for Paul's repeated μηδὲν ἀνακρίνοντες (10.25, 27) within the framework of Fee's interpretation. Fee has ruled out the weak as the addressees of this instruction, but he has not supplied any motive that would prompt the strong to make inquiries. If Paul is only forbidding temple dining, one is hard put to find a convincing reason why the strong would want to make inquiries about marketplace food or private meals. Witherington suggests that the strong would ask questions 'so that they might demonstrate the extent of their freedom and their moral awareness that food is food and idols are nothing'.[86] The situation Paul envisaged is 'that strong and weak together have gone to a dinner party, the weak not knowing in advance that "sacred food" would be served', so the strong 'would ask questions in order to demonstrate *their* moral awareness and freedom, especially

---

86. Witherington, *Conflict and Community*, p. 227; cf. Gardner, *Gifts*, pp. 175-78.

to the weak'.[87] Paul is again forbidding the strong to hurt the weak by flaunting their knowledge.

Such an explanation strikes one as very *ad hoc*—are we to suppose that strong and weak also go to the market and buy food together? Moreover, it turns the emphasis of Paul's instruction from one of tolerance (*eat* without inquiring) to one of further prohibition (eat *without inquiring*). This runs foul of 10.26 ('the earth is the Lord's, and everything in it'), which clearly serves to justify the eating in 10.25 rather than discourage asking questions.

Furthermore, if the Corinthians do indeed ask and find out that the marketplace food is idol food, then presumably Paul expects them to abstain, as in the case of private dining when the idolatrous origin of the food is pointed out. Otherwise, what is the point of telling them not to ask? Paul's intention is surely not to spare them the moral dilemma of eating or not eating, for if Paul himself has eaten food known to be idol food, why should they not? After all, they do not even have compunctions about dining in idol temples! But if Paul finds no problem with eating marketplace idol food, then there is absolutely no reason why they should abstain after they have found out the nature of the food by asking. The proponents of the traditional view, by taking Paul's addressees as the weak, can at least reason that Paul tells the weak not to ask so that their conscience may not suffer pain as they learn of the idolatrous origin of the food. But Fee, who argues that Paul is addressing the over-confident Corinthian church as a whole, does not have this option. Evidently, there is something wrong with Fee's premise that Paul disallows temple dining but not marketplace idol food.

3. *An Alternative Understanding of Paul's Approach to* εἰδωλόθυτα

I propose that Paul regards the eating of idol food, *with the awareness of their idolatrous origins*, as a sinful act rather than a mere ἀδιάφορον (*contra* the traditional view). Paul prohibits not only dining in idol temples but also eating any food, including marketplace food, that is identified as idol food (contra Fee). Paul never explicitly says that it is acceptable to eat idol food, he only says that one may eat anything without inquiring into the possibility of its being previously sacrificed to idols. If one is somehow informed of the idolatrous origins of the

87. *Conflict and Community*, p. 227 n. 31.

food, the only permissible action is to abstain. 1 Corinthians 8.1–11.1 must be seen as a two-stage argument to dissuade the Corinthian Christians from eating idol food. To eat idol food is both unloving and idolatrous. It will cause the weak to ruin *and* bring God's judgment against idolatry upon oneself. Such an understanding not only avoids the many exegetical difficulties associated with the other views, but it is also consistent with the early Christians' virtually unanimous prohibition of idol food evident in all extant sources, as we shall see in the next chapter. While the interpretation proposed here may seem novel in modern scholarship, it finds solid support in early Christianity. On the other hand, the (subsequent) traditional view did not once surface in a plethora of writings dealing with this extremely important subject in early Christianity.

As I pointed out in Chapter 1, 1 Cor. 8.1–11.1 could not have been the first time Paul discussed the issue with the Corinthians. Given the importance of the subject of idol food and the length of Paul's previous ministry in Corinth, it is historically unrealistic to think that the Corinthians were asking Paul for the first time whether they could eat idol food. Hurd has persuasively argued that Paul's response in 1 Cor. 8.1–11.1 must be related to the 'Previous Letter' and Paul's earliest preaching at Corinth. It will be instructive to examine the evidence in Acts and Paul's letters for his attitude toward idolatry about the time he wrote 1 Corinthians.

Regardless of their views on absolute Pauline chronology, most scholars agree that Paul first went to Corinth shortly after his mission in Thessalonica, and that he probably wrote 1 Thessalonians in Corinth.[88] Can 1 Thessalonians, then, shed some light on Paul's attitude to εἰδωλόθυτα? The answer is in the affirmative. According to Paul, the exemplary Christian conduct of the Thessalonians to 'all the believers in Macedonia and in Achaia' consists precisely in that, despite all the difficulties and hostility they suffered, 'they turned to God from idols, to serve a living and true God, and to wait for his son from heaven' (1 Thess. 1.7, 9, 10).[89] This is Paul's missionary teaching in a

---

88. See E.J. Richard, *First and Second Thessalonians* (Sacra Pagina, 11; Collegeville, MN: Liturgical Press, 1995), pp. 7-8.

89. Due to the unusual number of non- or rare Pauline terms and idioms clustered in vv. 9-10, some interpreters believe that the verses have pre-Pauline provenance in Jewish Christian missionary preaching, baptismal liturgy, or catechetical formulae, while others argue for Pauline composition that utilizes such

nutshell.[90] Thus Paul regards the rejection of idols the quintessence of pagan conversion to Christianity, as most Jews regard it the *sine qua non* of Gentile conversion to Judaism.[91] Now, how did the Thessalonian Christians turn from idols? In a culture where sharing meals was the mode and norm for social intercourse, arguably one of the first and most visible ways of turning from idols was to reject idol food!

Scholars also commonly agree that Paul penned 1 Corinthians (and perhaps the previous letter) in Ephesus, where Paul is primarily and vividly remembered as the preacher against idolatry. It is in this great city of many gods, in which idolatry always sells, that the idol manufacturing business fears a recession as a result of Paul's preaching (Acts 19.23-27). Not unlike Aseneth, who throws away her idols *and idol food* at her conversion, Paul's converts at Ephesus burn their idolatrous books as a visible and climactic renunciation of idolatry (Acts 19.19). The apocryphal *Acts of Paul* gives pretty much the same picture of Paul's assaults on idolatry in Ephesus: the pagan gods 'can neither take food nor see nor hear' and Paul's converts must 'no longer serve idols and the steam of sacrifices but the living God'.[92] We may also note that, according to Luke, just before Paul went to Corinth, the apostle was in Athens 'deeply distressed to see that the city was full of idols'

phraseology. See E. Best, *A Commentary on the First and Second Epistles to the Thessalonians* (HNTC; New York, Harper & Row, 1972), pp. 85-87; Richard, *Thessalonians*, pp. 53-56; C.A. Wanamaker, *The Epistles to the Thessalonians: A Commentary on the Greek Text* (NIGTC; Grand Rapids: Eerdmans; Exeter: Paternoster Press, 1990), pp. 84-85; T. Holtz, '"Euer Glaube an Gott": Zu Form und Inhalt von 1. Thess 1,9f', in E. Reinmuth and C. Wolff (eds.), *Geschichte und Theologie des Urchristentums: Gesammelte Aufsätze* (WUNT, 57; Tübingen: J.C.B. Mohr, 1991), pp. 270-96. In any case, the content of these verses are so thoroughly Pauline that the question of origin is ultimately irrelevant.

90. Note also that polemic against idolatry is the dominant theme of Paul's evangelistic speeches before Gentiles recorded in Acts. In his sociological study of Paul, Meeks outlines three major elements that encouraged group coherence and identity within Paul's letters, the first of which is 'You turned to God from idols' (W.A. Meeks, *The First Urban Christians: The Social World of the Apostle Paul* [New Haven: Yale University Press, 1983], pp. 91-93).

91. Note that Paul often characterizes the Christians' former pagan lives in terms of bondage to idols (Gal. 4.8; cf. 5.20; 1 Cor. 12.2; cf. 6.9).

92. *Acts of Paul* 7, in W. Schneemelcher (ed.), *New Testament Apocrypha* (trans. R.McL. Wilson; 2 vols.; Louisville, KY; Westminster/John Knox Press, rev. edn, 1991), II, pp. 251-52.

(Acts 17.16). Then a critique of idolatry is given in Paul's speech before the Areopagus (17.22-31).

Again, it is instructive to consider Paul's letter to the Roman church, written probably in Corinth a few years after he penned 1 Corinthians. In his survey of the sins of the Gentile world, idolatry not only tops the list of Gentile vices, it is also seen as the root of all evil, the vice that leads to all vices (Rom. 1.19-32). It is not enough to abhor idolatry, one must also in no way benefit from the pagan temples (Rom. 2.22).

All these indications make it virtually unimaginable that, during his lengthy ministry in Corinth, Paul had said nothing to the Corinthians regarding idol food. This impression is strengthened by the religious and social significance of idol food in Greco-Roman world and the strong association between εἰδωλόθυτα and εἰδωλολατρία in Jewish traditions. When one also takes into consideration Paul's consistent polemics against idolatry in his letters—not least in the vehement exclusivism of 2 Cor. 6.14–7.1, it does not appear that his converts would have been encouraged to eat idol food.[93]

It is probably not coincidental that the three items covered in the Previous Letter, namely, sexual immorality, greed-swindling and idolatry (5.9-10), are the subjects to which Paul devotes much discussion in the next few chapters in 1 Corinthians. As these are the subjects that Paul would have covered in his earliest preaching, Paul's previous letter to the Corinthians is probably occasioned by their moral behavior that conflicts with Paul's ethical teaching. The fact that Paul brings out those subjects again in 1 Corinthians suggests that the Corinthians have attempted to justify their behavior, taking exception to Paul's instructions in the Previous Letter. Fee, following Hurd, is surely correct in maintaining that 'whatever it is the Corinthians were *arguing for* in their letter, it is something Paul had already forbidden in his previous letter'.[94]

---

93. Unfortunately, we cannot discuss here the question of whether this passage is a (non-Pauline) interpolation. Note that Fee argues on the basis of many parallels with 1 Cor. 10.14-22 that the same issue of idol food is in view ('II Corinthians vi.14-vii.1 and Food Offered to Idols', *NTS* 23 [1977], pp. 140-61). Cf. W.J. Webb, 'Unequally Yoked Together with Unbelievers. Part 1: Who Are the Unbelievers (ἄπιστοι) in 2 Corinthians 6.14? Part 2: What Is the Unequal Yoke (ἑτεροζυγοῦν-τες) in 2 Corinthians 6.14?', *BSac* 149 (1992), pp. 27-44, 162-79. Webb thinks that the verses have a broader reference to metonymical idolatry, which includes attending cultic dinners.

94. Fee, 'Εἰδωλόθυτα', p. 179.

Focusing on the issue of εἰδωλόθυτα, we can briefly sketch the exchange between Paul and the Corinthians as follows. In his earliest preaching in Corinth, as in other cities, Paul had already given instructions prohibiting the eating of idol food (cf. Acts 16.4). However, after Paul had left Corinth, some Corinthian Christians (probably from the leadership of the church), perhaps because of their enlightened view of Christian freedom, but more likely due to social pressure, began to eat idol food. Some might have gone as far as dining in idol temples or even bringing idol food to the Lord's table for feasting. Paul had attempted to correct them in his previous letter (in somewhat unguarded language because of the urgency of the situation) but was rebutted with clever arguments constructed with exaggerations or distortions of his earlier teachings.[95] This led to Paul's present response in 1 Cor. 8.1–11.1, which is at once combative and cautious, uncompromising yet highly nuanced.

a. *The Broad Structure of Paul's Argument*
That Paul's attitude toward the eating of εἰδωλόθυτα is likely to be negative can be seen from a comparison with his treatment of πορνεία in 1 Corinthians 6.[96] There are strong linguistic and conceptual parallels: [96]

---

95. The way the Corinthians take Paul's command 'not to associate with πόρνοι' (5.9) seems to be a deliberate misinterpretation rather than an innocuous misunderstanding. Had the Corinthians understood Paul to mean that they should avoid all πόρνοι and tried to obey that virtually impossible injunction, there would have been less moral problems among them. It is more likely that they took advantage of the ambiguity of Paul's wording 'in order to discredit his whole authority by pointing out that what he advocates is in any case impracticable' (W.L. Knox, *St. Paul and the Church of Jerusalem* [Cambridge: Cambridge University Press, 1925], p. 320 n.9).

96. There is a strong biblical tradition linking πορνεία and εἰδωλόθυτα. While acknowledging Conzelmann's caution that temple prostitution in Corinth mentioned by Strabo belonged to an earlier period and probably did not continue to Paul's time, Fee suggests that 'these two sins really belong *together*' and find their connection in temple prostitution ('Εἰδωλόθυτα', p. 186). Likewise, Witherington claims that 'it is true that there is no clear evidence of sacred prostitution in Roman Corinth, but there certainly were numerous stories of sexual immorality in pagan temples' (*Conflict and Community*, p. 221). But the story in Josephus (*Ant.* 18.65-80), the only contemporary evidence cited by Fee, where Paulina 'after supper' had nightlong sex with Mundus (disguised as the god Anubis) in the temple, is irrelevant. Paulina, a *chaste woman* according to Josephus, was simply deceived. The

1. Most obvious is Paul's quotation of the Corinthian motto: πάντα [μοι] ἔξεστιν in 6.12 and 10.23, and his subsequent correction of it: ἀλλ' οὐ πάντα συμφέρει. The reference to food in 6.13 also foreshadows the discussion of idol food in chapters 8–10.
2. In 6.18 Paul urges the Corinthians: φεύγετε τὴν πορνείαν, as he urges them in 10.14: φεύγετε ἀπὸ τῆς εἰδωλολατρίας. A Christian must flee from both immorality and idolatry (epitomized by eating food sacrificed to idols) rather than employ clever arguments to indulge in them.
3. Paul's strongest reason against these sinful acts is the Christian's union with Christ in both cases. As πορνεία involves union with a prostitute, which is clearly unthinkable for one who has joined himself to the Lord (6.16-17), the eating of εἰδωλόθυτα involves fellowship with demons (10.20), which is unthinkable for one who is in fellowship with Christ (10.16-17, 21-22).

whole incident has nothing to do with temple prostitution or sexual immorality. When the deceit was discovered, Tiberius demolished the temple and crucified the priests involved in the plot, making clear that the whole matter was simply unacceptable. Like Fee, Witherington does not give any evidence for temple prostitution from the 'numerous stories' other than the story of Paulina and Anubis. I am not suggesting that there was no sexual activity in the temple precincts, for there probably was. But hetaerae and prostitutes could be present at *convivia* held in homes as well as in temples. Therefore the probable reference to sexual immorality in 1 Cor. 10.7 does not require a temple feast context. Murphy-O'Connor (*Corinth*, p. 56) believes that Strabo's account of sacred prostitution in classical Corinth was probably a fabrication based on Strabo's own experience of Comana in Pontus and the assumption that Corinth was a 'greater Comana'. He points out that 'sacred prostitution was never a Greek custom and, were Corinth an exception, the silence of all other ancient authors becomes impossible to explain'. Cf. H.D. Saffrey, 'Aphrodite à Corinthe: Reflexions sur une idée recue', *RB* 92 (1985), pp. 359-74. I think the reason idolatry and sexual immorality are often mentioned together in biblical traditions is that these two sins epitomize pagan perversion in the religious and social spheres. As Collins observes, in Diaspora Jewish literature, monotheism and sexual ethics are the two most accentuated items, much more prominent than circumcision, dietary laws, and the like (*Between Athens and Jerusalem*, *passim*; see especially the discussion of the 'Common Ethic' in chapter 4, pp. 137-74). More recently, J.T. Sanders, 'Jews and Gentiles', pp. 68-69, U. Heckel, 'Das Bild der Heiden', pp. 269-70 and J. Klawans, 'Notions of Gentile Impurity in Ancient Judaism', *AJS Review* 20 (1995), pp. 293-97, all point out that the primary Gentile sins in Jewish eyes were idolatry and sexual immorality.

4.　Both passages conclude with the motif of glorifying God (6.20, 10.31).

I have mentioned earlier that in his previous letter Paul had warned the Corinthians against eating idol food. But some have taken exception to Paul's injunctions. They argued that they all had the knowledge that 'an idol is nothing at all in the world and there is no God but one' (8.1, 4). Hence they could go through the motions of idolatry but without meaning what the idolaters meant. Some of them might go as far as dining in idol temples or bringing idol food to the Lord's Supper for feasting.

Paul would finally point out the flaw of this argument in 10.1-22. However, he wanted first to make the general point that there was a danger of being proud of having knowledge but devoid of love. Therefore he did not begin with a discussion about knowledge. He took the Corinthians' argument for granted for the moment and argued instead on the principle of love: 'Knowledge puffs up, but love edifies' (8.1).

Here we observe a striking similarity between Paul's way of arguing in this case and the case regarding πορνεία. Paul has also warned the Corinthians against sexual immorality, but they retorted with clever arguments, claiming that sexual behavior, like food, was an indifferent matter. In the end, Paul must say, φεύγετε τὴν πορνείαν (6.18), as he must eventually say, φεύγετε ἀπὸ τῆς εἰδωλολατρίας (10.14). Under no circumstances was πορνεία ever allowed for Christians. But why did Paul not forbid it at the outset? The reason, Fee suggests, is that

> πορνεία is not forbidden as Law; it is forbidden because it is incompatible with Life in Christ. Why then does he not begin here with the prohibition? Because that might turn ethical response into legal obligation. Therefore, it is not Law they need to hear, but a Christian understanding of freedom.
>
> ... Likewise...eating at the idols' table finally will be forbidden outright...it is incompatible with life in Christ as it is experienced at His table. *But their abuse of ἐξουσία in this matter, based on false γνῶσις and issuing in failing to love, is the far greater urgency.*[97]

Fee's suggestion does not satisfactorily explain why Paul has to emphasize his agreement with the Corinthians in the beginning of his discussion. Moreover, I do not think it is helpful to bring the Law–Gospel contrast into Paul's discussion here. If, as Fee believes, the Corinthians are engaging in sexually immoral and idolatrous activities,

97. Fee, 'Εἰδωλόθυτα', p. 197; emphasis added.

I am less certain than Fee that abuse of Christian freedom is of far greater urgency than fornication and idolatry. Paul takes the latter sins seriously enough to demand the excommunication of the immoral person and to forbid Christians to even eat with any professed Christian who is an idolater (1 Cor. 5)! He has serious questions about the spiritual state of those who commit sins of sexual immorality or idolatry (5.5; 6.9-10; 10.12). By contrast, without minimizing the sin of pride and unloving behavior, the apostle still recognizes the offenders as those who have the presence and power of the Spirit (1.3-8). They may be 'worldly, mere infants' (3.1), or shoddy workman (3.10-12), yet their salvation, though as through fire, is not in doubt (3.15).

Modern rhetorical analysis of persuasive discourses supplies a better explanation for the way Paul argues.[98] Perelman and Olbrechts-Tyteca define the rhetorical or argumentative situation as 'the influence of the earlier stages of the discussion on the argumentative possibilities open to the speaker'.[99] It includes both the goals of the speaker and the counter-arguments that are anticipated as the speaking progresses. The persuader who gives only one side of an argument is unlikely to convince those to be persuaded. If Paul is a competent persuader, he will gauge his audience as accurately as possible at every point. He will use their language and work from where they are in order to move them towards where he wants them to be. In no detail can he afford to ignore

98. For a good description of the rhetoric characteristic of 1 Corinthians from the perspective of the New Rhetoric, see A.C. Wire, *The Corinthian Women Prophets: A Reconstruction through Paul's Rhetoric* (Minneapolis: Fortress Press, 1990), pp. 12-38. Rhetorical studies have generally fallen into two broad categories. One line of approach is to analyze and classify Paul's letters in terms of Greco-Roman rhetorical models and devices. Another is to utilize modern (universal) rhetorical theory to understand Pauline argumentation without special regard to questions of genre. The division is not watertight, and there are many attempts to combine the approaches. Nevertheless, where one places the emphasis can lead to significantly different exegetical outcomes. While I do not want to minimize the importance of the rhetorical milieu within which Paul worked and wrote, I believe that it is more fruitful to focus on Paul's method of argumentation rather than attempt a sustained or comprehensive rhetorical analysis of 1 Corinthians in terms of ancient rhetoric. In the Appendix, I will outline the obstacles for using the first approach and will discuss in particular the work of Margaret Mitchell, a main representative of that approach.

99. C. Perelman and L. Olbrechts-Tyteca, *The New Rhetoric: A Treatise on Argumentation* (Notre Dame: University of Notre Dame Press, 1969), p. 491.

the arguments of those who need to be convinced, especially when the latter stand in opposition. This is plainly how Chrysostom, one of the most brilliant rhetoricians in ancient times, understands the way Paul argues (*1 Cor. Hom.* 20-25). This explains Paul's copious quotation of the Corinthians' slogans in his discussion and his emphasis on 'agreement in principle'. The persuasiveness of Paul's argument depends considerably on how well he reflects the views of his Corinthian opponents. He stresses his (real or apparent) agreement with them in principle as far as he can so that they will be open to his qualification in practice. In fact, *Paul's apparent agreement with them masks the extent of his qualification.*[100] What is offered as a simple qualification of the principle turns out to be an eventual prohibition in practice.[101]

It is not that Paul's plea for the weak is simply a foil for his real argument.[102] The principle that love for one's weak brother should be the motivating factor in contemplating Christian liberty is neither *ad hoc* nor purely *ad hominem*, but belongs to the core of Paul's Christian consciousness. He is genuinely and deeply concerned about the weak's welfare, else his emotional appeal on their behalf in 8.7-13 is inexplicable. His reiteration of the theme in the conclusion of the section, and his adaptation and generalization of it in Romans 14, are sufficient evidence for its importance. For Paul, love is indeed paramount in Christian behavior. Without love everything is reduced to nothing (1 Cor. 13). On the other hand, as far as persuasive strategy is concerned, consideration for the weak is perhaps not his strongest—and certainly not his only—argument against the Corinthian practice of eating idol food.[103] In effect, Paul is putting forward a two-stage argument against eating idol food. He first softens the Corinthians' resistance to the prohibition by appealing to their better nature: they should have been more considerate to the weak, the brothers for whom Christ died. This point is made with great pathos and is intended to cause guilt and shame. In an other-directed, honor-and-shame based culture, this is a very power-

---

100. Wire, *Women Prophets*, p. 13.

101. Cf. W.J. Brandt's observation that, in persuasive discourses, the ostensible object of an argumentation is often not the most important one (*The Rhetoric of Argumentation* [Indianapolis: Bobbs–Merrill, 1970], p. 22).

102. Contra Hurd, *Origins*, p. 125; Gooch, *Dangerous Food*, pp. 66-67; Smit, 'Rhetorical Disposition', p. 480 and n. 18.

103. We must also remember that the Corinthians' estimation of love is nowhere as high as Paul's.

ful argument in its own right. But, as Chrysostom observes, Paul saves his strongest argument for last: 'he began from the lesser topics, and so made his way to that which is the sum of all evils: since thus that last point also became more easily admitted, their mind having been smoothed down by the things said before'.[104]

b. *Exegetical Issues*

Terminology. Before I examine the pertinent exegetical issues of 1 Cor. 8.1–11.1 in detail, a note about terminology is in order. Those Christians in Corinth who ate idol food have been variously dubbed the 'strong', 'gnostics', or 'enthusiasts'. In order not to assimilate the terminology of Romans 14 or prejudge the relevance of gnosticism or over-realized eschatology, I will refrain from using such labels. Whatever their motive for eating, it is clear that those Corinthians justified their action on the basis of 'knowledge'. One may perhaps call them the 'knowledgeable'. However, such a label conveys something more positive than the passage suggests, as Paul is probably using γνῶσις in a somewhat sarcastic manner. For the lack of a better term, and to avoid encumbrance of expression (such as 'those who have knowledge'), I will henceforth call these Corinthians the 'knowers'. They might be a relatively small group, but their influence in the church certainly far out-proportioned their number. It seems that the majority of the church either stood on their side or at least tolerated their behavior. Therefore, I feel free to use the terms 'Corinthians' and 'knowers' interchangeably to refer to Paul's addressees in this section. I will also sometimes use terms like 'the strong' to refer to the knowers when I am discussing the views of other scholars.

Love and Knowledge. It is generally agreed that πάντες γνῶσιν ἔχομεν is a Corinthian slogan.[105] In response Paul reminds them that 'knowledge puffs up, but love edifies'. Paul is not disparaging knowledge per se, for he clearly values knowledge elsewhere (cf. Rom. 2.20; 11.33; 15.14; 1 Cor. 1.5; 12.8; 14.6; 2 Cor. 2.14; 4.6; 6.6; 8.7; 10.5; 11.6; Phil. 3.8; Col. 2.3). But he warns the Corinthians that without love, one can have too high an opinion of oneself and fail to consider the effects of

104. *1 Cor. Hom.* 24.
105. Willis (*Idol Meat*, pp. 67-70) maintains that οἴδαμεν ὅτι was also part of the Corinthian slogan. Whether this is correct or not does not materially affect my interpretation, for Paul is certainly trying to agree with the Corinthians here.

one's action on others. In fact, only the one who loves truly knows.[106]

It is not accurate to say that Paul begins by 'replying here to those "having knowledge" on their own grounds'.[107] Paul does not begin by arguing on the grounds of knowledge. On the contrary, he hopes to pre-empt the Corinthians' appeal to their knowledge in rebuttal of his argument. Therefore he agrees (or appears to agree) as far as he can regarding the content of their knowledge but diffuses their argument from knowledge by the argument from love. Thus, in merely stating his opinion that love is paramount and knowledge is unimportant—even harmful—in comparison, Paul cleverly and effectively rules out the very basis of the Corinthians' argument. The net effect is that they are unable to use knowledge, whether true or false, to justify their eating idol food. This then sets the stage for Paul's strong prohibition in 1 Corinthians 10.

Why Did the Knowers Eat Idol Food? All agree that the eating of εἰδ-ωλόθυτα by the knowers was related to their γνῶσις, but it is important how we understand this relationship. Since no clear indication is given from the text as to why they wanted to eat idol food, various back-grounds have been proposed.[108] Among the common options, the most controversial is probably Schmithals's argument that gnosticism pro-vided the context for understanding the Corinthians' ideology.[109] Also

---

106. I am adopting the reading of 𝔓[46] and understanding ἔγνωσται as a middle. Though the external witness for this shorter reading is not impressive, it clearly has the most claim of authenticity in terms of intrinsic and transcriptional probability. Not only does it most readily explain the other readings, it also fits Paul's overall argument best: love towards one's fellow Christians, rather than love for God, is certainly the issue here (cf. also the contrast between love [for others] and knowl-edge in ch. 13). See Fee, *The First Epistle to the Corinthians*, pp. 367-69 and notes.

107. G.W. Dawes, 'The Danger of Idolatry: First Corinthians 8.7-13', *CBQ* 58 (1996), p. 92.

108. See Gardner, *Gifts*, pp. 2-10 for a succinct discussion of various hypotheses that have been put forward.

109. Schmithals, *Gnosticism*, esp. pp. 141-55, 218-29. Schmithals has so force-fully advocated this theory that it pretty much sets the agenda for later discussion on Corinthian background. While there are endless debates on whether we can see in the position of the strong an early form of gnosticism, the majority of recent interpreters are properly skeptical of identifying the Corinthians as Gnostics. See, for example, H.O. Guenther, 'Gnosticism in Corinth?', in B.H. McLean (ed.), *Ori-gins and Method: Towards a New Understanding of Judaism and Christianity: Essays in Honour of John C. Hurd* (JSNTSup, 86; Sheffield: JSOT Press, 1993),

influential is Horsley's attempt to link the knowers' ideology with Hellenistic Judaism as exemplified in Philo and Wisdom of Solomon.[110] Yet others emphasize that an over-realized eschatology (and/or an enthusiastic theology) was the problem.[111]

pp. 44-81. Conzelmann (*1 Corinthians*, p. 15) argues that gnosticism is an unnecessary hypothesis for understanding 1 Corinthians. Nevertheless, he detects traces of the beginnings of what later was called gnosticism. In fact, it has become a scholarly trend to speak of proto-gnosticism in Corinth. I do not believe such terminology is helpful. While there are tendencies in the Corinthian ideology which resemble those of later gnosticism, one must remember that such tendencies can be found also in Judaism and Hellenistic culture in general. To speak of those tendencies which can be adequately explained on other grounds as proto-gnosticism does not advance our understanding. On the contrary, it is likely to mislead exegetes into unconscious and unfortunate equivocation by the importation of anachronistic conceptual categories and sources.

110. R.A. Horsley, 'Gnosis in Corinth: 1 Corinthians 8.1-6', *NTS* 27 (1980), pp. 32-51 and a number of other articles; cf. B.A. Pearson, *The Pneumatikos–Psychikos Terminology in 1 Corinthians: A Study in the Theology of the Corinthian Opponents of Paul in its Relation to Gnosticism* (Missoula, MT: Society of Biblical Literature, 1973). Horsley's theory is unconvincing. First, it fails to appreciate the extent of interpenetration of Judaism and Hellenism. Philo's writings were themselves heavily Hellenized. Secondly, the writings of Philo and *Wisdom of Solomon* take a clear stance against idolatry and the authors would not have been happy with the alleged application of their writings by the Corinthians to justify eating idol food. Thirdly, since Paul was also a Hellenistic Jew, is it surprising that the church he built showed Jewish features of theology such as nothingness of idols?

111. A. Thiselton, 'Realized Eschatology at Corinth', *NTS* 24 (1977–78), pp. 510-26. I think the case for such theology on the part of the Corinthians is considerably overstated. Even Paul's ironical statement in 1 Cor. 4.8-9, perhaps the strongest evidence for the over-realized eschatology of the Corinthians, is far from conclusive. As J.M.G. Barclay ('Thessalonica and Corinth: Social Contrasts in Pauline Christianity', *JSNT* 47 [1992], pp. 49-74 [64]) points out, such language may reflect Paul's own perspective, which is definitely eschatological, but it does not necessarily mean that the Corinthians themselves relate their experience to such an eschatological framework. As they seem quite contented with the present state of affairs and there is no evidence that they envisage radical disjunctions in the future, their theological framework may be more properly termed non-eschatological. D. Litfin (*St. Paul's Theology of Proclamation: 1 Corinthians 1–4 and Greco-Roman Rhetoric* [Cambridge: Cambridge University Press, 1994], p. 168) is probably justified in his complaint about the over-realized eschatology interpretation: 'its speculative character and its need to read so much between the lines serves to make one wary'.

It is clear that the knowers justified their eating on the basis of knowledge. The preponderance of the word γνῶσις and the verb γιν-ώσκω in 1 Corinthians, coupled with the appearance of words like σοφία and πνευματικός, is suggestive of an ideology that might be akin to later gnosticism. Nevertheless, we must not confuse justification with motive, rationalization with reason. The question 'why did they eat idol food?' is certainly not identical to the question 'on what grounds did they eat idol food?'

We do not have to imagine anything elaborate to understand why the knowers ate idol food. The problem of idol food in Corinth, as in many ancient and modern cities where Christianity was first introduced, was fundamentally a conflict between Christ and (polytheistic) culture.[112] As Niebuhr observes, 'not only pagans who have rejected Christ but believers who have accepted him find it difficult to combine his claims upon them with those of their societies'.[113] Similarly, J.T. Sanders rightly notes that 'Paul's idol-food and sex advice in 1 Corinthians...is "standing...against the dominant traditions of society and rejecting

112. Barclay, 'Social Contrasts', p. 59; R.B. Terry, *A Discourse Analysis of First Corinthians* (Dallas: Summer Institute of Linguistics, 1995), pp. 55-57. Since Theissen's ground-breaking social investigation of the Corinthian church, it has become fashionable to link the strong's behavior to their higher social status. It is perhaps true that 'those deeply enmeshed in the social networks of Corinthian life at a higher level would certainly have a lot to lose if they adopted too sectarian a mentality' (Barclay, 'Social Contrasts', p. 68). However, one must remember that those who have the more to lose usually also have more that they can afford to lose. Moreover, as Barclay observes, there is no necessary correlation between social status and sectarian perspective. The picture is much more complex and requires many qualifications. I will discuss Theissen's sociological interpretation in the Appendix. Here I just want to point out that from the evidence of 1 Corinthians, εἰδωλόθυτον seems something commonplace, as accessible to the weak as to the knowers. If the opportunities for the weak to eat εἰδωλόθυτον are really so limited, it is difficult to make sense of Paul's concern for the weak's danger in imitating the knowers.

113. H.R. Niebuhr, *Christ and Culture* (New York: Harper & Brothers, 1951), p. 10; cited in Terry, *Discourse Analysis*, p. 55. Terry (p. 57) observes that 'most, if not all, of the problems which Paul discusses in 1 Corinthians can be attributed to the influence of the Corinthian cultural setting on the Christians there': glorification of wisdom, eating of food offered to idols, and denial of a bodily resurrection were aspects of Greek culture; ecstatic utterances were probably features of Pythian and Dionysiac religions. Even moral problems such as fornication, drunkenness, and greed were culturally based, as they were not strongly condemned in Greek society.

prevailing patterns of belief and conduct"'.[114] For those converts who desired to retain their former public and social life in the city, compromise was almost inevitable.

It is instructive to compare the experience of Christians in Thessalonica and Corinth. Both congregations were founded by Paul in close succession, and both lived as Christian minorities in idolatrous pagan environments. But the contrast between them is highly significant. The Thessalonian Christians—well known for turning from idols—seem to have little problem obeying Paul's injunctions but face great hostility from their fellow countrymen.[115] The Corinthian Christians—notorious for eating idol food—have much difficulty in accepting Paul's advice but seem to be very at ease with the world.[116] Why were the Thessalonians having a much more difficult time? Barclay is surely correct in finding the answer in the Thessalonians' 'offensive abandonment…of traditional religious practices'.[117] They are like Aseneth, who laments being hated by family and fellow people for rejecting idols and idol food (*Jos. Asen.* 11.3-9).[118] Their uncompromising attitude to idolatry is the source of Paul's joy and the world's hostility, just as the Corinthians' compromising attitude is the source of Paul's grief and the world's acceptance.

This is not to deny that proto-gnosticism or over-realized eschatology or the like had any part to play in the Corinthians' behavior. I am only

114. J.T. Sanders, 'Jews and Gentiles', p. 79; citing B.R. Wilson, *The Social Dimensions of Sectarianism: Sects and New Religious Movements in Contemporary Society* (Oxford: Clarendon Press, 1990), p. 1.

115. 1 Thess. 2.14; cf. 1.6, 3.4.

116. As Barclay ('Social Contrasts', p. 57) notes, the Corinthians are ἔνδοξοι (1 Cor. 4.10) in their public reputation. There is no evidence of conflict in their relationship with outsiders. By contrast, there are many signs of their social acceptability.

117. Barclay, 'Social Contrasts', p. 53.

118. Such hostility, resulting from the abandonment of mainstream polytheistic culture, was faced by countless Christians in the Roman Empire and throughout the centuries. A.-J. Malherbe's (*Paul and the Thessalonians: The Philosophical Tradition of Pastoral Care* [Philadelphia: Fortress Press, 1987], p. 48) argument that the Thessalonians' suffering was an internal 'distress and anguish of heart experienced by persons who broke with their past' rather than external duress from their countrymen is hardly convincing. It is unlikely that Paul means that they become imitators of the Lord and an example for believers in Macedonia and beyond by believing in spite of such internal anguish. It seems clear that their exemplary conduct involved a public and courageous stand against external opposition.

stressing the point that the detrimental social effects of avoiding idol food were a sufficient cause for the Corinthians' action, which might then be justified *post hoc* by an ideology, be it gnosticism or realized eschatology, that was congenial to their position. Once the legitimacy of eating idol food was established, such ideology could and probably did bring along behavior not directly motivated by social expedience. Some might even go further to embark on an education of the weak, to bring the majority into similar behavior patterns to reduce any cognitive dissonance caused by compromise with the outside society.

In short, if avoiding idol food was something socially desirable, I seriously doubt that any Corinthian with any theology would have argued for the right to eat idol food. As J.T. Sanders puts it, 'if the majority of Graeco-Roman people had opposed polytheism and πορνεία, Paul would hardly have had to propose such lengthy arguments against them in 1 Corinthians'.[119] Therefore, the attempt to identify a particular ideology as the primary reason for the Corinthians' behavior is probably misguided effort.

The Content of the Knowers' γνῶσις. In 1 Cor. 8.1, Paul clearly reflects the knowers' assertion that 'we all have knowledge'. What is the content of this knowledge? It is generally agreed that it includes 'an idol is nothing in the world', and 'there is no God but one'. The confession of monotheism in v. 4 is reminiscent of the Shema. Its corollary, the nothingness of idols, which features prominently in Jewish apologetic literature, is already asserted in Deuteronomy, Psalms and Isaiah (e.g. Deut. 32.21; Ps. 115.4-8; 135.15-18; Isa. 40.19-20; 41.29; 44.9-17), which are among the most frequently quoted Jewish Scriptures in early Christianity. These beliefs are so fundamental to the Christian faith that no Christian can be ignorant of them. Paul agrees completely with the knowers here, as these statements must be a fundamental part of his own missionary preaching.

There is less consensus among scholars concerning the function of vv. 5-6 and the extent of possible Corinthian quotations in these verses. Many interpreters think that Paul's qualification of the Corinthian position begins here. According to such an understanding, Paul is in some ways affirming the existence of other gods despite the monotheistic confession of v. 4. Hurd sees here a 'henotheistic-sounding statement', 'as emphatic a qualification of the monotheism of [v. 4] as Paul could

119. J.T. Sanders, 'Jews and Gentiles', p. 82.

have made as a Christian'.[120] Fee thinks that Paul 'recognizes the existential reality of pagan worship' in anticipation of the argument of v. 7.[121] Witherington goes further and maintains that Paul is arguing for the objective rather than subjective reality of 'the so-called gods'.[122]

On the other hand, Willis argues that the whole of vv. 4-6, with the exception of v. 5b, is the argument of the Corinthians.[123] The Corinthian position is that though, at a hypothetical level, other gods may exist, the Christian God is all that matters for them. In response, Paul counters with a statement of the objective reality of other gods in v. 5b: 'as indeed there are many gods and many lords'.

In my opinion, vv. 5-6 is neither the Corinthians' statement nor Paul's qualification of the Corinthian position. The use of εἴπερ and λεγόμενος in v. 5a and ἀλλ᾽ ἡμῖν in v. 6 clearly suggests that the significance of those gods and lords are being downplayed.[124] As such the verses in fact lend support to, and explain, the position of v. 4 rather than qualify it. This is also the best way to understand the γάρ of v. 5a. Therefore Willis is correct in seeing that the whole of vv. 4-6, with the exception of the parenthetical v. 5b, is consistent with the Corinthian argument. On the other hand, there are major difficulties in understanding the verses as quotations from the Corinthian letter. As Fee points out, the explanatory γάρ is strictly a Pauline feature in 1 Corinthians and, more importantly, v. 6 seems to be constructed in response to v. 5b rather than the other way round.[125] Moreover, v. 5b does not seem to answer the argument of v. 5a and v. 6. As a qualification it is much too weak.

In fact, it is not necessary to see the ὥσπερ clause as a qualification at all. It may simply be explicative of the λεγόμενοι θεοί in v. 5a. It is

120. Hurd, *Origins*, p. 122.

121. Fee, *The First Epistle to the Corinthians*, pp. 372-73.

122. Witherington, *Conflict and Community*, p. 197.

123. Willis, *Idol Meat*, pp. 83-88; cf. F.W. Grosheide, *Commentary on the First Epistle to the Corinthians* (NICNT; Grand Rapids: Eerdmans, 1953), p. 192.

124. It makes little difference whether εἴπερ is used to imply that the supposition is contrary to fact (1 Cor. 15.15) or according to the fact (Rom. 3.30; 2 Thess 1.6) or uncertain (Rom. 8.9,17). The force of the word in this context is certainly concessive: 'even if' or 'granted that'.

125. Fee, *The First Epistle to the Corinthians*, p. 371 n. 10. The terms 'God' and 'Lord' in v. 6 correspond to the 'gods' and 'lords' of v. 5b. Therefore the ἀλλ᾽ ἡμῖν in v. 6 is a response to v. 5b rather than a continuation of v. 5a.

better to take the whole of vv. 5-6 as Pauline and understand its function in terms of Paul's persuasive strategy. At this point Paul is still engaging in the twofold task of building rapport and anticipating objections. He pre-empts their possible rebuttal to his prohibition of idol food by outlining and agreeing with their (perhaps unexpressed) argument, which is based largely on his own teaching. In this way, Paul steals the thunder of their objection before it is uttered, and hopefully prevents it from being uttered. Once it is recognized that Paul is not qualifying but supporting the monotheistic confession of v. 4, it is a moot point whether vv. 5-6 represents Pauline construction or Corinthian citation. Up to this point all is fine.

But in v. 7, Paul introduces an important qualification: ἀλλ᾽ οὐκ ἐν πᾶσιν ἡ γνῶσις. And he goes on to say, τινὲς δὲ τῇ συνηθείᾳ ἕως ἄρτι τοῦ εἰδώλου ὡς εἰδωλόθυτον ἐσθίουσιν, καὶ ἡ συνείδησις αὐτῶν ἀσθενὴς οὖσα μολύνεται. This verse raises a host of exegetical problems. Some Christians, called the weak, do not have this γνῶσις. Instead, they have weak συνείδησις. There is a series of interrelated issues: Who are the weak? What is the knowledge that the weak lack? What does συνείδησις mean?

Who are the Weak? Some commentators argue that the weak in v. 7 are 'Paul's invention, representing his own scruples'.[126] I do not share that view. While there is no evidence of actual 'weak' and 'strong' as parties in the church, the existence of weak individuals whose salvation is in jeopardy can scarcely be doubted. How else can one explain Paul's emotional plea on their behalf and his extreme statement that he will never eat meat if it causes the weak to stumble? In 9.19-22, where Paul describes his approach to win different kinds of (real) people, he insists that 'to the weak I become weak'. One may also consider Paul's statement in 2 Cor. 11.29, where the weak and their stumbling are definitely not hypothetical: 'Who is weak without I being weak? Who is led to fall (σκανδαλίζεται) and I do not burn?' To him, the weaker members of the body are indispensable (1 Cor. 12.22). Clearly, concern for the weak belongs to core of Paul's Christian consciousness. It reflects God's concern to give greater honor to those who are inferior (1 Cor. 12.24), rather than something created *ad hoc* because of the exigencies of the situation or because he wants to prove a point. Even the pursuit

126. Smit, 'Rhetorical Disposition', p. 480 n. 18; cf. Hurd, *Origins*, p. 125; Gooch, *Dangerous Food*, pp. 66-67.

and exercise of spiritual gifts in 1 Corinthians 12–14 must follow the fundamental guideline of self-limitation for the common good of the church.

If the weak are not hypothetical, then who are they? Divergent answers have been given to this question. The view that they are Jewish Christians can hardly be correct. All attempts, however ingenious, to identify the weak with Jewish Christians must run foul of Paul's description of them as 'until now accustomed to the idol' (8.7). Theissen's interpretation of weakness in terms of social status has gained not a few followers.[127] However, in 1 Corinthians 8–10 Paul does not discuss 'weakness' in connection with indicators of social status, but with reference to cognition.[128] While there may be correlation between cognitive weakness and inferior social status, the primary reference and connotation of weakness as used by Paul here is decisively not social in nature. More recently, some have sought to understand weakness in terms of its usage in Hellenistic moral philosophy. The weak are those who are intellectually and/or morally immature, unstable in their convictions, and who therefore easily give their assent to false judgments.[129] I believe this is probably how the knowers would have viewed those who had problems eating idol food. It is also likely that the designation of some people as weak stemmed from the knowers and that they thought these weak Christians needed to be 'built up'. On the other hand, while Paul does associate weakness with cognition and instability of conviction, we cannot simply assume that he accepts all the connotations of weakness as used by the knowers or Hellenistic philosophers. He may be singling out only those elements of weakness that are advantages to his argument, while rejecting other elements. It is therefore important for us to examine Paul's own description of the weak.

---

127. Theissen, *Social Setting*, pp. 70-73, 121-43; D.B. Martin, *Slavery as Salvation: The Metaphor of Slavery in Pauline Christianity* (New Haven: Yale University Press, 1990), pp. 118-24.

128. A.J. Malherbe, 'Determinism and Free Will in Paul: The Argument of 1 Corinthians 8 and 9', in T. Engberg-Pedersen (ed.), *Paul in his Hellenistic Context* (Edinburgh: T. & T. Clark, 1994), pp. 231-55 (233 n. 4).

129. For a large-scale treatment from this perspective, see Glad, *Philodemus*; cf. Malherbe, 'Determinism', pp. 233-35; *idem*, '"Pastoral Care" in the Thessalonian Church', *NTS* 36 (1990), pp. 375-91; S.K. Stowers, 'Paul on the Use and Abuse of Reason', in D.L. Balch *et al.* (eds.), *Greeks, Romans and Christians: Essays in Honor of Abraham J. Malherbe* (Minneapolis: Fortress Press, 1990), pp. 253-86.

In Paul's description in 1 Corinthians 8–10, the weak are 'accustomed to the idol'; they are 'brothers'; they are those 'for whom Christ died'; they have weak συνείδησις; they lack certain kind of knowledge; they are tempted to follow the knowers' lead in eating εἰδωλόθυτα, possibly as something that elevates their status before God (cf. 8.8a). Put together, we have a picture of recent Gentile converts who are somewhat insecure in their belief or convictions. Beyond this we cannot say much more. Conzelmann is properly cautious: 'The "weak" are neither Jewish Christians, nor any closed group at all. They do not represent a position. They are simply "weak".'[130] Whether or not the designation of some people as weak originates from the knowers, 'weak' is definitely not a pejorative word as used by Paul in 1 Corinthians 8–10. On the contrary, Paul exalts the value of weakness so often in the Corinthian correspondence that one wonders if he is not using the term with some irony here.[131] Unlike the moral philosophers or probably the knowers, Paul exhibits no concern to change the weak as he shows every concern to change the knowers.

The γνῶσις *that the Weak Lack.* The statement opening 8.7: ἀλλ' οὐκ ἐν πᾶσιν ἡ γνῶσις, resumes the thesis of 8.1: οἴδαμεν ὅτι πάντες γνῶσιν ἔχομεν. At the formal level, the two verses are clearly contradictory. However, most interpreters find it hard to believe that Paul would so blatantly contradict himself in the space of a few verses.[132] The resolution of the contradiction turns on understanding either 'all' or 'knowledge' differently in the two verses.

Some understand the knowledge in v. 7 to be identical to that in v. 1. Their solution is that in v. 1 the strong deny or callously ignore the existence of the weak by claiming that all have knowledge, when in fact the weak do not have such knowledge.[133] Paul responds by remind-

---

130. Conzelmann, *1 Corinthians*, p. 147.

131. On the importance of the concept of weakness in Paul's apostolic consciousness, see J.L. Sumney, 'Paul's "Weakness": An Integral Part of his Conception of Apostleship', *JSNT* 52 (1993), pp. 71-91; D.A. Black, *Paul, Apostle of Weakness: Asthenia and its Cognates in the Pauline Literature* (New York: Peter Lang, 1984).

132. As Mitchell (*Rhetoric*, p. 241) observes, 'it is interesting that no partition theorists, on the basis of their methodological principle of resolving contradictions, put these two verses in different letters!'

133. Mitchell, *Rhetoric*, p. 126 and n. 370 suggests that the strong consider γνῶσις their exclusive possession.

ing the strong that while their monotheistic statements are true and while 'we' (that is, the strong and Paul) all know them, the weak do not know them—and we must not forget they are there in the church. They still believe in the existence of gods and demons and we must respect their scruples.

This view must be abandoned. For one thing, to attribute the belief in demons to the weak alone introduces unbearable tension with 10.18-22, where Paul himself clearly believes in the reality of demons. The partition theories, which we have rejected, arose precisely to account for such alleged vacillation between two viewpoints on Paul's part. Much more importantly, such a view is historically unrealistic. In view of the emphatic denunciation of idolatry in early Christian preaching, can a Christian, however weak, not know that 'there is no God but one' and that 'an idol is nothing in the world'? Can one who is ignorant of such fundamental truths be called a 'brother for whom Christ died' at all? As Dunn points out, Paul never made much effort to expound his convictions about God because these beliefs were 'axioms', belonging to 'the foundations of his theology and so are largely hidden from view'.[134] More to the point, 'they were already common to and shared with his readers'.[135] This can only mean that Paul must have spent considerable time educating his Gentile converts about the God of the Jewish Scriptures, and concomitantly the biblical critique of idolatry. It is barely conceivable that some recent converts were unaware of Paul's teaching on idol food. But ignorance regarding the Christian monotheistic confession is simply unbelievable.

Other interpreters find the resolution of the contradiction between vv. 1 and 7 in the distinction between head knowledge (which all possess) and heart knowledge (which is not in all).[136] Intellectually the weak know the central truth of monotheism, but emotionally and experientially they still believe in the existence of many gods. They simply cannot bring themselves to accept that these gods, whom they have been worshipping for a long time, are in fact nothing.

However, to understand γνῶσις in the sense of 'emotional acceptance' does violence to the language. I am not aware of any parallel usage in the New Testament or other ancient Greek literature in which

---

134. Dunn, *Theology of Paul*, p. 28.
135. Dunn, *Theology of Paul*, p. 29.
136. Fee, *The First Epistle to the Corinthians*, p. 379; Conzelmann, *1 Corinthians*, p. 146; Dawes, 'Idolatry', p. 89; Murphy-O'Connor, 'Freedom', p. 554.

γνῶσις bears such an emotive force. Moreover, whether or not the weak experience emotional stress and strains, such a psychological reading misses Paul's major concern, which is the danger of idolatry. Paul's fear is not that the weak suffer emotional pains, but that they will be ruined by knowingly participating in what they regard as idolatry.[137] As Witherington observes: 'The problem of the weak is...that they rightly have qualms about eating...and yet are doing it, going along with the strong. The problem was not between the head and the heart of the weak but...the way in which the weak were violating their own moral awareness.'[138]

It is better to understand the knowledge of v. 7 as the knowledge of v. 1 *plus* the implication that such knowledge enables one to eat the sacrificed food οὐ ὡς εἰδωλόθυτον. To the knowers the sacrificed food is not εἰδωλόθυτον, but mere βρῶμα (v. 8) because idols are non-existent, but to the weak the food is εἰδωλόθυτον, the consumption of which constitutes a denial of their allegiance to Christ. In v. 7 the weak are said to eat (the food) ὡς εἰδωλόθυτον. By implication, the knowers do not eat the sacrificed food ὡς εἰδωλόθυτον. They do not regard the meal as idol food. This reveals a basic assumption that eating εἰδωλόθυτα was something unacceptable. The knowers are not arguing that they can eat εἰδωλόθυτα. Rather, they are arguing that they are not really eating εἰδωλόθυτον because, given the knowledge that God is one, idols and idol food are nothing (cf. 10.19). They cannot be accused of idolatry. On the basis of such beliefs the knowers claim that they can eat whatever they wish because they cannot be polluted by idols, which are nothing.

By contrast, the weak who lack such 'knowledge' eat the food ὡς εἰδωλόθυτον, the epitome of idolatry in Jewish and early Christian traditions.[139] The weak are thus defiled by idols. Such an open disobedience to God's will as they know it is nothing less than apostasy, which will lead to their destruction. This understanding is supported by Paul's use of σκανδαλίζω, which is probably allusive to Ps. 105.36-39: Israel's idolatry, which involves, *inter alia*, sacrificing their children to

137. Gardner notes that Paul does not link the defilement of conscience (v. 7) or the possibility of being 'destroyed' (v. 11) to immature or incomplete experiential knowledge (*Gifts*, p. 40).

138. Witherington, *Conflict and Community*, pp. 197-98 n. 40.

139. Cf. Dawes, 'Idolatry', p. 90: 'Such behavior can be described only as idolatry, pure and simple'.

demons (cf. 1 Cor. 10.18-22), is spoken of as a σκάνδαλον to them. It is the sin by which the Israelites defiled themselves.[140] Psalm 68.23 also speaks of pagan sacrificial meals as a σκάνδαλον for Israel.[141] Fee rightly perceives that 'what is in view is a former idolater falling back into the grips of idolatry'.[142] One must not minimize the force of ἀπόλλυμι (1 Cor. 8.11), which 'elsewhere in Paul…invariably refers to eternal ruin'.[143] Likewise, we should probably understand παρίστημι (v. 8) and πρόσκομμα (v. 9) in terms of one's status before God.[144] What Paul fears is not that the weak will suffer pains of conscience or some inner disunity, but that they will perish eternally.

The weak do not share the questionable part of the knowers' knowledge. In fact, neither does Paul. It is significant that while in v. 4 Paul includes himself in the οἴδαμεν, by vv. 9-12 he is clearly distancing himself from their knowledge. He attributes, with some sarcasm, such 'knowledge' exclusively to the Corinthians: σὲ τὸν ἔχοντα γνῶσιν (v. 10), ἐν τῇ σῇ γνώσει (v. 11). Moreover, to call the knowers' inconsiderate behavior ἡ ἐξουσία ὑμῶν (v. 9) is clearly sarcastic.[145] Paul

140. See below on other allusions to Ps. 105 in 1 Cor. 10.1-10.

141. As Willis (*Idol Meat*, pp 108-109) observes, the term σκάνδαλον means far more than 'offense' in the modern sense. It is seldom used metaphorically in Greek literature but often used in the LXX as a metaphor for being trapped into sinning, especially with reference to idolatry (e.g. Judg. 2.3; 8.27; Josh. 23.13; Ps. 105.36; Deut. 7.16). This is probably the source of Paul's usage.

142. Fee, *The First Epistle to the Corinthians*, p. 387.

143. Fee, *The First Epistle to the Corinthians*, p. 387. Granted that ἀπόλλυμι is probably hyperbolic, the prospect of destruction is, however remote, real.

144. Barrett, *The First Epistle to the Corinthians*, p 195; J. Héring, *The First Epistle of Saint Paul to the Corinthians* (trans. A.W. Heathcote and P.J. Allcock; London: Epworth Press, 1962), p. 73; Gardner, *Gifts*, p. 50.

145. Smit ('Rhetorical Disposition', p. 482) draws attention to the fact, often pointed out by grammarians, that οὗτος sometimes expresses contempt. A clear example is Lk. 15.30: 'that son of yours'. In support of Paul's dismissive use of ἐξουσία, Smit further observes that v. 10 is generally agreed to be sarcastic and that earlier in the letter 'Paul has already sarcastically exposed 'the royal dignity, wisdom, might and honour' of the Corinthians (4.6-13)'. Winter's view (*Welfare*, pp. 166-73) that ἐξουσία cannot mean freedom or authority, but refers specifically to the citizen's right to attend temple feasts during the quadrennial Caesarian games, is unconvincing. It fails to take account of Paul's use of ἔξεστιν and ἐξουσιασθήσομαι in 6.12, which has little to do with citizen's rights. Moreover, as I argued earlier, such a restrictive view does not square with the assumed frequency and accessibility of eating idol food in 1 Cor. 8–10.

himself has no part in such right or knowledge. He never suggests that
the weak should become more knowledgeable. On the contrary, he
demands that the knowers change their behavior because the weak did
not have *this* knowledge.

To see in the ἐξουσία of v. 9 Paul's implicit acknowledgment of the
Corinthians' freedom to eat idol food, as many scholars do, seriously
misjudges the rhetorical disposition of vv. 9-12. At this point Paul is
not yet interested in the theoretical legitimacy of eating idol food, but
in what harm such eating, even if legitimate, may cause. He is still
arguing from the perspective of love rather than knowledge. If the
knowers engage in an idolatrous act, then those weak brothers may be
encouraged to follow. To them this means participation in idolatry,
however the knowers view it. The Corinthians are therefore guilty in
using their so-called freedom and knowledge to bring their weak brothers down the path of destruction. By his sarcasm, his replacement of
'the weak' with 'the brother for whom Christ died', his repeated use of
the verb 'to sin', with the object changed from the brother to Christ,
and his own selfless conduct, Paul enlarges on the Corinthians' guilt.
The whole of 1 Cor. 8.9-12 is evidently meant to deter.[146] Whether or
not the eating is an ἀδιάφορον in the abstract, it is definitely not a neutral matter when it leads others into temptation and apostasy. The principle of love demands abstention, regardless of knowledge.

The Meaning of συνείδησις. Much scholarly energy has been spent on
the use of συνείδησις within the New Testament and in contemporary
literature. I will not rehearse the various views here.[147] Suffice it to say
that the word seems to be able to bear a meaning ranging from a minimal sense of (self) awareness to a very loaded sense of internal moral
arbiter, somewhat akin to our modern concept of conscience. Moreover,
there are indications that the connotation of the words related to
συνείδησις was still evolving in New Testament times. Rather than

146. Smit, 'Rhetorical Disposition', pp. 481-82. Heil (*Ablehnung*, pp. 301-302)
is clearly mistaken in his appeal to 1 Cor. 8.11 to support the view that Christ's
death is the basis for Paul's rejection of the food laws.

147. For a helpful survey with good bibliography see R. Jewett, *Paul's Anthropological Terms: A Study of their Use in Conflict Settings* (Leiden: E.J. Brill, 1971),
pp. 401-46; for a fuller treatment see H.-J. Eckstein, *Der Begriff Syneidesis bei
Paulus* (WUNT, 2.10; Tübingen: Mohr Siebeck, 1983). Brief discussions of the
major interpretations can be found in Willis, *Idol Meat*, pp. 89-92; and P.W.
Gooch, 'Conscience in 1 Corinthians 8 and 10', *NTS* 33 (1987), pp. 244-54.

attempting to find a 'basic' or 'original' meaning of the word, my task is to determine which sense suits the context of 1 Corinthians 8–10 best.

Judging from the evidence of 1 Corinthians 8–10, it seems that συνείδησις is the weak's counterpart to the knowers' γνῶσις. The knowers have γνῶσις but are not said to have συνείδησις. The weak have συνείδησις but lack γνῶσις. This suggests that we should probably look for the significance of συνείδησις in the cognitive domain.[148] It is instructive to consider Rom. 2.15, where συνείδησις and λογισμός are obviously set in apposition. Another clear example is Tit. 1.15, where Paul says that both the νοῦς and the συνείδησις of the corrupted and unbelieving are defiled.[149] Moreover, their defilement consists in their behaving contrary to their professed knowledge of God (Tit. 1.16). This suggests that συνείδησις is being used pleonastically and more or less synonymously to νοῦς. One may also note that, in his discussion of Paul's teaching about idol offerings, Chrysostom explains and elaborates the term συνείδησις using words like διανοία and προαίρεσις.[150]

---

148. Many scholars concur. Maurer states that 'the problem of conscience is especially one of knowledge' ('Συνείδησις', *TDNT*, VII, p. 905). Likewise, R.A. Horsley ('Consciousness and Freedom among the Corinthians: 1 Corinthians 8–10', *CBQ* 40 (1978), pp. 547-89 [586]) argues that 'the weak "consciousness" of some of the Corinthians was merely less secure in its *gnosis*'; cf. Willis, *Idol Meat*, p. 92. Following the lead of Michel Coune ('Le Probleme des idolothytes et l'education de la Syneidesis', *RSR* 51 [1963], pp. 497-534), Tomson relates συνείδησις to דעת (אלוהים) in the Jewish Scriptures and rabbinic literature and argues that συνείδησις should be translated 'consciousness' or 'intention' (*Jewish Law*, pp. 208-16). He also refers to Eckstein (*Syneidesis*, pp. 5-11), who discerns the following meanings: 'Mitwissen, Bewusstsein, Gewissen, Inneres' (p. 211 n. 110).

149. Whether or not one accepts Pauline authorship of the pastoral epistles, the usage of συνείδησις in Titus is a near contemporary parallel to that in 1 Cor. 8-10 by one who knows Paul's writings.

150. Tomson (*Jewish Law*, p. 211) claims that Chrysostom strikingly avoided the word συνείδησις apparently because 'in his vocabulary it did not express, or no longer expressed, what he understood to be meant, and described it using more appropriate words: intention (διανοία), mental aim (προαίρεσις)'. This is incorrect, for Chrysostom did not avoid the term even when he was not quoting or paraphrasing Paul (e.g. *TLG* 206.54; 208.4 [1 Cor. Hom. 25]). I think what Chrysostom did was try to explain or elaborate the term with the help of some other terms. In this respect, Tomson's observation still stands that Chrysostom understood the meaning of συνείδησις as consciousness or intention. But what Chrysostom did provides no evidence that the meaning of the word had changed by his time.

I propose that συνείδησις as used in 1 Corinthians 8–10 refers to one's moral consciousness or awareness with regard to the nature of the food.[151] As we shall see, this understanding provides a satisfactory explanation of all of Paul's usage of συνείδησις in 1 Corinthians 8–10.

In 1 Cor. 8.7, the weak person eats the food ὡς εἰδωλόθυτον, that is, in the consciousness that the food being eaten is idol food. The moral implication is that it is wrong to eat it, and in eating consciousness is defiled (μολύνεται). To understand what Paul means by the defiling of συνείδησις, it must be noted that the person and the συνείδησις are often set in apposition in 1 Corinthians 8–10. Consider the following parallels:

8.7   ἡ συνείδησις αὐτῶν ἀσθενὴς οὖσα μολύνεται
8.10   ἡ συνείδησις αὐτοῦ ἀσθενοῦς ὄντος οἰκοδομηθήσεται
8.12   τύπτοντες αὐτῶν τὴν συνείδησιν ἀσθενοῦσαν

In 8.7 and 8.12 the συνείδησις is said to be weak, whereas in 8.10 the masculine adjective and participle make it clear that it is the person who is weak. Since οἰκοδομηθήσεται, used ironically, is parallel to μολύνεται and τύπτοντες, Paul probably means something very similar in all three verses. Moreover, in 10.28, Paul instructs the Christians to abstain from eating δι' ἐκεῖνον τὸν μηνύσαντα καὶ τὴν συνείδησιν. As Gooch observes, the καί is 'explicative rather than conjunctive'.[152] One may also note that in Tit. 1.15-16, both the persons and their συνείδησις are said to be defiled.

We may further observe that οἰκοδομέω, μολύνω, and τύπτω are verbs which, like σκανδαλίζω in 8.13, can be appropriately applied to the person.[153] By contrast, it is somewhat difficult to see how they can be applied to a person's συνείδησις, however one understands συνείδησις. In the New Testament, μολύνω is used elsewhere only in Rev. 3.4 and 14.4, and the cognate noun μολυσμός is used in 2 Cor. 7.1. In all these cases it is employed metaphorically for defilement with

151. This is somewhat similar to Borgen's definition of the word as 'the conscious and existential classification of food on the basis of a person's experiences and of criteria held by him' ('How Far?', p. 34). Borgen's definition is based on Eckstein's general characterization of the word as 'das Bewusstsein, das rational oder affektiv die eigenen Taten moralisch oder unabhängig von sittlichen Kriterien verurteilt oder gutheisst' (*Syneidesis*, p. 56).

152. Gooch, 'Conscience', p. 247.

153. Willis is right on target in asserting that 'μολύνεται in 8.7 is explained by σκανδαλίζω in 8.13' (*Idol Meat*, p. 95).

sin. This metaphorical use of μολύνω for sin can also be found in a number of passages in the LXX (Prov. 24.9; 1 Esd. 8.80; Isa. 59.3; Jer. 23.11; Tob. 3.15; Sir. 21.28). Hence 1 Cor. 8.7 most probably refers to the defilement of the person by sin rather than some sort of falling apart of his 'conscience'.[154] The defilement of consciousness is thus a short-hand way of referring to the fact that the person sins in eating the food in the light of his consciousness that it is idol food. Though different purity terms are used, the same concept of defilement from eating idol food can be found in other Jewish and Christian writings.[155]

We may also understand the wounding of the συνείδησις as a short-hand way of saying that the person is wounded (metaphorically) in his relationship to Christ by acting contrary to the moral implications of his awareness that the food is idol food. Similarly, Paul's sarcastic state-ment of the building up of συνείδησις can be readily explained. Had the weak been treated in love, they would have been truly built up (1 Cor. 8.1). Instead, by the knowers' questionable knowledge, they are 'built up' to destruction as they go against their συνείδησις.[156]

Food as Neutral? Many commentators find 1 Cor. 8.8 puzzling with regard to its meaning and the extent of Corinthian quotations.[157] Whether or not one considers the slogans a reflection of what the

154. Cf. my earlier discussion of Paul's use of σκανδαλίζω in 8.13.

155. E.g. Dan. 1.8 (ἀλισγέω in the LXX); Acts 15.20 (ἀλίσγημα); *Jos. Asen.* 12.5 (μιάνω).

156. Dawes ('Idolatry', p. 94) argues that the weak's problem is not their eating despite having scruples but rather their wrongly believing that participation in temple meals is acceptable because their συνείδησις is 'built up'. Similarly, Borgen ('How Far?' pp. 34-35) suggests that this positive evaluation of the sacrificial meal leads to a 'syncretistic fusion of Christianity and polytheistic wor-ship' and the weak are in this way destroyed. This is a possible reading. By under-standing the defiling of συνείδησις in the sense of mistaken judgment which leads to idolatry, it has the advantage of staying closer to the wording of the text, which mentions συνείδησις, rather than the person, as the object of defilement. Neverthe-less, I judge this interpretation improbable, since it does not take sufficient account of the close relationship between a person and his συνείδησις, and it is thus unable to explain the wounding of συνείδησις satisfactorily. Moreover, it ignores the use of συνείδησις in other New Testament (and especially Pauline) passages, where συνείδησις does exist as a faculty of moral evaluation that can be defiled or vio-lated by actions contrary to its dictates (Tit. 1.15-16; Rom. 2.15; Acts 24.16; cf. 1 Pet. 3.16).

157. Fee, *The First Epistle to the Corinthians*, pp. 381-84.

Corinthians argued in their letter, it is often asserted that the point of the verse is that food is morally neutral.[158] It neither enhances nor harms our standing before God. Therefore, Paul does not dispute that the Corinthians have a right to eat idol food, as far as the food is concerned. On the other hand, precisely because food is morally indifferent, the Corinthians should realize that to eat sacrificial food is not a practice to be insisted on.

I believe that the idea of the indifference of food is simply read into the text of 1 Cor. 8.8 by the force of habitual interpretation under the influence of Romans 14. For Paul to assert the indifference of food at this point would be counterproductive to his rhetorical purpose of dissuasion. Moreover, the peculiarity of the way Paul phrases his statements functions to deter rather than accommodate.

The knowers may have the intellectual understanding that the power is with God rather than with the idol. It does not thereby follow that they should eat food sacrificed to idols. Granted that food does not commend one to God, there is *no benefit in eating* idol food and *no disadvantage in abstention*: 'We are no worse off if we do not eat, and no better off if we do' (8.8). Such a way of stating the issue does not indicate indifference. On the contrary, it makes clear where Paul's sympathy really lies: *do not eat!*[159]

Unlike many scholars who are puzzled by 1 Cor. 8.8 but seem oblivious to the challenges it raises for the traditional view, J. Murphy-O'Connor is keenly aware of the problem.[160] He agrees with the common interpretation that 1 Cor. 8.8 represents Paul's quotation of a slogan of the Corinthian strong: as a rebuttal to the criticism by the weak, the strong claim that they are not harmed by eating and the weak will not please God by abstention. But this is exactly opposite to what Paul actually says (one is not harmed by *not* eating and one will not please God by eating). Since Murphy-O'Connor cannot rewrite Paul's sentence for him, he opts instead for the *singular* reading of A*, which

---

158. Barrett, *First Epistle to the Corinthians*, p. 195; Gardner, *Gifts*, p. 49. Witherington, *Conflict and Community*, p. 199; Fee, *The First Epistle to the Corinthians*, pp. 383-84. R.A. Ramsaran, *Liberating Words: Paul's Use of Rhetorical Maxims in 1 Corinthians 1–10* (Valley Forge, PA: Trinity Press International, 1996), p. 50.

159. This verse is similar in import and rhetorical strategy to 6.12 and 10.23: πάντα [μοι] ἔξεστιν, ἀλλ' οὐ πάντα συμφέρει.

160. J. Murphy-O'Connor, 'Food and Spiritual Gifts in 1 Cor. 8.8', *CBQ* 41 (1979), pp. 292-98.

reverses the sense of the verse: 'We are no better off if we do not eat, and no worse off if we do'![161] But this singular reading, which has no pedigree, is extremely improbable on text-critical grounds and is unlikely to be anything more than a scribal blunder.[162]

It will be instructive to compare 1 Cor. 8.8 with Rom. 14.6, where Paul employs a similar principle of not causing fellow Christians to stumble, but where the issue is not idol food but Jewish food laws. Paul is completely even-handed on eating or abstention in that case: 'Those who eat, eat in honor of the Lord, since they give thanks to God; while those who abstain, abstain in honor of the Lord and give thanks to God'. The contrast of the rhetorical implications in the two passages can be seen clearly in the following table.

Text	Action	Result	Rhetorical Implication
Rom. 14.6	eat	give thanks; honor to God	let them eat; don't judge
1 Cor. 8.8	eat	no better off	why eat?
Rom. 14.6	do not eat	give thanks; honor to God	let them abstain; don't judge
1 Cor. 8.8	do not eat	no harm	why not abstain?

161. Recently I became aware of the great confusion in the listing of this singular reading in the Greek editions. Murphy-O'Connor lists the singular reading as A2, whereas Fee (*The First Epistle to the Corinthians*, p. 377 n. 6.) lists it as A[c]. However, NA[27] lists it as A* (its preferred reading [*txt*] as A, and the Majority reading as A[c]). Tischendorf's eighth edition lists the Majority reading as A*, but the singular reading as A with *two* asterisks! An examination of a (reduced) photographic plate of A shows that the reading of 1 Cor. 8:8b is Murphy-O'Connor's singular reading, but I could not see any sign of alteration of the verse on the plate. I am not sure if the later correction(s) are not visible in the photograph or are somewhere else. Or is it the case that the original reading was erased as a palimpsest, so that what I saw from the plate was a corrected reading (but which)? M. Silva suggests to me that, if Fee's description is accurate, the unique reading of A may be a correction that the original scribe made to his own writing. Presumably, the editors of NA[27] wish to distinguish corrected readings for which the original scribe was responsible from those for which later correctors were responsible. Therefore, they give A* for the unique reading and A[c] for a later corrected reading that inverts the clauses (i.e. the majority reading). I emailed to Fee for clarification. Unfortunately, at the time he was on an island with only NA[27] at hand. He said he would check it out when he went back to the city. I have not received his answer before I had to send off the manuscript.

162. See Fee, *The First Epistle to the Corinthians*, p. 377 n. 6. for a discussion of the text-critical problems involved.

The failure of interpreters to observe the difference in Paul's rhetoric in the two passages contributes to the confusion of Paul's approach to idol food in 1 Corinthians 8–10 with his approach to Jewish food laws in Romans 14.[163] Because Paul does treat Jewish food laws as an indifferent matter, this confusion gives some plausibility to the traditional view that Paul condones eating idol food. In this way, Paul's statement in Rom. 14.14 regarding *kashrut*—'nothing is unclean in itself'—is absolutized and applied to the issue of idol food. But Paul's treatments of the two issues are significantly different. In my survey of the early Christians' attitude to idol food in the next chapter, I shall show that the distinction between Jewish food laws and the idol food prohibition is made as early as Acts, and continues to be made by other early Christian authors in general. Here we may simply note that the decree in Acts 15 came *after* Peter's vision in Acts 10–11 which had already rejected the cleanliness food laws as a requirement for Gentiles to be accepted into the new covenant community. The extreme unlikelihood of Luke's reporting, in the space of a few chapters, both the abolition of the food laws and the ongoing obligation of the church to observe laws regarding some 'food', strongly suggests that the latter belong to a different category.

After pronouncing in v. 8 that eating idol food does not positively benefit the knowers' relationship with God, Paul's warning in vv. 9-12 becomes all the more persuasive. It is far better for the knowers to abstain: why should they eat if eating brings no benefit on the one hand, and it may 'cause the weak to fall, sin against Christ, and damage their relationship with God' on the other?[164]

Paul's hyperbolic statement in v. 13 follows naturally: 'If food causes my brother to fall, I would never ever eat meat'. It is interesting to note that Paul did not say he would never eat εἰδωλόθυτα again. If Paul had thought that idol food was something indifferent and if he himself had eaten idol food before, it would have been appropriate for him to say he would never eat idol food for the sake of the weak even though idol food was morally neutral. A probable inference is that Paul

---

163. E.g. Brunt suggests that 'the overall thrust of both passages is the same' ('Paul's Attitude', p. 183). Sawyer even argues that the 'weak' in 1 Cor. 8 were Jewish Christians ('Meat Sacrificed', pp. 122-40). But 1 Cor. 8.7 makes Sawyer's interpretation impossible: how could Paul describe a Jew as 'accustomed to idols until now'?

164. Smit, 'Rhetorical Disposition', p. 480.

himself does not eat, and has not eaten, idol food. For the apostle, to abstain from idol food is no sacrifice (no pun intended). To demonstrate his willingness to accommodate the weak, he needs to go a step further in abstaining from all meat. As we shall see, this observation also helps us to understand why Paul seems to have left the subject of εἰδωλόθυτα in chapter 9 when he illustrates the principle enunciated in chapter 8 by using his own example.

The Form and Function of 1 Corinthians 9. The form and function of chapter 9 is the subject of considerable debate.[165] Mitchell observes that scholarly opinion is divided into two broad camps.[166] On the one hand, those who favor compositional unity of 1 Corinthians 8–10 usually take the chapter to be an exemplary argument on the nature of Christian freedom, thus amplifying the principle enunciated in 1 Corinthians 8. On the other hand, those who opt for various partition theories—thus eliminating the need to fit the passage into its context—tend to see it as Paul's self-defense by focusing on the term ἀπολογία (9.3). Mitchell considers the two options mutually exclusive.[167]

For those who believe that Paul is using an exemplary argument, the greatest challenge is to explain his vigorous defense. The usual answer is that Paul is playing a rhetorical game here. Mitchell calls Paul's ἀπολογία a 'mock defense speech'.[168] Likewise Smit maintains that Paul is answering 'presumed questions which critical listeners might ask'.[169] Yet Paul's vigorous response seems to be an overkill unless there are some who have actually questioned, whether blatantly or subtly, his authority. In the end, the persuasion of the argument of Mitchell and others in her camp depends rather on the perceived failure of attempts to analyze 1 Corinthians 9 as a true defense against actual charges.

A related difficulty concerns the nature of Paul's digression. If Paul finds it beneficial to digress into a discussion of his apostolic rights,

---

165. For a discussion of the major issues see W.L. Willis, 'An Apostolic Apologia? The Form and Function of 1 Corinthians 9', *JSNT* 24 (1985), pp. 33-48; cf. Mitchell, *Rhetoric*, pp. 243-50 and notes; Martin, *Slavery*, pp. 68-80.

166. Mitchell, *Rhetoric*, pp. 243-44.

167. Mitchell is impatient with those who 'have propounded the dubious "kill two birds with one stone" position' (*Rhetoric*, p. 244 and n. 329).

168. Mitchell, *Rhetoric*, p. 130.

169. Smit, 'Rhetorical Disposition', p. 485. Similarly, Martin, *Slavery*, pp. 77-79; Willis, 'Apologia', p. 34.

why does he not take as an example his personal freedom to eat idol food? Surely this is closer to the subject at hand. Are there any common features that link Paul's diverse arguments for apostolic support to the context of idol food?

Witherington refines the exemplary argument position by arguing that a digression here is appropriate as part of Paul's rhetorical strategy in chapters 8–10.[170] According to Quintilian, digressions are often inserted when the goal is to admonish (*Inst. Or.* 4.3.16). The use of digressions can provide some relief for the audience when one's argument is long and has a very strong tone, lest they be put off (*Inst. Or.* 4.3.2). Based on this observation, Witherington suggests that 'Paul shifts the focus from the Corinthians' conduct to his own in ch. 9, giving them an opportunity to reflect…[on] the logical consequences of their un-Christian attitudes and actions, rather than just condemning them'.

Yet the staccato of rhetorical questions in rapid succession is hardly designed to provide relief for the audience! Even though there is an apparent change of subject, the apostle engages his audience as earnestly in chapter 9 as he does in chapters 8 and 10. Paul pulls no punches as he adduces support from every conceivable arena to prove that he has the right to be supported by the church: apostolic practice, ordinary social life, Scripture, justice, the Corinthians' debt to him, Israel's cult, and, finally, the Lord's command.

Fee rightly considers the exemplary argument answer inadequate because it 'scarcely accounts for the vigor of the rhetoric'.[171] But unlike those who favor partition theories, he does not agree that the chapter is only loosely connected to its context. Instead, he suggests that 1 Corinthians 9 is not a digression, but an integral part of Paul's response to the Corinthians' letter. Paul has to make a defense at this point because his failure to accept support while he was in Corinth and his apparently compromising stance on marketplace idol food raise doubts in the minds of many about whether he has the proper apostolic authority to forbid them to eat idol food.[172] By reasserting his apostolic authority, Paul accentuates the need for the Corinthians to heed his warnings in chapters 8 and 10.

---

170. Witherington, *Conflict and Community*, p. 191. Cf. Murphy-O'Connor , 'Freedom', p. 21.

171. Fee, *The First Epistle to the Corinthians*, p. 393.

172. Fee, *The First Epistle to the Corinthians*, pp. 362, 392-93.

Fee wisely insists that we must do justice to Paul's vigorous defense and situate it in the context of 1 Corinthians 8–10 without resorting to questionable partition theories. Nevertheless, his solution is not wholly convincing. That some in the Corinthian church might have attempted to undermine Paul's apostolic authority is scarcely to be doubted (v. 3),[173] else the vigor of Paul's rhetoric is inexplicable. Still, Paul seems to have taken for granted that most of the Corinthians will acknowledge his apostleship (the rhetorical questions in 9.1 all demand affirmative answers). This can be contrasted with Paul's elaborate defense in 2 Corinthians 10–13, when his apostleship seems to be much more seriously challenged. Moreover, that some opinion shapers of the Corinthian church (especially those from the upper social echelon) are affronted by Paul's rejection of their financial patronage is probable,[174] but it does not explain why Paul devotes so much space to the defense of his right to support, and so little to the defense of his refusal of support. In fact, Paul proclaims this right so loudly that he is afraid that the Corinthians may misunderstand his motive, that is, that he is subtly asking for their financial support (9.15)!

I think the exemplary argument interpretation is correct as far as it goes, but it needs a great deal of refinement because it leaves many questions unanswered. Moreover, to see 1 Corinthians 9 as a digression or excursus is unfortunate, for it obscures Paul's line of thought and suggests that there is only a loose connection between the chapter and its context.[175] To properly understand its function, ch. 9 must be seen as an integral part of Paul's response to the Corinthians.

173. Cf. also 1 Cor. 4.18; 11.16; 14.37-38.

174. On this, see E.A. Judge, 'Cultural Conformity and Innovation in Paul: Some Clues from Contemporary Documents', *TynBul* 35 (1984), pp. 3-24 (15-23). Judge observes that 'the Corinthian letters show [Paul] in a head-on confrontation with the mechanisms by which [the patronal system] imposed social power' (23). In an earlier study Judge has identified as many as forty persons of substance who might have been Paul's patrons ('The Early Christians as a Scholastic Community', *JRH* [1961], pp. 4-15, 125-37 [129-30]). For a recent thorough study on Paul's relationship with the Corinthians in the light of the phenomenon of patronage, see John K. Chow, *Patronage and Power: A Study of Social Networks in Corinth* (JSNTSup, 75; Sheffield: JSOT Press, 1992). See especially pp. 141-57 for Chow's discussion of 1 Cor. 8–10.

175. Of course, whether the chapter should be labeled a digression is to some extent a definitional question. Nevertheless, I agree with Mitchell (*Rhetoric*, pp. 249-50) that it is better to avoid the label because of its connotation.

Scholars often point out the ABA′ structure exhibited in several Pauline discourses. In 1 Corinthians, this feature is clearly seen in 7.1-40 (marriage, circumcision and slavery, marriage), 8.1–11.1 (eating food offered to idols, right to support, eating food offered to idols), and 12.1–14.40 (spiritual gifts, love, spiritual gifts).[176] What it is important to observe is that the B section in these discourses is neither a digression nor an excursus. On the contrary, it functions to provide further substantiation for the main thought of the A section.[177] There are two important implications for our understanding of Paul's argument in 1 Corinthians 8–10. First, ch. 8 (A) cannot be adequately understood apart from ch. 10 (A′). Thus it is unlikely that Paul allows freedom to eat idol food in ch. 8 if he clearly condemns the practice in ch. 10. Secondly, whether ch. 9 is an exemplary argument on Christian freedom or an apostolic defense, its rhetorical purpose is not to be understood in its own terms, but in terms of how it furthers Paul's argument against eating idol food.

Why does Paul not choose as an example his renouncement of the right to eat idol food? A possible answer is that Paul cannot use this example because he himself has eaten idol food before and the knowers are aware of it. However, the same consideration would also have precluded Paul, who probably did eat meat before, from making much of his willingness to become a vegetarian to avoid harming the weak (8.13). If Paul has no problem in using his self-sacrificial attitude in this matter to impress upon the Corinthians his readiness to accommodate the weak, why can he not do the same with respect to the eating of idol food, whether or not he has previously eaten such food?

There is a better explanation for Paul's failure to refer to his right of eating idol food: this right simply does not exist for Paul! Such a 'right' cannot be supported by apostolic behavior—Peter and James certainly do not eat idol food. Nor can it be substantiated by the Law—Scripture clearly condemns eating idol food. Justice does not require it. No word from the Lord permits it. Israel's cultus, with the implied incompatibility between the altar of Yahweh and that of the idols, demands not eating but abstention. To eat idol food is thus not even an option, let alone a right, for Paul. Had such an option existed, it would have served Paul's purpose to point out that though he had no problem with eating idol food, he would abstain for the sake of the weak. This observation

176. Terry, *Discourse Analysis*, p. 44.
177. Terry, *Discourse Analysis*, p. 44.

agrees with my assessment in the previous chapter that, given Paul's Jewish background and his continued (Jewish) hostility towards idolatry, it is difficult to find a motive for him to eat idol food.

As happens in 8.13, in order to exemplify his teaching on accommodating the weak, Paul needs to go a step further than simply saying he would not eat idol food. Therefore, the fact that Paul does not discuss idol food in ch. 9 must not be taken to mean that he has gone off to a tangent. On the contrary, it is clear that Paul still has the subject of idol food in mind. It is no accident that he begins the defense of his apostolic rights with reference to 'the right to food and drink' (9.4). Right to food, rather than apostolic rights in general, is the focus of the rich variety of Paul's examples in 9.4-14: apostles have the right to food; the planter of a vineyard should eat of its grapes; the tender of a flock should 'eat' (ἐσθίω) of its milk; the ox who treads the grain should not have its mouth muzzled; the plowman and the thresher are entitled to share in the harvest; the sower of spiritual seed ought to reap a material harvest; the priests receive their food from the temple; the preachers of the gospel should get their living by the gospel. Even the somewhat enigmatic 9.5 is best understood as a reference to the churches' support of the apostles' wives who accompany them in ministry.

Moreover, the repeated mention of ἐξουσία—arguably the keyword in ch. 9—harks back to the sarcastic reference to the knowers' ἐξουσία to eat idol food in 1 Cor. 8.9. It also provides a link to the unprofitable ἔξεστιν in 10.23.[178]

As Smit insightfully observes, over the common denominator of the right to food and drink, 'Paul cleverly couples the question of the sacrificial meals and the answer of his exemplary apostolic practice... suggesting that the example of his apostolic practice does apply to the question at hand'.[179] By making so much of his renunciation of the right to food and drink in order not to put any hindrance to the gospel, Paul's aim is not to teach the Corinthians the nature of Christian freedom. The rhetorical purpose is rather this: 'Go and do likewise. Renounce (idol) food.'

---

178. Cf. Willis, 'Apologia', pp. 39-40, for other verbal and thematic links between ch. 9 and its context.

179. 'Rhetorical Disposition', p. 486. Smit mentions Quintilian's observation that an example is drawn from without and pressed into the service of the case (*Inst. Or.* 5.11.1).

Here we may note that Paul's argument is complicated by the fact that he is probably killing two birds with one stone.[180] On the one hand, he highlights the voluntary renunciation of his apostolic rights to put pressure on the knowers: the greater the renounced rights of Paul, the more trivial the presumed rights of the Corinthians, and the more reason for them to let go of such presumed rights. On the other hand, Paul's vigorous affirmation of his rights gives his example a more secure base before those who might challenge him. For only on the basis of such assured rights can he exemplify one who voluntarily limits his freedom.

Once the association between his apostolic example and idol food is made, Paul can make more capital out of his behavior in other areas of life to further his argument against eating idol food. Thus in 9.19-23, he goes beyond his right to food and drink and discusses other areas of life in which he forfeits his right and adapts himself to many divergent groups, among whom are the weak. In imitation of Paul, the knowers ought also to accommodate the weak by forfeiting their so-called rights.

Paul mentions four groups of people: the Jews, those under the law, those without the law, and the weak. The identity of these groups seems clear enough, but their relationship to one another and Paul's rationale in selecting these four is far from obvious. I think it is probably not profitable to probe too deep into Paul's reason for choosing these particular groups. It is highly likely that, as far as his rhetorical strategy in ch. 9 is concerned, Paul is only interested in the last group. He selects the first three groups, which somewhat reflect the mixed composition of the Corinthian church, in a quasi-random manner mainly to set the stage for the climactic mention of the weak.[181] Moreover, it is perhaps significant that while in vv. 20-21 Paul states that he became τοῖς Ἰουδαίοις ὡς Ἰουδαῖος...τοῖς ὑπὸ νόμον ὡς ὑπὸ νόμον...τοῖς ἀνόμοις ὡς ἄνομος, in v. 22 he omits the word ὡς and simply says that he became τοῖς ἀσθενέσιν ἀσθενής.[182] This may be nothing more than

---

180. *Pace* Mitchell (*Rhetoric*, p. 244), who acknowledges that 'this is a very common argument'.

181. Cf. Willis, 'Apologia', p. 37; S.C. Barton, '"All Things to All People": Paul and the Law in the Light of 1 Corinthians 9.19-23', in J.D.G. Dunn (ed.), *Paul and the Mosaic Law* (WUNT, 89; Tübingen: Mohr Siebeck, 1996), pp. 271-85 (279-80).

182. ℵ², C, D, F, and other mss have added ὡς to v. 22. The omission has impressive support from 𝔓⁴⁶, a*, A, B, and others. It is likely that some early

a stylistic variation, but it is possible that Paul leaves out the caveat in v. 22 because he became 'weak to the weak' in a way that was not directly parallel to his accommodation to the other groups mentioned in vv. 20-21.[183] Much more significant is Paul's failure to say 'to the strong I became strong'. As in ch. 8, Paul is here clearly siding with the weak against the strong.[184]

There is some uncertainty regarding the identity of the weak in v. 22. It would be most natural to see them as identical to the weak Christians in ch. 8, given their importance in Paul's argument there. On the other hand, the use of κερδαίνω and σῴζω seems to imply that they are not believers. It is possible that Paul uses the terms in contrast with the stumbling and destruction of weak Christians. Hence the terms may be understood in a broader sense than simply 'conversion'.[185] In any case, since Paul's use of 'the weak' is primarily emotive and associative, exact identification of the weak in 9.22 with the weak in 8.7-13 is not necessary for his argument. It would have served Paul's rhetorical purpose as long as both shared some general features of weakness and could somehow have been described as the weak.

In 9.24-27 Paul generalizes further from his example of self-control and draws the parallel from the Isthmian or Caesarian games to show that the Christian race itself requires precisely such self-restraint and discipline. Then the argument takes a turn: while the exercise of self-control brings one the prize, the failure to exercise self-control leads to the danger of being 'disqualified' (9.27)! This danger is demonstrated from the history of Israel in the wilderness (10.1-10). Paul's argument is now shifted from the social to the theological, from avoiding causing others to stumble to avoiding destroying oneself. Correspondingly, the spotlight is no longer on the danger facing the weak, but on the danger facing the knowers.

scribes, consciously or unconsciously, added ὡς to bring the text into line with vv. 20-21.

183. Gardner, *Gifts*, p. 103. Fee (*The First Epistle to the Corinthians*, p. 431) and Conzelmann (*1 Corinthians*, p. 161 n. 28) agree that the missing ὡς is more significant than is often allowed.

184. G. Bornkamm, 'The Missionary Stance of Paul in 1 Corinthians and in Acts', in L.E. Keck and J.L. Martyn (eds.), *Studies in Luke–Acts* (Nashville: Abingdon Press, 1966), pp. 194-207 (203); Gardner, *Gifts*, p. 104.

185. Gardner, *Gifts*, p. 104.

The Danger of Idolatry. 1 Corinthians 10 begins with an explanatory γάρ, indicating the close connection of this chapter with what precedes. In 10.1-10, Paul weaves together a plethora of scriptural texts on Israel's wilderness experience to warn the Corinthians of the danger of idolatry.[186] Psalm 105, itself a commentary on the unfaithfulness of the fathers in the desert, seems to be prominent in Paul's mind. The verbal and thematic correspondence is impressive: The Israelites gave in to their craving (ἐπιθυμέω v. 14; 1 Cor. 10.6) and put God to test (πειράζω v. 14; 1 Cor. 10.9); they grumbled (γογγύζω v. 25; 1 Cor. 10.10) and grew envious of their leader Moses (v. 16); they committed idolatry (vv. 19, 28, 36-39; 1 Cor. 10.7, 14) and ate idol food (v. 28); God threatened to destroy them (ἐξολεθρεύω v. 23 [twice]; ὀλοθρευτής and ἀπόλλυμι 1 Cor. 10.9, 10; cf. 8.11) as a result of their idolatry. To these items we may add the use of σκάνδαλον (v. 36; σκανδαλίζω 1 Cor. 8.13) for idolatry, the mention of sacrificing to demons (δαιμόνιον v. 37; cf. 1 Cor. 10.18-22), and the figurative use of defilement for the sin of idolatry (vv. 38-39; 1 Cor. 8.7).

It is important to note that Paul alludes to Psalm 105 with primary reference to idolatry and that the allusions to the Psalm are made in 1 Cor. 8.1-13, 10.1-13, and 10.14-22. These observations support my contention that these three sections, contrary to what scholars often assert, all deal with the same subject of idolatry, expressed in the act of eating idol food.

Interestingly, in vv. 1-5 Paul draws a parallel between the Christian sacraments and their counterparts in the wilderness generation. It is difficult to know whether Paul is thereby disabusing the knowers of their hyper-sacramentalism which promises eternal security.[187] In any

186. It is sometimes suggested that Paul has made use of a Jewish or Christian midrash. See W.A. Meeks, '"And Rose Up to Play": Midrash and Paraenesis in 1 Corinthians 10.1-22', *JSNT* 16 (1982), pp. 64-78; cf. Conzelmann, *1 Corinthians*, p. 165; K.-G. Sandelin, *Wisdom as Nourisher: A Study of an Old Testament Theme, its Development within Early Judaism, and its Impact on Early Christianity* (Åbo: Åbo Akademi, 1986), p. 167; G.D. Collier, '"That we Might not Crave Evil": The Structure and Argument of 1 Corinthians 10.1-13', *JSNT* 55 (1994), pp. 55-75. However, as Fee (*The First Epistle to the Corinthians*, p. 442 n. 5) rightly maintains, Paul has adapted the material so thoroughly for his purpose that the question of origin is quite irrelevant.

187. Many commentators believe that the Corinthians adopted a magical view of the sacraments in Corinth that promised the participants immunity from the power of idols or demons. This hyper-sacramentalism resulted in an overconfidence that

case, his argument here is straightforward: just as the Israelites came out of Egypt with all the spiritual blessings but were judged by God with catastrophic judgment (1 Cor. 10.1-5) because they tested the Lord and fell into idolatry (and sexual immorality), the Corinthians with all their spiritual nourishment are courting the same disaster in their present participation in idolatry (and sexual immorality). And it does not help if, on top of that, they grumble against their God-appointed leader Paul, as the Israelites grumbled against their God-appointed leader Moses (10.10).[188] However much they want to say that an idol is nothing, or that idol food is nothing, there is the danger of losing. No one can get involved in idolatry with immunity.[189] There will be serious spiritual consequences. 'So, let him who thinks he stands take heed lest he falls' (10.12). By now it should be clear that, at the heart of Paul's argument, the ultimate danger is not the weak's weakness but the knowers' 'knowledge'.[190]

Whether 10.13 is understood as a promise or a warning, or both, commentators have no little difficulty in seeing how the verse fits into Paul's scheme of argument. It is often assumed that those who advocate eating idol food want to flaunt their gift of knowledge[191] or that they do

---

also accounted for their willingness to visit prostitutes, their denial of the resurrection, and so on. See von Soden, 'Sacrament', p. 259; Fee, 'Εἰδωλόθυτα', p. 180; and, less explicitly, Barrett, 'Things Sacrificed', pp. 54-55. This is really a moot point; the text itself does not suggest as much. We need only to note that what was uppermost in Paul's mind here was not the sacraments or their abuse, but the danger of idolatry to which the Corinthians were exposing themselves. For an extended and cogent argument against the hyper-sacramentalism interpretation, see K.-G. Sandelin, 'Does Paul Argue Against Sacramentalism and Over-Confidence in 1 Cor. 10.1-14?' in P. Borgen and S. Giversen (eds.), *The New Testament and Hellenistic Judaism* (Aarhus: Aarhus University Press, 1995), pp. 165-82.

188. Contrary to the assertion of many commentators (e.g. Willis, *Idol Meat*, p. 147; Barrett, *First Epistle to the Corinthians*, p. 226; Gardner, *Gifts*, p. 150), Paul's list of the four sins is not merely conventional, but applies specifically to the Corinthian situation.

189. As Sandelin (*Wisdom*, p. 171) points out, 'Paul also mentions other evil dees committed by the fathers, but almost all the Scriptural passages he alludes to contain references to idolatry... It thus seems incontrovertible that the main stress...is on idolatry'.

190. This may help explain why Paul deliberately avoids calling the Corinthians the 'strong', for in reality they are not (cf. the climax of Paul's argument in 10.22: 'Are we stronger than [God]?').

191. Gardner, *passim*. Cf. Wire, *Women Prophets*, p. 103: 'the Corinthians are

not want to miss out on 'occasions of good company, good food, and good fun'.[192] It has even been suggested that the temptation in view is factionalism, 'the ultimate human temptation... which now threatens the Corinthian community'![193] But such explanations seriously under-estimate the urgency of Paul's appeal. Mere fleshy desire to show off knowledge or social inconvenience or missing out on some fun hardly calls for Paul's emotional appeal to the Corinthians to trust in God's faithfulness in taking care of their situation. The testing envisioned in 10.13 must have seemed unbearable to some. The promise in 10.13 makes much better sense if the pressure for them to eat idol food is intense and comes from without. In view of the significance of social meals in the Greco-Roman world outlined earlier in Chapter 2, to refuse to eat idol food presented at such meals would mark one as anti-social and invite misunderstanding and hostility. Not only would one miss opportunities for social advancement, one would also risk being ostracized for refusing to eat idol food with friends, relatives, business associates, or other people of importance. Therefore, one's livelihood, and even life itself, would be in jeopardy.[194] This may be seen in the hostile treatments the Thessalonian Christians (who 'turn from idols to serve a living and true God') suffered from their own countrymen. As S. Mitchell puts it, 'it was not a change of heart that might win a Christian convert back to paganism, but the overwhelming pressure to conform imposed by the institutions of his city and the activities of his neighbours'.[195] It is highly probable that, instead of standing firm on Christian principles, the Corinthians rationalized their compromise by clever arguments and pretense to knowledge and rights (as they also did with regard to the issue of sexual immorality). But to those who take their stand against the idolatrous practice, the promise in 10.13 would have been necessary and precious.

By saying πειρασμὸς ὑμᾶς οὐκ εἴληφεν εἰ μὴ ἀνθρώπινος, Paul may be thinking of the testing endured by Christians all over the

choosing to make a public witness, even in cultic settings, that the sacrificed meat will not harm them, that "the stomach is for food and food for the stomach" because there is no God but one (6.13; 8.6)'.

192. Willis, *Idol Meat*, p. 63.

193. Mitchell, *Rhetoric*, p. 254.

194. See my earlier discussion on why the knowers ate idol food.

195. S. Mitchell, *Anatolia: Land, Men, and Gods in Asia Minor* (Oxford: Clarendon Press, 1993), II, p. 10. Mitchell's statement is made with special reference to the imperial cult.

Roman Empire who take their stand against idolatry. In any case, by stressing the fact that the Corinthians' testing, however severe, is never beyond human capacity to bear, and that God will provide the way out, v. 13 removes all excuses for them to compromise or test God in the matter of idol food.[196] This sets the stage for 10.14, 'the directive that all of chs. 8–10 has been arguing for'.[197] With the διόπερ Paul makes his strong appeal: flee from idolatry! Contrary to what is often asserted, there is no hint whatsoever that the subject of Paul's discussion suddenly changes from εἰδωλόθυτα to εἰδωλολατρία per se.[198] Rather, Paul is making clear the nature of εἰδωλόθυτον: to eat εἰδωλόθυτον is to participate in εἰδωλολατρία. Thus, in 10.19-20, he sets εἰδωλόθυτον and εἴδωλον in apposition: τί οὖν φημι; ὅτι εἰδωλόθυτόν τί ἐστιν; ἢ ὅτι εἴδωλόν τί ἐστιν; ἀλλ᾽ ὅτι ἃ θύουσιν, δαιμονίοις καὶ οὐ θεῷ.[199] If Paul were only attacking εἰδωλολατρία in contradistinction to εἰδωλόθυτα, then the phrase ὅτι εἰδωλόθυτόν τί ἐστιν would be irrelevant. That he mentions εἰδωλόθυτον before εἴδωλον is further indication that the former is the subject foremost in his mind. When we also take into account the total lack of evidence in early Jewish and Christian traditions for the dissociation of εἰδωλόθυτα from εἰδωλολατρία, the Corinthians cannot very well be expected to hear anything but a prohibition of εἰδωλόθυτα in Paul's warning to flee εἰδωλολατρία.[200]

Does Paul's strong stand against partaking of idol food imply that idols are real or that food can actually be defiled by them? How can such understanding be consistent with the monotheism Paul so strongly proclaims, that 'there is no God but one'? In 10.19-20 Paul anticipates such an objection by reaffirming the nothingness of idols. But he also

196. J.F.M. Smit ('"Do not be Idolaters": Paul's Rhetoric in First Corinthians 10.1-22', *NovT* 39 [1997], pp. 40-53 [44-45]) notes correctly: 'The unspoken, but unmistakable reverse of this encouragement is a last warning to the Corinthians not to become, for their part, unfaithful to God by participating in sacrificial meals'.

197. Witherington, *Conflict and Community*, p. 224.

198. E.g. Sawyer, 'Meat Sacrificed', pp. 165-66; Brunt, 'Paul's Attitude', p. 57, maintains that it is 'understandable that Paul would concern himself with the broader problem of idolatry in the course of discussing the problem of sacrificial meat'. However, such broadening of Paul's concern hardly calls for the vigor and urgency of Paul's appeal.

199. Note that in *Joseph and Aseneth*, Aseneth's conversion is expressed by the destruction of her idols *and* idol food.

200. Note that the Western text of Acts 15.29 obviously understands εἰδωλόθυτα in terms of εἰδωλολατρία.

introduces a new thought: irrespective of what has happened to the idol food, by partaking of it the Corinthians become 'sharers in demons' because the food is 'offered to demons and not to God' (10.20).[201]

I cannot, and do not deem it necessary, to go into Paul's theology of the Lord's Supper here. Most commentators acknowledge that the Lord's Supper is not Paul's main subject matter; it is only put to rhetorical use in rejecting sacrificial meals.[202] Nor can I explore the meaning of κοινωνία, or what precisely is involved in fellowship with demons.[203] For my purpose it is enough to point out that Paul obviously believes—and expects the Corinthians to agree—that 'fellowship with demons' is a grave sin.

In his argument against the Corinthians' involvement in πορνεία, Paul maintains that there is a basic incompatibility between one's union with Christ and one's union with a prostitute. The apostle uses a similar argument here against eating idol food: one cannot have a part in both the Lord's table and the table of demons. Participation in the Lord's Supper clearly involves the partakers in a fellowship with the blood and body of Christ, and it is unthinkable for one who has thus joined with the Lord to be joined with demons by eating idol food. It is possible that Paul's strong insistence on the incompatibility of the two tables is a reaction to the practice of some Corinthians of bringing idol food to the Lord's Supper for feasting. This understanding would be consistent with his stern warning against provoking God to jealousy. But we do not have enough contextual clues to be certain.

There is some question regarding the purpose of Paul's mention of Israel in 10.18. Most commentators understand θυσιαστήριον as a reference to the altar of Yahweh.[204] Thus the message Paul wants to convey is that 'the eating of sacrifice in the Jewish temple entails a

---

201. In pagan sources, the word δαιμόνιον normally referred to a supernatural being somewhat less than the gods. The term was not necessarily pejorative. But undoubtedly, in Paul's mind, as in biblical traditions, a malevolent spiritual being was meant, whatever its pagan connotations.

202. Smit, 'Idolaters', p. 41.

203. For a detailed discussion of the meaning and significance of the term see Willis, *Idol Meat*, pp. 167-220. Willis's claim that κοινωνία is primarily social and horizontal will be discussed in the appendix.

204. E.g. Fee, *The First Epistle to the Corinthians*, pp. 470-71; Witherington, *Conflict and Community*, p. 225; Talbert, *Reading Corinthians*, p. 59. H. Gressmann, 'Η ΚΟΙΝΩΝΙΑ ΤΩΝ ΔΑΙΜΟΝΙΩΝ', *ZNW* 20 (1921), pp. 224-30 (224) takes θυσιαστήριον as a metonym for Yahweh.

common participation in the altar'.[205] Fee thinks that Paul gives this example in addition to the example of the Lord's Supper because Jewish sacred meals are more closely analogous to pagan sacrificial meals.[206]

Alternatively, one can see θυσιαστήριον as the pagan altar rather than Yahweh's altar.[207] This option, seldom considered by scholars, is much preferable for the following reasons.[208]

1. Paul describes Israel with the phrase κατὰ σάρκα. His use of σάρξ in 1 Corinthians is primarily negative. This is particularly true of the κατὰ σάρκα in 1.26.

2. Verses 20 and 22 are quotations from Deuteronomy 32 which, in their original context, refer to Israel's participation in pagan sacrifices. Verses 1-11 focus on the idolatry of the wilderness generation of Israel. Most probably sinful Israel is also in view in v. 18.

3. As a positive example, v. 18 is much too brief and does not seem to add anything to Paul's more detailed reference to the Lord's Supper in vv. 16-17 and 21.

4. If Yahweh's altar is in view in v. 18, then the τί οὖν φημι, which begins v. 19, seems abrupt. Paul is qualifying something as yet unspoken. On the other hand, if mention is already made of pagan sacrifices in v. 18, then the qualification of v. 19 (ὅτι εἰδωλόθυτόν τί ἐστιν) is perfectly understandable.

5. The word δαιμόνιον is rare in the biblical portion of the LXX. When the term is used, it is employed exclusively in connection with Israel's idolatry. It is apostate Israelites who sacrifice their children to demons (Ps. 105.37) and it is they who prepare τῷ δαιμονίῳ τράπεζαν (Isa. 65.11).[209]

---

205. Witherington, *Conflict and Community*, p. 225. To illustrate this point, Philo is often quoted: 'The sacrificial meals...are the property...of him to whom the victim has been sacrificed,...who has made the convival company of those who carry out the sacrifices partners of the altar whose board they share' (*Spec. Leg.* 1.221).

206. Fee, *The First Epistle to the Corinthians*, p. 471.

207. To my knowledge, the only detailed defense of this position is given by Gardner (*Gifts*, pp. 165-69); for a similar but briefer argument, which focuses on the negative connotation of 'Israel according to the flesh', see Schrage, *Der erste Brief*, II, pp. 442-43.

208. The following is largely based on Gardner's arguments.

209. לגד שלחן in the MT.

6.   It is arguable that commentators are influenced by the gloss τὰ
      ἔθνη as a subject for θύουσιν in v. 20.[210] This almost auto-
      matically precludes one from seeing the possibility that Israel's
      participation in pagan sacrifices is in view in v. 18.

Paul is not concerned with pagans here, but with God's covenant
people. His point is not that pagans offer sacrifices to idols and are thus
in union with their demons. He is rather arguing that God's people cannot join themselves in union with both the Lord and the demons. The
Lord's table (Ezek. 44.16, Mal. 1.12) automatically excludes the
demon's table. As he has done so in vv. 1-10, Paul is using the example
of unfaithful Israel to warn the unfaithful Corinthians (vv. 6, 11). Like
Israel, the Corinthians have their spiritual food and drink, which join
them to the Lord; like Israel, they put the Lord to test and provoke him
to jealousy by eating idol food; like Israel, they thus become partners
with demons; and like Israel, unless they repent, they will face God's
severe judgment.

Paul's argument and terminology in 1 Corinthians 8–10 draw heavily
on biblical traditions. The biblical text uppermost in Paul's mind in
10.18-22 is Deuteronomy 32. The description of God as θεός πιστὸς
appears only in Deut. 32.4 and Deut. 7.9.[211] In Deut. 32.17, idol food is
deemed to be sacrifices to demons. Paul's final warning, 'Shall we provoke the Lord to jealousy?', echoes Deut. 32.21: 'They have provoked
me to jealousy with what is no god'.

Μὴ ἰσχυρότεροι αὐτοῦ ἐσμεν is the climactic rhetorical question
Paul poses to the Corinthians.[212] This question, like the previous one,
shows that Paul's mind is saturated with Deuteronomy 32. Rosner
notes that 'in Deuteronomy 32, especially in the Targumim, the question of Israel's participation in idolatry and the Lord's jealousy and
discipline is set in terms of strength and power'.[213] Already in Deut.
8.17-19, Israel is warned: 'Do not say to yourself, "My power (ἡ ἰσχύς

210. The external evidence is divided, with the Alexandrian witness favoring the
inclusion of τὰ ἔθνη. However, transcriptional probability clearly favors the omission. It is unlikely that early scribes omit the phrase in order to harmonize with the
LXX text.

211. Gardner, *Gifts*, p. 154.

212. It is this rhetorical question, Chrysostom observes, that reduces the
Corinthians' position to an absurdity (*1 Cor. Hom.* 24).

213. B.S. Rosner, '"Stronger than He?": The Strength of 1 Corinthians 10.22b',
TynBul 43 (1992), pp. 171-79 (177).

μου) and the might of my own hand have gotten me this wealth'. But remember the Lord your God, for it is he who gives you power (ἰσχύς)... If you do forget the Lord your God and follow other gods...you shall surely perish.'[214] Then in Deuteronomy 32, Moses threatens that if the Israelites provoke the Lord to jealousy with other gods, they will suffer God's judgment until 'their power is gone. Then he will say: Where are their gods...who ate the fat of their sacrifices and drank the wine of their libations?' (Deut. 32.36-37).

Though idols are nothing when conceived of as possible rivals to the Christian God, food sacrificed to them is nevertheless forbidden to Christians because it represents what is sacrificed to demons. Apparently Paul is able to hold such a dual world-view without attempting to dissolve the inherent tension. Tomson suggests that here Paul is combining a rational approach to idols in rabbinic traditions (which was influenced by Cynic–Stoic thoughts) with a realistic demonology in Qumran and apocalyptic thought.[215] This may be true, but is difficult to prove. My feeling is that one need not go beyond the biblical traditions for an explanation of such a dual world-view. It is important to note that, in the Jewish Scriptures, the 'nothingness' of pagan gods is not ontological, but in contrast to the power and glory of Yahweh.[216] Thus Isa. 44.9 says that idol *makers* (definitely real) are—like the idols they make—'nothings' (תהו; μάταιος in LXX). Similarly, nations (40.17) and princes and rulers (40.23) which set themselves against God are said to be 'nothing' (תהו; οὐδέν in LXX). Furthermore, we must note

214. Rosner, 'Stronger', p. 175.

215. Tomson, *Jewish Law*, pp. 156-58, 202. Earlier, Horsley ('Gnosis in Corinth') made the suggestion that the notion that demons are behind idols belongs to Palestinian and apocalyptic Judaism, whereas the notion of the non-existence of idols belongs to Hellenistic Judaism. He claims that the Corinthians followed the Hellenistic tradition, which Paul found it necessary to modify in line with the apocalyptic tradition. As Wright points out, such a division between Hellenistic and Palestinian Judaism is far too simplistic, and does not square well with the evidence—*Jub.* 22.17 is cited by Horsley as a witness for the 'demonic' view, and *Jub.* 12.1-5 for the 'non-existent' view (N.T. Wright, *The Climax of the Covenant: Christ and the Law in Pauline Theology* [Edinburgh: T. & T. Clark, 1991], p. 128 n. 20)! Tomson's discussion is more nuanced than Horsley's in that he allows for the possibility that such a combination of competing views of idols has come prepackaged to Paul via Pharisaic Judaism. But neither considers the fact that both world-views are already found in the Jewish Scriptures.

216. Gardner, *Gifts*, p. 36.

that in Deuteronomy, Psalms, and Isaiah, biblical books that Paul quotes frequently, both the nothingness of idols (Deut. 32.21; Ps. 115.4-8; 135.15-18; Isa. 40.19-20; 44.9-17) and the existence of demons and spirits (Deut. 18.11; 32.17; Ps. 106.37; Isa. 8.19; 19.3) are affirmed. More to the point, in Deuteronomy 32, which is foremost in Paul's thought, all the basic ingredients of the demonology in 1 Corinthians 8–10 are there: an idol is 'no god' (v. 21), yet idols are 'strange gods' that make the One God jealous (v. 16), and sacrifices to them are deemed sacrifices to demons (v. 16). In the final chapter I will argue that such a dual world-view on pagan gods and pagan sacrifices is in fact part and parcel of Israel's monotheistic faith.

Food of Unspecified Religious History (1 Corinthians 10.23-29a). Having clearly condemned the practice of eating idol food, Paul now deals with the question of whether Christians need also abstain from food that might have been previously sacrificed to idols. Before I look at the passage in detail, two general observations may be made:

1.   Of the permissible contexts for eating, temple dining is con-spicuous by its absence. Paul does not envisage any 'per-missible temple attendance',[217] but mentions only marketplace food and private meals, where the connection to idolatry is not self evident.

2.   The possibility of eating idol food in a private meal is envis-aged only when the invitation is offered by τις τῶν ἀπίστων (10.27). The implicit assumption is that οἱ πιστοί would not, or at least should not, be serving idol food in a meal.

Sometimes 10.23-29a (or part of it) is taken to be Paul's instruction to the weak. After severely limiting the strong's freedom, Paul now encourages the weak, it is argued, to take a broader view.

This view has little merits. As Fee points out, it is scarcely imagin-able that 'Paul would now command the "weak" of 8.7-13 to do the very thing that he acknowledges would destroy them'.[218] Moreover, some verses in the passage can hardly apply to the 'weak' (e.g. vv. 23-24, 28-29a).[219] Such a point of view would require Paul's audience to

217. Fisk, 'Eating', p. 62; cf. Oster, 'Archaeological Evidence', pp. 66-67.

218. Fee, *The First Epistle to the Corinthians*, p. 477 n. 10.

219. As Willis (*Idol Meat*, pp. 232-33) observes, v. 24 must be directed to the 'strong' because it answers their slogan πάντα ἔξεστιν and likewise v. 28 because

change three times in the short span of five verses—without any indication from Paul![220]

Most likely, Paul's discussion of marketplace food and pagan dinner invitations is a response to the Corinthians' challenge in their rebuttal of Paul's previous letter. Since Paul might not have carefully qualified his statements in the previous letter (which might well have been written on the spur of the moment when he learned of the Corinthians' immorality and idolatry), his prohibition was open to deliberate misinterpretation as something totally impracticable:[221]

> Paul, you say that idol food is off limits. But what about marketplace food? Since some of the food sold in the market has previously been sacrificed, are you saying that we should always avoid shopping in the market? And what about dinners with our pagan friends? You know sometimes they may serve us idol food. You see, your instructions are simply impractical. To follow them, we will have to go out of this world!

Paul responds that food which is possibly sacrificed to idols is not off limits—unless this possibility becomes a certainty. One who has unknowingly eaten idol food would not be defiled.[222] Therefore, one may eat anything that is sold in the marketplace μηδὲν ἀνακρίνοντες διὰ τὴν συνείδησιν. There is no need to inquire 'for the sake of consciousness', that is, for the sake of knowing the nature of the food with the entailed moral obligations. Since 'the earth is the Lord's, and all it contains' (10.26), συνείδησις need not be involved at all in the case of food of unspecified origin.

While it is clear that Paul maintains his Jewish hostility to idolatry, his relaxed attitude towards food of unspecified origin raises the

---

only the strong are likely to eat in spite of the known idolatrous origin of the food.

220. Fee, *The First Epistle to the Corinthians*, p. 477 n. 10. W.A. Meeks sees such a 'peculiar dialectic of affirmations and reversals', which leads to a practical compromise, as the mark of Paul's genius: 'his dialectical rhetoric subsumes and articulates a process in which conflicting factions of the congregation were trying to discover an appropriate manner of life' (*The Moral World of the First Christians* [LEC, 6; Philadelphia: Westminster Press, 1986], pp. 135-36). Such an understanding reflects more the fertility of Meeks's imagination than 'the ingenuity of Paul's rhetoric' (p. 135)!

221. The way the Corinthians take Paul's command 'not to associate with πόρνοι' (1 Cor. 5.9) seems to be another example of deliberate misinterpretation so that Paul's advice can be discarded as impractical.

222. See my discussion in the final chapter on the origins of Paul's approach.

question of whether he has disregarded his Jewish sensibilities at this point. Barrett's comments that 'in the matter of εἰδωλόθυτα...Paul was not a practising Jew' and that 'Paul is nowhere more un-Jewish than in this μηδὲν ἀνακρίνοντες' are extreme.[223] But Dunn may be correct in saying that 'Paul's traditional Jewish antipathy to idols was qualified at least to the extent that he put no obligation on his fellow believers to avoid idol food at all costs or to parade their consciences in the matter by making scrupulous enquiry beforehand'.[224]

Nevertheless, it is not at all clear that the scrupulous inquiry about food, supposedly encumbering upon devote Jews, was something prevalent in first-century Diaspora Judaism, or became only the stance of the most zealous Rabbis after the two revolts. Paul's advice might be no more liberal than that of many Diaspora Jews of his time who wished to maintain their participation in the wider community.[225]

There is some question regarding the proportion of marketplace food at Paul's Corinth that had been sacrificed to idols.[226] Hans Lietzmann argues in an excursus in his commentary on the Corinthian letters that all or most of the meat sold in the market was idol food previously sacrificed in nearby temples.[227] As Gooch notes, this early work continues to be the major discussion to which commentators refer.[228] But Lietzmann's rather slim evidence for linking idolatry to meat sold in Corinth's market is far from conclusive.[229] On the other hand, there are indications that non-sacrificed meat was readily available.[230] Therefore

223. Barrett, 'Things Sacrificed', p. 49.

224. Dunn, *Theology of Paul*, p. 705.

225. E.P. Sanders, *Jewish Law*, p. 281.

226. See Klauck, *Herrenmahl*, pp. 273-76 for secondary literature and discussions on *macella*.

227. H. Lietzmann, *An die Korinther I, II* (HNT 9; Tübingen: Mohr Siebeck, 1931), pp. 49-52.

228. Gooch, 'Food and Limits', p. 2.

229. Beside some brief general arguments, Lietzmann provides a diagram of a market adjacent to a Caesar cult shrine in Pompeii (*Korinther*, p. 52). As Cadbury points out, public buildings such as markets and temples were naturally found in city centers in the ancient world. Therefore their proximity to one another is no evidence for a close connection between the market and idolatry (H.J. Cadbury, 'The Macellum of Corinth', *JBL* 53 [1934], pp. 134-41 [141]). Incidentally, even today in Asia, one finds Buddhist and Taoist temples built next to Bible colleges in strategic locations in major cities!

230. Cadbury ('Macellum', pp. 134-41) draws attention to the fact that a shop in Pompeii had entire skeletons of sheep. Had the sheep been slaughtered in a temple,

one must not exaggerate the plight of the Corinthians as having *nothing* to eat unless it were sacrificial meat.[231] In any case, 1 Cor. 10.25 makes clear that not all food was previously sacrificed. Otherwise, what is the point of 'not asking'? Gooch wisely concludes: 'it is very doubtful that anything more can be known of food in the market than can be inferred from Paul's letter: some food had been offered, and probably some had not'.[232]

Idols have no magical power over the food per se because 'the earth is the Lord's, and all it contains' (10.26; cf. Ps. 24.1). It is often noted that Ps. 24.1 was used by the Rabbis to justify the use of benedictions over food (*t. Ber* 4.1).[233] In the Mishnah, the commandment to bless God at meal is associated with the prohibition of idolatry.[234] R. Shimon ben Yohai says: 'If three have eaten at one table and not spoken words of Torah on it, it is as though they had eaten of the sacrifices of the dead... But if three have eaten at one table and have spoken words of Torah on it, it is as if they had eaten from the table of God' (*m. Ab.*

the priestly portions would have been missing in the skeletons. We may also note Plutarch's comment that whenever the Pythagoreans ate meat, they usually ate from sacrificial animals—implying that others might eat non-sacrificial meat (*TLG, Quest. Conv.* 112.729.C.7-9; cf. Barrett, 'Things Sacrificed', p. 48). Furthermore, Tertullian says, 'We [Christians] live with you [pagans], enjoy the same food... We cannot dwell together in the world without the market-place, without your butchers' (*Apol.* 42). Yet Tertullian condemns eating idol food. Therefore it is clear that non-sacrificed meat was available in the markets in Tertullian's time. There is no reason to think that the situation would have been very different in Paul's time.

231. Sawyer, 'Meat Sacrificed', p. 99. Disputing Theissen's (*Social Setting*, p. 128) claim that the weak ate meat 'almost exclusively as an ingredient in pagan religious celebration', J.J. Meggitt ('Meat Consumption and Social Conflict in Corinth', *JTS* 45 [1994], pp. 137-41) observes that (lower quality) meat was readily available in the 'decidedly unsacral' *popinae* and *ganeae* ('cookshops') which were frequented by the common people and even by some members of the upper echelons of society, such as Nero, Commodus and Mark Anthony.

232. Gooch, 'Food and Limits', p. 7 n. 9. Gooch draws attention to M. Isenberg's study, which cites 1 Cor. 10.25 as one of a handful of references to sacrificed food in the market and yields only this minimal conclusion ('The Sale of Sacrificial Meat', *CP* 70 [1975], pp. 271-73).

233. E. Lohse ('Zu 1 Cor. 10.26.31', *ZNW* 47 [1956], pp. 277-80) thinks that Paul knew the tradition later codified in *t. Ber* 4.1 because of (1) the connection of Psalm 24 with meals in both Paul and the rabbinic text and of (2) the common theme of doing all things to God's glory (cited in Willis, *Idol Meat*, p. 235; Willis himself is uncertain). See also Barrett, 'Things Sacrificed', p. 52.

234. Tomson, *Jewish Law*, p. 205.

3.3).[235] The phrase 'sacrifices of the dead' recalls Ps. 105.28, a commentary on Israel's sin of eating idol food as recorded in Numbers 25. Presumably, then, food that has not been blessed is regarded as being like idol food. Could Paul be suggesting that Ps. 24.1 takes away the presumptive idolatrous character of the food?[236]

The invitation to a meal in v. 27 is sometimes understood to be to a social meal held in the temple's dining facilities. The difficulty with this interpretation is that, in 8.10, Paul has already discouraged temple dining. Moreover, it is difficult to understand why the nature of the food served in the temple needs to be pointed out by anyone. While we do not know if and how much non-sacred food was available in the temple dining facilities, the following considerations suggest that food served there would almost certainly include ἱερόθυτον.

1. If, as is commonly assumed, most sacrificed foods made their way to the marketplace, then how much more they would be consumed in the temple precincts!

2. The ancients had very limited means of keeping food from spoiling. Thus food sacrificed in the temple would most likely have been bought and eaten in the vicinity.

3. As mentioned in Chapter 2, the literary evidence strongly suggests that socially significant meals (and even not so significant ones), which were often held in homes, involved explicit religious rites. It would be highly unlikely that ἱερόθυτον was not served in meals at cultic settings where there was heightened consciousness of the gods.

We may also note that, if the invitation of 10.27 refers to temple meals, then Paul's advice for the Corinthians to eat without inquiring seems to conflict with his strong prohibition in 10.14-21. As Willis observes, most interpreters who think temple meals are in view in 10.27 also favor some kind of partition theories in order to ease the tension that results between these two pericopes.[237] Thus this interpretation is likewise subject to the many difficulties pertaining to the partition theories.

---

235. Note that the contrast between the sacrifices of the dead and the table of God is analogous to Paul's contrasting the table of demons to the table of the Lord.

236. Cf. 1 Tim. 4.4-5: 'For everything created by God is good, and nothing is to be rejected, provided it is received with thanksgiving; for it is sanctified by God's word and by prayer'.

237. Willis, *Idol Meat*, p. 237.

The majority of scholars rightly regard 10.27 as a reference to an invitation to eat in a private home.

Paul permits Christians to eat everything μηδὲν ἀνακρίνοντες διὰ τὴν συνείδησιν when invited for a meal by unbelievers (10.27). In Gooch's survey of the literature on Greco-Roman dining, there are many references to meals in private homes that included sacrificed food, but he also notes that meals are often mentioned without any overt or implicit reference to sacrifice or rites.[238] Therefore at meals in private homes, as in the case of marketplace food, there is no necessary or presumptive connection between food and idolatry. Further, it is possible that some of the foods being served are not εἰδωλόθυτα even though the rest have been hallowed (defiled) by sacrificial rites. This kind of meals is unlike both temple meals (in which εἰδωλόθυτα are most probably served) and meals hosted by Christians (in which εἰδωλόθυτα are not supposed to be served). Paul's advice in this case is the same as his instruction about marketplace food: simply eat; it is not necessary to know the nature of the food.

However, v. 28 introduces a qualification: if one is informed of the idolatrous origin of the food, the only proper Christian action is to abstain. This is not to say that the food has somehow become defiled through the Christian's knowledge of its prehistory. What is at stake is the Christian confession. By knowingly partaking of idol food, the Christian is tacitly condoning idolatry and thus lending a hand to the transgressors.[239]

There is a question about whether v. 28 should be connected with v. 27 or the whole of vv. 25-27. Commentators also do not agree over the question of what kind of person the τις who informs the Christian of the idolatrous origins of the food in 10.28 may be. Is that person the pagan host, a Christian fellow guest who has a 'weak' conscience, or a pagan fellow guest? The first option is somewhat unlikely because the host has already been referred to in 10.27 and this would make the use of τις in 10.28 curious. Moreover, were it the host's intention to inform

238. Gooch, 'Food and Limits', p. 124.

239. Tomson comes to a very similar understanding of Paul's approach to idol food by assuming that Paul operates within a halakhic framework: Paul 'does not teach a partial permission to eat idol food. He teaches a rational, halakhic definition of what should be considered an idol offering in uncertain cases and what should not' (*Jewish Law*, p. 217). I will address the difference between Tomson's view and mine in the Appendix.

his Christian guest of the prehistory of the food, he probably would have done so earlier rather than at the time of the meal (10.27 suggests that the food is already set before the Christian). On the other hand, the situation may be that both sacrificed food and non-sacrificed food are set on the table. The host, in keeping with the etiquette associated with inviting guests to a meal, informs the Christian of the origin of the particular food which may cause offense.[240] It is difficult to be certain.

Of the other options it may seem obvious that a fellow Christian is meant. The concern for the συνείδησις of the informant bears some resemblance to the situation in 8.7. Moreover, for those who accept the usual understanding of συνείδησις as conscience, it is not easy to see how a non-Christian's conscience could enter into the matter.[241] But the major difficulty with this option is that the informant refers to the idol food as ἱερόθυτον, the correct term for 'sacrificial food' from the pagan standpoint[242] rather than the standard Jewish-Christian (and pejorative) designation εἰδωλόθυτον, the term which Paul has been consistently using up to this point. It may be objected that the weak Christian simply wants to avoid offending the host, or perhaps he is speaking out of habit, or perhaps Paul's lexical choice is 'designed to reflect the informant's lingering pre-Christian perspective on things pagan'.[243] But the point remains that a Christian, especially if he objects to eating idol food, is highly unlikely to use the dignified pagan term to refer to something he finds abominable. In addition, as Fee rightly points out, this example is 'a Pauline creation, not a report of an actual event. Since Paul himself composed it so that the person speaking uses pagan terminology, it seems unlikely that he would thereby have understood the interlocutor to be a believer.'[244]

Moreover, the weak Christian who has known that sacrificial meat will be served, or possibly be served, is most unlikely to attend the dinner in the first place! Barrett attempts to salvage this view by conjecturing that the guest is a Christian, 'whose weak conscience, though it

240. Winter, *Welfare*, pp. 175-76. Gardner (*Gifts*, p. 177) objects to this interpretation on the ground that it assumes too noble a motivation on the part of a pagan. But such a 'noble' practice is in fact commonplace today in many Asian contexts.

241. Barrett, *First Epistle to the Corinthians*, p. 242.

242. Conzelmann, *1 Corinthians*, p. 177.

243. Fisk, 'Eating', p. 67.

244. Fee, *The First Epistle to the Corinthians*, p. 484.

permitted him to attend the meal, has led him to make inquiries (cf. vv. 25, 27) of his host or in the kitchen, and who, using the most courteous word available, now passes on the fruit of his researches to his stronger Christian brother'.[245] Barrett's conjecture, though imaginative, suffers from the fundamental weakness of being *ad hoc*—the conscience of the Christian in view is supposed to be just strong enough to permit him to attend the meal but weak enough to lead him to make inquiries later after he has arrived! And if he can privately make inquiries of the host, why can he not also pass on the information privately to his fellow Christian guest? But Paul's example is clearly meant to reflect fairly typical situations. Indeed, as Tomson points out, that Paul chooses to discuss the marketplace and the home of an unbeliever indicates that it is the Christian response in *pagan* surroundings that Paul is interested in.[246]

If a pagan fellow guest is intended, then what is the connection between his συνείδησις and the Christian's abstention? As argued earlier, συνείδησις is one's consciousness and knowledge with regard to the nature of food with moral implications for the rightness or wrongness of the act of eating. In the pagan's consciousness, the food is religiously significant and the moral implication is that it is wrong for the Christian to eat it. Lying behind the non-Christian informer's remark is the assumption that Christians have nothing to do with pagan gods and are not supposed to eat their sacrificed food. This may indicate that abstention from idol food has already become a fairly standard early Christian practice by the time Paul wrote 1 Corinthians.

Since the informant has already drawn the food into the sphere of pagan worship, Christians must abstain at this point.[247] Paul emphasizes that it is the informant's συνείδησις that counts. Why? It is because the knowers, unlike the weak, do not have the συνείδησις that the food is εἰδωλόθυτον. Hence they will see no moral problem in eating. Their obligation to abstinence is based on the pagan's συνείδησις, which classifies the food as ἱερόθυτον. If the Corinthians eat the food regardless, they will compromise their confession of the One God and abandon the basic Christian (and Jewish) critique of pagan gods. As Conzelmann puts it, the unbeliever 'would not only be strengthened in

245. Barrett, *First Epistle to the Corinthians*, p. 242.
246. Tomson, *Jewish Law*, p. 204.
247. Borgen, 'How Far?', p. 38.

his [idolatrous] conviction, but the Christian would objectify the power of the gods, and thereby "preach" faith in them'.[248]

It is possible that the informant is (purposely or otherwise) left indefinite because it does not matter who broaches the issue. On this understanding, '10.28, 29a need not be restricted to verse 27 and its situation but can be regarded as a general warning, applicable to either the dinner invitation of 10.27 or the meat purchased in a market (10.25), or presumably other occasions'.[249] This alternative interpretation would still be consistent with—and indeed strengthen—my thesis: if the prehistory of the food is unknown, one may eat without asking question; if its idolatrous prehistory is pointed out (by whatever means), one must abstain.

The Meaning of the Rhetorical Questions in 1 Corinthians 10.29b-30. To use Barrett's words, these two verses are 'notoriously difficult' to explain on any views.[250] The verses have sometimes been taken as Paul's response to the weak who were aggressively using their conscience as a pretext to limit the strong's freedom.[251] This interpretation is difficult to sustain in view of Paul's passionate concern for the weak throughout 1 Corinthians 8–10. Moreover, it presupposes a sudden change of audience without any indications of such.[252]

Some regard the interjections as a marginal gloss by an early scribe who found Paul's instructions in vv. 28-29a too restrictive.[253] From a similar perspective, others see the questions as the objection of the Corinthians rather than Paul's own view.[254] Thus the verses reflect the

248. Conzelmann, *1 Corinthians*, p. 178. Likewise, Willis (*Idol Meat*, p. 241) comments: 'the pagan who observes a Christian eating ἱερόθυτον might either think Christianity was syncretistic, or the Christian really is uncommitted in faith'.

249. Willis, *Idol Meat*, p. 243, following von Soden, 'Sakrament', p. 252.

250. Barrett, *First Epistle to the Corinthians*, p. 242.

251. Richardson, *Freedom*, p. 129: 'It seems that weak Christians were using their weakness aggessively to keep others from doing what offended them'. Similarly, Grosheide, *First Epistle*, p. 244; Héring, *First Epistle*, p. 99; Murphy-O'Connor, 'Freedom', p. 570.

252. Fee, *The First Epistle to the Corinthians*, p. 486 n. 52.

253. Weiss, *Der erste Korintherbriefe*, pp. 265-66; von Soden, 'Sakrament und Ethik', p. 252; G. Zuntz, *The Text of the Epistles: A Disquisition upon the Corpus Paulinum* (London: Oxford University Press, 1953), p. 17.

254. Witherington, *Conflict and Community*, p. 228; Lietzmann, *Korinther*, p. 51; H.D. Wendland, *Die Briefen die Korinther* (Göttingen: Vandenhoeck & Ruprecht, 1968), p. 83.

sentiment of the strong who may complain about Paul's demands for them to sacrifice their freedom to others' scruples. In anticipation, Paul offers this hypothetical objection only to neutralize it. As Barrett argues, this interpretation is unlikely for two reasons.[255]

1. If the questions were reactions, whether real or hypothetical, to Paul's strictures, one would expect the sentence to begin with δέ or ἀλλά, not γάρ.
2. Paul apparently gives no answer to the supposed complaint. As Zuntz puts it, 'a refutation is looked for in vain'.[256]

It seems best to see vv. 29b-30 as Paul's reasons for the restrictions in vv. 28-29a.[257] In effect, Paul says, 'Why eat, if eating causes so much trouble and misunderstanding?' Paul is not asking hypothetical questions but rhetorical questions for which no answer need to be provided, because the answer is clear: do not eat! This also explains the γάρ and the ἱνατί naturally: 'For to what purpose would my good become a cause of slander?' The likelihood of this understanding is significantly strengthened by the parallel statement in Rom. 14.16. There the rhetorical questions are condensed into statement form ('Do not let your good be brought into contempt') which no doubt serves as an argument for abstention. Therefore it seems that in 1 Cor. 10.29b-30, as in Rom. 14.16, Paul is stating his own view rather than voicing his opponents'.

Glory to God and Good Will to Men: 1 Corinthians 10.31–11.1. Commentators are agreed that Paul is here offering a summarizing conclusion, not just on 10.23-30, but on the whole of Paul's discussion on idol food. The exhortations in vv. 32-33, which reiterate major themes in chapters 8–10, are clear enough: believers should avoid causing anyone to stumble (ch. 8) and they should imitate Paul (ch. 9). There is less certainty on the import of v. 31. It is possible to see the 'glorifying God' in v. 31 as being defined in terms of seeking the good of others in vv. 32-33. But, more probably, here as in various places in Scripture, the injunction to give God the glory has something more specific in view, namely, to avoid sinning that affronts God's glory (cf. Josh. 7.19;

255. Barrett, *First Epistle to the Corinthians*, p. 243.

256. Zuntz, *Text*, p. 17. Willis (*Idol Meat*, p. 247) notes that this difficulty is admitted by many scholars who defend the diatribe interpretation.

257. Barrett, *First Epistle to the Corinthians*, p. 243; Willis, *Idol Meat*, pp. 246-50; more tentatively, Fee, *The First Epistle to the Corinthians*, pp. 485-87.

Jn 9.24; Rom. 4.20; 1 Cor. 6.20). Just as glorifying God in one's body means abstaining from πορνεία, eating and drinking to God's glory means avoiding εἰδωλόθυτα. In this way v. 31 summarizes the argument of ch. 10, which is primarily vertical, just as vv. 32-33 summarize the argument of chs. 8 and 9, which is basically horizontal.

4. *Conclusion*

I have demonstrated the inadequacy of the traditional understanding of Paul's approach to εἰδωλόθυτα. Far from mediating between the strong and the weak in an internal dispute, Paul's discussion in 1 Corinthians 8–10 is directed primarily to the whole church to warn them against eating idol food, leading to the climactic rhetorical questions: 'Shall we provoke the Lord to jealousy? Are we stronger than He?' (1 Cor. 10.22). There is no inconsistency between 1 Corinthians 8 and 1 Cor. 10.1-22. On the contrary, the two passages represent two stages of Paul's argument: not only will eating idol food cause the weak to stumble, but it will also make the Corinthians partners with demons. Inasmuch as food itself is something indifferent, Paul maintains that there is no need for the Corinthians to inquire about its origins before they eat, though they must abstain if the food is explicitly identified as idol food. Paul's position in a nutshell is this: to eat idol food knowingly is to participate in idolatry; therefore, for the sake of the weak and for the sake of yourselves, avoid any food if, and only if, you know that it is idol food.

Excursus:
Brief Scholarly Suggestions which Support my Interpretation

Tomson and Gooch are the only scholars of whom I am aware to argue in any detail for anything close to the interpretation I have put forward. But there are some other scholars who have made (undeveloped) suggestions that are akin to my view:

1. Several isolated statements by E.P. Sanders are noteworthy:

> One of Paul's responses as he wrestled with the problem of meat offered to idols was, When a guest, do not raise the question, but do not eat the meat if its origin is pointed out (I Cor. 10.27-29). This may well have been a common Jewish attitude when dining with pagan friends. Barrett

thinks that this is Paul's most *un*Jewish attitude. My own guess is that it too has a home somewhere in Judaism.[258]

Paul shows himself squeamish over meat offered to idols...and we may safely suppose that he, Barnabas, and other Jews would have been put off by being offered donkey or hare.[259]

In 1 Corinthians 8...he [Paul] tries to bring even the prohibition of idolatry under the rubric 'love thy neighbor'. This was not entirely satisfactory, as his further argument in 1 Corinthians 10 shows. His handling of...idolatry (including here 'food offered to idols') indicates both his deeply held Jewish convictions and his struggle to reformulate Jewish prohibitions in terms of Christian principles.[260]

2. Robert Grant comments in passing that Paul

was willing to let the stronger-minded Corinthian Christians eat meat that possibly had been sacrificed to a pagan deity if they did not know that it had been so 'consecrated'. In that case, they had to abstain.[261]

Unfortunately, Grant immediately goes on to affirm a major element of the traditional view in limiting the danger of consumption to the weak: 'Christians denied the reality and power of these gods, but they presented a threat to the "weaker" members'.[262]

3. In his discussion of the phrase *adhuc rarissimus emptor* in Pliny's letter, A.N. Sherwin-White mentions the suggestion of Vidman that Christians in Pontus followed Paul's advice in 1 Cor. 10.27-29 to 'turn a blind eye on occasion, to avoid giving offence'. But he immediately qualifies his agreement with Vidman: 'But this dispensation was strictly limited: the Christian need not inquire rigorously about the origin of his meat, but if he knows that it is from the temples he must refuse it'.[263]

4. In a short paper presented at the 1973 Oxford Biblical Congress,[264] F.M. Young defended the integrity of 1 Corinthians 8–10 by pointing

258. E.P. Sanders, *Jewish Law*, p. 281.

259. E.P. Sanders, 'Jewish Association', p. 172.

260. E.P. Sanders, *Paul, the Law*, p. 104.

261. Grant, *One God*, p. 25.

262. Grant, *One God*, p. 25.

263. A.N. Sherwin-White, *The Letters of Pliny: A Historical and Social Commentary* (Oxford: Clarendon Press, 1966), p. 710.

264. F.M. Young, 'Notes on the Corinthian Correspondence', in E.A. Livingstone (ed.), *Studia Evangelica* 7 (TU, 126; Berlin: Akademie Verlag, 1982), pp. 563-66.

out that Paul's inconsistent estimates of the significance of idols were in fact shared by early Jews and Christians alike:

> Paul is merely the first of a long line of Christian writers to maintain the non-existence of idols and the necessity of avoiding contact with the daemons. Both came from his Jewish attitudes. Jewish apologetic and polemic had developed the argument that the idols were only artefacts and non-existent; Judaism demanded uncompromising loyalty to its God, and any hint of contact with pagan religion was interpreted as idolatry.
>
> ... [Paul's] argument was one which apologists like Clement and Origen continued to use forcefully, in spite of the inconsistencies. ... The argument depends at once on the non-existence of idols and their dangerous power in the world; the source of the meat is irrelevant if Christians are unaware of it, but any conscious condoning of paganism ... implies disloyalty to the one true God. Paul's Jewishness is well-engrained, and this feature of Jewish exclusiveness remained an important characteristic of the Christian community.[265]

Young concluded that the inconsistencies in 1 Corinthians 8–10 'are not indications of a composite document, but of an attitude of mind which prevailed in the Church throughout succeeding centuries'.[266]

265. Young, 'Corinthian Correspondence', pp. 564-65. Young's brief statements encapsulate much of the substance of this study. I have little quarrel with Young apart from her questionable use of the adjective 'inconsistent' to describe Paul's dual world-view.

266. Young, 'Corinthian Correspondence', p. 565. In another short paper presented at the 1983 Oxford Patristics Conference, Young argues that since Chrysostom was sure that 'an idol is nothing' and yet was 'profoundly aware of the power of daemons', Paul probably would feel the same ('John Chrysostom on First and Second Corinthians', in E.A. Livingstone (ed.), *Studia Patristica. XVIII. 1. Historica–Theologica–Gnostica–Biblica* [Kalamazoo, MI: Cistercian, 1985], pp. 349-52 [350]).

Chapter 4

THE EARLY CHRISTIANS' UNDERSTANDING OF PAUL'S
ATTITUDE TO IDOL FOOD

1. *The State of Research*

I have shown in the previous chapter that the traditional understanding of Paul's approach cannot be supported by the internal evidence of 1 Corinthians 8–10. In this chapter I will examine the early Christians' understanding of Paul's attitude to idol food. In particular, I will see if the traditional understanding of Paul's position can be located on the map of early Christianity. Pertinent New Testament passages and other early Christian (including 'heretical') documents touching on the problem of idol food will be studied in detail.

To my knowledge, there is *no* scholarly study on Paul's influence on early Christian attitude towards idol food. In discussions of Paul's approach in 1 Corinthians 8–10, the position of early Christians towards idol food is typically disparaged, if not ignored altogether. Thus Willis writes not even a word on the subject in his dissertation on idol meat in Corinth.[1] Fee's commentary covers the whole issue in a brief footnote.[2] This lack of interest is also the case with most of the monographs that deal extensively with 1 Corinthians 8–10.

To be sure, several major studies on the influence of the idol food prohibition in early Christianity have been undertaken.[3] However, this

---

1. Willis, *Idol Meat*.
2. Fee, *The First Epistle to the Corinthians*, pp. 357-58 n. 1.
3. J.G. Sommer, *Das Aposteldekret: Entstehung, Inhalt und Geschichte seiner Wirksamkeit in der christlichen Kirche* (Theologische Studien und Skizzen aus Ostpreußen 4, 9; Königsberg: Hartung, 1887–89); K. Böckenhoff, *Das apostolische Speisegesetz in den ersten fünf Jahrhunderten: Ein Beitrag zum Verständnis der quasi-levitischen Satzungen in älteren kirchlichen Rechtsquellen* (Paderborn: Ferdinand Schöningh, 1903); Gotthold Resch, *Das Aposteldekret nach seiner außerkanonischen Textgestalt* (TU, NS 13.3; Leipzig: J.C. Hinrichs, 1905); H. Coppieters,

influence is studied primarily as part of the investigation of what scholars perceived to be a much more important issue, namely the spread and validity of the Apostolic Decree. The implicit assumption is that, in comparison with the influence of the decree, Paul's contribution to early Christians' prohibition of idol food is insignificant or nonexistent, with the result that the legacy of Paul's attitude towards idol food in early Christianity is not assessed.[4]

Even when scholars do comment on the relationship between the approaches of Paul and early Christianity, no serious attempt is made to explore the influence of Paul's teaching on early Christians. The discussion is invariably little more than a brief preface or postscript to the much more detailed exegesis of 1 Corinthians 8–10. Convinced that Paul treated idol food as a matter indifferent,[5] they usually do no more than point out the 'unreservedly negative attitudes' toward idol food in early Christianity by listing a few key texts (often based on secondary

'Le Décret des Apôtres (Act 15, 28. 29)', *RB* 4 (1907), pp. 31-58, 218-39; K. Six, *Das Aposteldekret (Act 15, 28.29): Seine Entstehung und Geltung in den ersten vier Jahrhunderten* (Veröffentlichungen des biblisch-patristischen Seminars zu Innsbruck, 5; Innsbruck: Felizian Rauch, 1912); R. Kidera, 'Les interdictions alimentaires du christianisme aux IIe et IIIe siècles: Etude du Décret Apostolique' (Thèse dactylographiée, Protestant Faculty of Theology, University of Strasbourg, 1973); M. Simon, 'De l'observance rituelle à l'ascèse: Recherches sur le Décret Apostolique', *RHR* 193 (1978), pp. 27-104 (cf. also its earlier and less developed version, 'The Apostolic Decree and its Setting in the ancient Church', *BJRL* 52 [1970], pp. 437-60). Heil (*Ablehnung*, pp. 269-94) briefly compares Paul's approach with other New Testament and early Christian writings, but largely in the context of Jewish food laws.

4.   J. Jervell notes that 'as a historic phenomenon [the decree] played a decisive role in the history of the church, for example, when it came to the question of the eating of consecrated food. No one followed what Paul recommended (1 Corinthians 8–9 and Romans 14–15), but we can see that Jewish-Christian policy gained ground' (*The Unknown Paul: Essays on Luke–Acts and Early Christian History* [Minneapolis: Augsburg, 1984], pp. 34-35). Brunt even suggests that Paul was interpreted by early Christians in the light of the Decree ('Rejected', pp. 117-18, 121).

5.   The only exceptions are Tomson (*Jewish Law*) and Gooch ('Food and Limits'), who argue that Paul urged the avoidance of idol food. But their discussions of idol food in early Christianity are undeveloped. They are content with establishing the (non-controversial) conclusion that idol food was universally prohibited, and therefore the eating of it was unlikely to have been condoned by Paul. They make no attempt to assess how or whether Paul's discussion played a role in this prohibition.

sources) and contrast such attitudes with 'Paul's uniquely tolerant attitude'.[6] In such views, only perhaps the Gnostics appreciated the indifferent character of idol food and came closest to understanding Paul, though they too went overboard in their libertinism.[7] The inevitable conclusion is that Paul's teaching was 'ignored, rejected, or misunderstood',[8] if not 'flatly repudiated', by the dominant Christian tradition.[9] Paul's approach, in short, is considered a singularity or anomaly in early Christianity.

How is this supposed singularity of Paul's approach explained? The only reasoned attempt is given by Brunt: Christians were ignorant of Paul's approach in the early stages and misunderstood it in the later stages.[10] This early ignorance, argues Brunt, 'is understandable on the basis of a lack of pervasive Pauline influence', whereas the later misunderstanding is due to the fact that early Christians retreated into a rigid legalism in their fight against the Gnostics (whose position on idol food came closer to Paul than the mainstream did).[11] In their moralistic mind they could 'focus merely on whether the act itself is right or wrong', thus failing to understand the complexity, or fathom the sublimity, of Paul's ethical approach, 'where the specific question of idol meat is transcended by the consideration of love's responsibility'.[12] While Paul successfully walked 'the tightrope between the legalism of Jewish Christianity and the false liberalism of gnostic rationalism',[13]

---

6.   Brunt, 'Paul's Attitude', p. 17.

7.   E.H. Pagels, *The Gnostic Paul: Gnostic Exegesis of the Pauline Letters* (Philadelphia: Fortress Press, 1975), p. 71; Klauck, *Herrenmahl*, p. 244; Brunt, 'Paul's Attitude', pp. 274-75. Brunt expresses more reserve in 'Rejected', pp. 119-20.

8.   Such a view is aptly captured by the title of Brunt's article: 'Rejected, Ignored, or Misunderstood?' (see especially Brunt's conclusions on pp. 120-22).

9.   L.E. Keck, 'Ethos and Ethics in the New Testament', in J. Gaffney (ed.), *Essays in Morality and Ethics* (New York: Paulist Press, 1980), pp. 29-49 (37). Barrett observes that 'if…we set aside the Pauline material it appears that the eating of εἰδωλόθυτα was reprobated in the strongest possible terms…this attitude persisted in the primitive Church for centuries' ('Things Sacrificed', p. 43). Segal also points out that 'throughout early church history, the dominant position is more like the Didache or the Apostolic Decree than Paul's ideological position' (*Paul*, p. 236).

10.   Brunt, 'Rejected', pp. 120-21.

11.   Brunt, 'Rejected', pp. 120-21; cf. Brunt, 'Paul's Attitude', p. 275.

12.   Brunt, 'Rejected', p. 121.

13.   Barrett, 'Things Sacrificed', p. 56. In Barrett's assessment, that Paul 'was

the next few generations of Christians fell headlong onto the side of legalism.[14] Amazingly, Jewish Christianity triumphed in this issue when 'Jewish Christians became less important in the church'![15]

I will attempt to show that such a negative assessment of the legacy of Paul's approach to idol food does scarce justice to the relevant sources. But before we look at those sources in detail, two preliminary observations may be made.

First, I suspect that because idol food is simply not an issue in contemporary Western society, some modern scholars fail to relate existentially to its impact. They, unlike early Christians, find it difficult to appreciate the circumstances and the dynamics of living as a Christian minority in cities like Corinth, where pagan religions were woven into the very fabric of everyday life. For example, Barrett suggests that 'the problem of εἰδωλόθυτα would never have arisen in a Gentile Church like that of Corinth if the Jewish Christians (the Cephas group perhaps) had not raised it'.[16] This cannot be further from the truth. In view of the tremendous religious and social significance of idol food in the Greco-Roman world, it would have been one of the very first issues to arise in a Gentile church! Again, contrary to Brunt's assertion, the ignorance of Paul's position on such an important and boundary-defining issue as idol food was not easily 'understandable'—especially when such a position supposedly went against basically the whole early Christian tradition. For early Christians—Paul and the Corinthian congregation included—a clear-cut answer to the rightness or wrongness of the act of consumption of idol food could not be shelved until all the ethical principles were worked out. Even if, for argument's sake, early Christians failed to grasp the complexity of Pauline ethical thinking *as a*

able to do this is one of the clearest marks of his greatness'—a greatness to which later Christians failed to measure up.

14. Barrett comments that 'in its quest for safety at any cost the church could see no way of excluding idolatry that did not include rigid abstention from heathen food and heathen dinner parties…the church as a whole retreated into a narrow religious shell' ('Things Sacrificed', p. 56). This is also the conclusion of Murphy-O'Connor's article bearing the suggestive title, 'Freedom or the Ghetto'. In the same vein, P. Richardson asserts that on the issue of idol food the church made 'the safer but much less satisfactory assertion that Christianity embraces a new Law' (*Israel in the Apostolic Church* [Cambridge: Cambridge University Press, 1969], p. 199).

15. Barrett, 'Things Sacrificed', p. 56.

16. Barrett, 'Things Sacrificed', p. 49.

system, they should have had much less difficulty in understanding whether or not Paul wanted them to abstain from idol food *in concrete circumstances*. Paul's instructions did not appear out of a space–time vacuum. He did not merely compose his letter as an ethical treatise and then disappear from the scene; he was a historical person who lived in the same era as the early readers of his letter, and whose opinion the latter could presumably consult when ambiguities arose (more on that below). The criticism of early Christians' moralistic attitude by modern scholars thus reflects perhaps not Paul's supposedly ethical approach but the scholars' own historical context (which is arguably much further away from that of Paul than was the early Christians').

Secondly, I believe that the negative assessment of early Christians' rejection of idol food is wholly consistent with—if not largely attributable to—the prevalent Protestant view (influenced especially by the works of Adolf Harnack and Walter Bauer) of Paul's legacy in early Christianity.[17] According to this view, the influence of Paul's thought in the pre-Marcion period was minimal.[18] Moreover, it was in the Gnostic streams of Christianity that Paul's theology was truly appreciated and came closest to being rightly understood. By contrast, Paul's teaching was either ignored or misconstrued by the 'orthodox', who reclaimed the apostle only belatedly from the 'heretics' after Marcion forced the issue.[19] The orthodox, with their moralistic emphasis, could accommodate only a domesticated and denatured Paul, whose gospel of freedom was restricted and transformed through institutionalizing. All was not well in the Latin West until Augustine came to the rescue. The Greek Christian tradition, however, was never significantly touched by the central themes of Pauline thought.

It is beyond the scope of this work (and well beyond my competence) to adjudge whether and to what extent Paul was rightly construed by

17. See W.S. Babcock (ed.), *Paul and the Legacies of Paul* (Dallas: Southern Methodist University Press, 1990) for a good outline of this view and recent efforts to correct it (note especially 'Introduction', pp. xiii-xxviii).

18. Cf. Overbeck's proverbial dictum that no one in early Christianity understood Paul except Marcion, who misunderstood him.

19. I am using the term 'orthodox' to refer to the emerging dominant tradition that would eventually define orthodoxy, without prejudging the question of its doctrinal or temporal priority over other early Christian traditions. Likewise, the term 'heretics' will be used as a shorthand for versions of Christianity that would eventually be judged heretical or marginal by the 'orthodox', without attempting to settle the question of whether heresy came before or after 'orthodoxy'.

the orthodox or heretical traditions.[20] Nevertheless, I do believe—and scholars like Wiles, Lindemann, and Dassmann have convincingly argued—that the prevalent Protestant view is too one-sided to reflect the true picture.[21] Lindemann and Dassmann have shown beyond a shadow of doubt that Paul was a potent influence on the emerging orthodox tradition *from the very beginning*. He was not the exclusive property of, nor the only authority for, those ultimately judged heretical.[22] Paul's letters were widely circulated and frequently cited as authority in cases of ecclesiastical dispute. The origin of the notion of a canon was from the beginning inextricably tied to the conception that 'zu einem solchen Kanon müßten auch die paulinischen Briefe gehören'.[23] Paul's person and works, real or imagined, were recounted in numerous traditions and legends. He was venerated early on as 'the Apostle' without need for further specification. In short, Paul was 'simply too vast a presence' in early Christianity to permit one 'to think

20. Note M.F. Wiles's comment: 'Whoever is confident that he knows the true exegesis of St Paul's thought will then be in a position to answer for himself the question how far the interpretation given by the Fathers is correct' (*The Divine Apostle: The Interpretation of St Paul's Epistles in the Early Church* [Cambridge: Cambridge University Press, 1967], p. 2).

21. Wiles, *Divine Apostle*; A. Lindemann, *Paulus im ältesten Christentum: Das Bild des Apostels und die Rezeption der paulinischen Theologie in der frühchristlichen Literatur bis Marcion* (BHT, 58; Tübingen: Mohr Siebeck, 1979); cf. *idem*, 'Paul in the Writings of the Apostolic Fathers', in Babcock (ed.), *Legacies*, pp. 25-45; Ernst Dassmann, *Der Stachel im Fleisch: Paulus in der frühchristlichen Literatur bis Irenäus* (Münster: Aschendorff, 1979). Cf. Babcock, *Legacies*; P. Gorday, 'Paul in Eusebius and Other Early Christian Literature', in H.W. Attridge and G. Hata (eds.), *Eusebius, Christianity, and Judaism* (Detroit: Wayne State University Press, 1992), pp. 139-165.

22. Dassmann, *Stachel*, pp. 316-20; Lindemann, *Paulus*, pp. 1-6. Dassmann (*Stachel*, p. 199) argues that the favorite of the Gnostic interpreters was John, not Paul. Lindemann concludes from his study of the *Paulusbild* in literature before Marcion, 'Daß das Paulusbild der Kirche durch den Widerstand gegen den "Paulus der Gnostiker" bestimmt worden wäre, läßt sich nicht belegen' (*Paulus*, pp. 36-113; quotation p. 113).

23. Lindemann, *Paulus*, p. 35; cf. H.Y. Gamble, *Books and Readers in the Early Church: A History of Early Christian Texts* (New Haven: Yale University Press, 1995), pp. 58-66. Gamble observes that Paul's letters were 'the earliest to be valued, imitated, to circulate beyond their original recipients, and to be collected' (p. 58). Gamble further argues that the need to collect and circulate Paul's letters provided the main impetus for the establishment of the codex as the preferred form of the Christian book by the early second century.

or speak as if Paul left little or no legacy in the Christianity of the patristic era (thus preserving him unscathed, as it were, for later legatees)'.[24]

To be sure, none of this proves or even implies that Paul's position on idol food was correctly understood by early Christians; that they (correctly) used Paul for support with regard to some issues is no conclusive evidence that they did so with regard to idol food. Nevertheless, it does make one hesitate to accept too easily the conclusion that Paul was misunderstood, let alone ignored or rejected, in the matter of idol food. It invites, if not demands, a detailed re-investigation of Paul's legacy on idol food which rests on more positive[25] or, at least, more neutral assumptions.[26]

2. *Assumptions and General Remarks*

The ostensible subject of Paul's discussion in 1 Corinthians 8–10 is idol food. While there are timeless ethical principles to be derived, one must resist the temptation of quickly bypassing the concrete historical problem in search for perennial principles. Paul did not write this 'treatise' to the Corinthians as the fruit of his quiet contemplation but as a vigorous response to urgent problems troubling the church. Such a response could not fail to leave its historical impact on early Christians who were facing similar problems in their daily lives.

To discover Paul's position regarding idol food, it is imperative that we examine not only 1 Corinthians 8–10, but also the early Christians' understanding of this position. In making such a statement, I am not disputing that Paul's extant letters must be investigated in their own right, but I am denying the assumption held by many modern scholars that the historical Paul is accessible only or primarily through his letters.

I think modern scholarship is justifiably wary of the danger of allowing other early Christian material to impose a predetermined meaning on Paul's letter, thus blunting the distinctiveness of, or even distorting, Paul's teaching. In particular, many feel that the *Paulusbild* of early

24. Babcock (ed.), *Legacies*, p. xv.

25. For example, most early Christians did genuinely attempt to understand Paul.

26. For example, most did not consciously ignore or reject Paul's teaching on the subject.

Christian writings is a far cry, at least on some important issues, from the Paul of the undisputed letters as understood in modern scholarship. However, there is also the opposite danger of attempting to treat Paul's letters in isolation from the rest of early Christian writings, as if the historical Paul can be simply identified with the epistolary Paul. The truth is, the extant letters preserve only fragments of the historical Paul.

From a human perspective, the survival of Paul's letters in their present extent and form was in part a matter of historical coincidence and in part due to the interests of the victors who preserved those letters. What would we make of Paul's theology if, say, 1 Thessalonians and 1 Corinthians were the only Pauline letters that we possessed? Moreover, all of Paul's letters are occasional literature, penned in situations often polemical. They do not readily reveal the non-polemical Paul or those aspects of his teaching that other Christian authorities, including the leaders of the church in Jerusalem, found unobjectionable. Jervell is certainly exaggerating when he suggests that the greatest part of Paul's life and work belongs to the 'unknown Paul', which is 'the irenic, non-controversial, and non-polemical apostle and missionary with the same preaching and practice as the other parts of the church'.[27] But perhaps not by much.

To compensate for the built-in selectivity of historical processes, we need to cast our net as widely as possible. Therefore an adequate assessment of Paul's position requires not only a careful historical exegetical investigation of 1 Corinthians 8–10, but also, *inter alia*, a sympathetic effort to situate Paul within the spectrum of other early Christian material as part of the context for the illumination of his attitude. How Paul's early legatees understood him must be a part of a valid historical reconstruction, because it tells us how Paul's immediate readers would likely have understood or misunderstood the text. This in turn could help us determine what Paul would likely have meant, assuming that he was a competent communicator.

This point takes on much greater significance when one recognizes the early, frequent, and widespread use of 1 Corinthians. By the end of the first century, 1 Corinthians became 'an approved weapon' in the orthodox fight against heresy and 'came to be firmly established and given special honor within churches of Rome, Smyrna, and Antioch'[28]—not to mention Corinth and other Greek cities. That the early

---

27. Jervell, *The Unknown Paul*, p. 10.
28. W. Bauer, *Orthodoxy and Heresy in Earliest Christianity* (Philadelphia:

use of 1 Corinthians can be established in such diverse geographical locations is no mean testimony to the letter's popularity. Bauer, convinced that Pauline theology had a minimal influence in the pre-Marcion period, suggests that 1 Corinthians was best loved and earliest employed by the orthodox because it is 'that unit among the major Pauline letters which yields the very least for our understanding of the Pauline faith'.[29] If Bauer's prejudicial opinion about the value of 1 Corinthians and the reason for its prominence must be strongly contested, the fact of orthodox reliance on the letter is indisputable.[30] As early as *1 Clement* one can see a developed use of 1 Corinthians with explicit citations. Likewise, Polycarp of Smyrna was steeped in the Corinthian correspondence.[31] It was the only Pauline letter 'which Ignatius assuredly had read'.[32] Bauer asserts that 'in our investigation of the impact of the Pauline writings, whenever we come from the marshy ground of "reminiscences" and "allusions" to firmer territory, again and again we confront 1 Corinthians'.[33] I have counted more than two thousand citations of or allusions to 1 Corinthians from diverse sources up to the time of Clement of Alexandria and Tertullian (about 250 of them are on 1 Corinthians 8–10) in the citation index of *Biblia Patristica*.[34] This is a density of citations and allusions unmatched by any other early Christian writing. In Barrett's words, 'the evidence for the use of 1 Corinthians is older, clearer, and more widespread than that of any other book of the New Testament'.[35] It is perhaps no accident

Fortress Press, 1971), p. 220. See pp. 213-28 for Bauer's discussion on the place of Paul's letters in the subapostolic age.

29. Bauer, *Orthodoxy*, p. 219.

30. Bauer's speculation is entirely unnecessary. The obvious explanation of the popularity of 1 Corinthians is that it deals with many practical situations to which the Gentile church can best relate existentially.

31. Dassmann, *Stachel*, pp. 149-58.

32. Bauer, *Orthodoxy*, p. 218. William Schoedel, *Ignatius of Antioch: A Commentary on the Letters of Ignatius of Antioch* (Hermeneia; Philadelphia: Fortress Press, 1985), pp. 9-10 argues that while there are many probable allusions to other Pauline letters, actual citation can be claimed only for passages from 1 Corinthians.

33. Bauer, *Orthodoxy*, p. 219.

34. *Biblia Patristica: Index des citations et allusions bibliques dans la littérature patristique* (4 vols.; Paris: Centre National de la Recherche Scientifique, 1975). By all accounts, the authority of Paul was firmly established by late second century. Thus it can be safely assumed that 1 Corinthians was known by virtually all early Christian writers from then on.

35. Barrett, *First Epistle to the Corinthians*, pp. 11-12.

that 1 Corinthians is listed first among Paul's letters in the Muratorian Canon.

In view of this special honor accorded to 1 Corinthians in early Christianity, it can safely be assumed that Paul's discussion about idol food in 1 Corinthians 8–10 was widely known from the beginning. The obvious implication is that the correct understanding of Paul's position would have left its mark on early Christian literature. It seems unlikely that what Paul really taught on this important subject was forgotten, ignored, rejected, or misunderstood by *every* early Christian author represented in our extant sources.

We may also assume that when early Christians used 1 Corinthians, many of them genuinely tried to understand the text rather than make it a waxen nose that could be pulled into any shape they pleased. They must have found 1 Corinthians congenial to their own position vis-à-vis the heretics. For if they knew well that Paul's position was opposed to their view, why would they appeal to him at all? If they felt no compunction about falsifying Paul's teaching, why did they stop at 1 Corinthians? After all, they were the ones who preserved Paul's discussion of idol food in its present form.[36] Paul's teaching might have been misunderstood, but it was not outright falsified. And it is highly unlikely that this misunderstanding—if there ever was misunderstanding—was universal. Again, this consideration leads us to believe that Paul's true position concerning idol food would not have vanished without trace.

The popularity of 1 Corinthians, and the numerous citations of 1 Corinthians 8–10 in particular, strongly suggest that an accurate understanding of Paul's attitude towards idol food would have been preserved somewhere in early Christian writings. Another consideration makes this inference almost conclusive: it is virtually impossible that 1 Corinthians 8–10 was the only occasion where Paul provided instructions concerning idol food. In certain locations, the first couple of generations of Christians not only had access to 1 Corinthians, but they also had access to very recent tradition and even to Paul himself or his living disciples. This impression is strengthened by the fact that, already in the apostolic period, Pauline churches appeared to take an interest in each other's situations. For instance, 'the churches in Asia'

---

36. There is no sign of tampering with the relevant texts in a very full manuscript tradition.

sent their greeting through Paul to the Corinthian church (1 Cor. 16.19).[37] I have earlier outlined the significant function idol food performed in pagan social and religious life. I have also noted the intimate association between εἰδωλόθυτα and εἰδωλολατρία in Jewish traditions and the strong polemics against idolatry in Jewish literature. I have come to the conclusion that it is highly probable, if not certain, that Paul would have paid considerable attention to this issue in his missionary preaching. He would have given practical instructions concerning idol food not only in writing, but also in person or through his associates, in every congregation he founded or to which he ministered. In particular, Paul could not have avoided making clear his position on the rightness or wrongness of the consumption of idol food. Moreover, he would have had ample opportunities to correct any misunderstanding or misconduct on this subject—before, during, and after he penned 1 Corinthians![38] Therefore it would have been almost impossible for the first generation of his disciples to have misunderstood Paul on this important subject. Since idol food was an issue that early Christians *continuously* faced in their daily lives, it was also unlikely that the next couple of generations would have entirely forgotten Paul's instructions. This virtually ensures that Paul's position would have been correctly understood by many, if not accepted or cherished by most.[39] We need not conclude that the true interpretation of Paul must be preserved in the dominant Christian tradition. But the least we can say is that the correct understanding of Paul's instruction, while perhaps not universally known (or not even known by the majority) was not likely to have vanished without trace.

37. The other greeting statements in the Pauline epistles and subapostolic literature confirm this impression.

38. I have argued in Chapter 3 that Paul's discussion about idol food in 1 Cor. 8–10 was called forth precisely by the arguments and behavior of some Corinthian Christians which conflicted with his missionary preaching.

39. Thus Brunt's explanation—which is also the only reasoned explanation—of how Paul's approach to idol food was (supposedly) misunderstood does not hold water. It is not historically plausible that most Christian leaders were ignorant of Paul's discussion at the early stages, given the popularity of 1 Corinthians and the importance of the subject. Nor is it realistic to think that Paul's later legatees completely misunderstood his position, as if the early legatees of Paul left absolutely no tradition to inform them of Paul's true position, especially since the time span separating the two groups is only a matter of a few decades.

Assuming, then, that an accurate interpretation of Paul's attitude towards idol food would have left its marks on early Christian sources, we will see whether Paul's true position can be discovered in those sources. As I have mentioned earlier, the virtually unanimous rejection of idol food by early Christians has been well documented. There is little point in my reworking well-trodden ground. My primary interest in the following survey is, therefore, not in the attitude of early Christians per se, which is hardly disputed. Rather, I am interested in how and whether the extant sources which mention the issue of idol food shed light on Paul's own position.[40] The study will be controlled by two overarching questions: (1) can any Pauline contact be discerned in early Christian rejection or consumption of idol food? and (2) in early Christian understanding and recollection, did Paul eat or permit the eating of idol food? To answer these questions our focus is not whether early Christians understood Paul correctly (for this assumes we already know what Paul actually taught) but how they understood him and what light their mention or non-mention of Paul is thrown on the apostle's attitude. Of course, it is hoped that our findings will help us in arriving at a more precise understanding of Paul on the issue of idol food.

Since all ancient documents available for us to examine are to a considerable extent the product of historical coincidence, they do not often directly answer our questions. We must also recognize that there are no 'brute' data in historical research. Like Paul's discussion in 1 Corinthians 8–10, early Christian writings are opened to a variety of interpretations, depending in some measures on the interpreter's presuppositions. The profuse use of qualifications like 'probably', 'likely', 'presumably', 'perhaps', 'possibly', 'conceivably', and so on, inelegant at best and wearisome at worst, is inevitable. Nevertheless, it does not mean that historical research is necessarily rendered impossible or unreliable. Provided that one handles the data responsibly, valid and

---

40. My approach fits what R.G. Collingwood (*The Idea of History* [Oxford: Clarendon Press, 1946], p. 275) describes as the methodology of a scientific historian: 'Confronted with a ready-made statement about the subject he is studying, the scientific historian never asks himself: "Is this statement true or false?"… [but] "what does this statement mean?" And this is not equivalent to the question "What did the person who made it mean by it?"… It is equivalent, rather, to the question, "What light is thrown on the subject in which I am interested by the fact that this person made this statement, meaning by it what he did mean?"'

useful conclusions may still be drawn. Moreover, in judgment of historical probability, there is safety in numbers. The persuasiveness of a hypothesis rests not upon any individual item, but upon the cumulative weight and overall pattern of the evidence, as well as the explanatory power of the hypothesis in accounting for all the evidence relative to competing hypotheses. I will discuss some methodological issues in more detail in an excursus at the end of this chapter.

3. *The Book of Acts*

a. *Luke's Account of the Jerusalem Council in Acts 15*

Luke's account of the Jerusalem Council furnishes one of the earliest extant references to the problem of εἰδωλόθυτα in early Christianity. Though the letter containing the decree was originally addressed only to Gentile Christians in Antioch and Syro-Cilicia (Acts 15.23), it was clearly intended that its terms should be valid for Gentile churches elsewhere (Acts 16.4; 21.25). The Apostolic Decree is first stated in Acts 15.19-20 as a proposal made by James. The text of NA[27] reads:

διὸ ἐγὼ κρίνω μὴ παρενοχλεῖν τοῖς ἀπὸ τῶν ἐθνῶν ἐπιστρέφουσιν ἐπὶ τὸν θεόν, ἀλλὰ ἐπιστεῖλαι αὐτοῖς τοῦ ἀπέχεσθαι τῶν ἀλισγημάτων τῶν εἰδώλων καὶ τῆς πορνείας καὶ τοῦ πνικτοῦ καὶ τοῦ αἵματος

In Acts 15.28-29 the decree is repeated, in a slightly different form, in the letter sent out by the apostles:

ἔδοξεν γὰρ τῷ πνεύματι τῷ ἁγίῳ καὶ ἡμῖν μηδὲν πλέον ἐπιτίθεσθαι ὑμῖν βάρος πλὴν τούτων τῶν ἐπάναγκες, ἀπέχεσθαι εἰδωλοθύτων καὶ αἵματος καὶ πνικτῶν καὶ πορνείας· ἐξ ὧν διατηροῦντες ἑαυτοὺς εὖ πράξετε.

We note that εἰδωλοθύτων is substituted for ἀλισγημάτων τῶν εἰδώλων and πορνείας is placed last in the second list.[41] This form is also used when the decree is given again in Acts 21.25.

It is a well-known fact that major textual problems exist in the passages quoted above. The most significant variants are the omission of the reference to πνικτόν in all three lists of the decree and the addition of the 'Golden Rule' in its negative form (καὶ ὅσα μὴ θέλουσιν ἑαυτοῖς γίνεσθαι ἑτέροις μὴ ποιεῖτε) in 15.20 and 15.29 in the so-called

---

41. There is no need to speculate why those changes from James's oral proposal were made in the official letter. Such minor variations in formalizing a proposal are natural and can even be considered marks of the authenticity of the account of the council.

Western Text (notably, D).[42] When αἷμα is then taken to mean 'bloodshed' rather than 'blood', an ethical interpretation of the decree becomes possible. The resulting three prohibitions form a triad which is commonly thought to be 'practically identical to the three cardinal sins of Judaism, "idolatry, illicit sexuality and bloodshed"'.[43] Together these prohibitions presumably represent the minimum ethical standard Hellenistic Jews required of proselytes, which the decree adopts for Gentile converts to Christianity.

Does the Western reading represent a secondary emendation of the original at a time when the church could no longer understand those ritual requirements, or is the Alexandrian reading a secondary ritualization of the original moral code? Or are these two alternative versions both traceable to Luke?[44]

It is beyond the scope of this investigation to discuss the details of these textual problems. I concur with most scholars in rejecting the Western reading as secondary.[45] Aside from the fact that the textual

42. Another significant variant is the omission of καὶ τῆς πορνείας in the 𝔓[45] text of Acts 15.20. This enables a purely ritual interpretation of the decree, and some consider it the original form. However, it is difficult to see why a scribe would add the phrase to a supposedly purely ritual list. Unfortunately, a comparison with the texts of 15.29 and 21.25 cannot be performed because those texts are not extant in 𝔓[45]. See Hurd, *Origins*, pp. 250-53 for a survey of the secondary literature on the textual problems.

43. Tomson, *Jewish Law*, p. 179; cf. H. Sahlin, 'Die drei Kardinalsünden und das Neue Testament', *ST* (1970), pp. 93-112, for a good discussion of the issues.

44. Tomson (*Jewish Law*, p. 179) suggests that 'we should drop the opposition of ritual and morals and consider the Eastern text an alternative, stricter version which shortly after the Jerusalem meeting rose to acceptance in Asia minor'. See also the following note.

45. The recent attempts of M.-E. Boismard and A. Lamouille (*Le texte occidental des Actes des Apôtres: Reconstitution et réhabilitation* [2 vols.; Paris: Editions Recherche sur les Civilisations, 1984]), E. Delebecque (*Les deux Actes des Apôtres* [EBib, NS 6; Paris: J. Gabalda, 1986]) and W.A. Strange (*The Problem of the Text of Acts* [Cambridge: Cambridge University Press, 1992]) to rehabilitate the Western Text deserve careful evaluation. Nevertheless, in view of the notorious difficulty in defining and identifying 'Lukanisms', as well as the apparently secondary character of many Western variants, one remains to be convinced that the Western Text ultimately goes back to Luke. In particular, through a detailed literary analysis of the narrative of the Jerusalem Council, I have demonstrated that several important Western variants destroy or lessen Luke's intended literary effects, thus revealing their secondary nature (A.T.M. Cheung, 'A Narrative Analysis of Acts 14.27–15.35: Literary Shaping in Luke's Account of the Jerusalem Council', *WTJ* 55

evidence weighs heavily against it, the supposed parallel with the 'ancient Jewish triad' is flimsy at best. In spite of repeated mentions of this triad in scholarly literature, its existence in first century CE is probably no more than a figment of the scholars' imaginations. One searches in vain for concrete evidence. For instance, Tomson claims without supplying any evidence from primary sources that those three universal commands were accepted around the beginning of the first century and that 'later traditions mention four, six, seven or more items'.[46] Segal, who maintains that there is a close relationship between the decree and the Noachide Commandments, frankly admits that 'rabbinic doctrine, enumerating from six to ten Noahide Commandments depending on the version, cannot be traced to earlier than the third century'.[47] Nevertheless, he ventures to suggest that 'Luke... helps demonstrate that a positive use of the Noahide Commandments was known in first-century Judaism'.[48] This is tantamount to admitting that there is no evidence for the triad apart from the decree itself!

The only pre-Christian version of the so-called Noachide Commandments is found in *Jub.* 7.20-21, which encourages carrying out justice, honoring parents and loving neighbors, and prohibits incest, fornication and pollution. As a catalog of vices and virtues, it no doubt bears some resemblance to the decree (and to other New Testament lists of vices and virtues). But to call it a parallel to the decree is quite a stretch. Moreover, the function of the catalog is not to establish a minimum ethical standard for Gentiles but to form the basis of the judgment against the giants in the flood narrative (hence also a basis of judgment on Gentiles for constant breaking of the commands).[49]

The closest rabbinic parallel to the decree is found in the decisions of

[1993], pp. 141 n. 18, 146 n. 33, 147 n. 41, 149 nn. 46 and 49). See also the helpful brief discussions by G. Schneider, 'Zum "westlichen Text" der Apostelgeschichte', *BZ* 31 (1987), pp. 138-44 and T.C. Geer, 'The Presence and Significance of Lucanisms in the "Western" Text of Acts', *JSNT* 39 (1990), pp. 59-76. For a thorough discussion see Eldon Jay Epp, *The Theological Tendency of Codex Bezae Cantabrigiensis in Acts* (SNTSMS, 3; Cambridge: Cambridge University Press, 1966); cf. P. Head, 'Acts and the Problem of Its Text', in A.D. Clarke and B.W. Winter (eds.), *The Book of Acts in its Ancient Literary Setting* (AIIFCS, 1; Grand Rapids: Eerdmans; Carlisle: Paternoster Press, 1994), pp. 415-44.

46. Tomson, *Jewish Law*, pp. 50, 179.
47. Segal, *Paul*, p. 195.
48. Segal, *Paul*, p. 197.
49. Segal, *Paul*, p. 196.

a synod held in Lydda during the second Jewish revolt.[50] In determining the limits of what a Jew under the menace of persecution might do to escape death, the Rabbis decided that only three things were off limits: idolatry, dissolute living (probably incest and adultery), and murder. In Simon's opinion, 'there is no connection between the solution of the Lydda Synod and that of the decree', though the apparent analogy between the two solutions may contribute to the acceptance of the moral interpretation in some sectors of the early church.[51] In any case, one must remember that the so-called synod of Lydda was considerably later than the promulgation of the decree, and the codification of the decisions of that synod was much later.[52] Moreover, the exclusion of dissolute living as a means to escape persecution strikes me as very odd and betrays the hands of a later redactor.

In any case, even those early Christians who bore witnesses to the Western reading nevertheless observed the prohibitions against idol food and blood literally. Thus, for the purpose of this survey, it is a moot point which version is authentic.

There is also endless debate about the intent of the decree, in particular the meaning of πορνεία. Much scholarly energy is spent in tracing the origins of the decree in Leviticus 17–18 as the Mosaic laws which are applicable to Gentiles, or in the Noachide Commandments, or elsewhere. In my opinion, the search for an exact parallel in early Judaism as a precedent for the decree may turn out to be a futile exercise. The decree is probably rooted in the missionary preaching of Paul and other early Christians, which in turn was influenced by (Hellenistic) Jewish apologetic literature.[53] Its function is not so much to establish a minimal standard of morality—for then prohibition of murder, stealing, lying, and other sins, would have to be mentioned—as to keep Gentile believers away from certain major vices which were not generally frowned upon in the Gentile world.[54] It would not need 'a solemn

50. Simon, 'Observance rituelle', pp. 33-36.

51. Simon, 'Observance rituelle', pp. 35-36.

52. *B. Šab.* 7b; *b. Sanh.* 74a; they do not appear in the *Mishnah* or the *Tosefta*.

53. This understanding has some similarity to the position of P. Borgen, 'Catalogues of Vices, the Apostolic Decree, and the Jerusalem Meeting', in J. Neusner *et al.* (eds.), *The Social World of Formative Christianity and Judaism* (Philadelphia: Fortress Press, 1988), pp. 126-41, though Borgen denies that the decree was issued at the time of the Jerusalem meeting.

54. Cf. M. Simon, 'The Apostolic Decree and its Setting in the Ancient Church', *BJRL* 52 (1970), pp. 437-60 (442-43). E.P. Sanders (*Jewish Law*, p. 82)

conclave of apostles and elders to insist that the Gentiles should abstain from murder'.[55] On the other hand, to condemn idolatry and sexual immorality would have been both appropriate and necessary to ensure that the freedom Gentile believers had acquired did not degenerate into antinomianism.[56] The somewhat cryptic v. 21 can be readily explained by the fact that condemnation of idolatry and sexual immorality is indeed the focus of the preaching of Mosaic law in Hellenistic Judaism.

Whatever the exact intent of the decree, there is no question that Luke views the eating of idol food with disfavor and wants to register a plain and unambiguous prohibition against it. The terms of the decree are described as τὰ ἐπάναγκες, 'necessary things' which 'seemed good to the Holy Spirit'. Now, according to Luke, Paul was a participant in the Jerusalem meeting which issued the decree. Moreover, right after the meeting, Paul dutifully delivered the decree to the churches he founded on his first missionary journey (Acts 16.4). If Luke's account is historically accurate, it will be an early and important witness to Paul's negative attitude towards idol food. It will pose tremendous difficulty for the traditional understanding of Paul's stance in this matter.[57]

points out that 'what Paul and most other Jews would call πορνεία was generally accepted among the Graeco-Roman population in Paul's day'. Sanders cites the example from Plutarch, who explains that Marcus Cato married again in his old age because his son was embarrassed by Cato's consorting with a slave girl every night. Plutarch otherwise makes it fairly clear that he generally disapproves of the son.

55. W. Neil, *The Acts of the Apostles* (Grand Rapids: Eerdmans, 1987), p. 174.

56. The difficulty of keeping Gentile converts from these vices is evident in 1 Cor. 6–10 and Rev. 2. The prohibition of blood is more difficult to assess because of the lack of data in the New Testament and subapostolic literature on the subject. It is quite possible that strangulation or eating blood has something to do with pagan religion. In *Jos. Asen.* 8.5-7, Joseph refuses to kill Aseneth because she is 'a strange woman who will bless with her mouth dead and dumb idols and eat from their table bread of strangulation (ἄρτον ἀγχόνης)'. Though a different word is used, the strangulation is clearly performed in connection with idol sacrifices. Probably the eating of blood did not emerge as a major issue in early Christianity because, as Sanders (*Jewish Law*, pp. 278-79) observes, Greeks used the same slaughtering technique as Jews, so that meat sold in the marketplace would normally be free of blood in any case. Later authors prohibited blood consumption on the ground that it was demon's food (i.e. idol food). In this way, the blood-prohibition was justified (and made sense of) by the prohibition against eating idol food.

57. Brunt, who thinks Paul condones the eating of εἰδωλόθυτα, is understandably puzzled that 'Luke writes in support of Paul, addresses an issue which Paul

Of course, it is precisely at this point that the historicity of Acts is most strongly challenged by scholars. Since Paul's attitude to idol food would have been understood very differently depending on whether he accepted, rejected, ignored, or was ignorant of the decree, I must explore Paul's historical relationship with the decree in some detail.[58]

It is clear that one's opinion about the authenticity of Luke's version of the Jerusalem meeting, as that of any other stories in Acts, will be strongly affected by one's view of the larger issue of the historical trustworthiness of Luke–Acts as a whole. Nevertheless, in view of the enormous literature elicited by the subject, to assess Luke's historical trustworthiness (or even the more limited question of the *Paulusbild* in Acts) will go well beyond the scope of this investigation.[59] We will simply focus on the specific difficulties in accepting the authenticity of the Jerusalem Council account. There are four major difficulties which make Luke's account appear problematic:

1. Paul's law-free gospel is incompatible with the legal require-
    ments, albeit minimal, of the decree. He would not have had
    any use for any regulations which might shackle or obscure
    his gospel of liberty. Furthermore, in his letters Paul speci-
    fically rejects the validity of Jewish food laws for Gentile
    believers (Rom. 14.1-6, 17, 20; 1 Cor. 8.8; Col. 2.16; cf.
    1 Tim. 4.3-5; Tit. 1.15).
2. In Acts 21.25, James informs Paul of the decree as if for the
    first time.[60] That implies that Paul was absent when the

discussed, yet makes no mention of Paul's discussion, does not even show awareness of it, and appears to take an attitude which is very different from it' ('Rejected', pp. 115-16).

58. Almost every conceivable suggestion regarding this relationship has been
made. See Hurd, *Origins*, pp. 250-59, for a good survey.

59. See Gasque, *History*, esp. chapter 10, for a good survey of the problem. See
also C.H. Talbert, 'Luke–Acts', in E.J. Epp and G.W. MacRae (eds.), *The New
Testament and its Modern Interpreters* (Philadelphia: Fortress Press, 1989) for bibliography on secondary literature. For a survey of recent studies of *Paulusbild* in
Acts, see R. Maddox, *The Purpose of Luke–Acts* (FRLANT, 16; Göttingen: Vandenhoeck & Ruprecht, 1982), pp. 66-90. See also Jervell, *The Unknown Paul* (esp.
chs. 3 and 4), J.C. Lentz, Jr, *Luke's Portrait of Paul* (ed. M.E. Thrall; SNTSMS,
77; Cambridge: Cambridge University Press, 1993) and Lindemann, *Paulus*, pp. 49-
68. For a recent careful attempt to situate Paul's life within the chronological
framework of Acts, see Riesner, *Die Frühzeit*.

60. J.N. Sanders, 'Peter and Paul in Acts', *NTS* 2 (1955), pp. 133-43 (140);

decisions were made. Moreover, in Luke's account of the council, Paul certainly appeared more like a passive onlooker than an active participant. The failure of Luke to record any speech by Paul is due to the fact that Paul did not give one, and he did not give one because he was not there to make one.[61]

3. It is difficult to understand why Paul did not mention the decree in his account of the Jerusalem meeting in Galatians 2, as it would have helped his position tremendously in the controversy over circumcision. Worse, Paul said specifically that nothing was added to his gospel (Gal. 2.6). In addition, it is not easy to harmonize the Acts accounts of Paul's visits to Jerusalem with Galatians 1–2.[62] This suggests that Luke has confused or is not playing straight with his sources.

4. It is also difficult to understand why Paul never referred to the decree in his letters. In particular, in the Corinthian controversy over idol food, he did not mention the decree nor is his attitude in harmony with it.

These difficulties have led most critics to discard Luke's version of the Jerusalem meeting as inauthentic in some way.[63] Barrett claims that 'nothing is more striking than that Luke can make Paul himself part-author of the Decree'.[64] Conzelmann asserts that at this point 'there is an open contradiction between Paul's account [in Gal. 2] and that of the

K.F. Nickle, *The Collection* (London: SCM Press, 1966), p. 55; M. Hengel, *Acts and the History of Earliest Christianity* (Philadelphia: Fortress Press, 1979), p. 117; R.E. Brown and J.P. Meier, *Antioch and Rome* (New York: Paulist Press, 1983), p. 42; P.J. Achtemeier, *The Quest of Unity in the New Testament Church* (Philadelphia: Fortress Press, 1987), pp. 14-15 and notes; cf. G. Bornkamm, *Paul* (London: Hodder & Stoughton, 1971), p. 42; H. Conzelmann, *History of Primitive Christianity* (Nashville: Abingdon Press, 1973), p. 89; P.F. Esler, *Community and Gospel in Luke–Acts: The Social and Political Motivations of Lucan Theology* (SNTSMS, 57; Cambridge: Cambridge University Press, 1987), p. 99.

61. Sanders, 'Peter and Paul', p. 142; cf. Achtemeier, *Quest*, p. 16; M.-E. Boismard, 'Le "Concile" de Jerusalem', *ETL* 64 (1988), pp. 433-40 (435).

62. Cf. Knox, *Chapters*, pp. 13-88.

63. Even a conservative scholar like Fee notes that Paul's approach to idol food makes 'Paul's own relationship with the Decree a matter of some historical difficulty' (*The First Epistle to the Corinthians*, p. 360 n. 10). Unfortunately, Fee does not explore this relationship any further.

64. Barrett, 'Things Sacrificed', p. 59.

book of Acts'.[65] Even Hengel, who has quite a high regard for the historical trustworthiness of Acts on the whole, cannot accept that the decree was promulgated in a council in which Paul took part.[66]

While the authenticity of the decree itself is not seriously questioned,[67] many contemporary critics believe that the decree was formulated in Paul's absence to heal the rifts that resulted from the Antioch incident.[68] Paul might have learned of the decree later, but he did not submit to its authority and it made no difference to his ministry.[69]

There is a minority of scholars who think that Paul knew and

65. Conzelmann, *Primitive Christianity*, p. 88.

66. Hengel, *Acts*, pp. 115-16: 'Paul knows nothing of legal concessions of this kind; indeed, he asserts that no obligations were laid on Barnabas and himself (Gal. 2.6). Here we may trust him, rather than Luke's account.'

67. A notable exception is Borgen, 'Catalogues', pp. 126-41. Borgen has argued, on account of the textual variations, that there never were specific provisions appended to the Apostolic Decree (p. 135). The essential purpose of the decree was to confirm the waiver of circumcision for Gentile converts (p. 137) and this was embellished with various versions of the catalogues of pagan vices which proliferated in the Jewish world at the time. However, the variation between the different accounts in Acts and between various textual traditions is really too small for Borgen's thesis to be plausible.

68. Hengel provides a clear statement of this view: 'In reality, the "Apostolic Decree" which Luke attributes to James—probably not by chance—goes back to a compromise achieved some time later without Paul, which after the clash in Antioch (Gal. 2.11ff.) was intended to restore the broken table-fellowship between Gentile Christians and Jewish Christians who observed the law. Possibly James was able to assert his position here. In contrast to Paul, Barnabas and the Antiochene community seem to have accepted this compromise… Paul, by contrast, never acknowledged it or practised it' (*Acts*, p. 117). See also Nickle, *Collection*, p. 67; Brown and Meier, *Antioch and Rome*, p. 42; J.D.G. Dunn, 'The Incident at Antioch', *JSNT* 18 (1983), pp. 3-57 (38); N. Taylor, *Paul, Antioch and Jerusalem: A Study in Relationships and Authority in Earliest Christianity* (JSNTSup, 66; Sheffield: JSOT Press, 1991), pp. 140-42. D.R. Catchpole, on the other hand, argues that the decree was introduced by James and was the *cause* of the Antioch incident in Gal. 2 ('Paul, James and the Apostolic Decree', *NTS* 23 [1977], pp. 428-44). He suggests that Paul's hostile reaction in Gal. 2 is consistent with what his reaction would have been to the theology of the decree, which is fundamentally Mosaic and hence inimical to Paul. Catchpole further claims that 'the correspondence between the demands involved in the Gal. 2.11-14 situation and the demands expressed in the decree' is 'precise' and 'exact' (p. 442). Such claims are surely exaggerated, for one is not even sure what exactly happened in the Antioch incident!

69. Taylor, *Paul*, p. 140; cf. Sawyer, 'Meat Sacrificed', p. 37.

accepted the decree. Their interpretation usually turns on understanding the decree as limited in its intent and extent. Paul did not mention the decree because it was merely a temporary or local compromise motivated by 'a due consideration for the prejudices of the Jews', instead of having a fundamental and abiding character.[70] It is also common for those scholars to adopt the South Galatians theory with a pre-council dating, to lessen any difficulties that Galatians 2 may impose on this interpretation.

Such an understanding of the decree is no doubt prompted by the desire to maintain consistency with the traditional understanding of Paul's approach to idol food. But this solution convinces few critics because it glosses over many difficulties (such as those mentioned above). It also requires a very unnatural reading of Acts 16.4 and 21.25, as Luke does not seem to understand the decree as geographically or temporally limited. Moreover, if Jewish scruples are the main consideration, it is hard to see why ceremonial commands regarding Sabbaths, pork, and so on, are not included in the decree. More difficult to understand is why a temporary pragmatic compromise could command such widespread early Christian observance in all parts of the Roman Empire.

I cannot accept the common evangelical interpretation as doing justice to the historical problems involved. On the other hand, I do not think that the difficulties that lead scholars to conclude that Paul could not have participated in the formation and distribution of the decree are insurmountable, provided one removes the unproven assumption that Paul condoned eating idol food in 1 Corinthians 8–10. I will tackle the four difficulties mentioned above in order:

1. The first difficulty is much less formidable now than it was in previous generations, thanks mainly to the increasing emphasis on ecumenical Jewish–Christian dialogues in New Testament scholarship in recent years. The current intensive effort on the part of Pauline scholars to reassess Paul's relationship to the Jewish Scriptures and early Judaism results in a much more positive appreciation of Paul's

---

70. W.J. Conybeare and J.S. Howsen, *The Life and Epistles of St. Paul* (Hartford: S.S. Scranton, 1902), p. 193. This is the predominant view of evangelical scholars. See, for example, I.H. Marshall, *Acts* (Leicester: IVP, 1980); F.F. Bruce, *The Acts of the Apostles* (Grand Rapids: Eerdmans, Leicester: IVP, 2nd edn, 1987); R.P. Martin, *New Testament Foundations* (2 vols.; Grand Rapids: Eerdmans, 1978); E.F. Harrison, *Interpreting Acts* (Grand Rapids: Zondervan, 1986).

attitude towards the Jewish law than scholars in previous generations would have cared to think or admit. In particular, the assertion that Paul has no use for Jewish laws after his conversion is shown to be patently untrue.[71] Paul clearly expects his converts to observe a high standard of ethics that is largely derived from the Jewish Scriptures, however informed and transformed it is by the Christ event.[72] His law-free gospel is not incompatible with legal requirements. Not only does he quote the decalogue freely, he even claims that 'circumcision is nothing, and uncircumcision is nothing; but obeying the commandments of God is everything' (1 Cor. 7.19).

That Paul specifically rejects the validity of Jewish food laws for Gentile believers is no difficulty for his acceptance of the decree once we remove the unwarranted assumption that the prohibitions of idol food and blood (and hence πνικτόν, from which the blood has not been drained) are dietary regulations in the sense of the *kashrut*. In the Jewish Scriptures, it is clear that the consumption of idol food or blood is much more offensive than the violation of *kashrut*. Eating idol food provokes God's jealousy and brings down divine judgment—a point that Paul also makes in 1 Corinthians 10.[73] Moreover, in my survey of Jewish literature, I found that the idol food prohibition is considered so fundamental that, unlike the case with *kashrut*, there is no evidence that rationalization or justification of the command has been made through allegory. It is not considered a stumbling-block that needs to be removed, but the quintessence of Jewish faith that needs to be strongly affirmed.

The prohibition against consumption of blood is also asserted with full force in the Torah. In Gen. 9.3-4, it is stated that one may eat any living thing (probably including unclean animals at that time) but the blood must not be consumed. While the eating of unclean food merely constitutes a person unclean (Lev. 11.42-43), the person eating blood is threatened to be 'cut off'—death by divine agency (Lev. 17.10). While

71. See Tomson's (*Jewish Law*) thorough discussion of the subject.

72. E.P. Sanders (*Paul* ['Past Masters' Series; Oxford: Oxford University Press, 1991], pp. 115-16) suggests that 'when forced to think, [Paul] was a creative theologian: but on ethical issues [like idolatry and sexual transgression] he was seldom forced to think, and simply sought to impose Jewish behavior on his Gentile converts'.

73. Exod. 34.12-16; Num. 25; Deut. 32.16-23; Ps. 106.28-29. These passages are clearly in Paul's mind as he warns the Corinthian Christians about God's jealousy and judgment in 1 Cor. 10. See my discussion in Chapter 3.

aliens sojourning in Israel are forbidden to eat blood, they may eat unclean animals (uncleanness caused by death). The Israelites may also sell unclean animals to foreigners (Deut. 14.21). In Lev. 17.10-14, within five verses the blood prohibition occurs six times. 'Such staccato of repetition is unprecedented in law; it betrays the strident alarm of the legislator lest this fundamental principle be violated'.[74]

Such a distinction between the idol food and blood prohibitions on the one hand, and the dietary laws on the other, is also patent in the decree itself. According to Luke's report of Peter's visions, the food laws pertaining to cleanliness, which have symbolized the holiness of Israel apart from the Gentiles, were done away with (10.9-16, 34-35; 11.5-10). Significantly, the Apostolic Decree in Acts 15 came *after* Peter's visions in Acts 10–11 which had already abolished the cleanliness food laws and had established a new basis for Jewish and Gentile communion.[75] Indeed, the extreme unlikelihood of Luke's reporting, in the space of a few chapters, both the abolition of the food laws and the ongoing obligation of the church to observe laws regarding some 'food' strongly suggests that the latter belongs to a different category. Otherwise, how is Acts 15 possible after Acts 10–11?[76] It is no surprise that

74. J. Milgrom, 'Ethics and Ritual: The Foundation of the Biblical Dietary Laws', in E.B. Firmage (ed.), *Religion and Law: Biblical-Judaic and Islamic Perspectives* (Winona Lake, IN: Eisenbrauns, 1990), p. 162.

75. For those who view the prohibitions in the decree in ceremonial categories, the tension between Acts 10–11 and Acts 15 is keenly felt. S.G. Wilson is puzzled as to 'why pork and blood...equally abhorrent to a Jew and both unequivocally prohibited by the law, should be treated differently?' (*Luke and the Law* [Cambridge: Cambridge University Press, 1983], p. 75). Similarly, E. Haenchen, *The Acts of the Apostles* (Oxford: Westminster Press, 1971), p. 450; J.C. O'Neil, *The Theology of Acts in its Historical Setting* (London: SPCK, 2nd edn, 1970), p. 108; Brunt, 'Rejected', p. 121. However, once the 'food laws' in Acts 15 are understood to be different in character and purpose from the other dietary laws, the difficulty disappears.

76. It is commonly recognized that varied repetition (e.g. on Paul's call and Peter's preaching to Cornelius) plays a significant role in the scheme of Acts. Nevertheless, the degree of variation between Acts 10–11 and Acts 15 is simply too great for the two accounts to be doublets of one incident (cf. the much smaller, and much more typical, variation between Acts 10 and Acts 11 regarding the Cornelius incident). Jervell thinks that there is another 'simple' answer: in the intervening years, 'a hardening of Jerusalem in its attitude to Gentiles took place', which resulted in new demands imposed on Gentile Christians—'demands which were not there from the beginning' (*The Unknown Paul*, pp. 23, 30). But Jervell's

early Christians continued to observe those prohibitions even when
there was a widespread rejection of Jewish food laws in general.[77]

In view of this distinction, Paul's statement in Rom. 14.14 regarding
Jewish food laws—'nothing is unclean in itself'—cannot be absolutized and applied to the issue of idol food. On the contrary, as I have
argued in the previous chapter, Paul in fact treats the two issues very
differently.

2. In a literary analysis of the Jerusalem council narrative, I have
dealt in some detail with the major historical problems raised by Luke's
reiteration of the decree in Acts 21.25 and Paul's passiveness in the
council.[78] I have shown how Luke underscores the subordinate role of
Paul in the council through the literary shaping of the account and that,
in view of Paul's dominance in the two missionary journeys which
frame the council narrative, such literary shaping is deliberate. Had
Luke wanted to fake Paul's presence in the council, he could have easily made up a prominent speech and put it in Paul's mouth, as many
critics have no difficulty in believing that Luke did make up speeches
for Peter and James which have Pauline rings. But far from faking
Paul's presence, Luke's purpose was to make Paul look passive, in
spite of what was perhaps common knowledge—that Paul did participate in the council. In his apologetic interest, Luke wanted to

speculation goes contrary to the evidence in Acts, which seems rather to portray a
gradual softening of Jewish Christian hesitation about the Gentile mission through
the special guidance of the Holy Spirit. In the scheme of Acts, the decree signifies
the completion of this process of softening, as Paul's Gentile mission was fully
legitimized for the first time. Henceforth Paul was virtually given a free hand. Peter
completely disappears from the scene and Paul becomes the only figure of importance (cf. Cheung, 'Narrative Analysis', pp. 152-53). Haenchen (*Acts*, p. 462)
remarks incisively that even though Jerusalem is once more the stage in ch. 21, it is
'strictly within the context of the Pauline story: no sooner is Paul arrested than the
congregation of Jerusalem vanishes without trace'. This can be compared with
Jerusalem's earlier concern to closely 'monitor' the Gentile mission: when the
apostles 'heard that Samaria had accepted the word, they sent Peter and John' to
check things out (8.14-17); it took supernatural visions to convince Peter to go to
the Gentile Cornelius (Acts 10) and afterwards his action drew severe criticism
from Jewish Christians (11.1-18); again, when the Jerusalem church heard about
Gentile conversion in Antioch, they were concerned and sent Barnabas to check
things out (11.19-26).

77. See the discussions on Didache, Justin, Tertullian, Origen and Novatian
below.

78. Cheung, 'Narrative Analysis' (esp. pp. 142-43, 147-49).

accentuate the role of Jerusalem in the legitimizing of the Gentile mission and to avoid giving the impression that Paul was a leading voice in the debate. If Paul did not participate in the council, Luke could simply tell us that the decision was made by the Jerusalem apostles without Paul—that would have served his purpose really well—and did not need to go to extraordinary lengths to emphasize Paul's subordinate role. Therefore, Luke's portrayal of Paul's passiveness need not raise doubts about the apostle's presence there. On the contrary, it may even lend support for the authenticity of the account.

Critics who consider Acts 21.25 evidence that Paul was informed of the decree for the first time must assume that Luke has forgotten what he has written a few chapters earlier. This is highly unlikely in view of the central significance of the decree in Acts. Moreover, there are strong literary links between Acts 15 and 21. For example, the recognition of the role of the four mission reports in the council (Acts 14.27, 15.3, 4, 12) provides a good literary rationale for Luke's reiteration of the decree in Acts 21.25, where the only other mission report recorded in Acts is given (21.19).[79] With his literary sophistication, it is unlikely that Luke bungles at this point.

Why, then, did James not refer back to the decision of the council (Luke could have easily made him do so)? We cannot be certain here. Probably the decree was originally addressed only to churches in Antioch and Syro-Cilicia (Acts 15.23), but between the time of the council and Paul's visit to Jerusalem in Acts 21, the same ruling of the decree was given to other Gentile churches which were uncertain about their obligation to the Mosaic law. Realistically, disputes over circumcision, like the dispute in Antioch, did not happen only once. It is natural to assume that other Gentile churches (not necessarily established by Paul) would have encountered similar problems and sought counsel from Jerusalem, which at that stage still commanded considerable authority. In this way, the decision in Acts 15, though at first formulated to resolve a specific dispute, could easily have become a standard solution to the problem of Gentile obligations to the law.

3. Paul's failure to mention the decree in Galatians 2, coupled with his explicit claim that nothing was added to him, is perhaps the decisive factor in many scholars' rejection of Luke's account of the council. Conzelmann maintained that Paul 'could not have argued thus if the

79. Cheung, 'Narrative Analysis', p. 143.

decree had actually been issued by the council. Otherwise he would have played trump cards right into the hands of his opponents.'[80] Therefore, either Paul did not know the decree at all, or if he did know it, he denied that it is a part of the agreement at Jerusalem, or he was not very savvy about what his opponents might do.

A common response from conservative scholars is to date Galatians before the council: Paul could not have mentioned the decree because it had not been formulated at the time of the writing of Galatians. As mentioned above, I do not accept this solution because the similarities between Acts 15 and Galatians 2 are too strong and numerous for them to be describing two different meetings in the space of a few years.[81] Moreover, this solution contributes nothing to answering the question of why Paul did not quote the decree in any of his letters. It would ultimately be more satisfactory to show if there is any incompatibility between Acts 15 and Galatians 2 whether or not they refer to the same meeting.

The difficulty perceived by scholars rests on an assumption that is seldom questioned, namely, that the decree was something that was imposed on Paul by the 'pillars' as a concession to Jewish scruples. But what if the decree was not merely a concession but in fact reflected an ethical standard which Paul himself has been preaching to the Gentiles since the beginning of his ministry? What if it was something totally

---

80. Conzelmann, *Primitive Christianity*, p. 89.

81. The relationship between Paul's two Jerusalem visits mentioned in Galatians and his three visits to Jerusalem detailed in Acts is exceedingly complex. The numerous issues involved are covered in standard commentaries and introductions, and need not be rehearsed here (for a good summary and discussion of the options, see R.N. Longenecker, *Galatians* [WBC, 41; Dallas: Word Books, 1990], pp. lxxii-lxxxviii). I can do scarce justice, within the constraint of this work, to the various theories proposed. I shall simply state my agreement with the majority of scholars that Gal. 2.1-10 and Acts 15 report the same visit. In my opinion, J.B. Lightfoot's argument that 'a combination of circumstances so striking is not likely to have occurred twice within a few years' has remained unanswered—and almost unanswerable (*Saint Paul's Epistle to the Galatians* [London: Macmillan, 10th edn, 1890], p. 124). The alleged inconsistencies between the two accounts are capable of being explained when one appreciates the different perspectives of the authors and the literary shaping of the accounts. In fact, the differences between the two accounts are no more (and the similarities, no less) than those between the various resurrection accounts in the Gospels, yet no one would argue for more than one resurrection of Jesus. I owe this last observation to Moisés Silva.

non-controversial, about which Paul was in total agreement with the Jerusalem apostles? Then it would not have been something imposed on him![82]

In the immediate preceding context of Paul's claim that nothing was added to him, he mentioned that he had laid before the Jerusalem leaders the gospel that he had proclaimed among the Gentiles (Gal. 2.2). What was the content of this gospel? Presumably there would have been a condemnation of vices, including πορνεία and εἰδωλολατρία, which characterized the pagan way of life (Gal. 5.19-21). Such a condemnation of pagan vices seemed a core element in Paul's missionary preaching, for Paul said: ἃ προλέγω ὑμῖν καθὼς προεῖπον ὅτι οἱ τὰ τοιαῦτα πράσσοντες βασιλείαν θεοῦ οὐ κληρονομήσουσιν (5.21). This understanding is considerably strengthened when one looks at 1 Cor. 6.9-10, another list of vices which shows clear connections to Gal. 5.19-21: ἢ οὐκ οἴδατε ὅτι ἄδικοι θεοῦ βασιλείαν οὐ κληρονομήσουσιν; μὴ πλανᾶσθε·[83] οὔτε πόρνοι οὔτε εἰδωλολάτραι... βασιλείαν θεοῦ κληρονομήσουσιν.

Other lists of vices of Paul (or early Paulinists) also corroborate this impression (Eph. 5.5; Col. 3.5; 2 Cor. 12.20-21; cf. Rev. 22.15; 2.14-15, 20; Acts 15.20). While the number and kind of vices differ from list to list, idolatry and sexual immorality are the most prominent items.[84] Again, 1 Thess. 1.9-10 and Rom. 1.18-32, which must belong to the core part of Paul's preaching to Gentiles, confirm this understanding.[85] Avoidance of idolatry in any form was not a concession on Paul's part to appease ultraconservative Jewish Christians, but was part and parcel of Gentile conversion to the Christian faith.

The condemnation of idolatry and sexual immorality was also a central concern in Jewish propagandistic literature.[86] In Chapter 3 I

---

82. Cf. M. Bockmuehl, 'The Noachide Commandments and New Testament Ethics with Special Reference to Acts 15 and Pauline Halakhah', *RB* 102 (1995), pp. 72-101 (96): 'Paul may well fail to mention the Decree in Gal. 2 because its meaning indeed "contributed nothing"...to the Gentile mission other than the laws which would apply to it in any case—and which Paul takes for granted and consistently upholds, even in Galatians (5.19ff.)'.

83. Cf. also the μὴ πλανᾶσθε of Gal. 6.7.

84. Cf. Borgen, 'Catalogues'.

85. Note also Paul's clear polemics against idolatry in both of his evangelistic speeches to Gentiles in Acts (14.15-18; 17.16-29).

86. J.J. Collins (*Athens and Jerusalem*, pp. 137-74) observes that in Diaspora Jewish literature commending or defending Judaism before Gentiles or Hellenistic

mentioned the close connection between Paul's missionary preaching and Jewish apologetic/proselyte traditions. When one remembers that in Jewish literature no effort has been made to dissociate εἰδωλόθυτα from εἰδωλολατρία, the prohibitions in the decree cannot very well be understood as something 'added' to Paul's gospel.[87]

Such an understanding is also consistent with Paul's own claim that he preached the gospel among Gentiles shortly after his conversion (Gal. 1.15-16) and that, until the Judaizers forced the issue of circumcision many years later, his preaching was approved by churches in Judea (Gal. 1.23-24). This claim could hardly have been made had the Jerusalem leaders thought that Paul condoned eating idol food.

Therefore, Paul's statement that the Jerusalem leaders added nothing to him must be understood to mean that they did not add the requirement of circumcision (and all that it entails) to Paul's gospel. Understood thus, Gal. 2.6 cannot be construed as Paul's renunciation of the decree and constitutes no problem for Luke's account of the council.

But what about the failure of Paul to appeal to the decree, which would have helped his position? My answer is that *Paul did refer to the decree* (namely, the waiving of the demand of circumcision)—but not the part that Luke (and most scholars) focused on (namely, the prohibitions). The failure to distinguish the differing concerns of Paul and Luke results in much misunderstanding.

In his apologetic concern to conciliate Jewish Christians, Luke is very reticent regarding the abolition of the requirement of circumcision for Gentile Christians. The overruling of the Pharisaic demand for circumcision is phrased in a very circumlocutory manner—the term 'circumcision' is not even mentioned in Peter's and James's speeches, nor in the decree![88] On the other hand, he highlights the prohibitions of the decree to reassure his Jewish readers that the Gentile Christians' freedom from the Mosaic law would not result in antinomianism.

Jews (or bolstering Jewish self-identification), monotheism and social ethics are the most accentuated topics. They are much more prominent than circumcision, dietary laws, and the like. This point is more recently emphasized by J.T. Sanders ('Jews and Gentiles', pp. 68-69) and J. Klawans ('Gentile Impurity', pp. 293-97).

87. Note that if the Jerusalem leaders maintained that Gentile converts should refrain from those vices listed in Gal. 5.19-21, Paul could still have easily said that they added nothing to him.

88. Cheung, 'Narrative Analysis', pp. 151-52.

For Paul, however, in his polemics against the Judaizers, the most important part of the decree was not the prohibitions but the agreement that Gentile believers were not required to be circumcised.[89] The prohibitions, on the other hand, were totally non-controversial because they were common elements in both Paul's missionary preaching and that of the other apostles. Paul had no occasion to mention such non-controversial items (which would not have advanced his argument) in his urgent and emotional appeal to the Galatians.

The waiving of the demand for circumcision was a totally different matter. It was a hard fought victory for Paul. There is strong evidence in the text that the Jerusalem leaders did put pressure on Paul to comply with the Pharisaic demand. Otherwise Paul's somewhat derogatory attitude towards the pillars and his proud pronouncement that not even Titus was forced to be circumcised, not to mention his claim that nothing was added to him, would be inexplicable. Paul's emotion ran so high that 'the sense of the passage is well-nigh lost'.[90]

Therefore, I submit that Paul's statement in Gal. 2.6 that the Jerusalem leaders 'added (προσανέθεντο) nothing' to him is indeed a direct reference to the Jerusalem council agreement regarding the waiving of the obligation of circumcision. It is instructive to compare Acts 15.10, where Peter argued that they should not impose (ἐπιθεῖναι) the yoke of the Mosaic law on the neck of the disciples.[91]

4. In Chapter 3 I have already demonstrated that Paul's approach to idol food in 1 Corinthians 8–10 is indeed consistent with the decree. As for the failure of Paul to quote the decree explicitly in 1 Corinthian 8–10, it becomes a pseudo-problem when one recognizes that the decree is consistent with (and is a part of) Paul's earliest missionary preaching.

In Chapter 2 I underlined Paul's vigorous polemics against idolatry in his missionary preaching. I have argued that, given the prominent function idol food performed in the Corinthian society, the issue of idol food could not have failed to come up during Paul's lengthy ministry in

89. Note that Martin Dibelius considers the essential purpose of the decree as a confirmation that circumcision was not integral to Christian teaching (*Studies in the Acts of the Apostles* [London: SCM Press, 1956], p. 97). See also Borgen, 'Catalogues', p. 137.

90. Lightfoot, *Galatians*, p. 104.

91. Cf. also Acts 15.19: 'Therefore I have reached the decision that we should not trouble those Gentiles who are turning to God'.

Corinth. In particular, if Paul had condoned eating idol food or given ambiguous instructions on the subject, the supposed dispute between the strong and the weak would have arisen long before Paul left Corinth![92]

As I have shown earlier, the most likely scenario is that, in his first visit to Corinth, Paul prohibited—perhaps without any qualification—the consumption of idol food. He thus acted in accordance with the decree, whether he appealed to it or not.[93] However, after Paul had left Corinth, some from the leadership of the church, perhaps because of their enlightened view of Christian freedom, but more likely due to social pressure, began to eat idol food. Paul attempted to correct them in the previous letter but was rebutted with clever arguments which were constructed with distortions of his earlier teachings and which seized on the potential impracticality of Paul's unguarded language. This led to Paul's response in 1 Cor. 8.1–11.1, which is both strongly combative and highly nuanced. To quote the decree there would not have served Paul's purpose.

To sum up, I have shown that the arguments advanced against the historical accuracy of Luke's account of the Jerusalem council are not insurmountable.[94] On the contrary, they readily fall apart if we are allowed to make one major assumption—that the decree is consistent with Paul's missionary preaching, that Paul indeed prohibited eating idol food. As we shall see, this assumption also allows us to make sense of a plethora of early Christian writings touching on Paul's stance in the matter of idol food.

---

92. Any Christian who lives in a place where 'there are many gods and many lords', or anyone acquainted with the history of mission in such places, understands that idol food is one of the earliest and most important issues confronting new converts. The issue demands a clear-cut standard and approach from the church leadership, or else controversies will immediately arise. It is thus totally unrealistic and historically detached to think that Paul did not give clear instructions regarding idol food in his earliest preaching in Corinth.

93. As the important part of the decree for Paul is the waiver of circumcision, he did not really have to appeal to it if he saw no sign of troubles caused by Judaizers.

94. Of course, there are still other obstacles such as problems of chronology and (in)completeness of reference which may call Acts' accuracy into question. Unfortunately, I cannot discuss these issues here.

b. *The Significance of Acts 21.18-26 for our Understanding of Paul's Approach*

I have argued above that if Luke's account is historically accurate, as I believe it is, Acts 15 would be a virtually decisive witness to Paul's negative attitude towards idol food, and an almost insuperable difficulty for the traditional understanding of Paul's position. I will now attempt to show that even if one has questions about the historical trustworthiness of Acts 15, there is still another passage in Acts that would constitute a powerful testimony against the traditional view. This passage is Acts 21.18-26, which is quoted here from the NRSV.

> [18]The next day Paul went with us to visit James; and all the elders were present. [19]After greeting them, he related one by one the things that God had done among the Gentiles through his ministry. [20]When they heard it, they praised God. Then they said to him, 'You see, brother, how many thousands of believers there are among the Jews, and they are all zealous for the law. [21]*They have been told about you* (κατηχήθησαν δὲ περὶ σοῦ) that you teach all the Jews living among the Gentiles to forsake Moses, and that you tell them not to circumcise their children or observe the customs. [22]What then is to be done? *They will certainly hear* that you have come. [23]So do what we tell you. We have four men who are under a vow. [24]Join these men, go through the rite of purification with them, and pay for the shaving of their heads. *Thus all will know that there is nothing in what they have been told about you* (ὧν κατήχηνται περὶ σοῦ), but that you yourself observe and guard the law. [25]But as for the Gentiles who have become believers, we have sent a letter with our judgment that they should abstain from what has been sacrificed to idols and from blood and from what is strangled and from fornication.' [26]Then Paul took the men, and the next day, having purified himself, he entered the temple with them, making public the completion of the days of purification when the sacrifice would be made for each of them.

Presumably, at the time Luke was writing, he was still dealing with a very lively and powerful Jewish Christianity.[95] This alone will explain

---

95. This may suggest an early dating of Acts, but no confident conclusion can be drawn, as the dominance of Gentile Christianity (especially in the east) probably took place much later than earlier scholarship tended to think. In particular, the early model and dating of the 'parting of the ways' are almost certainly wrong. See A.J. Saldarini, 'Jews and Christians in the First Two Centuries: The Changing Paradigm', *Shofar* 10 (1992), pp. 16-34 and J.D.G. Dunn (ed.), *Jews and Christians: The Parting of the Ways: AD 70 to 135* (WUNT, 66; Tübingen: J.C.B. Mohr [Paul Siebeck], 1992).

why Luke was so concerned about the Jewish Christians' opinion about Paul.

Luke realizes that Jerusalem is well informed about Paul's preaching among Diaspora Jews and that there are rumors that Paul has been teaching them to forsake Moses. Whatever the factual content of such rumors, they are an indication of the reservations of the Jerusalem Christians regarding Paul.[96] Extremely anxious to dispel such rumors, Luke strives to demonstrate that Jewish traditions have not been impugned by Paul's preaching. In fact, Paul himself is faithful to the law and fulfills it himself, as shown by his participation in the rite of purification with four Nazirites. This much is clear.

Now v. 21 and v. 25 clearly distinguish the Jews and Gentiles regarding their relation to the Mosaic law. Supposedly, Jewish Christians are to continue to circumcise their children and observe the customs of Moses. Gentile Christians, on the other hand, will have to observe the prohibitions in the decree. Here we may pose a rhetorical question: if Luke is concerned to dispel rumors that Paul has taught Jewish Christians to forsake Moses, would he not be equally concerned to dispel any rumors—if there are such rumors—that Paul has taught Gentile Christians not to observe the decree?

That Luke makes no effort to dispel any such rumors suggests that he is probably not aware of such. This implies—in Luke's personal recollections or in traditions he has received—not only that Paul has not taught Gentile Christians to neglect the decree, but also that Paul's teaching has not been (wrongly) construed in this way by friends or foes.

According to Luke, he was present when Paul met with James (Acts 21.18). If the author of Acts was indeed Paul's travel companion Luke the physician, Acts 21.18-26 is little short of decisive evidence that Paul did not condone eating idol food. But even if this is not true, even if Acts is not always historically accurate, Acts 21.18-26 would still be a near-contemporary indication of the nonexistence of the traditional

---

96. Gerd Lüdemann, *Paulus, der Heidenapostel. II. Antipaulinismus im frühen Christentum* (Göttingen: Vandenhoeck & Ruprecht, 1983), p. 93. Lüdemann points out 'daß der Apostel von geborenen Juden im Verkehr mit Heidenchristen die Nichtbeachtung von Speisegesetzen verlangte (vgl. Gal. 2, 11ff) und in seinen Briefen mehrfach die Indifferenz des Gesetzes gegenüber der neuen Schöpfung in Christus lehrte (1Kor 7,19; Gal. 6,15)'. It is thus a small step for such Jewish Christians to stop circumcising their children.

understanding of Paul's stance in the matter of idol food.

If Paul had taught, or been (mis)understood to teach, that idol food is a matter of indifference, such an outlandish view would hardly have gone unnoticed in early Christianity. In view of his diligent research and extensive use of sources (cf. Lk. 1.3-4) Luke would have heard it if Paul had done it! Had Luke attempted to exonerate Paul from the charge that he taught something contrary to the decree, one who takes a skeptical view might infer that Paul was indeed guilty of such but Luke was falsifying history because he or his readers could not accept such a Paul.[97] This is the attitude many scholars take regarding Luke's portrait of Paul as a faithful Jew. However, in the matter of the decree, there was not even any perceived need for Luke to defend Paul's position.[98] Therefore, unless one pushes the date of Acts well into the second century,[99] this lack of any awareness of the traditional understanding of Paul's attitude towards idol food at such an early stage would be an extremely powerful testimony that is almost impossible to dismiss.

4. *Revelation*

In Revelation, the issue of idol food surfaces in the letters to the churches in Pergamum and Thyatira (Rev. 2.14, 20). In both cases φαγεῖν εἰδωλόθυτα is condemned together with πορνεῦσαι:[100]

---

97. Certain sections of Jewish Christianity indeed refused to accept Paul because of his apparent repudiation of some Jewish laws.

98. If there had been any such need, Luke could have made Paul a much more active participant in formulating the decree, or he could have made Paul actively spreading the decree everywhere. But instead he went very low key concerning Paul's relation to the decree. Paul was passive in the council. The only occasion Luke mentioned Paul's teaching the decree was right after the council, and it was strictly to follow 'the decisions that had been reached by the apostles and elders who were in Jerusalem' (16.4). This serves to underscore Paul's submission to the Jerusalem leaders but does not give the impression that Luke needed to defend Paul's compliance with the decree against any rumors to the contrary.

99. Notably O'Neill (*Theology of Acts*, pp. 1-47), who dates Acts between 115 CE and 130 CE. His arguments are based mostly on the supposed theological parallels between Luke–Acts and other early Christian writers. But this is far too inadequate as a criterion for dating. Theological parallels are often in the eyes of the beholder. In my view, the kind of parallels O'Neill mentions, such as the theme of jealousy and the concept of salvation history, can also be found between Luke–Acts and many other New Testament writings.

100. For the purpose of this investigation, it is a moot point whether πορνεῦσαι

ἀλλ' ἔχω κατὰ σοῦ ὀλίγα, ὅτι ἔχεις ἐκεῖ κρατοῦντας τὴν διδαχὴν Βαλαάμ, ὃς ἐδίδασκεν τῷ Βαλὰκ βαλεῖν σκάνδαλον ἐνώπιον τῶν υἱῶν Ἰσραήλ, φαγεῖν εἰδωλόθυτα καὶ πορνεῦσαι· οὕτως ἔχεις καὶ σὺ κρατοῦντας τὴν διδαχὴν [τῶν] Νικολαϊτῶν ὁμοίως (Rev. 2.14-15).

ἀλλὰ ἔχω κατὰ σοῦ ὅτι ἀφεῖς τὴν γυναῖκα Ἰεζάβελ, ἡ λέγουσα ἑαυτὴν προφῆτιν, καὶ διδάσκει καὶ πλανᾷ τοὺς ἐμοὺς δούλους πορνεῦσαι καὶ φαγεῖν εἰδωλόθυτα (Rev. 2.20).

The church at Pergamum is rebuked for having some people there holding 'the teaching of Balaam'. Balaam became a prototype and symbol of false prophets who promoted compromise with paganism in idolatry and sexual immorality when he counseled Balak to entice the Israelites to 'play the harlot with the daughters of Moab' and to eat 'the sacrifices of their gods' and 'bowed down to their gods' (Num. 25.1,2; cf. 31.6). It is significant that John singles out φαγεῖν εἰδωλόθυτα for mention as the representative act of Israel's idolatry.

In the letter to Thyatira, the figure of Jezebel is substituted for that of Balaam. Jezebel, like Balaam, also led Israel into idolatry and immorality (cf. 1 Kgs 16.31-33; 2 Kgs 9.22; 2 Chron. 21.13). It is noteworthy that whereas 1 Kgs 16.31 only describes Jezebel's sin of leading Ahab (and subsequently, Israel) into idolatry in general terms, Rev. 2.20 makes specific reference to the eating of εἰδωλόθυτα. Probably, therefore, John considers the consumption of idol food the prime and representative act of Israel's idolatry.[101]

In a possible allusion to the Apostolic Decree, it is said that no other βάρος is to be placed upon those who refuse to hold the teaching of Jezebel (2.24; cf. Acts 15.28).[102] If the tradition that attributes the Apocalypse to the apostle John is correct, then this is hardly surprising: according to Gal. 2.9, John was present in the Jerusalem Council and probably had some influence on the formulation of the decree there. Since there is no other evidence of the use of Acts in Revelation, this

should be taken literally or figuratively for participating in idolatry.

101. It is interesting to note here Ehrhart's observation that, in the Spanish synod of Elvira in AD 306, εἰδωλόθυτα is used 'as a comprehensive term for all the various dues to idols, which the Christians refused to pay' (*Framework*, pp. 288-89).

102. Note the verbal analogy between μηδὲν πλέον ἐπιτίθεσθαι ὑμῖν βάρος (Acts 15.28) and οὐ βάλλω ἐφ' ὑμᾶς ἄλλο βάρος (Rev. 2.24). Cf. R.H. Charles, *A Critical and Exegetical Commentary on the Revelation of St. John* (ICC; 2 vols.; Edinburgh: T. & T. Clark, 1920), I, p. 74.

points to an independent circulation of the decree and lends credence to its historicity.

Revelation presents unmistakable evidence that there were some who advocated eating idol food. But the tone of 2.13-14 and 2.19-20 suggests that the Christians in those churches who followed such teaching, while perhaps a sizeable number, were not the majority. This can be compared with Rev. 3.4, which says that only a few remained faithful in the church of Sardis.[103] Moreover, the accusation in Rev. 2.20, 'you tolerate (ἀφεῖς) that woman Jezebel', seems to reflect the situation of a majority tolerating a minority teaching. John's point is that the church in Thyatira already knew the wrongness of that teaching but did nothing about it.

John's condemnation of the eating of idol food is unequivocal. Since John does not seem to feel the need to substantiate his case against eating idol food at all, the prohibition bears the marks of a well-established 'official' position. Thus we have in Revelation an early witness of the general prohibition of idol food in Asia Minor. On the other hand, because John nowhere mentions Paul, the bearing of Revelation 2 on Paul's position regarding idol food is far from obvious. Inferences must be drawn from indirect evidence and a measure of cautious speculation is unavoidable. In practice, one's view of Paul's attitude regarding idol food, one's own theological commitment, and one's overall construction of the theology and historical context of Revelation strongly influence the conclusion. Given the lack of direct evidence, this phenomenon is not necessarily to be deplored. However, it does call for greater methodological self-consciousness and care in approaching the indirect evidence.

Since Revelation was addressed to some of the churches in Asia Minor which Paul founded or influenced, a comparison of the approaches of John and Paul is both possible and profitable. In the assessment of the Tübingen school, Revelation is a Judaistic counterpart to the universalism of Paul and its theology is deficient when compared to Pauline theology.[104] Bauer claims:

---

103. Unfortunately, we have very little idea what the problems of the church of Sardis were. In particular, we do not know whether their sins included eating idol food.

104. E. Schüssler Fiorenza, *The Book of Revelation: Justice and Judgment* (Philadelphia: Fortress Press, 1985), p. 115.

The Apocalypse does not leave us with a particularly impressive idea of what sought to replace the Pauline gospel in the 'ecclesiastically oriented' circles at Ephesus...there remains for the most part a Jewish Christianity...[that] was undoubtedly better suited for the anti-gnostic struggle than was the Pauline proclamation, but in other respects it is hardly comparable.[105]

Within this framework of understanding, and assuming the validity of the traditional view of Paul's attitude toward idol food, Simon finds conscious polemics against Paul in Revelation 2: (1) John's denouncement of 'those who say they are apostles, and are not' (Rev. 2.2) echoes the controversies about Paul's apostleship (Rom. 11.13; 1 Cor. 9.1-2; 15.9; Gal. 1.1, 16-19; 2.6-9, etc.); (2) the strong emphasis on the concept of 'works' (2.2, 19) leaves the same impression; (3) the 'deep things of Satan' (τὰ βαθέα τοῦ Σατανα) in 2.24 perhaps alludes to 'the deep things of God' (τὰ βάθη τοῦ θεοῦ) mentioned in 1 Cor. 2.10.[106] In the same vein, though more guardedly, Hoffmann maintains that while active opposition to Paul's teaching cannot be substantiated as the reason for John's failure to mention him, the polemic of Rev. 2.14, 20, 24 and 3.14 is directed to an 'exaggerated or "heretical" paulinism in the churches of Asia Minor'.[107]

On the whole, I do not find the above interpretation persuasive. The verbal analogy between τὰ βαθέα τοῦ Σατανᾶ and τὰ βάθη τοῦ θεοῦ is interesting but proves little. Even if there is indeed an allusion, it does not prove Simon's point, for the allusion can be as easily construed in an opposite sense. John could be parodying 1 Cor. 2.10: failing to learn

---

105. Bauer, *Orthodoxy*, p. 84

106. Simon, 'Apostolic Decree', p. 452. Simon suggests that, against the extremes of Judaizers and Paul, Revelation represents a mitigated Jewish Christianity that clings to 'the authentic form of apostolic Christianity as expressed and summarized in the Apostolic Decree' (pp. 451-52). Note that Bauer considers Paul the 'target' of Rev. 2.2, 9, 20 and 3.9 and concludes that 'it was precisely orthodoxy that rejected Paul' (*Orthodoxy*, p. 233; cf. pp. 214-15).

107. R.J. Hoffmann, *Marcion: On the Restitution of Christianity: An Essay on the Development of Radical Paulinist Theology in the Second Century* (AAR Academy Series, 46; Chico, CA: Scholars Press, 1984), p. 238. Cf. C.J. Hemer, *The Letters to the Seven Churches of Asia in their Local Setting* (JSNTSup, 11; Sheffield: JSOT Press, 1986), pp. 94, 123. Hemer suggests that the libertines may have pressed Pauline phrases insisting on the Christian's liberty from the law into their service. Nicolaitanism was an antinomian movement whose antecedents can be traced in the misrepresentation of Pauline liberty.

the deep things of God which were revealed by the Spirit, the Nicolaitans learned instead the deep things of Satan. This can be supported by the fact that the deep things of Satan include participation in immorality and the eating of idol food, from which vices Paul urges Christians to flee (1 Cor. 6.18; 10.14). Again, the emphasis on works proves little. Paul can also exhort the Corinthian Christians to 'be steadfast, immovable, always excelling in the work of the Lord, because you know that in the Lord your labor is not in vain' (1 Cor. 15.58). As for Rev. 2.2, it is strange that the plural is used if Paul is the target of John's attack on false apostles. On the other hand, if we can trust Acts 20.28-31, Paul warns the church elders in Ephesus to be alert against false teachers. Revelation 2.2 may thus reflect the fruit of Paul's ministry in Ephesus rather than any opposition to him.

Therefore, unless one assumes the traditional understanding of Paul's attitude toward idol food, it is hard to see any polemic against Paul in Revelation 2. In other words, Revelation 2 does not furnish us with any evidence that Paul was understood to condone eating idol food.

The notion that it is an 'exaggerated Paulinism' that underlies John's polemic in Revelation 2 is more difficult to assess, for the phrase can mean different things. If by 'exaggerated' one means 'perverted' or 'distorted', then I have no quarrel with it: I believe that was exactly what the Corinthian knowers did when they ate idol food, but their behavior did not represent Paul's true position and was in fact at odds with his explicit teaching. But if by 'exaggerated Paulinism' is meant the logical development of Paul's attitude with which Paul agrees in principle but does not carry out in practice for some reason, then I would strongly dispute such a notion.

Instead of quibbling about terminology, it seems more fruitful to look at the concrete question of whether the 'false teachers' explicitly appealed to Paul in their advocacy to eat idol food. To answer this question, it is important to know something about those false teachers and the nature of their teaching.

The Nicolaitans, 'Jezebel', and 'Balaam' were, as Schüssler Fiorenza points out, the only opponents John directly named in his letters to the seven churches.[108] All three groups were presented as holding the same basic teaching and practice.[109] Therefore they were closely related, if

108. Schüssler Fiorenza, *Revelation*, p. 115.
109. Note the emphatic parallel between Balaam and the Nicolaitans in 2.15: οὕτως... καὶ σύ... ὁμοίως (Hemer, *Seven Churches*, p. 88). Moreover, since

not identical.[110] What was the nature of their teaching?

Hardly any commentator fails to recognize the relevance of the local settings of the three cities to the false teaching of the Nicolaitans.[111] Ephesus was a great city of trades and pagan cults; Thyatira had a great number of trade guilds; and Pergamum was the center of various pagan cults, including perhaps the emperor cult.[112] In short, they were cities of 'many gods and many lords'—not unlike Paul's Corinth. And it is no surprise to see that idol food emerged as one of the main issues Christians in cities like these had to face. To avoid idol food would be not only socially awkward, but would also pose a severe threat to a Christian's livelihood, or even life itself. Therefore compromise and accommodation were very tempting indeed.

It is thus very probable that the false teaching of the Nicolaitans consisted precisely in their attempt to conform to the pagan cult without giving up faith in the one true God.[113] Perhaps like the Corinthian knowers, they claimed that 'an idol is nothing' and their understanding of Christian freedom allowed them to eat idol food without qualms, thus enabling them to participate in the social and economic life of the society, or even adapt to the syncretistic Roman culture and religion.[114]

Can something more specific be learned about the Nicolaitans? There is considerable scholarly debate about whether they should be regarded as Pauline in tendency, as (Jewish) Gnostics, as a 'hostile Judaizing group', or as related to the Corinthian enthusiasts (or early Christian enthusiasts in general).[115] Such identification would be very helpful if

'Jezebel' teaches the same vices of which 'Balaam' is accused (2.14, 20), they probably belong to the same group.

110. Schüssler Fiorenza (*Revelation*, p. 116) thinks that the false apostles who spread the teaching of the Nicolaitans are migrant missionaries in Ephesus, whereas the Nicolaitans seem to be an integral part of the churches of Thyatira and Pergamum.

111. See Hemer, *Seven Churches*, pp. 33-56, 78-128 (and the abundant secondary literature cited).

112. Though there is no hard evidence to suggest that the imperial cult has already become a widespread problem for Christians in the first century.

113. Schüssler Fiorenza, *Revelation*, p. 117.

114. Cf. W.H.C. Frend, 'The Gnostic Sects and the Roman Empire', *JEH* 5 (1954), pp. 25-37.

115. See Schüssler Fiorenza, *Revelation*, pp. 117-18 and notes, for secondary literature. Schüssler Fiorenza's own belief is that the Nicolaitans were related to the Corinthian enthusiasts whom Paul opposed, as she finds some 'striking parallels' between the two groups (pp. 119-20). Though I agree with Schüssler Fiorenza that

possible. However, in view of the limited data in Revelation 2, precise identification seems difficult and precarious. My own objective is more modest. I want to see what specific information can be extracted from early Christian writers that may shed light on Paul's attitude toward idol food.

Several church fathers mention the Nicolaitans.[116] Irenaeus says that they were followers of Nicolas, one of the seven Hellenists ordained to the diaconate by the apostles (*Adv. Haer.* 1.26.3). They were said to lead lives of unrestrained indulgence, exemplified by eating idol food and practising sexual immorality. He quotes Revelation 2 in denouncing them. In another passage (*Adv. Haer.* 3.11.1), where he condemns the cosmology of Cerinthus, he claims that the error of Cerinthus was also represented 'a long time previously by those called Nicolaitans, who are an offset of that "knowledge" falsely so called'—a clear reference to 1 Tim. 6.20.[117] Thus the Nicolaitans were apparently linked with the opponents in 1 Timothy.

Clement of Alexandria also condemns the licentiousness of the Nicolaitans and explains how they abused the name and perverted the words of Nicolas (*Strom.* 2.20). He relates an interesting story about Nicolas (*Strom.* 3.4) which is later quoted by Eusebius (*Hist. Eccl.* 3.29). When accused of jealousy, Nicolas once brought his attractive wife in the midst of the apostles and said that anyone who wished might have her, because 'the flesh must be treated with contempt' (παραχρήσασθαι τῇ σαρκὶ δεῖ). Nicolas intended this as a statement of his mastery of pleasure and renunciation of desire, but the Nicolaitans took it literalistically (ἁπλῶς καὶ ἀβασανίστως) as a call to practice immorality. Clement exonerates Nicolas by maintaining that he had heard nothing immoral about Nicolas or his children.

Tertullian also denounces the Nicolaitans in a number of places (*Praescr.* 33.10; *Pud.* 19.4; *Adv. Marc.* 1.29.2). But the Nicolaitans are traced to Nicolas only in the (probably) spurious work *Against All Heresies*. In that work, the author denounces their concupiscence and

the teaching of the Nicolaitans was in line with that of Paul's opponents in Corinth, the parallels she cites are neither striking nor really parallel on close examination.

116. Cf. R. Heiligenthal, 'Wer waren die "Nikolaiten"? Ein Beitrag zur Theologiegeschichte des frühen Christentums', *ZNW* 82 (1991), pp. 133-37.

117. The original Greek is not extant. The Latin translation has *vulsio eius quae falso cognominatur scientiae*.

mentions briefly their (Gnostic) cosmology, and quotes Revelation 2 in condemning them (*Adv. Haer.* 1.6).

Hippolytus (*Refut.* 7.24) also traces the Nicolaitans to Nicolas, who departed from true doctrine and became a cause of widespread heresy. That was why John had to reprove his disciples in Revelation 2. He also attributes the denial of the resurrection of the body to the Nicolaitans (*de Resurr.*, frag. 1), thus linking them to Paul's opponents in 1 Corinthians 15 and 2 Tim. 2.18.

In the long recension of the letters of Ignatius, the readers are warned to 'flee...the impure Nicolaitans, falsely so called, who are lovers of pleasure' (*Trall.* 11; cf. *Phld.* 6).[118] Thus it seems that the editor condemns the Nicolaitans but denies that Nicolas was the founder of this school of heretics. The Nicolaitans are also mentioned by later authors but they add little to the above picture.

The testimony of the church fathers concerning Nicolaitans is usually dismissed by scholars as mere guesswork.[119] For example, it is often claimed that Irenaeus himself only knows about the sect from the references in Revelation 2, as his portrait of the Nicolaitans has nothing which might not be inferred from the passage, to which Irenaeus explicitly refers. The reference to Cerinthus and 1 Tim. 6.20 is also dismissed as a speculation prompted by a tradition connecting John's opponents with the 'gnosis falsely so-called'.[120] Likewise, the testimonies of Clement and others are summarily dismissed because of the impression that they are guesswork based on Revelation 2 and the mention of Nicolas in Acts.

It is difficult to be sure whether the fathers are following reliable sources or merely speculating. Though I suspect most scholars may have dismissed the witnesses of the fathers too sweepingly, it is pointless merely to pit my impression against theirs. It is quite conceivable

118. These references to Nicolaitans are missing from the middle recension of the texts, which are regarded as authentic and prior to the long recension by most scholars. See W.R. Schoedel, *Ignatius of Antioch: A Commentary on the Letters of Ignatius of Antioch* (Hermeneia; Philadelphia: Fortress Press, 1985), pp. 3-7, for a summary of scholarly debates regarding issues of authenticity and priority of the three recensions.

119. E.g. Charles, *Revelation*, I, p. 52; Brunt, 'Paul's Attitude', p. 268; A.Y. Collins, 'Insiders and Outsiders in the Book of Revelation and its Social Context', in J. Neusner and E.S. Frerichs (eds.), *'To See Ourselves as Others See Us': Christians, Jews, 'Others' in Late Antiquity* (Chico, CA: Scholars Press, 1985), p. 210.

120. Hemer, *Seven Churches*, p. 88.

that nothing reliable is known about the Nicolaitans beyond what is said in Revelation 2 and Acts 6. But what I have not seen is any convincing reason why the testimonies should be guesswork.

Take the example of Irenaeus. It is not true that his portrait of the Nicolaitans adds nothing not inferable from Revelation and Acts. The connection between the Nicolaitans and Nicolas or Cerinthus is not something deducible from those passages. Moreover, if the spiritual descendants of the Nicolaitans still existed in Irenaeus's time and were still advocating the eating of idol food, it was only reasonable for Irenaeus to rebuke them with a ready-made weapon, namely, Revelation 2. For an analogous situation, Clement of Rome also rebuked the factionalism of the Corinthian Christians in his own time by employing a ready-made weapon, namely, Paul's rebuke of Corinthian Christians for the same sin in the apostle's time (1 Cor. 1–4). Thus Irenaeus's condemnation of the Nicolaitans with reference to Revelation 2 does not imply that the Nicolaitans of his own time had no historical relation to the Nicolaitans in the time of the apocalypse, or that he had no reliable information about the latter, any more than Clement's rebuke of the Corinthian Christians with reference to 1 Corinthians implies that the Corinthian Christians in his time bore no historical relation to their counterpart in Paul's time, or that he knew nothing about the Corinthian church in Paul's time. Of course, it does not prove that Irenaeus is following a reliable tradition. There might be other features in his testimony which indicate its speculative nature; but the fact that he appeals to Revelation 2 for his condemnation of the Nicolaitans is not one of them.

Moreover, whatever the historical relationship the Nicolaitans of Revelation had with the second-century sect of the Nicolaitans,[121] it seems clear that the latter did appeal to Nicolas for their teaching. Such circumstantial details as those mentioned by Clement of Alexandria are unlikely to have been products of pure invention. In particular, if the Nicolaitans (in Clement's time or in his sources) never appealed to Nicolas, why would Clement have felt obliged to defend Nicolas's good name? On the other hand, Hippolytus's refusal to exonerate Nicolas (perhaps suggesting that it is an independent testimony) also

---

121. Harnack maintains that the Nicolaitans of Revelation and the second-century sect of the Nicolaitans are the same continuously existing gnostic sect ('The Sect of the Nicolaitans and Nicolaus, the Deacon in Jerusalem', *JR* 3 [1923], pp. 413-22).

strengthens this impression. In any case, what must be acknowledged is that no other tradition about the Nicolaitans has the support of the church fathers; rightly or wrongly, they point to Nicolas, not Paul or any other figure in early Christianity.

If the second century sect of the Nicolaitans were historically continuous with the Nicolaitans of Revelation, then this point has an important bearing on Paul's attitude toward idol food. For it suggests that— contrary to the opinion of many scholars—the Nicolaitans did not appeal to Paul's teaching in justifying the consumption of idol food. When the Nicolaitans appealed to Nicolas, Clement was concerned to explain how they falsely interpreted Nicolas's teaching. Now if Clement felt obliged to clear the name of a relatively minor figure like Nicolas, whom Hippolytus failed to exonerate, would he not have been much more obliged to defend the good name of Paul, if the Nicolaitans did appeal to the apostle? Surely much more was at stake in the latter case! That Clement did not feel any need to correct any 'false' interpretation of Paul suggests that he was not aware of any such interpretation.

Moreover, Asia Minor, and especially Ephesus, was one of Paul's most important mission fields. There Paul's teaching was surely known and his authority was surpassed by no one except perhaps John. Why did the Nicolaitans not appeal to Paul there, if they found Paul's teaching congenial to their behavior? Their failure to appeal to Paul does not encourage us to believe that Paul was understood to permit eating idol food.

Even if the Nicolaitans of the second century had no historical relation to the Nicolaitans of Revelation, the testimony of Clement and other fathers is still a significant indicator that the second-century Gnostic sect of the Nicolaitans (which were related to many other Gnostic sects) did not appeal to Paul's teaching to justify their eating idol food. In light of the Gnostics' apparent fondness of Paul, this probably means that even at this early stage, any memory or understanding of Paul's condoning of idol food—if it ever existed—was long lost. I will address the Gnostics' attitudes toward idol food below.

It is also interesting to note that, of the three churches troubled by the Nicolaitans, it was the church of Ephesus which rejected their teaching. Apart from the brief mention of Lydia, a native of Thyatira who listened to Paul's preaching in Philippi (Acts 16.14-15), there is no tradition linking Paul with Pergamum or Thyatira. They were not among the many cities named in Acts in which Paul was said to minister or intend to minister. While Acts 19.10 suggests that 'all the residents of Asia heard the word of the Lord' through Paul's ministry, it seems that the impact of Paul (or his disciples) on the churches in these two cities is not very noteworthy compared to Paul's influence on churches in many other cities. Thus the fact that those who advocated eating idol food were tolerated in those two churches in no way implicates Paul.

By contrast, the church at Ephesus, which was praised for rejecting false apostles and hating the works of the Nicolaitans, was the site where Paul had his most intensive and extensive ministry.[122] Already in Acts Paul's impact on Ephesus is strongly emphasized. Not only did Paul minister there more than in any other city, *he also stirred up troubles with his preaching against paganism and idolatry.* As a result of his preaching, Gentile Christians in Ephesus gave up their magical practices (19.11-20). In Ephesus, a great center of trades and pagan cults, where idolatry always sold, the silversmiths who made shrines of Artemis had to fear for their livelihood because of Paul (19.21-41).

About two decades after Revelation was written,[123] Ignatius, who was deeply influenced by Paul, also praised the church in Ephesus for refusing to listen to false teachers who passed by on their way (*Eph.* 9.1; cf. 6.2; 8.1). He charged the church to avoid them as wild beasts (θηρία), a possible reference to Paul's fight with wild beasts (ἐθηριομάχησα) in Ephesus (*Eph.* 7.1; cf. 1 Cor. 15.32). Thus it seems that the church in Ephesus in Ignatius's time was still faithful to Paul's

122. In Hoffmann's opinion, there is 'no reason to believe that Paul encountered any *initial* success whatever in Ephesus, being rejected both by synagogue and by the Gentile population. The "paulinism" of the Ephesus-community must have been marginal from the first, and the *prominence* of Paul a byproduct of the struggle to reclaim his teaching from the heretics' (*Marcion*, p. 270; emphasis original). Thus Hoffmann goes even further than Bauer in his negative assessment of Pauline influence in early Christianity. But insofar as a main factor in his argument is the incorrect notion that Rev. 2 contains polemic against Paul or Paulinism, Hoffmann's assessment is seriously flawed.

123. It is generally believed that Revelation was written around the end of the reign of Domitian (c. 95 CE), though there are scholars who would date it later (or, less often, earlier). See A.Y. Collins, *Crisis and Catharsis: The Power of the Apocalypse* (Philadelphia: Westminster Press, 1984), pp. 54-83 for a thorough defense of the majority view and L.L. Thompson, *The Book of Revelation: Apocalypse and Empire* (Oxford: Oxford University Press, 1990), pp. 13-17, for a brief summary. For a good description of the current state of scholarship on the issue of dating see D.A. deSilva, 'The Social Setting of the Revelation to John: Conflicts Within, Fears Without', *WTJ* 54 (1992), pp. 273-302 (281).

teaching. Since the church in Ephesus in Luke's time was also evidently loyal to Paul, there is little reason to believe that the church in
Ephesus in Revelation 2 (probably temporally situated between Acts
and Ignatius) would have been going against the perceived teaching of
Paul when it rejected the Nicolaitans.

In the apocryphal *Acts of Paul*, Paul's denouncement of idolatry is
again the focus of his activity in Ephesus. 'Paul' tells his hearers to
'repent and believe that there is only one God... For your gods...can
neither take food nor see nor hear, nor even stand'[124] and urges
Artemilla to 'trust in God...that you may no longer serve idols and the
steam of sacrifices but the living God'.[125]

It may also be mentioned that the church at Smyrna, in which idol
food seemed not a problem, was soon to give rise to the great Polycarp,
who admired Paul deeply and certainly knew 1 Corinthians.

It is perhaps no accident that in the testimony of the fathers, if Nicolaitans had anything to do with Paul at all, they were linked to his
opponents. The Balaam incident to which John refers in Revelation 2
also underlies Paul's discussion of idol food in 1 Corinthians 10.[126]
While John may not have consciously followed Paul in his condemnation of those who advocate eating idol food, the correspondence
between Revelation 2 and 1 Corinthians 10 probably reflects a common
Christian tradition shared by both Paul and John. If one may be allowed
to speculate a little further, the 'hidden manna', in contrast to idol food,
which is promised to the victor (Rev. 2.17) may reflect a common tradition underlying Paul's opposing the table of the Lord to the table of
demons in 1 Corinthians 10.[127] We may also note that this contrast

124. *Acts of Paul* 7, in *NTApoc*, II, p. 251.

125. *NTApoc*, II, p. 252.

126. Barrett, 'Things Sacrificed', p. 42, points out this correspondence and suggests that the use of the Balaam motif in Jude 11 and 2 Pet 2.15 also connects these
passages to the issue of idol food. This is difficult to prove or disprove because of
limited data. Brunt dismisses the correspondence between 1 Cor. 10 and Rev. 2 as
'coincidental' ('Paul's Attitude', p. 267 n. 1).

127. The possibility of these links is strengthened if John knew and used Paul's
letter. For possible literary influence of Paul on Revelation, see A.E. Barnett, *Paul
Becomes a Literary Influence* (Chicago: University of Chicago Press, 1941),
pp. 106-107. Barnett lists a dozen passages in Revelation where there is 'a high
degree of probability' of allusion to the Pauline corpus, and dozens more with
reasonable probability of literary indebtedness. For the affinity of vocabulary
between Revelation and Paul's letters see Schüssler Fiorenza, *Revelation*, p. 94.

between the manna and idol food is also found in Aseneth's conversion account, which bears a striking resemblance to 1 Cor. 10.16-17 in its antithesis between the idol's table and the Lord's table.[128]

All in all, Revelation gives us no reason to believe that Paul was understood to condone eating idol food. If he was understood to take a liberal attitude toward idol food, it is strange that the church in Ephesus (where he labored hard) rejected outright the Nicolaitans and their teaching regarding idol food while those churches on which he seemed to have less influence took a more tolerant attitude. It is even stranger that the Nicolaitans appeal to Nicolas rather than Paul in justifying their teaching and that the church fathers apparently made no attempt to defend Paul against the heretics on this issue, whereas there was a felt need to exonerate Nicolas.

5. *6 Ezra*

The prohibition of idol food is mentioned in *6 Ezra* (= 2 Esd. 15–16): 'For behold, the wrath of a great multitude will burn against you and they will carry away captive some of you and make you eat food that is sacrificed to idols. And those are led astray by them will be ridiculed, reproached and mistreated' (16.69-70). The passage suggests that the Christian prohibition of idol food was well known to pagans. If they wanted to be really nasty to God's people, they would force them to eat idol food! So it seems that the majority of Christians would normally have refused to eat idol food. In all probability, such a refusal to eat idol food was generally considered, if only in theory, an outstanding mark of Christian faithfulness.

There is no certainty regarding the dating of *6 Ezra*. Estimates range from the late first century CE to the early third century CE.[129] In any

---

128. After her rejection of idols and idol food, Aseneth received a honeycomb which was 'big and white as snow and full of honey. And that honey was like dew from heaven and its exhalation like breath of life' (*Jos. Asen.* 16.8; cf. Exod. 16.13-14, 31). This comb represents the bread of life and cup of immortality (*Jos. Asen.* 16.16) which are earlier contrasted with the bread of strangulation and cup of insidiousness from the idol's table (8.5). The comb's resemblance to manna is pointed out by many scholars; see Sandelin, *Wisdom*, p. 152 n. 11.

129. W. Schmithals, *The Apocalyptic Movement: Introduction and Interpretation* (trans. J.E. Steely; Nashville: Abingdon Press, 1975), p. 197; H. Duensing and A. de Santos Otero, 'The Fifth and Sixth Books of Esra', in *NTApoc*, II, p. 641 n. 3; B. Metzger, 'The Fourth Book of Ezra', in *OTP*, I, p. 520.

case, in order for the prohibition to be so well known, the practice must have been considerably earlier than the composition of the chapters. The popularity of the book among early Christians also suggests widespread observance of the prohibition, which is also mentioned in early Christian interpolations in *Pseudo-Phocylides* 31 and *Sib. Or.* 2.96.

6. *The Apostolic Fathers*

The fact that Paul's name is not often mentioned and that his letters are not often explicitly cited in the writings of the Apostolic Fathers is sometimes taken as an indication of ignorance of, or even hostility toward, the apostle. But this conclusion is unwarranted when we put such a lack of explicit appeal to Paul in perspective. Surprising as it may seem, no other early Christian figure is mentioned as often as Paul in the writings of the Apostolic Fathers.[130] Peter is mentioned only four times, two of them in conjunction with Paul.[131] James, the brother of Jesus, is not even mentioned. More to the point, Paul's letters are alluded to far more often than other New Testament traditions or texts.[132] It is important to bear these facts in mind as we approach the texts.

a. *The Didache*

This primitive church manual is an important witness to early Christians' attitude to dietary laws and food offered to idols. Drawing heavily on traditional Christian and Jewish material,[133] it is commonly

---

130. See A. Lindemann, 'Paul in the Writings of the Apostolic Fathers', in Babcock (ed.), *Legacies*, pp. 27-28.

131. Lindemann ('Apostolic Fathers', p. 29) also points out that the mention of Peter is brief compared to that of Paul. Of Peter, *1 Clement* mentions only that he 'endured not one or two but many labors' (5.4). In contrast, the portrait of Paul is far more detailed and impressive: 'seven times he was in bonds, he was exiled, he was stoned', he 'preached in the East and in the West' and 'taught righteousness unto the whole world'.

132. Lindemann, 'Apostolic Fathers', p. 28.

133. However, as Klaus Wengst ([ed. and trans.] *Didache [Apostellehre], Barnabasbrief, Zweiter Klemensbrief, Schrift an Diognet* [Schriften des Urchristentums, 2; Munich: Kösel, 1984], pp. 20-32) and Kurt Niederwimmer (*Die Didache* [Kommentar zu den Apostolischen Vätern 1; Göttingen: Vandenhoeck & Ruprecht, 1989], pp. 48-78) have shown, the use of traditional material in the *Didache* is by no means unoriginal and unreflective.

thought of as a Jewish-Christian work which emerged from a Syrian or Palestine (or, somewhat less likely, Egyptian) milieu around the beginning of the second century.[134] While it is possible that the *Didache* did not reach its present form earlier than the mid-second century, it certainly contains a great deal of material which derives from very early forms of (Eastern) Christianity.[135] Thus the dating of the final version is largely irrelevant when one discusses specific items,[136] which might even be almost contemporaneous with Paul's discussion of εἰδω-λόθυτα. The oft-quoted passage about idol food reads (*Did.* 6.3):[137]

Περὶ δὲ τῆς βρώσεως, ὃ δύνασαι, βάστασον· ἀπὸ δὲ τοῦ εἰδωλοθύτου λίαν πρόσεχε, λατρεία γάρ ἐστιν θεῶν νεκρῶν.

Now concerning food: bear what you are able. But keep strictly away from idol food, for that is the worship of dead gods.

It is impossible to know for sure whether the περὶ δὲ τῆς βρώσεως in *Did.* 6.3 has to do with Jewish dietary laws or is rather a recommendation for an ascetic abstention from all meat. Böckenhoff opts for the second interpretation and claims that the first interpretation is long abanandoned.[138] A major factor in his argument is the anti-Judaistic tendency apparent in some of the Apostolic Fathers.[139] However, given

134. The question of the date and provenance of the Didache is a very difficult one. For a classic discussion of the main issues, see J.-P. Audet, *La Didachè: Instructions des Apôtres* (EBib; Paris: J. Gabalda, 1958), pp. 187-210; For a cautious (and almost skeptical) approach, see R.A. Kraft, *Barnabas and the Didache* (AFNTC, 3; New York: Thomas Nelson, 1965), pp. 72-77. For recent discussions see Wengst, *Didache*, pp. 61-63; Niederwimmer, *Didache*, pp. 78-80; and W.R. Schoedel, 'The Apostolic Fathers', in J. Epp and G.W. MacRae (eds.), *The New Testament and its Modern Interpreters* (Philadelphia: Fortress Press, 1989), pp. 457-98 (467-68).

135. Audet, on the basis of internal evidence, places the *Didache* in the first century. In his opinion, the *Didache* is 'contemporaine des premiers écrits évangeliques' (*Didachè*, p. 197).

136. Kraft, *Barnabas*, pp. 76-77.

137. Audet considers 6.3 a later interpolation, but without any textual evidence. Few scholars follow Audet's theory about the composition of the Didache, which is based primarily on internal, not external, evidence; cf. R.M. Grant, *The Apostolic Fathers: An Introduction* (AFNTC, 1; New York: Thomas Nelson, 1964), p. 74.

138. *Speisegesetz*, pp. 22-23. Böckenhoff's claim is surely exaggerated. Karl Six, writing shortly after him, argues for precisely the opposite (*Aposteldekret*, pp. 90-91).

139. Böckenhoff, *Speisegesetz*, pp. 24-27.

the very Jewish character of the book and the lack of polemic against Judaism for the most part,[140] Böckenhoff's argument loses force considerably.

Moreover, if the point of the recommendation is to take as little food as possible, the warning against consumption of εἰδωλόθυτα would seem out of place. For then one would rather expect a warning against gluttony. On the other hand, such a warning makes perfect sense if observance of dietary laws is being urged (in other words, tolerance of laxity in food laws does not extend to idol food). In any case, since much of the ascetic practice in early Christianity arose from Jewish-Christian quarters, observance of Jewish food laws would be at least part of the recommendation in *Did.* 6.3.[141]

The attitude of the *Didache* in regard to food is clearly one of concession and adaptations.[142] The observance of Jewish dietary laws is desirable but by no means obligatory. The bottom line is to stay away from idol food, on which no compromise can be entertained.

It appears that the *Didache* is addressing a community for whom strict observance of all Jewish dietary laws is no longer considered practical by the majority. On the other hand, the author seems to be confident that those Christians, like the Gentile Christians in Acts, would at least be persuaded to adhere to the prohibition of idol food. It is significant that the author, like Luke (and, I would argue, Paul), makes an important distinction between Jewish food laws and the idol food prohibition.

---

140. The main exception is *Did.* 8.1-2, where the author attacks the hypocrites' (i.e. non-Christian Jews') manner of praying and fasting; see Andrew Chester, 'The Parting of the Ways: Eschatology and Messianic Hope', in J.D.G. Dunn (ed.), *Jews and Christians: The Parting of the Ways. AD 70 to 135* (WUNT, 66; Tübingen: J.C.B. Mohr [Paul Siebeck], 1992), p. 278; cf. O. Knoch, 'Die Stellung der Apostolischen Väter zu Israel und zum Judentum: Eine Übersicht', in J. Zmijewski and E. Nellessen (eds.), *Begegnung mit dem Wort: Festschrift für H. Zimmermann* (BBB, 53; Bonn: Heinstein, 1979), pp. 356-59; Wengst, *Didache*, pp. 29-30; Niederwimmer, *Didache*, pp. 165-68.

141. Six, *Aposteldekret*, p. 91; cf. Simon, 'Observance Rituelle', pp. 90-91; Hans Joachim Schoeps, *Theologie und Geschichte des Judenchristentums* (Tübingen: J.C.B. Mohr, 1949), pp. 188-90.

142. Note similar concessions/adaptations in 6.2 and 7.2-3. It is probable that 6.3 represents a softening of older, more conservative material (Kraft, *Barnabas*, pp. 61, 163).

Thus *Did.* 6.3 gives evidence that Christians abstained from idol food at a very early stage. The popular reception of the work by early Christians[143] further suggests that the prohibition was widespread.

That the author urges avoidance of idol food in the context of his recommendation to observe the dietary laws suggests that his focus is on the idol food itself rather than on the setting of eating. There is no hint whatever in the text about temple attendance, and the matter is introduced by περὶ δὲ τῆς βρώσεως. The instruction is clearly concerning the nature of food rather than the context of eating. Therefore, as is often recognized by commentators, the abstention commanded in our text has a more general reference than just consumption in a cultic setting. If only formal consumption of idol food in cultic setting is meant, it would be superfluous to explain that such eating represents λατρεία θεῶν νεκρῶν: given the (conservative) Jewish character of the book, one's mere presence in pagan temples would have already been seen as idolatry.[144]

The relation of the *Didache* to the Pauline letters is difficult to assess. Barnett finds 29 possible literary connections, of which 13 are in 1 Corinthians.[145] In particular, the verbal and thematic analogy between *Did.* 6.3 and statements from 1 Corinthians is remarkable. The introduction of various topics by the formula περὶ δέ (*Did.* 6.3; 7.1; 9.1-3; 11.2) finds parallels in 1 Cor. 7.1, 25; 8.1; 12.1; 16.1, 12.[146] The

---

143. See F.L. Cross, *The Early Christian Fathers* (London: Gerald Duckworth, 1960), pp. 8-9, for evidence of the work's popularity. Cross notes that 'Eusebius and Athanasius even regarded it as on the fringe of the Scriptural canon' (p. 8).

144. Borgen ('How Far?' p. 40 n. 46) refers to Josephus's account of the meeting of Jewish envoys before a council gathered by Augustus in the temple of Apollo in his palace (*War* 2.80-83 and *Ant.* 17.301-303) and suggests that Jews may enter pagan temples. However, the two passages in Josephus are ambiguous. The meeting might have taken place in the palace or the area outside the temple. It is worth noting that in rabbinic writings there is some discussion about whether one can go to places like public bath houses which may have tenuous connection with idolatry, but no discussion on the permissibility of a Jew attending pagan temples. Even bath houses that are 'owned by idols' are forbidden. As Tomson points out, according to some sages, a Jew may not even bow down towards a pagan temple in order to pick up a coin dropped on the ground (*t. 'Abod. Zar.* 6.4-6; *Jewish Law*, pp. 162-63). See §2.7 above.

145. Barnett, *Literary Influence*, pp. 207–212.

146. Barnett (*Literary Influence*, p. 210) notes that such a parallel use of Περὶ δέ does not necessarily imply the *Didache*'s acquaintance with 1 Corinthians, as this same parallel can be observed in the epistle of 'Claudius to the Alexandrians' and

correspondence between the περὶ δὲ τῆς βρώσεως of *Did.* 6.3 on the one hand, and the περὶ τῆς βρώσεως of 1 Cor. 8.4 and περὶ δὲ τῆς εἰδωλοθύτων of 1 Cor. 8.4 on the other, is almost philologically exact. The idea of accommodation expressed in ὃ δύνασαι, βάστασον has some similarity to 1 Cor. 7.7-10, 39-40.[147] The phrase λατρεία θεῶν νεκρῶν may be a variation of the Pauline κοινωνοὺς τῶν δαιμονίων and τραπέζης δαιμονίων (1 Cor. 10.20, 21).

In view of the above, a case for the *Didache's* acquaintance with 1 Corinthians can certainly be made, although the evidence is hardly conclusive. Lindemann points out that there is a near consensus that there is some affinity between the two writings, and, in particular, between Did. 6.3 and 1 Cor. 8–10.[148] The least that can be said is that Paul and the *Didache* are following some common traditions. Nevertheless, direct literary dependence remains difficult to prove. In fact, the opinion of modern scholarship leans against direct acquaintance because the *Didache* on the whole seems untouched by Pauline theology and never mentions the apostle.[149]

In response, it must be noted that the *Didache* does not mention any other apostle either and whether its theology has any contact with Pauline theology depends a lot on how Jewish one allows Paul to be. Since Antioch, where the *Didache* was perhaps written, was the traditional site of the origin of Paul's Gentile mission, the possibility of direct literary dependence cannot be dismissed out of hand. But because of the relative lack of data, I am not willing to push my point further than this. In any case, the fundamental reason for the rejection of idol food is the same for both the *Didache* and Paul: idol food is demonic. Whether this is due to literary dependence or earlier common traditions, it points to Paul's negative attitude toward idol food. Moreover, since the *Didache* draws a distinction between Jewish food laws and the idol food prohibition, it raises somewhat the likelihood that Paul also draws such a distinction. At the very least, it shows that

Claudius's dependence on Paul is out of the question. Still, insofar as such a use of the formula is not found in other early Christian material, the parallel between the *Didache* and 1 Corinthians on this point is striking.

147. Cf. Lindemann, *Paulus*, p. 175.

148. Lindemann, *Paulus*, p. 174 n. 5 for opinions of other scholars.

149. This is also the assessment of Lindemann (*Paulus*, p. 177); cf. Dassmann, *Stachel*, p. 99.

Paul's rejection of Jewish dietary laws is no reason for his rejection of the idol food prohibition.

There is no further mention of εἰδωλόθυτα in the rest of the Apostolic Fathers. However, based on the evidence in Acts 21, Revelation 2, Pliny's letter, Celsus's *True Doctrine*, and *Did.* 6.3, there is no reason to believe that the prohibition of idol food was not upheld by the rest of the Apostolic Fathers and their communities. There are also some indirect indications that the prohibition was widely observed.

b. *Clement of Rome*

In *1 Clement*, which was written probably at the end of the first century to the church in Corinth, the influence of 1 Corinthians is unmistakable.[150] As Lindemann points out, Clement could simply assume that the Corinthian church still possessed (a copy of?) the letter which Paul sent to them four decades earlier.[151] Moreover, the author felt no need to comment on the fact that the Roman church also had a copy of 1 Corinthians, as if it was something surprising.

1 Clement discusses a number of major topics, including resurrection, justification, and ecclesiology, which show clear contacts with Paul's letters.[152] Significantly, there is no trace of any debate about the food laws. In Heil's opinion, this shows how soon the problem of food laws became a non-issue for the Christian churches in the West.[153] This lack of mention of any debate about idol food has some bearing on the view and practice of the Corinthian Christians on this issue. To be sure, *1 Clement* was probably written with the main purpose of rebuking the 'abominable and unholy schism' (1.1) in the church. Yet given the general climate of early Christian prohibition of idol food and the prominence of Paul's discussion of the matter in 1 Corinthians, it does seem unlikely that Clement would have failed to say a single word on the issue, had he been informed that some Corinthians ate or condoned eating idol food.[154] Clement claims that 'we knew well that we were

---

150. See A. Lindemann, *Die Clemensbriefe* (HNT, 17; Tübingen: Mohr Siebeck, 1992); *idem*, 'Apostolic Fathers', pp. 29-36; also L. W. Barnard, 'Clement of Rome and the Persecution of Domitian', *NTS* 10 (1963–64), pp. 251-60.

151. Lindemann, 'Apostolic Fathers', p. 31.

152. Lindemann, 'Apostolic Fathers', p. 32.

153. Heil, *Ablehnung*, p. 281.

154. Probably because of the leading position of the Corinthian church in Acaia, Clement seems to consider the behavior of the Corinthian Christians to have far reaching consequences for others. He complains that their factionalism 'has led

writing to men who are faithful and highly regarded and have diligently searched into the oracles of the teaching of God' (62.3). Except on the issue of the ousting of the presbyters because of jealousy, the author seems to regard the Corinthian church as pretty much in agreement with the church in Rome.[155]

If 1 Corinthians 8–10 allow, even if only in principle, the eating of idol food, then it is somewhat difficult to understand why there is no evidence that some members of the Corinthian church took advantage of Paul's permission. It is very unlikely that everyone misunderstood the apostle. After all, 1 Corinthians was followed by the personal visit to the church by Paul, who would have cleared up any ambiguity of his attitude on this issue. Therefore, unless there was a strong discontinuity in the Corinthians' understanding of Paul's position between the time of the apostle and the time of Clement for some unknown reason, it does not appear that Paul's was understood by the Corinthians to permit the eating of idol food.

c. *Ignatius*

Not long after John's commendation of the church in Ephesus for rejecting the teaching of the Nicolaitans who advocated eating idol food, Ignatius wrote to the same church and praised her for rejecting false teachers (*Eph.* 9.1; cf. 6.2; 8.1). It is thus somewhat likely that Ignatius, like John, would have condemned the eating of idol food. Moreover, if, as many scholars hold, the *Didache* was composed in Syria, then its negative attitude toward idol food would probably reflect that of Ignatius, bishop of Antioch. The likelihood of this is increased by the great popularity of the *Didache* among early Christians.

Since Ignatius's letters are largely concerned with the problem of heterodoxy in the various churches he addresses,[156] his lack of mention of idol food suggests that in his time no major challenge to the idol food prohibition was perceived in those Asia Minor churches, including Ephesus.

Now, Ignatius's theological outlook was strongly influenced by

---

many astray; it has made many despair; it has made many doubt; and it has distressed us all' (46.9). Worst of all, they 'heap blasphemies on the name of the Lord' (47.7).

155. Lindemann, 'Apostolic Fathers', p. 31.

156. R.M. Grant, *Ignatius of Antioch* (AFNTC, 4; New York: Thomas Nelson, 1966), p. 54.

Paul—not surprisingly, given Paul's prominence in Antioch. Moreover, Ignatius frequently alludes to the Pauline letters, the most important of which is 1 Corinthians, with at least forty-six quotations or allusions.[157] This means that Ignatius was definitely aware of Paul's discussion on idol food. Since Ignatius regarded the church of Ephesus, which did not compromise on the issue of idol food, as faithful to Paul's teaching (*Eph.* 7.1; cf. 1 Cor. 15.32), it suggests that Paul was not understood to condone eating idol food.

Ignatius's antagonistic stance against Judaism is also worth noting (*Phld.* 6.1; *Magn.* 8.1, 10.3). It is another indication that the widespread Christian observance of the idol food prohibition was not conditional upon the acceptance of Jewish Christianity.

d. *Polycarp*

According to Irenaeus, Polycarp was personally acquainted with the apostle John (*Adv. Haer.* 3.3.4; cf. Eusebius, *Hist. Eccl.* 5.20.6; Tertullian, *Praesc.* 32). Polycarp was at least in his mid-twenties when John wrote Revelation.[158] And when Ignatius wrote to him around 110 CE, Polycarp had already become bishop of Smyrna, a stronghold of Christian faithfulness according to Revelation 2. Therefore, even if one questions the veracity of Irenaeus's testimony about Polycarp's personal acquaintance with John, it is likely that Polycarp would have adopted the seer's attitude toward idol food. His eventual martyrdom also indicates his uncompromising stance with regard to idolatry.

Even a cursory reading of Polycarp's letter to the Philippians reveals the bishop's deep admiration of Paul.[159] He urges them to read the letters of 'the blessed and glorious Paul' who 'accurately and reliably taught the word concerning the truth' (*Phil.* 3.2). Would Polycarp have held Paul in such a high regard if he had believed that the apostle had condoned eating idol food? Moreover, Polycarp said that he had not

157. Grant, *Ignatius*, p. 57. Lindemann ('Apostolic Fathers', p. 40) points out that 'there was nothing in the situation [of Ignatius] to compel reference to Paul or use of the Pauline epistles or of Pauline theology' and therefore 'the allusions to Paul are all the more remarkable; they demonstrate just how far-reaching the Pauline influence on Ignatius apparently was'.

158. This can be deduced from Polycarp's statement that he had served Christ eighty-six years (*Mart. Pol.* 9.3) at his trial around 155 CE; cf. Cross, *Fathers*, p. 19.

159. Grant notes that his letter seems to reflect all the Pauline epistles except Philemon (*Introduction*, p. 67).

heard of idolatry among the Philippians (11.2-3). He could hardly have written thus if Paul had condoned, or had been understood to condone, eating idol food in Philippi.[160]

e. *Epistle of Barnabas*

A document related to the *Didache*, the *Epistle of Barnabas* also enjoyed great popularity among early Christians.[161] *Barnabas* does not refer to idol food, but it comments extensively on Mosaic food regulations. The author interprets the Mosaic food prohibitions in terms of ethical allegories: 'It is not God's commandment that they [the Israelites] should not eat; rather Moses spoke spiritually' (10.2). For instance, the true meaning of the prohibition against eating pork was that one should not associate with 'men who are like swine' (10.3). We have seen similar ethical interpretations in Pseudo-Aristeas and Philo. But in contrast to them, it seems that *Barnabas* no longer considers literal observance of the dietary laws obligatory or even desirable: 'Moses received three doctrines concerning food and thus spoke of them in the Spirit; but they received them as really referring to food, owing to the lust of their flesh' (10.9).[162]

It is altogether a different question whether *Barnabas* condones the eating of food offered to idols. It may be noted that later representatives of the Alexandrian stream of Christian assessment of the Jewish Scriptures (including Origen), who read and venerated *Barnabas,* still kept the idol food prohibition when they, like *Barnabas,* rejected the literal keeping of the ritual and dietary laws.

Barnabas clearly sees idolatry as something detestable: it puts idolatry as the first item in its list of the way of death (20.1c). It suggests that the Jews lost the covenant 'when they turned to idols' (4.8).

---

160. It is true that Polycarp's main point was to warn the Philippians against covetousness, which would lead to defilement by idolatry. Nevertheless, had they been committing actual idolatry—which was far worse than the metaphorical idolatry of coverteousness, Polycarp could hardly have said that 'I have neither seen nor heard of any such thing among you, in the midst of whom the blessed Paul labored'.

161. See W. Horbury, 'Jewish-Christian Relations in Barnabas and Justin Martyr', in Dunn (ed.), *Jews and Christians*, pp. 315-46 (316).

162. Note that *Barnabas* explicitly sets aside literal circumcision (9.4b-8b). In fact, his interpretation of the food laws is a natural consequence of his understanding of the meaning and significance of circumcision. See Kraft, *Barnabas,* pp. 106-107.

Significantly, it also follows the early Jewish (and Christian) tradition of equating idols with demons (16.7b). Therefore, *Barnabas*'s contempt for idolatry, coupled with its apocalyptic outlook, makes it somewhat unlikely that the author would have condoned the eating of idol sacrifices. However, the evidence is not sufficient to warrant a definite conclusion.

There are no direct citations or clear allusions to the Pauline letters in *Barnabas*.[163] Though the author did make use of traditions in which Pauline ideas are reflected, direct literary influence cannot be proven.[164] Therefore, no confident inference on Paul's attitude toward idol food can be drawn.

e. *Conclusion*
The above examination of the attitude toward idol food in the writings of the Apostolic Fathers indicates the following.

1. The avoidance of idol food was considered a *sine qua non* of the Christian faith at a very early stage. The lack of evidence for any controversy over this issue in Pauline churches suggests that Paul did not or was not understood to condone eating idol food.

2. The fundamental reason for the *Didache*'s rejection of idol food has close affinities to Paul's argument. This points to Paul's negative attitude toward idol food.

---

163. Barnett, *Literary Influence*, pp. 203-207. Although Barnett thinks that the author of *Barnabas* probably knew Paul's writings and he finds a few possible allusions, he concludes that there are 'no instances that require explanation in terms of literary indebtedness to Paul's letters on the part of Barnabas' (p. 207).

164. In earlier generations, *Barnabas* was often regarded, with confidence, as a representative of Pauline theology and even a precursor to Marcion. But the major factor in this assessment is the supposed parallel of *Barnabas*'s anti-Judaism with Paul's criticism of the law. Ever since the more exact text-investigations of the Oxford Committee (*NTAF* project) and A.E. Barnett, a near consensus has been reached among scholars that Paul's literary influence on *Barnabas* was negligible. See Lindemann, *Paulus*, pp. 272-82 for a good survey of recent as well as older scholarly opinions on this issue. Lindemann himself takes a somewhat middle position: 'Unmittelbarer paulinischer Einfluß ist kaum anzunehmen; aber ein von paulinischer Überlieferung berührtes Milieu scheint offenbar im Hintergrund zu stehen' (p. 280). See also R. Hvalvik, *The Struggle for Scripture and Covenant: The Purpose of the Epistle of Barnabas and Jewish–Christian Competition in the Second Century* (WUNT, 2.82; Tübingen: Mohr Siebeck, 1996).

3. With the avoidance of idol food there was a concomitant relaxation or rejection of Jewish dietary practice among the Apostolic Fathers. Thus a distinction was clearly drawn between Jewish food laws and the idol food prohibition. This again substantiates my contention that Paul's rejection of the observance of Jewish food laws for Gentile believers does not imply that he condoned eating idol food.

7. Pagan References to Early Christian Attitudes toward Idol Food

a. Pliny

Pliny's letter to Trajan (*Ep.* 10.96), written somewhere between Amisus and Amastris in northern Pontus around 112 CE, affords us the first non-Christian reference to the avoidance of idol food by early Christians.[165] In this letter Pliny sought clarification of his duty as governor of Bithynia–Pontus in proceedings against Christians. He said he had executed Christians for their 'inflexible obstinacy'. On the other hand, those who denied that they were or had been Christians were released after they had invoked the gods and offered incense and wine to Trajan's image, and 'finally cursed Christ—none of which acts, it is said, those who are really Christians can be forced into performing'.

After interrogating the accused Christians, Pliny admitted that he 'could find nothing worse than a depraved and excessive superstition'. In view of this, he suspended the trial. But there was something else that bothered him (perhaps this was his true concern) and he could not simply let the matter drop. Therefore he sought Trajan's advice, for

> The question seems to me worthy of your consideration, especially in view of the number of persons endangered; for a great many individuals of every age and class, both men and women, are being brought to trial, and this is likely to continue. It is not only the towns, but villages and rural districts too which are infected through contact with this wretched cult. I think though that it is still possible for it to be checked and directed to better ends, for there is no doubt that people have begun to

---

165. Discussion of Pliny's letter to Trajan is extensive. The standard treatment is Sherwin-White, *Commentary*, pp. 690-710; cf. A.N. Sherwin-White (ed.), *Fifty Letters of Pliny* (Oxford: Oxford University Press, 1969), pp. 68-70, 171-78. For a brief treatment and bibliography see Stephen Benko, 'Pagan Criticism of Christianity', *ANRW*, II.23.2, pp. 1055–118. For a lucid description of Pliny's political career, see R.L. Wilken, *The Christians as the Romans Saw Them* (New Haven: Yale University Press, 1984), pp. 1-30.

throng the temples which had been almost entirely deserted for a long time; the sacred rites which had been allowed to lapse are being performed again, and flesh of sacrificial victims is on sale everywhere, though up till recently scarcely anyone could be found to buy it (*Certe satis constat prope iam desolata templa coepisse celebrari, et sacra sollemnia diu intermissa repeti passimque venire <carnem> victimarum, cuius adhuc rarissimus emptor inveniebatur*).[166]

This passage is very significant in that it is one of the earliest pagan witnesses of the Christian observance of the prohibition of idol food. Moreover, it makes clear that idol food sold in markets—*not just idol food in cultic banquets*—was generally avoided by Christians in Bithynia and Pontus in Pliny's time, and indeed before Pliny's time, for Pliny was writing about a phenomenon that had existed for a long time (*diu*). This is consistent with my earlier observation that, by the time Paul wrote 1 Corinthians, the avoidance of idol food had apparently become a standard Christian practice of which even pagans took notice.[167]

Pliny's witness is particularly valuable and trustworthy because of his background and interest. Before he became governor of Pontus and Bithynia, Pliny was appointed an augur, a position he desired and held with pride.[168] Therefore he would have had a great interest in the tradi-

---

166. This is the reading in the standard editions (such as Loeb Classical Library and Oxford Classical Texts series). The choice of *passim* from the Aldine prototype with Körte's addition of *carnem* is generally preferred by scholars. It makes much more sense in the context than the alternative 'fodder for sacrificial animals' in some earlier editions which reflects the reading *pastum victimarum* in Avantius's text. As Sherwin-White (*Commentary*, p. 709) points out, it would make the identity and function of the *emptor* obscure. Moreover, 'there is a rhetorical balance and contrast throughout this sentence, which *passim* preserves—answering to *adhuc rarissimus* as *prope iam* to *diu*—and *pastum* destroys'. Cf. W. Schmid, 'Ein verkannter Ausdruck der Opfersprache in Plinius' Christenbrief' *VC* 7 (1953), pp. 75-78. It is somewhat difficult to think of what, if not sacrificial meat, was the something related to sacrificial animals that Christians refused to buy. In any case, even if sacrificial meat was not specifically meant in the original text, the fact of Christian desertion the temples and refusal to buy something related to sacrificial animals is certainly consistent with, and highly indicative of, an abhorrence of idol food.

167. Cf. the discussion in Chapter 3 on 1 Cor. 10.28-29.

168. When he was congratulated by his friend for the appointment, he compared himself with the great Cicero and noted with pride that he had 'reached the same priesthood and consulship at a much earlier age than [Cicero] did' (*Ep.* 4.8). Cf.

tional religions with their sacrifices and rites, and the disruption caused by Christians would have been more than just a political matter to him.[169] Pliny was also skilled in finance and management. Indeed, a primary reason for Trajan's sending of Pliny to Bithynia-Pontus was that he might inspect the cities and help them solve their financial problems.[170] It is thus no surprise to find Pliny so interested in the impact of Christians on the meat trade. Not unlike the silversmiths in Acts 19,[171] Pliny found the Christians both sacrilegious and bad for business. We can be fairly certain that Pliny's description of the Christian contribution to the recession in the idol food business was largely factual, even if we allow for some exaggeration.

We may also infer that Gentile Christians, not Jewish Christians, were being discussed in Pliny's letter. There is no mention of anything peculiarly Jewish in the letter. Moreover, since Jews always opposed idol food anyway, Jewish Christianity would not have done much additional damage to the market; it required a Gentile Christianity to bring about the slump in idol meat business.

In order for the desertion of the temples with their related business to have had the kind of impact described by Pliny, the Christians would have had to be numerically very strong and not confined to the lower classes. This fits with Pliny's complaint that Christians consisted of people from all ranks and ages.

First-century Bithynia and Pontus are on the outskirts of the sphere of Christian influence. They are not areas known in early Christian tradition for intensive missionary activities to Gentiles.[172] In view of this,

Wilken, *Christians*, pp. 6-7. However, Wilken does not point out the relevance of this appointment to Pliny's concern about the disruption of traditional religions by Christians.

169. Note that in *Ep.* 8.24, the first principle Pliny urged Maximus, the governor of Achaia, to observe in governing was to 'revere their Divine Founders'.

170. Wilken, *Christians*, pp. 7-10. But Wilken does not point out the relevance of this observation to the disruption to the meat trade.

171. S. Benko and J.J. O'Rourke (*Pagan Rome and the Early Christians* [Bloomington: Indiana University Press, 1986], p. 8) observe that the local citizenry who brought charges against the Christians were motivated by the same concerns as those of the Ephesian silversmiths.

172. The only reference to such activities is Eusebius's statement that Peter 'wrote to the Hebrews in the Dispersion of Pontus and Galatia, Cappadocia, Asia, and Bithynia' because he had preached Christ 'to those of the circumcision' in that part of the world (*Hist. Eccl.* 3.4.2-3; cf. 3.1.2). It is clear that Eusebius took 1 Pet.

it would probably have taken at least a few decades for Gentile Christians to have become so numerous, well represented in all classes, and obnoxious that they provoked the local citizenry to bring widespread charges against them. Therefore, it seems safe to assume that the teaching about the avoidance of marketplace idol food must have been current as early as, if not earlier than, 80 CE. This impression is strengthened by the fact that Pliny mention those who had quitted Christianity 'as many as twenty [or twenty-five, depending on whether *quinque* is read] years ago'. This may point to an early spread of the decree, but there is no other hint of the influence of the decree in Pliny's letter (for example, the blood-prohibition is not mentioned). In any case, dependent on the decree or not, the prohibition of idol food seems to have been an integral part of early missionary preaching to Gentiles in that area.

I will explore Pliny's letter a bit further to see if it may shed any light on Paul's attitude toward idol food. It is usually suggested that, in abstaining from marketplace idol meat, Christians in Bithynia and Pontus went much further than what Paul had demanded.[173] However, this observation is solely based on the assumption that Paul permitted the eating of marketplace idol food. Pliny's letter itself gives no evidence which may validate this assumption. On the contrary, insofar as Paul was the apostle to the Gentiles, the behavior of Gentile Christians at such an early stage presumably reflects Paul's teaching on the subject. If Gal. 2.7-9 means what it says, then, at the beginning of the

1.1 at face value and assumed that Peter's audience were Jewish Christians. However, there is now a near consensus that 1 Peter was addressed to a predominantly Gentile Christian audience, as some features of the book seem scarcely intelligible in relation to a Jewish Christian audience (e.g. 4.3-5; cf. 1.14, 18, 2.10). If Peter wrote to Gentile Christians, then Eusebius's testimony about Peter's evangelistic efforts there, being an incorrect inference from 1 Pet 1.1, is of doubtful value. If Peter did preach and write to Jewish Christians, as Eusebius asserted, it is still no evidence for missionary activities to *Gentiles*, except to the extent that Jewish Christians evangelized by Peter might then preach to Gentiles. See J.R. Michaels, *1 Peter* (WBC, 49; Waco, TX: Word Books, 1988), pp. xlix–lv for the issue of audience.

173. Commenting on the significance of Pliny's letter, Six asserts: 'Die Christen waren also bedeutend über das hinausgegangen, was Paulus von ihnen verlangt hatte' (*Aposteldekret*, pp. 87-88). Gooch sees it as 'a stark indication of the extent to which Paul's attempted accommodation of the Corinthians' position was disregarded' by early Christians ('Food and Limits', p. 391 n. 15).

second half of the first century, Gentile Christians were still considered primarily the domain of Paul's apostleship both by Paul himself and by the Jerusalem leaders. Moreover, even though Paul was not the only one who preached to the Gentiles, it seems that other Jewish Christians who cared enough to evangelize Gentiles shared Paul's attitude and practice when they went to Gentile cities. Even Peter 'lived like a Gentile' in Antioch (Gal. 2.14).[174] But we need more evidence.

It is perhaps no accident that Aquila and Marcion, the two earliest and most notable Christian figures from Pontus, were both closely associated with Paul's name. Acts 18.2 mentions that when Paul came to Corinth, he found Aquila and stayed with him. As many commentators point out, Aquila was probably already a Christian then, otherwise Luke would have reported his conversion by Paul. A question that has not been explored, however, is whether Paul knew Aquila before he came to Corinth. εὑρίσκω can bear the sense of either 'find' or 'discover'. That Paul stayed with Aquila right away seems to suggest they were old acquaintances. On the other hand, the use of the indefinite τινα points to the opposite conclusion.

If Aquila knew Paul before he came to Corinth, it would be suggestive of early Pauline influence in Pontus. In any case, he and Priscilla remained staunch friends of the apostle. They endangered their lives for Paul's sake (Rom. 16.3) and accompanied him back to Asia Minor from Corinth (Acts 18.18). They were still in Ephesus when 1 Corinthians was written (1 Cor. 16.19). A church was meeting in their house and Paul was probably again their guest, as a gloss claims.[175] They were the only individuals Paul named when sending greetings to the Corinthian church. They took great interest in the church (cf. 1 Cor. 16.19: ἀσπάζεται ὑμᾶς… ἐν κυρίῳ πολλα) and were presumably aware of their problems and Paul's response. Some time later, they were back in Rome, well known and loved by 'all the churches of the Gentiles' (Rom. 16.3). We do not know if they ever returned to Pontus. In view of their propensity for travel, it is quite possible. Certainly Luke considers Aquila's association with Pontus noteworthy enough

---

174. Thus Peter's possible influence on Gentile Christians there need not have been of an anti-Pauline nature. In fact, those who doubt Petrine authorship of 1 Peter tend to see it as written by a (deutero-)Paulinist because of Pauline features in the book. Cf. Barnett, *Literary Influence*, pp. 51-68, which argues for 1 Peter's literary indebtedness to Paul's letters.

175. D* F G it vg^cl.

that when he explains why Aquila came to Corinth from Italy, he gives an incidental remark about Aquila's native home. The strength of Aquila's association with Pontus in early Christianity can be seen in the fact that his namesake, the translator, was made a native of Pontus!

The case of Marcion is also revealing. I will discuss his attitude toward idol food later. Here I simply note that Marcion was a wealthy shipowner from Sinope of Pontus. He was the son of a bishop.[176] He was already well established in his business, a keen Christian, probably in his forties or fifties, prior to his arrival at Rome some time before 140 CE. While we cannot know for sure whether and to what extent Marcion's theology deviated from 'orthodoxy' before he met Cerdo, there is no reason to doubt that he was already acquainted with Paul's writings before he came to Rome. If Polycarp's letter to the Philippians (c. 125 CE) was written partly as a response to the early spreading of Marcion's teaching, then it would put Pauline influence in Pontus beyond doubt. In any case, since Pliny's letter was written only 20 years or so before Marcion's arrival at Rome, it is highly likely that Paul's teaching was already known in the Pontus region.

According to Acts 16.7, Paul arrived at the border of Bithynia and *intended* (ἐπείραζον) to preach the gospel there but was prevented by the Holy Spirit at that time. R. Jewett, referring to an earlier study by V. Weber, draws attention to the fact that 'the imperfect verb indicates several efforts to travel in that direction'.[177] While an imperfect by itself does not necessarily imply multiple efforts, Weber's understanding is probably correct in this case because the imperfect is embedded in a host of aorists, thus forming a significant contrast. Therefore it seems that the evangelization of Bithynia was part of Paul's mission plan.[178] It

176. As Lüdemann (*Heretics: The Other Side of Early Christianity* [trans. J. Bowden; Louisville, KY: Westminster/John Knox Press, 1996], p. 159) argues, there is no reason to doubt this piece of information as it is not tendentious.

177. R. Jewett, 'Mapping the Route of Paul's Second Missionary Journey' from Dorylaeum to Troas' *TynBul* 48 (1997), pp. 1-22 (5 n. 20); V. Weber, *Des Paulus Reisenrouten bei der zweimaligen Durchquerung Kleinasiens: Neues Licht für die Paulusforschung* (Würzburg: Becker, 1920), p. 33.

178. Here we may note Riesner's (*Frühzeit*, pp. 213-25) interesting suggestion that in Rom. 15.7-24, Paul views his mission as the eschatological fulfilment of the prophetic promise for the ingathering of Gentiles in Isa. 66.18-21. Moreover, the choice of geographical routes in Paul's mission plan was influenced (though not determined) by Isa. 66.19. Riesner argues that in the most probable contemporary Jewish understanding, the nations listed in Isa. 66.19 (Tarshish, Put, Lud, Meshech,

is not known whether he subsequently did go there. This is not impossible, as he did return to preach the gospel to Asia, where he had been formerly 'forbidden by the Holy Spirit to speak the word' (Acts 16.6). On the so-called third missionary journey, Paul traveled from Antioch from Syria to the region of Galatia and Phrygia (18.22-23). Then, on his way to Ephesus, he crossed into τὰ ἀνωτερικὰ μέρη, 'the upper parts' (19.1). Considering the geography, the 'upper parts' would probably be a reference to the region of Pontus, Bithynia, or Mysia.[179] Moreover, after Paul returned to Asia, and particularly during his lengthy ministry in Ephesus (Acts 19–20), he could have taken a short trip to Bithynia (like his trip to Corinth, of which there is no record in Acts). In any case, in view of Paul's prodigious missionary efforts in Asia, it is at least probable that some of Paul's disciples would have carried Paul's teaching to Gentiles in Bithynia and Pontus (cf. Acts 19.10: 'all the residents of Asia heard the word of the Lord, both Jews and Greeks'). The fact that Paul could greet by name so many Christians in a church he had never visited (Rom. 16.1-16) is an eloquent testimony both to the mobility of early Christians and to the extent of Pauline influence in Gentile churches.

Again, it is probably no fluke that the earliest known correspondence to Christians in the region, aside from 1 Peter (whose 'Paulinism' is notable), was written by Dionysius of *Corinth* in the second century. Thus even if the Gentile churches in Bithynia and Pontus were not founded by Paul or his disciples, Pauline teaching on idol food would hardly have been unknown in that province.[180] The question then

Tubal, Javan, and the farthest islands) correspond to Cilicia, Lydia, Mysia, *Bithynia*, Macedonia, and the far West. This would help explain why Paul next speaks about the collection for the Jerusalem saints (Rom. 15.25-28), which might be 'eine materielle Konkretion' of the eschatological offerings of the Gentiles to Jerusalem prophesied in Isa. 66.20 (cf. 60.5). Riesner notes that R.D. Aus ('Paul's Travel Plans to Spain and the "Full Number of the Gentiles" of Rom. XI 25', *NovT* 21 [1979], pp. 232-62) has reached similar conclusions independently.

179. This possibility is noted in passing by D. French, 'Acts and the Roman Roads of Asia Minor', in D.W.J. Gill and C. Gempf (eds.), *The Book of Acts in its Graeco-Roman Setting* (AIIFCS, 2; Grand Rapids: Eerdmans; Carlisle: Paternoster Press, 1994), pp. 49-58 (55).

180. Note that a major conclusion of Lindemann's study on Paul's legacy to early Christianity is that 'es im ehemahls paulinischen Missionsgebiet (Kleinasien und Griechenland) sowie in Rom. eine nahezu geschlossene Paulus-Tradition gegeben zu haben scheint' (Lindemann, *Paulus*, p. 396). If the North Galatian

becomes: if avoiding idol food caused so much trouble, why did Christians in Bithynia and Pontus disregard Paul's advice which would have allowed them to eat?

There are some other details in Pliny's letter which may suggest Pauline influence. Pliny mentioned that the Christians 'sang a hymn antiphonally to Christ as God' (*carmenque Christo quasi deo dicere secum invicem*). This bears a striking resemblance to Paul's exhortation to Christians to sing to one another in singing to Christ as Lord: λαλοῦντες ἑαυτοῖς [ἐν] ψαλμοῖς καὶ ὕμνοις καὶ ᾠδαῖς πνευματικαῖς, ᾄδοντες καὶ ψάλλοντες τῇ καρδίᾳ ὑμῶν τῷ κυρίῳ (Eph. 5.19). In the parallel teaching of Col. 3.16, Christ and God are all but identified. Such a high christology would not be found in much of (post-apostolic) Jewish Christianity unsympathetic to Paul.[181]

Pliny also mentioned that to curse Christ was something true Christians could not be forced to do. Here again is a possible link to Paul. For in the context of denouncing idolatry (1 Cor. 12.2), the apostle to the Gentiles taught that οὐδεὶς ἐν πνεύματι θεοῦ λαλῶν λέγει, Ἀνάθεμα Ἰησοῦς, καὶ οὐδεὶς δύναται εἰπεῖν, Κύριος Ἰησοῦς, εἰ μὴ ἐν πνεύματι ἁγίῳ (1 Cor. 12.3).

It is fair to ask, and to attempt to answer, this question: in view of the lack of (documentation of) intensive Gentile mission in first-century

theory is correct, the likelihood of Pauline influence would be increased, for then Bithynia and Pontus would be closely surrounded by churches founded by Paul. R.E. Brown (*An Introduction to the New Testament* [New York: Doubleday, 1997], p. 476) thinks that the North Galatian Theory is 'still the majority theory', though I think its case is not impressive.

181. We may also note here the interesting proposal of A. Cabaniss, 'The Harrowing of Hell, Psalm 24, and Pliny the Younger: A Note', *VC* 7 (1953), pp. 65-74. On the basis of some remarkable verbal and thematic links between Ps. 24 and Pliny's description of early Christian worship, Cabaniss argues that the *carmen* Pliny described might be (an adaptation of) Ps. 24. Cabaniss also sees a connection between Ps. 24 and two Pauline passages in early Christian liturgy commemorating Christ's victorious conquest of Hades (p. 71). The first passage is 1 Cor. 2.8, where Christ is referred to as 'the Lord of glory'. Cabaniss points out that 'apart from James 2.1...[the phrase] is the only verbal identification of Christ with the Shekinah: it seems to be a very strong reminiscence of the Psalmist's "King of glory" (a phrase which interestingly enough appears nowhere else in the Old Testament)'. The second passage is Col. 2.15 , 'where Christ is said to have displayed [the rulers of darkness] as captives in a public triumphal procession'. In addition to Cabaniss's passages we may also mention 1 Cor. 10.26, where Paul quotes Ps. 24.1: 'the earth is the Lord's and all that is in it'.

Bithynia and Pontus, which early Christian figure would have exerted the greatest influence there? It seems that the Apostle to the Gentiles is our best guess. And this inference is consistent with other supportive evidence in Pliny's letter. It is freely admitted that none of the above considerations, not even their cumulative effect, unmistakably links the avoidance of idol meat by Christians in Bithynia and Pontus to Pauline teaching. But as virtually all available evidence points to Paul, I think a plausible case has been made that the behavior of those Christians is consistent with, and perhaps reflective of, Paul's negative attitude toward idol food.

b. *Lucian*

The satirist Lucian (c. 115–c. 190), in his attacks on charlatans in Asia Minor, provides a very interesting account of a Christian community credulously taken advantage of by the charlatan philosopher Peregrinus (c. 100–65). However, Peregrinus was finally rejected.[182]

> For a time he [Peregrinus] battened himself thus; but then, after he had transgressed in some way even against them—he was seen, I think, eating something that is forbidden them (ὤφθη γάρ τι … ἐσθίων τῶν ἀπορρήτων αὐτοῖς)—they no longer accepted him.

From the above remark it appears that there was a certain kind of food prohibition that was strictly held among the oriental Christians. It is usually taken to be an indirect reference to idol food, but it could also support a number of alternative interpretations. For example, G. Bagnani suggests that Ebionite dietary laws were involved, on the assumption that the Christian community where Peregrinus belonged was of an Essene–Ebionite type.[183] Moreover, we must also reckon with the possibility that Lucian's account is not altogether factual, as his description of Christians is fairly stereotypical,[184] and there are indications of the

---

182. *De morte Peregrini* 16, in *Lucian* (trans. A.M. Harmon; LCL; Cambridge, MA: Harvard University Press; London: Heinemann, 1919), V, p. 19.

183. G. Bagnani, 'Peregrinus Proteus and the Christians', *Historia* 4 (1955), pp. 107-12.

184. They are 'convinced they are immortal, so that they despise death'; they considered one another brothers; they had 'denied the Greek gods'; they worshiped 'that executed Sophist and live according to his laws'. Benko quips that 'everybody who knew Christians probably knew as much about them as [Lucian] mentions ('Pagan Criticism', p. 1095).

confusion of Judaism with Christianity.[185] In particular, scholars have observed that Lucian's description of Peregrinus is reminiscent of the picture of Christian life found in Ignatius's letters, and that Lucian might have parodied the letters themselves and added further Christian traits from his own observations.[186]

In any case, whether or not Lucian's account of the rejection of Peregrinus is stereotypical, it attests to a general prohibition of a certain food, for (1) if the account is factual, then the prohibition must be sacrosanct in the Christian community, or else they would not have rejected Peregrinus (who used to be their hero) for this single transgression, and (2) if the account is stereotypical, then the prohibition must be well-known enough for Lucian to take it as the reason for Peregrinus's rejection. Now, there is no way to be sure that this forbidden food was indeed idol food. But since the community's attitude toward the Greek gods was definitely negative, this interpretation is certainly possible. It is also consistent with other evidence that the idol food prohibition was already widespread by the end of the first century, whereas we have no evidence of widespread observance of Jewish dietary laws. It may also be noted that Lucian spoke of the numerical strength of Christians in Pontus (*Alex.* 25, 38) and was perhaps aware of their attitude towards idol food.[187]

Therefore, Lucian's account gives further indications that the idol food prohibition was generally observed by Christians at an early stage. This again makes it somewhat unlikely that Paul was thought to condone eating it. Unfortunately, due to the non-specificity of Lucian's account, no firm conclusion can be drawn and no further light can be shed on Paul's attitude toward idol food.

c. *Celsus*

Celsus's 'True Doctrine', which was written some time between 177 and 180 CE, represents the first major systematic attack on Christianity. Because Origen quotes copiously from Celsus's treatise, it is possible to reconstruct the main lines of Celsus's argument and even his specific

185. For example, Lucian mentions that Peregrinus 'learned the wondrous lore of the Christians, by associating with their priests and scribes in Palestine'.

186. R.M. Grant, *A Historical Introduction to the New Testament* (New York: Harper & Row, 1963), p. 95.

187. Note that Christians were lumped together with 'atheists'.

words. Celsus's criticism of Christian avoidance of idol food is important because it is not based on hearsay or unsubstantiated charges but
on personal observations and a study of Jewish-Christian literature.[188]

In showing the unreasonable nature of the Christians' avoidance of
the public feasts, Celsus argues: 'If these idols are nothing, what harm
will there be in taking part in the feast?' (*Contra Celsum* 8.24).[189] Then
he focuses on their abstention from idol food:[190]

> If in obedience to the traditions of their fathers they abstain from particu-
> lar sacrificial victims (ἱερείων τινῶν ἀπέχονται), surely they ought to
> abstain from all animal food—such is the view taken by Pythagoras, on
> the premise that he thereby honored the soul and its bodily organs. But
> if, as they say, they abstain to avoid eating together with demons (ὅπως
> μὴ συνεστιῶνται δαίμοσι), I congratulate them on their wisdom,
> because they are slowly coming to understand that they are always
> associating with demons (συνέστιοι δαιμόνων). They take pains to
> avoid this only when they see a sacrificial victim (ἱερεῖον θυόμενον
> βλέπωσιν). But whenever they eat food, and drink wine, and taste fruits,
> and drink even water itself, and breathe even the very air, are they not
> receiving each of these from certain demons, among whom the adminis-
> tration of each of these has been divided? (8.28)

We will not concern ourselves with Origen's response at this juncture.
Rather, we will see what information can be extracted from Celsus's
criticism that may shed light on the attitude of early Christians (and
Paul) toward idol food. It is clear that by Celsus's time, the Christian
avoidance of idol food had become a standard approach which was well
known enough to draw the pagan Celsus's sophisticated attack. In particular, Celsus's criticism reveals that the Christians were abstaining
from idol food 'in obedience to the traditions of their fathers'. This
could only mean that the prohibition of idol food was a long established
practice. This is consistent with what we have seen in 1 Cor. 10.28 as
well as Pliny's letter and Lucian's treatise.

---

188. Benko, 'Pagan Criticism', p. 1101.

189. The quotation is prefaced by ἃ δὲ λέγει [ὁ Κέλσος] τοιαῦτά ἐστιν. This
suggests that Origen is quoting Celsus's words more or less exactly here.

190. The quotation is prefaced by Origen's comment that he is now proceeding
to τὴν ἑξῆς λέξιν of Celsus. Again, this gives the impression that Origen is following a written source and suggests that his quotation of Celsus at this point is probably exact. This impression is strengthened when one notes that Celsus refers to
idol food with a variety of pagan expressions, but not εἰδωλόθυτα, which is the
term Origen himself uses in his refutation of Celsus.

Much more important for my purpose is the fact that Celsus's criticism reveals striking links with Paul's discussion on idol food in 1 Corinthians 8–10. It seems that, following Paul, the Christians whom Celsus criticizes affirm both that idols are nothing (cf. 1 Cor. 8.4) and that eating idol food is eating together with demons (cf. 1 Cor. 10.19-21). The notion of the 'nothingness' of idols is in all probability an essential ingredient of early Christian (and Jewish) missionary preaching. As such it is not exclusive to Pauline teaching. But insofar as this concept finds its mention in the New Testament only in Paul's writings, it is probably Paul who gives the concept its widespread currency among early Christians. Moreover, the argument that eating idol food implies a fellowship with demons (συνεστιῶνται δαίμοσι) is distinctively Pauline. It is not found in any writing before Paul and, as we shall see, every early Christian writer who uses this argument is aware of Paul's discussion on idol food.[191] In fact this argument of Paul is so persuasive and definitive that it becomes *the* Christian argument against eating idol food—and even the basis for the justification of the blood prohibition! No other argument is deemed necessary, not even the argument about the weaker brethren, which is sometimes (but not always) mentioned as a supporting argument. This is strong evidence that the second-century Christian approach to idol food was deeply influenced by Paul. Hence, it is extremely unlikely that Paul was understood to condone eating idol food.

191. Cf. Baur's claim that Paul's arguments concerning the avoidance of tables of demons became the standard early Christian approach (F.C. Baur, *Paul, the Apostle of Jesus Christ, his Life and Work, his Epistles and his Doctrine: A Contribution to a Critical History of Primitive Christianity* (2 vols.; London: Williams & Norgate, 2nd edn, 1873–75), II, p. 140). Of course, Paul's connecting idol food with demons is not completely novel. In the Jewish Scriptures, food sacrificed to idols is considered food sacrificed to the dead or demons. In (later) rabbinic literature, a contrast between the sacrifice of the dead and the table of the Holy One is found. The same contrast can be found in *Joseph and Aseneth*, though I believe the author or redactor of *Joseph and Aseneth* has borrowed the notion from Paul. Origen (*Contra Celsum* 8.31) seems to suggest that this contrast is adduced by Jews and Christians alike. Thus it is entirely possible that Paul had adopted the argument from the Jewish Scriptures or contemporary Jewish sources. But he developed it and gave it a distinctive shape (e.g. in terms of the contrast between *fellowship* with the Lord and *fellowship* with demons; cf. Paul's command to separate from idolators: τῷ τοιούτῳ μηδὲ συνεσθίειν [1 Cor. 5.11]). In any case, the fact is that later writers borrowed this argument from Paul, not from the Jews. They inevitably appealed to *Paul's* formulation.

There is some uncertainty about whether Celsus's attack on the Christian avoidance of idol food has reference only to pagan feasts. While complete certainty is not possible, it seems that in Celsus's first argument (*Contra Celsum* 8.24) the target of his attack is the Christian avoidance of the feasts, and the second argument is concerned with a more general abstention from idol food (8.28).[192] In the first argument, Celsus wants to prove that Christians should join the feasts and believe in the demons, sacrifice to them, and pray to them for the general good of the people. Celsus does not even mention idol food. On the other hand, neither Celsus's second argument nor Origen's reply refers to the feasts. Celsus's comparison of Christian abstention of idol food with Pythagorean vegetarianism seems to presuppose a general setting. He also suggests that even if Christians abstain from idol food, they still cannot avoid contacting demons as they drink water and breathe. He is unlikely to argue thus if Christians have no qualms about eating idol food in a non-cultic setting. He could easily have pointed out that in their private consumption of idol food they would be associating with demons anyway.

Moreover, in his reply to Celsus, Origen compares the Christian abstention from idol food with Jewish abstention from certain foods. Origen also justifies the blood prohibition on the basis that it is demons' food. Thus Origen seems to be thinking of more than just cultic settings when he examines Celsus's argument. Therefore, presumably, Celsus is attacking Christian avoidance of idol food in general, not just in cultic occasions. This is of course consistent with the evidence in Pliny's letter that marketplace idol food was avoided by Christians. It is also consistent with the later witnesses of Clement of Alexandria and Tertullian that Christians avoided market place idol food.

d. *Porphyry*

Porphyry, 'the most learned of philosophers' according to Augustine, was also the most formidable critic early Christians had to face. Never before has a pagan critic claimed so much attention of generations of Christian intellectuals. Almost two hundred years after his attack on

---

192. This distinction is implicit in R.J. Hoffmann's reconstruction of Celsus's *True Doctrine* (*Celsus: On the True Doctrine: A Discourse Against the Christians* [Oxford: Oxford University Press, 1987], pp. 117-18). The way Origen replies to Celsus also seems to presuppose this distinction.

Christianity, Augustine was still wrestling with his arguments. In Wilken's assessment, not only did Porphyry show 'wide learning in history, philosophy, religion, chronography, and literary criticism', he also 'knew the Bible almost as well as [the Christians] knew it themselves'.[193]

A passage quoted by Macarius Magnes probably preserves a fragment of Porphyry's *Contra Christianos*.[194] This passage is very instructive because of its direct and significant interaction with Pauline teaching on idol food in 1 Corinthians 8–10:[195]

> Ἀμέλει τὴν βρῶσιν τῶν ἱεροθύτων ἀπαγορεύων πάλιν ἀδιαφορεῖν περὶ τούτων διδάσκει, λέγων μὴ δεῖν πολυπραγμονεῖν μηδ᾽ ἐξετάζειν, ἀλλ᾽ ἐσθίειν κἄν ἱερόθυτα ᾖ, μόνον ἐάν τις μὴ προείπῃ.

> While [Paul] forbids the eating of sacrificial food, he also teaches that one may treat it as something indifferent. He says that one need not scrupulously inquire, but just eat, even if it might be idol food—except when somebody tells one in advance that it is sacrificial food.

Like modern critics who partition 1 Corinthians 8–10 because of the perceived inconsistency in Paul's arguments, this author quotes seemingly contradictory passages in 1 Corinthians 8–10 to prove his point:

---

193. Wilken, *Christians*, p. 127.

194. Böckenhoff, *Speisegesetz*, pp. 57-58 (following the studies by Wagenmann and Bardenhewer [57 n. 3]). *TLG* also lists the passage as a fragment of Porphyry's work. However, some doubts must be entertained. Wilken (p. 135) points out that while most scholars have assumed that such a work *Contra Christianos* did exist, the title is first mentioned only c. 1000 CE. Moreover, about half of the fragments that Harnack considers as originating from *Contra Christianos* are taken from Macarius's *Apocriticus*, though Macarius himself never says he has excerpted his material from Porphyry. Therefore, the Macarian fragments may not be used to reconstruct Porphyry's work with confidence. For this point, see T.D. Barnes, 'Porphyry against the Christians: Date and the Attribution of Fragments', *JTS* NS 24 (1973), pp. 424-42. For a more positive assessment, see R. Waelkens, *L'Economie, thème, apologétique et principe herméneutique dans l'Apocriticos de Macarios Magnes* (Recueil de Travaux d'Histoire et de Philologie, 6.4; Louvain: University of Louvain Press, 1974). In any case, since Macarius is quoting an earlier work, the passage, if not from Porphyry, is probably not much later than Porphyry.

195. Porphyrius, *Contra Christ.*, in *TLG* 23.32. I attempted a fairly literal translation of this and the following passages in order to bring out the flavor of Porphyry's argument and verbal links to Paul.

[Paul] says: 'What the Gentiles offer, they offer to the devil. Now I do not want you to have fellowship with the devil...' But again he speaks and writes indifferently concerning this food: 'Now we know that an idol is nothing in the world, and that there is no God but one', and shortly after: 'But food does not commend us to God... Buy and eat everything in the market, asking no question for consciousness' sake'.[196]

'Porphyry' concludes that Paul's teaching is confusing: he is like one who lifts up his sword against himself and an outlandish archer whose arrow returns and hits himself.[197]

We need not concern ourselves with Macarius's reply here. What is clear is that we have a third-century attempt to show the contradictory nature of Paul's teaching on idol food. Paul is understood as teaching two things: (1) to eat idol food is to have fellowship with demons; and (2) one might eat food that is possibly idol food, unless someone else informs one of the nature of the food. This dual attitude is precisely what we have shown to be Paul's true position vis-à-vis idol food: avoid idol food if and only if one knows it is such! But such an attitude is not necessarily contradictory unless Paul believes that the defilement is in the food itself.[198]

e. *Imperial Edicts of Persecution*
Ehrhardt points out that, already in the first general persecution of Christians under Decius (249–251 CE), special provision for the compulsory consumption of idol food was made.[199] Similar provisions also appeared in other imperial edicts of persecution of Christians and the martyrs' refusal to eat idol food was narrated in many martyrological

196. Porphyrius, *Contra Christ.*

197. Porphyrius, *Contra Christ.*

198. Thus Böckenhoff, *Speisegesetz*, p. 58: 'Man muß gestehen, daß seine [Porphyry's] Ausführung allerdings das beweist, daß man die κοινωνία τῶν δαιμονίων, von welcher der Apostel spricht, nicht im Sinne des Origenes usw. und des Porphyrius selbst als eine physische Wirkung jedweden Genusses von Opferfleish auffassen kann, ohne den Apostel mit sich selbst in Widerspruch zu setzen'. But I would argue that not even Origen believes that the defilement is in the food itself (see my discussion of Origen's view in §15).

199. *Framework*, p. 286. Cf. Justin's claim that true Christians 'would rather endure every torture and pain, even death itself, than worship idols, or eat idol food' (*Dial.* 34.8).

accounts.[200] There is no need to recite the witnesses here. Such provisions for the stuffing of idol food only made sense if the Christians' abstention from idol food was fundamental and widespread. This is thus a clear confirmation of the picture we have obtained from earlier pagan sources.

It is also interesting to note that, in 314 CE, shortly after the edict of Milan, a group of bishops assembled in Ancyra to discuss the re-organization of the church after a decade of persecution. They made the following decision, recorded in the third canon of that synod, concerning the compulsory stuffing of idol food:[201]

> If people...have been forced...*by having been made to swallow some food*, yet constantly protesting that they were Christians, and have always shown their grief at what had happened,...those people being without sin shall not be turned away from Communion.

This canon really shows how severely the prohibition of idol food was held, for it appears that there was some question whether those who were forced to swallow idol food could be re-admitted to the church. It is deemed necessary to explain that being forced to eat idol food does not constitute a sinful consumption of idol food! Incidentally, it also shows that the Christians avoided idol food not only in cultic settings, and that any consumption of idol food was forbidden, except when it was forced upon one while one was protesting. It is also clear that those bishops did not take a magical view of idol food: those Christians who swallowed idol food were *without sin* provided they protested.

f. *Conclusion*

The above examination of pagan sources touching on early Christians' attitude toward idol food reveals the following.

1. Idol food was generally prohibited among Christians at a very early stage. It is possible that Paul's teaching contributed to this early and widespread avoidance.

2. Those early Christians who avoided idol food did so not only in cultic settings, but in all contexts, including the markets.

3. There is no evidence that early Christians' avoidance of idol food had anything to do with Jewish dietary practice. This

---

200. Ehrhardt, *Framework*, pp. 286-88.
201. Cited in Ehrhardt, *Framework*, pp. 289-90.

substantiates my contention that Paul's rejection of Jewish food laws does not imply that he condoned eating idol food.

4.   Paul's argument against eating idol food was known even to pagan critics. This suggests that early Christians might have been deeply influenced by Paul's teaching in their avoidance of idol food.

8. *The Apologists*

a. *Aristides*

Aristides' *Apology* was written either at the end of Hadrian's reign (117–138 CE) or in the first years of Antoninus Pius (138–161 CE).[202] In it Aristides the philosopher-apologist set forth the case for monotheism and Christian morality before the emperor.[203] In chapter 15, arguably the most important part of the *Apology*, Christian customs are described: 'They do not worship idols (made) in the image of man; and whatever they would not that others should do unto them, they do not to others; and of the food which is consecrated to idols they do not eat, for they are pure' (15.2).[204]

The ease with which Aristides refers to the idol food prohibition is indicative of its widespread currency among Christians in the first half of the second century. Furthermore, it appears that the avoidance of idol food, described after the mention of the negative golden rule, was of a very general kind and not limited to cultic settings, for Aristides

202. Cf. R.F. Grant, *Greek Apologists of the Second Century* (Philadelphia: Westminster Press, 1988), pp. 36-39, 45; Cross, *Fathers*, pp. 45-47.

203. It is of course very unlikely that Pius would be expected to read the work. More probably, the work is written for Christians to bolster self-definition under the guise of an apologia presented to the emperor. Note that Tertullian, speaking of Christian apologetical literature, says, 'to which [literature] no one comes for guidance unless he is already a Christian' (*De Test. Animae* 1).

204. Syriac version. The references to idol food and the worship of idols are lacking in the Greek version as preserved in the eighth century work *Barlaam and Josaphat*. However, the Greek version is an abbreviated text adapted to the circumstances of an Indian court and there is a clear tendency towards simplifying the descriptions of Christian customs. Therefore, the references to Christian refusal to be involved in idolatry most probably belong to the original text. That such references are not the result of later interpolation is confirmed by the fact that other items of the apostolic decree are not mentioned here.

had already said that Christians did not participate in worship of idols.[205]

Aristides also makes it clear that the idol food prohibition has nothing to do with Jewish dietary laws or ascetic practices, for he claims that the Jews 'erred from true knowledge' and that they are not rendering their service to God 'when they celebrate Sabbaths, new moons, Passover, *fasting*, circumcision, and *the purification of meats*' (14.3). Since Aristides does not mention the Jews' refusal to eat idol food, he probably does not consider such a refusal something peculiarly Jewish.

Again, it is difficult to be certain whether Aristides knew Paul's writings. Barnett thinks that 'the resemblance in idea and language is sufficiently striking to make literary reminiscence possible'.[206] In particular, strong similarities can be found between Aristides' polemics against idolatry and Paul's condemnation of idolatry in Romans 1. Nevertheless, literary dependence is difficult to prove.

b. *Justin*

Whether Justin's *Dialogue* is an authentic record of his meeting with Trypho or purely a literary creation, it is generally considered to reflect genuine contact with Jews. Like *Barnabas*, Justin rejects the validity of Jewish laws for Christians. But unlike *Barnabas*, Justin is willing to see a temporal function of the laws for the Jews prior to Jesus' coming. He even suggests that Christians who, 'through weakmindedness', continue to keep the Mosaic laws will be saved, as long as they do not insist on other Christians doing the same as a condition for salvation (*Dial.* 47). This tolerant attitude is remarkable and can be compared with Paul's statements in Romans 14. Yet Justin condemns the eating of εἰδωλόθυτα. Evidently, he does not view the idol food prohibition as belonging to the category of Jewish dietary laws.

Justin's contempt for idolatry is unmistakable. He holds that all the nations who practiced idolatry—apparently above all other crimes that they might have committed—deserved God's curse (*Dial.* 95.1). He boasts that 'Gentiles who know God, the Creator of the world, through the crucified Jesus, would rather endure every torture and pain, even death itself, than worship idols, or eat idol food (περὶ τοῦ μήτε εἰδ-

---

205. Böckenhoff, *Speisegesetz*, pp. 33-34.

206. Barnett, *Literary Influence*, pp. 219-21. But Barnett is unwilling to commit himself to certain literary dependence. Lindemann, *Paulus*, pp. 350-52 and Dassmann, *Stachel*, p. 259 are similarly uncommitted.

ωλαλητρῆσαι μήτε εἰδωλόθυτα φαγεῖν)' (*Dial.* 34.8). Trypho's response to Justin's claim and Justin's subsequent rejoinder are very significant (*Dial.* 35):

> At this point, Trypho interrupted me by saying, 'I know that there are many who profess their faith in Jesus and are considered to be Christians, yet they claim there is no harm in their eating idol food (ἐσθίειν τὰ εἰδωλόθυτα καὶ μηδὲν ἐκ τούτου βλάπτεσθαι λέγειν)'.

> 'The fact that there are such men', I replied, 'who pretend to be Christians and admit the crucified Jesus as their Lord and Christ, yet profess not His doctrines, but those of the spirits of error, only tends to make us adherents of the true and pure Christian doctrine more ardent in our faith and more firm in the hope He announced to us ... we see events actually taking place which He predicted would happened in His name. Indeed, He foretold: "Many shall come in My name, clothed outwardly in sheep's clothing...' And: 'There shall be schisms and heresies' [1 Cor. 11.19]...

> 'My friends, there were, and still are, many men who, in the name of Jesus, come and teach others atheistic and blasphemous doctrines and actions; we call them by the name of the originator of each false doctrine... Some of these heretics are called Marcionites, some Valentinians, some Basilidians, and some Saturnilians, and others by still other names'.

A number of important observations may be made. First, for Justin and the type of Christianity that he represented, refusal to eat εἰδωλόθυτα was a prominent mark of Christian courage and faithfulness. It was also a touchstone of orthodoxy to distinguish true Christians from false prophets.

Secondly, Justin implies that Christians who refused to worship idols or eat idol food might be persecuted. Justin's language indicates that such persecutions were probably official. This means that the practice of refusing to eat idol food was very widespread, well known enough even to the Christians' persecutors, who had to force the consumption of idol food upon the Christians. This picture agrees with what we have established from the examination of references to idol food by pagan authors.

Thirdly, while Trypho's objection was admittedly *ad hominem*, it nevertheless suggests an essential point of agreement between Trypho and Justin: both did not approve of the eating of εἰδωλόθυτα. Whatever may be said about the historicity of the figure of Trypho, it seems that, according to Justin's perception, a typical Jew would not have been disposed to eating idol food. This supports my contention that nothing in Paul's Jewish background would have encouraged him to eat idol food.

Fourthly, instead of denying Trypho's charge that many professing Christians ate food offered to idols, Justin concedes the correctness of his opponent's observation but claims that such a phenomenon only confirms the faith of true Christians. So it seems that the number of professing Christians who ate idol food was noticeable. Of course, Justin considered those people not true Christians but false prophets. Justin's rebuttal somewhat begs the question. Much more important is his earlier remark that true Christians refused to eat idol food even under all sorts of torture and on the pain of death. Therefore it seems that many of those who ate did so only under coercion. Presumably, most Christians would not normally eat idol food.

Fifthly, in asserting that Jesus had already foretold the coming of false prophets, Justin specifically names some of them: Marcionites, Valentinians, Basilidians, Saturnilians, and 'others by still other names'. Thus it appears that these groups (mostly Gnostic) advocated eating idol food, as is usually concluded by scholars. However, while Justin certainly implicated those groups with such a teaching, he fell short of saying this explicitly. I shall discuss this point more fully after I deal with the comments of other heresiologists on the attitude of Marcion and the Gnostics to idol food.

Justin's knowledge of Paul is one of the most controversial items in the issue of *Paulusrezeption* in early Christianity and an untold amount of scholarly energy has been expended on the subject.[207] It is well

---

207. Lindemann, *Paulus*, pp. 353-67 lists and discusses, with extensive biblography, four major options: (1) Justin knew nothing of the Pauline tradition; (2) Justin knew Paul thoroughly, but deliberately suppressed this knowledge because of his battle with Marcion; (3) Justin did not mention Paul because of his regard for his Jewish Christian interlocutors; and (4) Justin, contrary to first impressions, was in fact an advocate of Pauline theology, though for tactical reasons he did not mention Paul by name. After examining a host of probable Pauline parallels in Justin, Lindemann himself becomes certain that Justin knew Paul's letter. Lindemann then suggests an alternative reason for the non-mention of Paul: 'Daß er Paulus dennoch nicht erwähnt, ist Folge seines theologischen Prinzips: Die Wahrheit des Christentums wird aus dem Alten Testament erwiesen; von Bedeutung sind daneben nur noch Worte Jesu, wie sie in den ἀπομνημονεύματα τῶν ἀποστόλων, d.h. den Evangelien aufgezeichnet sind' (p. 366); cf. Barnett, *Literary Influence*, pp. 231-47; Dassmann, *Stachel*, pp. 244-48. I do not find Lindemann's reasoning persuasive: an

beyond the scope of this work to go into it in any detail. Suffice it to say that, in view of the extensive contacts with Pauline teaching in Justin's writings, there is little doubt that Justin knew and used Paul's letters. It is scarcely conceivable that Justin, who spent a considerable time in Rome, should have been ignorant of Paul, who wrote to the Roman church and whose letters were regarded as authoritative already by the time of Clement of Rome. The only serious question is why Justin nowhere mentions the apostle by name.

The non-mention of Paul is sometimes seen as an indication of Justin's anti-Paulinism.[208] This is probably incorrect, for there would have been plenty of opportunity for Justin to raise objections against Paul, had it been his intention to do so.[209] On the other hand, Justin's failure to defend Paul against heretics who claimed the apostle as their own makes our apologist an unlikely candidate for a Pauline advocate. It is perhaps more likely that, in his battle with Marcion, Justin was or became somewhat ambivalent towards the apostle. But it is difficult to be certain.

In any case, that Justin was presumably familiar with Paul's teaching has a very important implication for our investigation of Paul's attitude toward idol food. Since Justin saw the issue of idol food as a fairly black and white issue, his silence was not likely due to the fact that he was disturbed by Paul's (ambiguous) stance. Had Justin thought that Paul tolerated eating idol food, he would hardly have kept an ambivalent or neutral attitude towards the apostle. Given his insistence on the idol food prohibition as a touchstone of orthodoxy and his claim that only heretical groups treated idol food as something indifferent, he would likely have denounced Paul as a heretic. This observation takes on additional significance as Justin might have had 1 Corinthians 8–10 in the back of his mind when he answered Trypho's charge that some Christians ate idol food.[210] He refers not only to Jesus' warning that false prophets would come in sheep's clothing but also to the statement

emphasis on the dominical traditions may account for relatively infrequent mentions of Paul, but is inadequate to account for a total lack of mention of Paul.

208. See Lüdemann, *Antipaulinismus*, p. 209 n. 18 for representative works arguing for or against such a position.

209. A. von Harnack, *Judentum und Judenchristentum in Justins Dialog mit Trypho* (Leipzig: J.C. Hinrichs, 1913), p. 51; Lüdemann, *Antipaulinismus*, p. 209 n. 19.

210. Lindemann, *Paulus*, p. 360.

that 'there shall be schisms and heresies'—a possible allusion to 1 Cor. 11.19—to support his argument that such a false doctrine had been foretold. Besides the key terms σχίσματα καὶ αἱρέσεις, the mention of ψευδαπόστολοι in *Dial.* 35.3 betray contacts with the Corinthian letters (2 Cor. 11.13).[211] One may also note that in *Apol.* 14.5, Justin makes the lack of sophistic eloquence a virtue, almost paraphrasing 1 Cor. 1.18-25.[212] Thus it seems reasonable to conclude that Justin was probably not aware of any construe of Paul's position which permitted eating idol food as something indifferent. Nevertheless, since we are not sure why Justin did not mention Paul in any of his writings, his failure to mention Paul in *Dialogue* 35 must not be pressed too hard.

c. *Letter to Diognetus*
This Christian apology is usually printed with the Apostolic Fathers, but it belongs rather to the period of the apologists or later.[213] The author issues a scathing attack on Jewish food laws. The Jews' 'scruples about food', the author asserts, 'are ridiculous and unworthy of any argument. For how can it be anything but unlawful to receive some of the things created by God for the use of man as if well created, and to reject others as if useless and superfluous?' (4.1-2). Such liberal attitude regarding the food laws has affinity with, but go somewhat beyond, Romans 14 (cf. Col. 2.16 and 1 Tim. 4.3-5). This is not surprising, as there is no question that Paul's letters are known to the author of *Diognetus*, even if the apostle is not mentioned by name.[214] Whether through explicit citations or paraphrasing, the letter clearly shows the influence of Paul's writings.[215]

---

211. See A. le Boulluec, 'Remarques à propos du problème de 1 Cor. 11, 19 et du "logion" de Justin, Dialogue 35', *Studia Patristica* 12 (1975), pp. 328-31 for arguments that there is a clear reference to 1 Cor. 11.19 in *Dial.* 35.

212. N. Hyldahl, 'Paul and Hellenistic Judaism', in P. Borgen and S. Giversen (eds.), *The New Testament and Hellenistic Judaism* (Nashville: Abingdon Press, 1995), pp. 204-16 (13).

213. Grant, following H.-I. Marrou, thinks that the work should be ascribed to Pantaenus (*Greek Apologists*, p. 178). For a fine survey of the arguments for various datings, see Wengst, *Didache*, pp. 305-309; Wengst himself places *Diognetus* at the end of the second century or later.

214. Dassmann, *Stachel*, pp. 254-59; cf. Lindemann, *Paulus*, pp. 343-50. Dassmann points out that, aside from the addressee, the letter mentions nobody by name, not even Christ or Jesus (p. 258).

215. Thus Dassmann, *Stachel*, p. 255: 'nicht allein die Fülle paulinischer

Would the author of the letter have objected to eating idol food? It is difficult to be certain. While *Diognetus* ridicules Jewish dietary laws, there is no ridicule of the abstention from εἰδωλόθυτα in the letter. Further, there is a strong denunciation of pagan idolatry. To be sure, the author does mention that Christians lived in 'Greek and barbarian cities' and followed 'the local customs, both in clothing and in food and in the rest of life' (5.4). However, the import of the statement is that Christians—unlike Jews—do not set themselves apart from pagans in social customs; it does not necessarily mean that idol food was consumed by Christians. As we will see below, Tertullian can say very similar things of Christians and yet condemns the eating of idol food.

9. *Irenaeus*

Irenaeus's use of Pauline letters, especially 1 Corinthians, is extensive and unmistakable.[216] In particular, there are multiple references to 1 Corinthians 8–10 in *Adversus Haereses*.[217] More importantly, as Norris observes, 1 Cor. 8.4-6 'seems to have dictated...the basic out-

---

Wendungen, die der Verfasser zitierend oder paraphrasierend in die eigene Darstellung einfließen läßt, sondern ein Eingehen auf zentrale Anliegen der paulinisher Theologie'.

216. Scholarly assessment of Irenaeus as an interpreter of Paul has been, until recently, largely negative. R. A. Norris, Jr ('Irenaeus' Use of Paul in His Polemic Against the Gnostics', in Babcock [ed.], *Legacies*, p. 79) notes that 'since the influential 1889 monograph of...Werner...a great deal of stress has been laid on his role as a legitimizer or domesticator of the Pauline and deutero-Pauline letters at a time when...their principal advocates and exponents were followers of Marcion or of Valentinus'. Happily, a number of recent studies provide a much needed corrective to such a negative assessment of Irenaeus's use of Paul. See Norris, 'Irenaeus' Use of Paul', pp. 79-98; M.J. Olson, *Irenaeus, the Valentinian Gnostics, and the Kingdom of God (A.H. Book V): The Debate about 1 Corinthians 15.50* (Lewiston, NY: Mellen Biblical Press, 1992); Dassmann, *Stachel*, pp. 292-315; D.L. Balás, 'The Use and Interpretation of Paul in Irenaeus's Five Books *Adversus Haereses*', *Second Century* 9 (1992), pp. 27-39; R. Noormann, *Irenäus als Paulusinterpret* (WUNT, 2.66; Tübingen: Mohr Siebeck, 1994). Norris ('Irenaeus' Use of Paul', p. 79) argues that 'Irenaeus, as he cites, alludes to, and muses over Paul's writings, is not merely engaged, as Werner thought, in an unwelcome apologetic task that circumstances have more or less forced upon him'. Olson (*Irenaeus*, p. 62) concurs: 'Werner's case crumbles beneath the accumulated weight of hundred upon hundreds of Pauline citations'.

217. Olson, *Irenaeus*, p. 137.

line of Book 3 from the sixth chapter on'.[218] In *Adv. Haer.* 3.6.5 he points out that while Paul acknowledged the existence of 'so-called gods', he referred to these pagan idols as 'no gods' in contrast with the one true God.[219] Yet for Irenaeus, the nothingness of those gods was no reason for liberty in the matter idol food. He could scarcely have understood Paul to condone eating such food.

On the other hand, Irenaeus mentions heretical groups of Christians who had no qualms about eating idol food. They were all of Gnostic persuasion: Valentinians, Saturnilians, Basilidians, Carpocratians, and Nicolaitans. *Adv. Haer.* 1.6.3 is a very revealing passage.

Διὸ δὴ καὶ τὰ ἀπειρημένα πάντα ἀδεῶς οἱ τελειότατοι πράττουσι αὐτῶν, περὶ ὧν αἱ γραφαὶ διαβεβαιοῦνται, τοὺς ποιοῦντας αὐτά βασιλείαν θεοῦ μὴ κληρονομήσειν. Καὶ γὰρ εἰδωλόθυτα διαφόρως [ἀδιαφόρως] ἐσθίουσι, μηδὲ [μηδὲν] μολύνεσθαι ὑπ' αὐτῶν ἡγούμενοι[220]

Wherefore also it comes to pass, that the 'most perfect' among them [Valentinians] indulge themselves without fear in all those kinds of forbidden deeds of which the Scriptures [αἱ γραφαὶ] assure us that 'they who do such things shall not inherit the Kingdom of God' [Gal. 5.21; 1 Cor. 6.9-10]. For they eat idol food with indifference, thinking that they are not in any way defiled thereby.[221]

The accusation of eating idol food is then followed by denunciations of attendance at pagan feasts and spectacles, greed, and sexual immorality. It is significant that Irenaeus puts the eating of idol food at the top of the rather lengthy list of forbidden deeds.[222]

Similarly, Irenaeus accuses Basilides that 'he attaches no importance to idol food...and makes use of them without any hesitation; he holds

218. Norris, 'Irenaeus' Use of Paul', p. 85.

219. Olson, *Irenaeus*, p. 87.

220. The quotation of this passage of Irenaeus in Epiphanius, *Panar.* 29 (8,6) [*TLG, Adv. Haer.* 25.417.19-22] corresponds exactly to the emended text.

221. Cf. *Adv. Haer.* 2.14.5: 'Again, their opinion as to the indifference of meats and other actions, and as to their thinking that, from the nobility of their nature, they can in no degree at all contract pollution, whatever they eat or perform, they have derived it from the Cynics, since they do in fact belong to the same society as do these'.

222. Incidentally, Irenaeus's separate mention of the heretics' attending a 'heathen festival celebrated in honour of the idols' may suggest that there is a distinction between the consumption of idol food and attendance at idol feasts; the former may take place apart from the latter. Both are condemned.

also...the practice of every kind of lust a matter of perfect indifference' (*Adv. Haer.* 1.24.5).[223] Examples of other vices then follow. Again, the eating of idol food is put at the head of the list of vices.

Irenaeus apparently thinks that the Nicolaitans' practice of fornication and eating εἰδωλόθυτα is enough to prove that they 'lead lives of unrestrained indulgence' (*Adv. Haer.* 1.26.3). He does not deem it necessary to furnish other examples of their vices. Again, in his description of the followers of Basilides and Carpocrates, fornication and eating idol food epitomize their vices (*Adv. Haer.* 1.28.2).

It is fairly evident that Irenaeus regarded the Gnostics' practice of eating idol food as a strong selling point in his polemics against them, for it showed to what evils their teaching would lead. Moreover, the fact that Irenaeus could, without any argument, denounce the practice as a self-evident wickedness *par excellence* suggests that his readers were unlikely to have had any sympathy with those who ate idol food.

The vigorous apologetic of Irenaeus (and other heresiologists) indicates that the prohibition of idol food was violated by Gnostic groups. Is it possible that Paul's attitude, for the topic of εἰδωλόθυτα at least, fits better with that of, say, some Valentinian Christians?[224]

It seems that the answer is No. While Irenaeus's statements show unmistakably that some Gnostics ate idol food freely, it does not necessarily prove that they specifically appealed to Paul to justify their action. If one believes Irenaeus's witness on the Gnostics' attitude toward idol food, one will also have to believe that those Gnostics who ate idol food were libertines in regard to sexual morality. After all, Irenaeus accused the Gnostics, in the same breath, of eating idol food and committing sexual immorality, the latter being a practice which Paul clearly detested. This makes those Gnostics who ate idol food more like the 'gnostics' in Corinth—namely, Paul's opponents—than Paul himself.

---

223. *Contemnere autem et idolothyta, et nihil arbitrari, sed sine aliqua trepida-tionne uti eis: habere autem et reliquarum operationum usum indifferentem et uni-versae libidnis.* Eusebius learns from Agrippa Castor's refutation of Basilides that the heresiarch 'taught that there was no objection to eating idol food, or to cheerfully forswearing the Faith in times of persecution' (*Hist. Eccl.* 4.7.7).

224. In Brunt's opinion, the Valentinian position on idol food came closer to Paul than the mainstream did ('Paul's Attitude', p. 275; cf. *idem*, 'Rejected', pp. 120-21).

Since Irenaeus was obviously well versed in Paul's letters, his condemnation of the practice of eating idol food is a very important indication of his understanding of Paul's attitude. If Irenaeus believed that Paul condoned eating idol food, it would have been impossible for him to have treated Paul's letters as γραφή[225] and to have used them to denounce the practice. His statements in *Adv. Haer.* 1.6.3 rather imply that Paul forbade eating idol food. However, how the Gnostics understood Paul is a totally different matter.

There is an evident fondness for Paul among the Gnostics, whether or not we accept Dassmann's opinion that John rather than Paul was the favorite of the Gnostic interpreters.[226] In particular, the massive attention to Pauline texts on the part of Valentinian Gnostic exegetes is indisputable.[227] Therefore it seems a priori likely that the Gnostics would have appealed to 1 Corinthians 8 to support their eating of idol food, whether or not such an appeal agreed with Paul's intention. However, other considerations lead to a conclusion that go against this intuition.

Throughout *Adversus haereses*, Irenaeus details the various ways in which the Gnostics subvert the natural meaning of Pauline texts.[228] Moreover, on various occasions in Book 1 of the *Adversus haereses*, Irenaeus indicates the drift of Valentinian exegeses of Pauline passages (mostly from 1 Corinthians!) for his readers.[229] If the traditional view is correct, the Gnostics could easily have appealed to 1 Cor. 8.1 ('we all have knowledge'), 8.4 ('an idol is nothing'), 10.23 ('all things are lawful'), or 10.25, 27 ('eat anything...without asking questions for consciousness' sake') to justify their action. But there is no indication that they did. To be sure, Elaine H. Pagels claims that 'the Valentinians cite this passage [1 Cor. 8.7] to show that those who *do* have gnosis need not hesitate to eat meat sacrificed to idols, "since they cannot incur defilement"'.[230] However, she does not substantiate her claim with any

---

225. For a good discussion on Irenaeus's attitude to the status of Paul's letter, see Dassmann, *Stachel*, pp. 298-305.

226. *Stachel*, p. 199.

227. Gorday, 'Paul', p. 161 n. 20 notes that in *Adv. Haer.* 1.1-8, where Irenaeus describes Ptolemaeus's version of Valentinian gnosis, Paul is cited 19 times, more than any other New Testament writers. See Pagels, *Gnostic Paul*, for a general survey.

228. Olson, *Irenaeus*, pp. 70-80.

229. Norris, 'Irenaeus' Use of Paul', p. 81.

230. Pagels, *Gnostic Paul*, p. 71; emphasis original.

evidence that the Valentinians did indeed appeal to Paul's discussion of idol food. She merely *assumes* that the charges by Irenaeus and Justin are indications of Valentinian exegesis of Pauline texts. Brunt rightly objects that Pagels's suggestions

> go far beyond the evidence... It can in no way be concluded from Ire-
> naeus' statement that the Valentinians specifically used 1 Cor. 8 in sup-
> port of their practice; it can only be said that the Valentinians felt free to
> eat idol-meat. While Pagels' work is successful in showing that the
> Gnostics used Paul for support with regard to many issues, she offers no
> evidence that they did so with regard to idol-meat.[231]

The only possible evidence of Gnostic appeal to Paul is the use of μολύνω in *Adv. Haer.* 1.6.3 (cf. 1 Cor. 8.7). But the statement μολύν-εσθαι ὑπ' αὐτῶν ἡγούμενοι represents *Irenaeus's* assessment (employ-ing Pauline terms) of their practice rather than any explicit claim on the Valentinians' part. When Irenaeus quotes the Gnostics, there are usually explicit indicators such as λέγουσι (*Adv. Haer.* 1.6.3; *TLG* 001.1.1.12.11); ἀποκαλοῦντες, λέγουσι, αὐταῖς λέξεσι λέγοντες (*Adv. Haer.* 1.6.4; *TLG* 001.1.1.12.25, 26, 31). Furthermore, Paul's ·point in 1 Cor. 8.7 is that the weaker brother who eats idol food *is* defiled.

It is noteworthy that, in denouncing the evil of eating idol food, Ire-naeus apparently felt no need to defend his understanding of Paul's teaching against any heretical interpretation. The uncontroversial, matter-of-fact manner with which Irenaeus denounced the Gnostics suggests that he was probably not aware of any alternative interpreta-tion of Paul on this point. Given Irenaeus's frequent practice of provid-ing alternative interpretations of Paul in order to refute the Gnostics' misuse of the apostle, he would likely have defended Paul, had the Gnostics adduced support from Paul in their advocacy of eating idol food. The force of this argument is considerably strengthened when one recognizes that on numerous occasions in his condemnation of idol food, Irenaeus consistently fails to attack the Gnostics on the level of exegesis. Nor does he feel the need to elaborate his own theological position, which is rather treated as a given. This is in clear contrast to

---

231. Brunt, 'Rejected', p. 119. Similarly, Klauck (*Herrenmahl*, p. 244) argues that Paul's position concerning idol food in 1 Cor. 8 and 10.23–11.1 gave the Gnostics their justification for eating idol food, but is unable to produce evidence from primary texts.

Irenaeus's engagement with gnostic exegesis of other Pauline texts, such as 1 Cor. 15.50.

It may also be noted that, immediately after he has discussed Irenaeus's works, Eusebius remarks that '*Large numbers* of short works composed with commendable zeal by churchmen of that early time [i.e. around Irenaeus's time] are still *preserved in many libraries*' (*Hist. Eccl.* 5.27.7). The first example he gives is Heraclitus's *The Epistles of Paul*, which he claims to have read himself. If even Eusebius seems to know of a tradition of interpretation of Paul's epistles by Irenaeus's contemporaries, it is unlikely that Irenaeus himself is not aware of deviant interpretations of Paul's attitude toward idol food, given the importance of the issue for him.[232]

Therefore, the evidence leads us to believe that 1 Corinthians 8–10 was understood neither by Irenaeus nor by his Gnostic opponents as a text which supports eating idol food. Of course, it is not impossible that Irenaeus was implicitly refuting Gnostic exegesis when he denounced their practice, or that the Gnostics for some unknown reason did not see the need to appeal to Paul despite their belief that 1 Corinthians 8–10 supported their behavior. But what concerns us in this investigation is evidence, not mere possibilities that cannot be substantiated. I will address the Gnostics' attitude to idol food in more detail below.

10. *Marcion*

As noted earlier, Justin seemed to implicate the Marcionites for eating idol food and link them with gnostic sects. Now Marcion and his followers held Paul in extremely high regard. Tertullian went as far as calling Paul 'the Apostle of the heretics', apparently because of the way in which Marcion used the apostle (*Adv. Marc.* 3.5.4). Therefore, if the Marcionites indeed advocated eating idol food as something indifferent, this might be taken as an indirect indication (though certainly no proof) that Paul condoned eating idol food. Conversely, any negative attitude toward idol food on the part of the Marcionites might be reflective of Paul's attitude. In view of its significant implication, we will explore

---

232. As G. Vallee (*A Study in Anti-Gnostic Polemics: Irenaeus, Hippolytus, and Epiphanius* [Waterloo, ON: Wilfrid Laurier University Press, 1981], p. 9) points out, Irenaeus knew some heretics personally, read their writings and the writings of other heresiologists.

Marcion's attitude toward idol food in detail.[233] Though Marcion did not directly comment on idol food, there is plenty of indirect evidence which suggests that he did not eat idol food:[234]

1. *Marcionite Asceticism*. Harnack notes that 'the severity of Marcionite asceticism was second to none in early christianity'.[235] This severe asceticism expressed itself in, *inter alia*, strict abstention from enjoyment of food.[236] According to Epiphanius, the Marcionites 'reject the enjoyment of food as something dishonorable (*Escarum usum quasi inhonestum criminant*)' (*Panar*. 42). Tertullian considers their abstention from food as a way of repudiating the Creator (*Adv. Marc*. 1.14). Such a severe asceticism in relation to food made it very unlikely that Marcion would have eaten idol food. Another passage by Tertullian, not mentioned by Harnack, is virtually decisive on this point:

> [Paul] condemns also those who command abstention from food [1 Tim. 4.3?], through the foresight of the Holy Spirit, condemning beforehand the heretics who would enjoin *perpetual* abstention in order to destroy and despise the works of the Creator; such as I may find in the person of a *Marcion*, a Tatian, or a Jupiter, the Pythagorean heretic of today, but not in the person of the Paraclete (*De ieiunio* 15.1).

Since *De ieiunio* was written after Tertullian became a Montanist, it seems that the Marcionites were even stricter than the Montanists in their asceticism with regard to food.[237] Tertullian, with his ascetic

---

233. For the purpose of this investigation, I need not and will not address the primarily definitional question whether, and to what extent, Marcion is to be considered a Gnostic. Nor are we concerned with whether, as Harnack suggests, Marcion was the propagator of a Paulinism more authentic than that of the Great Church.

234. In searching for evidence that may shed light on Marcion's attitude towards idol food, I am greatly helped by A. von Harnack's magisterial work, *Marcion: Das Evangelium vom fremden Gott: Eine Monographie zur Geschichte der Grundlegung der katholischen Kirche* (TU, 45; Leipzig: J.C. Hinrichs, 2nd edn, 1924), which collects and sets forth an enormous amount of primary texts touching on Marcionite faith and practice. In particular, the lengthy appendices (which are omitted in the recent English translation) are invaluable.

235. Harnack, *Marcion*, p. 148.

236. Stuart G. Hall sums up Marcionite morality in terms of 'sexual continence, sparse diet, and commitment to martyrdom in the face of persecution, as they did battle against the law and the flesh in the name of pure Spirit' (*Doctrine and Practice in the Early Church* [Grand Rapids: Eerdmans, 1991], p. 38).

237. In the *Fihrist* we also read about uninterrupted fasts among the Marcionites (Harnack, *Marcion*, Appendix VI, p. 384*).

inclination, was obviously troubled by the apparent piety of those he considers heretics.[238] Thus he directed his attack not against Marcionite abstention per se but against the permanency of it.[239]

It is also significant that the Marcionites apparently made an exception for fish, the *sanctiorem cibum*, in their abstention from meat (Tertullian, *Adv. Marc.* 1.14.). According to Esnik, one of the main reasons why the Marcionites ate fish was that fish would not have been offered in sacrifices.[240] Such an explanation is unlikely to have been made up by Marcion's opponents, as it presents the Marcionites in very good light indeed. This is as direct an evidence as one can get that Marcionites would not have eaten idol food.

2. *Marcionite Martyrs.* The readiness to suffer martyrdom is another hallmark of Marcionite morality.[241] Since idol worship and compulsory eating of idol food were constant elements in the trials of martyrs, the Marcionites' willingness to suffer martyrdom was indicative of their uncompromising stand against idolatry and does not square well with a permissive attitude toward idol food.

238. Note that, in *De praescr.* 30.5, Tertullian refers to Marcion, perhaps ironically, as Apelles' *sanctissimi magistri.*

239. It is interesting to compare this with Tertullian's opposition to Marcionite proscription of marriage: Tertullian says that the orthodox Christians, unlike the Marcionites, did not reject marriage; they simply refrained from it. In this way they were also unlike the Nicolaitans, who indulged in their passion (*Adv. Marc.* 1.29.2). Thus Tertullian seemed to consider the Marcionites the opposite extreme of the Nicolaitans (who ate idol food!) in terms of strictness of discipline.

240. Source: Harnack, *Marcion*, Appendix VI, p. 373*. In Harnack's opinion, Esnik had not read Marcion's *Antithesis*, but derived his knowledge of Marcion's teaching from a later Marcionite writing which would have been strongly influenced by the *Antithesis* (*Marcion*, p. 77 n. 2). The notion that 'fish is not fit for dedication or sacrifice' can be found in Plutarch's table-talk: ἰχθύων δὲ θύσιμος οὐδεὶς οὐδ' ἱερεύδιμός ἐστιν (*Quest. Conv.* 729C; *TLG* 112.729.C.9-10)

241. The unnamed anti-Montanist author in Eusebius admits that the Marcionites 'claim an immense number of Christian martyrs' (*Hist. Eccl.* 5.16.21). Hoffmann (*Marcion*, p. 18) points out that, according to Eusebius, the Marcionites were also affected by the Smyrnean persecution of 156, in which Polycarp suffered (*Hist. Eccl.* 4.15.46). Cf. Clement, *Strom.* 4.4.17; Irenaeus, *Adv. Haer.* 4.33.9; Tertullian, *Adv. Marc.* 1.24, 27; and Pionius's *Acts of the Martyrs* (sources listed in Harnack, *Marcion*, p. 150 n. 4). Harnack comments that 'sie müssen in besonders großer Zahl vorhanden gewesen sein, und den Gegnern war es augenscheinlich peinlich, daß sie das nicht übersehen und vertuschen konnten' (p. 150).

3. *Marcion's Proscription of Sacrifices and Tendentious Emendations of Pauline Texts.*[242] Epiphanius twice points out that in 1 Cor.
10.19, Marcion has substituted ἱεροθύτον τι ἐστιν ἤ ὅτι εἰδωλόθυτον
τι ἐστιν for εἴδωλόν τί ἐστιν κτλ.[243] Harnack thinks that it is because,
for Marcion, the non-existence of idols was unthinkable.[244] A similar
tendency is seen in Gal. 4.8, where Marcion has replaced τοῖς φύσει μὴ
οὖσι θεοῖς with τοῖς ἐν τῇ φύσει οὖσι θεοῖς.[245] If Harnack is correct
about the motive of Marcion's emendation, then Marcion's insistence
on the reality of idols (gods) makes it somewhat improbable that he
would have advocated eating idol food.

Judging from what Epiphanius himself actually says in *Panarion* 42,
I think that the reason for Marcion's emendation of 1 Cor. 10.19 (if
there was a emendation) seems to be other than what Harnack suggests.
But whatever the true reason, Epiphanius's critique of the alleged
Marcionite emendation makes it almost impossible that Marcion con-
doned eating idol food.

According to Epiphanius, Marcion adds ἱεροθύτον to justify the proscription of all sacrifices (including biblical sacrifices) by equating
ἱερόν (in the sense of 'sacred', pertaining to God) with εἴδωλον.[246] In
this way the prohibition of εἰδωλόθυτα becomes the basis for rejection
of all sacrifices. Epiphanius, in his critique of Marcion, is concerned to
show that while Paul forbade sacrifices to demons, he did not reject the
sacrifices in Jerusalem from ancient times up to his own day. The

242. There is considerable debate about how to detect Marcionite tendentious
emendations. John J. Clabeaux is critical of Harnack's 'maximalist' approach in
attributing textual variants to Marcionite theological tendency (Clabeaux, *A Lost
Edition of the Letters of Paul: A Reassessment of the Text of the Pauline Corpus
Attested by Marcion* [CBQMS, 21; Washington, DC: Catholic Biblical Association
of America, 1989]). Clabeaux himself takes a 'minimalist' approach and accepts
fewer than half the readings that Harnack presents. But he does not dispute Harnack's findings on 1 Cor. 10.19 and Gal. 4.9. The variants in these two verses listed
by Harnack are not included in Clabeaux's list of 'secure' and 'probable' pre-Mar-
cionite readings. Hence, by implication, Clabeaux considers it possible that those
variants were results of Marcionite alterations.

243. *Panar.* 42 (*TLG, Adv. Haer.* 31.122.13-15; 31.165.15-17; cf. 31.165.26-27).

244. Harnack, *Marcion*, p. 47 and Appendix III, p. 88*.

245. Harnack, *Marcion*, p. 46 and Appendix III, p. 75*.

246. ...σὺ δέ, ὦ Μαρκίων, προσέθηκας τὸ ἱεροθύτον, νομίσας ἀπὸ τοῦ
μεμίχθαι τὰ δύο ὀνόματα, ἱεροῦ τε καὶ εἰδώλου, συνάπτεσθαι τῶν δύο τρόπων
τὴν σχέσιν (*TLG, Adv. Haer.* 31.165. 26-28).

apostle only condemned those who sacrificed to idols instead of to the true God.

We need not concern ourselves with the finer details of Epiphanius's refutation of Marcion. It is not even sure whether his sources for Marcion's actual text are reliable.[247] What is important is not the precise wording of Marcion's text, but the general tradition that Marcion proscribed all sacrifices and that he probably attempted to justify this by the idol food prohibition. Since it in no way helps the cause of anti-Marcionite writers represented in Epiphanius's sources as depicting Marcion as one who condemned idolatry, there is little reason to doubt the overall veracity of Epiphanius's presentation of Marcion's teaching on this point. Thus it seems that Marcion did observe the idol food prohibition and even made it the basis for his controversial proscription of sacrifice.

4. Tertullian's Silence Concerning Marcion's Attitude toward Idol Food. Book 5 of Tertullian's *Adversus Marcionem* is devoted to a detailed refutation of Marcionite teaching by way of an exposition of all Pauline letters regarded by Marcion as genuine. We need not concern ourselves with whether it was Marcion or Tertullian who had a better understanding of Pauline teaching. The important point is that in *Adv. Marc.* 5.7.9-14, where Tertullian attempts to refute many Marcionite doctrines by setting forth the evidence in 1 Corinthians 8–10, he gives no hint whatsoever that eating idol food was part of Marcionite teaching. Given Tertullian's strong condemnation of idol food (see below, §12), his penchant for polemic, and his tendency to seize every opportunity of demonstrating the absurdity of Marcion's belief— sometimes even availing himself of his opponents' unfortunate use of language—there is no way Tertullian could have passed over Marcion's teaching on idol food in silence if Marcion indeed condoned eating idol food. It is also significant that while Irenaeus accused some Gnostics of eating idol food without qualms, he completely failed to attack Marcionites on this issue. The only reasonable explanation is that Marcion

---

247. In *Panar.* 42, Epiphanius lists passages which he claims are from the Marcionite Gospel and Apostolikon and then argues against Marcion's interpretation of them. But the text presented by Epiphanius as Marcionite contains significant disagreements with that presented in Tertullian, *Adv. Marc.* 5, which is considerably earlier than *Panarion*. See Clabeaux, *Lost Edition*, pp. 13-14, 65. Clabeaux thinks that Epiphanius has compiled his list from citations made in other anti-Marcionite works.

did not disagree with Tertullian or Irenaeus on this issue. By implication, in Marcion's understanding, Paul did not condone eating idol food either.

The evidence I have presented above does not harmonize well with Justin's statement, which implies that some professing Christians who eat idol food are Marcionites. It seems that at this point Justin's statement must be taken with a heavy measure of skepticism. He does not say explicitly that Marcionites eat idol food. It is probable that he knows well they do not, but he is so carried away by his polemics against heretics that his accusations become indiscriminate. If one takes a less charitable view, Justin may even be deliberately slandering Marcion by insinuation. That Justin is capable of doing this can be seen in *1 Apol.* 26, where he complains that

> all those who take their opinions from [the heretics, chief among them Marcionites] are called Christians... Whether they perpetrate those fabulous and shameful deeds—the upsetting of the lamp, and promiscuous intercourse, and eating human flesh—we know not. But we do know that they are neither persecuted nor put to death by you, at least on account of their opinions.

Thus Justin seems willing to let these allegations of the heretics' moral depravity stand. But he is 'probably too well aware of [the heretics'] reputation for moral ascesis to do more than implicate them in the slander by a profession of ignorance'.[248] Again, contrary to fact, Justin claims that Marcionites are not persecuted, though what he means, of course, is that the Marcionites, inasmuch as they die for false doctrine, are not considered *true* martyrs.[249] Though Justin is not technically lying, his words can hardly be taken at face value.

Since, apart from Justin's questionable statement in *Dial.* 35, no early Christian author ever suggested Marcion condoned eating idol food, the Marcionites in all probability observed the idol food prohibition. This means that one cannot find in this great admirer of Paul any indication that the apostle ever taught the indifference of idol food. On the contrary, the Marcionite abstention from idol food was probably reflective of Paul's own attitude.

---

248. Hoffmann, *Marcion*, p. 32.
249. Hoffmann, *Marcion*, p. 32; cf. Clement of Alexandria, *Strom.* 4.4.17.

11. *The Gnostics*

I have earlier concluded (§9) that there is little evidence to suggest Gnostic use of Paul to justify eating idol food. I will now attempt to show that it is not even sure that the majority of Gnostics ate idol food.

I have noted that Justin implied, and Irenaeus explicitly charged, that the Gnostics ate idol food. Yet current scholarly assessment of anti-Gnostic charges tends to question whether the heresiologists' charges of Gnostic antinomian behavior were not merely conventional polemics.[250] In Filoramo's opinion, 'there could not be a more radical contrast between external sources and direct documentation'.[251] Therefore, a brief examination of the factual content of the antinomian charges is in order.

The evidence of Gnostic libertinism is virtually confined to the Christian polemical literature. Gnostic writings from Nag Hammadi contain little material to support the heresiologists' allegations. In fact, when ethical practices are dealt with directly, the norm is asceticism rather than antinomianism.[252] One searches in vain to find Gnostic texts openly advocating libertinism.[253]

In particular, there is no reference to the Gnostics' eating of idol food. On the other hand, *The Prayer of Thanksgiving* (NHC 6.7), a Hermetic work, mentions the eating of 'holy food, which has no blood in it' (65.5).[254] As the prohibition of eating blood often accompanies—and is frequently justified by—the prohibition of idol food, it may indicate that some Gnostic groups would not have approved of eating idol food. Furthermore, we read in *The Sentences of Sextus* (NHC 7.1):

It is better to die [than] to darken the soul because of [the] immoderation of the belly...the body is the garment of your soul; keep it, therefore,

250. Cf. George W. MacRae, 'Why the Church Rejected Gnosticism', in E.P. Sanders and A.I. Baumgarten (eds.), *Jewish and Christian Self-Definition* (3 vols.; Philadelphia: Fortress Press, 1980), I, pp. 126-33.

251. Giovanni Filoramo, *A History of Gnosticism* (Oxford: Basil Blackwell, 1990), p. 186.

252. Kurt Rudolph asserts that 'the overwhelming majority of the sources give unequivocal support to this aspect of gnostic morality [asceticism or abstinence]' (*Gnosis: The Nature and History of Gnosticism* [San Francisco: Harper & Row, 1983], p. 257).

253. MacRae, 'Gnosticism', p. 129; cf. Filoramo, *Gnosticism*, pp. 185-89.

254. In *NHL*, p. 329.

pure since it is innocent... Unclean demons do lay claim to a polluted
soul; a faithful (and) good soul evil demons will not be able to hinder in
the way of God (30.10-21).[255]

This again suggests ascetic abstention from food. The reference to
avoiding pollution by demons is certainly consistent with, if not indicative of, abstention from idol food.

As is the case with Justin, the possibility of tendentious presentation
of evidence by Irenaeus cannot be ruled out.[256] Irenaeus himself admits
that many who belong to the school of Saturninus abstain from meat,
but he argues that such temperance is 'feigned'.[257] Likewise Epiphanius
writes of the Archontics: 'Some of them ruin their bodies by dissi-
pation, but others feign ostensible fasts and deceive simple people
whilst they pride themselves with a sort of abstinence, under the dis-
guise of monks' (*Panar.* 40.1.4). The *Didascalia*, in the context of
polemics against Gnostic heresy, admits that some heretics abstain
from pork and eat only what the law declares pure (*Didasc.* 6.10.4).[258]
We may also note the comment by Clement of Alexandria that
Basilides saw in the martyr's death a punishment for sin (*Strom.* 4.12);
this makes the charge of Basilides's libertinism somewhat difficult to
believe.

On the other hand, it would be unwise to conclude that the antinomian charges are devoid of any factual basis. The vigorous apologetic
of the heresiologists would be difficult to explain unless there were
indeed those among the Gnostics who advocated (or at least permitted)
eating idol food. We must remember that the Nag Hammadi 'library'
comprises a great variety of religious traditions, not just that of the
Gnostics. If ethical teaching in the Nag Hammadi texts tends to be
ascetic rather than libertine, that may be due to the ascetic–monastic
setting for the production or transmission of the texts.

255. *NHL*, p. 506.

256. Rudolph comments that '[the heresiologists] either resorted to the simple
expedient of slander or made out the asceticism to be sheer dissimulation and dup-
licity' (*Gnosis*, p. 256).

257. 'Marriage and procreation, they maintain, are of Satan. Many of his followers abstain from animal food, and through this feigned continence they lead many
astray' (*Adv. Haer.* 1.24.2). Cf. Tertullian's mention of heretics like Marcion 'who
would enjoin *perpetual* abstinence' from meat (*De ieiunio* 15).

258. Georg Strecker, 'On the Problem of Jewish Christianity' (Appendix to
Walter Bauer, *Orthodoxy and Heresy in Earliest Christianity* [ed. R.A. Kraft; trans.
R.A. Kraft *et al.*; Philadelphia: Fortress Press, 1971]), pp. 241-85 (244-57).

In any case, there are texts that seem to advocate a radical relativity of moral categories, which might then lead to an ethic of indifference. In *The Gospel of Philip* (NHC 2.3) we read: 'In this world there is good and evil. Its good things are not good, and its evil things are not evil' (66.10).[259] Another example is *The Thunder: Perfect Mind* (NHC 6.2): 'I am the whore and the holy one' (13.19); 'Do not hate my obedience and do not love my self-control' (15.18-19); 'I am the one whom they call Law, and you have called Lawlessness' (16.15-16); 'I am sinless, and the root of sin derives from me. I am lust in (outward) appearance, and interior self-control exists within me' (19.16-20).[260] The indifference of food seems to be taught in *Gospel of Thomas* (NHC 2.2), logion 14: 'If you fast, you will give rise to sin for yourselves… When you go into any land… eat what they will set before you… For what goes into your mouth will not defile you, but that which issues from your mouth—it is that which will defile you' (35.16-26).[261] This is, however, no proof that the author advocates eating idol food.[262] The object of attack in the logion is most probably Jewish laws (fasting gives rise to sin, praying to condemnation, the giving of alms to harming one's spirit).[263]

A significant passage which may shed some light on the Valentinians' attitude toward idol food is *The Testament of Truth* (NHC 9.3), a document which attacks both catholic Christianity and other Gnostic groups.[264] The fragmentary text reveals that the disciples of Valentinus 'leave the good, [but] they have [worship of] the idols' (56.5-17).[265] If

259. *NHL*, p. 149.

260. *NHL*, pp. 297–301.

261. *NHL*, p. 128.

262. Citing this logion, Ehrhardt claims that Justin's statement against the Gnostics ('they eat sacrificial meat and say that it does not hurt them') 'does indeed appear in… the Gospel of Thomas' (*Framework*, p. 279 n. 2). This is a huge stretch. Barrett thinks that the logion is of only marginal relevance ('Things Sacrificed', p. 57 n. 12). Since the logion consists mostly of quotations from sayings of Jesus and Paul, it is evidence for the author's indifference toward idol food only if both Jesus and Paul were indifferent toward idol food.

263. Cf. Rudolph, *Gnosis*, p. 236: 'Jewish laws made out to be of no consequence, indeed as detrimental to salvation'.

264. This sort of Gnostic infighting can be compared with the accusations of immorality in *Pistis Sophia* 147 against other Gnostics. On this point see Filoramo, *Gnosticism*, p. 186.

265. *NHL*, p. 456.

the reference to 'idols' is not metaphorical, this passage suggests that some Valentinians had committed acts that might have been viewed as the worship of idols. Could it be that they had eaten idol food?

In conclusion, it cannot be denied that some Gnostics did eat idol food without qualms. But what evidence there is does not encourage us to think that their attitude was the prevalent one among Gnostic groups. It is likely that, in the context of vehement polemics, the heresiologists' charges were exaggerated for the sake of scoring a palpable debating point. Even Irenaeus revealed—inadvertently—that probably only οἱ τελειότατοι among the Valentinians did partake of idol food (*Adv. Haer.* 1.6.3).[266] Thus it appears that only in the rarefied atmosphere of spiritual elitism was idol food treated as something indifferent. Those Gnostic elitists (like the Corinthian knowers) who ate idol food simply ignored or rejected Paul's instruction. Those who did not eat were following the practice of the majority and hence no question was raised on the issue.

12. *Tertullian*

Tertullian's hatred of idolatry is so evident in his writings as to require little comment. In the opening statement of his treatise on idolatry, he labels it 'the principal crime of the human race' and suggests that it is the root of those mortal sins which are *exitiosa* and *devoratoria salutis* (*De idol.* 1; cf. *De pud.* 19.25). Little wonder he puts idolatry at the top of his list of seven capital sins (*Adv. Marc.* 4.9).

It is true that Tertullian, like the anonymous author of *Diognetus*, rejects the Jewish purity and dietary laws in general. He claims that 'faith, free in Christ, owes no abstinence from particular food to the Jewish Law' (*De ieiun.* 2). Moreover, Tertullian (in his pre-Montanist days) is concerned to show that while Christians have moral goals different from those of pagans, there is a general coincidence between their life-styles. We Christians, Tertullian claims, 'live with you, enjoy

266. Irenaeus goes on to mention that, in Valentinus's teaching, those who have not yet attained perfection must continue to live ascetic lives: 'they tell us that it is necessary for us whom they call animal men, and describe as being of the world, to practise continence and good works, that by this means we may attain to the intermediate habitation, but that to them who are called "the spiritual and perfect" such a course of conduct is not all necessary. For it is not conduct of any kind which leads into the Pleroma' (*Adv. Haer.* 1.6.4).

the same food, have the same manner of life... We cannot dwell together in the world, *without the market-place, without butchers,* without your baths' (*Apol.* 42). But such an apparently open attitude to the pagan world should not lead us to conclude that Tertullian would have condoned eating idol food. For he says specifically that Paul 'has delivered you [Christians] the keys of the meat-market, permitting the eating of all things, with a view to establishing *the exception of idol food*' (*De ieiun.* 15.5; more on this below).[267] It cannot be clearer that Tertullian did not condone eating marketplace idol food.

There is no question that Tertullian considers the apostolic decree to have abiding authority for Christians.[268] He argues that since the gospel 'shook the things of old to their foundations' and removed 'so heavy a yoke from our necks', it is all the more necessary to keep, 'at all times (*semper*), these compendia of discipline [i.e. the decree]'. The transgression of the prohibitions in the decree is deemed irremissible sin. For 'why do they [the apostles] relax so many bonds, if not to bind us in perpetuity (*perpetuo*) to duties which are more imperative?' (*De pud.* 12.3-4, 7; cf. *De idol.* 24.3). In particular, the moral dangers in partaking of idol food are strongly emphasized in various contexts. The Pauline argument that those who eat idol food become partakers of the table of demons is reiterated (*De spec.* 13.4; cf. *De Cor.* 10).[269] We may also note that Tertullian regards blood as the food of demons, thus providing a basis for the justification of the blood prohibition in terms of the prohibition of idol food (*Apol.* 22.6; 23.14).

267. Tertullian also makes the point that Christians do not attend pagan ceremonies (*Apol.* 42); cf. *Apol.* 38: 'We have left you nothing but the temples'.

268. Tertullian knows the decree in its Western version and interprets blood as a metaphor for murder (*De pud.* 12.5). Nevertheless, he observes the blood prohibition literally (in *Apol.* 9.13, he defends Christians against the accusation of eating children by pointing out that they would not even eat blood and things strangled), apparently independent of the decree. Or does Tertullian know both the Eastern and the Western versions? Note that Justin defends the blood prohibition with reference to Gen. 9 rather than to the decree (*Dial.* 20).

269. J.H. Waszink and J.C.M. van Winden point out that, for Tertullian, 'idolatry is in fact demonolatry' because the real object of worship are the demons rather than the idols (*Tertullianus: De Idololatria. Critical Text, Translation and Commentary* [VCSup, 1; Leiden: E.J. Brill, 1987], p. 75). See also their introductory remarks on Tertullian's concept of idolatry (pp. 73-79); cf. J.C.M. van Winden, '*Idolum* and *idololatria* in Tertullian', *VC* 36 (1982), pp. 108-14.

I have noted earlier that the silence of Tertullian about Marcion's teaching on the issue of idol food indicates that the Marcionites did not eat idol food. This in turn suggests that Paul had not been (mis)understood to condone eating idol food. There is a passage in Tertullian (*De spec.* 13) which indicates that such a (mis)understanding was not found among the orthodox Christians either:

> [1]I have, I think, adequately carried out my plan by showing in how many and in what ways the spectacles involve idolatry. I discussed their origins, their names, their equipment, their locations, and their arts—all that we may be certain that the spectacles in no way become us who twice renounce idols. [2]'Not that an idol is anything', as the Apostle says, 'but because what they do, they do in honor of demons' [1 Cor. 8.4; 10.19] who take up their abode there at the consecration of idols, whether of the dead, or, as they think, of gods. [3]It is for this reason, therefore, since both kinds of idols belong to one and the same category (the dead and the gods being the same thing) that we refrain from both types of idolatry. [4]Temples and tombs, we detest both equally; we know neither kind of altar, we adore neither kind of image, we offer no sacrifice, we celebrate no funeral rites. Nor do we eat of what is sacrificed (*neque de sacrificio edimus*), or offered at funeral rites, because 'we cannot share the Lord's supper and the supper of demons' [1 Cor. 10.21]. [5]If we keep, then, our palate and stomach free from defilement, how much more should we guard our nobler organs, our ears and eyes, from pleasures connected with sacrifices to idols and sacrifices to the dead—pleasures which do not pass through the bowels, but are digested in the very spirit and soul with whose purity God is more concerned than with that of the bowels.

In *De spectaculis* Tertullian sought to persuade both catechumens and baptized Christians that participation in pagan spectacles was incompatible with Christian faith and morality. The persuasion consists in two parts. The first part, chapters 1–13, is theological: spectacles are idolatrous in origin and spirit, therefore injurious to the Christians' own faith, making them guilty of idolatry. The second part, chapters 14–27, is practical: the enjoyment of spectacles is detrimental to moral discipline and arouses violent passions. *De spectaculis* 13 represents the clinching argument for the first part of Tertullian's persuasion.

It is clear that the Pauline notion that to eat idol food is to have fellowship with demons underlies Tertullian's argument. What is significant is that Tertullian felt absolutely no need to defend his understanding of Paul. That Christians would not eat idol food in order not to be defiled by demons was regarded as a given. It was the unquestioned premise of Tertullian's argument that he should dissuade his audience from going to theaters.

Such non-contentiousness over the idol food prohibition is in marked contrast to the vigorous disputes about how far a Christian could participate in the social and economic life of the Roman world without being guilty of idolatry. Tertullian's opinion that Christians should not attend theaters was challenged by laxer Christians with an appeal to Christian teaching: 'all things have been created by God and handed over to man—*just as we Christians teach*—and that they are undoubtedly good' (*De spec.* 2.1). In a similar treatise, no doubt inspired by Tertullian's, Novatian revealed such scriptural arguments in more details:

> Where are such things [attending theaters] prohibited? On the contrary, was not Elijah the charioteer of Israel? Did not even David himself dance before the ark?...A struggling apostle [i.e. Paul] paints for us the picture of a boxing match and of our own wrestling against the spiritual forces of wickedness [1 Cor. 9.26-27]. Furthermore, when he makes use of illustrations taken from the foot race, he also mentions the prize of the wreath [1 Cor. 9.24-25]. Why, then, should a faithful Christian not be free to be a spectator of things that the divine writings are free to mention? (*De spec.* 2.3).

Similarly, in his treatise *De idololatria*, Tertullian had to argue against those Christian manufacturers of idols who justified their refusal to leave the trade by appealing to the Pauline texts, 'Let everyone remain in the calling in which he was called' [1 Cor. 7.20] and 'let each one work with his own hands for a living' [1 Thess. 4.11] (*De idol.* 5.1-2). Such people also pointed out that Moses made a serpent in the desert (*De idol.* 5.4).

Thus it is clear that those Christians who were not as strict as Tertullian had no problem in quoting or misquoting Pauline texts to their advantage. In particular, passages from 1 Corinthians 7 and 9 were quoted. This means they could not have been ignorant of 1 Corinthians 8–10. Therefore, if Paul had taught, or been understood to teach, that idol food was something indifferent in 1 Corinthians 8–10, the laxer Christians could hardly have failed to appeal to this text to justify the eating of idol food, the avoidance of which was socially awkward and economically detrimental.[270] The reason they did not appeal to

---

270. Tertullian gives evidence of violations of the prohibition of idol food by heretical groups of Christians whom he calls 'another sort of Nicolaitans' (*De praescr.* 33.10). But there is no reference whatsoever to 1 Cor. 8–10.

1 Corinthians 8–10 is probably that the passage was not readily understood as permitting the eating of idol food. The point bears much more weight when one also considers the great range of matters pertaining to idolatry that Tertullian covered: spectacles, feasts, convivial gatherings, trades, astrology, education, usury, civic appointments, military offices, use of expletives, pledges or oaths, and so on. Tertullian had to argue at length to win his audience to his position, and at times it seems he was fighting a losing battle.[271] Yet apparently he did not feel obliged to defend the idol food prohibition except by reiterating Paul's argument.

It is worth noting that, for Tertullian, the strict prohibition of idol food is compatible with the liberty to treat food in general as indifferent. In chapter 15 of his treatise on fasting, Tertullian quotes Romans 14 extensively to refute both the libertine heretics who indulge in food and the ascetic heretics who enjoin strict abstention. He specifically mentions the Pauline principle of having concern for the weak by not causing them to stumble (*De ieiun.* 15.4). He claims that orthodox Christians 'abstain from things which [they] do not reject, but defer (*abstinentes ab eis quae non reicimus, sed differimus*)' (*De ieiun.* 15.2). Like Paul, he urges his readers not to destroy the work of God for the sake of food. This is a clear counter-example to the prevailing scholarly opinion that early Christians, with their legalistic attitude, are too interested in the mere rightness or wrongness of their acts to understand Paul's ethic of love.[272]

Then, in a remarkable statement similar to *Strom.* 4.15 (Clement of Alexandria), he says that Paul 'has delivered you the keys of the meat-market (*claues macelli tibi tradidit*), permitting the eating of all things, with a view to establishing the exception of idol food (*ad constituendam idolothytorum exceptionem*)' (*De ieiun.* 15.5).

Therefore, it is clear that, in Tertullian's understanding, Romans 14 and 1 Corinthians 8–10 are talking about different things. Paul's liberal attitude towards food in general in the former passage does not require

---

271. Cf. A. von Harnack's helpful discussion of the early Christians' conflict with idolatry in *The Mission and Expansion of Christianity in the First Three Centuries* (Gloucester, MA: Peter Smith, 1972), pp. 290-311 (esp. pp. 300-309, with extensive discussion of Tertullian).

272. We will find another roughly contemporary counter-example in Clement of Alexandria's *Paed.* 2.1.8-10, and many others after them. Really, in a communal and other-directed culture, the Pauline principle of having regard for the weak is not that difficult to understand, however difficult it is to practice.

that he holds a similar attitude regarding idol food in the latter. Moreover, while Tertullian clearly understands Paul's argument about not causing the weak to stumble, he does not see this as the true basis of Paul's abstention from idol food. Rather, in contrast to 'all things' in the market, idol food is absolutely non-negotiable.[273] This suggests that he urges avoidance of idol food not because he fails to understand Paul's ethic of love, but because he perceives that Paul's attitude toward idol food is far more negative than modern scholars tend to think. The non-controversial manner in which Tertullian refers to the idol food prohibition—in a polemical context concerning food and given Tertullian's penchant for polemics—suggests that his understanding of Paul's view on this issue has not been disputed at all. There is simply no competing interpretation. This is consistent with my earlier observation that, in Tertullian's detailed exegesis of 1 Corinthians 8–10, with specific focus in countering heretical views, he does not mention any deviant interpretation of Paul's teaching on idol food.

13. *Minucius Felix*

Minucius Felix also wrote about Christian avoidance of idol food in the *Octavius*. The clear and close literary connections between the *Octavius* and Tertullian's *Apology* necessarily raise the question of literary dependence. But there is no certainty about whether Minucius depends on Tertullian or vice versa.[274] In any case, if the *Octavius* was not written before the *Apology*, it could not have been very long after: Lactanius, already writing in the late third century, considered Minucius the earlier author. Lactanius could not have made such a mistake if Minucius had written in the second half of the third century. Thus the *Octavius* must have been written by the mid-third century at the latest. As such it is another early witness of the fundamental and widespread rejection of idol food by Christians.

Caecelius, Octavius's opponent, criticizes the Christians' notorious withdrawal from popular aspects of social life with fairly stereotypical pagan accusations:

273. Incidentally, this shows that marketplace idol food, not just idol food in cultic settings, is prohibited.

274. Opinions were divided as early as the fourth century. Lactantius apparently regarded Minucius as the elder, whereas Jerome maintained the exact opposite. Cf. Cross, *Fathers*, pp. 146-47, on this point.

> In your anxious state of expectation, you refrain from honest pleasures: you do not go to our shows, you take no part in our processions, you are not present at our public banquets, you shrink in horror from our sacred games, from food ritually dedicated, and from drink hallowed by libation poured upon our altars. Such is your dread of the very gods you deny (*Oct.* 12.5).

Octavius's response is significant:

> Now you claim that we reject food left over from sacrifices and cups from which libations have been poured. This is no admission of fear; it is a declaration of real independence. It is not that anything that comes into existence as an inviolable gift of God can possibly be spoiled; nevertheless we do abstain, for fear it might be thought that we make submission to the demons, to whom libation has been poured, or that we are ashamed of our own religion (*Oct.* 38.1).

Thus Christians rejected idol food not because they believed that the physical defilement by demons was in the food itself. No gift of God could be spoiled—this expresses a monotheistic belief akin to 1 Tim. 4.4 and 1 Cor. 10.26. Rather, the reason for their abstention was a confessional one: they wanted to avoid being thought of as participating in idolatry or as failing to stand up for their monotheistic faith. This also seems to have connections with Paul's discussion in 1 Corinthians 10.

14. *Clement of Alexandria*

Considering Clement's moral austerity and disposition towards vegetarianism, it is little surprise to find him condemning eating idol food. What is significant, however, is that whereas he concedes that the partaking of meat and wine is not a sin, he makes it absolutely clear that such liberty concerning food and drink does not extend to idol food, on which no compromise can be entertained. There are two important passages (*Paed.* 2.1.8-10; *Strom.* 4.15) in which he comments specifically on the problem of idol food.[275]

1. *Paedogogus 2.1.8-10*. In the second book of the *Paedagogus*, Clement gives advice on temperance concerning food and drink on various dining occasions. In 2.1.8-10 we read:

---

275. He mentions εἰδωλόθυτα almost in passing in two other places. In *Paed.* 2.1.17 the prohibition is mentioned as an example of Jewish frugality. In *Paed.* 2.7.56 the decree is quoted as a proof that one should shun drinking parties.

Now we will turn our attention to the so-called idol food, in order to show how we are enjoined to avoid it... ' I do not want you to be in fellowship with demons', the apostle says [1 Cor. 10.20]. The food of those who are saved is different from that of those who perish [1 Cor. 10.21?]. We should abstain from [the latter sort], not out of fear (for there is no power in such food), but we detest it for the sake of our consciousness— which is holy—and for the sake of our contempt for the demons (διὰ τὴν συνείδησιν τὴν ἡμετέραν ἁγίαν οὖσαν καὶ τῶν δαιμονίων διὰ τὴν βδελυρίαν), to whom the food has been dedicated. Another reason is the instability of those who interpret many things in a way that harms themselves, 'whose consciousness, being weak, is defiled. Now, food does not commend us to God' [1 Cor. 8.8], nor does 'what goes into a man defile him, but what comes out of the mouth' [Mt. 15.11], in the words of Scripture. The physical act of eating is indifferent (ἀδιάφορος ἄρα ἡ φυσικὴ χρῆσις τῆς τροφῆς)... But it is illogical for those made worthy of partaking of divine and spiritual food to partake of the table of demons (ἀλλὰ οὐκ εὔλογον τραπέζης δαιμονίων μεταλαμβάνειν τοὺς θείας μετέχειν καὶ πνευματικῆς κατηξιωμένους τροφῆς) [1 Cor. 10.21].

... And 'if some unbeliever invites us to a banquet and we decide to go'—although it is well not to associate with the disorderly—[Paul] bids us 'eat what is set before us, asking no question for the sake of consciousness' [1 Cor. 10.27]... 'Let not him who eats despise him who does not eat, and let not him who does not eat judge him who eat' [Rom. 14.3]. A little later [Paul] explains the reason for his command: 'He who eats', he says, 'eats for the Lord and he gives thanks to God. And he who does not eat, abstains for the Lord and give thanks to God' [Rom. 14.6].

Clement's attitude toward food is remarkably similar to that of the *Didache*. He regards ascetic abstention from food something desirable and praises Pythagoras in this regard (2.1.11). But he refers to Peter's visions in Acts 10 to show that it is by no means obligatory to adhere to any food laws (2.1.16). As is the case with the *Didache*, the bottom line is to stay away from idol food, which is absolutely not negotiable.

The reasons Clement gives for the avoidance of idol food are also remarkable. The prohibition is not motivated by fear of defilement in the food itself. According to Clement, both Paul and Jesus have taught that the physical act of eating is indifferent. The prohibition is rather motivated by two concerns outlined by Paul: to avoid having fellowship with demons and to avoid causing the weaker brethren to stumble. Unlike many modern scholars, Clement sees no tension or contradiction between the two concerns. They are just two separate arguments used by Paul to achieve the same goal of dissuading Christians from eating idol food. It is also noteworthy that Clement makes no reference to the decree in the passage, but solely bases his argument on Pauline discussions of idol food and dietary laws.[276] This is another example of how whenever early Christians give explicit arguments against eating idol food, they inevitably appeal to Paul. Again, this suggests that Paul's stance on idol food might be far more negative than it is usually thought to be.

We may also point out that, like Tertullian, Clement clearly understands Paul's argument of having concern for the weak but does not consider it the main reason for the abstention from idol food. This shows that he urges avoidance of idol food not because he fails to understand Paul's ethic of love, but because he perceives that an even stronger basis for abstention is the Christian refusal to have fellowship with demons. I am far from suggesting that Clement fully understood all the details of Paul's argument in 1 Corinthians 8–10—who does? In particular, his statement that 'we detest [idol food] for the sake of our consciousness' cannot find support in the text, which says rather that it is the other person's consciousness that counts (1 Cor. 10.29). Nevertheless, the noncontroversial manner in which Clement appeals to 1 Corinthians 8–10 to forbid eating idol food suggests that he was probably not aware of any interpretation of Paul which would allow eating. However, because of the peaceful and generally non-contentious character of Clement's writings, this point has less force than is the case with Tertullian.

2. *Stromateis* 4.15. In *Strom.* 4.15 Clement discusses the issue of avoiding offense. The passage, which consists mostly of quotations from 1 Corinthians 8–10, reads:

> (97.1) 'We know that we all have knowledge'—common knowledge in common things, and the knowledge that there is one God. For he was writing to believers; whence he adds, 'But knowledge is not in all', being communicated to few. And there are those who say that the knowledge about idol food is not promulgated among all, 'lest our freedom prove a stumbling-block to the weak. For by your knowledge the weak is destroyed'.

---

276. Clement quotes Paul 15 times in *Paed.* 2.1.8-10 (12 from 1 Cor. 8–10; 2 from Rom. 14); the only non-Pauline biblical text quoted is Mt. 15.11. He also quotes *Odyss.* 11.37 ([to the blood of idol food fly] 'the souls from out of Erybus now dead') to reinforce the Pauline argument that eating idol food is to have fellowship with demons.

(97.2) If they say, 'It is necessary to buy everything being sold in the market by way of inquiry [i.e. it is necessary to inquire before buying any food in the market]', thus making the 'asking no questions' into the equivalent of 'asking questions', they give a ridiculous interpretation (κἄν φάσκωσι πᾶν τὸ ἐν μακέλλῳ πωλούμενον ἀγοράζειν δεῖ κατὰ πεῦσιν[,] ἐπάγοντες τὸ μηδὲν ἀνακρίνοντες ἐπ᾽ ἴσης τῷ ἀνακρίνοντες, γελοίαν ἐξήγησιν παραθήσονται).

(97.3) For the apostle says, 'All other things buy out of the market, asking no questions'—with the exception of the things mentioned in the Catholic epistle of all the apostles [i.e. the decree], 'with the consent of the Holy Spirit', which is written in the Acts of the Apostles, and conveyed to the faithful by the hands of Paul himself. For they intimated 'that they must of necessity abstain from idol food, from blood, from things strangled, and from sexual immorality...' [Acts 15.29].

(97.4) It is a different matter, then, which is expressed by the apostle: 'Have we not power to eat and drink?...' [1 Cor. 9.4-5, 12]. (98.1) 'For the earth is the Lord's, and the fulness thereof'. (98.2) For the sake of consciousness, then, we are to abstain from what we ought to abstain. 'Consciousness, I say, not his own', for it is endued with knowledge, 'but that of the other', lest he be trained badly, and by imitating in ignorance what he knows not, he become a despiser instead of a strong-minded man. (98.3) 'For why is my liberty judged of by other's consciousness?...' [10.29-31].

The exact sense of (97.2) is somewhat difficult to determine. It turns on whether the κατὰ πεῦσιν should be construed together with ἐπάγοντες or δεῖ. The *GCS* text has the comma between δεῖ and κατὰ πεῦσιν, thus linking the latter to ἐπάγοντες. This understanding is reflected, for example, in the *ANF* translation: 'Should they say, "Whatever is sold in the shambles, ought that to be bought?" adding, by way of interrogation, "asking no questions", as if equivalent to "asking questions", they give a ridiculous interpretation'. I am unable to figure out precisely what sense the translator has made out of the sentence. I think the sentence makes much better sense if κατὰ πεῦσιν is linked to δεῖ (placing the comma between κατὰ πεῦσιν and ἐπάγοντες), thus producing my own translation above.[277]

Furthermore, the flow or focus of Clement's argument in *Strom.* 4.15, as in much of the material in the *Stromata*, is difficult to ascertain

277. It is also possible to link κατὰ πεῦσιν to φάσκωσι, giving: 'If they say by way of question, "whatever is sold in the market, ought that to be bought?" thus making the "asking no questions" into the equivalent of "asking questions", they give a ridiculous interpretation'. But this makes the statement a *non sequitur*.

because he does not make a point fully before passing onto another point.[278] There is a plethora of quotations from Pauline texts to prove or illustrate what he says, but the logical connections between those texts are far from clear. Moreover, *Strom.* 4.14 and 4.16 cover completely different topics from 4.15 and thus offer no help at all. Hence my understanding of this passage is put forward with no small degree of tentativeness.

In *Strom.* 4.15 (97.1), Clement mentions 'those who say that the knowledge about idol food is not promulgated among all'. It seems that those people have a relatively strict attitude towards idol food and they appeal to the Pauline principle of not causing the weak to stumble in order to discourage eating idol food. In 97.2 their attitude is further revealed: they assert that it is necessary to inquire before buying market food.[279] Clement quips that this is tantamount to making Paul's μηδὲν ἀνακρίνοντες into ἀνακρίνοντες! For Paul explicitly says that one may buy all things in the market, μηδὲν ἀνακρίνοντες. But Clement hastens to add, 'except idol food', lest his (and Paul's) liberal attitude concerning food be misunderstood.[280] That Paul did not allow buying idol food follows from the fact that the apostle himself spread the decree. Then, quoting Paul liberally to support his view, Clement returns to his point that Christians do enjoy liberty in the matter of food, but they also need to have restraint and temperance.

Therefore, Clement appears to understand Paul's position to be this: buy any food you want in the market without questioning, as long as

278. Cf. Jülicher's opinion that the reason Clement was not repudiated as a heretic in the fifth and sixth centuries is the fact that he was unintelligible (mentioned by Simon P. Wood, *Clement of Alexandria: Christ the Educator* [FC, 23; Washington, DC: Catholic University of America Press, 1954], p. xiii). Wood himself thinks that *Stromata* 'is a patchwork treatment rather than a consistent systematic explanation, proceeding at random... His mind never seems completely disciplined, or at home with logic' (xii).

279. The only possible plural subject for φάσκωσι in (97.2) is the οἵ φασι in (97.1). Thus Clement seems to be talking about the same group of people in both. However, it is also possible that φάσκωσι is an impersonal plural.

280. Compare Tertullian, *De ieiun.* 15.5: '[Paul] has delivered you the keys of the meat-market, permitting the eating of all things, with a view to establishing the exception of idol food'. Since there does not seem to be direct contact between the statements of Tertullian and Clement, they are probably appealing to a more or less 'official' position in early Christianity. Cf. Novatian, *De cib. jud.* 7: 'one must not think for a moment that freedom [from dietary laws] has also been granted to partake of idol food'.

you do not know that it is idol food, but any food that is specified as idol food is off limits.

Holding the traditional view of Paul's attitude toward idol food, Brunt sees *Strom.* 4.15 as a clear example that 'by Clement's time Paul's argument in 1 Corinthians 8–10 is not understood and his views are interpreted in light of the Apostolic Decree'.[281] But, as I have already argued, Paul and the decree in fact speak with one voice on the issue of idol food, so the question of which is interpreted in light of which is moot. Moreover, from our examination of early Christian texts, the prohibition of idol food is much more often justified by appealing to Paul's discussion in 1 Corinthians 8–10 than by appealing to the decree. A case in point is the first passage discussed above, *Paed.* 2.1.8-10, where Clement argues for abstention from idol food with no reference to the decree at all. This is the same with Tertullian and some later authors.[282] The evidence clearly shows that Paul's argument in 1 Corinthians 8–10 is capable of being understood (and is in fact universally understood in all verifiable cases) as prohibiting the consumption of idol food apart from the decree. This is especially true with regard to the Latin Fathers, most of whom know only the Western version of Acts. It is mere supposition that Paul is interpreted according to decree (if by that it is meant that early Christians use the decree to adjust or correct their understand of Paul's position regarding idol food). The historical evidence suggests rather the reverse: Paul's argument that to eat idol food is to have fellowship with demons becomes the rationale underlying the prohibitions of idol food (and even blood!) in the decree.

15. *Origen*

As already noted (pp. 229-32) the pagan critic Celsus argues that if Christians abstain from idol food they should also abstain from all food, since they cannot avoid coming into contact with demons when they eat or drink or breathe. In reply, Origen maintains that it is only when one eats idol food or blood that he is in fellowship with the demons.

281. Brunt, 'Paul's Attitude', p. 271.

282. For example, Novatian made an exception to idol food in his opposition to Jewish food laws but did not mention blood and strangled animals. This could hardly have been the case if he was reading Paul in the light of the decree (which of course has the Western reading).

That which is offered to idols is sacrificed to demons, and a man of God ought not to become a partaker of the table of demons. The Bible forbids things strangled because the blood has not been removed, which they say, is the food of demons who are nourished by the vapours rising from it, in order that we may not be fed on demons' food, perhaps because if we were to partake of things strangled some spirits of this nature might be fed together with us (*Contra Celsum* 8.30; cf. 8.24).

Like Clement, Origen also explains the prohibition of εἰδωλόθυτα on the grounds of pollution by demons. The *locus classicus* for this argument is, of course, Paul's discussion of idol food in 1 Corinthians 10. Origen also justifies the blood prohibition on the basis that it is demons' food, thus reading the decree in the light of Paul's discussion.[283]

Moreover, Origen maintains a distinction between Jewish food laws and the idol food prohibition. Again, like Clement (*Paed.* 2.1.8-10), Origen appeals to both Mt. 15.11 and 1 Cor. 8.8 to show that food itself is an indifferent matter. Because of the indifferent nature of food, Origen opposes mandatory observance of Jewish food laws in general (*Contra Celsum* 8.29).[284] In *Contra Celsum* 8.32 he further quotes 1 Cor. 10.31 and 1 Tim. 4.4-5 in refuting Celsus's argument that demons are in charge of what Christians eat and drink and breathe. Yet Origen strongly condemns partaking of idol food and never makes any attempt to allegorize the prohibition. Evidently, for Origen, the idol food prohibition is not understood in the framework of dietary laws but in the framework of idolatry.

It is also significant that Origen clearly understands Paul's discussion about the weak,[285] but does not draw the conclusion which modern

283. Cf. *Contra Celsum* 3.29, 37; 4.32; 7.5; 8.60. The notion that demons, being sensual and gluttonous, were attracted by the aroma of roasting meat and the blood, is also found in Justin *Apol.* 2.5; Tertullian *Apol.* 22.6, 23.14. Since this concept is also mentioned in Porphyry *De abst.* 2.42 and other pagan passages, it must have been commonplace in this period, though it is not clear whether Paul himself also held such concept. See Schoeps, *Theologie*, pp. 52-59; Böckenhoff, *Speisegesetz*, pp. 56-57; Resch, *Aposteldekret*, pp. 155-57.

284. Cf. also Origen's commentary on Mt. 15.2, where he demonstrates the nullity of the Jewish Law after Christ.

285. Cf. Origen's commentary on Rom. 14.20-21: πάντα μὲν καθαρά, ἀλλὰ κακὸν τῷ ἀνθρώπῳ τῷ διὰ προσκόμματος ἐσθίοντι (*TLG* 039.14.20-21). See also R. Roukema, *The Diversity of Laws in Origen's Commentary on Romans* (Amsterdam: Free University Press, 1988), pp. 75-77 for Origen's discussion (as transmitted by Rufinus) on Rom. 14.1-4, 16-18, 20-21.

commentators draw regarding the indifference of idol food. Rather, he sees Paul as employing a two-step argument against eating idol food:

> In reference to this statement [i.e. Celsus's: 'if idols are nothing, what harm…?'], it would be profitable for us to take up and clearly explain the whole passage of 1 Corinthians, in which Paul treats of offerings to idols. The apostle draws from the fact that 'an idol is nothing in the world' the consequence that it is harmful to eat idol food (ἐν ᾧ καὶ πρὸς τὸ μηδὲν εἶναι εἴδωλον ἐν κόσμῳ ἀπαντῶν τὴν ἀπὸ τοῦ χρῆσθαι τοῖς εἰδωλοθύτοις βλάβην κατεσκεύασεν); and he shows…that he who partakes of idol food is worse than a murderer, for he destroys his own brethren, for whom Christ died.[286] Further, he maintains that the sacrifices are made to demons; and from that he proceeds to show that those who join the table of demons become associated with the demons; and he concludes that a man cannot both be a partaker of the table of the Lord and of the table of demons (*Contra Celsum* 8.24).

Thus Origen argues for the avoidance of idol food not because he fails to understand Paul's concern for the weak. Rather, he realizes that it is only the first stage of Paul's argumentation leading to the clinching argument that one cannot partake both of the table of the Lord and of the table of demons.

In his commentary on Matthew (11, 12), Origen mentions that Jews and Ebionites accuse Christians (with whom Origen is associated) of transgression because they follow Pauline teaching in rejecting the distinction between pure and impure, and treating food indifferently. In response, Origen says that 'manifestly we are not defiled when we eat those things which the Jews who desire to be in bondage to the letter of the law declare to be unclean', quoting many Pauline texts on the indifferent status of food (1 Cor. 8.8; 10.31; Col. 2.16; Tit. 2.15).[287] Significantly, while Origen defends the indifferent status of dietary laws, he warns against eating idol food and puts forward a very important interpretation of Paul's teaching regarding food which might have been sacrificed to idols:

> But as for us who know that some things are used by demons, or if we do not know, but suspect it, and are in doubt about it (ὑπονοοῦντες δὲ

---

286. Cf. Origen's homilies on 1 Corinthians: 'Even if one's knowledge promises that one will not be harmed by the consumption of idol food, to another it is harmful; therefore one ought to be considerate to one's neighbor, lest others perish because of such an excuse (ἵνα μὴ τῇ προφάσει αὐτοῦ ἄλλοι ἀπολλύωνται)' (fragment of Homily on 1 Cor. 9.7-9 in *TLG* 034.40.14-17).

287. He also quotes Mt. 15.11 and Mk 7.19.

καὶ διακρινόμενοι περὶ τούτου), if we use such things, we have used them not to the glory of God... for not only does the belief that the foods have been sacrificed to idols condemn him who eats, but even the doubt concerning this (οὐ μόνον τῆς περὶ τοῦ εἰδωλόθυτα εἶναι ὑπολήσεως κατακρινούσης τὸν ἐσθίοντα, ἀλλὰ καὶ τῆς περὶ τούτου διακρίσεως)... He then eats in faith who believes that that which is eaten has not been sacrificed in the temples of idols... And the man who knowing that they have been sacrificed to demons nevertheless uses them, becomes a communicant with demons (καὶ κοινωνὸς δὲ τῶν δαιμονίων γίνεται ὁ καὶ αὐτὰ εἰδὼς δαιμονίοις τεθύσθαι), while at the same time, his imagination is polluted with reference to demons participating in the sacrifice. And the apostle, however, knowing that it is not the nature of the foods which is the cause of harm to one who uses them, or of advantage to one who refrains from their use, but beliefs and the reason which is in them (ἐπιστάμενος μὴ τὴν φύσιν τῶν βρωνάτων αἰτίαν εἶναι βλάβης τῷ χρωμένῳ, ἢ ὠφελείας τῷ ἀπεχομένῳ, ἀλλὰ τὰ δόγματα καὶ τὸν ἐνυπάρχοντα λόγον), said, 'But food does not commend us to God, for we are no better if we eat, and no worse if we do not eat'.

Therefore, in the understanding of Origen, a native Greek speaker, Paul's position is this: one may treat any food indifferently so long as one does not know or suppose that it is idol food; but one who knowingly eats idol food becomes a communicant with demons.[288] Eating idol food is harmful not because the food is physically defiled but for confessional reasons (that is, because of the idolatrous connotation of the act).[289] Again, Origen perceives a difference between Romans 14

288. The implementation of such an understanding may be seen in the practice of Antiochian Christians during the reign of Julian the apostate. When Julian began his policy of persecuting Christians, he conducted an experiment to find out how far the Christians would go in their abstention from idol food. He contaminated the springs and the market foodstuffs in Antioch with idol food. According to Theodoret (*Hist. Eccl.* 3.11), the Christians in Antioch continued to buy and eat food from the market that might have been contaminated, because they relied on Paul's instruction in 1 Cor. 10.25 that one might buy and enjoy everything on the market. See Böckenhoff, *Speisegesetz*, p. 74. Böckenhoff also notes that the same experiment yielded different results in Constantinople, where the Christians avoided any food that was possibly contaminated (p. 75). Cyril of Jerusalem took a similar stand (pp. 75-77). But such stricter prohibition seems to have been the exception rather than the rule, and was always prompted by persecution.

289. This can be compared with Minicius Felix, *Oct.* 38.1: 'It is not that anything that comes into existence as an inviolable gift of God can possibly be spoiled; nevertheless we do abstain, for fear it might be thought that we make submission to the demons, to whom libation has been poured, or that we are ashamed of our own

and 1 Corinthians 8–10: while the former condemns those who do not eat any food in faith, the latter condemns all who eat any food known to be idol food.

Origen was an extremely important witness for the nature of early Christian avoidance of idol food because of his great learning and enormous literary productivity. The great library that he built in Caesarea made the city a major center of Christian learning. Since Origen was steeped in Scripture and was familiar with the Christian—and even Jewish—exegetical traditions before him, he was presumably aware of the various ways early Christians or heretics had understood 1 Corinthians 8–10. As noted earlier (§9), Eusebius seemed to know of a tradition of interpretation of Paul's epistles by Irenaeus's contemporaries that was still preserved in Eusebius's time. If Eusebius, who was primarily a transmitter of traditions rather than an exegete and who was a century later than Origen, read second-century interpretative works on Paul, it seems reasonable to assume that Origen must have read as least as much, if not much more. Moreover, since Origen was such a prolific writer, there were many occasions when he could have mentioned or hinted at variant understandings of the apostle on the issue of idol food. This point bears more weight when one recognizes that 1 Corinthians was among his favorite biblical books.[290] Yet Origen's writings give us no hint whatsoever that Paul had ever been misunderstood as condoning eating idol food. Moreover, Origen did not find it necessary to defend Paul's teaching or the behavior of Christians associated with himself in the matter of idol food, while he did need to defend Pauline teaching and Christian behavior against the Ebionites' accusation in the matter of dietary laws. This confirms my contention that the usual understanding of Paul's position on idol food cannot be found in early Christianity and is thus probably wrong.[291]

religion'. Tomson (*Jewish Law*, p. 185), following Böckenhoff (*Speisegesetz*, pp. 53-58), thinks that Origen holds a 'physical demonology' which believes in 'real contamination' (as opposed to 'spiritual contamination') of food by demons. This is certainly incorrect.

290. Gorday, 'Paul', pp. 149 and 162 n. 47.

291. Of course, one may argue that Origen, Clement, Tertullian, Irenaeus, etc. might have chosen to suppress Gnostic interpretation. This is not impossible in principle. Yet one is not sure what sort of evidence would be allowed to count against such a view. As in scientific studies, a virtually unfalsifiable hypothesis, whose veracity bears little relation to evidence, is generally suspect.

16. *Novatian*

In his treatise on Jewish foods, Novatian emphatically argues for the passing away of all Jewish dietary laws and allegorizes a good number of them. However, he makes an important exception for idol food by appealing to the Pauline argument that to eat idol food is to have fellowship with demons (*De cib. jud.* 7):

> But concerning the use of foods one must be especially on his guard and not think for a moment that freedom has also been granted to partake of what has been offered to idols. If we have regard only to God's creation every food is clean: but once it has been offered to demons, it is defiled for God, insofar as it is offered to idols. As soon as this has been done, the food belongs not to God, but to an idol. When this is taken as food, it nourishes the one who partakes of it for the devil, not for God, and makes him a table-companion of an idol, not of Christ, as the Jews also rightly hold.

17. *The Apostolic Constitutions*

For the author of the *Apostolic Constitutions*, only the Ten Commandments are considered binding on Christians. The dietary regulations and other legislations which were given after the golden calf incident are not binding. Therefore he advises the eating of all sorts of food, but—again alluding to Paul—ends with a caution against partaking of idol food (7.2.20-21). This suggests that eating idol food is considered an idolatrous act rather than a mere breaking of the dietary laws.

The idol food prohibition was also upheld by other third-century writers such as Hippolytus, Cyprian, and Methodius of Olympus (a hostile critic of Origen). But their testimonies need not be rehearsed here as they add little to what we already know from other patristic writers.

18. *Jewish Christianity2*[292]

In the ascetic milieu of Jewish Christianity, it is no surprise to find idol food prohibited. Jewish Christians regarded, perhaps independently of

292. The history and nature of Jewish Christianity is one of the most difficult topics in early Christian studies. For an excellent account of the main issues involved, see Strecker's essay, 'Jewish Christianity'. See also A.F. Segal, 'Jewish Christianity', in H.W. Attridge and G. Hata (eds.), *Eusebius, Christianity, and*

Acts, the prohibitions in the decree as normative.[293] Indeed they tended to go beyond the requirements of the decree and recommend obser-vance of *kashrut* (and even vegetarianism).[294] This tendency can already be seen in the early Jewish-Christian *Didache* (see pp. 211-12).

The Pseudo-Clementine *Homilies* and *Recognitions* contain many explicit references to the prohibition of idol food.[295] In *Hom.* 7.3-4, Peter explains to the congregation in Tyre that the demons have no power over them unless they have first sat down at the demons' table and partaken of things sacrificed to them. Therefore he urges them 'to abstain from the table of demons; not to taste dead flesh; not to touch blood (τραπέζης δαιμόνων ἀπέχεσθαι, νεκρᾶς μὴ γεύεσθαι σαρκός, μὴ ψαύειν αἵματος)' (*Hom.* 7.4.2; cf. *Hom.* 7.8, 8.19, 8.23, 11.15; *Recogn.* 4.19, 4.36, 8.56). In *Hom.* 7.8.1 and *Recogn.* 4.36 the table of demons is explicitly equated with idol food, dead carcasses, things strangled, and blood. Thus there is a single underlying reason for the prohibition of all these items, namely, that the Christians may not, through consumption of these things, be enslaved by demons.

The prohibition of idol food is also found in other Jewish-Christian works (or Christian interpolations of Jewish works).[296] There is no need

Judaism (Detroit: Wayne State University Press, 1992), pp. 326-51 for a brief dis-cussion of the character of Jewish Christian groups in various geographical and temporal locations. Segal also lists some of the most important monographs on the issue. For the purpose of this investigation, I am using the term to denote the vari-ous Jewish-Christian groups discussed in A.F.J. Klijn and G.J. Reinink, *Patristic Evidence for Jewish-Christian Sects* (Leiden: E.J. Brill, 1973) and Lüdemann, *Antipaulinismus*.

293. E. Molland, 'La circoncision, le baptême et l'autorité du décret apostolique (Actes xv, 28 sq.) dans les milieux judéo-chrétiens des Pseudo-Clémentines', *ST* 9 (1955), p. 34.

294. Simon, 'Observance Rituelle', p. 90.

295. For more detailed discussions of the relationship between the Pseudo-Clementines and the decree, see Six, *Aposteldekret*, pp. 109-18; A.F.J. Klijn, 'The Pseudo-Clementines and the Apostolic Decree', *NovT* 10 (1978), pp. 305-12; and Molland, 'La circonsision'. Molland thinks that the community who produced the Pseudo-Clementines were Jewish Christians from Jerusalem who imposed the decree on Gentile converts. He thus rejects the view that associates them with the Ebionites. For a helpful review of the issues of sources and the character of the Pseudo-Clementines see F. S. Jones, 'The Pseudo-Clementines: A History of Research', *SecCent* 2 (1982), pp. 1-33, 63-96.

296. *Pseudo-Phocylides* 31; *Sib. Or.* 2.95-96; *6 Ezra* 16.69 and *Jos. Asen.* 8.5, 11.8-9, 12.5, 21.13-14.

Idol Food in Corinth

to rehearse such uncontroversial evidence here. For the purpose of this investigation, what is important is not the avoidance of idol food by Jewish Christians—which is understandable and expected. Rather, what is of supreme importance is the silence of Jewish Christians on Paul's attitude toward idol food.

Despite the relative paucity of first-hand reports, certain characteristics of Jewish Christianity are unmistakable: Jewish Christians were devout monotheists; they had a strong interest in dietary regulations and ritual purifications; and they often expressed deep hostility toward Paul.[297] Given such characteristics, one would have expected them to have attacked Paul vehemently had they known, believed, or imagined that the apostle condoned eating idol food. However, none of the sources collected by Klijn and Reinink and Lüdemann about Jewish Christians give the slightest hint that such was the case.[298]

Moreover, Origen mentions that Christians in his community are accused of transgressing the dietary laws by Jews and Ebionites because they follow Pauline teaching in rejecting the distinction between pure and impure, and treating food as indifferent (*Comm. Matt.* 11, 12).[299] Origen feels obliged to answer their accusations. However, he feels no need to defend Paul's teaching or the Christians' behavior in the matter of idol food. It seems that Paul is not known to Origen or his Jewish Christian opponents for treating idol food as a matter of indifference.

In the *Kerygmata Petrou*, which has been embedded in the later Pseudo-Clementine literature,[300] Paul is attacked in the guise of Simon Magus (*Hom.* 18.13-19). The account of the contest between Simon and the apostle Peter contains unmistakable allusions to Paul's letters, including 1 Corinthians.[301] If Paul regarded idol food as a matter of

297. The denigration of Paul is characteristic of Jewish Christianity in the reports of Irenaeus, Origen, Eusebius, Epiphanius, and other writers. In the Pseudo-Clementines Paul is attacked in the guise of Simon Magus. Nevertheless, it is not true that Paul was rejected unanimously by Jewish Christianity. Paul was accepted, for instance, by the Nazoreans.

298. Klijn and Reinink, *Patristic Evidence*, and Lüdemann, *Antipaulinismus*.

299. Origen also makes it clear that Christians do not reject the idol food prohibition. See my earlier discussion on Origen.

300. On this subject see G. Strecker's introduction to 'The Kerygmata Petrou', in *NTApoc*, II, pp. 488-91; cf. Strecker, 'Jewish Christianity', pp. 257-72.

301. Barrett notes that the expression τράπεζα τῶν δαιμόνων (*Hom.* 7.4, 7.8,

indifference, there would have been plenty of opportunities for the author to discredit Paul by pointing that out. But the author never avails himself of such opportunities.

Indeed, for Jewish Christians antagonistic towards Paul, the slightest evidence or rumors that Paul had condoned eating idol food would have made the apostle a ready target for their attack. The same can be said if they merely thought Paul's teaching could conceivably be construed to mean that. Therefore the failure on the part of anti-Pauline Jewish Christians to attack Paul on this important issue is a very strong indication that Paul was not understood to condone eating idol food, nor could his teaching be readily so construed. This conclusion is consistent with my earlier observation of Luke's lack of awareness of accusations of Paul by Jews (or Jewish Christians) concerning the matter of idol food.[302]

19. *Later Patristic Writers*

Further evidence for the prohibition of idol food is found in the works by Lactantius, Eusebius of Caesarea, Cyril of Jerusalem, Athanasius of Alexandria, Basil of Caesarea, Gregory of Nyssa, Amphilochius of Iconium, Epiphanius, Chrysostom, Jerome, Augustine, Cyril of Alexandria, and other writers.[303] It is tempting indeed to list all the relevant passages to show how pervasive such a prohibition was in early Christianity. But such an exercise hardly makes for elegant prose and does not advance my arguments any further. It 'would amount to chewing the cud without the allegorical meaning attached to it!'[304] Therefore, I will spare my readers the tedium of going through all these materials and will briefly discuss only two significant authors.

8.19, 8.23) may owe something to Paul, though the borrowing is likely indirect ('Things Sacrificed', p. 45).

302. Robert Kraft pointed out to me that my argument from the evidence of Jewish Christianity might be extended to the picture of Paul in Acts.

303. Some of these writers are discussed by Six (*Aposteldekret*, pp. 139-53) and Böckenhoff (*Speisegesetz*, pp. 71-107), though they focus on the influence of the decree rather than Paul.

304. S. Stein, 'The Dietary Laws in Rabbinic and Patristic Literature', in K. Aland and F. L. Cross (eds.), *Studia Patristica*, II (Berlin: Akademie Verlag, 1957), pp. 141-54 (151). The statement is made with regard to the insignificant payoff in discussing all references to the dietary laws in patristic literature.

Idol Food in Corinth

a. *Chrysostom*

Chrysostom is relatively late in the extensive list of authors commenting on the issue of idol food. However, his understanding of Pauline teaching on idol food is very significant because of his sensitivity to the historical meaning of the texts and his awareness of possible ambiguities in Paul's language. His rhetorical training contributes to a concern for context, logical thought-progression, and clear exposition as he deals with the text.[305]

Like many writers before him, Chrysostom argues for the passing away of Jewish food laws and yet maintains the idol food prohibition. He also sees Paul as using a two-stage argument to dissuade the Corinthians from eating idol food: the concern for the weak and the danger of having fellowship with demons (*1 Cor. Hom.* 20-24).[306] In his *Discourse Against Judaizing Christians*, Chrysostom even mimics this two-stage argument of Paul to dissuade his audience from attending Jewish festivals (*Adv. Jud.* 1.6.7; 1.7.5)!

Concerning food that has possibly been sacrificed to idols, Chrysostom, like Origen before him, understands that Paul permits one to eat any food bought at the market or offered in a private home, as long as nobody points out the religious history of the food. One need not be overscrupulous, nor should one be concerned if one eats in ignorance. 'Such things are not in their nature evil, but through the intention become unclean. Wherefore [Paul] says, "Asking no question"'.[307]

---

305. Chrysostom's education as a classically trained rhetorician is well known. He studied with the famous pagan rhetorician, Libanius, who claimed Chrysostom would have been his successor if the Christians had not stolen him (F.M. Young, 'The Rhetorical Schools and their Influence on Patristic Exegesis', in R. Williams [ed.], *The Making of Orthodoxy* [Cambridge: Cambridge University Press, 1989], p. 189). The straightforward, if somewhat unspectacular and common-sense approach of Chrysostom is commonly held to be one of the chief virtues of the Antiochian school of interpretation (P. Gorday, *Principles of Patristic Exegesis* [Lewiston, NY: Edwin Mellen Press, 1987], p. 104).

306. In *1 Cor. Hom.* 25.2 (on 1 Cor. 10.30), Chrysostom sums up the Pauline argument: 'You say, "Why then abstain?" Not as though I am becoming unclean, far from it; but for my brother's sake, and lest I become a communicant with demons, and lest I be judged by an unbeliever'. In Chrysostom's understanding, the third reason was put forward by Paul after he had already led the Corinthians away from the table of demons.

307. τοιαῦτα γὰρ τὰ μὴ τῇ φύσει πονηρά, ἀλλ' ἀπὸ τῆς διανοίας ποιοῦντα τὸ ἀκάθαρτον κτλ. (*PG* 61.205.52-59 [*1 Cor. Hom.* 25.1]; cf. *PG* 61.207.38-41 [*1 Cor. Hom.* 25.2]). Cf. Origen, *Matt. Hom* 11.12: ἐπιστάμενος μὴ τὴν φύσιν τῶν

Chrysostom, who has an innate sense of the language and who is well trained in Greek rhetoric, is often most helpful when he fails to perceive any possible ambiguity in a passage.[308] If he consciously argues for one interpretation against another, his view may be important but must not be given excessive weight, for the very existence of different interpretations indicates that the Pauline text is capable of being (mis)construed in more than one way. But if he does not seem to be aware of any ambiguities or alternative interpretations, then his reading of the text ought to be highly valued, for it gives us a good indication of how the text was likely understood by Paul's first readers. Assuming that Paul was a competent communicator, this also helps us to determine what he probably meant. Thus Chrysostom's straightforward and non-controversial reading of Paul's discussion of idol food, without the slightest awareness of the usual understanding, shows that Paul is unlikely to have condoned eating idol food.

b. *Ambrosiaster and Augustine*
The approach of Origen and Chrysostom to the problem of idol food finds its counterpart in the Western Church in Ambrosiaster's commentary on 1 Corinthians. While Ambrosiaster clearly prohibits idol food, he allows the consumption of unspecified food bought at the market or offered at private dinners. It is not a sin to eat idol food in ignorance.[309] Similarly, Augustine allows the eating of food possibly sacrificed, but maintains that to eat food known to be idol food is to have communion with the demon, which will pollute one's conscience. His position is wonderfully illustrated in his reply to a hypothetical question of the appropriate behavior of a starving Christian traveler who finds nothing to eat but some food placed in an idol temple while no one is around:[310]

> Since in this question it is not assumed that the food thus found was offered to the idol (for it might have been left by mistake or designedly

βρωνάτων αἰτίαν εἶναι βλάβης τῷ χρωμένῳ, ἤ ὠφελείας τῷ ἀπεχομένῳ, ἀλλὰ τὰ δόγματα καὶ τὸν ἐνυπάρχοντα λόγον. Note also Chrysostom's judgment that 'if you eat *in ignorance*, you are not subject to the punishment [which came upon Israel for idolatry]' (*PG* 61.205.43-44 [*1 Cor. Hom.* 25.1]). This seems to suggest that Chrysostom did not approves of knowingly eating marketplace idol food.

308. As Professor Moisés Silva points out repeatedly in his doctoral seminar on 'The History of Interpretation' at Westminster Theological Seminary.

309. *PL* 17.251 (1 Cor. 10.25-29).

310. *Ep.* 47.6, mentioned in Böckenhoff, *Speisegesetz*, pp. 101-102.

by persons who, on a journey, had turned aside there to take refresh-
ment; or it might have been put there for some other purpose), I answer
briefly thus: Either it is certain that this food was offered to the idol, or it
is certain that it was not, or neither of these things is known. If it is certain, it is better to reject it with Christian fortitude. In either of the other
alternatives, it may be used for his necessity without any conscientious
scruple.

20. *Conclusions*

The above survey of the primary sources has shown unmistakably the
early, fundamental, and pervasive nature of the idol food prohibition in
early Christianity. Given the diverse nature of the sources, the picture
that emerges from these texts is remarkably consistent. The existence of
such a virtual unanimity among early Christians gives credence to my
contention that Paul at root urges the avoidance of idol food. After all,
it was early Christians who preserved Paul's discussion of idol food in
its present form![311] Thus the well-entrenched scholarly view that Paul
condoned eating idol food is seen to be highly unlikely.

Scholars tend to explain the universal opposition to idol food as a
result of the influence of the decree. Of course, it is undeniable that
early Christians were concerned to maintain consistency between Paul
and the decree. Moreover, once the link between the decree and
1 Corinthians 8–10 had been made, it might have become unnecessary
to mention the former when speaking about the latter. Nevertheless, if
for argument's sake we accept such an explanation, we may still pose
the question: yet what gave the decree its universal appeal? As many
scholars maintain, Acts was not in wide circulation until well into the
second century—and one of its main purposes was to promote Paul!
Further, the decree is not recorded in the Gospel traditions or other
Christian documents in apostolic or subapostolic times. It is recorded
only in Acts, a document that testifies to Paul's agreement to, and pro-
motion of, the decree. Moreover, much of early Christian condemnation of idol food, if traceable at all, is traceable to the influence of the
apostle to the Gentiles rather than to that of other apostles. So what

---

311. As Tomson puts it, 'If [Paul] did [condone eating idol food] he would not
just have been the first, but in effect the only early Christian authority to defend this
position. Indeed it would have been a miracle, resulting from pure misunderstanding, that First Corinthians was preserved at all by the early Church in its extant
form' (*Jewish Law*, p. 185).

figure in early Christianity was responsible for the decree's widespread currency? I think Paul may not be a bad guess!

Moreover, as I have argued in the introduction to this survey, in view of the immense popularity of 1 Corinthians in early Christianity, Paul's discussion about idol food in 1 Corinthians 8–10 must have been widely known from the beginning. If the decree—independent of or contrary to Paul—indeed exercised such pervasive influence—though its use in early Christianity is far less documented than that of 1 Corinthians—then it is difficult to understand how Paul's supposedly contrary attitude on this boundary-defining issue went completely unnoticed. More difficult to comprehend is how Paul's name became so firmly attached to the decree.

The implication of the popularity of 1 Corinthians and the importance of the issue of idol food in early Christianity is that Paul's true position would hardly have vanished without trace. And indeed our sources reveal plenty of evidence, direct and indirect, positive and negative, for the understanding of Paul's attitude.

In Acts we find a very early testimony that Paul was involved in the formulation and promulgation of the decree. This means that the apostle would not have condoned eating idol food. For those who accept the historicity of Luke's account of the Jerusalem council, this evidence is virtually decisive. But other early Christian sources also give strong indications that the widespread prohibition of idol food owed something to Paul's teaching. Paul's argument against eating idol food was known even to pagan critics, implying that early Christians were widely influenced by his teaching in their avoidance of idol food. In fact the Pauline argument that to eat idol food is to have fellowship with demons is so persuasive and definitive that it becomes *the* Christian argument against eating idol food and even the basis for the justification of the blood prohibition.

It is also clear that early Christians' avoidance of idol food did not entail a concomitant observance of Jewish dietary practice. On the contrary, our sources reveal that a distinction was generally made between Jewish dietary laws and the idol food prohibition. This gives us reason to believe that Paul indeed treated the two issues differently and substantiates our contention that Paul's rejection of Jewish food laws does not imply that he condoned eating idol food.

Contrary to the prevailing scholarly conception, early Christians who opposed eating idol food did show some understanding of the Pauline principle of putting aside one's freedom for the sake of weaker brethren. They were not so moralistic as to become merely interested in the rightness or wrongness of the act. This makes the notion of their ignoring or misconstruing Paul more difficult to accept. Their rejection of idol food in absolute terms is thus all the more significant, for despite their familiarity with this principle, they did not draw the conclusion that they had freedom to eat idol food provided no one would be harmed. They perceived that Paul's attitude toward idol food was far more negative than modern scholars tend to think. In their understanding, Paul's appeal for the weak was only the first part of a two-stage argument to dissuade Christians from eating idol food. The second and clinching argument is to avoid having fellowship with demons.

All early Christian writers who commented on the problem of food that was possibly sacrificed to idols (such as marketplace food) invariably referred to Paul's discussion in 1 Cor. 10.25-31. Like Paul, they believed that food itself was indifferent. Because no inviolable gift of God could be spoiled, their rejection of idol food was not the result of the mistaken belief that there was physical defilement by demons in the food itself. Rather, the reason for their abstention was a confessional one: they wanted to avoid being thought of as participating in idolatry or as failing to stand up for their monotheistic faith. With such an understanding, they generally permitted the eating of any food that was possibly, but not definitely, sacrificed, following Paul's advice to buy and eat any food in the market without questioning. Yet when the religious history of the food was known, the only permissible action was to abstain. Such an attitude is consistent with what we have shown to be Paul's true position vis-à-vis idol food: avoid any food if, and only if, one knows that it is idol food.

None of the individual sources in this survey is unassailable or incapable of supporting alternative interpretations. But taken together they give us powerful and unambiguous *prima facie* evidence that the early Christian attitude toward idol food was significantly influenced by, and strongly reflective of, Paul's own attitude in 1 Corinthians 8–10.

The negative evidence arguing against the traditional understanding of Paul's position vis-à-vis idol food is also early and pervasive. It is obvious from our sources that what is usually taken to be the heart of Paul's argument regarding idol food—that idol food was a matter of indifference and should be avoided only for the sake of the weak—did not once surface in any discussion about this extremely important issue in early Christianity. This is truly remarkable in view of the not infrequent mention of this same principle of having concern for the weak when Jewish dietary laws were in view. This suggests that many scholars may have confused Paul's rhetoric in 1 Corinthians 8–10 and Romans 14, and read into Paul's discussion of idol food his attitude toward Jewish dietary laws.

Given the vehemence with which the prohibition of idol food was held by orthodox Christians, they were unlikely to have been sympathetic to Paul if they knew or thought that Paul condoned eating idol food. Yet not only did they appeal to Paul to support their own position, but they also felt absolutely no need to defend their understanding of Paul against any alternative interpretation. They did not even seem to have been aware of any rumors that Paul condoned eating idol food or that his discussion had been construed to mean that. The non-controversial and matter-of-fact manner in which they appealed to Paul's teaching suggests that there was simply no competing interpretation. This means that the traditional understanding of Paul's position was either long forgotten at a very early stage or—more probably—never existed in early Christianity.

It is also significant that those opponents of idol food who were antagonistic towards Paul never gave any hint that Paul condoned eating idol food. Given their deepseated suspicion and even hostility towards Paul, any slightest evidence or rumors that Paul had condoned eating idol food would have made him a ready target for their attack. The same can be said if they merely thought that Paul's teaching could conceivably be construed to mean that. At the very least, such a teaching would hardly have gone unnoticed. This suggests that early Christians, whether they were sympathetic or antagonistic toward the apostle, did not readily understand 1 Corinthians 8–10 to permit eating idol food. Thus the usual understanding of Paul's teaching on this subject is unlikely to be a natural reading of 1 Corinthians 8–10.

To be sure, some members of marginal Christian groups (perhaps like some of the Corinthian Christians, who were opposed to Paul in this matter) apparently ate idol food without qualms, but this is no evidence for the usual interpretation of Paul's position. Those Christians who advocated eating idol food invariably failed to appeal to Paul's discussion in justifying their position regarding idol food, even though they did appeal to Paul frequently to justify other heterodox behavior or teaching. If they venerated Paul and appealed to Paul in other areas, why then did they not also appeal to Paul on this issue, especially when their position was vehemently condemned by the orthodox and could not be supported by other Christian writings? The true explanation may never be known, but the least we can say is that Paul's teaching was not readily understood to provide liberty in eating idol food.

It is true that much of the argument against the usual understanding of Paul's position is an argument from silence. However, its force is not thereby lessened. How else does one prove the non-existence of an interpretation in early Christianity except by showing that there is no positive evidence for it? If it was indeed the case that no one appealed to 1 Corinthians 8–10 to justify eating idol food, how can we prove it? What could a Tertullian or an Irenaeus have written? They would have had no reason to write that the heretics did not quote Paul on this matter. It seems the only reasonable approach is to show that Tertullian, say, did not refer to the heretics' use of 1 Corinthians 8 in justifying idol food, whereas he did refer to their use of 1 Corinthians 8 and other Pauline passages in justifying other behavior or doctrines. In the very nature of the case, one cannot very well expect early Christians to have said explicitly that the subsequent traditional interpretation is wrong. Indeed, the refutation, or mere mention, of such an interpretation would be evidence of its existence and would make it a possible interpretation!

It is important to remind the reader that I do not just rely on argument from silence. I have provided much positive evidence for the early Christians' reading of Paul that is consistent with my thesis. However, I have not focused or relied too much on such evidence because it is all too easily dismissed by scholars who, without support from primary sources, attribute early Christian understanding to the influence of the decree or other unspecified traditions. Since I am not sure what kind of positive evidence would prove convincing, I have concentrated on negative evidence, which can sometimes be more revealing. I have tried to show how inherently improbable it is that diverse streams of early Christianity all reinterpreted Paul according to certain tradition and in the result left no trace of Paul's true teaching.

It is also important for the reader to appreciate the nature and the force of my argument from silence. I conclude that early Christians were unaware of the usual reading of Paul not merely because they did not argue with it, but because *they did not argue with it when one can reasonably expect them to have done so*. Not unlike Sherlock Holmes's inference from 'the curious incident of the dog which did nothing in the night-time' that the midnight visitor was someone the dog knew well, mine is an argument from silence when silence is not expected. It is a testing of a hypothesis that has many controls. The following table lists some of the major controls and significant omissions:

Control	*Significant Omission*
1. Luke was extremely anxious to dispel rumors that Paul's preaching had impugned Jewish traditions.	He was not concerned to dispel rumors that Paul had taught Gentile Christians not to observe the decree.
2. Paul's weaker brethren principle is mentioned in early Christian writings in relation to Jewish food in order to argue for abstention while acknowledging the right to eat.	The permissibility of eating is never acknowledged when the same principle was mentioned in the context of idol food.
3. Irenaeus refuted Gnostic exegesis of many Pauline texts.	He did not refute Gnostic interpretation of 1 Cor. 8–10 when he attacked the Gnostics eating of idol food.
4. Tertullian provided detailed refutation of heretical interpretations of 1 Cor. 8–10.	He never hinted at, nor did he feel necessary to refute, any interpretation which understood Paul to condone idol food.
5. Tertullian had to argue vigorously for his position on a wide range of matters pertaining to idolatry—in part because some appealed to Paul's teaching (especially 1 Corinthians) to justify their deviant behavior.	He did not need to argue for his understanding of Paul on idol food.
6. Clement tried to exonerate Nicholas, a relatively minor figure, for providing justification for the heretics to eat idol food.	He felt no need to exonerate Paul, when much more would have been at stake.
7. Some heretics appealed to Paul frequently to justify various heterodox behavior or teaching.	They invariably failed to appeal to Paul's discussion to justify their eating idol food.
8. Some Jewish Christians attacked those who followed Pauline teaching in rejecting the distinction between pure and impure.	They failed to attack them or Paul on the issue of idol food.

It is of course impossible to quantify the probability that such omissions are all gratuitous. However, some simple arithmetic will help one get a feel of the inherent implausibility of the scenario. Let the hypothesis be that it was known among early Christians that Paul permitted, or was thought to permit, the eating of idol food. Now, in each of the above eight cases, one can reasonably expect Paul's view to be mentioned. Let us assume that in each case it is, on average, just as likely for such a view to be mentioned as for it to be not mentioned for some reasons. Then the overall probability that such a view is not mentioned at all will be $(0.5)^8 = 0.004$, that is, less than 0.5 per cent.[312] Thus the hypothesis is extremely unlikely to be true. As a corollary, the probability that such a view is mentioned in at least one of the eight cases will be greater than 99.5 per cent. This means that, if the traditional understanding of Paul were known in early Christianity, it would almost certainly have been mentioned somewhere. This conclusion will be stronger still if we consider additional negative evidence.

If we are talking about the lack of mention of a particular interpretation on an obscure subject by a few writers, that silence may raise some doubts in one's mind about the correctness of such an interpretation. It could even become a disturbing ring in hermeneutically sensitive ears, but no more than that. However, we are here talking about the complete lack of attestation to the existence of the traditional understanding of Paul's position in a plethora of ancient writings. With a whole chorus of witnesses, representing an extremely wide spectrum of Christian communities in almost all parts of the Roman Empire, on one of the most important issues in early Christianity, such resounding silence is simply deafening!

Excursus: Some Methodological Remarks

The evaluation of evidence and hypotheses involves many judgments of historical probability. While my expertise prior to biblical studies was in the field of applied mathematics and statistics,[313] I decided it would be more profitable to present my arguments at an informal and

312. I am assuming that these omissions are independent events, as there is no reason to believe that there are necessary links between one omission and another.

313. For my study and research in applied mathematics, I received numerous awards, including the University Medal and Postgraduate Award of University of Sydney, and Medical Engineering Research Association Award of the Commonwealth government of Australia. I also worked in the actuarial field for a number of years.

intuitive level.[314] After all, logical reasoning is in large measure good application of common sense. Nevertheless, for those readers who desire greater methodological rigor, it is appropriate here to address in some detail some factors affecting historical probability, argument from silence, and evaluation of hypotheses.[315] While some examples will be given for illustrative purposes, they should not be seen as attempts to reargue my case exhaustively.

The Importance of the Majority Attitude

I have concluded that most pious Jews in Paul's time would not have condoned eating idol food. The same can be said of most early Christians. This virtual unanimity in the rejection of idol food makes it *prima facie* unlikely that Paul condoned eating idol food, because the majority attitude has an important conditioning effect on the probability of events. Simply put, all things being equal, the majority view is what any one individual is most likely to hold. Even when things are not equal, it skews the conditional probability of whether one holds a certain view.

It may be objected that in early Christianity (and elsewhere) many 'victorious' ideas and practices were 'minority' viewpoints at one time or another, even within their own more local situations. Moreover, there are too many unknown variables that affect the view of any individual on any matter. Therefore, the 'majority' factor does not bear much weight in historical arguments, beyond describing some situations at some times and in some places.

In response, we readily agree that history deals with particulars and many 'improbable' events could and did occur. But we must also remember that many more ideas and practices, perhaps seldom noticed because they are non-controversial, are majority and 'probable' view-

314. The facile uses of logical apparatus in criticizing the reasoning of opponents, especially accusations of logical fallacies (such as *non sequitur*, question begging, inconsistency, etc.), often have the harmful effect of blowing the debate off the rails. It is true that examples of bad reasoning do abound in the literature, and some deserved to be thus labeled. Nevertheless, one must recognize that a lot of 'lapses' in logic and methodology are due to ambiguities of language or unstated premises which the author does not feel necessary to justify. To quickly label them fallacies is most unfortunate.

315. I would like to remind my readers, though, that good historical reasoning is a very complex skill which requires sound judgment and broad knowledge about the subject matter. It is an art that cannot be reduced to rules and methodologies.

points. Much more to the point, to appeal to historical particularity in
dismissing majority viewpoints is to misunderstand the nature of probability argument. We are not equating probability with truth. Some conjecture can be highly probable without being true or could be true
without being very probable. Probability (in inductive reasoning) is
really the degree to which it is reasonable to believe something depending on how much we already know, regardless of how much we do not
know.[316] If 99.99 per cent of people in Paul's day believed in demons,
the probable inference is that Paul believed in demons, even if we know
nothing about his particular family upbringing, educational background, psychological disposition, and a host of other factors. If we do
not have figures as high as 99.9 per cent, it only makes the argument
weaker, but not worthless.

Consider another example. It is reasonable to infer that Tom probably believes in a round earth because almost everyone else believes
that. But if we know that Tom is a member of the 'flat-earth society',
the probability will be reduced drastically. Nevertheless, the conditional probability of Tom's believing in a round earth, even given the
knowledge of his membership in the flat-earth society, will still be
higher than it would have been had almost everyone else believed in a
flat earth.

The significance of the virtually unanimous early Christian attitude
cannot be downplayed by an uncritical appeal to ignorance regarding
historical particularities. Not knowing all the variables is not a valid
reason to exclude a probability approach. In fact, it is a major reason
for such an approach. If one knows all the variables, no resort to probability is necessary, for then the conclusion is wholly contained in the
premises.

Inductive Generalization

A typical inductive generalization takes the form:[317]

1.   a, b, c...each has been observed to be S and P.

316. Therefore the 'probability' of a certain event is a shorthand way of speaking
of the degree to which it is reasonable to believe that such an event occurred. This
notion of probability as rational credibility is quite different from the sense of the
term 'probability' in physical science, such as the probability of radioactive decay
of a particle. In the latter, the probability has the sense of 'relative frequency', a
definite numerical value which can be measured.

317. A good introduction to logical argumentation which successfully combines

2.   Nothing has been observed to be S without being P.

3.   Therefore, probably, all S are P.

In our case, S = 'early Christians' and P = 'they did not indicate that 1 Corinthians 8–10 had been understood to allow eating food known to be idol food'. The variables a, b, c and so on are Luke, *Didache*, Justin, Irenaeus, and so on. The conclusion is that, probably, no early Christian indicated that 1 Corinthians 8–10 had been understood to allow eating idol food.

The credibility of the conclusion in an inductive generalization depends on how reasonable it is to suppose that the things observed constitute a 'fair sample' of S, with regard to being P. There are five important factors:[318]

1.   *Positive analogy*: the degree to which a, b, c...have been observed to be alike (besides the mere fact that each is both S and P). For example, let S be 'swans' and P be 'white'. If all the observed were female and American, then our inference that 'all swans are white' would be quite weak, for we would not have excluded the possibility that it is only female swans, or perhaps only American swans, that are white. Similarly, if only Christians in the Western part of the Roman empire failed to mention Paul's tolerance of idol food, my case that the traditional understanding of Paul is not known in early Christianity would be very weak. As a rule of thumb, the greater the positive analogy among the observed instances, the weaker the inference, other things being equal.

2.   *Negative analogy*: the degree to which a, b, c...have been observed to differ one from another. If we have observed swans in winter and in summer, in the wilds and in captivity, young and fully grown, then our argument that 'all swans are white' is strengthened, because we have increased the probability that the observed entities constitute a fair sample as regards color. Now, the non-mention of the traditional understanding of 1 Corinthians 8–10 is observed among Christians from the East and from the West, among supporters and

symbolic logic and informal logic can be found in S.F. Barker, *The Elements of Logic* (New York: McGraw–Hill, 1989). On the concept of inductive generalization, see pp. 186-90.

318. Barker, *Logic*, pp. 187-88. The swan example below is taken from Barker.

antagonists of Paul, among those who were somewhat neutral or ambivalent, among those who condemned idol food and those who advocated eating it. Therefore the conclusion that this lack is universal in early Christianity is considerably strengthened. In general, the greater the negative analogy among the observed instances, the stronger the argument.

3. *The character of the generalization.* The more sweeping the generalization, the less is its probability relative to our evidence. 'No early Christian condoned eating idol food' is a more sweeping generalization than 'no early Christian appealed to 1 Corinthians 8–10 to condone eating idol food'. 'All early Christians ignored/misunderstood Paul on the issue of idol food' is a generalization that says a lot more than 'some sections of early Christianity ignored/misunderstood Paul on the issue'.

4. *The number of observed instances.* In general, the greater the number of observed instances, the stronger the inference.[319] Inductive generalization is more probable on an important matter on which there are much discussion, such as idol food in early Christianity, than an obscure matter, such as baptism for the dead.

5. *The relevance of S to P.* In formulating our inference, we must ask: can we reasonably expect a connection between S and P? In our case, the matter seems quite clear cut. Given the importance of the issue of idol food in early Christianity and the popularity of 1 Corinthians, it is reasonable to expect some correlation between one's status as a Christian and one's mention or lack of mention of 1 Corinthians 8–10 in any discussion of idol food.

Intuition and Conditional Probability

The assessment of the probability of Justin's or 'Gnostics' ' or anyone else's use of Paul is not a simple statistical matter. Because of the many

---

319. There is some question whether the increase in the number of observed instances in itself necessarily makes the generalization more probable. Instead, the generalization may have become more probable on account of an increase in the extent of the negative analogy which ordinarily accompanies an increase in the number of observed instances. Fortunately, in real life, this matter is largely academic, for additional observed instances almost always lead to an increase of negative analogy.

unknown variables, it often comes down to one's general knowledge, intuition and presuppositions. While this phenomenon is unavoidable, and not necessarily to be deplored, we must attempt to seek controls which may qualify or adjust our 'raw' beliefs.

For example, some scholars, such as Pagels, find it natural to assume that Gnostics who did eat idol food would have appealed to 1 Corinthians 8 for support.[320] The reasoning seems to be:

1. Gnostics were fond of Paul
2. some Gnostics ate idol food
3. therefore, they would have used Paul to support their eating idol food.

This assumption that gnostics would have used Paul in support of eating idol food seems, *prima facie*, reasonable enough.[321] In abstract, this could have been a probable event. But here is where our raw perception of the probability needs to be modified by other factors. In probability theory, an event that is probable in isolation may have an extremely low conditional probability depending on the observed instances of other related events.

For example, not knowing much about cats, and based on the commonly observed results of the tossing of many objects, one may intuitively believe that a toss of a black cat, like a coin toss, will have a 50–50 chance of its landing on its legs or its back. But if we know that the previous ten tossings of a white cat, a yellow cat, and so on, always has the cat landing on its legs, we will have to conclude that, contrary to our initial judgment, the next toss of a black cat will probably result in a legs landing rather than a back landing.[322] This modified belief is the most reasonable one to take even if—and precisely because—we do not know all the variables.

So what are the events that affect the conditional probability that

320. Pagels, *Gnostic Paul*, p. 71.

321. I was in fact quite surprised to find out in my research that there was no evidence for their use of Paul in this matter.

322. This applies even to the case of a coin toss, which presumably has a 50–50 chance of turning up a head or a tail. In real life, the 50–50 chance is only an intuition, for we do not know all the variables (e.g. whether coin is loaded or fair, wind factors, tossing techniques, etc.). If one knows that the previous ten tosses had not turned up a head, the conditional probability of a toss turning up a head will be much lower than the value we originally assumed. In short, probability is always relative to evidence.

gnostics uses 1 Corinthians 8 to justify eating idol food? One such notable event is that, in his detailed exposition of 1 Corinthians 8–10 with very specific focus to refute deviant interpretations of Paul on a range of behavior and doctrines, Tertullian failed to mention any view that Paul might have allowed idol food. There is no reason to believe that Tertullian suppressed this but not other heretical interpretations. Given his penchant for polemics and ridicule, the heretics would have played trump cards right into his hands had they indeed interpreted Paul as condoning idol food. Similarly, Irenaeus indicated the drift of Valentinian exegeses of many Pauline passages (many from 1 Corinthians!) and then refute them by discussing the 'natural' meaning of these passages, but he did not quote Gnostic use of 1 Corinthians 8 on all occasions of his condemnation of eating idol food (which eating was for him, as for Tertullian, almost the chief of vices). Another factor which may significantly affect the probability is the fact that while most Gnostics were fond of Paul, apparently only a minority ate idol food. Therefore the Gnostics' fondness for Paul did not seem to be strongly or clearly correlated to the behavior of eating idol food. This will reduce the likelihood of conscious appeal to Paul by those who ate idol food. These and other factors make the conditional probability of Gnostic use of 1 Corinthians 8 in justifying eating idol food far lower than if the issue is considered in isolation.

Let us consider another example. The virtually unanimous rejection of idol food by early Christians suggests that, *prima facie*, Paul is unlikely to have condoned eating idol food. Now, are there related events which would have significantly affected this probability? One obvious factor we need to take into account is the fact that there are clear instances where, in my judgment, Paul was misunderstood by early Christians. Does the knowledge of this fact reduce the probability of my original inference? It depends. If we know that early Christians always misunderstood Paul on all other issues, that conditional probability will be drastically reduced to virtual impossibility. On the other hand, if we know that early Christians always understood Paul correctly on all other issues, the conditional probability that Paul did not condone eating idol food will be significantly increased to virtual certainty. Now, what we know is that some early Christians misunderstood Paul on some issues and some understood him correctly on some issues. Therefore, the fact of Pauline misunderstanding in early Christianity seems to have a relatively neutral effect on the conditional probability, unless it can be shown that there is a strong disparity between the instances of correct understanding and the instances of misunderstanding.

The Role of Negative Evidence

The virtually unanimous prohibition of idol food by early Christians, and particularly their universal appeal to Paul, is very strong positive evidence for my understanding of Paul's position. Nevertheless, such evidence is usually dismissed rather quickly by scholars who attribute early Christian (mis)understanding to the influence of the decree or other undocumented factors. As Thomas Kuhn insightfully points out (with respect to scientific observations), data are never brute facts. What counts as data or evidence depends on the paradigm, or disciplinary matrix, that researchers use.[323] Once the assumption of orthodox misunderstanding of Paul is taken for granted as a part of the disciplinary matrix within which scholars operate, no amount of positive evidence will prove convincing. The usual view of Paul thus becomes almost unfalsifiable and invulnerable against all attacks from early Christian evidence. Therefore, for strategic purpose, I have concentrated on the use of negative evidence, which can sometimes be more revealing, in the hope that anomalies that are difficult to ignore may lead to changes in the disciplinary matrix itself.[324]

It is sometimes objected that arguments from silence are necessarily weak and speculative. This is simply not true. Such arguments are weak only when the silence has no probabilistic significance. But an argument from silence can be most persuasive when silence is not expected. One of the most famous experiments of modern physics, the Michelson–Morley experiment, which sought to measure the velocity of the earth's motion through the luminiferous ether at different times of the year, gained its celebrated reputation by its notorious failure to detect

---

323. T.S. Kuhn, *The Structure of Scientific Revolutions* (Chicago: University of Chicago Press, 2nd edn, 1970). Kuhn uses the word 'paradigm', especially in the first edition of his work, in many different senses. In the second edition, he recommends using the term 'disciplinary matrix' for 'paradigm' in the sense of 'the entire constellation of beliefs, values, techniques, and so on shared by the members of a given community' (p. 175; cf. pp. 182, 187). For an excellent discussion on the implications of Kuhn's theory for biblical exegesis, see V.S. Poythress, *Science and Hermeneutics: Implications of Scientific Method for Biblical Interpretation* (Grand Rapids: Zondervan, 1988).

324. Cf. Kuhn, *Scientific Revolutions*, p. 83.

any effects of the ether. The null result for ether-drift measurements, which apparently was an embarrassment to the experimenters, was entirely unexpected and inexplicable. Yet this negative evidence set the stage for Einstein's special theory of relativity, which declared the ether to be superfluous. The effects of the ether cannot be detected because there is no ether. Without this negative evidence, it is extremely doubtful whether Einstein's theory would have found such quick and ready acceptance in the scientific community.

Likewise, in modern textual criticism, the lack of evidence for the existence of Byzantine text types in the first three centuries is one of the strongest arguments for their secondary character. Another example, much closer to home, is Bauer's challenge of the then widely accepted traditional view of the relationship between orthodoxy and heresy in early Christianity. Whether or not one accepts Bauer's comprehensive reconstruction, his thesis of the relative dominance of heretics is arguably most persuasive precisely in the chapters on Edessa and Alexandria, where he makes extensive use of argument from silence regarding orthodox presence and influence.

It is true that argument from silence can be easily misused, but the potential for misuse is no reason for rejecting the argument—especially when much positive evidence points to similar or compatible conclusions.

Asymmetry in the Use of Negative Evidence

My own argument from silence takes the following typical form (where x stands for Justin, Irenaeus, Tertullian, Gnostics, Jewish Christians, etc.).

1. x did not quote or implicate Paul in condoning idol food.
2. x had good reasons to do so if they had understood Paul to teach that.
3. Therefore, probably, in the understanding of x, Paul was not thought to condone idol food.

This form of the argument is, as far as I am aware, consistently applied across the board. However, since an argument from silence is a good argument only if silence is somewhat unexpected, there is an asymmetry involved when the probability of conclusion is concerned. On any important issue, one is more likely to write in response when one is disturbed than when one is not aware of any problems.

Regarding those who held the issue of idol food as a touchstone of orthodoxy (e.g. Tertullian), it is very difficult to imagine that they understood Paul to condone idol food and still accepted the apostle. If they knew or thought that some used Paul to justify eating idol food, it is also unlikely that they gave no indication of such use on every occasion that they condemned the practice. Regarding those who were hostile to Paul, silence was even more improbable. If Paul was interpreted, or could have been interpreted, as condoning idol food, he would have been a ready target for their attack. Therefore, when they were silent, the almost inevitable inference is that they were not aware of such teaching, provided their views are reflected in our sources.

Regarding those who ate idol food, the situation was very different. There was simply no compulsion for them to justify every behavior or doctrine by appealing to Pauline teaching. When 1 Corinthians 8–10 did not suit their purpose, it might be simply ignored. Even if 1 Corinthians 8–10 would have suited their purpose, it might also have been be ignored in the context of a broader perspective. Therefore, when we do not have positive evidence of their use of Paul, the proper inference is that we do not know. It is possible that they did use 1 Corinthians 8–10, but the probability must be assessed by taking into account other factors, such as whether the majority did eat idol food. Obviously, the greater the number of eaters, the higher the chance that such eating has been seen to be congruent to 1 Corinthians 8–10.

Evaluating Hypotheses

The lack of attestation of the traditional understanding of Paul's approach to idol food in early Christianity can hardly be disputed. But this fact is open to various interpretations. Indeed, for any set of data there are always different ways in which the data might conceivably be explained. If we are imaginative enough in thinking of auxiliary hypotheses, we can succeed in making virtually any hypothesis fit the observed facts. Of course, some hypotheses are judged to be more probable than others. But when we ask how good an explanation is, more than probability is involved. Other factors, such as explanatory power, simplicity, and falsifiability, make one explanatory hypothesis better than others. While we cannot define those factors in a thoroughly rigorous manner, we can say something about them.[325]

325. Cf. Barker, *Logic*, pp. 209-15.

1. *Explanatory Power*. The hypothesis that is most probable may not be a good hypothesis, if it lacks explanatory power, which is the ability of the hypothesis to illuminate the phenomena to be explained. Consider the hypothesis 'early Christians for some reason did not appeal to 1 Corinthians 8–10 to justify eating idol food'. As an explanation for the non-attestation it is highly probable but rather trivial. It merely describes the fact in a different way and does not illuminate anything in the process. The hypothesis 'they first completely ignored Paul and later completely misunderstood him' is much better because it does illuminate the issue of Pauline reception in early Christianity. However, it is still unsatisfactory because its auxiliary hypothesis 'early Christians were ignorant of Paul's approach because of the lack of Pauline influence'[326] is not far from tautological. It does not explain how they could be ignorant of Paul's approach on such an important subject matter discussed in such length in such a popular letter as 1 Corinthians. By contrast, the hypothesis 'they did not read Paul that way' not only explains the non-attestation, but also sheds light on Paul's own attitude that relates to his Jewish hostility to idolatry.

2. *Simplicity*. Other things being equal, the simpler a hypothesis, the more acceptable it is as an explanation of the data. Simplicity is in some measures a subjective criterion, but it has some fundamental characteristics. A simple hypothesis is one that minimizes the need to supplement the hypothesis with auxiliary hypotheses, or to postulate the existence of any entities that have not been observed. A simple hypothesis also attributes usual and direct operations to the observed phenomena, rather than elaborate and *ad hoc* ones. For example, 'everyone interpreted Paul according to some tradition that takes an approach different from Paul's' introduces an entity for which we have little evidence in the primary sources, for virtually all early Christians who discussed idol food referred primarily to Paul's teaching. Moreover, even if such a tradition played an important role, the hypothesis still needs an auxiliary hypothesis that no one noticed or made a point of its difference to Paul's own approach. Likewise, the hypothesis 'all early Christians misunderstood Paul's approach' attributes to the non-attestation the unusual operation of universal misunderstanding by

---

326. This is the explanation of Brunt ('Rejected', pp. 120-21), the only reasoned attempt to explain the singularity of Paul's approach in early Christianity.

those who were close to the thought world of Paul. There is no indication from 2 Corinthians or Clement of Rome that 1 Corinthians 8–10 was misunderstood by the first generation of its recipients. To postulate that the next few generation of Christians all misunderstood the passage introduces a significant and unusual discontinuity in early Christian reading of Paul.

3. *Falsifiability.* Strange as it may seem, a good hypothesis is one that is highly falsifiable, that is, one that is vulnerable to being overthrown by a highly definable set of potential evidence. A moment of reflection shows that it is an eminently reasonable criterion. It is another way of saying that statements must be testable by observation. On the other hand, an unfalsifiable hypothesis (even if it might be true in theory) is generally a bad hypothesis because its veracity bears no relation to evidence. A hypothesis that does not rule out anything, but rather is compatible with any conceivable state of affairs, is vacuous. One needs to be able to specify what would count as a falsification of the claim. The hypothesis 'Paul's approach was not attested because it was misunderstood by all early Christians in our sources', even if totally false, is virtually unfalsifiable. If there is fresh evidence that a newly discovered early Christian writing appeals to Paul to condemn eating idol food, it will be seen as another instance of misunderstanding, for which we have so much evidence already. If instead the writing appeals to Paul to justify eating idol food, then it can be seen as evidence of Paul's true position, which most early Christians misunderstood. It is difficult to think of any kind of evidence (short of interviewing Paul himself on the subject) that could, at least in theory, disconfirm the claims for the misunderstanding theory. The hypothesis thus gains an invulnerable status against all attacks. But the high cost of this invulnerability is that one cannot hope to win over those who are not already convinced of the truth of the hypothesis. In the end, it is accepted only by those who find it expedient to do so, and by those who can see no alternatives.

By contrast, the hypothesis 'the traditional view of Paul's approach to idol food is not attested in early Christianity because it is an unnatural reading of 1 Corinthians 8–10 that is incompatible with Paul's well-known position' is highly falsifiable. Even relatively sparse evidence for early Christian use of Paul in justifying eating idol food would have significantly weakened, if not decisively refuted, the hypothesis.

Chapter 5

SUMMARY AND CONCLUDING REFLECTIONS

1. *Summary*

This historical and exegetical investigation strongly challenges the widely held view that Paul regards idol food as a matter of indifference, to be avoided only if it causes the weak to stumble. An alternative understanding is proposed: Paul considers conscious consumption of idol food a denial of the Corinthians' allegiance to Christ and urges them to avoid idol food if, and only if, it is identified as such.

After outlining the significant social meaning of idol food in the Greco-Roman world, I argued that an objective separation between purely social meals eaten ἐν εἰδωλείῳ and meals involving τραπέζης δαιμονίων μετέχειν was highly improbable in Paul's Corinth. Because of the frequent performance of idolatrous rites over food in most formal meals in private homes, let alone those in temples, it is highly unrealistic to think that social meals in temples could have been purely secular or only nominally connected to idolatry. On the contrary, such dinners would naturally have been perceived as idolatrous by early Christians, including Paul. Many interpreters have simply underestimated the religious import of most social meals in antiquity.

The examination of a wide spectrum of Jewish sources in the Hellenistic period shows that a negative attitude toward idol food was pervasive, despite a general willingness on the part of many Jews to participate in the social life of the Gentile world. In contrast to the *kashrut*, which often required justification through allegorization, the idol food prohibition was held as the *sine qua non* of Jewish faith. Eating idol food was considered the epitome of idolatry.

Since Paul spoke vociferously of his Jewish and Pharisaic credentials, and since he had a strong disdain for idolatry, it is difficult to find a motive for him to condone eating idol food. That Paul rejected the continuing validity of *kashrut* in making way for Gentiles to be accepted into God's covenant community is no reason for his condoning the eating of idol food. Such rejection of *kashrut* for Gentile believers is in accord with the downplaying of the dietary laws in favor of monotheism and sexual ethics in Jewish apologetic literature, which shows close connection with Paul's own missionary preaching. Moreover, Paul did not see the issue of idol food as one concerning sociological interaction between Jews and Gentiles. Rather, he set his discussion of idol food squarely in the context of idolatry. Because of this, one would not expect Paul to condone eating idol food without some strong reasons yet unknown to us. Thus the significance of the pervasive negative attitude toward idol food in early Judaism for Paul's own position cannot legitimately be downplayed by an uncritical appeal to Paul's rejection of the validity of Jewish dietary laws for Gentile Christians. If Paul was influenced by his Jewish hostility to idolatry in any significant ways, his attitude toward idol food was likely to be negative.

An exegetical examination of 1 Corinthians 8–10 shows that Paul is not settling an internal dispute between the strong and weak parties in Corinth. Many scholars seemed to have confused Paul's rhetoric in 1 Corinthians 8–10 with that in Romans 14, and read into Paul's discussion of idol food his attitude toward Jewish dietary laws. While Paul did remove the requirements of *kashrut* for Gentiles, he still insisted on an exclusive allegiance to the God of Israel expressed in the avoidance of idol food. His discussion in 1 Corinthians 8–10 is directed primarily to those who compromised this allegiance by eating idol food, leading to the climactic rhetorical questions: 'Shall we provoke the Lord to jealousy? Are we stronger than He?' (1 Cor. 10.22).

Contrary to the opinion of those who deny the literary integrity of 1 Corinthians 8–10, there is no inconsistency between 1 Corinthians 8 and 1 Cor. 10.1–22. The two passages represent two stages of Paul's argument to dissuade the Corinthian Christians from eating idol food. To eat idol food is both unloving and idolatrous. It will cause the weak to be ruined *and* bring God's judgment against idolatry upon oneself. Paul never explicitly permits eating idol food, he only says that one may eat anything without inquiring into the possibility of its being previously sacrificed to idols. Though food itself is neutral and there is no need to inquire about its origins, one is expected to abstain if the food is somehow identified as idol food. Paul's position in a nutshell is thus: idol food is dangerous; therefore avoid any food if, and only if, one knows that it is idol food.

A virtually exhaustive survey of early Christian writings turns up no evidence that any early Christian writer had any inkling of what would become the traditional understanding of Paul's approach. Significantly, what is usually considered the heart of Paul's argument—that idol food is something indifferent and should be avoided only for the sake of the weak—did not once surface in a plethora of writings about this extremely important issue in early Christianity. This is truly remarkable in view of the not infrequent mention of this same principle of having concern for the weak when Jewish dietary laws are in view. This renders the well-entrenched scholarly view highly unlikely.

Given the status of the idol food prohibition as a boundary-defining issue, many early Christians would hardly have been sympathetic with Paul if they thought that he condoned eating idol food. Yet not only did they had frequently and almost exclusively appeal to Paul to support their own position, but they also felt absolutely no need to defend their understanding of him against others who saw no problem in eating. They did not even seem to have any inkling that Paul condoned eating idol food or that his discussion had been construed to mean that. There is simply no evidence for any competing interpretation. This means that the usual scholarly understanding of Paul's position was either long forgotten at a very early stage or—more probably—never existed in early Christianity.

Opponents of idol food who were suspicious of, or antagonistic towards, Paul gave no hint that he condoned eating idol food, when any slightest evidence or rumors that Paul had taught thus would have made him a ready target for their attack. The same can be said if they merely thought that Paul's teaching could conceivably have been construed to mean that. Thus the traditional interpretation is very unlikely to be a natural reading of 1 Corinthians 8–10.

Those few who advocated eating idol food invariably failed to enlist 1 Corinthians 8–10 to support their position, even though they did appeal to it and other Pauline texts to justify other heterodox behavior or teaching. Their lack of appeal to Paul in this issue, especially when their position was vehemently condemned by the orthodox and could not be supported by other Christian writings, shows that 1 Corinthians 8–10 was not readily understood as a passage which would permit eating idol food.

It is also significant that most early authors who discussed the issue were strongly influenced by Paul's discussion. The Pauline argument that to eat idol food was to have fellowship with demons was so persuasive and definitive that it became *the* Christian argument against eating idol food and even the basis for the justification of the blood prohibition. This argument was known even to early pagan critics of Christianity.

When there is absolutely no evidence for any competing interpretations, such an early, widespread, and uniform understanding of Paul's approach cannot be dismissed except by internal evidence of the most persuasive sort. But, as argued earlier, the internal evidence of 1 Corinthians provides no clear support for the traditional view but is consistent with the view that Paul at root urged the avoidance of idol food. It is highly unlikely that the early Christians failed completely to understand what Paul wanted them to do because his argument was too complicated. After all who, early Christians or modern scholars, would be most likely to understand better the circumstances and the dynamics of living as a Christian minority in a city like Corinth, where pagan religions were woven into the very fabric of everyday life? Who, early Christians or modern scholars, would have been more likely to have had a deeper existential appreciation of Paul's discussion about demons and 'many gods and many lords'?

If the conclusions of my study are valid, then Paul, in the matter of idol food at least, was reconciled to his Jewish background and Christian legacy. Contrary to Barrett's claim, Paul's attitude is not un-Jewish at all. And contrary to Brunt's claim, Paul's approach has not been rejected, ignored, or misunderstood by early Christians. Instead, Paul stands firmly together with other Jews and Christians in seeing the conscious consumption of idol food as a denial of their allegiance to their Lord. The concord of Paul's thinking with that of early Judaism and Christianity on this issue should make one wary of extravagant claims of the *sui generis* nature of Paul's legal understanding.

2. *The Origins of Paul's Approach*

It is strictly beyond the scope of this investigation to trace the origins of Paul's attitude toward idol food. Nevertheless, it seems to me that this study would be somewhat incomplete (if there ever is a 'complete' study) if I did not register and briefly defend my own conjecture: the formative influence on Paul's approach was the Jewish Scriptures.

Early in his discussion on idol food, the theme of the *shema*, 'there is no God but one', is introduced as a fundamental principle underlying the whole discussion.[1] Paul's prohibition of idol food indeed brings us to the heart of Israel's monotheistic faith: there is only one God, the creator and redeemer of his people; yet false gods and powerful demons exist and are to be shunned. For Paul, as for Israel, the nothingness of idols is not ontological, but is to be understood in contrast with the power and glory of the one true God. Insofar as these false gods do not possess the same level of existence and power as the true God does, they are unreal. They are no rivals to the true God, however powerful they are for those who worship them and affirm their reality. Nevertheless, the non-reality of false gods does not make worshipping them a matter of indifference for God's people. On the contrary, precisely because these gods are unreal, they are to be shunned. Any act that might foster or condone their worship is simultaneously a denial of the confession of the One God. It detracts from God's glory that cannot be shared with any other. Therefore, as I have suggested earlier, in Deuteronomy, Psalms, and Isaiah, biblical books that Paul quotes often, both the nothingness of idols and the evil power of demons are affirmed with equal intensity. In fact, one cannot be separated from the other. It is precisely such a dual world-view that informs Paul's critique of idol food. Like idols themselves, idol food can be both indifferent (unreal) and demonic. Just as the non-reality of idols does not mean that one can participate in idolatry, the indifference of food does not mean one can eat idol food. The reason for shunning idolatry is the same reason that eating idol food is proscribed. Paul's logic is Jewish monotheistic logic. It is no accident that underlying Paul's discussion in 1 Corinthians 8–10 are classic passages in the Torah against eating idol food, Deuteronomy 32 and Numbers 25.

Not only is Paul's theological framework that of the Jewish Scriptures, but his practical instructions also have the unmistakable stamp of the biblical legal rulings.[2] I have argued that Paul urges abstention from idol food if it is known to be such, but one is not guilty if one eats idol food unknowingly. This somewhat casuistic approach to marketplace

---

1. On this point, see Wright, *Climax*, pp. 120-36.

2. Cf. the thorough study of B.S. Rosner (*Paul, Scripture and Ethics: A Study of 1 Corinthians 5–7* [AGJU, 22; Leiden: E.J. Brill, 1994]), which seeks to demonstrate that Scripture was the formative influence on Paul's ethical teaching in 1 Cor. 5–7. It is difficult to read his book and not be persuaded that Paul's reliance on Scripture for his ethical instructions was much more positive than most scholars tend to think.

food and dinner invitations by unbelievers finds strong parallels in biblical case laws. A clear example is Exod. 21.28-29: 'When an ox gores a man or a woman to death...the owner of the ox shall *not* be liable. But if the ox has been accustomed to gore in the past, and *its owner has been warned* but has not restrained it, and it kills a man or a woman...its owner shall be put to death.' Thus, the guilt or innocence of the owner depends on whether he knows the history of the ox's behavior, just as the guilt or innocence of the consumer of idol food depends on whether he knows the history of the food.

Similarly, the guilt or innocence of a man-slaughterer depends on whether he knowingly strikes the person: 'Whoever strikes a person mortally shall be put to death. If it was not premeditated, but came about by an act of God, then I will appoint for you a place to which the killer may flee' (Exod. 21.12-13). It is important to note that the passage is not here making an exception to the law on murder. The law remains that a murderer is to be put to death. What the passage does is to define more clearly what is meant by murder by giving a specific example of what is not murder: unknowingly striking a person to death is not murder and hence not subject to the general punishment for murder.

Exodus 22.2 offers another example of what is not murder: 'If a thief is found breaking in, and is beaten to death, no bloodguilt is incurred'. Thus killing a thief while he is breaking in at night is not subject to the law on murder—presumably because there is no premeditated intention to kill. But it is interesting that 'if it happens after sunrise, bloodguilt is incurred'—presumably because there is intention to kill or because the 'thief' who 'breaks in' after sunrise may not be a thief after all (Jer. 2.34)! The status of the killing changes and the case is now subject to the original law on murder.

In the same way, Paul affirms the general prohibition against eating idol food, but attaches an explanation that eating food of unknown origins does not constitute eating idol food. But once the idolatrous status of the food is known, the status of such eating changes accordingly and is then subject to the original general prohibition.

The exceptions in biblical laws are often not so much exceptions to the rule as clarifications of the rule. Specific examples are given lest one erroneously extrapolate beyond the intention of the general rule and make the rule impracticable or stricter than it ought to be. Leviticus 11.29-36 is a case in point:

> These are unclean for you among the creatures that swarm upon the
> earth: the weasel, the mouse... And anything upon which any of them
> falls when they are dead shall be unclean... And if any of them falls into
> any earthen vessel, all that is in it shall be unclean, and you shall break
> the vessel... Any food that could be eaten shall be unclean if water from
> any such vessel comes upon it; and any liquid that could be drunk shall
> be unclean if it was in any such vessel... *But a spring or a cistern hold-*
> *ing water shall be clean.*

In this example, there is a general rule that water in any vessel which
comes into contact with unclean creatures becomes unclean. And the
objection will surely arise: 'What about major water sources like
springs or cisterns? Since it is almost inevitable that some part of it will
come into contact with these creatures sometimes, are you saying,
Moses, these water sources are unclean too? Then where shall we find
water to use?' This objection is anticipated in the clarification of the
rule: that a small part of the water source has come into contact with
unclean creatures does not render the whole source unclean. The rule is
to teach the people of Israel to distinguish between clean and unclean;
it is not to make life impossible for them.

In the same way, Paul clarifies his general prohibition of idol food:
all marketplace food is not off limits simply because some of the food
sold in the market has previously been sacrificed. Paul recognizes that
believers need not go out of this world in order to fulfill God's commandments. The logic and spirit of Paul's instruction is thus strikingly
similar to that of many biblical case laws.

Of course, it is foolhardy to think that Paul could have bypassed
centuries of Jewish interpretive traditions and approached the Scriptures with a *tabula rasa*. His understanding of Scripture would have
been, to a considerable extent, conditioned by his upbringing and
training in Judaism of his day, as well as by interaction with other early
Christians. Yet the fact remains that, for 1 Corinthians 8–10 at least, it
is the Scriptures—not the sages or other traditions—to which Paul
made his most conscious, direct, and frequent appeal. Whatever unconscious influence the broad interpretive milieu of first-century Judaism
might have had on Paul's approach, there is no doubt that he relied on
the Scriptures, 'which were written down for our instructions' (1 Cor.
10.11), to provide support and authority for his own teaching.

3. *Concluding Hermeneutical Reflections*

I believe that this study has established beyond reasonable doubt that the usual understanding of Paul's attitude toward idol food cannot be correct. Yet the question is bound to arise: what makes the usual understanding of Paul's approach so attractive and plausible—to modern Western scholars at least?

Philosophers like Gadamer have made it abundantly clear that interpretation without pre-understanding is impossible. Our own historicality entails that the very questions we ask (or fail to ask) of a text, and the answers we expect from it, reflect the limitations and biases imposed by our present concern and the cultural baggage we carry. As I have hinted in the introduction to this study, the modern Christian preoccupation with ethical principles rather than with the concrete problem of idolatry has to a considerable extent determined what exegetes expect from the text. The desire to have a general scheme which provides values and principles that form a consistent system and cover all possible situations is evident in, for example, the English common law, a legal system with a minimum of statutes and a maximum of moral and legal reasoning. As D. Patrick puts it, 'genuine law, as opposed to arbitrary commands, must convince the conscience'.[3] Moreover, a rational and masterly Paul who bravely rejected narrow religious rules and superstition, and skillfully mediated between the opposing extremes of legalism and antinomianism, is certainly attractive to the modern mindset which regards it a virtue to avoid extremes. I am not suggesting that such a picture of Paul is wrong. I am only saying that it is incomplete, for it does not reveal the Paul who fiercely denounced idolatry and seriously reckoned with the power of demons. As the apocalyptic side of Paul is suppressed in favor of the rational, the results of the exegesis are easily skewed.

On a more fundamental level, I think Western secular materialism has subtly led commentators to overestimate the 'nothingness' of idols and hence underestimate the sinfulness of eating idol food. The Enlightenment and the development of modern science have shaped the modern perception of reality. The world is to be understood in secular terms without reference to the supernatural or the spiritual. Hence the typical attitude toward food is: 'Food is food, what's the matter?'

---

3.   D. Patrick, *Old Testament Law* (Atlanta: John Knox Press, 1985), p. 4.

Whether it is idol food, or even the Lord's Supper, the transcendental meaning of eating is almost completely evaporated. And Christians do not totally escape the influence of this secular world-view.

To be sure, there is some truth in the statement 'food is food' from the biblical perspective. The Scriptures affirm that God is sovereign and idols are no real rivals to him, hence they do not have the power to defile any food sacrificed to them. So far so good. But coupled with the atheistic or deistic framework of the Enlightenment, what begins as a legitimate insight into biblical truth easily degenerates into an imposition of alien conceptual structures. Because idolatry is not a problem in the Western church, Christians may simply not hear the Bible when it warns us of the power and darkness of demonic forces. Idols are so 'demythologized' into existential categories that they now come to mean one's wealth, fame, family, or any other objects of one's pursuit. It is not my purpose to dispute whether these are valid applications of scriptural teaching. My point is that when the Bible speaks about idols it almost always means real idols—idols associated with real demonic forces. There is spiritual warfare on planes other than the existential.

In cultures more sensitive to demonic forces (such as the Asian culture or the Biblical culture), many Christians by instinct have regarded idol food as abominable. I have already observed how abhorrent idol food was to early Christians. I have also come across many Asian Christians who literally cannot stomach idol food, even after they have been told that it is all right to do so after giving thanks, and even when their attitude is fairly 'free' regarding other issues.[4] Though experience is no sure guide to truth, I cannot help feeling that there is probably something to the way they instinctively react. Can it be that, having been educated by the Holy Spirit, they intuitively feel the evil of eating idol food, even though they are not able to articulate the reason for their abstinence?[5]

---

4.   Unlike the case with Jewish aversion to pork or the food taboos which exist in every culture, Asian Christians are not brought up to treat idol food as something 'sickening'. The decisive factor in their aversion to idol food is their turning from dumb idols to serve the living God.

5.   I believe Frame is right in maintaining that emotion, or feeling, is a valid existential perspective from which we apprehend truth, and that 'a right (i.e. justified and true) feeling is a right belief, that is knowledge' (J.M. Frame, *The Doctrine of the Knowledge of God: A Theology of Lordship* (Phillipsburg, NJ: Presbyterian & Reformed, 1987], p. 338).

Of course, the above general argument of the influence of culture cuts both ways. If Western emphasis on rational consistency and individual freedom may provide grounds for rationalization and the seeking of legal loopholes, Eastern emphasis on authority and rules may result in the imposition of arbitrary commands that engenders legalism. On a more fundamental level, if Western culture tends to underestimate the power of demonic forces, Eastern culture tends to overestimate it. Eastern mysticism can easily lead to the overrating of the transcendental meaning of eating. The influence of dualism can also create the conception of demons as real rivals to God and lead to undue fear of them and anything associated with them, thus losing sight of the truth that the earth is the Lord's and everything therein. Therefore this heightened awareness of the spiritual can be a liability as well as an asset. Without proper biblical control, it can degenerate into an oppressive bondage. I know of Christians who used to smell idols everywhere and smash expensive antiques because they thought these were the locale of demons. Such people did not fully enjoy the victory and liberty which Christ's redemptive work has achieved.

An idol is nothing when conceived of as God's rival, yet food sacrificed to it is associated with demons which are real and powerful. There is an undeniable tension, and indeed a paradox, in such a belief. Some may even call it an inconsistency. However, it is a charge to which faith in a God who creates everything and yet hates evil is inevitably susceptible. A theological conundrum of this kind is inherent in any Christian theology which takes seriously the sovereignty of God and the reality of evil. Like sin and evil, demons entered the world both contrary to God's will and according to God's plan. They are powerless and yet destructive. Christians have victory over them and yet need constantly be watchful in avoiding them. Satan is bound (Mt. 12.29) and yet prowls around as a roaring lion, seeking someone to devour (1 Pet. 5.8). We need to maintain both biblical perspectives in all their tension and ambiguities rather than flatten them to suit our cultural framework or limited rational minds.

Appendix

EVALUATION OF SOME MAJOR STUDIES

While I have interacted with various scholarly opinions in more or less detail in the course of this investigation, it is appropriate to discuss here briefly some major studies of Paul's approach and to indicate important areas of my disagreement with them. The views of John Hurd and Gordon Fee have already been evaluated in Chapter 3 and hence will not be discussed here. The authors whose views I will address are Tomson, Gooch, Willis, Theissen (an example of sociological study of 1 Cor. 8–10), Mitchell (an example of rhetorical study), and Witherington.

1. *Peter J. Tomson*

Like my interpretation, Tomson's understanding of Paul's approach to idol food strongly challenges the well-entrenched scholarly consensus. Tomson argues that while Paul is not a systematic thinker, he is not incoherent. It is unlikely that Paul contradicts himself in 1 Corinthians 8 and 1 Corinthians 10. Nor is Paul discussing two different situations. Tomson's understanding is that 'while 1 Cor. 8 introduces the problem and 10.1-22 reiterates the general prohibition of food known to be consecrated to idols, 10.25-29 deals with food of unspecified nature in a pagan setting'.[1]

By affirming Paul's essential Jewishness and assuming that Paul operates within a halakhic framework, Tomson comes to the conclusion that Paul 'does not teach a partial permission to eat idol food. He teaches a rational, halakhic definition of what should be considered an idol offering in uncertain cases and what should not.'[2] This interpretation and mine can be seen as corollaries to each other.

Tomson also points out that the uniformity with which idol food was prohibited among both Jews and early Christians makes it highly unlikely that Paul would have condoned eating such food.[3] But he makes no attempt to assess how or whether the diverse Jewish material has influenced Paul, or how or whether Paul has influenced early Christian attitudes toward idol food.

I think Tomson is essentially correct in seeing Paul in the context of his Jewish, and in particular, Pharisaic background. But his investigation of 1 Corinthians 8–10

---

1. Tomson, *Jewish Law*, p. 208.
2. Tomson, *Jewish Law*, p. 217.
3. Tomson, *Jewish Law*, pp. 151-86.

is too heavily weighted toward a consideration of the influence of Tannaitic halakha on Paul to be fully convincing.[4] This heavy focus on the halakha tends to minimize the dynamic variety of expressions of first-century Judaism that recent scholarship has rightly emphasized. To take an obvious problem, the fundamental role eschatology plays in Paul's thinking does not easily square with the supposition that Paul's Jewishness must be seen primarily in terms of rabbinic halakha, in which eschatological discussions are conspicuously absent.

Moreover, because of the lateness of the codification of rabbinic teachings, any discussion of rabbinic halakha in Paul's time—even if one can legitimately speak of 'Rabbis' as an institution in the first century—necessarily raises the question of anachronism. For example, the so-called Noachic commandments, which bear some resemblance to the apostolic decree in Acts 15, cannot be traced to earlier than the third century CE.[5] Therefore, I am less certain than Tomson to what extent rabbinic halakhot governing idolatry and relations with Gentiles reflect the situation in first-century Judaism.

It cannot be denied that Paul's 'casuistic' reasoning in 1 Cor. 10.25-29 is, as Tomson argues, consistent with halakhic procedures. Yet casuistry is such a necessary feature of human legal thinking that it is hardly unique to rabbinic halakha. After all, Augustine, who has little acquaintance with Jewish halakha, discusses in a 'casuistic' manner the proper response of an imaginary hungry traveler who finds food in front of a statue or altar with nobody around.[6] On the other hand Segal, who basically holds the usual view of Paul's approach, makes precisely the same assumption as Tomson does that Paul's approach is halakhic—and explains Paul's 'accommodationist position' with reference to the halakha![7] The fact is that the halakha encompasses so broad a spectrum of practical wisdom that one is able to adduce parallels to almost any type of thinking.

Tomson's broadening of halakha to include not only other Jewish ethical instructions but also those derived from Jesus and the other apostles, and even Paul's personal ethical teaching, further weakens the persuasiveness of his thesis. For if halakha is defined so broadly, then, almost by definition, the texture of Paul's ethical thinking must be halakhic. But the problem is more than mere tautology. Unfortunately, Tomson sometimes tends to slip back to the narrower definition of halakha as being *rabbinic* halakha. This produces the fallacious argument that because Paul's thinking finds strong parallels in halakha (broad definition), the formative influence on his ethical thinking is rabbinic halakha (narrow definition).

I do not want to re-argue here my contention that the formative influence on Paul's approach to idol food is the Jewish Scriptures. I simply want to note that Paul's approach, for which Tomson provides halakhic parallels, can be otherwise

4.   Tomson covers non-rabbinic Jewish material on idol food in a mere paragraph (*Jewish Law*, pp. 153-54), in contrast to his extensive discussion of Tannaitic halakha on the issue, which spans two dozen pages (pp. 154-77).

5.   Segal, *Paul*, p. 195.

6.   Note that the recent policy on gays in the US military, 'Don't ask; don't tell; don't pursue', represents a striking example of similar casuistic reasoning.

7.   Segal, *Paul*, pp. 192, 237.

explained and paralleled by biblical case laws. It is possible that the scriptural influence on Paul was partly via rabbinic halakha (and other strands of Jewish literature). But it is also possible that Paul's ethical advice and rabbinic halakha represent parallel developments of legal teaching in the Jewish Scriptures (perhaps mediated through first-century Pharisaic teaching, which is not necessarily identical to rabbinic halakha). We cannot be sure. What seems indisputable is that, in his discussion in 1 Corinthians 8–10 at least, Paul made his conscious and direct appeals to the Scriptures rather than to the sages.

2. *Peter D. Gooch*

Gooch's social-historical investigation of Paul's response to the Corinthian Christians concerning idol food reaches conclusions with which I find little to disagree. From his thorough analysis of archaeological and literary data concerning the concrete settings and social meaning of idol food in Paul's Corinth, he concludes that it is highly improbable that eating social meals in temples was perceived in any other way than taking part in idolatry. Based on his own συνείδησις as a Jew, Paul at root considered idol food dangerous and therefore attempted to dissuade the Corinthian Christians from eating any food infected by non-Christian religious rites. Paul's advice against eating idol food on grounds that it might harm the weak was only the first stage of his argument toward that goal.

On the whole, my work differs from Gooch's not so much in what he does, but in what he does not do. For example, given Gooch's conviction that Paul's attitude toward idol food is conditioned by his self-understanding as a Jew, it is surprising that Gooch does not make any effort at all to explore the relevance of Paul's Jewish background. Again, he may be criticized for not exploring the influence of Paul's attitude in early Christianity. But it would be unfair to dwell on what he fails to do in a dissertation which has other objectives and which has already done so much.

My main disagreement with Gooch concerns his denial that Paul's approach is consistent or principled. He sees Paul's advice regarding marketplace food as an accommodation to the strong which goes against Paul's own conception of idol food as a vector of contagion.[8] Since 'what he [Paul] says does not reveal any distinction at all between idolatry and food', a basic conflict remains between Paul's prohibition of idol food and permission to eat marketplace food which might well have been offered to idols.[9] In my opinion, Gooch pushes Paul's warning about the danger of eating idol food too far when he argues that

8. Gooch, 'Food and Limits', pp. 250-58. 'In my [Gooch's] view, the inconsistency between 10.25 and chapter 8 and 10.27-28 remains unaccounted for, except as an instance of Paul's lack of perception of inconsistency or lack of concern over it' (p. 258).

9. Gooch, 'Food and Limits', p. 255. Gooch also notes that 'the claim that Paul makes a distinction between food as food and the idolatry which food sometimes expresses cannot be supported cleanly from the text of 1 Corinthians 8.1–11.1. Paul instead says both things—that food can be just food, but that idol-food as food can kill. If commentators shy at admitting that Paul says the latter, it may be that they are embarrassed for him; if commentators argue an underlying consistency to Paul's views on the status of food as food, they go further than the text allows.'

Paul's warnings in 10.14-22, read together with 11.17-34, show very clearly that Paul sees the *koinônia* (which can lead either to God's blessing or God's rejection) *inherent* in food; the cup and the bread *are* partnership in the blood and body of Christ (10.16), and it is the *table* of demons—not the allegiance to demons expressed by this rite or some such more abstract concept, but the concrete cup and table of *daimonia*—that breaks *koinônia* with the Lord.[10]

While 1 Cor. 11.17-34 threatens (and documents) divine judgment upon wrongful behavior in association with eating, it does not provide support for the idea that food itself can have such dangerous effects. I believe that Paul's approach is much more consistent than Gooch thinks. Contrary to Gooch's assertion, Paul does make 'a distinction between food as food and food as instrument of idolatry'.[11] For Paul, the danger of eating idol food is not in the food itself but in the implicit denial of the Christian confession of the One God by affirming the reality of idols in any way. This alone will explain why Paul can be so relaxed about the eating of food possibly, but not definitely, sacrificed to idols.[12]

3. *Wendell L. Willis*

Willis's study, which has exercised great influence on scholarly discussion of the topic, on the whole affirms the traditional understanding of Paul's approach to idol food. I will not repeat my criticism of the traditional view. Here I simply want to address in some detail a central feature of Willis's interpretation, namely, that meals in temple precincts, and even most cultic meals, were basically social in character and were only nominally or minimally religious.

Willis rejects earlier interpretations of Greco-Roman sacrificial meals as 'sacramental' in the sense of magical or quasi-magical consumption of the god which effects salvation. Instead, he sees most of these meals as occasions where 'the focus is on the social relationship among the worshippers. The deity is more an observer than a participant.'[13] As an extension of this understanding, Willis stresses that 'κοινωνία means the relationship established among members of a covenant and the obligations ensuing from it'.[14] Therefore κοινωνία with the demons or Christ does not refer to mystical participation in the demons or Christ but covenant relationship with other idolaters or Christians.[15] Paul's objection to eating idol food is not on the basis that such eating effects partnership with demons but on the basis

10. Gooch, 'Food and Limits', p. 255; emphases original.

11. Gooch, 'Food and Limits', p. 254.

12. In Gooch's opinion, the reason for Paul's relaxed attitude about marketplace food is that, inconsistently with his aversion to idol food, Paul genuinely saw no danger in marketplace food, and hence did not challenge the Corinthians' views of it. Even if, for argument's sake, Paul's advice about marketplace food is unprincipled, Gooch's understanding is unlikely to be correct. Why does Paul need to tell the Corinthian Christians not to inquire, when a simple permission to 'buy and eat whatever in the market' will do? Surely the strong are not having a weak conscience which leads them to inquire!

13. Willis, *Idol Meat*, pp. 7-64 (20).

14. Willis, *Idol Meat*, p. 209.

15. Willis, *Idol Meat*, pp. 188-212.

of how such eating affects the body of Christ. This understanding of Paul's argument in 1 Cor. 10.1-22 is then seen as consistent with Paul's advice in 1 Corinthians 8, which urges abstention from idol food on the grounds that it might hurt the weak.

I think Willis is correct in stressing the social character of most meals in temples. But he is seriously mistaken in thinking that the secular nature of those meals is thereby established. In setting up a false dichotomy between the social and the religious, he is seeing the matter as a strictly 'either–or' rather than 'both–and'.[16] He grossly underestimates the religious import of Greco-Roman social meals by failing to see that the social and the religious aspects of meals are often intermingled and mutually enforcing. Why could not 'occasions of good company, good food and good fun' have been authentic religious occasions at the same time?[17]

While many ancients might not have had a sacramental understanding of sacrificial food in the sense of crude theophagy (even this point is debatable),[18] they would not have thought of it in purely social terms without some consciousness of the gods. Undoubtedly, there were atheists then as now and Willis has provided examples of misconduct in cultic meals which show disregard of the gods. But Gooch's survey of social meals in the Greco-Roman period shows that these people were definitely in the minority. Plutarch can say as a matter of fact that 'it is not the abundance of wine or the roasting of meat that makes the joy of the festivals, but the good hope and belief that the god is present in his kindness and graciously accepts what is offered' (*Mor.* 1102A). Moreover, even people who did not pay much respect to the gods could still be very superstitious and would go through at least some of the rituals. In any case, since their personal assessment of the religious significance of the meals was not known to Paul, they could only be judged on their outward involvement in sacrificial rites. And Paul would not have perceived their actions as anything but idolatry.[19]

---

16. To be sure, Willis concedes that 'even in the social understanding of these meals, it is granted that due regard was given, and a portion allotted, to the deity. Their presence at such meals was assumed' (*Idol Meat*, p. 48). Yet he continues to maintain the distinction by arguing that the important issue is whether the 'focus' of the participants was religious or social. Against this it may be noted that the mind or focus of the participants was not accessible to Paul, who would have judged them idolators because of their outward acts.

17. Willis, *Idol Meat*, p. 63.

18. According to Klauck, some sacred meals were indeed theophagy (*Herrenmahl*, pp. 50-52).

19. In the second part of his important monograph on the origins of the *Herrenmahl* (pp. 31-233), Klauck examines an immense variety of evidence for different forms and functions of sacred meals in the environment of early Christianity from a phenomenological perspective and classifies those meals into eleven different types: (1) *Göttermahl*; (2) *Götterspeisung*; (3) *Opfermahl*; (4) *Kommunionopfer*; (5) *Gottessen (Theophagie)*; (6) *Bündnismahl*; (7) *Vereinsmahl*; (8) *Totenmahl*; (9) *Tägliches Mahl*; (10) *Mysterienmahl*; (11) *Sakrament.* Klauck recognizes that his classification is not rigid and there is overlapping between types. But the general picture that emerges is clear: as far as phenomenology is concerned, most of these meals are indeed religious in character. That even daily meals are sacralized speaks strongly about the religious mindset of the populace.

Likewise, Willis's essentially secular reading of Paul's understanding of the Lord's Supper cannot be sustained. While Paul holds nothing like a crass theophagy, there is a fundamental and pervasive Christ-mysticism in his teaching on the believers' union with Christ, which effects their union with one another. Willis has unjustifiably dichotomized κοινωνία with Christ and κοινωνία with other Christians.

Willis also greatly underestimates Paul's concern about the danger of partaking of the table of demons. In effect, he substitutes the idolatrous community for demons and makes Paul say, 'though idols are nothing, the idolatrous community is everything'. But Paul's expressed statement is that eating idol food provokes *the Lord's*—not other believers'—jealousy and incurs severe judgment. Therefore the problem he attacks is much more serious than mere wrongful association with idolaters, the eating with which is, incidentally, permitted by Paul provided no explicitly identified idol food is served (1 Cor. 5.9-11, 10.27-29).

4. *Gerd Theissen*

Theissen's study on the strong and the weak in Corinth represents the first major attempt to apply sociological theory to the problem of idol food.[20] Theissen challenges a 'common' assumption that the 'strong' and the 'weak' in 1 Corinthians 8–10 refer to Gentile and Jewish Christians respectively.[21] He proposes instead that this distinction reflects differences of economic and social status: the rich and powerful had frequent occasions to eat meat offered to idols with their business and social contacts. They tended to see little problem in eating such meat. On the other hand, the poor, who rarely ate meat, would have done so almost exclusively on cultic occasions and so associated eating idol meat with the worship of the pagan gods. The social stratification of the Corinthian Christian community was thus the main cause of the conflict.[22] 1 Corinthians 8–10 is Paul's attempt to mediate between these two socially stratified groups.[23]

According to Theissen, Paul is in basic agreement with the strong's position.[24] 'Paul's recommendation, based on love, that the higher classes accommodate their behavior to the lower classes, only mitigates the tension between the two but allows

20. Gerd Theissen, 'Die Starken und Schwachen in Korinth: Soziologische Analyse eines theologische Streites', *EvT* 35 (1975), pp. 155-72. This article is translated and collected by John H. Schultz in *The Social Setting of Pauline Christianity. Essays on Corinth by G. Theissen* (trans. J.H. Schultz; Philadelphia: Fortress Press, 1982), pp. 121-43. Translations of Theissen's other articles dealing with 1 Corinthians are also collected in the same volume.

21. This view which Theissen opposes is in fact common only in works that refer to 1 Cor. 8–10 in passing. Most scholars who examine the passage in detail do not hold this view. Most indeed point out that 1 Cor. 8.7 implies that the weak are Gentiles.

22. Theissen argues that the majority of the Christians in Corinth were from the lower classes, but the church was basically led by a minority from the upper classes (*Social Setting*, pp. 69-119).

23. Theissen, *Social Setting*, pp. 138-39. Cf. pp. 35-40, where Theissen sees Paul's role as a community organizer who sought to win the support of both the rich and the poor.

24. Theissen, *Social Setting*, p. 138.

the differing customs to continue to exist'.[25] In this way Paul preserves the 'factual privileges of status enjoyed by the higher strata' of the Corinthian church: 'private meals with consecrated meat continue to be allowed in principle... Nor is participation in cultic meals excluded in principle'.[26] Thus eating idol meat is an indifferent matter as long as the weak brother is not harmed.

It is clear that Theissen affirms many elements of the traditional understanding of Paul's approach while providing further support to them by sociological reasoning. This fact alone goes a long way in explaining the positive reception Theissen's work has received. On the other hand, his explanation is therefore subject to much of the same criticism I have made against the traditional view in Chapter 3. I do not want to reiterate my misgivings about the traditional view here. I simply want to note that the failure on Theissen's part to challenge the major elements of the traditional understanding shows clearly the descriptive nature of the sociological approach. *If* one knows what had actually occurred between Paul and the Corinthian Christians, the application of different sociological models can provide new perspectives and insights in looking at the problem. But such an approach is least helpful when the actual historical situation is unclear or misconstrued.

Upon my first reading of Theissen's ground-breaking work, I was struck by the simplicity, elegance and explanatory power of his thesis. It has demonstrated the tremendous potential benefits of a sociological approach to the study of Paul's letters. Nevertheless, Theissen's thesis must in the end be judged unconvincing because it rests on a number of highly questionable, and probably mistaken, assumptions.

First, Theissen argues that the rich would have been more seriously affected by an avoidance of idol food. This could be true, but is difficult to prove. In view of the ubiquitous use of religious rites over meals in the Greco-Roman period, avoiding idol food would not have been easy for the poor either. One cannot assume that the rich in Corinth would have been more reluctant than the poor to reject idol food simply on the ground that they had the more to lose, for they also had more that they could afford to lose! If the history of missions is any guide, the avoidance of idol food seemed to affect the poor Christians more severely than the wealthier ones, whose economic power might serve as a buffer in mitigating hostility from social acquaintances.

Moreover, Theissen assumes that εἰδωλόθυτον was meat. But actually many non-meat products were offered to the gods.[27] Therefore, even if the poor hardly ate meat, they would still have had ample opportunities to eat idol food. And it is not true that the poor hardly ate meat. As Meggitt points out, literary evidence shows clearly that (lower quality) meat was 'frequently consumed by [the non-elite] in settings which were decidedly unsacral' and was thus 'a familiar enough part of

---

25. Theissen, *Social Setting*, p. 139.

26. *Social Setting*, p. 139. Theissen thinks that, in 1 Cor. 10.1-22, Paul perhaps only forbids a strong Christian 'to extend a reciprocal invitation for the same kind of meal. To do so would make him the initiator of "idol worship" ' (p. 122).

27. Cf. Gooch, 'Food and Limits', pp. 180-83.

everyday life of the "non-elite" that "numinous" qualities could not have been ascribed to it'.[28] The evidence listed by Meggitt corroborates the impression we gain from the reading of 1 Corinthians 8–10. In Paul's discussion, idol food seems to have been something commonplace, as accessible to the weak as to the knowers. We need not dispute Theissen's claim that wealthier people ate meat more often. Nevertheless, if the opportunities for the weak to eat idol food were really as limited as Theissen suggests, it is difficult to make sense of Paul's urgent concern for the weak, since they could hardly have followed the knowers' example even if they wanted to.[29]

Secondly, Theissen assumes that 'the spokesmen of the Corinthian parties, that is, protagonists among the followers of other missionaries, belong to the upper classes' and that Paul only defends himself before such an elite group in 1 Cor. 9.3.[30] Now there is evidence that *some* wealthy members were the cause of some problems in Corinth like litigation (ch. 6) and abuse of the Lord's Supper (ch. 11). But can we assume that the majority of the well-to-do were responsible for all the problems, including the problem of idol food? Some arithmetic shows that it is very unlikely that this was the case.

Theissen's study yields a list of names of seventeen people who were probably active in the Corinth church. Of these nine clearly belonged to the upper classes. This also may have been true of three others. The rest are uncertain.[31] Now, as Witherington points out, it is reasonable to suppose that most of them were married and had children.[32] So the households of those socially better off individuals whose names we know would have accounted for perhaps thirty members in the church. We do not have a head count of the Corinthian congregation, but it was almost certainly under a hundred. Based on his calculation of the average space of four large houses excavated in Corinth, Murphy-O'Connor thinks that fifty is a realistic limit, considering the difficulty of accommodating 'the whole church' (1 Cor. 14.23) in even a well-to-do house.[33] Given Paul's statement in 1 Cor. 1.26-28 that not many of the Corinthians are 'wise', 'powerful', or 'of noble birth', the number of those who belonged to high status families (excluding slaves) is unlikely to have been much bigger than thirty. This means that we may already have most of the names of high status members in Corinth. But most of these people, except perhaps Apollos, seem to have been in Paul's camp! None of them appears to have been the

---

28. Meggitt, 'Meat Consumption', pp. 137-40. Note also Witherington's incidental remark that both Claudius and Nero attempted to ban selling of meat in the *popinae* and *taberna* (referred to by J.E. Stambaugh, *The Ancient Roman City* [Baltimore: The Johns Hopkins University Press, 1988], pp. 208-209). Such attempts would have been unnecessary had meat not been widely available in those establishments. Witherington's remark is made for a different point.

29. Note that probably only citizens had the right to receive the public distribution of sacrificed meat on significant ceremonial occasions. This would have limited even further the opportunities for the poor to eat meat, if the only source of meat for them was sacrificed meat from cultic feasts.

30. Theissen, *Social Setting*, p. 97.

31. Theissen, *Social Setting*, pp. 69-96.

32. Witherington, *Conflict and Community*, p. 32.

33. Murphy-O'Connor, *Corinth*, pp. 153-58.

target of Paul's vehement rhetoric. As Wire observes, Paul considers them his reliable sources (Chloe, 1.11), converts (Crispus, Gaius, Stephanus, 1.14-16) co-workers (Apollos, Prisca, Aquila, and Stephenus 3.5-6; 16.15,19) and helpers worthy of respect (Stephenus, Fortunatus, Achaicus, 16.17-18).[34] She quips that 'Theissen should have asked whether those claiming Apollos might not have lower social status'.[35]

Thirdly, the correspondence between theological view and social status that Theissen proposed seems to me a retrojection of modern Western cultural behavior patterns onto the ancient world.[36] Most anachronistic and culturally insensitive is his suggestion that Paul 'would not contest the right to participate in temple meals with *the appropriate mental reservations*'.[37] This kind of introspection-governed behavior was hardly common in ancient Mediterranean (and much of modern non-Western) culture, which is primarily non-introspective, other-directed, and honor-and-shame based. In other words, Theissen's explanations may be culturally ill-suited to the social world he describes so well.[38]

5. *Margaret Mitchell and Rhetorical Analyses of 1 Corinthians 8–10*

Mitchell's study analyzes 1 Corinthians 8–10 in terms of the literary and rhetorical conventions of the first century. Arguing that 1.10 is the *propositio* of the whole letter, she identifies anti-factionalism as Paul's rhetorical choice and reads Paul's discussion on idol food against the background of responses to factionalism in Greco-Roman political texts.

Mitchell's erudition and mastery of ancient rhetorical theories are beyond doubt. She has shown that 1 Corinthians 8–10 has some traits found in works of deliberative rhetoric. However, it is doubtful whether her designation of 1 Corinthians as a letter of deliberative rhetoric is justified. It is much less certain that anti-factionalism is the main issue of 1 Corinthians 8–10.

Before addressing the specifics of Mitchell's study, I want to draw attention to some general problems in applying ancient rhetorical categories to the analysis of letters. It is not my purpose—and strictly beyond my competence—to discuss the relevance of classical rhetorical criticism to the study of Paul's letters. The advantage of this approach is clear: it helps us situate Paul's letters in their literary con

---

34. Wire, *Women Prophets*, p. 66.

35. Wire, *Women Prophets*, p. 218. Wire does allow for P. Marshall's (*Enmity in Corinth: Social Conventions in Paul's Relations with the Corinthians* [WUNT, 2.23; Tübingen: J.C.B. Mohr, 1987], pp. 341-48) argument that rhetorical convention rather than low status prevents Paul from naming his opponents. However, if we are right in concluding that most of the wealthy individuals have already been named and they are sympathetic to Paul, then there are not that many people who could have been named as Paul's opponents.

36. Such a correspondence is not even always true in modern society. Wealthy Christians can be very conservative theologically.

37. Theissen, *Social Setting*, p. 122.

38. Cf. W.F. Taylor's review of Theissen's study in *Dialog* 23 (1984), pp. 151-52.

text and facilitates a comparative study with other texts in the same period. But there are also major obstacles:[39]

1. Ancient rhetorical theorists hardly discussed letter writing until the fourth century CE. Categories appropriate to oratory probably did not influence epistolography to any significant degree. Witherington tries to sidestep this problem by arguing that 'letters in the hand of a Cicero or a Paul became surrogates for and extensions of oral speech ... and the rhetorical conventions of public speech and discourse were carried over into such letters'.[40] The first assertion may well be correct. Paul's letters did at times appear to function as speeches *in absentia*. But the second assertion flies in face of Cicero's own understanding of the (lack of) relationship between speech and letters: *'quid enim simile habet epistula aut iudicio aut contioni?'* (*Fam.* 9.21.1).[41]

2. 1 Corinthians is much lengthier than typical Greco-Roman letters. It is not even certain whether *Gattungen* pertaining to ancient letter writings are appropriate for 1 Corinthians. Moreover, if Paul could deviate so much from the typical letters in terms of length, there is no reason to think that he would not deviate significantly from classical models in matters of structure and style.

3. It is true that Paul would have been acquainted with the broad stance of Greco-Roman rhetoric.[42] He was definitely no cultural Philistine. However, to argue for the close conformity of Paul's letters to ancient rhetorical models assumes a much more specific training in, and use of, Greco-Roman rhetoric on Paul's part. Such an assumption does not sit well with Paul's characterization of himself as an ἰδιώτης τῷ λόγῳ (2 Cor. 11.6), suggesting a lack of finesse and eloquence in public speaking.[43] His

39. See S.E. Porter, 'The Theoretical Justification for Application of Rhetorical Categories to Pauline Epistolary Literature', in S.E. Porter and T.H. Olbricht (eds.), *Rhetoric and the New Testament: Essays from the 1992 Heidelberg Conference* (JSNTSup, 90; Sheffield: JSOT Press, 1993), pp. 100-22; R.D. Anderson, Jr, *Ancient Rhetorical Theory and Paul* (Kampen: Pharos, 1996), pp. 93-104, 249-56; A.J. Malherbe, *Ancient Epistolary Theorists* (SBLSBS, 19; Atlanta: Scholars Press, 1988).

40. Witherington, *Conflict and Community*, p. 45.

41. As Anderson (*Rhetorical Theory*, pp. 101-102) observes, Cicero's question also makes G.A. Kennedy's assertion (*New Testament Interpretation through Rhetorical Criticism* [Chapel Hill: University of North Carolina Press, 1984], p. 141) that 'the structure of a Greco-Roman letter resembles a speech' *prima facie* suspect.

42. See M.A. Bullmore, *St. Paul's Theology of Rhetorical Style: An Examination of I Corinthians 2.1-5 in Light of First Century Graeco-Roman Rhetorical Culture* (San Francisco: International Scholars Press, 1995), esp. chapter 4, on the level of Paul's rhetorical awareness. Bullmore's thesis is that Paul chose a simple and unaffected style in his preaching even though he was fully aware of the aesthetics style of the orators.

43. It is well beyond the scope of this investigation to discuss Paul's educational background, which is a highly controversial subject. In regard to rhetorical training, I think Hengel ('Vorchristliche Paulus', pp. 212-39) is probably correct that Paul's rhetorical art was not derived directly from Greco-Roman rhetorical models, but through frequent speaking and teaching in Greek-

downplaying of ὑπεροχή λόγος (1 Cor. 2.1) may be likewise understood.[44]

4. In contrast to Diaspora Jews like Philo, Paul wrote reasonable, but unsophisticated, Greek.[45] This fact was not lost in the comments of early church fathers, many of whom were well trained in rhetorical theory and thus in a much better position to judge the level of Paul's literary sophistication.[46] The relatively low literary quality of Paul's writing represented for Augustine a test of faith and humility.

I do not want to minimize the importance of the rhetorical milieu within which Paul worked and wrote. Nevertheless, until we have more understanding of ancient epistolography and the degree to which Paul's writings conform to classical models, it is probably more fruitful to focus on Paul's method of argumentation rather than attempt a sustained or comprehensive rhetorical analysis of 1 Corinthians in terms of ancient rhetoric.

When we come to specifics, Mitchell's identification of 1 Corinthians as a work of anti-factionalism deliberative rhetoric is clearly problematic. In view of the multifarious nature of the problems and conflicts revealed in 1 Corinthians, to see the thematic and rhetorical unity of the letter under the categories of factionalism and reconciliation seems reductionistic. For an obvious example, Paul's discussion on the topic of resurrection in ch. 15 has little if anything to do with factionalism in the church. Still, Mitchell is undaunted. She argues that Paul 'appeals to the resurrected life to minimize the importance of the present striving to supremacy within the community' and 'to urge concord in the present'.[47] The 'different views on the resurrection which various groups within the church hold' is considered evidence for factionalism that Paul seeks to combat.[48] But the problem is that Paul does not make any such connections to factionalism in the text. The division of the Corinthians on the issue of resurrection is very different in nature to the factionalism which

---

speaking synagogues. This is not to deny that oral training for synagogue teaching was itself influenced to some degree by classical models, but to insist that Hellenistic rhetorical traditions had only a general and indirect influence on Paul. In obvious contrast to his contemporary orators, Paul makes little use of Greek and Latin authors or external rhetorical artifices. The fabric of his letters is fundamentally Jewish and scriptural. Cf. C.J. Classen, 'Paulus und die antike Rhetorik', *ZNTW* 82 (1991), pp. 1-33; N.A. Rosaeg, 'Paul's Rhetorical Arsenal and 1 Corinthians 1–4', *Jian Dao* 3 (1995), pp. 51-75.

44. It is sometimes argued that the disavowal of rhetorical techniques is itself a rhetorical ploy used by clever rhetoricians! But Paul's lack of sophistication in speech is not just a Pauline statement, but also his opponents' impression. More importantly, as Litfin (*Proclamation*, pp. 259-60) observes, 'Paul grounds his disavowal in his deepest convictions regarding God, the Spirit, and the cross of Christ. To see this as nothing more than a rhetorical ploy misconstrues not only the Apostle's motives but the argument of 1 Cor. 1–4 as well.'

45. Judging from the contrast between Paul's Greek and Philo's, I think Paul's Greek is probably not much better than my English, of which I am not a native speaker.

46. Anderson, *Rhetorical Theory*, p. 251. Anderson refers to the study of E. Norden on the church fathers' views on Paul's style (*Die antike Kunstprosa: Vom vi Jahrhundert v. Chr. Bis in die Zeit der Renaissance* [2 vols; Darmstadt: Wissenschaftliche Buchgesellschaft, 1898], pp. 501-506).

47. Mitchell, *Rhetoric*, pp. 175-76.

48. Mitchell, *Rhetoric*, p. 176.

Paul rebukes in 1 Corinthians 1–4. If Paul says anything about divisions at all in 1 Corinthians 15, he urges separation rather than concord in dealing with those who hold deviant views on the resurrection (15.33)![49] Likewise, Mitchell can relate issues of fornication and marriage to that of anti-factionalism only by highly imaginative and associative reasoning that is not based on textual data she purports to analyze so carefully.

In the chapter on the thematic and rhetorical unity in 1 Corinthians, Mitchell discusses 1 Corinthians 8–10 under the heading 'Factionalism, Freedom and Compromise' and subheadings 'offense and factionalism', 'freedom and accommodation', 'the negative example of the wilderness generation', 'unity in sharing the same rituals', 'factionalism and the common advantage', and '"pleasing everyone"—the description of the non-factionalist'.[50] But 'idol food' or 'idolatry', the ostensible issue which provokes Paul's response, does not make the headlines. Such lack of interest in the concrete historical issue of idol food seems deliberate. In her words, 'Paul treats the issue of idol meat, not just as a behavioral issue, but as a case which requires the proper definition of Christian freedom in order to ensure the unity of the church body'.[51] After this opening statement in her analysis of the theme of 1 Corinthians 8–10, the behavioral issue of idol food is largely forgotten, and the discussion is primarily concerned with the topics of factionalism, freedom, and compromise. She merely assumes that factionalism is the problem but spends little effort to determine whether the problem arises from an internal discord among the Corinthian Christians or from Paul's own objection to their behavior. The same analysis could almost be written for Romans 14–15.

The a priori assumption that factionalism is the problem that underlies every problem in 1 Corinthians gets Mitchell involved in tendentious use of sources and no small measure of equivocation. Her treatment of 1 Cor. 10.1-10 is a *tour de force*.[52] She claims that Paul here offer examples of factious behavior from the Scriptures. She cites Josephus (*Ant.* 3.295) to the effect that the episode recorded in Numbers 11 (cf. 1 Cor. 10.5) is an example of factionalism (στασιάζω) and that Philo (*Post.* 182-85) describes the Baal Peor incident (cf. 1 Cor. 10.8) as a 'faction' (στάσις). She also draws attention to the fact that both Josephus (*Ant.* 4.12) and Philo (*Vit. Mos.* 2.174, 283) refer to the Korah episode in Numbers 16 (Cf. 1 Cor. 10.10) as an instance of στάσις.[53] Never mind that the 'factionalism' mentioned in those passages refers not to divisions among the Israelites, but to their murmurs against their leader Moses. The analogy for Corinth is surely not quarrels within the

---

49. Cf. I. Saw, *Paul's Rhetoric in 1 Corinthians 15: An Analysis Utilizing the Theories of Classical Rhetoric* (Lewiston, NY: Edward Mellen Press, 1995). It is interesting that Saw, whose study is strongly influenced by Mitchell, suggests that the Corinthians function as the 'adjudicator' between Paul and his opponents who deny the resurrection (p. 194), that is, the 'division' is not within the congregation, but between Paul and the deniers of resurrection.

50. Mitchell, *Rhetoric*, pp. 126, 128, 130, 138, 141, 142, 147.

51. Mitchell, *Rhetoric*, p. 126.

52. Mitchell, *Rhetoric*, pp. 138-40.

53. This understanding is followed by Witherington in his major rhetorical commentary on the Corinthian letters (*Conflict and Community*, p. 218).

church, but quarrels between the Corinthians and their founder Paul! Thus Mitchell uses 'factionalism' (between the congregation and their leader) in the Jewish Scriptures as examples for factionalism (among the members).

It is a pity that Mitchell's tremendous erudition is pressed into such hard labor to defend what is plainly indefensible. In the end, I feel that she has merely taken over many elements of the traditional understanding of Paul's approach and offered ingenious rhetorical explanations of those elements in terms of political factionalism. Her interpretation of 1 Corinthians 8–10 is therefore subject to much of the same criticism I have made against the traditional view in Chapter 3. Mitchell's failure to engage concrete historical issues reflects the nature of many rhetorical studies, which are concerned with the rhetorical rather than the historical situation.[54] As in the case with sociological approaches, if one knows what has actually occurred between Paul and the Corinthian Christians, rhetorical analyses can

54. Such problems are not confined to works which utilize ancient rhetorical categories. Yeo's rhetorical study of 1 Cor. 8–10 (*Rhetorical Interaction*), which employs a combined approach of ancient and modern rhetoric, is similarly plagued. Yeo rightly insists that our understanding of the rhetorical situation should be informed by the socio-historical context. However, while major historical critical issues are discussed, it is clear that Yeo's primary interest lies elsewhere. The historical issues only serve as a foil for his rhetorical analysis that moves towards a reader-oriented Chinese hermeneutic. His downplaying of 10.1-22 as Paul's failed attempt in an earlier letter has less to do with literary criteria than with the awkwardness of the passage for his cross-cultural reading of 1 Cor. 8–10 which emphasizes dialog and mutual transformation. Moreover, in spite of numerous footnotes and an extensive bibliography, there is a lack of first-hand acquaintance and substantive engagement with primary (ancient and modern) sources, resulting in an annoying array of incorrect or irrelevant citations. For example, accepting the common but unproven and undocumented view that εἰδωλόθυτον is a Jewish term, he remarks that 'Paul uses the customary Jewish pejorative εἰδωλόθυτον' and lists the references of *3 Macc.* 4.16; *Sib. Or.* 4.7, 3.30, all of which concern idolatry but none of which contain the word εἰδωλόθυτον (p. 99). To bolster his claim that 'one does not have to perceive NT writings either as the authoritative proclamation or persuasive argument', Yeo refers not only to the literary studies of the New Testament by Jasper and Caird, but also Sternberg, who 'speaks of the Bible as "ideological literature" which may represent a bold attempt to combine ... art and truth' (p. 61). But Yeo does not seem to realize that, unlike Jasper and Caird, Sternberg is speaking of the *Hebrew* bible and his focus is biblical *narratives*. Sternberg's comments are of little relevance to the rhetorical conventions or peculiarities of Paul's letters. Furthermore, Yeo's use of secondary sources at times borders on plagiarism. In his description of Greek sacrificial practices (p. 97 nn. 21, 22), Yeo copies lavishly, and almost verbatim, from M. Harding ('Church and Gentile Cults at Corinth', *GTJ* 10 [1989], pp. 203-23), pp. 206-207 and notes. He not only fails to acknowledge his debt to Harding, but also glaringly reproduces Harding's mistaken reading of Burkett! Harding quotes Burkett to the effect that the city officials had their share of 100 sheep and cows and the remaining meat was given to the people, but what Burkett says is that the city officials 'all being accorded their share of the meat; *then* more than a hundred sheep and cows are slaughtered ... and the meat is distributed to the whole populace' (W. Burkett, *Greek Religion* [trans. J. Raffan; Cambridge, MA: Harvard University Press, 1985], p. 232).

By contrast, Witherington's socio-rhetorical commentary (*Conflict and Community*) is much more successful in appropriating the benefits of the newer social and rhetorical disciplines in the context of older grammatical historical approaches. Though I disagree with Witherington in not a few places, I think that, on the whole, his exegetical results are far more convincing than Mitchell's or Yeo's.

be most helpful in discerning and explaining the logic and structure of Paul's argument. But they can be very misleading when the actual historical situation is unclear or misconstrued. In short, they may limit or open the range of possibilities in understanding Paul's approach, but they cannot by themselves determine what is the correct understanding of Paul's position.

7. Ben Witherington, III

In a 1993 article, Witherington suggests that εἰδωλόθυτα does not refer to market-place idol food. Instead, it is a technical term for that which is eaten ἐν εἰδωλείω.[55] This new understanding of εἰδωλόθυτον clearly competes with my interpretation that Paul urges avoidance of known marketplace idol food. There are two major theses in Witherington's article:

1. The common assumption that εἰδωλόθυτον is a polemical term created by early Jews to refer to idol food is very doubtful. An exhaustive search of the data in the *TLG* and the papyri reveals no reference to the term that antedates 1 Corinthians. This suggests that it is a Jewish-Christian term, possibly coined by Paul himself.

2. Εἰδωλόθυτον means meat sacrificed to and eaten in the presence of an idol, or in the temple precincts. This is the meaning in Acts 15 and other early Christian literature. Εἰδωλόθυτον is thus distinguishable in meaning from ἱερόθυτον, 'the proper term for food that has come from the temple, but is not being eaten in the temple or as part of temple worship'.[56] This distinc-tion underlies Paul's different approaches to meals in temples on the one hand, and marketplace idol food and pagan dinner invitations on the other.

I have little disagreement with the first thesis. In fact, I have independently reached a similar, though less articulated, conclusion regarding the provenance of the term εἰδωλόθυτον with the help of the same Ibycus search on the *TLG*.[57] How-ever what I find objectionable is that Witherington seems to discard the relevance of Jewish attitudes toward idol food because the term εἰδωλόθυτον was not used by early Jews.[58] That the term was not used does not mean there was no equivalent designation for the object. A common-sense approach would be to equate, if only tentatively, εἰδωλόθυτα with the rabbinic זבחי מתים. One can also relate the com-pound term to the phrase θυσίαι τῶν εἰδώλων/θεῶν and its variants, which are found already in the LXX and other Jewish and Christian writings to denote idol food.[59]

---

55. Witherington, 'Idle Thoughts'.

56. Witherington, 'Idle Thoughts', p. 246.

57. See my discussion of *4 Macc*. 5.2 in Chapter 2.

58. Witherington does not make this claim explicitly, but he nowhere explores the relevance of Jewish attitude for determining the semantic range of εἰδωλόθυτον.

59. E.g. Exod. 34.15; Lev. 17.7, Num. 25.2, *Jos. Asen.* 12.5. Dr. Simon Wong, a linguist and classical Greek scholar, has drawn my attention to F. Zorell's *Lexicon Graecum Novi Testamenti* (Rome: Biblical Appendix Press; Chicago: Loyola University Press, 1978), which cites Exod. 34.15

This leads me to Witherington's second point, with which I strongly disagree. It is the result of doubtful interpretation of unrepresentative evidence. Apart from his reading of 1 Cor. 10.28, he offers no evidence for his interpretation of ἱερόθυτον. A similar *TLG* search on ἱερόθυτον (or the equivalent θεόθυτον) would have yielded a different conclusion. Epiphanius, discussing the alleged addition of ἱερόθυτον in the text of 1 Cor. 10.18 by Marcion, comments that anyone with a sound mind would treat ἱερόθυτον and εἰδωλόθυτον as one and the same![60] In a pagan critique of Paul's discussion of idol food in 1 Corinthians 8–10 cited by Macarius, ἱερόθυτον is substituted for Paul's pejorative εἰδωλόθυτον with no apparent change of meaning as far as the locale for eating is concerned.[61] The idea that ἱερόθυτον, in contradistinction to εἰδωλόθυτον, denotes specifically sacrificed food removed from the sacrificial context, cannot be found in any early Christian writing which discusses 1 Corinthians 8–10. On the other hand, in his table-talk, Plutarch mentions that the Pythagoreans ἐγεύοντο τῶν ἱεροθύτων ἀπαρξάμενοι τοῖς θεοῖς.[62] Clearly, conscious idol worship could happen in the eating of ἱερόθυτον. There is no need to insist that the two terms are strictly synonymous; it is enough to recognize that they both refer to the same reality in 1 Cor 10.28, namely, sacrificed food in a private home, which is a non-sacral setting.

The evidence that Witherington cites to prove that εἰδωλόθυτον meant meat sacrificed to and eaten in the presence of an idol is unconvincing. He appeals to the mention of 'a certain high place' in *4 Macc.* 5.1 to show that Antiochus was trying to force the Jewish martyrs to eat εἰδωλόθυτα 'in a setting where it would obviously carry the clear connotations of participating in an act of idol worship'.[63] Strangely, he seems to have forgotten his earlier suggestion that εἰδωλόθυτα is a Christian gloss on the basis that there is no reference to idolatry in the context anywhere (thus strengthening his argument that εἰδωλόθυτα is not used in Jewish sources). But if the 'high place' were cultic as he suggests, then it would be a clear reference to idolatry in the immediate context. He cannot have his cake and eat it.

In any case, as I have shown in my earlier discussion of *4 Maccabees*, the 'high place' is very unlikely to have had any cultic significance. The use of προκαθίσας...ἐπί with τινος ὑψηλοῦ τόπου suggests that the 'high place' is probably a reference to something like a raised platform. Moreover, in numerous references to high places, the LXX never uses the phrase ὑψηλός τόπος, but uses the simpler τὸ ὑψηλόν or other non-cognate terms.

---

and Lev. 17.7 to show the equivalence between the phrase and the compound word. However, Wong adds that the semantic focus of the two representations is different: for the phrase, it is usually the event (i.e. sacrificing to the gods/idols) which is in focus, but for the compound, it is the 'food' that receives the major attention. Therefore, if anything, the compound is the more natural term than the phrase to refer to food that has been removed from its sacrificial setting.

60.   *TLG, Haer.* 31.166.6-7: ὅμως ἓν καὶ τὸ αὐτὸ ἐκρίνετο παρὰ τοῖς τὸν εὔλογον λογισμὸν κεκτημένοις.

61.   Porphyrius, *Contra Christ.*, in *TLG* 23.32.

62.   *TLG, Quest. Conv.* 112.729.C.8-9. Cf. *Reg. et imper.* 081.192.C.8.

63.   Witherington, 'Idle Thoughts', p. 241.

Witherington's appeal to *Did.* 6.3 is also unpersuasive. I refer the reader to my discussion in Chapter 4 on the semantic reference of εἰδωλόθυτα in the passage. Other early Christian passages (which are not many) to which he appeals do not really support his interpretation. For example, he begs the question in asserting that the phrase τῶν ἀλισγημάτων τῶν εἰδώλων in Acts 15.20 'is curious if the issue is simply avoiding meat that has been sacrificed in a temple but is to be eaten elsewhere. The most natural way to interpret "abstain from the pollutions of idols" is surely that he is referring to what happens when one is in the presence of idols.'[64] Aside from the clearly circular reasoning, this understanding in fact goes against what evidence there is for the meaning of ἀλίσγημα τῶν εἰδώλων (ἀλίσγημα is a *hapax legomenon*). In Daniel 1, where the setting is clearly in the king's palace rather than idol temples, we read that 'Daniel resolved that he would not defile (ἀλισγέω in the LXX) himself with the royal rations of food and wine' but asked instead for vegetables and water. If the eating were in the idol temple, then even vegetables would have been defiling for Daniel! The point is probably that vegetables and water, in contrast to the royal rations, would not have been previously contaminated by idolatrous rites. Therefore, the natural meaning of ἀλίσγημα τῶν εἰδώλων is simply food defiled through idol worship, wherever it is eaten.[65]

Witherington is perhaps correct to see in the phrase 'Satan's throne' (Rev. 2.13) an allusion to the pagan temple built to Augustus at Pergamum.[66] But the presence of a pagan temple is no proof that εἰδωλόθυτα must have been eaten there. In fact it proves nothing, for even marketplace idol food needs a temple for its supply!

The only other evidence Witherington cites is Chrysostom's homilies on 1 Corinthians. He asserts that 'of…meat eaten outside a temple…[Chrysostom] says at the beginning of Homily 20 on 1 Corinthians that Jesus' words in Matthew 15.11 apply: "not the things that enter in defile a person…"'[67] But Chrysostom does not say this at all and he does not discuss marketplace idol food until Homily 25.[68] His point is rather that some Corinthians, having learnt the indifference of food in Mt. 15.11, went to dine in idol temples, thus leading the weak into idolatry and harming themselves by partaking in the tables of demons. To be sure, Chrysostom focuses on the problem of eating idol food in temples. But this simply reflects the change of the contexts for eating idol food since the Christianization of the Roman Empire. By Chrysostom's time, paganism has rapidly dwindled and there were few

---

64. Witherington, 'Idle Thoughts', p. 248. That Gregory of Nyssa uses this phrase to describe abominable things happening in pagan feasts (*Vita Greg. Thaumaturg* PG 46:944) does not mean that he equates the two. Witherington has confused meaning and referent here.

65. The author of *Joseph and Asenath* regards eating any idol food as (sinful) eating from the table of the idols, even when the idols are no longer present (cf. my discussion on p. 53). Note also that the rabbis call 'what comes forth from a temple' sacrifices to the dead (*m. 'Abod. Zar.* 2.3). Idol food need not be eaten in the temples to be polluting.

66. Witherington, 'Idle Thoughts', p. 250.

67. Witherington, 'Idle Thoughts', p. 251.

68. Witherington (*Acts*, p. 462 n. 419) also claims that his conclusion is confirmed by examining Chrysostom's treatment of Acts 15. But I am unable to find anything in Chrysostom's homilies on Acts 15 that supports such a claim.

opportunities for Christians to eat idol food except in pagan temples.[69] It is also clear that Chrysostom regards eating marketplace idol food as a sin because it damages the Christian witness before unbelievers.[70] Witherington has simply overlooked the bulk of early Christian evidence (e.g. Clement of Alexandria, Tertullian, Origen, etc.) that makes his view untenable. The persuasiveness of his interpretation is further undermined by his failure to explore the relevance of Jewish sources on this topic.

69. In the so-called Canon of the Apostles, a fourth-century document, the dietary prescriptions of the decree are enforced: 'If a bishop ... or any other cleric eat meat with its own blood, the flesh of an animal torn by a wild beast, or an animal which died of itself, they shall be dismisses; if it is a layman, he shall be excommunicated'. The Canon also discussed vegetarianism and teetotalism. But no mention is made of εἰδωλόθυτα. Marcel Simon argues that this shows that the occasions for eating such food were very rare by mid-fourth century ('Apostolic Decree', pp. 457-58).

70. Chrysostom's attitude on eating marketplace food is that 'if you eat [idol food] in ignorance, you are not subject to the punishment [which came upon Israel for idolatry]' (*PG* 61.205.43-44 [*1 Cor. Hom.* 25.1]). This suggests that knowingly eating marketplace idol food is wrong in Chrysostom's opinion. See Chapter 4 for more detailed discussion on Chrysostom.

BIBLIOGRAPHY

The Greek texts used in this work are from the *Thesaurus Linguae Graecae* CD–ROM disk unless otherwise specified. Information about the editions of the primary texts can be found in L. Berkowitz and K.A. Squitier, *Thesaurus Linguae Graecae: Canon of Greek Authors and Works* (Oxford: Oxford University Press, 3rd edn, 1990). Christian Latin texts are from *Corpus christianorum* Series Latina, and *Corpus scriptorum ecclesiasticorum latinorum* (CSEL). Other texts and translations are listed below.

Achtemeier, P.J., *The Quest for Unity in the New Testament Church* (Philadelphia: Fortress Press, 1987).
Aland, K., 'Neutestamentliche Textkritik und Exegese', in Aland and Meurer (eds.), *Wissenschaft und Kirche*, pp. 132-48.
Aland, K., and B. Aland, *The Text of the New Testament: An Introduction to the Critical Editions and to the Theory and Practice of Modern Textual Criticism* (Grand Rapids: Eerdmans; Leiden: E.J. Brill, 2nd edn, 1989).
Aland, K., and S. Meurer (eds.), *Wissenschaft und Kirche: Festschrift für Eduard Lohse* (Bielefeld: Luther-Verlag, 1989).
Alexander, P.S., 'Rabbinic Judaism and the New Testament', *ZNW* 74 (1983), pp. 237-46.
Allo, E.-B., *Saint Jean: L'Apocalypse* (Paris: J. Gabalda, 4th edn, 1933).
Alon, G., *Jews, Judaism and the Classical World: Studies in Jewish History in the Times of the Second Temple and the Talmud* (Jerusalem: Magnes Press, 1977).
Altaner, B., *Patrology* (Freiburg: Herder, 1960).
Amir, Y., 'Authority and Interpretation of Scripture in the Writings of Philo', in M.J. Mulder (ed.), *Mikra: Text, Translation, Reading and Interpretation of the Hebrew Bible in Ancient Judaism and Early Christianity* (CRINT, 2.1; Assen: Van Gorcum; Philadelphia: Fortress Press, 1988), pp. 421-53.
Anderson, R.D., Jr, *Ancient Rhetorical Theory and Paul* (Kampen: Pharos, 1996).
Atkins, R.A., Jr, *Egalitarian Community: Ethnography and Exegesis* (Tuscaloosa: University of Alabama Press, 1991).
Attridge, H.W., *The Interpretation of Biblical History in the Antiquitates Judaicae of Flavius Josephus* (HDR, 7; Missoula, MT: Scholars Press, 1976).
Attridge, H.W., and G. Hata (eds.), *Eusebius, Christianity, and Judaism* (Detroit: Wayne State University Press, 1992).
Attridge, H.W. *et al.* (eds.), *Of Scribes and Scrolls: Studies on the Hebrew Bible, Intertestamental Judaism, and Christian Origins Presented to John Strugnell on the Occasion of his Sixtieth Birthday* (Lanham, MD: University Press of America, 1990).
Audet, J.-P., *La Didachè: Instructions des apôtres* (EBib; Paris: J. Gabalda, 1958).

Aubert, R., *Dictionnaire d'histoire et de géographie ecclésiastiques* (Paris: Letouzey & Ané, 1912–).

Aus, R.D., 'Paul's Travel Plans to Spain and the "Full Number of the Gentiles" of Rom. XI 25', *NovT* 21 (1979), pp. 232-62.

Babcock, W.S. (ed.), *Paul and the Legacies of Paul* (Dallas: Southern Methodist University Press, 1990).

Bagnani, G., 'Peregrinus Proteus and the Christians', *Historia* 4 (1955), pp. 107-12.

Baird, W., ' "One Against the Other": Intra-Church Conflict in 1 Corinthians', in R.T. Fortna and B.R. Gaventa (eds.), *The Conversation Continues: Studies in Paul and John in Honor of J. Louis Martyn* (Nashville: Abingdon Press, 1990), pp. 116-36.

Balás, D.L., 'The Use and Interpretation of Paul in Irenaeus's Five Books *Adversus Haereses*', *SecCent* 9 (1992), pp. 27-39.

Balch, D.L. *et al.* (eds.), *Greeks, Romans, and Christians: Essays in Honor of Abraham J. Malherbe* (Minneapolis: Fortress Press, 1990).

Bandstra, A., 'Interpretation in 1 Cor. 10.1-11', *Calvin Theological Journal* 6 (1971), pp. 5-21.

Barclay, J.M.G., 'Thessalonica and Corinth: Social Contrasts in Pauline Christianity', *JSNT* 47 (1992), pp. 49-74.

Barker, S.F., *The Elements of Logic* (New York: McGraw–Hill, 1989).

Barnard, L.W., 'Clement of Rome and the Persecution of Domitian', *NTS* 10 (1963–64), pp. 251-60.

Barnes, T.D., 'Porphyry against the Christians: Date and the Attribution of Fragments', *JTS* NS 24 (1973), pp. 424-42.

Barnett, A.E., *Paul Becomes a Literary Influence* (Chicago: University of Chicago Press, 1941).

Barnett, P.W., 'Opposition in Corinth', *JSNT* 22 (1984), pp. 3-17.

Baron, S.W., *A Social and Religious History of the Jews* (2 vols.; New York: Columbia University Press, 2nd edn, 1952–80).

Barrett, C.K., *The First Epistle to the Corinthians* (HNTC; New York: Harper & Row, 1968).

—*The Second Epistle to the Corinthians* (HNTC; New York: Harper & Row, 1973).

—'Cephas and Corinth', in *idem*, *Essays on Paul* (Philadelphia: Westminster Press, 1982), pp. 28-39.

—'Things Sacrificed to Idols', in *idem*, *Essays on Paul*, pp. 40-59.

—'The Apostolic Decree of Acts 15.29', *AusBR* 35 (1987), pp. 50-59.

—*The New Testament Background* (New York: Harper & Row, rev. edn, 1989).

Barton, S.C., ' "All Things to All People": Paul and the Law in the Light of 1 Corinthians 9.19-23', in J.D.G. Dunn (ed.), *Paul and the Mosaic Law* (WUNT, 89; Tübingen: Mohr Siebeck, 1996), pp. 271-85.

Batey, R., 'Paul's Interaction with the Corinthians', *JBL* 84 (1965), pp. 139-46.

Bauckham, R., 'James and the Gentiles (Acts 15.13-21)', in B. Witherington, III (ed.), *History, Literature, and Society in the Book of Acts* (Cambridge: Cambridge University Press, 1996), pp. 154-84.

Bauer, W., *Orthodoxy and Heresy in Earliest Christianity* (Philadelphia: Fortress Press, 1971).

Baur, F.C., *Paul, the Apostle of Jesus Christ, his Life and Work, his Epistles and his Doctrine: A Contribution to a Critical History of Primitive Christianity* (2 vols.; London: Williams & Norgate, 2nd edn, 1873–75).

Beker, J.C., *Paul the Apostle: The Triumph of God in Life and Thought* (Philadelphia: Fortress Press, 1980).

Benko, S., 'Pagan Criticism of Christianity', *ANRW*, II.23.2, pp. 1055-118.

Benko, S., and J.J. O'Rourke (eds.), *The Catacombs and the Colosseum: The Roman Empire as the Setting of Primitive Christianity* (Valley Forge, PA: Judson Press, 1971).

—*Pagan Rome and the Early Christians* (Bloomington: Indiana University Press, 1986).

Benoit, A. *et al.*, *Biblia Patristica: Index des citations et allusions bibliques dans la littérature patristique* (4 vols.; Paris: Editions du Centre National de la Recherche Scientifique, 1975–87).

Bentwick, N., *Josephus* (Philadelphia: Jewish Publication Society of America, 1926).

Bergren, T.A., *Sixth Ezra: The Text and Origin* (New York: Oxford University Press, 1998).

Berkowitz, L., and K.A. Squitier, *Thesaurus Linguae Graecae: Canon of Greek Authors and Works* (Oxford: Oxford University Press, 3rd edn, 1990).

Best, E., *A Commentary on the First and Second Epistles to the Thessalonians* (HNTC; New York: Harper & Row, 1972).

Betz, H.D., '2 Cor. 6.14-7.1: An Anti-Pauline Fragment?', *JBL* (1973), pp. 88-108.

—'The Literary Composition and Function of Paul's Letter to the Galatians', *NTS* 21 (1975), pp. 353-79.

Betz, O. *et al.*, *Josephus-Studien* (Göttingen: Vandenhoeck & Ruprecht, 1974).

Biblia Patristica: Index des citations et allusions bibliques dans la littérature patristique (4 vols.; Paris: Centre National de la Recherche Scientifique, 1975–).

Bieringer, R. (ed.), *The Corinthian Correspondence* (BETL, 125, Leuven: Peeters, 1996).

Bilde, P., *Flavius Josephus between Jerusalem and Rome: His Life, his Works and their Importance* (Sheffield: Sheffield Academic Press, 1988).

Black, D.A., *Paul, Apostle of Weakness: Asthenia and its Cognates in the Pauline Literature* (New York: Peter Lang, 1984).

Black, M., *Romans* (NCB; Greenwood, SC: Attic Press, 1973).

Blidstein, G.J., 'The Sale of Animals to Gentiles in Talmudic Law', *JQR* 61 (1970–71), pp. 188-98.

Böcher, O, 'Das sogennannte Aposteldekret', in H. Frankemölle and K. Kertelge (eds.), *Von Urchristentum zu Jesus: Für Joachim Gnilka* (Freiburg: Herder, 1989), pp. 325-36.

Böckenhoff, K., *Das apostolische Speisegesetz in den ersten fünf Jahrhunderten: Ein Beitrag zum Verständnis der quasi-levitischen Satzungen in älteren kirchlichen Rechtsquellen* (Paderborn: Ferdinand Schöningh, 1903).

Bockmuehl, M., 'The Noachide Commandments and New Testament Ethics with Special Reference to Acts 15 and Pauline Halakhah', *RB* 102 (1995), pp. 72-101.

Boer, M.C. de., 'Comment: Which Paul?', in W.S. Babcock (ed.), *Paul and the Legacies of Paul* (Dallas: Southern Methodist University Press, 1990), pp. 45-54.

Boismard, M.-E., 'Le "Concile" de Jerusalem', *ETL* 64 (1988), pp. 433-40.

Boismard, M.-E., and A. Lamouille, *Le texte occidental des Actes des Apôtres: Reconstitution et réhabilitation* (2 vols.; Paris: Editions Recherche sur les Civilisations, 1984).

—*Les actes des deux Apôtres* (EBib, 12–14; 3 vols.; Paris: J. Gabalda, 1990).

Boman, T., 'Das textkritische Problem des sogennannten Aposteldekrets', *NovT* 7 (1964), pp. 26-36.

Borgen, P., 'Philo of Alexandria', in M. Stone (ed.), 'Catalogues of Vices, the Apostolic Decree, and the Jerusalem Meeting', in J. Neusner *et al.* (eds.), *The Social World of Formative Christianity and Judaism* (Philadelphia: Fortress Press, 1988), pp. 126-41.

—' "Yes", "No", "How Far?":The Participation of Jews and Christians in Pagan Cults', in *idem, Early Christianity and Hellenistic Judaism* (Edinburgh: T. & T. Clark, 1996), pp. 15-43.

Borgen, P., and S. Giversen (eds.), *The New Testament and Hellenistic Judaism* (Aarhus: Aarhus University Press, 1995).

Borgen, P., and R. Skarsten, *'Quaestiones et Solutiones*: Some Observations on the Form of Philo's Exegesis', *Studia Philonica* 4 (1976–77), pp. 1-16.

Boring, E. *et al.*, *Hellenistic Commentary to the New Testament* (Nashville: Abingdon Press, 1995).

Bornkamm, G., 'The Missionary Stance of Paul in 1 Corinthians and in Acts', in L.E. Keck and J.L. Martyn (eds.), *Studies in Luke–Acts* (Nashville: Abingdon Press, 1966), pp. 194-207.

—*Paul* (London: Hodder & Stoughton, 1971).

Boulluec, A. le, 'Remarques à propos du problème de 1 Cor. 11, 19 et du "logion" de Justin, Dialogue 35', *Studia patristica* 12 (1975), pp. 328-31.

Bousset, W., *Die Religion des Judentums im späthellenistischen Zeitalter* (HNT, 21; Tübingen: J.C.B. Mohr, 1926).

Bradley, D.G., 'The Origins of the Hortatory Materials in the Letters of Paul' (PhD dissertation, Yale University, 1947).

—'The *Topos* as a Form in the Pauline Paraenesis', *JBL* 72 (1953), pp. 238-46.

Brandt, W.J., *The Rhetoric of Argumentation* (Indianapolis: Bobbs–Merrill, 1970).

Brown, R.E., and J.P. Meier, *Antioch and Rome* (New York: Paulist Press, 1983).

Brown, R. *et al.* (Programmers), *MacBible. Texts: UBS, BHS, NRSV w/apocrypha, LXX* (Grand Rapids: Zondervan Electronic Publishing, 1990–).

Bruce, F.F., *Biblical Exegesis in the Qumran Texts* (Philadelphia: Fortress Press, 1960).

—*Jesus and Christian Origins Outside the New Testament* (London: Hodder & Stoughton, 1974).

—'Biblical Exposition in Qumran', in R.T. France and D. Wenham (eds.), *Gospel Perspectives.* III. *Studies in Midrash and Historiography* (Sheffield: JSOT Press, 1983), pp. 77-98.

—*The Acts of the Apostles* (Leicester: IVP, 2nd edn, 1987).

Brunt, J.C., 'Paul's Attitude Toward and Treatment of Problems Involving Dietary Practice: A Case Study in Pauline Ethics' (PhD dissertation, Emory University, 1978).

—'Rejected, Ignored, or Misunderstood? The Fate of Paul's Approach to the Problem of Food Offered to Idols in Early Christianity', *NTS* 31 (1985), pp. 113-24.

Bullmore, M.A., *St. Paul's Theology of Rhetorical Style: An Examination of I Corinthians 2.1-5 in Light of First Century Graeco-Roman Rhetorical Culture* (San Francisco: International Scholars Press, 1995).

Bultmann, R., *Theology of the New Testament* (trans. K. Grobel; 2 vols.; New York: Charles Scribner's Sons, 1951–55).

—'Gnosis', *JTS* 3 (1952), pp. 10-26.

Bünker, M., *Briefformular und rhetorische Disposition im 1 Korintherbrief* (Göttingen: Vandenhoeck & Ruprecht, 1984).

Burchard, C., *Untersuchungen zu Joseph und Aseneth* (WUNT, 8; Tübingen: Mohr Siebeck, 1965).

—'Joseph and Aseneth', *OTP*, II, pp. 175-247 (187).

—'Ein vorläufiger griechischer Text von Joseph und Aseneth', *Dielheimer Blätter zum Alten Testament* 14 (1979), pp. 2-53.

—'Verbesserungen zum vorläufigen Text von Joseph und Aseneth', *Dielheimer Blätter zum Alten Testament* 16 (1982), pp. 37-39.

—'The Importance of Joseph and Aseneth for the Study of the New Testament: A General Survey and a Fresh Look at the Lord's Supper', *NTS* 33 (1987), pp. 102-34.

Burford, A., *The Greek Temple Builders at Epidauros* (Toronto: University of Toronto Press, 1969).

Burger, D.C., *Bibliotheca Chrysostomica: Bibliographia analytica corporis Chrysostomici* (Portland: Bibliotheca Chrysostomica, 1982–).

Burton, E. de W., *A Critical and Exegetical Commentary on the Epistle to the Galatians* (ICC; Edinburgh: T. & T. Clark, 1959).

Cabaniss, A., 'The Harrowing of Hell, Psalm 24, and Pliny the Younger: A Note', *VC* 7 (1953), pp. 65-74.

Cadbury, H.J., 'The Macellum of Corinth', *JBL* 53 (1934), pp. 134-41.

Callan, T., 'The Background of the Apostolic Decree (Acts 15.20,29; 21.25)', *CBQ* 55 (1993), pp. 284-97.

Campbell, J.Y., 'Κοινωνία and its Cognates in the New Testament', in *idem, Three New Testament Studies* (Leiden: E.J. Brill, 1965), pp. 1-28.

Carpenter, R., *Ancient Corinth: A Guide to Excavations* (rev. R.L Scranton; Athens: American School of Classical Studies, 1960).

Catchpole, D.R., 'Paul, James and the Apostolic Decree', *NTS* 23 (1977), pp. 428-44.

Cazeaux, J., *La trame et la chaîne: Structures littéraires et exégèse dans cinq traités de Philon d'Alexandrie* (ALGHJ, 15; Leiden: E.J. Brill, 1983).

Chadwick, H. *Contra Celsum* (rev. and repr.; Cambridge: Cambridge University Press, 1965 [1953]).

Charles, R.H., *A Critical and Exegetical Commentary on the Revelation of St John* (ICC; 2 vols.; Edinburgh: T. & T. Clark, 1920).

Charlesworth, J.H., *The Old Testament Pseudepigrapha and the New Testament: Prolegomena for the Study of Christian Origins* (2 vols.; Cambridge: Cambridge University Press, 1985).

Chester, A., 'The Parting of the Ways: Eschatology and Messianic Hope', in Dunn (ed.), *Jews and Christians*, pp. 239-313.

Chestnutt, R.D., 'Conversion in Joseph and Aseneth: Its Nature, Function, and Relation to Contemporaneous Paradigms of Conversion and Initiation' (PhD dissertation, Duke University, 1986).

—'The Social Setting and Purpose of Joseph and Aseneth', *JSP* 2 (1988), pp. 21-48.

Cheung, A.T.M., 'The Priest as a Redeemed Man: A Biblical-Theological Study of the Priesthood', *JETS* 29 (1986), pp. 265-75.

—'A Narrative Analysis of Acts 14.27–15.35: Literary Shaping in Luke's Account of the Jerusalem Council', *WTJ* 55 (1993), pp. 137-54.

Chow, J.K., *Patronage and Power: A Study of Social Networks in Corinth* (JSNTSup, 75; Sheffield: JSOT Press, 1992).

Clabeaux, J.J., *A Lost Edition of the Letters of Paul: A Reassessment of the Text of the Pauline Corpus Attested by Marcion* (CBQMS, 21; Washington, DC: Catholic Biblical Association of America, 1989).

Classen, C.J., 'Paulus und die antike Rhetorik', *ZNW* 82 (1991), pp. 1-33.

Cohen, N.G., 'The Jewish Dimension of Philo's Judaism: An Elucidation of the *Spec. Leg.* IV 132-150', *JJS* 38 (1987), pp. 164-86.

Cohen, S., *From the Maccabees to the Mishnah* (Philadelphia: Westminster Press, 1987).

Collier, G.D., ' "That we Might not Crave Evil": The Structure and Argument of 1 Corinthians 10.1-13', *JSNT* 55 (1994), pp. 55-75.

Collingwood R.G., *The Idea of History* (Oxford: Clarendon Press, 1946).

Collins, A.Y., *Crisis and Catharsis: The Power of the Apocalypse* (Philadelphia: Westminster Press, 1984).

—'Insiders and Outsiders in the Book of Revelation and its Social Context', in J. Neusner and E.S. Frerichs (eds.), *To See Ourselves as Others See Us': Christians, Jews, 'Others' in Late Antiquity* (Chico, CA: Scholars Press, 1985), pp. 187-218.

Collins, J.J., *The Apocalyptic Vision of the Book of Daniel* (HSM, 16; Missoula, MT: Scholars Press, 1977).

—*Between Athens and Jerusalem: Jewish Identity in the Hellenistic Diaspora* (New York: Crossroad, 1983).

—*The Apocalyptic Imagination: An Introduction to the Jewish Matrix of Christianity* (New York: Crossroad, 1987).

—'The Development of the Sibylline Tradition', *ANRW*, 20.1, pp. 421-59.

Colson, F.H. *et al.* (eds. and trans.), *Philo, with an English Translation* (10 vols. and 2 supps.; LCL; London: Heinemann, 1929–64).

Conybeare, W.J., and J.S. Howsen, *The Life and Epistles of St. Paul* (Hartford: S.S. Scranton, 1902).

Conzelmann, H., 'Korinth und die Mädchen der Aphrodite', *Nachrichten von der Akademie der Wissenschaft in Göttingen* 8 (1967–68), pp. 247-61.

—*History of Primitive Christianity* (Nashville: Abingdon Press, 1973).

—*1 Corinthians* (Hermeneia; Philadelphia: Fortress Press, 1975).

Coote, R.B., 'Sibyl: Oracle', *JNSL* 5 (1977), pp. 3-8.

Cope, O.L., 'First Corinthians 8-10: Continuity or Contradiction?', *ATR* 11 (1990), pp. 114-23.

Coppieters, H., 'Le Décret des Apôtres (Act 15, 28. 29)', *RB* 4 (1907), pp. 31-58, 218-39.

Coune, M., 'Le Probleme des idolothytes et l'education de la Syneidesis', *RSR* 51 (1963), pp. 497-534.

Countryman, L.W., *Dirt, Greed, and Sex* (Philadelphia: Fortress Press, 1988).

Cranfield, C.E.B., *The Epistle to the Romans* (ICC; 2 vols.; Edinburgh: T. & T. Clark, 1979).

Cross, F.L., *The Early Christian Fathers* (London: Gerald Duckworth, 1960).

Crouzel, H., *Origen* (San Francisco: Harper & Row, 1989).

Cullmann, O., and F.J. Leenhardt, *Essays on the Lord's Supper* (Ecumenical Studies in Worship, 1; Richmond, VA: John Knox Press, 1958).

Culp, J., 'The Impact of Modern Thought upon Biblical Interpretation', in J.E. Hartley (ed.), *Interpreting God's Word for Today* (Anderson: Warner, 1982), pp. 111-34.

Dahl, N., *Studies in Paul* (Minneapolis: Augsburg, 1977).

Danby, H. (ed.), *The Mishnah: Translated from the Hebrew with Introduction and Brief Explanatory Notes* (London: Oxford University Press, 1933).

Daniélou, J., *The Dead Sea Scrolls and Primitive Christianity* (Baltimore: Helicon, 1958).

—*A History of Early Christian Doctrine before the Council of Nicea* (3 vols.; London: Darton, Longman & Todd; Philadelphia: Westminster Press, 1964–77).

Dassmann, E., *Der Stachel im Fleisch: Paulus in der frühchristlichen Literatur bis Irenäus* (Münster: Aschendorff, 1979).

Daube, D., *The New Testament and Rabbinic Judaism: Some Rabbinic Elements in Pauline Theology* (London: Athlone Press, 1956).

Dauer, A., *Paulus und die christliche Gemeinde im syrischen Antiochia: Kritische Bestandsaufnahme der modernen Forschung mit einigen weiterführenden Überlegungen* (Weinheim: Beltz Athenäum, 1996).

Davies, W.D., *Torah in the Messianic Age* (Philadelphia: Fortress Press, 1952).

—'Paul and the Dead Sea Scrolls: Flesh and Spirit', in K. Stendahl (ed.), *The Scrolls and the New Testament* (New York: Harper & Brothers, 1957), pp. 157-82, 276-82.

—'The Moral Teaching of the Early Church', in J.W. Efird (ed.), *The Use of the Old Testament in the New and Other Essays* (Durham, NC: Duke University Press, 1972), pp. 310-32.

—*Paul and Rabbinic Judaism* (Philadelphia: Fortress Press, 4th edn, 1980 [1948]).

Davies, W.D., and L. Finkelstein (eds.), *The Cambridge History of Judaism* (4 vols.; Cambridge: Cambridge University Press, 1984–).

Dawes, G.W., 'The Danger of Isolatry: First Corinthians 8.7-13', *CBQ* 58 (1996), pp. 82-98 (92).

Dean, J.T., *Saint Paul and Corinth* (London: Lutterworth, 1947).

Deissmann, A., *New Light on the New Testament from Records of the Graeco-Roman Period* (Edinburgh: T. & T. Clark, 1908).

Delebecque, E., *Les deux Actes des Apôtres* (EBib, NS 6; Paris: J. Gabalda, 1986).

Delling, G., 'Die Kunst des Gestaltens in "Joseph und Aseneth" ', *NovT* 26 (1984), pp. 1-42.

Denis, A.-M., *Concordance grecque des Pseudépigraphes d'Ancien Testament* (Leiden: E.J. Brill, 1987).

Deselaers, P., *Das Buch Tobit* (Düsseldorf: Patmos, 1990).

deSilva, D.A., 'The Social Setting of the Revelation to John: Conflicts Within, Fears Without', *WTJ* 54 (1992), pp. 273-302.

Dibelius, M., *Studies in the Acts of the Apostles* (London: SCM Press, 1956).

Dix, G., *Jew and Greek: A Study in the Primitive Church* (London: A. & C. Black, 1953).

Donfried, K.P., 'A Short Note on Romans 16', *JBL* 89 (1970), pp. 441-49.

—'False Presuppositions in the Study of Romans', *CBQ* 36 (1974), pp. 332-55.

—*The Setting of Second Clement in Early Christianity* (Leiden: E.J. Brill, 1974).

Donovan, M.A., 'Irenaeus in Recent Scholarship', *SecCent* 4 (1984), pp. 219-41.

Doran, R., 'Narrative Literature', in R.A. Kraft and G.W.E. Nickelsburg (eds.), *Early Judaism and its Modern Interpreters* (Philadelphia: Fortress Press; Atlanta: Scholars Press, 1986), pp. 287-310.

Douglas, M., *Purity and Danger: An Analysis of the Concepts of Pollution and Taboo* (London: Routledge & Kegan Paul, 1966).

Downing, F.G., 'Pliny's Prosecutions of Christians', *JSNT* 34 (1988), pp. 105-24.

Drane, J.W., 'Tradition, Law and Ethics in Pauline Theology', *NovT* 16 (1974), pp. 167-78.

Duensing, H., and A. de Santos Otero, 'The Fifth and Sixth Books of Esra', *NTApoc*, II, pp. 641-52.

Dugmore, C.W., 'Sacrament and Sacrifice in the Early Fathers', *JEH* 2 (1951), pp. 24-37.

Dunn, J.D.G., 'The Incident at Antioch', *JSNT* 18 (1983), pp. 3-57.

—*Romans 9–16* (WBC, 38B; Dallas: Word Books, 1988).

—*Jesus, Paul and the Law: Studies in Mark and Galatians* (Louisville, KY: Westminster/ John Knox Press, 1990).

—'What was the Issue between Paul and "Those of the Circumcision"?', in M. Hengel and U. Heckel (eds.), *Paulus und das antike Judentum: Tübingen–Durham-Symposium im Gedenken an den 50. Todestag Adolf Schlatters* (Tübingen: Mohr Siebeck, 1991), pp. 295-317.

—*The Theology of Paul the Apostle* (Grand Rapids: Eerdmans, 1998).

Dunn, J.D.G. (ed.), *Jews and Christians: The Parting of the Ways: AD 70 to 135* (Tübingen: WUNT, 66; J.C.B. Mohr [Paul Siebeck], 1992).

—*Paul and the Mosaic Law: The Third Durham–Tubingen Research Symposium on Earliest Christianity and Judaism* (WUNT, 89; Tübingen: Mohr Siebeck, 1996).

Dupont, J., *Gnosis: La connaissance religieuse dans les épîtres de S. Paul* (Universitas Catholica Lovaniensis, Dissertationes in Facultate Theologica, 2.40; Louvain: Nauwelaerts, 1960).

Dupont-Sommer, A. (ed.), *The Essene Writings from Qumran* (Oxford: Basil Blackwell, 1961).

Eckstein, H.-J., *Der Begriff Syneidesis bei Paulus* (WUNT, 2.10; Tübingen: Mohr Siebeck, 1983).

Ehrhardt, A., *The Framework of the New Testament Stories* (Manchester: Manchester University Press, 1964).

Ellis, E.E., 'A Note on First Corinthians 10.4', *JBL* 56 (1957), pp. 53-56.

Elmslie, W.A.I., *The Mishna on Idolatry: 'Aboda Zara'* (trans. J.A. Robinson; Text and Studies, 8.2; Cambridge: Cambridge University Press, 1911).

Engels, D.W,. *Roman Corinth: An Alternative Model for the Classical City* (Chicago: University of Chicago Press, 1990).

Enslin, M.,S., *The Ethics of Paul* (Nashville: Abingdon Press, 1962).

Epp, E.J., *The Theological Tendency of Codex Bezae Cantabrigiensis in Acts* (SNTSMS, 3; Cambridge: Cambridge University Press, 1966).

—'Textual Criticism in the Exegesis of the New Testament, with an Excursus on Canon', in S.E. Porter (ed.), *Handbook to Exegesis of the New Testament* (Leiden: E.J. Brill, 1997), pp. 45-97.

Epstein, I. (ed.), *The Babylonian Talmud* (18 vols.; repr.; Hindhead Surrey: Soncino, 1961).

Esler, P.F., *Community and Gospel in Luke–Acts: The Social and Political Motivations of Lucan Theology* (SNTSMS, 57; Cambridge: Cambridge University Press, 1987).

Eusebius, *Ecclesiastical History* (trans. H.J. Lawlor and J.E.L. Oulton; New York: Macmillan, 1928).

Falk, Z.W., *Introduction to Jewish Law of the Second Commonwealth*, I (Leiden: E.J. Brill, 1972).

Farrar, F.W., 'The Rhetoric of St. Paul', *Expositor* 10 (1979), pp. 1-27.

Fee, G.D., 'II Cor. vi.14–vii.1 and Food Offered to Idols', *NTS* 23 (1977), pp. 140-61.

—'Eἰδωλόθυτα Once Again: An Interpretation of 1 Corinthians 8-10', *Bib* 61 (1980), pp. 172-97.

—*The First Epistle to the Corinthians* (Grand Rapids: Eerdmans, 1987).

Feeley-Harnik, G., *The Lord's Table* (Philadelphia: University of Pennsylvania Press, 1981).

Feldman, L.H., *Jew and Gentile in the Ancient World: Attitudes and Interactions from Alexander to Justinian* (Princeton, NJ: Princeton University Press, 1993).

Feldmeier, R., and U. Heckel (eds.), *Die Heiden: Juden, Christen und das Problem des Fremden* (WUNT, 70; Tübingen: Mohr Siebeck, 1992)

Ferguson, E., *Backgrounds of Early Christianity* (Grand Rapids: Eerdmans, 1987).

Filoramo, G., *A History of Gnosticism* (Oxford: Basil Blackwell, 1990).

Firmage, E.B. (ed.), *Religion and Law: Biblical-Judaic and Islamic Perspectives* (Winona Lake, IN: Eisenbrauns, 1990).

Fishbane, M., *Biblical Interpretation in Ancient Israel* (Oxford: Oxford University Press, 1985).

Fisk, B.N., 'Eating Meat Offered to Idols: Corinthian Behavior and Pauline Response in 1 Corinthians 8–10', *Trinity Journal* 10 NS (1989), pp. 49-70.

Fitzgerald, J.T., 'Paul, the Ancient Epistolary Theorists, and 2 Corinthians 10-13: The Purpose and Literary Genre of a Pauline Letter', in Balch *et al.* (eds.), *Greeks, Romans, and Christians*, pp. 190-200.

Fitzmyer, J.A., *The Dead Sea Scrolls: Major Publications and Tools for Study* (Missoula, MT: Scholars Press, 1977).

Flusser, D., 'Paganism in Palestine', in Safrai and Stern (eds.), *The Jewish People in the First Century*, II, pp. 1065-100.

Flusser, D., and S. Safrai, 'Das Aposteldekret und die Noachitischen Gebote', in E. Brocke and H.J. Barkenings (eds.), *'Wer Tora vermehrt, mehrt Leben': Festgabe für Heinz Kremers zum 60 Geburtstag* (Neukirchen–Vluyn: Neukirchener Verlag, 1986), pp. 173-92.

Foerster, W. (ed.), *Gnosis* (2 vols.; Oxford: Clarendon Press, 1972).

Frame, J.M., *The Doctrine of the Knowledge of God: A Theology of Lordship* (Phillipsburg, NJ: Presbyterian & Reformed, 1987).

French, D., 'Acts and the Roman Roads of Asia Minor', in D.W.J. Gill and C. Gempf (eds.), *The Book of Acts in its Graeco-Roman Setting* (AIIFCS, 2; Grand Rapids: Eerdmans; Carlisle: Paternoster Press, 1994), pp. 49-58.

Frend, W.H.C., 'The Gnostic Sects and the Roman Empire', *JEH* 5 (1954), pp. 25-37.

Freudenberger, R., *Das Verhalten der römischen Behörden gegen die Christen im 2. Jahrhundert* (Munich: Beck, 1967).

Friedrich, Gerhard., 'Freiheit und Liebe im ersten Korintherbrief', *TZ* 26 (1970), pp. 81-98.

Furnish, V.P., *Theology and Ethics in Paul* (Nashville: Abingdon Press, 1968).

—*The Love Command in the New Testament* (Nashville: Abingdon Press, 1972).

Gabba, E., 'The Growth of Anti-Judaism or the Greek Attitude towards Jews', in W.D. Davies and L. Finkelstein (eds.), *The Cambridge History of Judaism*. II. *The Hellenistic Age* (Cambridge: Cambridge University Press, 1989), pp. 614-56.

Gager, J., *Kingdom and Community: The Social World of Early Christianity* (Englewood Cliffs, NJ: Prentice–Hall, 1975).

Gamble, H.Y., *Books and Readers in the Early Church: A History of Early Christian Texts* (New Haven: Yale University Press, 1995).

Gardner, P.D., *The Gifts of God and the Authentication of a Christian: An Exegetical Study of 1 Corinthians 8.1–11.1* (Lanham, MD: University Press of America, 1994).

Gasque, W.W., *A History of the Interpretation of the Acts of the Apostles* (Peabody, MA: Hendrickson, 1989).

Gaston, L., 'Paul and the Law in Galatians 2-3', in P. Richardson (ed.), *Anti-Judaism in Early Christianity* (Waterloo, ON: Wilfred Laurier University Press, 1986), pp. 37-57.

Geer, T.C., 'The Presence and Significance of Lucanisms in the "Western" Text of Acts', *JSNT* 39 (1990), pp. 59-76.

Glad, C.E., *Paul and Philodemus: Adaptability in Epicurean and Early Christian Psychagogy* (NovTSup, 81; Leiden: E.J. Brill, 1995).

Gnilka, J., '2 Cor. 6.14-7.1 in the Light of the Qumran Texts and the Testaments of the Twelve Patriarchs', in J. Murphy-O'Connor (ed.), *Paul and Qumran: Studies in New Testament Exegesis* (London: Geoffrey Chapman, 1968), pp. 48-68.

Goldin, J. (ed.), *The Fathers According to Rabbi Nathan* (New Haven: Yale University Press, 1955).

Goldingay, J.E., *Daniel* (WBC, 30; Dallas: Word Books, 1989).

Goldstein, J.A., *I Maccabees* (AB, 41; New York: Doubleday, 1976).

—*II Maccabees* (AB, 41A; New York: Doubleday, 1983).

—'Jewish Acceptance and Rejection of Hellenism', in E.P. Sanders and A.I. Baumgarten (eds.), *Jewish and Christian Self-Definition* (3 vols.; London: SCM Press, 1981), II, pp. 64-87.

Gooch, P.D., 'Food and the Limits of Community: I Corinthians 8 to 10' (PhD dissertation, University of Toronto, 1988).

—*Dangerous Food: 1 Corinthians 8–10 in its Context* (Studies in Christianity and Judaism, 5; Waterloo, ON: Wilfred Laurier University Press, 1993).

Gooch, P.W., 'Conscience in 1 Corinthians 8 and 10', *NTS* 33 (1987), pp. 244-54.

Goodenough, E.R., *Jewish Symbols in the Greco-Roman Period* (13 vols.; New York: Bollingen Foundation, 1953–68).

—*An Introduction to Philo Judaeus* (New Haven: Yale University Press, 1962).

Goodenough, E.R., and A.T. Kraabel, 'Paul and the Hellenization of Christianity', in J. Neusner (ed.), *Religions in Antiquity* (NumenSup, 14; Leiden: E.J. Brill, 1968), pp. 23-68.

Goppelt, L., 'Paul and Heilsgeschichte: Conclusions from Romans 4 and 1 Cor. 10.1-13', *Int* 21 (1967), pp. 315-26.

Gorday, P., *Principles of Patristic Exegesis* (Lewiston, NY: Edwin Mellen Press, 1987).

—'Paul in Eusebius and Other Early Christian Literature', in H.W. Attridge and G. Hata (eds.), *Eusebius, Christianity, and Judaism* (Detroit: Wayne State University Press, 1992), pp. 139-65.

Grant, R.M., *Gnosticism: A Source Book of Heretical Writings from the Early Christian Period* (New York: Harper & Brothers, 1961).

—'Hellenistic Elements in I Corinthians', in A. Wikgren (ed.), *Early Christian Origins* (Chicago: Quadrangle Books, 1961), pp. 60-66.

—*A Historical Introduction to the New Testament* (New York: Harper & Row, 1963).

—*The Apostolic Fathers: An Introduction* (New York: Thomas Nelson, 1964).

—*Ignatius of Antioch* (AFNTC, 4; New York: Thomas Nelson, 1966).

—'Dietary Laws among Pythagoreans, Jews, and Christians', *HTR* 73 (1980), pp. 299-310.

—*Gods and the One God* (ed. W.A. Meeks; LEC, 1; Philadelphia: Westminster Press, 1986).

—*Greek Apologists of the Second Century* (Philadelphia: Westminster Press, 1988).

Gressmann, H., 'Η ΚΟΙΝΩΝΙΑ ΤΩΝ ΔΑΙΜΟΝΙΩΝ', *ZNW* 20 (1921), pp. 224-30.

Grosheide, F.W., *Commentary on the First Epistle to the Corinthians* (NICNT; Grand Rapids: Eerdmans, 1953).

Guenther, H.O., 'Gnosticism in Corinth?', in B.H. Mclean (ed.), *Origins and Method: Towards a New Understanding of Judaism and Christianity: Essays in Honour of John C. Hurd* (JSNTSup, 86; Sheffield: JSOT Press, 1993), pp. 44-81.

Gunther, J.J., *St. Paul's Opponents and their Background* (NovTSup, 35; Leiden: E.J. Brill, 1973).

Guttmann, A., *Rabbinic Judaism in the Making: A Chapter in the History of the Halakhah from Ezra to Judah I* (Detroit: Wayne State University Press, 1970).

Hadas, M., *The Third and Fourth Books of Maccabees* (New York: Harper & Brothers, 1953).

Haenchen, E., *The Acts of the Apostles* (Oxford: Westminster Press, 1971).

Hall, S.G., *Doctrine and Practice in the Early Church* (Grand Rapids: Eerdmans, 1991).

Halpérin, J., and G. Lévitte (eds.), *Idoles: Données et débats, actes du XXIVue colloque des intellectuels juifs de langue française* (Paris: Editions Denoël, 1985).

Harding, M., 'Church and Gentile Cults at Corinth', *Grace Theological Journal* 10 (1989), pp. 203-23.

Harnack, A. von, *Marcion: Das Evangelium vom fremden Gott: Eine Monographie zur Geschichte der Grundlegung der katholischen Kirche* (TU, 45; Leipzig: J.C. Hinrichs, 2nd edn, 1924).

—*The Mission and Expansion of Christianity in the First Three Centuries* (Gloucester, MA: Peter Smith, 1972).

—'The Sect of the Nicolaitans and Nicolaus, the Deacon in Jerusalem', *JR* 3 (1923), pp. 413-22.

Harris, B.F., 'ΣΥΝΕΙΔΗΣΙΣ (Conscience) in the Pauline Writings', *WTJ* 24 (1962), pp. 173-86.

Harrison, E.F., *Interpreting Acts* (Grand Rapids: Zondervan, 1986).

Hartley, J.E., *Interpreting God's Word for Today* (Anderson: Warner, 1982).

Harvey, V.A., *The Historian and the Believer: The Morality of Historical Knowledge and Christian Belief* (New York: Macmillan, 1966).

Head, P., 'Acts and the Problem of its Text', in A.D. Clarke and B.W. Winter (eds.), *The Book of Acts in its Ancient Literary Setting* (AIIFCS, 1; Grand Rapids: Eerdmans; Carlisle: Paternoster Press, 1994), pp. 415-44.

Heckel, U., 'Das Bild der Heiden und die Identität der Christen bei Paulus', in Feldmeier and Heckel (eds.), *Die Heiden*, pp. 269-96.

Heil, C. *Die Ablehnung der Speisegebote durch Paulus: Zur Frage nach der Stellung des Apostels zum Gesetz* (BBB, 96; Weinheim: Beltz Athenäum, 1994).

Heiligenthal, R., 'Wer waren die "Nikolaiten"? Ein Beitrag zur Theologiegeschichte des frühen Christentums', *ZNW* 82 (1991), pp. 133-37.

Hemer, C.J., *The Letters to the Seven Churches of Asia in their Local Setting* (JSNTSup, 11; Sheffield: JSOT Press, 1986).

Hengel, M., *Judaism and Hellenism: Studies in their Encounter in Palestine during the Early Hellenistic Period* (2 vols.; Philadelphia: Fortress Press, 1974).

—*Acts and the History of Earliest Christianity* (Philadelphia: Fortress Press, 1979).

—'Der vorchristliche Paulus', in Hengel and Heckel (eds.), *Paulus und das antike Judentum*, pp. 177-293.

Hengel, M., and A.M. Schwemer, *Paul between Damascus and Antioch: The Unknown Years* (Louisville, KY: Westminster/John Knox Press, 1997).

Hengel, M., and U. Heckel (eds.), *Paulus und das antike Judentum: Tübingen-Durham-Symposium im Gedenken an den 50. Todestag Adolf Schlatters* (WUNT, 58; Tübingen: Mohr Siebeck, 1991).

Hennecke, E., and W. Schneemelcher (ed.), *New Testament Apocrypha* (trans. R.McL. Wilson; 2 vols.; Philadelphia: Westminster Press, rev. edn, 1991).

Herford, R.T., *The Ethics of the Talmud: Sayings of the Fathers* (New York: Ktav, rpt edn, 1962).

Héring, J., *The First Epistle of Saint Paul to the Corinthians* (trans. A.W. Heathcote and P.J. Allcock; London: Epworth Press, 1962).

Herondas, *The Mines of Herondas* (trans. Guy Davenport; San Francisco: Grey Fox, 1981).

Hill, C., *Hellenists and Hebrews: Reapraising Division with the Earliest Church* (Minneapolis: Fortress Press, 1992).

Hoffmann, R.J., *Marcion: On the Restitution of Christianity: An Essay on the Development of Radical Paulinist Theology in the Second Century* (AAR Academy Series, 46; Chico, CA: Scholars Press, 1984).

—*Celsus: On the True Doctrine: A Discourse Against the Christians* (Oxford: Oxford University Press, 1987).

Holladay, C.R., *Fragments from Hellenistic Jewish Authors. I. Historians* (Pseudepigrapha Series, 10; Chico, CA: Scholars Press, 1983).

Holladay, W.L., *A Concise Hebrew and Aramaic Lexicon of the Old Testament* (Grand Rapids: Eerdmans, 1971).

Holmberg, B., *Sociology and the New Testament* (Minneapolis: Fortress Press, 1990).

Holtz, T., ' "Euer Glaube an Gott": Zu Form und Inhalt von 1. Thess 1,9f', in E. Reinmuth and C. Wolff (eds.), *Geschichte und Theologie des Urchristentums: Gesammelte Aufsätze* (WUNT, 57; Tübingen: J.C.B. Mohr, 1991), pp. 270-96.

Horbury, W., 'Jewish–Christian Relations in Barnabas and Justin Martyr', in Dunn (ed.), *Jews and Christians*, pp. 315-346.

Horrell, D.G., *The Social Ethos of the Corinthian Correspondence: Interests and Ideology from 1 Corinthians to 1 Clement* (Edinburgh: T. & T. Clark, 1996).

Horsley, G.H.R. (ed.), *New Documents Illustrating Early Christianity* (8 vols.; Sydney, Australia: Macquarie University Press, 1981–).

Horsley, R.A., 'Pneumatikos vs. Psychikos: Distinctions of Spiritual Status among the Corinthians', *HTR* 69 (1976), pp. 269-88.

—'Wisdom of Words and Words of Wisdom in Corinth', *CBQ* 39 (1977), pp. 224-39.

—'The Background of the Confessional Formula in 1 Kor 8.6', *ZNW* 69 (1978), pp. 130-35.

—'Consciousness and Freedom Among the Corinthians: 1 Corinthians 8–10', *CBQ* 40 (1978), pp. 574-89.

—'Gnosis in Corinth: 1 Corinthians 8.1-6', *NTS* 27 (1980), pp. 32-51.

Horsley, R.A., and M. Myers, 'Idols, Demons, and the Hermeneutics of Suspicion: Biblical Traditions informing Ethics', *SBLSP* (1989), pp. 634-55.

Horst, P.W. van der, *The Sentences of Pseudo-Phocylides* (VTSup, 4; Leiden: E.J. Brill, 1978).

Houston, W., *Purity and Monotheism: Clean and Unclean Animals in Biblical Law* (JSOTSup, 140; Sheffield: JSOT Press, 1993).

Howard, G., *Paul: Crisis in Galatia* (Cambridge: Cambridge University Press, 1990).

Hughes, P.E., *Paul's Second Epistle to the Corinthians* (Grand Rapids: Eerdmans, 1962).

Hulen, A.B., *Porphyry's Work against the Christians: An Interpretation* (Yale Studies in Religion, 1; Scottdale, PA: Mennonite Press, 1933).

Hurd, J.C., Jr, *The Origins of 1 Corinthians* (Macon, GA: Mercer University Press, new edn, 1983).

Hvalvik, R., *The Struggle for Scripture and Covenant: The Purpose of the Epistle of Barnabas and Jewish–Christian Competition in the Second Century* (WUNT, 2.82; Tübingen: Mohr Siebeck, 1996).

Hyldahl, N., 'The Corinthian "Parties" and the Corinthian Crisis', *ST* 45 (1991), pp. 19-32.

—'Paul and Hellenistic Judaism', in Borgen and Giversen, *Hellenistic Judaism*, pp. 204-16.

Isenberg, M., 'The Sale of Sacrificial Meat', *CP* 70 (1975), pp. 271-73.

Jervell, J., *Luke and the People of God: A New Look at Luke–Acts* (Minneapolis: Augsburg, 1972).

—*The Unknown Paul: Essays on Luke–Acts and Early Christian History* (Minneapolis: Augsburg, 1984).

Jewett, R., *Paul's Anthropological Terms: A Study of their Use in Conflict Settings* (Leiden: E.J. Brill, 1971).

—'Mapping the Route of Paul's Second Missionary Journey from Dorylaeum to Troas', *TynBul* 48 (1997), pp. 1-22.

Jonas, H., *The Gnostic Religion: The Message of the Alien God and the Beginnings of Christianity* (Boston: Beacon Press, 2nd rev. edn, 1963).

Jones, F.S., 'The Pseudo-Clementines: A History of Research', *SecCent* 2 (1982), pp. 1-33, 63-96.

Jourdan, G.V., 'ΚΟΙΝΩΝΙΑ in 1 Corinthians 10.16', *JBL* 67 (1947), pp. 111-24.

Judge, E.A., *The Social Patterns of Christian Groups in the First Century* (London: Tyndale Press, 1960).

—'The Early Christians as a Scholastic Community', *JRH* (1960–61), pp. 4-15, 125-37.

—'Cultural Conformity and Innovation in Paul: Some Clues from Contemporary Documents', *TynBul* 35 (1984), pp. 3-24.

Juel, D., *Messianic Exegesis: Christological Interpretation of the Old Testament in Early Christianity* (Philadelpha: Fortress Press, 1988).

Karris, R.J., 'Romans 14.1–15.3 and the Occasion of Romans', *CBQ* 35 (1973), pp. 155-78.

—*Luke: Artist and Theologian* (New York: Paulist Press, 1985).

Keck, L.E., 'Ethos and Ethics in the New Testament', in J. Gaffney (ed.), *Essays in Morality and Ethics* (New York: Paulist Press, 1980), pp. 29-49.

Kee, H.C., 'The Social–Cultural Setting of Joseph and Aseneth', *NTS* 29 (1983), pp. 394-413.

Kennedy, C.A., 'The Cult of the Dead in Corinth', in J.H. Marks and R.M. Good (eds.), *Love and Death in the Ancient Near East: Essays in Honor of Marvin H. Pope* (Guilford, CN: Four Quarters, 1987), pp. 227-36.

Kennedy, G.A., *New Testament Interpretation through Rhetorical Criticism* (Chapel Hill: University of North Carolina Press, 1984).

Kent, J.H. *Corinthian VIII. III. The Inscriptions 1926–1950* (Princeton, NJ: American School of Classical Studies, 1966).

Kidera, R., 'Les interdictions alimentaires du christianisme aux IIe et IIIe siècles: Etude du décret apostolique' (Thèse dactylographiée; Protestant Faculty of Theology, University of Strasbourg, 1973).

Klauck, H.-J., *Herrenmahl und hellenistischer Kult: Eine religionsgeschichtliche Untersuchung zum ersten Korintherbrief* (NTAbh, NS 15; Münster: Aschendorff, 1982).

—*1 Korintherbrief* (NEB, 7; Würzburg: Echter Verlag, 1984).

Klawans, J., 'Notions of Gentile Impurity in Ancient Judaism', *AJS Review* 20 (1995), pp. 285-312.

Klijn, A.F.J., 'The Pseudo-Clementines and the Apostolic Decree', *NovT* 10 (1978), pp. 305-12.

Klijn, A.F.J., and G.J. Reinink, *Patristic Evidence for Jewish–Christian Sects* (Leiden: E.J. Brill, 1973).

Klumbies, P.-G., *Die Rede von Gott bei Paulus in ihrem zeitgeschichtlichen Kontext* (Göttingen: Vandenhoeck & Ruprecht, 1992).

Knoch, O., 'Die Stellung der Apostolischen Väter zu Israel und zum Judentum: Eine Übersicht', in J. Zmijewski and E. Nellessen (eds.), *Begegnung mit dem Wort: Festchrift für H. Zimmermann* (BBB, 53; Bonn: 1980), pp. 347-78.

Knox, J., *Chapters in a Life of Paul* (London: A. & C. Black, 1954).

Knox, W.L., *St Paul and the Church of Jerusalem* (Cambridge: Cambridge University Press, 1925).

Koester, H., *New Testament Introduction* (2 vols.; Philadelphia: Fortress Press; Berlin: W. de Gruyter, 1982).

Koester, H., and J.M. Robinson, *Trajectories through Early Christianity* (Philadelphia: Fortress Press, 1971).

Kraft, R.A., *Barnabas and the Didache* (AFNTC, 3; New York: Thomas Nelson, 1965).

—'Judaism on the World Scene', in S. Benko and J.J. O'Rourke (eds.), *The Catacombs and the Colosseum: The Roman Empire as the Setting of Primitive Christianity* (Valley Forge, PA: Judson Press, 1971), pp. 81-98.

—'The Multiform Jewish Heritage of Early Christianity', in J. Neusner (ed.), *Christianity, Judaism and Other Greco-Roman Cults: Studies for Morton Smith at Sixty* (3 vols.; Leiden: E.J. Brill, 1975), III, pp. 174-99.

—'Tiberius Julius Alexander and the Crisis in Alexandria According to Josephus', in Attridge *et al.* (eds.), *Of Scribes and Scrolls*, pp. 175-84.

Kraft, R.A., and G.W.E. Nickelsburg (eds.), *Early Judaism and its Modern Interpreters* (Philadelphia: Fortress Press; Atlanta, GA: Scholars Press, 1986).

Krause, G. (eds.), *Müller theologische Realenzyklopädie* (Berlin: W. de Gruyter, 1977–).

Krupp, R.A., *Saint John Chrysostom: A Scriptural Index* (Lanham, MD: University Press of America, 1984).

Kuenning, L., 'Would Early Christians Care whether Joseph Married an Outsider? A Possible Context for Joseph and Aseneth' (unpublished paper for Robert Kraft's doctoral seminar on 'Joseph and Aseneth', University of Pennsylvania, 1991).

Kuhn, T.S., *The Structure of Scientific Revolutions* (Chicago: University of Chicago Press, 2nd edn, 1970).

Kümmel, W.G., *The New Testament: The History of the Investigations of its Problems* (Nashville: Abingdon Press, 1970).

—*Introduction to the New Testament* (Nashville: Abingdon Press, 3rd edn, 1975).

Laato, T., *Paul and Judaism: An Anthropological Approach* (trans. T. McElwain; Atlanta: Scholars Press, 1995).

Lake, K., 'The Judaistic Controversy and the Apostolic Council', *CQR* 71 (1911), pp. 345-70.

Lake, K., and H.J. Cadbury, *The Beginning of Christianity*. I. *The Acts of the Apostles* (5 vols.; repr.; London: Macmillan, 1933; Grand Rapids: Baker Book House, repr., 1979).

Lake, K. (ed. and trans.), *The Apostolic Fathers* (LCL; 2 vols.; New York: Macmillan, 1914–24).

Lang, M., *Cure and Cult in Ancient Corinth: A Guide to the Asklepieion* (American Excavations in Old Corinth, Corinth Notes, 1; Princeton, NJ: American School of Classical Studies in Athens, 1977).

Lange, N.R.M. de, *Origen and the Jews: Studies in Jewish–Christian Relations in Third-Century Palestine* (Cambridge: Cambridge University Press, 1976).

Lentz, J.C., Jr., *Luke's Portrait of Paul* (ed. M.E. Thrall; SNTSMS, 77; Cambridge: Cambridge University Press, 1993).

Lieberman, S., *Hellenism in Jewish Palestine: Studies in the Literary Transmission, Beliefs, and Manners of Palestine in the I Century BCE–IV Century CE* (New York: Jewish Theological Seminary of America, 1950).

Lietzmann, H., *An die Korinther I, II* (HNT, 9; Tübingen: Mohr Siebeck, 1931).

Lightfoot, J.B., *Saint Paul's Epistle to the Galatians* (London: Macmillan, 10th edn, 1890).

—*The Apostolic Fathers: Clement, Ignatius, and Polycarp: Revised Texts with Introductions, Notes, Dissertations, and Translations* (2 parts in 5 vols.; Grand Rapids: Baker Book House, 2nd edn, 1981).

Lindemann, A., *Paulus im ältesten Christentum: Das Bild des Apostels und die Rezeption der paulinischen Theologie in der frühchristlichen Literatur bis Marcion* (BHT, 58; Tübingen: Mohr Siebeck, 1979).

—'Paul in the Writings of the Apostolic Fathers', in Babcock (ed.), *Legacies*, pp. 25-45.

—*Die Clemensbriefe* (HNT, 17; Tubingen: Mohr Siebeck, 1992).

Lisle, R., 'Cults of Corinth' (PhD dissertation, John Hopkins University, 1955).

Litfin, D., *St. Paul's Theology of Proclamation: 1 Corinthians 1–4 and Greco-Roman Rhetoric* (Cambridge: Cambridge University Press, 1994).

Logan, A.H.B., and A.J.M. Wedderburn (eds.), *The New Testament and Gnosis: Essays in Honour of Robert McL. Wilson* (Edinburgh: T. & T. Clark, 1983).

Lohse, E., 'Zu 1 Cor. 10.26.31', *ZNW* 47 (1956), pp. 277-80.

—*The New Testament Environment* (Nashville: Abingdon Press, 1976).

Longenecker, R.N., *Paul: Apostle of Liberty* (New York: Harper & Row, 1964).

—*Biblical Exegesis in the Apostolic Period* (Grand Rapids: Eerdmans, 1975).

—*Galatians* (WBC, 41; Dallas: Word Books, 1990).

Lovering, E.H., Jr, and J.L. Sumney (eds.), *Theology and Ethics in Paul and his Interpreters: Essays in Honor of Victor Paul Furnish* (Nashville: Abingdon Press, 1996).

Lüdemann, G., *Paulus, der Heidenapostel*. II. *Antipaulinismus im frühen Christentum* (Göttingen: Vandenhoeck & Ruprecht, 1983).

—*Heretics: The Other Side of Early Christianity* (trans. J. Bowden; Louisville, KY: Westminster/John Knox Press, 1996).

—*Das Unheilige in der Heiligen Schrift: Die andere Seite der Bibel* (Stuttgart: Radius-Verlag, 1996).

MacMullen, R., *Roman Social Relations 50 BC to AD 284* (New Haven: Yale University Press, 1974).

—*Paganism in the Roman Empire* (New Haven: Yale University Press, 1981).

MacRae, G.W., 'Why the Church Rejected Gnosticism', in E.P. Sanders and A.I. Baumgarten (eds.), *Jewish and Christian Self-Definition* (3 vols.; Philadelphia: Fortress Press, 1980), I, pp. 126-33.

Maddox, R., *The Purpose of Luke–Acts* (FRLANT, 16; Göttingen: Vandenhoeck & Ruprecht, 1982).

Magee, B.R., 'A Rhetorical Analysis of First Corinthians 8.1–11.1 and Romans 14.1–15.13' (ThD dissertation, New Orleans Baptist Theological Seminary, 1988).

Malherbe, A.J., *Social Aspects of Early Christianity* (Philadelphia: Fortress Press, 2nd edn, 1983).

—*Ancient Epistolary Theorists* (SBLSBS, 19; Atlanta: Scholars Press, 1988).

—' "Pastoral Care" in the Thessalonian Church', *NTS* 36 (1990), pp. 375-91.

—'Determinism and Free Will in Paul: The Argument of 1 Corinthians 8 and 9', in T. Engberg-Pedersen (ed.), *Paul in his Hellenistic Context* (Edinburgh: T. & T. Clark, 1994), pp. 231-55.

Malina, B.J., *The New Testament World: Insights from Cultural Anthropology* (London: SCM Press, 1981).

—*Christian Origins and Cultural Anthropology* (Atlanta: John Knox Press, 1986).

Manson, T.W., 'The Corinthian Correspondence (1)', in M. Black (ed.), *Studies in the Gospels and Epistles* (Philadelphia: Westminster Press, 1962), pp. 109-209.

Marcus, R., *Philo. Suppliment I. Questions and Answers on Genesis* (Cambridge, MA: Harvard University Press, 1953).

Mark, O., *Handeln aus Glauben: Die Motivierungen der Paulinischen Ethik* (Marburger Theologische Studien; Marburg: Elwert, 1968).

Marshall, I.H., *The Acts of the Apostles* (Grand Rapids: Eerdmans; Leicester: IVP, 1980).

Marshall, P., *Enmity in Corinth: Social Conventions in Paul's Relations with the Corinthians* (WUNT, 2.23; Tübingen: J.C.B. Mohr, 1987).

Martin, D.B., *Slavery as Salvation: The Metaphor of Slavery in Pauline Christianity* (New Haven: Yale University Press, 1990).

Martin, R.A., *Studies in the Life and Ministry of the Early Paul and Related Issues* (Lewiston, NY: Edward Mellen Press, 1993).

Martin, R.P., *New Testament Foundations* (2 vols.; Grand Rapids: Eerdmans, 1978).

Mason, S.N., 'Josephus on the Pharisees Reconsidered: A Critique of Smith/Neusner', *SR* 17 (1988), pp. 455-69.

—'Was Josephus a Pharisee: A Re-examination of Life 10-12', *JJS* 40 (1989), pp. 31-45.

—*Flavius Josephus on the Pharisees: A Composition–Critical Study* (Leiden: E.J. Brill, 1991).

Matlock, R.B., *Unveiling the Apocalyptic Paul: Paul's interpreters and the Rhetoric of Criticism* (JSNTSup, 127; Sheffield: Sheffield Academic Press, 1996).

Maurer, 'Συνείδησις', *TDNT*, VII, pp. 898-919 (905).

McCullough, W.S., *A Short History of Syriac Christianity to the Rise of Islam* (Scholars Press General Series, 4; Chico, CA: Scholars Press, 1982).

McKnight, S., *A Light among the Gentiles: Jewish Missionary Activity in the Second Temple Period* (Minneapolis: Fortress Press, 1991).

McLean, B.H. (ed.), *Origins and Method: Towards a New Understanding of Judaism and Christianity: Essays in Honour of John C. Hurd* (JSNTSup, 86; Sheffield: JSOT Press, 1993).

McNamara, M., *Palestinian Judaism and the New Testament* (GNS, 4; Wilmington, DE: Michael Glazier, 1983).

Meeks, W.A., ' "And Rose Up to Play": Midrash and Paraenesis in 1 Corinthians 10.1-22',
JSNT 16 (1982), pp. 64-78.

—*The First Urban Christians: The Social World of the Apostle Paul* (New Haven: Yale
University Press, 1983).

—*The Moral World of the First Christians* (LEC, 6; Philadelphia: Westminster Press,
1986).

Meeks, W.A. (ed.), *The Writings of St Paul* (New York: W.W. Norton, 1972).

Meggitt, J.J., 'Meat Consumption and Social Conflict in Corinth', *JTS* 45 (1994), pp. 137-
41.

Melnick, R., 'On the Philonic Conception of the Whole Man', *JSJ* 11 (1980), pp. 1-32.

Mendelson, A., *Philo's Jewish Identity* (BJS, 161; Atlanta: Scholars Press, 1988).

Metzger, B., 'The Fourth Book of Ezra', in *OTP*, I, pp. 517-59.

Michaels, J.R., *1 Peter* (WBC, 49; Waco, TX: Word Books, 1988).

Milgrom, J., 'Ethics and Ritual: The Foundation of the Biblical Dietary Laws', in E.B.
Firmage (ed.), *Religion and Law: Biblical-Judaic and Islamic Perspectives* (Winona
Lake, IN: Eisenbrauns, 1990), pp. 159-91.

Minear, P.S., 'Paul's Teaching on the Eucharist in First Corinthians', *Worship* 44 (1970),
pp. 83-92.

—*The Obedience of Faith: The Purpose of Paul in the Epistle to the Romans* (SBT Second
Series; Naperville, IL: Allenson, 1971).

Mitchell, M.M., *Paul and the Rhetoric of Reconciliation: An Exegetical Investigation of
the Language and Composition of 1 Corinthians* (Tübingen: Mohr Siebeck, 1991).

Mitchell, S., *Anatolia: Land, Men, and Gods in Asia Minor* (2 vols.; Oxford: Clarendon
Press, 1993).

Molland, E., 'La circoncision, le baptême et l'autorité du décret apostolique (Actes xv, 28
sq. dan les milieux judéo-chrétiens des Pseudo-Clémentines', *ST* 9 (1955), pp. 1-39.

Moore, G.F., *Judaism in the First Three Centuries of the Christian Era: The Age of the
Tannaim* (Cambridge, MA: Harvard University Press, 1927–30).

Mühlenberg, E., 'Griechische Patristik. I. Textausgaben, Hilfsmittel, Kommentare und
Übersetzungen', *TRu* 56 (1991), pp. 140-75.

Mulder, M.J. (ed.), *Mikra: Text, Translation, Reading and Interpretation of the Hebrew
Bible in Ancient Judaism and Early Christianity* (CRINT, 2.1; Assen: Van Gorcum;
Philadelphia: Fortress Press, 1988).

Munck, J., *Paul and the Salvation of Mankind* (Richmond, VA: John Knox Press, 1959).

Murphy-O'Connor, J., 'Freedom or the Ghetto (1 Cor. viii, 1-13; x, 23-xi.1)', *RB* 85
(1978), pp. 543-74.

—'Food and Spiritual Gifts in 1 Cor. 8.8', *CBQ* 41 (1979), pp. 292-98.

—*St Paul's Corinth: Text and Archaeology* (GNS, 6; Wilmington, DE: Michael Glazier,
1983).

Murphy-O'Connor, J. (ed.), *Paul and Qumran: Studies in New Testament Exegesis*
(London: Geoffrey Chapman, 1968).

Murray, G., *Five Stages of Greek Religion* (Oxford: Clarendon Press, 1925).

Mussner, F., *Der Galaterbrief* (HTKNT; Freiburg: Herder, 1974).

Nabers, N., 'The Architectural Variations of the Macellum', *Opuscula Romana* 9 (1973),
pp. 173-76.

Neil, W., *The Acts of the Apostles* (Grand Rapids: Eerdmans, 1987).

Neusner, J., *Rabbinic Traditions about the Pharisees before 70* (3 vols.; Leiden: E.J. Brill,
1971).

—*From Politics to Piety: The Emergence of Pharisaic Judaism* (Englewood Cliffs, NJ: Prentice–Hall, 1973).

—*The Idea of Purity in Ancient Judaism* (Leiden: E.J. Brill, 1973).

—*A History of the Mishnaic Law of Purities*. XXII. *The Mishnaic System of Uncleanness: Its Context and History* (Leiden: E.J. Brill, 1977).

—'The Use of the Later Rabbinc Evidence for the Study of Paul', in W.S. Green (ed.), *Approaches to Ancient Judaism* (6 vols.; BJS, 9; Chico, CA: Scholars Press, 1980), II, pp. 43-63.

—*Formative Judaism: Religious, Historical and Literary Studies, Torah, Pharisees, and Rabbis* (Chico, CA: Scolars Press, 1983).

—*Judaism and Christianity in the Age of Constantine: History, Messiah, and Israel, and the Initial Confrontation* (Chicago: University of Chicago Press, 1987).

—*Judaism: The Evidence of the Mishnah* (Atlanta: Scholars Press, 1988).

Neusner, J. (ed.), *The Mishnah* (New Haven: Yale University Press, 1988).

—*The Talmud of the Land of Israel* (Chicago: University of Chicago Press, 1982–).

Neusner, J. *et al.* (eds. and trans.), *The Tosefta* (6 vols.; Hoboken, NJ: Ktav, 1977–86).

Neusner, J., and E.S. Frerichs (eds.), *'To See Ourselves as Others See Us': Christians, Jews, 'Others' in Late Antiquity* (Chico, CA: Scholars Press, 1985).

Newsome, J.D., *Greeks, Romans, Jews: Currents of Culture and Belief in the New Testament World* (Philadelphia: Trinity Press International, 1992).

Newton, M., *The Concept of Purity at Qumran and in the Letters of Paul* (SNTSMS, 53; Cambridge: Cambridge University Press, 1985).

Neyrey, J.H., 'Ceremonies in Luke–Acts: The Case of Meals and Table-Fellowship', in J.H. Neyrey (ed.), *The Social World of Luke–Acts: Models for Interpretation* (Peabody, MA: Hendrickson, 1991), pp. 361-87.

Nickelsburg, G.W.E., *Jewish Literature between the Bible and the Misnah: A Historical and Literary Introduction* (Philadelphia: Fortress Press, 1981).

Nickelsburg, G.W.E, and M.E. Stone (eds.), *Faith and Piety in Early Judaism: Texts and Documents* (Philadelphia: Fortress Press, 1983).

Nickle, K.F., *The Collection* (London: SCM Press, 1966).

Niebuhr, H.R., *Christ and Culture* (New York: Harper & Brothers, 1951).

Niederwimmer, K., *Die Didache* (Kommentar zu den Apostolischen Vätern, 1; Göttingen: Vandenhoeck & Ruprecht, 1989).

Nikiprowetzky, V., 'La Sibylle juive et le "Troisième Livre" des "Pseudo-Oracles Sibyllins" depuis Charles Alexandre', *ANRW* 20.1, pp. 460-542.

—*Le commentaire de l'écriture chez Philon d'Alexandrie* (ALGH, 11; Leiden: E.J. Brill, 1977).

Nilson, J., 'To Whom Is Justin's Dialogue with Trypho Addressed?', *ThStud* 38 (1977), pp. 538-46.

Nilsson, M.P., *Greek Folk Religion* (New York: Harper Torchbooks, 1961).

Nock, A.D., *Early Gentile Christianity and its Hellenistic Background* (New York: Harper Torchbooks, 1964).

Noormann, R., *Irenäus als Paulusinterpret* (WUNT, 2.66; Tübingen: Mohr Siebeck, 1994).

Norden, E., *Die antike Kunstprosa: Vom vi Jahrhundert v. Chr. Bis in die Zeit der Renaissance* (12 vols.; Darmstadt: Wissenschaftliche Buchgesellschaft, 1898).

Norris, R.A., Jr, 'Irenaeus' Use of Paul in his Polemic Against the Gnostics', in W.S. Babcock (ed.), *Paul and the Legacies of Paul* (Dallas: Southern Methodist University Press, 1990), pp. 79-98.

O'Malley, T.P., *Tertullian and the Bible* (Utrecht: Nijmegen, 1967).

O'Neil, J.C., *The Theology of Acts in its Historical Setting* (London: SPCK, 2nd edn, 1970).

Olson, M.J., *Irenaeus, the Valentinian Gnostics, and the Kingdom of God (A.H. Book V): The Debate about 1 Corinthians 15.50* (Lewiston, NY: Edward Mellen Press, 1992).

Orr, W.F., and J.A. Walther, *1 Corinthians* (AB, 32; Garden City, NY: Doubleday, 1976).

Oster, R.E., Jr, 'Use, Misuse and Neglect of Archaeological Evidence in Some Modern Works on 1 Corinthians (1 Cor. 7, 1-5; 8, 10; 11, 2-16; 12, 14-26)', *ZNW* 83 (1992), pp. 52-73.

Pagels, E.H., *The Gnostic Paul: Gnostic Exegesis of the Pauline Letters* (Philadelphia: Fortress Press, 1975).

Pak, J.Y.-S., *Paul as Missionary: A Comparative Study of Missionary Discourse in Paul's Epistles and Selected Contemporary Jewish Texts* (European University Studies, 23; New York: Peter Lang, 1991).

Parker, R., *Miasma: Pollution and Purification in Early Greek Religion* (Oxford: Oxford University Press, 1983).

Parkes, J., *The Conflicts of the Church and Synagogue: A Study in the Origins of Anti-Semitism* (Cleveland: Meridian, 1977).

Patrick, D., *Old Testament Law* (Atlanta: John Knox Press, 1985).

Pearson, B.A., 'Hellenistic-Jewish Wisdom Speculation and Paul', in R.L. Wilken (ed.), *Aspects of Wisdom in Judaism and Early Christianity* (Notre Dame: Notre Dame University Press, 1975).

—*The Pneumatikos–Psychikos Terminology in 1 Corinthians: A Study in the Theology of the Corinthian Opponents of Paul in its Relation to Gnosticism* (Missoula, MT: Society of Biblical Literature, 1973).

—'Philo, Gnosis and the New Testament', in Logan and Wedderburn (eds.), *The New Testament and Gnosis*, pp. 73-89.

Pelikan, J., *The Christian Tradition: A History of the Development of Doctrine. I. The Emergence of the Catholic Tradition (100–600)* (Chicago: University of Chicago Press, 1971).

Perelman, C., *The Realm of Rhetoric* (Notre Dame: University of Notre Dame Press, 1982).

Perelman, C., and L. Olbrechts-Tyteca, *The New Rhetoric: A Treatise on Argumentation* (Notre Dame: University of Notre Dame Press, 1969).

Pervo, R.I., 'Joseph and Aseneth and the Greek Novel', *SBLSP* (1976), pp. 171-81.

Philonenko, M. *Joseph et Aséneth: Introduction, texte critique et notes* (Leiden: E.J. Brill, 1968).

Pierce, C.A., *Conscience in the New Testament* (SBT, 1.15; London: SCM Press, 1955).

Pogoloff, S.M., *Logos and Sophia: The Rhetorical Situation of 1 Corinthians* (Atlanta: Scholars Press, 1992).

Porter, S.E., 'The Theoretical Justification for Application of Rhetorical Categories to Pauline Epistolary Literature', in S.E. Porter and T.H. Olbricht (eds.), *Rhetoric and the New Testament: Essays from the 1992 Heidelberg Conference* (JSNTSup, 90; Sheffield: JSOT Press, 1993), pp. 100-22.

Porter, S.E. (ed.), *Handbook to Exegesis of the New Testament* (Leiden: E.J. Brill, 1997).

Porton, G.G., 'Diversity in Postbiblical Judaism', in R.A. Kraft and G.W.E. Nickelsburg (eds.), *Early Judaism and its Modern Interpreters* (Philadelphia: Fortress; Atlanta: Scholars Press, 1986), pp. 57-80.

Poythress, V.S., *Science and Hermeneutics: Implications of Scientific Method for Biblical Interpretation* (Grand Rapids: Zondervan, 1988).

Probst, H., *Paulus und der Brief: Die Rhetorik des antiken Briefes als Form der paulinischen Korintherkorrespondenz (1 Kor 8–10)* (WUNT, 2.45; Tübingen: Mohr Siebeck, 1991).

Quast, K., *Reading the Corinthian Correspondence: An Introduction* (New York: Paulist Press, 1994).

Quasten, J., *Patrology* (Newman, MD: Westminster Press, 1951–86).

Rainbow, P.A., 'Monotheism and Christology in 1 Corinthians 8.4-6', (PhD Thesis, Oxford University, 1987).

Ramsaran, R.A., *Liberating Words: Paul's Use of Rhetorical Maxims in 1 Corinthians 1–10* (Valley Forge, PA: Trinity Press International, 1996).

Rauer, M., *Die 'Schwachen' in Korinth und Rom nach dem Paulusbriefen* (Biblische Studien, 21; Freiberg: Herder, 1923).

Reicke, B., '*Syneideisis* in Rom. 2.15', *TZ* 12 (1956), pp. 157-61.

Reitzenstein, R., *Hellenistic Mystery Religions* (PTMS, 15; Pittsburgh: Pickwick Press, 1978).

Rengstorf, K.H., *A Complete Concordance to Flavius Josephus* (Leiden: E.J. Brill, 1973–83).

Rensberger, D.K., 'As the Apostle Teaches: The Development of the Use of Paul's Letters in Second-Century Christianity' (PhD Thesis, Yale University, 1981).

Resch, G., *Das Aposteldekret nach seiner außerkanonischen Textgestalt* (TU, NS 13.3; Leipzig: J.C. Hinrichs, 1905).

Richard, E.J., *First and Second Thessalonians* (Sacra Pagina, 11; Collegeville, MN: Liturgical Press, 1995), pp. 7-8.

Richardson, P., *Israel in the Apostolic Church* (Cambridge: Cambridge University Press, 1969).

—*Paul's Ethics of Freedom* (Philadelphia: Westminster Press, 1979).

Richardson, P., and P.W. Gooch., 'Accommodation Ethics', *TynBul* 29 (1978), pp. 89-142.

Ridderbos, H., *Paul: An Outline of his Theology* (Grand Rapids: Eerdmans, 1975).

Riesner, R., *Die Frühzeit des Apostels Paulus: Studien zur Chronologie, Missionsstrategie und Theologie* (Tübingen: J.C.B. Mohr, 1994).

Rivkin, E., *A Hidden Revolution: The Pharisees' Search for the Kingdom Within* (Nashville: Abingdon Press, 1978).

Roberts, A., and J. Donaldson (eds.), *Ante-Nicene Fathers* (10 vols.; American repr. edn, Grand Rapids: Eerdmans, 1977).

Roebuck, C.A. *Corinth: Results of Excavations Conducted by the American School of Classical Studies in Athens. XIV. The Asklepieion and Lerna* (Princeton, NJ: American School of Classical Studies in Athens, 1951).

Ropes, J.H., *The Text of Acts* (repr.; Grand Rapids: Baker Book House, 1979).

Rosaeg, N.A., 'Paul's Rhetorical Arsenal and 1 Corinthians 1–4', *Jian Dao* 3 (1995), pp. 51-75.

Rosner, B.S., ' "Stronger than He?": The Strength of 1 Corinthians 10.22b', *TynBul* 43 (1992), pp. 171-79.

—*Paul, Scripture and Ethics: A Study of 1 Corinthians 5–7* (AGJU, 22; Leiden: E.J. Brill, 1994).

Rosner, B.S. (ed.), *Understanding Paul's Ethics: Twentieth Century Approaches* (Grand Rapids: Eerdmans, 1995).

Roukema, R., *The Diversity of Laws in Origen's Commentary on Romans* (Amsterdam: Free University Press, 1988).

Rudolph, K., *Gnosis: The Nature and History of Gnosticism* (San Francisco: Harper & Row, 1983).

Saffrey, H.D., 'Aphrodite à Corinthe: Reflexions sur une idée reçue', *RB* 92 (1985), pp. 359-74.

Safrai, S. (ed.), *The Literature of the Sages* (CRINT, 2.3; 2 parts; Assen: Van Gorcum; Philadelphia: Fortress Press, 1974–76).

Safrai, S., and M. Stern (eds.), *The Jewish People in the First Century: Historical Geography, Political History, Social, Cultural and Religious Life and Institutions* (CRINT, 1; 2 vols.; Assen: Van Gorcum; Philadelphia: Fortress Press, 1974–76).

Sahlin, H., 'Die drei Kardinalsünden und das Neue Testament', *ST* 24 (1970), pp. 93-112.

Saldarini, A.J,. *Scholastic Rabbinism* (Chico, CA: Scholars Press, 1982).

—*Pharisees, Scribes and Sadducees in Palestinian Society: A Sociological Approach* (Wilmington, DE: Michael Glazier, 1988).

—'Jews and Christians in the First Two Centuries: The Changing Paradigm', *Shofar* 10 (1992), pp. 16-34.

Sandelin, K.-G., *Wisdom as Nourisher: A Study of an Old Testament Theme, its Development within Early Judaism, and its Impact on Early Christianity* (Åbo: Åbo Akademi, 1986).

—'Does Paul Argue Against Sacramentalism and Over-Confidence in 1 Cor. 10.1-14?', in P. Borgen and S. Giversen (eds.), *The New Testament and Hellenistic Judaism* (Aarhus: Aarhus University Press, 1995), pp. 165-82.

Sanders, E.P., *Paul and Palestinian Judaism: A Comparison of Patterns of Religion* (Philadelphia: Fortress Press, 1977).

—*Paul, the Law and the Jewish People* (Philadelphia: Fortress Press, 1983).

—'Jewish Association with Gentiles and Galatians 2.11-14', in R.T. Fortna and B.R. Gaventa (eds.), *The Conversation Continues: Studies in Paul and John in Honor of J. Louis Martyn* (Nashville: Abingdon Press, 1990), pp. 170-88.

—*Jewish Law from Jesus to the Mishnah: Five Studies* (London: SCM Press; Philadelphia: Trinity Press International, 1990).

—*Paul* ('Past Masters' Series; Oxford: Oxford University Press, 1991).

—*Judaism: Practice and Belief 63 BCE–66 CE* (London: SCM Press; Philadelphia: Trinity Press International, 1992).

Sanders, J.N., 'Peter and Paul in Acts', *NTS* 2 (1955), pp. 133-43.

Sanders, J.T., *Ethics in the New Testament* (Philadelphia: Fortress Press, 1975).

—'Paul between Jews and Gentiles in Corinth', *JSNT* 65 (1997), pp. 67-83.

Sandmel, S., *The Genius of Paul: A Study of History* (New York: Schocken Books, 1970).

—*Philo's Place in Judaism* (New York: Ktav, 1971).

—*Philo of Alexandria: An Introduction* (Oxford: Oxford University Press, 1979).

Sänger, D., *Antikes Judentum und die Mysterien: Religionsgeschichtliche Untersuchungen zu Joseph und Aseneth* (WUNT, 2.5; Tubingen: J.C.B. Mohr, 1980).

Savage, T.B., *Power through Weakness: Paul's Understanding of the Christian Ministry in 2 Corinthians* (Cambridge: Cambridge University Press, 1995).

Saw, I., *Paul's Rhetoric in 1 Corinthians 15: An Analysis Utilizing the Theories of Classical Rhetoric* (Lewiston, NY: Mellen Biblical Press, 1995).

Sawyer, W.T., 'The Problem of Meat Sacrificed to Idols in the Corinthian Church' (ThD dissertation, Southern Baptist Theological Seminary, 1968).

Schaff, P. (ed.), *Nicene and Post-Nicene Fathers* (American repr. edn; Grand Rapids: Eerdmans, 1979).

Schenke, H.-M. *et al.*, *Einleitung in die Schriften des Neuen Testaments*. I. *Die Briefe des Paulus und Schriften des Paulinismus*; II. *Die Evangelien und die anderen neutestamentlichen Schriften* (2 vols.; Berlin: Evangelische Verlagsanstalt, 1978–79).

Schlatter, A., *Die korinthische Theologie* (Gütersloh: C. Bertelsmann, 1914).

Schmid, W., 'Ein verkannter Ausdruck der Opfersprache in Plinius' Christenbrief', *VC* 7 (1953), pp. 75-78.

Schmithals, W., *Paul and James* (London: SCM Press, 1965).

—*Gnosticism in Corinth* (Nashville: Abingdon Press, 1971).

—*Paul and the Gnostics* (Nashville: Abingdon Press, 1972).

—*The Apocalyptic Movement: Introduction and Interpretation* (trans. J.E. Steely; Nashville: Abingdon Press, 1975).

Schnackenburg, R., *The Moral Teaching of the New Testament* (London: Burns & Oates, 1965).

Schneemelcher, W. (ed.), *New Testament Apocrypha* (trans. R. McL. Wilson; 2 vols.; Louisville, KY: Westminster/John Knox Press, rev. edn, 1991).

Schneider, G., 'Zum "westlichen Text" der Apostelgeschichte', *BZ* 31 (1987), pp. 138-44.

Schoedel, W.R., *Ignatius of Antioch: A Commentary on the Letters of Ignatius of Antioch* (Hermeneia; Philadelphia: Fortress Press, 1985).

—'The Apostolic Fathers', in J. Epp and G.W. MacRae (eds.), *The New Testament and its Modern Interpreters* (Philadelphia: Fortress Press, 1989).

Schoedel, W.R., and R.L. Wilken (eds.), *Early Christian Literature and the Classical Intellectual Tradition: In Honorem Robert M. Grant* (Paris: Editions Beauchesne, 1979).

Schoeps, H.J., *Theologie und Geschichte des Judenchristentums* (Tübingen: J.C.B. Mohr, 1949).

—*Aus frühchristlicher Zeit: Religionsgeschichtliche Untersuchungen* (Tübingen: Mohr Siebeck, 1950).

—*Jewish Christianity: Factional Disputes in the Early Church* (Philadelphia: Fortress Press, 1969).

Schrage, W., *Der erste Brief an die Korinther*. II. *1Kor 6, 12–11, 16* (EKKNT, 7.2; Zürich: Benziger Verlag, 1995).

Schürer, E., *The History of the Jewish people in the Age of Jesus Christ (175 BC–AD 135)* (3 vols.; Edinburgh: T. & T. Clark, rev. edn, 1973–87).

Schüssler Fiorenza, E., *The Book of Revelation: Justice and Judgment* (Philadelphia: Fortress Press, 1985).

—'Rhetorical Situation and Historical Reconstruction in 1 Corinthians', *NTS* 33 (1987), pp. 386-403.

Schweitzer, A., *Paul and his Interpreters* (New York: Schocken Books, 1964).

Segal, A.F., *Paul the Convert: The Apostolate and Apostasy of Saul the Pharisee* (New Haven: Yale University Press, 1990).

—'Jewish Christianity', in H.W. Attridge and G. Hata (eds.), *Eusebius, Christianity, and Judaism* (Detroit: Wayne State University Press, 1992), pp. 326-51.

Sherwin-White, A.N., *The Letters of Pliny: A Historical and Social Commentary* (Oxford: Clarendon Press, 1966).

Sherwin-White, A.N. (ed.), *Fifty Letters of Pliny* (Oxford: Oxford University Press, 1969).

Shotwell, W.A., *The Biblical Exegesis of Justin Martyr* (London: SPCK, 1965).

Sider, R.D., 'Approaches to Tertullian: A Study of Recent Scholarship', *SecCent* 2 (1982), pp. 22-60.

Siegert, F., 'Die Heiden in der pseudo-philonischen Predigt *De Jona*', in Feldmeier and Heckel (eds.), *Die Heiden*, pp. 55-59.

—*Drei hellenistisch-jüdische Predigten*, II (WUNT, 61; Tubingen: Mohr Siebeck, 1992).

Sigal, P., *Judaism: The Evolution of a Faith* (Grand Rapids: Eerdmans, 1988).

Silva, M., *Explorations in Exegetical Method: Galatians as a Test Case* (Grand Rapids: Baker Book House, 1996).

Simon, M., 'The Apostolic Decree and its Setting in the Ancient Church', *BJRL* 52 (1970), pp. 437-60.

—'De l'observance rituelle à l'ascèse: Recherches sur le décret apostolique', *RHR* 193 (1978), pp. 27-104.

—*Le Christianisme antique et son contexte religieux: Scripta Varia*, II (WUNT, 23; 2 vols.; Tübingen: Mohr Siebeck, 1981).

Six, K., *Das Aposteldekret (Act 15, 28. 29): Seine Entstehung und Geltung in den ersten vier Jahrhunderten* (Veröffentlichungen des biblisch-patristischen Seminars zu Innsbruck, 5; Innsbruck: Felizian Rauch, 1912).

Smit, J.F.M., '1 Corinthians 8, 1-6, a Rhetorical Partitio: A Contribution to the Coherence of 1 Cor. 8, 1–11, 1', in R. Bieringer (ed.), *The Corinthian Correspondence* (BETL, 125; Leuven: Peeters, 1996), pp. 577-91.

—' "Do not Be Idolaters": Paul's Rhetoric in First Corinthians 10.1-22', *NovT* 39 (1997), pp. 40-53.

—'The Rhetorical Disposition of First Corinthians 8.7–9.27', *CBQ* 59 (1997), pp. 476-91.

Smith, D.E., 'The Egyptian Cults at Corinth', *HTR* 70 (1977), pp. 201-31.

—'Meals and Morality in Paul and his World', *SBLSP* 20 (1981), pp. 319-39.

Soden, H.F. von., 'Sakrament und Ethik bei Paulus: Zur Frage der literarischen und theologischen Einheitlichkeit von 1 Kor. 8–10', in H. von Campenhausen (ed.), *Urchristentum und Geschichte Gesammelte Aufsätze und Vortrage* (2 vols.; Tübingen: Mohr Siebeck, 1951–56), I, pp. 239-75.

—'Sacrament and Ethics in Paul', in Meeks (ed.), *The Writings of St Paul*, pp. 257-68.

Sommer, J.G., *Das Aposteldekret: Entstehung, Inhalt und Geschichte seiner Wirksamkeit in der christlichen Kirche* (Theologische Studien und Skizzen aus Ostpreußen, 4.9; Königsberg: Hartung, 1887–89).

Songer, H.S., 'Problems Arising from the Worship of Idols: 1 Corinthians 8.1–11.1', *RevExp* 80 (1983), pp. 363-75.

Souter, A., *The Earliest Commentaries on the Epistles of St Paul: A Study* (Oxford: Clarendon Press, 1927).

Sparks, H.F.D. (ed.), *The Apocryphal Old Testament* (Oxford: Oxford University Press, 1984).

Staab, K., *Pauluskommentare aus der griechischen Kirche aus Kettenhandschriften gesammelt und herausgegeben* (NTAbh, 15; Münster: Aschendorff, 1933).

Stambaugh, J.E., *The Ancient Roman City* (Baltimore: The Johns Hopkins University Press, 1988).

Stanton, G.N., 'Aspects of Early Christian–Jewish Polemic and Apologetic', *NTS* 31 (1985), pp. 377-92.

Stein, R., 'The Relationship of Galatians 2.1-10 and Acts 15.1-35: Two Neglected Arguments', *JETS* 17 (1974), pp. 239-42.

Stein, S., 'The Dietary Laws in Rabbinic and Patristic Literature', in K. Aland and F.L. Cross (eds.), *Studia Patristica*, II (Berlin: Akademie Verlag, 1957), pp. 141-54.

Steltzenberger, J., *Syneidesis im Neuen Testament* (Paderborn: Ferdinand Schöningh, 1961).

Stern, M., *Greek and Latin Authors on Jews and Judaism* (3 vols.; Jerusalem: Israel Academy of Sciences and Humanities, 1974–84).

Stone, M. (ed.), *Jewish Writings of the Second Temple Period: Apocrypha, Pseudepigrapha, Qumran, Sectarian Writings, Philo, Josephus* (CRINT, 2.2; Assen: Van Gorcum; Philadelphia: Fortress Press, 1984).

Stowers, S.K., 'Paul on the Use and Abuse of Reason', in D.L. Balch *et al.* (eds.), *Greeks, Romans and Christians: Essays in Honor of Abraham J. Malherbe* (Minneapolis: Fortress Press, 1990), pp. 253-86.

Strange, W.A., *The Problem of the Text of Acts* (Cambridge: Cambridge University Press, 1992).

Strecker, G., *Das Judenchristentum in den Pseudoclementinen* (TU, 70; Berlin: Akademie Verlag, 1958).

—'On the Problem of Jewish Christianity', Appendix to W. Bauer, *Orthodoxy and Heresy in Earliest Christianity* (ed. R.A. Kraft; trans. R.A. Kraft *et al.*; Philadelphia: Fortress Press, 1971), pp. 241-85.

Strobel, A., 'Das Aposteldekret in Galatien: Zur Situation von Gal. I und II', *NTS* 20 (1974), pp. 177-90.

Sumney, J.L., 'Paul's "Weakness": An Integral Part of his Conception of Apostleship', *JSNT* 52 (1993), pp. 71-91.

Sundberg, A., *The Old Testament and the Early Church* (HTS, 20; Cambridge, MA: Harvard University Press, 1964).

Talbert, C.H., *Reading Corinthians: A Literary and Theological Commentary on 1 and 2 Corinthians* (New York: Crossroad, 1987).

—'Luke–Acts', in E.J. Epp and G.W. MacRae (eds.), *The New Testament and its Modern Interpreters* (Philadelphia: Fortress Press, 1989), pp. 297-320.

Taylor, C. (ed.), *Sayings of the Jewish Fathers* (New York: Ktav, 1969).

Taylor, N., *Paul, Antioch and Jerusalem: A Study in Relationships and Authority in Earliest Christianity* (JSNTSup, 66; Sheffield: JSOT Press, 1991).

Taylor, R.E., 'Attitudes of the Fathers towards Practices of the Jewish Christians', *Studia patristica* 4 (1961), pp. 141-54.

Taylor, W.F., Review of *The Social Setting of Pauline Christianity*, by Gerd Theissen, in *Dialog* 23 (1984), pp. 151-52.

Tcherikover, V.A., 'The Third Book of Maccabees as a Historical Source', in A. Fuks and I. Halpern (eds.), *Studies in History: Scripta Hierosolymitana* 7 (1961), pp. 1-26.

Tcherikover, V., *Hellenistic Civilization and the Jews* (New York: Atheneum, 1977).

Tcherikover, V.A., and A. Fuks (eds.), *Corpus Papyrorum Judaicarum* (3 vols.; Cambridge, MA: Harvard University Press; Jerusalem: Magnes Press, 1957, 1960 and 1964).

Terry, R.B., *A Discourse Analysis of First Corinthians* (Dallas: Summer Institute of Linguistics, 1995).

Thackeray, H. *et al.* (eds. and trans.), *Josephus, with an English Translation* (10 vols.; LCL; London: Heinemann, 1926–65).

Thackeray, H. St. J., *Josephus, the Man and the Historian* (with an introduction by S. Sandmel; New York: Ktav, rpt edn, 1968).

Theissen, G., 'Die Starken und Schwachen in Korinth: Soziologische Analyse eines theologischen Streites', *EvT* 35 (1975), pp. 155-72.

—*The Social Setting of Pauline Christianity: Essays on Corinth* (trans. J.H. Schultz; Philadelphia: Fortress Press, 1982).

Thiselton, A., 'Realized Eschatology at Corinth', *NTS* 24 (1977–78), pp. 510-26.

Thompson, L.L., *The Book of Revelation: Apocalypse and Empire* (New York: Oxford University Press, 1990).

Thrall, M.E., *I and II Corinthians* (CBC; Cambridge: Cambridge University Press, 1965).

—'The Pauline Use of Συνείδησϊ', *NTS* 14 (1968), pp. 118-25.

Tobin, T.H., *The Creation of Man: Philo and the History of Interpretation* (CBQMS, 14; Washington, DC: Catholic Biblical Association of America, 1983).

Tomlinson, R.A., *Epidauros* (Archaeological Sites; London: Granada, 1983).

Tomson, P.J., *Paul and the Jewish Law: Halakha in the Letters of the Apostle to the Gentiles* (CRINT, 3.1; Jewish Traditions in Early Christian Literature; Assen: Van Gorcum; Minneapolis: Fortress Press, 1990).

Trigg, J.W., *Origen: The Bible and Philosophy in the Third-Century Church* (Atlanta: John Knox Press, 1983).

Unnik, W.C. van, *Tarsus or Jerusalem: The City of Paul's Youth* (London: Epworth Press, 1962).

Urbach, E.E., 'The Rabbinical Laws of Idolatry in the Second and Third Centuries in the Light of Archaeological and Historical Facts', *IEJ* 9 (1959), pp. 149-65, 229-45.

—*The Sages: Their Concepts and Beliefs* (2 vols.; Jerusalem: Magnes Press, 2nd edn, 1979).

Vallee, G., *A Study in Anti-Gnostic Polemics: Irenaeus, Hippolytus, and Epiphanius* (Waterloo, ON: Wilfrid Laurier University Press, 1981).

Vermes, G., *Scripture and Tradition in Judaism* (Studia Post-Biblica, 4; Leiden: E.J. Brill, 1961).

—*Jesus the Jew: A Historian's Reading of the Gospel* (Philadelphia: Fortress Press, 1973).

—*The Dead Sea Scrolls: Qumran in Perspective* (Cleveland: Collins World, 1978).

—'A Summary of the Law by Flavius Josephus', *NovT* 24 (1982), pp. 289-303.

—*The Dead Sea Scrolls in English* (Baltimore: Penguin Books, 1988).

Vielhauer, P., 'On the "Paulinism" of Acts', in L.E. Keck and J.L. Martyn (eds.), *Studies in Luke–Acts* (Nashville: Abingdon Press, 1966), pp. 33-50.

Waelkens, R., *L'Economie, thème, apologétique et principe herméneutique dans l'Apocriticos de Macarios Magnes* (Recueil de Travaux d'Histoire et de Philologie, 6.4; Louvain: University of Louvain Press, 1974).

Walker, W., Jr, 'The Burden of Proof in Identifying Interpolations in the Pauline Letters', *NTS* 33 (1987), pp. 610-18.

Walter, N., 'Christusglaube und heidnische Religiosität in paulinischen Gemeinden', *NTS* 25 (1979), pp. 422-42.

Wanamaker, C.A., *The Epistles to the Thessalonians: A Commentary on the Greek Text* (NIGTC; Grand Rapids: Eerdmans; Exeter: Paternoster Press, 1990).

Waszink, J.H., and J.C.M. van Winden, *Tertullianus: De Idolatria: Critical Text, Translation and Commentary* (VCSup, 1; Leiden: E.J. Brill, 1987).

Watson, D.F., '1 Corinthians 10.23–11.1 in the Light of Greco-Roman Rhetoric: The Role of Rhetorical Questions', *JBL* 108 (1989), pp. 301-18.

Watson, F.B., *Paul, Judaism and the Gentiles* (Cambridge: Cambridge University Press, 1986).

Webb, W.J., 'Unequally Yoked Together with Unbelievers. I. Who are the Unbelievers (ἄπιστοι) in 2 Corinthians 6.15?; II. What is the Unequal Yoke (ἑτεροζυγοῦντες) in 2 Corinthians 6.14?', *BSac* 149 (1992) pp. 27-44, 162-79.

Weber, V., *Des Paulus Reisenrouten bei der zweimaligen Durchquerung Kleinasiens: Neues Licht für die Paulusforschung* (Würzburg: Becker, 1920).

Weingreen, J., *From Bible to Mishna: The Continuity of Tradition* (Manchester: Manchester University Press, 1976).

Weiss, J., *Der erste Korintherbrief* (MeyerK; Göttingen: Vandenhoeck & Ruprecht, 1910).

—*Earliest Christianity: A History of the Period AD 30–150*, II (New York: Harper Torchbooks, 1965).

Wendland, H.D., *Die Briefen die Korinther* (Göttingen: Vandenhoeck & Ruprecht, 1968).

Wengst, K., *Didache (Apostellehre), Barnabasbrief, Zweiter Klemensbrief, Schrift an Diognet* (Schriften des Urchristentums, 2; Munich: Kösel, 1984).

Wenham, G.J., 'The Theology of Unclean Food', *EvQ* 53 (1981), pp. 6-15.

West, S., 'Joseph and Aseneth: A Neglected Greek Romance', *Classical Quarterly* 24 (1974), pp. 70-81.

Westerholm, S., *Israel's Law and the Church's Faith: Paul and his Recent Interpreters* (Grand Rapids: Eerdmans, 1988).

White, J.L., 'Saint Paul and the Apostolic Tradition', *CBQ* 45 (1983), pp. 433-44.

Whittaker, M., *Jews and Christians: Graeco-Roman Views* (Cambridge: Cambridge University Press, 1984).

Wiles, M.F., *The Divine Apostle: The Interpretation of St Paul's Epistles in the Early Church* (Cambridge: Cambridge University Press, 1967).

Wilken, R.L., *The Christians as the Romans Saw Them* (New Haven: Yale University Press, 1984).

Williams, F., *The Panarion of Epiphanius of Salamis: Book I, Sects 1-46* (NHS, 35; Leiden: E.J. Brill, 1987).

Williams, R. (ed.), *The Making of Orthodoxy* (Cambridge: Cambridge University Press, 1989).

Willis, W.L., 'An Apostolic Apologia? The Form and Function of 1 Corinthians 9', *JSNT* 24 (1985), pp. 33-48.

—*Idol Meat in Corinth: The Pauline Argument in 1 Corinthians 8 and 10* (SBLDS, 68; Chico, CA: Scholars Press, 1985).

Wilson, B.R., *The Social Dimensions of Sectarianism: Sects and New Religious Movements in Contemporary Society* (Oxford: Clarendon Press, 1990).

Wilson, R.McL., 'How Gnostic Were the Corinthians', *NTS* 19 (1972), pp. 65-74.

Wilson, S.G., *The Gentiles and the Gentile Mission in Luke–Acts* (SNTSMS, 23; Cambridge: Cambridge University Press, 1973).

—*Luke and the Law* (Cambridge: Cambridge University Press, 1983).

Winden, J.C.M. van, '*Idolum* and *idololatria* in Tertullian', *VC* 36 (1982), pp. 108-14.

Winston, D., and J. Dillon, *Two Treatises of Philo of Alexandria: A Commentary on De Gigantibus and Quod Deus Sit Immutabilis* (BJS, 25; Chico, CA: Scholars Press, 1983).

Winter, B.W., 'Theological and Ethical Responses to Religious Pluralism: 1 Corinthians 8-10', *TynBul* 41 (1990), pp. 209-25.

—*Seek the Welfare of the City: Early Christians as Benefactors and Citizens* (Grand Rapids: Eerdmans, 1994).

—'The Achaean Federal Imperial Cult, II: The Corinth Church', *TynBul* 46 (1995), pp. 169-81.

Wire, A.C., *The Corinthian Women Prophets: A Reconstruction through Paul's Rhetoric* (Minneapolis: Fortress Press, 1990).

Wischnitzer, M., 'Notes to a History of the Jewish Guilds', *HUCA* 23.2 (1938), pp. 246-53.

Witherington, B., III, 'Not so Idle Thoughts about *Eidolothuton*', *TynBul* 44 (1993), pp. 237-54.

—'Why not Idol Meat? Is it What You Eat or Where You Eat it?', *BR* 10 (1994), pp. 38-43, 54-55.

—*The Acts of the Apostles: A Socio-Rhetorical Commentary* (Grand Rapids: Eerdmans; Cambridge: Paternoster Press, 1998).

Witherington, B., III (ed.), *History, Literature, and Society in the Book of Acts* (Cambridge: Cambridge University Press, 1996).

Wolfson, H.A., *Philo: Foundations of Religious Philosophy in Judaism, Christianity, and Islam* (2 vols.; Cambridge, MA: Harvard University Press, rev. edn, 1962).

Wood, S.P., *Clement of Alexandria: Christ the Educator* (FC, 23; Washington, DC: Catholic University of America Press, 1954).

Wright, N.T., *The Climax of the Covenant: Christ and the Law in Pauline Theology* (Edinburgh: T. & T. Clark, 1991).

Wuellner, W., 'Greek Rhetoric and Pauline Argumentation', in W.R. Schroedel and R.L. Wilken (eds.), *Early Christian Literature and the Classical Intellectual Tradition: In Honorem Robert M. Grant* (Theologie Historique, 53; Paris: Beauchesne, 1979), pp. 177-88.

—'Where is Rhetorical Criticism Taking Us?', *CBQ* 49 (1987), pp. 448-63.

Yarbrough, O.L., *Not Like the Gentiles: Marriage Rules in the Letters of Paul* (SBLDS, 80; Atlanta: Scholars Press, 1985).

Yeo, K., *Rhetorical Interaction in 1 Corinthians 8 and 10: A Formal Analysis with Preliminary Suggestions for a Chinese, Cross-Cultural Hermeneutic* (Biblical Interpretation Series, 9; Leiden: E.J. Brill, 1995).

Yerkes, R.K., *Sacrifice in Greek and Roman Religions and Early Judaism* (New York: Charles Scribner's Sons, 1952).

Young, F.M., 'Notes on the Corinthian Correspondence', in E.A. Livingstone (ed.), *Studia Evangelica 7* (TU, 126; Berlin: Akademie Verlag, 1982), pp. 563-66.

—'John Chrysostom on First and Second Corinthians', in E.A. Livingstone (ed.), *Studia patristica. XVIII. 1. Historica–Theologica–Gnostica–Biblica* (Kalamazoo, MI: Cistercian, 1985), pp. 349-52.

—'The Rhetorical Schools and their Influence on Patristic Exegesis', in R. Williams (ed.), *The Making of Orthodoxy* (Cambridge: Cambridge University Press, 1989), pp. 182-99.

Zorell, F., *Lexicon Graecum Novi Testamenti* (Rome: Biblical Institute Press; Chicago: Loyola University Press, 1978).

Zuntz, G., *The Text of the Epistles: A Disquisition upon the Corpus Paulinum* (London: Oxford University Press, 1953).

INDEXES

INDEX OF REFERENCES

OLD TESTAMENT

Genesis

2.8	63
3.1	63
9.3-4	186

Exodus

16.13-14	209
16.31	209
20.5	41
21.12-13	301
21.28-29	301
22.2	301
34.12-16	186
34.14	41
34.15	42, 319

Leviticus

11.29-36	301, 302
11.42-43	186
17–18	180
17.7	320
17.10-14	187
17.10	186

Numbers

16	317
25	42, 57, 156, 186, 300
25.1	198
25.2	42, 43, 198, 319
25.11	42
31.6	198

Deuteronomy

7.9	150
7.16	129
8.17-19	150
14.21	187
18.1-4	68
18.11	152
32	149, 150, 151, 152, 300
32.4	150
32.16-23	186
32.16	152
32.17	42, 55, 150, 152
32.21	122, 150, 152, 152
32.36-37	151

Joshua

2.3	129
7.19	161
8.27	129
23.13	129

2 Samuel

3.6	77

1 Kings

16.31-33	198
16.31	198

2 Kings

9.22	198

2 Chronicles

21.13	198

Esther

14.17	43

Psalms

24	155, 227
24.1	155, 156, 227
68.23	129
105	129, 144
105.14	144
105.16	144
105.19	144
105.23	144
105.25	144
105.28	55, 144, 156
105.36-39	128, 144
105.36	129, 144
105.37	144, 149
105.38-39	144
106.28-29	186
106.28	42
106.37	152
112.5	47
115.4-8	122, 152
135.15-18	122, 152

Proverbs

24.9	133

Isaiah

8.19	152
14.13	47

19.3	152	66.18-21	225	*Daniel*	
40.17	151	66.19	225	1	42, 321
40.19-20	122, 152	66.20	226	1.8	42, 133
40.23	151			3	43
41.29	122	*Jeremiah*		5.2-4	43
44.9	151	2.34	301	6	43
44.9-17	122, 152	23.11	133		
59.3	133			*Malachi*	
60.5	226	*Ezekiel*		1.12	150
65.11	149	44.16	150		

APOCRYPHA

1 Esdras		3.15	133	*Ecclesiasticus*	
8.80	133	13.6	48	21.28	133
2 Esdras		*Judith*		*Bel and the Dragon*	
15–16	209	10.5	42, 49	3	43
16.69-70	209	12.2	42, 49		
16.69	273	12.9	49	*1 Maccabees*	
		12.19	49	1.11-15	45
6 Ezra				1.42-43	44, 45
16	43	*Additions to Esther*		1.62-3	45
16.9	43, 273	14.17	49		
				2 Maccabees	
Tobit		*Wisdom of Solomon*		4.18-20	45
1.10-11	43, 48	13–16	49	7	46

NEW TESTAMENT

Matthew		*John*		11.5-10	187
11	269	6.35	55	11.19-26	188
12	269	6.48	55	14.15-18	191
12.29	305	6.51	55	14.27	189
15.2	268	9.24	162	15	15, 69, 103,
15.11	263, 268,				136, 177,
	269, 321	*Acts*			187, 189,
		8.14-17	188		190, 195,
Mark		10–11	22, 136, 187		319
7.19	269	10	187, 188,	15.3	189
			263	15.4	189
Luke		10.9-16	187	15.10	193
1.3-4	197	10.34-35	187	15.12	189
15.30	129	11	187	15.19	193
		11.1-18	188		

Acts (cont.)

15.20	133, 177, 178, 191, 321
15.21	181
15.23	177, 189
15.28-29	177
15.28	198
15.29	147, 177, 178, 265
16.4	112, 177, 181, 185
16.7	225
16.14-15	206
16.14	197
17.16-29	191
17.16	111
17.22-31	111
18.2	224
18.18	224
19.10	207
19.11-20	207
19.19	110
19.21-41	207
19.23-27	110
20.28-31	201
21	189, 215
21.18-26	195, 196
21.18	196
21.19	189
21.21	196
21.25	177, 178, 182, 185, 188, 189, 196
22.3	77
24.16	133
26.5	77

Romans

1	237
1.18-32	191
1.19-32	111
1.21-32	80
1.21-23	80
1.24-32	80
2.15	131, 133
2.20	117
2.22	80, 111
3.30	123
4.20	162
8.9	123
8.17	123
9.1-3	57
9.3	77
11.1	77
11.13	200
11.33	117
14–15	18, 166, 317
14.1–15.13	87, 88
14	21, 79, 87, 90, 91, 92, 116, 117, 134, 136, 237, 241, 260, 270, 281
14.1-6	182
14.1-4	268
14.3	263
14.6	135, 263
14.14	20, 136, 188
14.16-18	268
14.16	161
14.17	182
14.20-21	268
14.20	182
14.23	20
15.1	88
15.7-24	225
15.14	117
15.25-28	226
16.3	224

1 Corinthians

1–4	87, 88, 205, 317
1.3-8	115
1.5	117
1.10	314
1.11	314
1.14-16	314
1.18-25	241
1.26-28	313
1.26	149
2.1	316
2.8	227
2.10	200
2.15	227
3.1	115
3.5-6	314
3.10-12	115
3.15	115
4.8-9	119
4.10	121
4.18	139
5–7	300
5	115
5.5	115
5.9-11	311
5.9-10	111
5.9	98, 112, 153
5.11	231
6	112, 313
6.9	110
6.9-10	115, 191, 243
6.12	90, 113, 129, 134
6.13	113, 146
6.16-17	113
6.18	113, 114, 201
6.20	114, 162
7	259
7.1-40	140
7.1	213
7.7-10	214
7.19	186, 196
7.20	259
7.25	213
7.39-40	214
8–10	16-20, 22-25, 36, 38, 43, 47, 79, 87, 88, 90-92, 98, 102, 103, 113, 125, 126, 129, 131, 132, 136-40, 147, 150, 152, 160-66, 171-74, 176,

185, 193,
214, 216,
233, 242,
247, 251,
259, 260,
261, 264,
267, 271,
278, 279-83,
287, 288,
290, 293-95,
297, 298,
300, 302,
308, 311,
313, 314,
317, 318,
320

8.1–11.1 82, 83, 87,
88, 92, 94,
99, 101, 109,
112, 117,
140, 194,
308

8–9   166
8   22, 92, 93,
137, 138,
140, 143,
161-63, 245,
246, 282,
289, 290,
306, 310
8.1-13   32, 82, 85,
89, 91, 96,
102, 103,
144
8.1-4   86
8.1   114, 122,
126, 128,
133, 213,
245
8.4   114, 122-24,
129, 214,
231, 245,
258
8.4-6   85, 92, 123,
242
8.5-6   122-24
8.5   15, 123
8.6   123, 146

8.7–9.27
8.7-13

8.7-10
8.7

8.8

8.9-12

8.9

8.10

8.11
8.12
8.13

9

9.1-23
9.1-2
9.1
9.3

9.4-14
9.4-5
9.4
9.5
9.12
9.15
9.19-23
9.19-22
9.20-21
9.22

96
20, 86, 91,
100, 116,
143, 152
88
22, 38, 124-
26, 128, 132,
133, 144,
158, 245,
246
126, 128,
134-36, 182,
263, 268,
269
129, 130,
136
129, 130,
141
31, 83, 86,
93-95, 101,
104-106,
129, 132,
156
128-30, 144
132
15, 105, 132,
133, 136,
140, 141,
144
82, 86, 137-
39, 140-42,
161, 162,
259
82
200
139
102, 137,
139, 313
141
265
141
141
265
139
83, 102, 142
124
142, 143
142, 143

9.24–10.22
9.24-27
9.24-25
9.26-27
9.27
10

10.1-22

10.1-13
10.1-11
10.1-10

10.1-5
10.5
10.6
10.7
10.8
10.9
10.10

10.11
10.12
10.13
10.14-22

10.14-21
10.14

10.16-17
10.18-22
10.18

10.19-22
10.19-21

83
83, 143, 144
259
259
143
93, 118, 138,
140, 144,
162, 163,
186, 208,
262, 268
32, 82, 83,
85, 86, 89,
91, 92, 95,
96, 100, 102,
103, 114,
162, 297,
306, 310,
312, 318
42, 144
149
129, 143,
144, 150,
317
144, 145
317
144, 150
144
317
144
144, 145,
317
150, 302
115, 145
145-47
83, 86, 92,
95, 102, 104,
111, 144,
309
156
113, 114,
147, 201
113, 209
126, 129,
144, 150
107, 148,
149, 320
93
231

1 Corinthians (cont.)
10.19-20	92, 93, 147
10.19	85, 128, 250, 258
10.20	42, 95, 107, 113, 148, 149, 150, 263
10.21-22	113
10.21	28, 31, 54, 94, 258, 263
10.22	42, 83, 145, 149, 162, 297
10.23–11.1	82, 87, 89, 92, 102
10.23-30	91, 161
10.23-29	88, 91, 152
10.23-28	95
10.23-24	152
10.23	83, 90, 101, 113, 134, 141, 245
10.24	152
10.25-31	280
10.25-29	277, 306, 307
10.25-27	157
10.25	20, 91, 106-108, 155, 159, 160, 245, 270
10.26	108, 153, 155, 227, 262
10.27-29	162, 163, 311
10.27	20, 35, 83, 107, 152, 156-60, 245, 263
10.28-29	152, 160, 161, 221
10.28	87, 102, 132, 152, 157, 160, 230, 320
10.29-31	265
10.29-30	160, 161
10.29	102, 160, 264
10.30	276
10.31–11.1	161
10.31	114, 161, 162, 268, 269
10.32-33	161, 162
11	313
11.16	139
11.17-34	309
11.19	238, 241
12–14	125
12.1–14.40	140
12.1-2	54
12.1	213
12.2	15, 80, 110, 227
12.3	227
12.8	117
12.22	124
12.24	124
13	116
14.1–15.13	95
14.6	117
14.23	313
14.37-38	139
15	316
15.9	200
15.15	123
15.32	207, 217
15.33	317
15.50	247
15.58	201
16.1	213
16.12	213
16.15	314
16.17-18	314
16.19	175, 224, 224, 314

2 Corinthians
2.14	117
4.6	117
6.6	117
6.14–7.1	111
6.14	111
6.16	80
7.1	132
8.7	117
10–13	139
10.5	117
11.6	117, 315
11.13	241
11.22	77
11.29	124
12.20-21	191

Galatians
1–2	183
1.1	200
1.14	78
1.15-16	192
1.16-19	200
1.23-24	192
2	183-85, 189, 190
2.2	191
2.6-9	200
2.6	183, 184, 192, 193
2.9	198
2.11-14	184
2.11	184
2.14	224
2.15	77
4.8	80, 110, 250
4.9	250
5.1	191
5.19-21	191, 192
5.20	110
5.21	191
6.7	191
6.15	196

Ephesians
5.5	191
5.19	227

Philippians
3.5	77
3.8	117

Colossians
2.3	117

2.16	182, 241,	*Titus*			207, 208,
	269	1.15-16	132, 133		215, 217
3.5	191	1.15	131, 182	2.2	200, 201
3.16	227	1.16	131	2.9	200
		2.15	269	2.13-14	199
1 Thessalonians				2.13	321
1.6	121	*1 Peter*		2.14-15	191, 198
1.7	109	1.1	222	2.14	197, 200,
1.9-10	54, 78, 191	1.14	223		202
1.9	15, 80, 109	1.18	223	2.15	201
1.10	109	2.10	223	2.17	208
2.14	121	3.16	133	2.19-20	199
3.4	121	4.3-5	223	2.19	200
4.11	259	5.8	305	2.20	191, 197-
					200, 202
2 Thessalonians		*2 Peter*		2.24	198, 200
1.6	123	2.15	208	3.4	132, 199
				3.9	200
1 Timothy		*Jude*		3.14	200
4.3-5	182, 241	11	208	6	205
4.4-5	156, 268			14.4	132
4.4	262	*Revelation*		22.15	191
6.20	203, 204	2	15, 199-201,		
			203-205,		

PSEUDEPIGRAPHA

3 Maccabees		*Letter of Aristeas*		11.3-9	121
3.3-4	45	128	50	11.8-9	43, 53, 104,
3.7	45	139	50		273
3.22-23	45	142	50	11.9	53
4.16	318	16	49	12.5	43, 53, 133,
5.31	45	180-86	50		273, 319
6.25	45	181	50	13.8	43, 53
7.7	45	184	50	15.5	55
		284-85	50	16.8	209
4 Maccabees				16.14	55
5.1	47, 320	*Joseph and Asenath*		16.16	55, 209
5.1-4	46	1.3	52	19.4-5	54
5.2	43, 47, 319	3.3	52	19.5	55
5.4	48	8.5-7	43, 52-54,	20.9	52
5.5–18.23	46		104, 181	21.13-14	43, 53, 104,
5.9	47	8.5	55, 209, 273		273
5.13	47	8.9	55	21.21	55
5.17	46	10.1-13	104		
5.20	47	10.11-13	43	*Jubilees*	
		10.11-12	53	1.9	55
		10.13	43, 53	1.19	55

Jubilees (cont.)

6.35	55
7.20-21	179
12.1-5	151
22.16	55
22.17	43, 55, 151
23.24	55

Pseudo-Phocylides

31	43, 210, 273

Sibylline Oracles

1.15-22	80
2.56-148	43
2.95-96	273

2.96	43, 210
3.29-35	80
3.30	318
3.762-66	80
4.7	318

DEAD SEA SCROLLS

1QH

14.21-22	56

1QS

1.4	56
5.1-02	56
5.10-11	56
6.15	56
9.5	56

9.8-09	56
9.20-21	56

4QD

6.14	56
6.15	56
7.13	56
8.4	56
8.8	56
8.16	56

11.4-05	56
12.6-11	56
13.14	56
16.9	56
19.17-29	56

11QT

48.7-13	56
60.16-21	56

PHILO

Agric.

97	63, 64

Ebr.

177	58

Flacc.

95-6	59

Leg. All.

1.43	63

Leg. Gai.

115-18	57
162-64	57
209	41, 57
361	59
362	59
363	59

Migr. Abr.

89	58
93	58

Omn. Prob. Lib.

26	58
141	58

Op. Mund.

1–2	66

Poster. C.

182-85	317

Quaest. in Gen.

1.3	63, 63
1.6	62
1.8	62, 63
1.10-13	62
1.10	63
1.11	62
1.12	63
1.13	63
1.14	63
1.18	63, 64
1.19	63, 64
1.21	63, 64
1.25	62

1.31	62
1.32	63, 64
1.33	64
1.37	62
1.38	62
1.39	62, 63
1.41	62
1.44-50	62
1.45	63
1.48	62
1.49	62
1.52	62
1.53	62, 63
1.55	63
1.56	62
1.57	62, 63
1.58	63
1.59	63
1.68	63
1.70	62
1.74	63
1.75	62
1.76	62
1.77	62, 64

1.82	62	2.58	63	*Spec. Leg.*	
1.83	64	2.64	63	1.54-55	57
1.87	62, 63	2.79	63	1.56-57	57
1.88	62	3.8	63	1.315-16	57
1.90	62	3.11	63	4.100-101	59
1.91	64	3.13	63	4.100-31	59
1.93	63	3.52	63		
1.94	62	4.2	63	*Vit. Mos.*	
1.95	62	4.64	63	2.174	317
2.28	63	4.145	63	2.283	317

JOSEPHUS

Ant.		20.100	41, 67	2.237-38	65
3.295	317	20.181	68	2.239-49	65
3.320	68	20.206-207	68	2.258	76
4.12	317			2.271-72	66
9.99	66	*Apion*		2.283	66
9.205	66	1.60	66		
9.243	66	1.190	66	*Life*	
9.273	66	2.66-67	66	1–12	66
10.50	66	2.128-29	65	13–14	68, 69
10.65	66	2.137	66	66–67	68
10.69	66	2.148	75	74	68
12.120	68	2.168-76	66		
12.276	67	2.173	66	*War*	
13.246	75	2.177-78	67	1.641-50	68
17.149-54	68	2.179	67	1.648-50	68
17.301-303	213	2.183	66	2.80-83	213
18.55-59	68	2.184	66	2.119-63	56
18.65-80	112	2.232-35	68	2.184-203	68
18.141	41, 67	2.234-35	66	2.220	67
18.257-309	68	2.235	66	2.591	68

EARLY CHRISTIAN WRITINGS

1 Clem.		*Barn.*		24	117, 150
1.1	215	4.8	218	25	131
62.3	216	10.2	218	25.1	276, 277,
		10.3	218		322
Apostolic Constitutions		10.9	218	25.2	276
7.2.20-21	272	16.7	219		
		20.1	218	Clement	
Apology				*Paed.*	
14.3	237	Chrysostom		2.1.8-10	260, 262,
15.2	236	*1 Cor. Hom.*			263, 264,
		20–25	116		267, 268
		20–24	276	2.1.11	263

Paed. (cont.)
2.1.16   263
2.1.17   262
2.7.56   262

Strom.
2.20   203
3.4   203
4.12   254
4.14   266
4.15   260, 262,
                264, 265,
                267
4.16   266
4.4.17   249, 252

Didache
6.2   212
6.3   211, 212,
                213, 214,
                215, 321
7.1   213
7.2-3   212
8.1-2   212
9.1-3   213
11.2   213

Didasc.
6.10.4   254

Epiphanius
Panar.
40.1.4   254
42   248, 250,
                251

Eusebius
Hist. Eccl.
3.29   203
3.1.2   222
3.4.2-3   222
4.7.7   244
4.15.46   249
5.16.21   249
5.20.6   217
5.27.7   247

Hippolytus
De Resurr.
frag. 1   204

Refut.
7.24   204

Ignatius
Eph.
6.2   207, 216
7.1   207, 217
8.1   207, 216
9.1   207, 216

Letter to Diognetus
4.1-2   241
5.4   242

Magn.
8.1   217
10.3   217

Phld.
6   204
6.1   217

Trall.
11   204

Irenaeus
Adv. Haer.
1.1-8   245
1.6.3   243, 245,
                246, 256
1.6.4   246, 256
1.24.5   244
1.26.3   203, 244
1.28.2   244
2.14.5   243
3.3.4   217
3.6.5   243
3.11.1   203
4.33.9   249
25.417.19-22   243

Justin
1 Apol.
2.5   268

14.5   241
26   252

Dial.
20   257
34.8   238
35   238, 241
35.3   241
47   237
95.1   237

Minucius
Oct.
12.5   262
38.1   262, 270

Novatian
De cib. jud.
7   266, 272

Origen
Adv. Jud.
1.6.7   276
1.7.5   276

Comm. Matt.
11   269, 270,
                274
12   269, 270,
                274

Contra Celsum
3.29   268
3.37   268
4.32   268
5.41   75
7.5   268
8.6   268
8.24   230, 232,
                268, 269
8.28   230, 232
8.29   268
8.30   268
8.31   231
8.32   268

Matt. Hom.
11.12   276

Polycarp
Phil.
3.2   217
11.2-3   218

Pseudo-Clementine
Hom.
7.3-4   273
7.4   274
7.4.2   273
7.8   273, 274
7.8.1   273
8.19   273, 275
8.23   273, 275
11.15   273
18.13-19   274

Recogn.
4.19   273
4.36   273
8.56   273

Tertullian
Adv. Haer.
1.6   204
1.24.2   254

Adv. Marc.
1.27   249

1.14   248, 249
1.24   249
1.29.2   203, 249
3.5.4   247
4.9   256
5.7.9-14   251

Apol.
9.13   257
22.6   257, 268
23.14   257, 268
38   257
42   155, 257

De Cor.
10   257

De Test. Animae
1   236

De idol.
1   256
5   72
5.1-2   259
5.4   259
24.3   257

De ieiunio
2   256

15   254
15.1   248
15.2   260
15.4   260
15.5   257, 260,
             266

De praescr.
30.5   249
32   217
33.10   203, 259

De pud.
12.3-4   257
12.5   257
12.7   257
19.4   203
19.25   256

De spec.
2.1   259
2.3   259
13   258
13.4   257

Theodoret
Hist. Eccl.
3.11   270

NAG HAMMADI

Gos. Phil.
66.10   255

Gos. Thom.
35.16-26   255

Pr. Thanks.
65.5   253

Sent. Sextus.
30.10-21   253, 254

Testim. Truth
56.5-17   255

Thund.
13.19   255
15.18-19   255
16.15-16   255
19.16-20   255

CLASSICAL

Cicero
Fam.
9.21.1   315

Diodorus
Bibliotheca historica
34.1.2   75

Epictetus
Encheiridion
25.4-05   35

Fragment
17   35

Herondas
Mime
4.19   32
4.88-95   32

Horace
Satire
2.2.115-25   34
2.6.65-66   34

Plautus
Twin Menaechmi
1.1.90-95   35

Juvenal
Satire
301   75

Lucian
Alex.
25   229
38   229

De morte Peregrini
16   228

Parasite
22   35

Mart. Pol.
9.3   217

Pausanias
Description of Greece
2.4.5   29

Plutarch
Mor.
1102A   310

Quest. Conv.
112.729.C.7-9   155
612D   35
621C   35
642F   34
726E   35

Pliny
Ep.
4.8   221
8.24   222
10.96   220

Porphyry
De abst.
2.42   268

Seneca
Letter
5.4   36

Quintilian
Inst. Or.
4.3.2   138
4.3.16   138
5.11.1   141

Tacitus
Historiae
5.5.1-4   76

Vitruvius
On Architecture
1.2.7   29

RABBINIC

Mishnah
Ab.
3.3   104, 106,
                    155, 156

'Abod. Zar.
1.5   73
2.3   74, 104, 321
3.4   71
4.3   71
4.4-5   72
4.4   72
4.6   71

4.9–5.10   43, 44
5.5   34, 44

Ḥul.
2.7   73

Talmud
b. 'Abod. Zar.
48b   53
50a   53

b. Šab.
7b   180

b. Sanh.
74a   180

Tosefta
'Abod. Zar.
6.4-6   213

Ber.
4.1   155

Ḥag.
3.3   72

INDEX OF AUTHORS

Achtemeier, P.J. 183
Aland, K. 84
Alexander, P.S. 69
Alon, G. 43, 44, 53
Amir, Y. 61
Anderson, R.D. 315, 316
Audet, J.-P. 211
Aus, R.D. 226

Babcock, W.S. 169-71
Bagnani, G. 228
Baird, W. 87
Balás, D.L. 242
Barclay, J.M.G. 119-21
Barker, S.F. 287, 293
Barnard, L.W. 215
Barnes, T.D 233
Barnett, A.E. 208, 213, 219, 224, 237, 239
Barrett, C.K. 20, 21, 39, 83, 86, 87, 89, 97, 129, 134, 145, 154, 155, 158-61, 167, 168, 173, 183, 208, 274, 275
Barton, S.C. 142
Bauer, W. 172, 173, 200, 254
Baur, F.C. 231
Benko, S. 220, 222, 228, 230
Best, E. 110
Bildstein, G.J. 73
Black, D.A. 126
Böckenhoff, K. 165, 211, 233, 234, 237, 268, 270, 271, 275, 277
Bockmuehl, M. 191
Boismard, M.-E. 178, 183
Borgen, P. 40, 61, 132, 133, 159, 180, 184, 191, 193, 213
Bornkamm, G. 143, 183

Boulluec, A. le 241
Brandt, W.J. 116
Brown, R.E. 183, 184, 227
Bruce, F.F. 185
Brunt, J.C. 16, 19, 21, 22, 83, 84, 91, 93, 95, 104, 136, 147, 166, 167, 181, 182, 187, 204, 208, 244, 246, 267, 294
Bullmore, M.A. 315
Burchard, C. 51, 52, 54, 55
Burford, A. 30
Burkett, W. 318

Cabaniss, A. 227
Cadbury, H.J. 154, 155
Catchpole, D.R. 184
Cazeaux, J. 61
Charles, R.H. 198, 204
Chester, A. 212
Cheung, A.T.M. 77, 178, 179, 188, 189, 192
Chow, J.K. 139
Clabeaux, J.J. 250
Classen, C.J. 316
Collier, G.D. 144
Collingwood, R.G. 176
Collins, A.Y. 204, 207
Collins, J.J. 40-42, 46, 52, 54, 113, 191
Conybeare, W.J. 185
Conzelmann, H. 85, 89, 90, 92, 93, 119, 126, 127, 143, 144, 158, 160, 183, 184, 190
Coppieters, H. 165, 166
Coune, M. 131
Cranfield, C.E.B. 91
Cross, F.L. 213, 217, 236, 261

deSilva, D.A. 207
Dassmann, E. 170, 173, 214, 237, 239, 241, 242, 245
Davies, W.D. 20
Dawes, G.W. 118, 127, 128, 133
Deissmann, A. 36
Delebecque, E. 178
Deselaers, P. 48
Dibelius, M. 193
Dillon, J. 61
Doran, R. 51
Douglas, M. 77
Duensing, H. 209
Dunn, J.D.G. 17, 91, 97, 106, 127, 142, 154, 184, 195

Eckstein, H.-J. 130, 131
Ehrhardt, A. 234, 235, 255
Elmslie, W.A.I. 44
Epp, E.J. 84, 179
Esler, P.F. 183

Fee, G.D. 17, 20, 85, 86, 88, 91, 96, 100-102, 111, 114, 118, 123, 127, 129, 133, 135, 138, 143, 144, 148, 149, 152, 153, 158, 160, 161, 165, 183
Feldman, A.H. 68
Filoramo, G. 253, 255
Fisk, B.N. 93, 102, 152, 158
Frame, J.M. 304
French, D. 226
Frend, W.H.C. 202

Gabba, E. 75
Gaffney, J. 167
Gamble, H.Y. 170
Gardner, P.D. 17, 102, 103, 107, 118, 128, 143, 145, 149-51
Gasque, W.W. 100, 182
Geer, T.C. 179
Glad, C.E. 89
Goldingay, J.E. 42
Goldstein, J. 75
Gooch, P.D. 15, 17, 23, 27-34, 36, 37, 80, 91, 94, 96, 116, 124, 154, 155, 157, 223, 308, 309, 312
Gooch, P.W. 130, 132

Goodenough, E.R. 57, 71
Gorday, P. 170, 245, 271, 276
Grant, R.M. 75, 81, 163, 211, 216, 217, 229, 236, 241
Gressmann, H. 148
Grosheide, F.W. 160
Guenther, H.O. 118

Hadas, M. 46, 47
Haenchen, E. 187, 188
Hall, S.G. 248
Harding, M. 318
Harnack, A. von 205, 240, 248-50, 260
Harrison, E.F. 185
Head, P. 179
Heckel, U. 113
Heil, C. 17, 130, 166, 215
Heiligenthal, R. 203
Hemer, C.J. 200, 202, 204
Hengel, M. 69, 71, 77, 78, 100, 183, 184, 315
Héring, J. 129, 160
Hoffmann, R.J. 200, 207, 232, 249, 252
Holtz, T. 110
Horbury, W. 218
Horsley, G.H.R. 37
Horsley, R.A. 119, 131, 151
Horst, P.W. van der 43
Houston, W. 58, 77
Howsen, J.S. 185
Hurd, J.C. 82, 83, 85, 88, 89, 95, 97-101, 116, 123, 124, 178, 182
Hvalvik, R. 219
Hyldahl, N. 241

Isenberg, M. 155
Ishmael, R. 71

Jervell, J. 166, 172, 182, 187, 188
Jewett, R. 89, 130, 225
Jones, F.S. 273
Judge, E.A. 139

Karris, R.J. 90
Keck, L.E. 143, 167
Kennedy, C.A. 102
Kidera, R. 166
Klauck, H.-J. 17, 27, 55, 154, 246, 310

Klawans, J. 44, 113, 192
Klijn, A.F.J. 273, 274
Klumbies, P.-G. 54, 55, 81
Knoch, O. 212
Knox, J. 78, 183
Knox, K.L. 112
Kraft, R.A. 39, 51, 62, 67, 211, 212,
  218, 275
Kuenning, L. 51
Kuhn, T.S. 291
Kümmel, W.G. 83

Lamouille, A. 178
Lang, M. 29
Lentz, J.C. 182
Lieberman, S. 70
Lietzmann, H. 154, 160
Lightfoot, J.B. 190, 193
Lindemann, A. 170, 182, 210, 214-16,
  219, 226, 237, 239-41
Lisle, R. 27
Litfin, D. 119, 316
Lohse, E. 155
Longenecker, R.N. 62, 190
Lüdemann, G. 196, 225, 240, 273

MacMullen, R. 27, 37
MacRae, G.W. 253
Maddox, R. 182
Magee, B.R. 17, 90
Malherbe, A.J. 121, 125, 315
Marcus, R. 61
Marshall, I.H. 185
Marshall, P. 314
Martin, D.B. 137
Martin, R.P. 185
Martyn, J.L. 143
Mason, S.N. 66
McKnight, S. 40, 55, 56, 81
Meeks, W.A. 110, 144, 153
Meggitt, J.J. 155, 313
Meier, J.P. 183, 184
Melnick, R. 64
Mendelson, A. 57, 65
Metzger, B. 209
Michaels, J.R. 223
Milgrom, J. 187

Mitchell, M.M. 17, 83, 86, 126, 137,
  139, 142, 146, 316, 317
Mitchell, S. 146
Moffatt, J. 89
Molland, E. 273
Murphy-O'Connor, J. 18, 29, 30, 37, 94,
  95, 113, 127, 134, 135, 138, 160,
  168, 313

Neil, W. 181
Neusner, J. 34, 51, 74
Nickelsburg, G.W.E. 39, 51
Nickle, K.F. 183, 184
Niebuhr, H.R. 120
Niederwimmer, K. 211
Nikiprowetzky, V. 60, 61
Noorman, R. 242
Norden, E. 316
Norris, R.A. 242, 243, 245

O'Neil, J.C. 187, 197
O'Rourke, J.J. 222
Olbrechts-Tyteca, L. 115
Olson, M.J. 242, 243, 245
Oster, R.E. 32

Pagels, E.H. 167, 245, 289
Pak, J.Y.-S. 80
Patrick, D. 303
Pearson, B.A. 119
Perelman, C. 115
Philonenko, M. 51
Porter, S.E. 315
Poythress, V.S. 291
Probst, H. 17, 83, 84

Ramsaran, R.A. 134
Reinink, G.J. 273, 274
Resch, G. 165, 268
Richard, E.J. 109, 110, 160
Richardson, P. 168
Riesner, R. 100, 182, 225, 226
Rivkin, E. 74
Roebuck, C.A. 29
Rosaeg, N.A. 316
Rosner, B.S. 150, 151, 300
Roukema, R. 268
Rudolph, K. 253-55

Saffrey, H.D. 113
Sahlin, H. 178
Saldarini, A.J. 195
Sandelin, K.-L. 144, 145, 209
Sanders, E.P. 17, 40, 47, 69, 74, 154,
  162, 163, 181, 186
Sanders, J.T. 79, 113, 120-22, 182, 183,
  192
Sandmel, S. 63, 64
Saw, I. 317
Sawyer, W.T. 16, 22, 136, 147, 155, 184
Schmid, W. 221
Schmithals, W. 82, 83, 118, 209
Schneemelcher, W. 110
Schneider, G. 179
Schoedel, W. 173, 204, 211
Schoeps, H.J. 212, 268
Schrage, W. 17, 149
Schüssler Fiorenza, E. 199, 201, 202,
  208
Schwemer, A.M. 100
Segal, A.F. 21, 69, 167, 179, 272, 307
Sherwin-White, A.N. 163, 220, 221
Siegert, F. 81
Silva, M. 277
Simon, M. 166, 180, 200, 273, 322
Six, K. 166, 211, 212, 223, 273, 275
Skarsten, R. 61
Smit, J.F.M. 88, 96, 116, 124, 129, 130,
  136, 137, 141, 147, 148
Smith, D.E. 33
Soden, H.F. von 19, 93, 145, 160
Sommer, J.G. 165
Stambaugh, J.E. 313
Stein, S. 275
Stern, M. 74
Stowers, S.K. 125
Strange, W.A. 178
Strecker, G. 254, 272, 274
Sumney, J.L. 126

Talbert, C.H. 148, 182
Taylor, N. 184
Taylor, W.F. 314
Tcherikover, V.A. 42, 46, 70
Terry, R.B. 120, 140
Thackeray, H. 67
Theissen, G. 17, 125, 155, 311-14

Thiselton, A. 119
Thompson, L.L. 207
Tobin, T.H. 62, 63
Tomlinson, R.A. 30
Tomson, P.J. 17, 20-23, 70-73, 105,
  106, 131, 151, 155, 157, 159, 166,
  178, 179, 186, 213, 271, 278, 306,
  307

Urbach, E.E. 70-72

Vallee, G. 247

Waelkens, R. 233
Walker, W. 84
Wanamaker, C.A. 110
Waszink, J.H. 257
Webb, W.J. 111
Weber, V. 225
Weiss, J. 85, 89, 160
Wendland, H.D. 160
Wengst, K. 210-12
Whittaker, M. 75
Wiles, M.F. 170
Wilken, R.L. 220, 222, 233
Willis, W.L. 16, 17, 22, 27, 36, 93, 101,
  106, 117, 123, 129-32, 137, 141,
  142, 145, 146, 148, 152, 155, 156,
  160, 161, 165, 309, 310
Wilson, B.R. 121
Wilson, S.G. 187
Winden, J.C.M. van 257
Winston, D. 61
Winter, B.W. 27, 47, 73, 94, 129, 158
Wire, A.C. 115, 116, 145, 314
Wischnitzer, M. 60
Witherington, B. 79, 102, 103, 107, 108,
  112, 123, 128, 138, 147-49, 160,
  313, 315, 317-21
Wood, S.P. 266
Wright, N.T. 151, 300

Yeo, K. 17, 318
Young, F.M. 163, 164, 276

Zorell, F. 319
Zuntz, G. 160, 161

JOURNAL FOR THE STUDY OF THE NEW TESTAMENT
SUPPLEMENT SERIES

64   Henry Wansborough (ed.), *Jesus and the Oral Gospel Tradition*

65   Douglas A. Campbell, *The Rhetoric of Righteousness in Romans 3.21-26*

66   Nicholas Taylor, *Paul, Antioch and Jerusalem: A Study in Relationships and Authority in Earliest Christianity*

67   F. Scott Spencer, *The Portrait of Philip in Acts: A Study of Roles and Relations*

68   Michael Knowles, *Jeremiah in Matthew's Gospel: The Rejected-Prophet Motif in Matthaean Redaction*

69   Margaret Davies, *Rhetoric and Reference in the Fourth Gospel*

70   J. Webb Mealy, *After the Thousand Years: Resurrection and Judgment in Revelation 20*

71   Martin Scott, *Sophia and the Johannine Jesus*

72   Steven M. Sheeley, *Narrative Asides in Luke–Acts*

73   Marie E. Isaacs, *Sacred Space: An Approach to the Theology of the Epistle to the Hebrews*

74   Edwin K. Broadhead, *Teaching with Authority: Miracles and Christology in the Gospel of Mark*

75   John K. Chow, *Patronage and Power: A Study of Social Networks in Corinth*

76   Robert W. Wall & Eugene E. Lemcio, *The New Testament as Canon: A Reader in Canonical Criticism*

77   Roman Garrison, *Redemptive Almsgiving in Early Christianity*

78   L. Gregory Bloomquist, *The Function of Suffering in Philippians*

79   Blaine Charette, *The Theme of Recompense in Matthew's Gospel*

80   Stanley E. Porter & D.A. Carson (eds.), *Biblical Greek Language and Linguistics: Open Questions in Current Research*

81   In-Gyu Hong, *The Law in Galatians*

82   Barry W. Henaut, *Oral Tradition and the Gospels: The Problem of Mark 4*

83   Craig A. Evans & James A. Sanders (eds.), *Paul and the Scriptures of Israel*

84   Martinus C. de Boer (ed.), *From Jesus to John: Essays on Jesus and New Testament Christology in Honour of Marinus de Jonge*

85   William J. Webb, *Returning Home: New Covenant and Second Exodus as the Context for 2 Corinthians 6.14–7.1*

86   B.H. McLean (ed.), *Origins of Method: Towards a New Understanding of Judaism and Christianity—Essays in Honour of John C. Hurd*

87   Michael J. Wilkins & T. Paige (eds.), *Worship, Theology and Ministry in the Early Church: Essays in Honour of Ralph P. Martin*

88   Mark Coleridge, *The Birth of the Lukan Narrative: Narrative as Christology in Luke 1–2*

89   Craig A. Evans, *Word and Glory: On the Exegetical and Theological Background of John's Prologue*

90   Stanley E. Porter & Thomas H. Olbricht (eds.), *Rhetoric and the New Testament: Essays from the 1992 Heidelberg Conference*

91   Janice Capel Anderson, *Matthew's Narrative Web: Over, and Over, and Over Again*

92   Eric Franklin, *Luke: Interpreter of Paul, Critic of Matthew*

93   Jan Fekkes III, *Isaiah and Prophetic Traditions in the Book of Revelation: Visionary Antecedents and their Development*

94   Charles A. Kimball, *Jesus' Exposition of the Old Testament in Luke's Gospel*

95   Dorothy A. Lee, *The Symbolic Narratives of the Fourth Gospel: The Interplay of Form and Meaning*

96   Richard E. DeMaris, *The Colossian Controversy: Wisdom in Dispute at Colossae*

97   Edwin K. Broadhead, *Prophet, Son, Messiah: Narrative Form and Function in Mark 14–16*

98   Carol J. Schlueter, *Filling up the Measure: Polemical Hyperbole in 1 Thessalonians 2.14-16*

99   Neil Richardson, *Paul's Language about God*

100   Thomas E. Schmidt & M. Silva (eds.), *To Tell the Mystery: Essays on New Testament Eschatology in Honor of Robert H. Gundry*

101   Jeffrey A.D. Weima, *Neglected Endings: The Significance of the Pauline Letter Closings*

102   Joel F. Williams, *Other Followers of Jesus: Minor Characters as Major Figures in Mark's Gospel*

103   Warren Carter, *Households and Discipleship: A Study of Matthew 19–20*

104   Craig A. Evans & W. Richard Stegner (eds.), *The Gospels and the Scriptures of Israel*

105   W.P. Stephens (ed.), *The Bible, the Reformation and the Church: Essays in Honour of James Atkinson*

106   Jon A. Weatherly, *Jewish Responsibility for the Death of Jesus in Luke–Acts*

107   Elizabeth Harris, *Prologue and Gospel: The Theology of the Fourth Evangelist*

108   L. Ann Jervis & Peter Richardson (eds.), *Gospel in Paul: Studies on Corinthians, Galatians and Romans for R.N. Longenecker*

109   Elizabeth Struthers Malbon & Edgar V. McKnight (eds.), *The New Literary Criticism and the New Testament*

110   Mark L. Strauss, *The Davidic Messiah in Luke–Acts: The Promise and its Fulfillment in Lukan Christology*

111   Ian H. Thomson, *Chiasmus in the Pauline Letters*

112   Jeffrey B. Gibson, *The Temptations of Jesus in Early Christianity*

113   Stanley E. Porter & D.A. Carson (eds.), *Discourse Analysis and Other Topics in Biblical Greek*

114   Lauri Thurén, *Argument and Theology in 1 Peter: The Origins of Christian Paraenesis*

115   Steve Moyise, *The Old Testament in the Book of Revelation*

116   Christopher M. Tuckett (ed.), *Luke's Literary Achievement: Collected Essays*

117 Kenneth G.C. Newport, *The Sources and Sitz im Leben of Matthew 23*

118 Troy W. Martin, *By Philosophy and Empty Deceit: Colossians as Response to a Cynic Critique*

119 David Ravens, *Luke and the Restoration of Israel*

120 Stanley E. Porter & David Tombs (eds.), *Approaches to New Testament Study*

121 Todd C. Penner, *The Epistle of James and Eschatology: Re-reading an Ancient Christian Letter*

122 A.D.A. Moses, *Matthew's Transfiguration Story in Jewish-Christian Controversy*

123 David Lertis Matson, *Household Conversion Narratives in Acts: Pattern and Interpretation*

124 David Mark Ball, *'I Am' in John's Gospel: Literary Function, Background and Theological Implications*

125 Robert Gordon Maccini, *Her Testimony is True: Women as Witnesses According to John*

126 B. Hudson Mclean, *The Cursed Christ: Mediterranean Expulsion Rituals and Pauline Soteriology*

127 R. Barry Matlock, *Unveiling the Apocalyptic Paul: Paul's Interpreters and the Rhetoric of Criticism*

128 Timothy Dwyer, *The Motif of Wonder in the Gospel of Mark*

129 Carl Judson Davis, *The Names and Way of the Lord: Old Testament Themes, New Testament Christology*

130 Craig S. Wansink, *Chained in Christ: The Experience and Rhetoric of Paul's Imprisonments*

131 Stanley E. Porter & Thomas H. Olbricht (eds.), *Rhetoric, Scripture and Theology: Essays from the 1994 Pretoria Conference*

132 J. Nelson Kraybill, *Imperial Cult and Commerce in John's Apocalypse*

133 Mark S. Goodacre, *Goulder and the Gospels: An Examination of a New Paradigm*

134 Larry J. Kreitzer, *Striking New Images: Roman Imperial Coinage and the New Testament World*

135 Charles Landon, *A Text-Critical Study of the Epistle of Jude*

136 Jeffrey T. Reed, *A Discourse Analysis of Philippians: Method and Rhetoric in the Debate over Lierary Integrity*

137 Roman Garrison, *The Graeco-Roman Contexts of Early Christian Literature*

138 Kent D. Clarke, *Textual Optimism: The United Bible Societies' Greek New Testament and its Evaluation of Evidence Letter-Ratings*

139 Yong-Eui Yang, *Jesus and the Sabbath in Matthew's Gospel*

140 Tom Yoder Neufeld, *Put on the Armour of God: The Divine Warrior from Isaiah to Ephesians*

141 Rebecca I. Denova, *The Things Accomplished Among Us: Prophetic Tradition in the Structural Pattern of Luke–Acts*

142 Scott Cunningham, *'Through Many Tribulations': The Theology of Persecution in Luke–Acts*

143 Raymond Pickett, *The Cross in Corinth: The Social Significance of the Death of Jesus*

144 S. John Roth, *The Blind, the Lame and the Poor: Character Types in Luke–Acts*

145 Larry Paul Jones, *The Symbol of Water in the Gospel of John*

146 Stanley E. Porter & T.H. Olbricht (eds.), *Rhetorical Analysis of Scripture: Essays from the 1995 London Conference*

147 Kim Paffenroth, *The Story of Jesus According to L*

148 Craig A. Evans and James A. Sanders (eds.), *Early Christian Interpretation of the Scriptures of Israel: Investigations and Proposals*

149 J. Dorcas Gordon, *Sister or Wife?: 1 Corinthians 7 and Cultural Anthropology*

150 J. Daryl Charles, *Virtue Amidst Vice: The Function of the Catalog of Virtues in 2 Peter 1.5-7*

151 Derek Tovey, *Narrative Art and Act in the Fourth Gospel*

152 Evert-Jan Vledder, *Conflict in the Miracle Stories*

153 Christopher Rowland & Crispin H.T. Fletcher-Louis (eds.), *Understanding, Studying and Reading: New Testament Essays in Honour of John Ashton*

154 Craig A. Evans and James A. Sanders (eds.), *The Function of Scripture in Early Jewish and Christian Tradition*

155 Kyoung-Jin Kim, *Stewardship and Almsgiving in Luke's Theology*

156 I.A.H. Combes, *The Metaphor of Slavery in the Writings of the Early Church: From the New Testament to the Begining of the Fifth Century*

158 Jey. J. Kanagaraj, *'Mysticism' in the Gospel of John: An Inquiry into its Background*

159 Brenda Deen Schildgen, *Crisis and Continuity: Time in the Gospel of Mark*

160 Johan Ferreira, *Johannine Ecclesiology*

161 Helen C. Orchard, *Courting Betrayal: Jesus as Victim in the Gospel of John*

162 Jeffrey T. Tucker, *Example Stories: Perspectives on Four Parables in the Gospel of Luke*

163 John A. Darr, *Herod the Fox: Audience Criticism and Lukan Characterization*

164 Bas M.F. Van Iersel, *Mark: A Reader-Response Commentary*

165 Alison Jasper, *The Shining Garment of the Text: Gendered Readings of John's Prologue*

166 G.K. Beale, *John's Use of the Old Testament in Revelation*

167 Gary Yamasaki, *John the Baptist in Life and Death: Audience-Oriented Criticism of Matthew's Narrative*

168 Stanley E. Porter and D.A. Carson, *Linguistics and the New Testament: Critical Junctures*

169 Derek Newton, *Deity and Diet: The Dilemma of Sacrificial Food at Corinth*

173 Stanley E. Porter and Richard S. Hess (eds.), *Translating the Bible: Problems and Prospects*

174 J.D.H. Amador, *Academic Constraints in Rhetorical Criticism of the New Testament: An Introduction to a Rhetoric of Power*

176 Alex T. Cheung, *Idol Food in Corinth: Jewish Background and Pauline Legacy*